HTML

Complete Concepts and Techniques

Gary B. Shelly
Thomas J. Cashman
Denise M. Woods

COURSE TECHNOLOGY
ONE MAIN STREET
CAMBRIDGE MA 02142
Thomson Learning™

Australia • Canada • Denmark • Japan • Mexico • New Zealand • Philippines
Puerto Rico • Singapore • South Africa • Spain • United Kingdom • United States

Printed in the United States of America

For more information, contact:

Course Technology
One Main Street
Cambridge, Massachusetts 02142, USA

or find us on the World Wide Web at: www.course.com

Asia (excluding Japan)
Thomson Learning
60 Albert Street, #15-01
Albert Complex
Singapore 189969

Japan
Thomson Learning
Palaceside Building 5F
1-1-1 Hitotsubashi, Chiyoda-ku
Tokyo 100 0003 Japan

Australia/New Zealand
Nelson/Thomson Learning
102 Dodds Street
South Melbourne, Victoria 3205
Australia

Latin America
Thomson Learning
Seneca, 53
Colonia Polanco
11560 Mexico D.F. Mexico

South Africa
Thomson Learning
Zonnebloem Building,
Constantia Square
526 Sixteenth Road
P.O. Box 2459
Halfway House, 1685
South Africa

Canada
Nelson/Thomson Learning
1120 Birchmount Road
Scarborough, Ontario
Canada M1K 5G4

UK/Europe/Middle East
Thomson Learning
Berkshire House
168-173 High Holborn
London, WC1V 7AA United Kingdom

Spain
Thomson Learning
Calle Magallanes, 25
28015-MADRID
ESPANA

PHOTO CREDITS: *Project 1, pages HTM 1.2-3* Basketball, CD-ROM, open book, Courtesy of PhotoDisc, Inc.; baseball, sunflower, Courtesy of KPT Metatools; *Project 2, pages HTM 2.2-3* Brandy snifter, computer monitor, flagstone, Courtesy of KPT Metatools; people in park, Courtesy of Adobe Systems, Inc.; Storyspace map, Storyspace logo, *afternoon, a story*, quotation, Courtesy of Eastgate Systems, Inc.; *Project 3, pages HTM 3.2-3* illustrations, Ken Russo; *Project 4, pages HTM 4.2-3* Globe, world map, Courtesy of PhotoDisc, Inc.; *Project 5, pages HTM 5.2-3* Heart, wedding couple, Courtesy of Corel Professional Photos CD-ROM Image Usage; kids drinking milkshakes, woman graduate, Courtesy of Digital Stock, Inc.; old school memorabilia, students under tree, teacher and chalkboard, Courtesy of PhotoDisc, Inc.; *Project 6, pages HTM 6.2-3* Keyboard, mouse, reading glasses, typewriter, circuit board, Courtesy of PhotoDisc, Inc.; Alex Haley, Courtesy of Christian Viouiard/The Gamma Liaison Network; Allen Ginsberg, Courtesy of UPI/Corbis-Bettman; Ernest Hemingway, Courtesy Archive Photos.

ISBN 0-7895-4723-6

2 3 4 5 6 7 8 9 10 BC 04 03 02 01 00

HTML

Complete Concepts and Techniques

CONTENTS

PROJECT ONE

CREATING AND EDITING A WEB PAGE

PROJECT TWO

CREATING A WEB SITE WITH LINKS

PROJECT FIVE

Creating Frames on a Web Page

PROJECT SIX

Creating Forms on a Web Page

Preface

The Shelly Cashman Series® Internet books reinforce the fact that you made the right choice when you use a Shelly Cashman Series book. Earlier Shelly Cashman Series Internet books were used by more schools and more students than any other series in textbook publishing. Yet, the Shelly Cashman Series team wanted to produce an even better book for HTML, so the step-by-step pedagogy was refined to include larger screens (800 x 600) to present material in an even easier-to-understand format. Features such as OtherWays and More Abouts, with links to HTML Web sites, enhance the book to give students an in-depth knowledge of HTML. Each project opens with a fascinating perspective of the subject covered in the project. Completely redesigned student assignments include the unique Cases and Places. This book provides the finest educational experience for students learning about how to create Web pages using HTML.

The World Wide Web

In the several years since its birth, the World Wide Web, or Web for short, has grown beyond all expectations. During this short period of time, the Web has increased from a limited number of networked computers to more than twenty million computers offering millions of Web pages on any topic you can imagine. Schools, businesses, and the computing industry all are taking advantage of this new way of delivering information. Web pages do not just happen. Someone must create and manage them. This book shows you how to create Web pages using HTML.

Objectives of This Textbook

HTML: Complete Concepts and Techniques is intended for use as a stand-alone textbook or in combination with other books in an introductory course on creating Web pages. This book also is suitable for use in a two- to three-credit hour course or a continuing education course. Specific objectives of this book are as follows:

- To expose students to creating Web pages
- To teach students how to use HTML
- To expose students to common Web page formats and functions
- To encourage curiosity and independent exploration of World Wide Web resources
- To develop an exercise-oriented approach that allows students to learn by example
- To encourage independent study and help those who are learning how to create Web pages in a distance education environment

Organization of This Textbook

HTML: Complete Concepts and Techniques is comprised of six projects that introduce students to creating Web pages. Neither World Wide Web nor Internet experience is necessary. Each project begins with a statement of Objectives. The topics in the project are presented in a step-by-step, screen-by-screen manner.

Each project ends with a Project Summary and a section titled What You Should Know. Questions and exercises are presented at the end of each project. Exercises include Test Your Knowledge, Use Help, Apply Your Knowledge, In the Lab, and Cases and Places. The projects are organized as follows:

Project 1 - **Creating and Editing a Web Page** In Project 1, students are introduced to World Wide Web terminology, basic HTML tags, and the various parts of a Web page. Topics include starting and quitting Notepad and a browser; entering headings and text into an HTML file; creating a bulleted list with HTML; adding background color and a horizontal rule; saving the HTML file and viewing it in the browser; printing the HTML file and the Web page; and Web page design.

Project 2 - **Creating a Web Site with Links** In Project 2, students are introduced to linking terms and definitions. Topics include adding an e-mail link; linking to another page on the same Web site; linking to another Web site; setting link targets within a page; linking to targets; types of image files; alternative text for images; defining image size; wrapping text around an image; and inserting images onto Web pages.

Project 3 - Creating Tables in a Web Site In Project 3, students learn how to create tables using HTML tags. First, students assess table needs and then plan the table. Topics include table definitions and terms; table uses; creating borderless tables; inserting images into tables; vertical and horizontal alignment within a table; adding color to a cell; adding links to another page; adding an e-mail link; using the ROWSPAN and COLSPAN attributes; adding captions; and spacing within and between cells.

Project 4 - Creating an Image Map In Project 4, students learn how to use an image map to create more advanced Web pages. Topics include image mapping purpose and considerations; selecting images for mapping; dividing an image into hotspots; creating links with hotspots; and using text to describe links. Students also use graphics software to determine the coordinates needed for image mapping.

Project 5 - Creating Frames on a Web Page In Project 5, students are introduced to using frames for Web page creation. Topics include purpose and considerations when using frames; resizing frames; frame headers; scroll bars; frame navigation; linking frames; and two-frame and three-frame Web pages. Additional topics include using the NORESIZE attribute and creating four-frame Web pages.

Project 6 - Creating Forms on a Web Page In Project 6, students create a form that will allow readers to complete a survey online and send information via e-mail. Topics include form purposes and basics; selecting check boxes on a form; choosing menu items on a form; form text boxes for free-form text; and creating an e-mail link to transfer the form information back to the Web page developer. Students also are introduced to using advanced selection menus.

End-of-Project Student Activities

A notable strength of the Shelly Cashman Series Internet books is the extensive student activities at the end of each project. Well-structured student activities can make the difference between students merely participating in a class and students retaining the information they learn. These activities include all of the following sections.

- **What You Should Know** A listing of the tasks completed within a project together with the pages where the step-by-step, screen-by-screen explanations appear. This section provides a perfect study review for students.
- **Test Your Knowledge** Four or five pencil-and-paper activities designed to determine students' understanding of the material in the project. Included are true/false questions, multiple-choice questions, and two short-answer exercises.
- **Use Help** Any user of HTML must know how to use Help. Therefore, this book contains two Help exercises per project. These exercises alone distinguish the Shelly Cashman Series from any other set of instructional materials.
- **Apply Your Knowledge** A substantive exercise intended to be completed in a few minutes that provides practice with project skills.
- **In the Lab** Several assignments per project that require students to apply the knowledge gained in the project to solve problems.
- **Cases and Places** Up to seven unique case studies per project allow students to apply their knowledge to real-world situations.

Shelly Cashman Series Teaching Tools

A comprehensive set of Teaching Tools accompanies this textbook in the form of a CD-ROM. The CD-ROM includes an electronic Instructor's Manual and teaching and testing aids. The CD-ROM (ISBN 0-7895-5622-7) is available through your Course Technology representative or by calling one of the following telephone numbers: Colleges and Universities, 1-800-648-7450; High Schools, 1-800-824-5179; and Career Colleges, 1-800-477-3692. The contents of the CD-ROM are listed below.

- **Instructor's Manual** The Instructor's Manual is made up of Microsoft Word files that include lecture notes, solutions to laboratory assignments, and a large test bank. The files allow you to modify the lecture notes or generate quizzes and exams from the test bank using you own word processing software. The Instructor's Manual includes the following for each project: project objectives; project overview; detailed lesson plans with page number references; teacher notes and activities; answers to the end-of-project exercises; test bank of 110 questions (50 true/false, 25 multiple-choice, and 35 fill-in-the blanks); transparency references; and selected transparencies. The transparencies are available on the Figures in the Book described below. The test bank questions are numbered the same as in Course Test Manager. Thus, you can print a copy of the project and use the printed test bank to select your questions in Course Test Manager.

- **Figures in the Book** Illustrations for every figure in the textbook are available. Use this ancillary to create a slide show from the illustrations for lecture or to print transparencies for use in lecture with an overhead projector.
- **Course Test Manager** Course Test Manager is a powerful testing and assessment package that enables instructors to create and print tests from the large test bank. Instructors with access to a networked computer lab (LAN) can administer, grade, and track tests online. Students also can take online practice tests, which generate customized study guides that indicate where in the textbook students can find more information for each question.
- **Lecture Success System** The Lecture Success System is a set of files that allows you to explain and illustrate the step-by-step, screen-by-screen development of a project in the textbook. The Lecture Success System requires that you have a copy of Notepad, a browser, a personal computer, and a projection device.
- **Instructor's Lab Solutions** Solutions and required files for all the Apply Your Knowledge and In the Lab assignments at the end of each project and the projects themselves are available.
- **Student Data Files** All the files that are required by students to complete the Apply Your Knowledge exercises are included.
- **Interactive Labs** Eighteen hands-on interactive labs that take students from ten to fifteen minutes to step through help solidify and reinforce computer concepts. Student assessment requires students to answer questions about the contents of the interactive labs.

Shelly Cashman Online

Shelly Cashman Online is a World Wide Web service available to instructors and students of computer education. Visit Shelly Cashman Online at www.scseries.com.

Acknowledgments

The Shelly Cashman Series would not be the leading computer education series without the contributions of outstanding publishing professionals. First, and foremost, among them is Becky Herrington, director of production and designer. She is the heart and soul of the Shelly Cashman Series, and it is only through her leadership, dedication, and tireless efforts that superior products are made possible. Becky created and produced the award-winning Windows series of books.

Under Becky's direction, the following individuals made significant contributions to these books: Doug Cowley, production manager; Ginny Harvey, series specialist and developmental editor; Ken Russo, senior Web designer; Mike Bodnar, associate production manager; Mark Norton, Web designer; Stephanie Nance, graphic artist and cover designer; Marlo Mitchem, Chris Schneider, Ellana Russo, and Hector Arvizu, graphic artists; Jeanne Black and Betty Hopkins, Quark experts; Nancy Lamm and Laura Michaels, copyeditors; Cherilyn King, proofreader; Cristina Haley, indexer; Sarah Evertson of Image Quest, photo researcher; and Susan Sebok and Ginny Harvey, contributing writers.

Special thanks go to Richard Keaveny, managing editor; Jim Quasney, series consultant; Lora Wade, product manager; Meagan Walsh, associate product manager; Francis Schurgot, Web product manager; Tonia Grafakos, associate Web product manager; Scott Wiseman, online developer; Rajika Gupta, marketing manager; and Erin Bennett, editorial assistant.

Gary B. Shelly
Thomas J. Cashman
Denise M. Woods

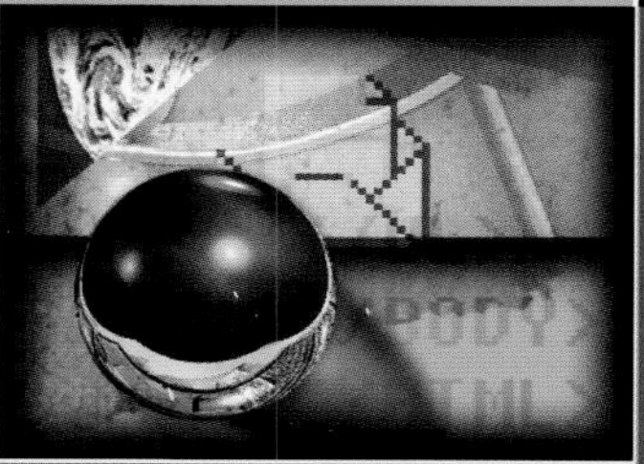

HTML

Creating and Editing a Web Page

OBJECTIVES

You will have mastered the material in this project when you can:

- Describe the Internet and its associated key terms
- Describe the World Wide Web and its associated key terms
- Start Notepad
- Describe the Notepad window
- Enter the HTML, HEAD, TITLE, and BODY tags
- Enter a paragraph of text, a bulleted list, and HTML tags
- Save an HTML file
- Change the background color of a Web page
- Center a heading
- Start Your Browser
- View the HTML file in Your Browser
- Print an HTML file from Notepad
- Print a Web page from Your Browser
- Access information about Web page design via the Internet
- Quit Notepad
- Quit Your Browser

Click 'till You Drop

Online Shopping Is Gaining Customers

Check out the new mall opening in your neighborhood. It is filled with thousands of stores, open 24 hours every day, and loaded with the season's newest merchandise. Best of all, you can head there without getting in your car. Just boot up your computer, connect to the Internet, and shop to your heart's content.

Merchants have discovered Web surfers across the world love to shop online. Although the actual number of consumers and their spending habits are difficult to track, one thing is for certain: e-commerce is flourishing. Yahoo!, the largest subject-directory search tool on the Internet, reports more than 1,000 merchants sign up on its service each day. In 1997, one-third of Internet users shopped online and bought $4.3 billion of services and products, most commonly apparel, books, and music. By 2002, one-half of Internet users are predicted to buy products online and to spend an estimated $54 billion.

Programmers developed the first cybershop sites, but these pioneers had

little insight of how shoppers actually would use the pages. Their goal was to get the files to load and work properly, not necessarily to attract visitors with an attractive design and meaningful content. In the past few years, however, researchers have become involved by analyzing the shoppers and scrutinizing their shopping behaviors.

Typical cybershoppers are middle-aged, male, wealthy, married, and educated. They go to movies, concerts, plays, and museums, do charity or volunteer work, and garden. Above all, they want mastery of the Web sites and instant fulfillment. They want to browse, read product descriptions, and comparison shop with ease. When cybershopping, they look at only four of the hundreds of thousands of cybershop Web pages. When a page loads, they look at the material and make a speedy decision to continue or to click the Back button. When they are ready to buy, they want to purchase the product quickly and pay securely.

As a result of this shopping behavior, marketing professionals often work actively with HTML (hypertext markup language) programmers to create effective Web pages. They realize that a merchant's Web site should contain tables, frames, and colors to lead surfers in a focused direction to the items they want to buy. The pages ask visitors to get involved by clicking various options. They contain Help, a frequently asked questions (FAQ) section, a telephone number, an e-mail address, and a physical company address.

In this textbook you will learn to create dazzling Web pages that contain the same components as those you see in the cybermalls. In Project 1, you will use HTML tags and design a Web page with a bulleted list and background color. In later projects, you will add tables and links to other Web sites. As you work through these projects and exercises, consider how visitors would use your Web pages. With practice and patience, you will develop pages that even a power shopper would love.

HTML

Creating and Editing a Web Page

PROJECT 1

CASE PERSPECTIVE

Jared Smith is the owner of Chiaravalle Pizza, a local pizza place where you work when you are not attending classes. Recently, Mr. Smith called you into his office to ask some questions about the Internet and World Wide Web (also called the Web). He had been reading about the Web lately and wondered if Chiaravalle Pizza should develop its own Web site for advertising.

With this in mind, you have decided to design and develop a Web page that advertises Chiaravalle Pizza's variety of traditional and specialty pizzas (Figure 1-1a). To develop this Web page, you will use hypertext markup language (HTML), as shown in Figure 1-1b. You also have decided to make the Web pages more appealing by using various text sizes and formats, adding color and an image in the form of a horizontal rule. Once you have completed this Web page, you will show it to Mr. Smith to get his feedback on future development.

Introduction

Quick access to information is vitally important. Each day, you make decisions in all areas of your life. Today, computers and networks have become the tools people use to gather, analyze, and use information to make informed decisions and to communicate with others around the world. The world's largest network is the Internet — a worldwide network of computers that houses information on a multitude of subjects.

What Is the Internet?

The **Internet** is a worldwide collection of networks that links together millions of businesses, the government, educational institutions, and individuals using modems, telephone lines, and other communication devices and media (Figure 1-2 on page HTM 1.6). More than 125 million people in more than 150 countries are connected to the Internet in their homes, offices, or schools. Users with computers connected to the Internet have access to a variety of services including e-mail, newsgroups, and the World Wide Web.

page1 - Notepad
File Edit Search Help
<HTML>
<HEAD>
<TITLE>Chiaravalle Pizza Home Page</TITLE>
</HEAD>
<BODY BGCOLOR=#94D6E7>
<H1 ALIGN="CENTER">Chiaravalle Pizza</H1>
<HR>
<P>Chiaravalle Pizza has been in business for the past 50 years. We specialize in unique pizzas
and other Italian dishes. Located on Main Street, Chiaravalle Pizza is proud to be on the city's
"Ten Best Restaurants" list for the past seven years. Call 1-219-555-2510 for reservations or
orders today!</P>
<H2>Our services include:</H2>
<UL>
<LI>A 100 seating capacity restaurant</LI>
<LI>Take out orders</LI>
<LI>Delivery services at no charge</LI>
</UL>
</BODY>
</HTML>
Start
page1
(b)
Chiaravalle Pizza
Chiaravalle Pizza has been in business for the past 50 years. We specialize in unique pizzas and other Italian dishes. Located on Main Street, Chiaravalle Pizza is proud to be on the city's "Ten Best Restaurants" list for the past seven years. Call 1-219-555-2510 for reservations or orders today!
Our services include:
A 100 seating capacity restaurant
Take out orders
Delivery services at no charge
(a)

FIGURE 1-1

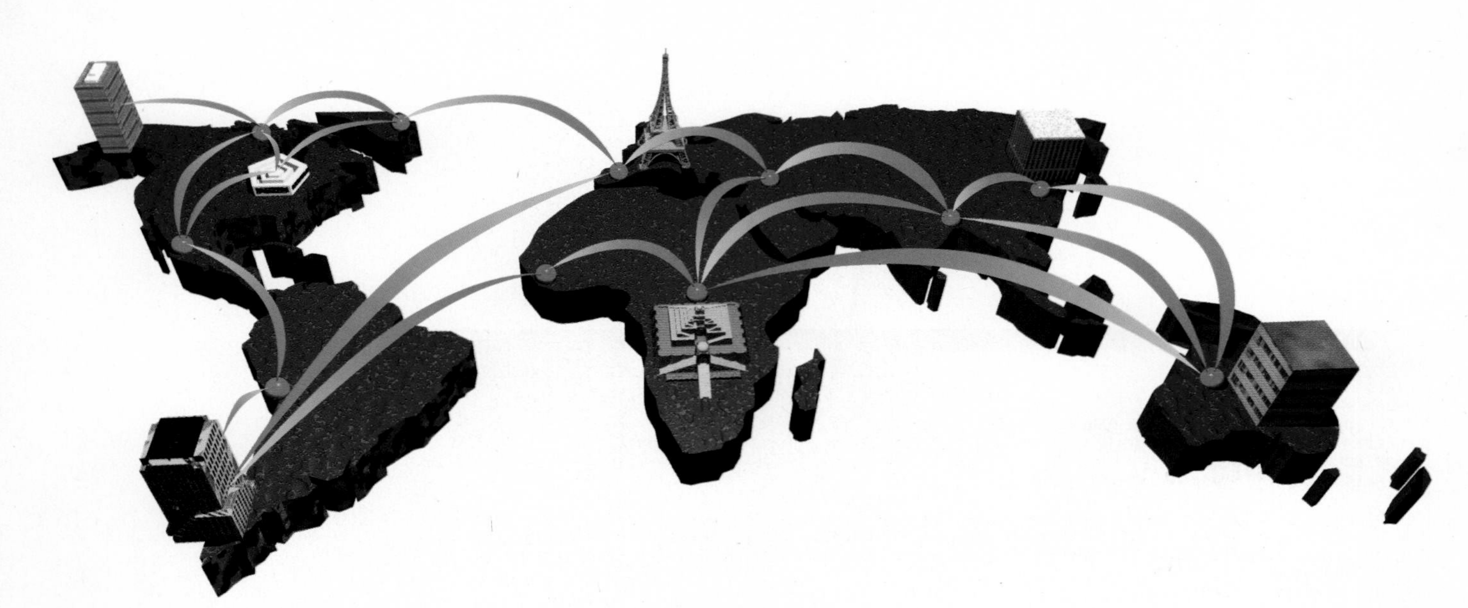

FIGURE 1-2

> **More About**
>
> **Web Law**
>
> As new Web developers, it is helpful to understand intellectual property issues that may affect your Web development. For more information about HTML standards, visit the HTML More About page (www.scsite.com/html/more.htm) and click Web Law.

What Is the World Wide Web?

The **World Wide Web**, also called the **Web**, is the part of the Internet that supports multimedia and consists of a collection of linked documents. These documents, or pages of information, are known as **Web pages**. Because the Web supports multimedia, text, graphics, sound, and video, they all can be included on a Web page. A **Web site** is a collection of Web pages that are created and maintained by a company, a university or college, a government agency, or even an individual. Web sites are used at universities and colleges to distribute information about major areas of study, to display course information from professors for students to view, and to allow students to register for classes online. Companies use Web sites to advertise their products worldwide as well as to provide 24-hour online support for their customers.

Web pages are stored on a **Web server** or **host**, which is a computer that sends (serves) requested Web pages. Any computer that has server software installed and is connected to the Internet can act as a Web server. Every Web site is stored on and runs from one or more Web servers.

Copying files onto a Web server is known as **publishing** the Web pages. Once a Web page is published, anyone who has access to the Internet can view it. Figure 1-3 shows a Web site maintained by Indiana University. Although this site is housed on a Web server in Bloomington, Indiana, it is available for viewing by anyone in the world.

Indiana University Bloomington Home Page - Microsoft Internet Explorer provided by MSN
Welcome to Bloomington
Student life: Admissions, housing, financial aid,
Academic programs and research: Courses,
People and groups: Names, e-mail addresses,
Recreation and entertainment: Athletics, culture
Services used often: Computing, library, health,
Undergraduate Program - Microsoft Internet Explorer provided by MSN
Welcome
Profile of the Undergraduate Program
Areas of Study
Admission Information/Application
Student Honor Code
Direct Freshman Admission
Grad Pact Program
Honors Program
Overseas Studies Program
Minorities in Business Program
Community Service & Learning
Internships, Co-ops, Placement
Indiana University - Microsoft Internet Explorer provided by MSN
INDIANA UNIVERSITY
ADMISSIONS INFORMATION
ABOUT IU
CAMPUSES
UNITS & SERVICES
FINDING IU PEOPLE
SEARCHING IU BY TOPIC

FIGURE 1-3

A Web page can be linked to other Web pages by the use of hyperlinks. A **hyperlink,** also called a **link**, is used to connect a Web page to another Web page on the same, or a different, Web server located anywhere in the world. Clicking a hyperlink allows you to move quickly from one Web page to another. You also can use hyperlinks to move to a different section of the same Web page. Figure 1-4 shows examples of different types of hyperlinks.

FIGURE 1-4

What Is Hypertext Markup Language?

Web pages are created using **hypertext markup language** (or **HTML**), which is a set of special instructions called **tags** or **markups** that specify links to other documents, as well as how the page is displayed. A Web page is a file that contains both text and

HTML tags. HTML tags *mark* the text to define how it displays when viewed as pages on the World Wide Web. Examples of tags are <B> to indicate bold text, <P> to indicate a new paragraph, and <HR> to display a horizontal rule across the page. Figure 1-1b on page HTM 1.5 shows how the Web page shown in Figure 1-1a on page HTM 1.5 looks as text coded with HTML tags.

To view a Web page written in HTML, you use a Web browser. A **Web browser**, also called a **browser**, is a program that interprets and displays Web pages and enables you to link to other Web pages. The two more popular browsers are Internet Explorer and Netscape® Navigator.

One of the greatest benefits of HTML is that it is *platform independent*. Because HTML is platform independent you can create or *code* an HTML file on one type of computer and then view that file as a Web page on another type of computer. To ensure that browsers can interpret HTML, an organization called the World Wide Web Consortium maintains HTML standards. Several versions of HTML are in use today; each new version expands the capabilities of HTML. In this project, you will learn how to create a Web page by typing text and HTML tags in Notepad — a simple text editor. You also will learn how to view your Web page using a browser.

More About

HTML Standards

Standards are important in any programming language. Several versions of HTML are in use today for Web page creation. The standards used for HTML tags are maintained by the World Wide Web Consortium. For more information about HTML standards, visit the HTML More About page (www.scsite.com/html/more.htm) and click HTML Standards.

Project One – Chiaravalle Pizza Web Page

To illustrate the capabilities of HTML, this book presents a series of projects that use HTML to develop a variety of Web pages. This project uses HTML to create a Web page for Chiaravalle Pizza, as shown in Figure 1-1a. Although you previously have never created a Web page, you are excited to learn this very marketable skill. Before you start building your first Web page, you must decide what content to include — in this case, general information about Chiaravalle Pizza. To make the page interesting, you will use various HTML tags to format the paragraphs and add a bulleted list. You also will insert a horizontal rule and a colored background to make the Web page more appealing.

To edit text and HTML tags used to create the Web page, you will use a program called Notepad as shown in Figure 1-1b. Notepad is a standard program on most computers, so you should have access to it. If not, any other text editor will work. You also will use a browser to view your Web page as you create it.

Web Page Development

Today, many people are developing Web pages including students, business executives, and teachers, as well as professional Web developers. Each person has his or her own style and the resulting Web pages are as diverse as the people who create them. Most Web pages, however, include several common elements and parts. Figure 1-5 on the next page lists the standard elements and parts of a Web page.

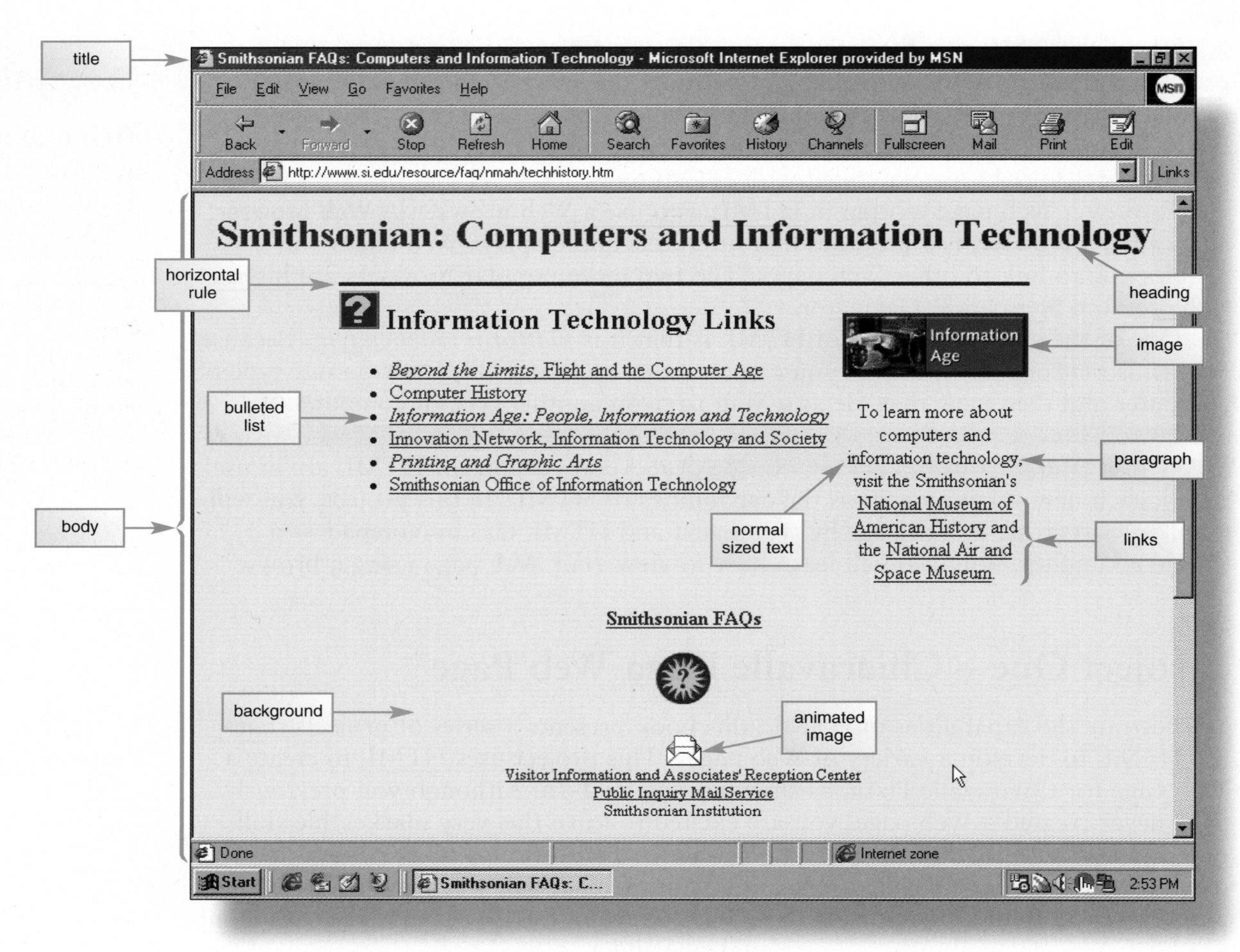

FIGURE 1-5

The Elements of a Web Page

The title of a Web page usually is the first element you see (Figure 1-5). A Web page's **title** identifies the subject or purpose of the page; when you view the page in a browser, the title displays on the browser's title bar. The title also is the name assigned to the page if you added the page to your browser's list of favorites or **bookmarks**. Because of its importance, you always should include a title on your Web page. The title should be concise yet descriptive and briefly explain the page's content or purpose to the visitor.

The **body** of the Web page contains the information that displays in the browser window. The **background** of a Web page is similar to the wallpaper in Windows. A background can be a solid color, a picture or graphic, or the default standard white or gray background. When choosing your background, be sure it does not overpower the information on the Web page.

Normal text is the text that makes up the main content of a Web page. Normal text can be used on a Web page in many formats, such as a standard **paragraph** format or a **bulleted** (or numbered) list. Normal text also can be formatted to display as bold (<B>), italic (<I>), or underlined (<U>) text, in different colors, and so on.

Headings, such as those in Figure 1-5, are used to set off different paragraphs of text or different sections of a page. Headings are a larger font size than normal text and usually are bold or italic. HTML has six different sizes, or levels, of headings numbered 1 through 6, with 1 being the largest. Headings can help you organize content and emphasize key points on a Web page. When using them to break up information on a page, be sure to use headings consistently. That is, if you use a Heading 2 (<H2>) style for a specific category of text, you always should use a Heading 2 style to break up information at that level. Also, do not skip levels of headings in your document. For example, do not start with a Heading 1 (<H1>) style and next use a Heading 3 (<H3>) style.

Another important element of a Web page is any graphic or **image**, such as an icon, bullet, line, photo, illustration, or other picture. Also referred to as **inline images**, such images include any graphics or picture files that are not part of the HTML file. **Horizontal rules** are inline images that display lines across the page to separate different sections. Instead, these separate graphic and picture files are merged into the Web page as it is displayed. The HTML file contains <IMG> tags that tell the browser which graphic file to request from the server, where to locate it on the page, and how to display it. On a Web page, inline images can serve merely as graphical representations or as hyperlinks. Whatever its function, an image should serve a purpose; be cautious not to overuse images that may give your Web page a cluttered look.

An **image map** is a special type of inline image in which you define one or more areas as hotspots. A **hotspot** is an area of an image that activates a function when selected. For example, each hotspot in a Web image map can link to a different Web page. Some inline images are animated, meaning they include motion and can change in appearance. Such images, called **animated images**, can make a Web page more exciting. You must ensure, however, that they do not distract the visitor from the purpose of the Web page.

One of the more important elements of a Web page is a **hyperlink**, or **link**. Links not only serve as the primary way to navigate between pages, they distinguish the Web page as a unique repository of information. Clicking a link instructs the browser to go to a location in a file or to request a file from a server. The requested file might be a Web page or a graphic, sound, multimedia, or even a program file. You also can use links to trigger e-mail messages to be sent to you or to other people associated with the Web page. As noted, you can identify the hyperlinks in a Web page using text or images. The most commonly used hyperlinks are text links (also called *hypertext links*). When text is used to identify a hyperlink, it usually is given a color different from the normal text.

Web Page Considerations

Creating an attractive and functional Web page layout is an important aspect of Web page development. One of the goals of designing Web pages is to capture the attention of the Web page visitor. When initiating your Web page layout, you must consider many formatting styles and techniques. For more information about Web page layout, visit the HTML More About page (www.scsite.com/html/more.htm) and click Web Page Considerations.

Starting Notepad

Follow the steps on the next page to start Notepad, or ask your instructor how to start Notepad for your system.

Steps To Start Notepad

1 Click the Start button on the taskbar and then point to Programs on the Start menu. Point to Accessories on the Programs submenu and then point to Notepad on the Accessories submenu (Figure 1-6).

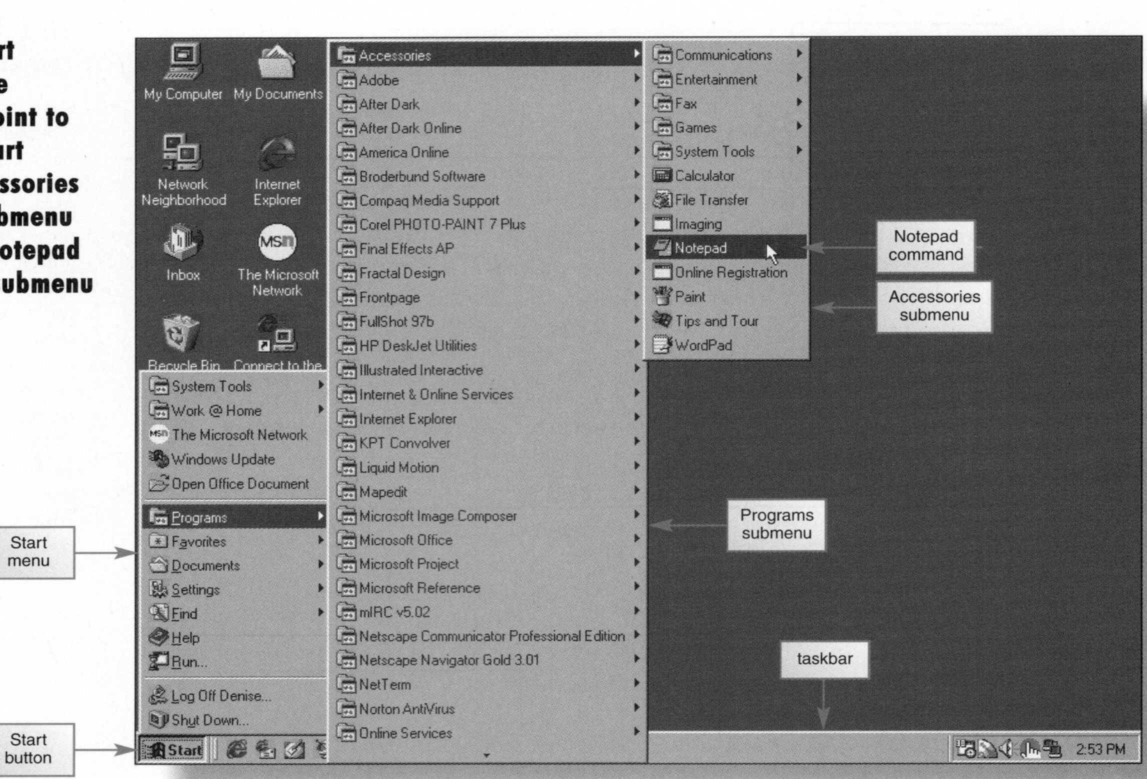

FIGURE 1-6

2 Click Notepad.

The Notepad window opens (Figure 1-7).

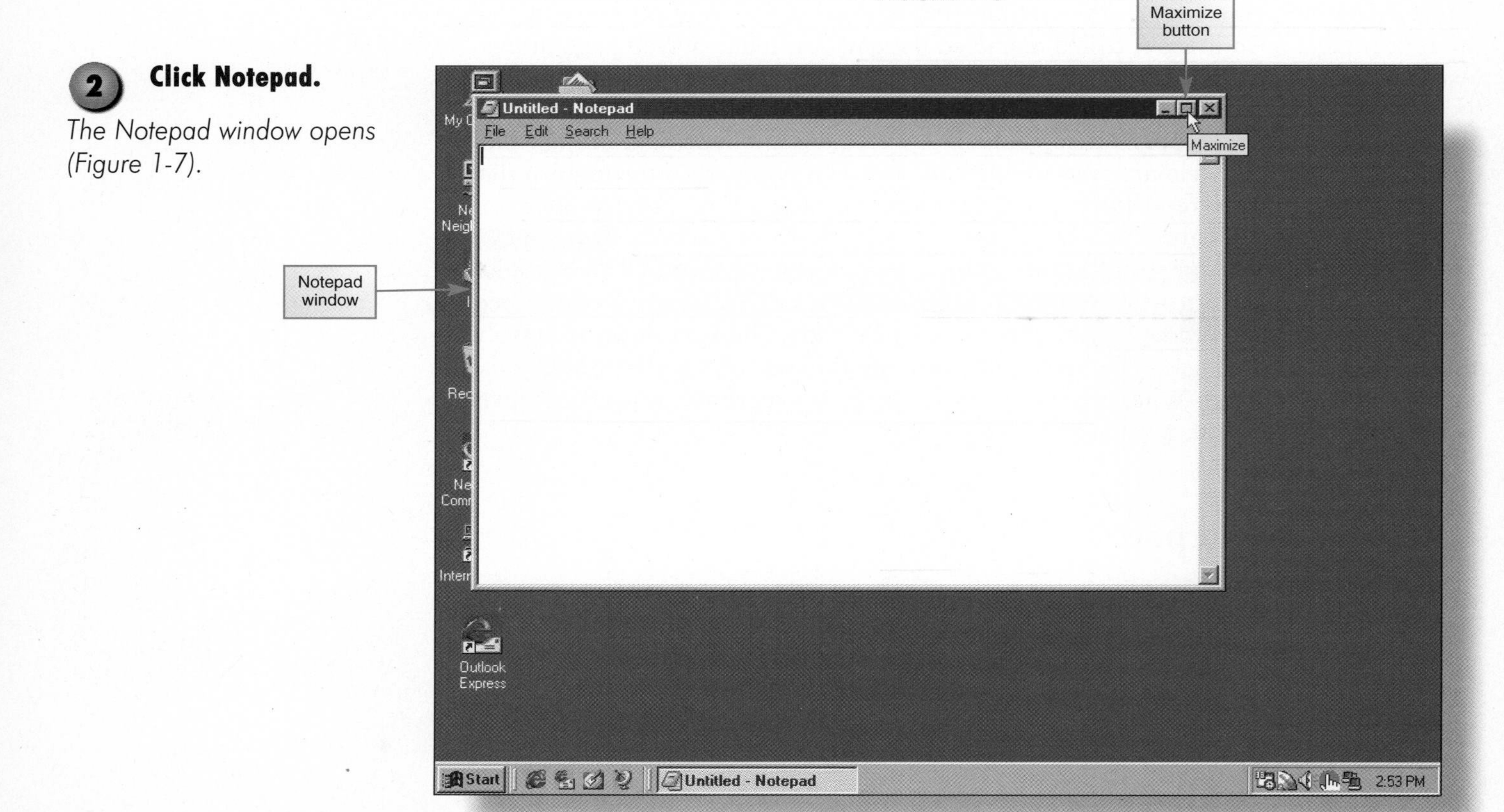

FIGURE 1-7

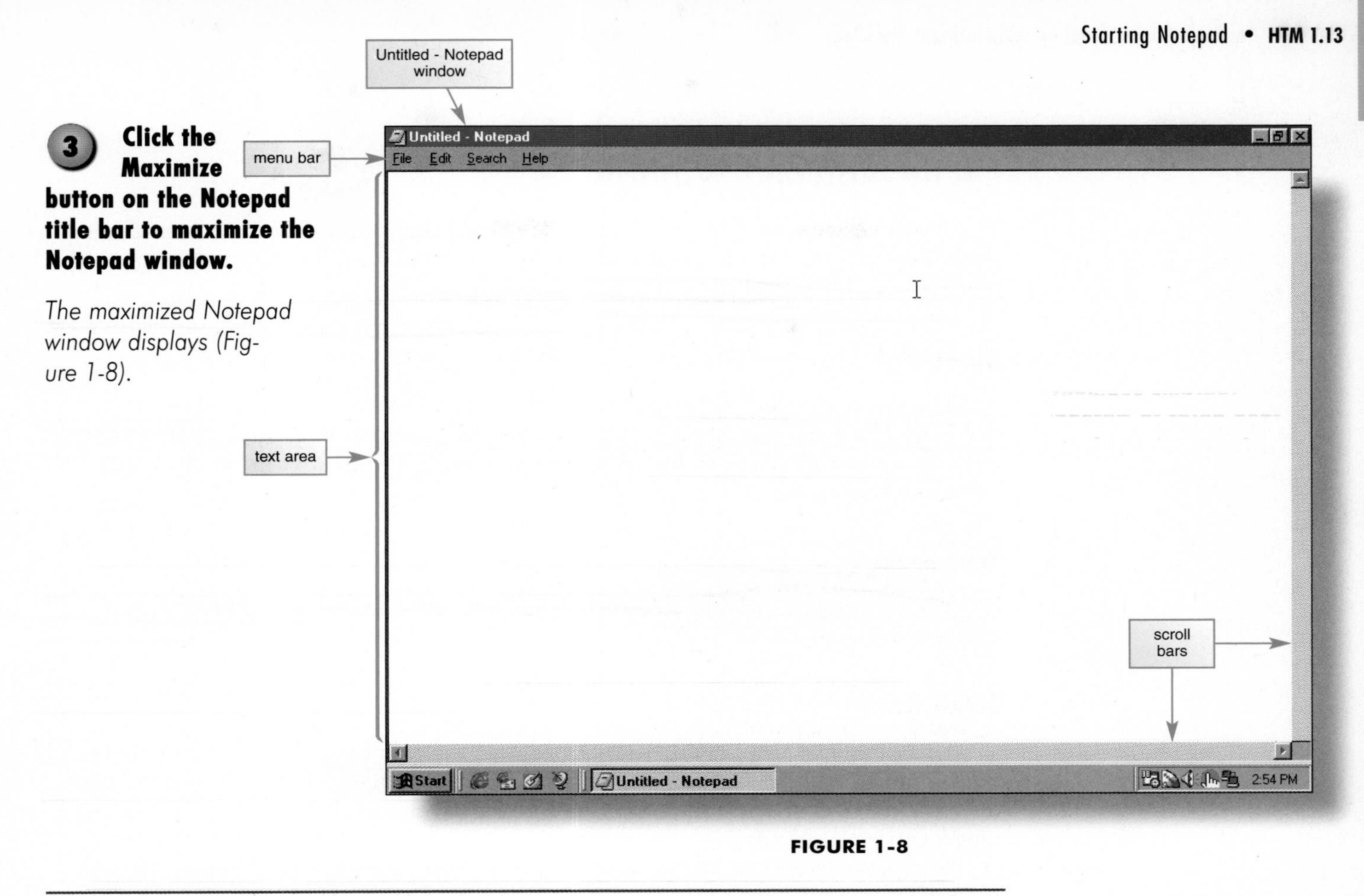

3 Click the Maximize button on the Notepad title bar to maximize the Notepad window.

The maximized Notepad window displays (Figure 1-8).

FIGURE 1-8

Wrapping Text in the Notepad Window

In Notepad, the text you type will scroll continuously to the right unless the WordWrap feature is turned on. **WordWrap** makes all the text visible in the window, but does not affect the way text appears when it is printed. When the **WordWrap command** is turned on, a check mark precedes the command on the Edit menu. Follow these steps to enable the WordWrap command.

Steps To Turn on WordWrap in Notepad

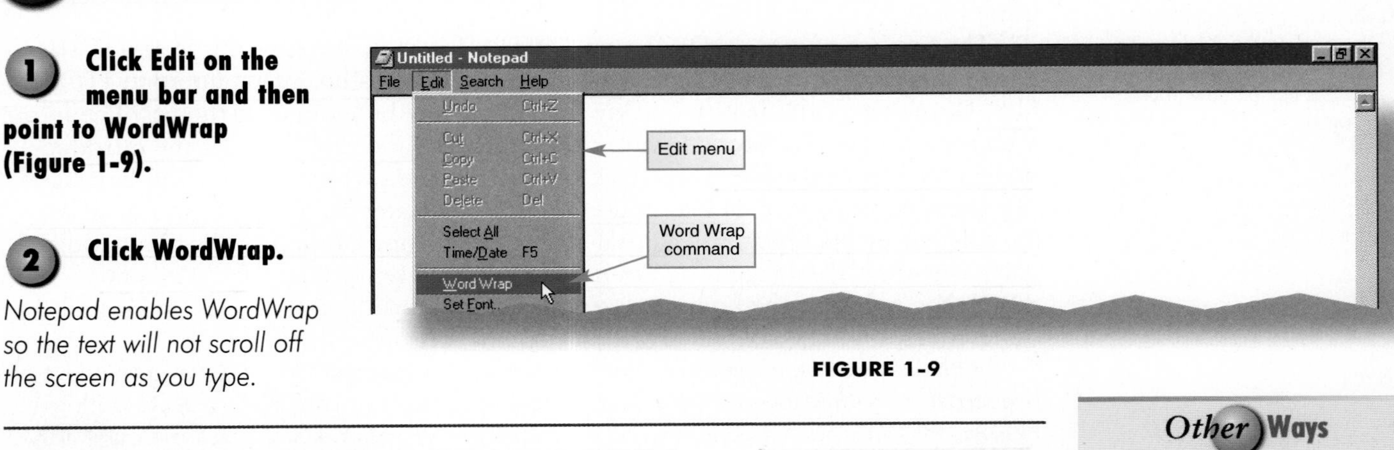

1 Click Edit on the menu bar and then point to WordWrap (Figure 1-9).

2 Click WordWrap.

Notepad enables WordWrap so the text will not scroll off the screen as you type.

FIGURE 1-9

Other Ways

1. Press ALT+E, W

The Notepad Window

The Notepad window contains several elements similar to document windows in other applications. The main elements of the Notepad window are the menu bar, the text area, and the scroll bars (Figure 1-8 on page HTM 1.13).

Menu Bar

The menu bar displays at the top of the screen just below the title bar (Figure 1-8). The **menu bar** displays the Notepad menu names. Each menu name offers a list of commands you can use to open, save, and print the text in the file, and perform other tasks.

Text Area

The **text area** is another element of the Notepad window. As you type, text displays in the text area.

Scroll Bars

The **scroll bars** display different portions of the text file in the window. At the right-hand side of the window is a vertical scroll bar, and at the bottom of the window is a horizontal scroll bar. On both scroll bars, the **scroll box** indicates your current location in the file.

Notepad is preset to use standard 8.5-by-11-inch paper, with .75-inch left and right margins and 1-inch top and bottom margins. Only a portion of the text file, however, displays on the screen at one time. You view the portion of the file displayed on the screen in the **Notepad window** (Figure 1-8).

More About

Text Editing

WordPad is another text editor that you can use to create HTML files. To start WordPad, click the Start button on the taskbar, point to Programs on the Start menu, point to Accessories on the Programs submenu, and then click WordPad on the Accessories submenu. WordPad Help provides tips on how to use the product.

Entering HTML Tags and Text

In Project 1, you will begin by inserting four sets of tags (<HTML>, <HEAD>, <TITLE>, and <BODY>) that define the overall structure of a standard Web page. These tags are not required, so your browser can display your Web page without them. The projects in this book always will include these tags in HTML pages because they are a good standard to follow. In the future these tags may become required Web page components; therefore, you should develop the habit of always using them.

The first set of tags, <HTML> and </HTML>, indicates that this is an HTML document. Using this set of tags, software tools, such as browsers, interpret HTML files. Developers can identify quickly the HTML file by looking at the first line in the Web page source. The second set of tags, <HEAD> and </HEAD>, is the introduction to the rest of the file. These tags indicate the area where the title will be placed. The third set of tags, <TITLE> and </TITLE>, indicates the title that will display on the title bar of the browser. The title also is the portion of the HTML file that displays when the Web page is bookmarked. The final set of tags, <BODY> and </BODY>, indicates the boundaries of the Web page. All text, images, links, and other content will be contained within this final set of tags.

HTML is not case sensitive; therefore, you can enter HTML tags in uppercase or lowercase or a mixture of both. The project directions in this book always will type HTML tags in uppercase. It is good form to be consistent when you type tags, adhering to a standard practice in your own HTML development.

Entering Initial Tags

As you can see, the four tags <HTML>, <HEAD>, <TITLE>, and <BODY> also have corresponding ending tags, </HTML>, </HEAD>, </TITLE>, and </BODY>. Table 1-1 lists the functions of those tags as well as other tags that you will use in this project.

Table 1-1

HTML TAG	FUNCTION
<HTML> </HTML>	Indicates the beginning and end of an HTML document.
<HEAD> </HEAD>	Indicates the beginning and end of a section of the document used for the title and other document header information.
<TITLE> </TITLE>	Indicates the beginning and end of the title; the title does not display in the body of the Web page, but displays on the title bar of the browser.
<BODY> </BODY>	Indicates the beginning and end of the Web page body.
<HN> </HN>	Indicates the beginning and end of the text section called a heading; sizes range from <H1> through <H6>. See Figure 1-12a on page HTM 1.17 for heading size samples.
<P> </P>	Indicates the beginning of a new paragraph; inserts a blank line above the new paragraph.
<UL> </UL>	Indicates the beginning and end of an unordered (bulleted) list.
<LI> </LI>	Indicates that the item that follows the tag is an item within a list.
<HR>	Inserts a horizontal rule.
 	Breaks a line of text at the point where the tag appears.

Perform the following steps to enter the initial tags for the Web page, using all uppercase as you enter the HTML.

Steps To Enter Initial HTML Tags

1 Type <HTML> **and then press the ENTER key. Type** <HEAD> **and then press the ENTER key. Type** <TITLE> Chiaravalle Pizza Home Page</TITLE> **and then press the ENTER key. Type** </HEAD> **and then press the ENTER key.**

The HTML tags display in the Notepad window (Figure 1-10). The text between the title tags will display when you view the Web page using a browser. The </TITLE> *tag indicates the title is complete and the* </HEAD> *tag indicates the headings are complete.*

```
<HTML>
<HEAD>
<TITLE>Chiaravalle Pizza Home Page</TITLE>
</HEAD>
```


FIGURE 1-10

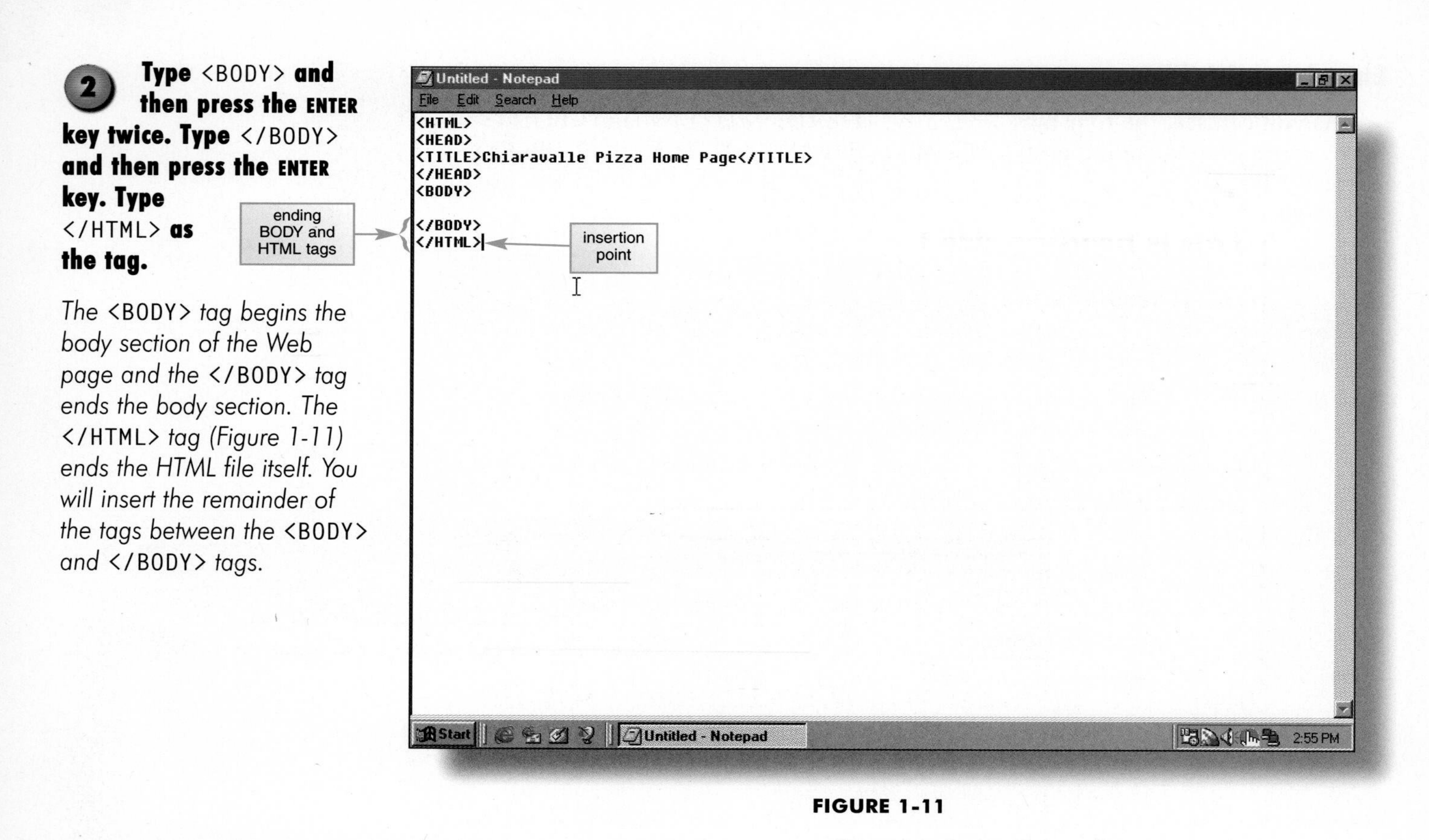
Untitled - Notepad
File Edit Search Help
<HTML>
<HEAD>
<TITLE>Chiaravalle Pizza Home Page</TITLE>
</HEAD>
<BODY>
</BODY>
</HTML>
ending BODY and HTML tags
insertion point
Start
Untitled - Notepad
2:55 PM

2 **Type** <BODY> **and then press the ENTER key twice. Type** </BODY> **and then press the ENTER key. Type** </HTML> **as the tag.**

The <BODY> *tag begins the body section of the Web page and the* </BODY> *tag ends the body section. The* </HTML> *tag (Figure 1-11) ends the HTML file itself. You will insert the remainder of the tags between the* <BODY> *and* </BODY> *tags.*

FIGURE 1-11

Correcting Errors

If you notice an error in the text, use the BACKSPACE key to erase all the characters back to and including the one that is incorrect and then continue typing.

More About

HTML Tags

Many Web developers use the popular programming language HTML. The World Wide Web has a number of excellent sources on HTML. For more information about HTML tags, visit the HTML More About page (www.scsite.com/html/more.htm) and click HTML Tags.

Entering Headings in an HTML File

Headings serve to separate text and introduce new topics on Web pages. The heading tags used for this purpose vary in size. The sizes range from <H1> through <H6>, with <H1> being the largest. Figure 1-12a shows a Web page displaying the various sizes of headings. One method of maintaining a consistent look to your Web site is to use the same sized heading for the same level of topic (Figure 1-12b). The following step explains how to enter the first heading for the Web page.

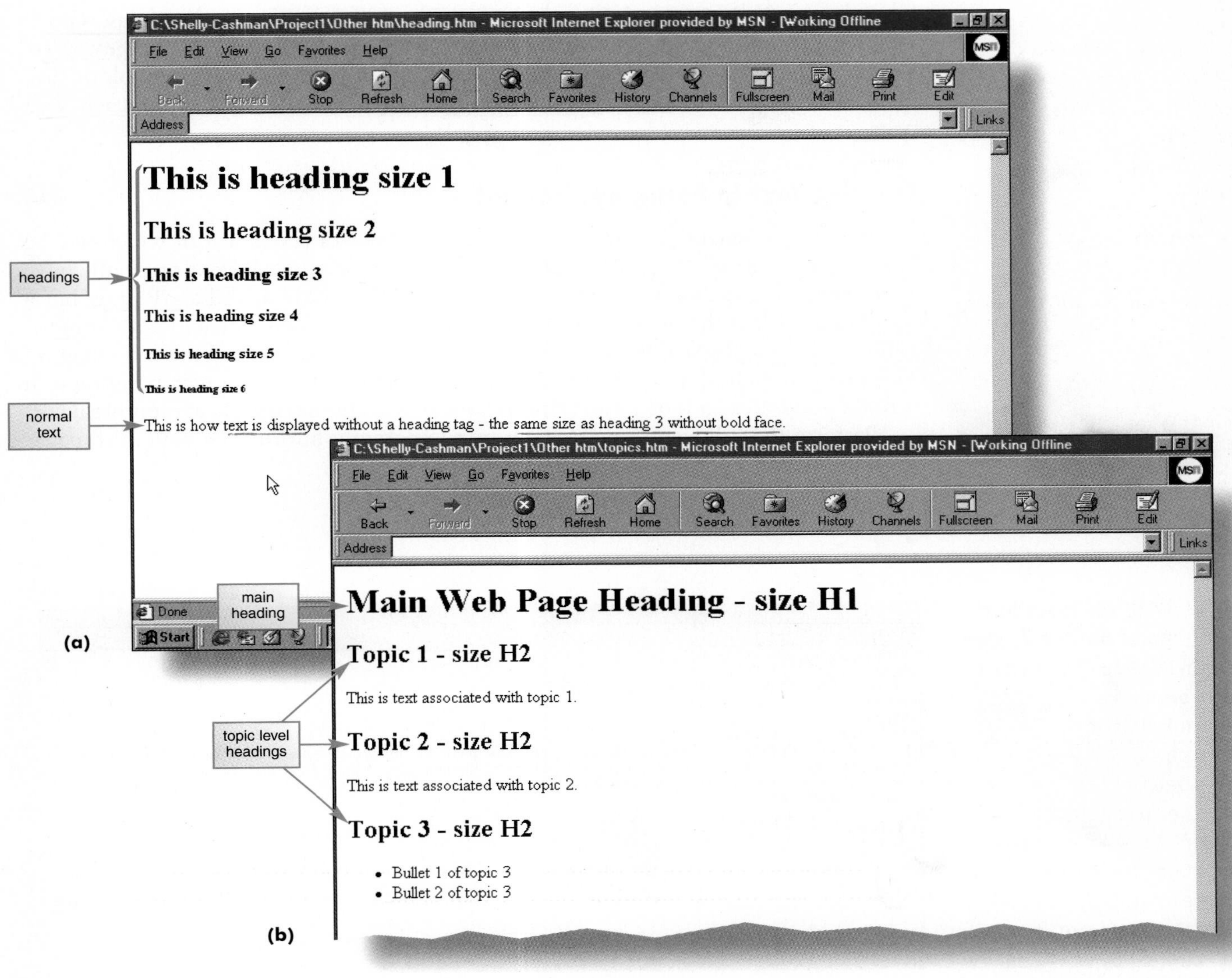

FIGURE 1-12

To Enter a Heading in the HTML File

1 **Click the blank line below <BODY>, type** `<H1>Chiaravalle Pizza</H1>` **and then press the ENTER key.**

The HTML code displays (Figure 1-13).

Untitled - Notepad

```
<HTML>
<HEAD>
<TITLE>Chiaravalle Pizza Home Page</TITLE>
</HEAD>
<BODY>
<H1>Chiaravalle Pizza</H1>

</BODY>
</HTML>
```

main heading

insertion point

FIGURE 1-13

As just stated, six sizes of heading tags are used when entering headings. The <H1> tag is used for the main heading on a Web page because it is the largest sized heading. The main heading may contain the name of the business or school, or the main idea of that Web page. You usually will have only one <H1> tag on each Web page.

Entering Text in Paragraph Format

Web pages generally contain a significant amount of text, most of which will be in paragraph format. The <P> tag is one of the few tags that did not originally have a corresponding ending tag. Newer versions of HTML have added a </P> tag, but it is optional. When the browser finds a <P> tag, it starts a new line and adds some additional vertical space between the line that it just displayed and the following line. This gives enough of a break in the text to indicate that there is a new paragraph. It is not a good idea to type large sections of text without having paragraph breaks.

Perform the following step to enter text in paragraph format in your Web page.

To Enter Text in Paragraph Format

1. With the insertion point on line 7, type `<P>Chiaravalle Pizza has been in business for the past 50 years. We specialize in unique pizzas and other Italian dishes. Located on Main Street, Chiaravalle Pizza is proud to be on the city's "Ten Best Restaurants" list for the past seven years. Call 1-219-555-2510 for reservations or orders today!</P>` **and then press the ENTER key (Figure 1-14).**

Untitled - Notepad

File Edit Search Help

```
<HTML>
<HEAD>
<TITLE>Chiaravalle Pizza Home Page</TITLE>
</HEAD>
<BODY>
<H1>Chiaravalle Pizza</H1>
<P>Chiaravalle Pizza has been in business for the past 50 years. We specialize in unique pizzas
and other Italian dishes. Located on Main Street, Chiaravalle Pizza is proud to be on the city's
"Ten Best Restaurants" list for the past seven years. Call 1-219-555-2510 for reservations or
orders today!</P>

</BODY>
</HTML>
```

line 7

paragraph tag and text

Start | Untitled - Notepad | 2:58 PM

FIGURE 1-14

Another tag that is used to break text is the <BR> tag. This tag breaks a line of text exactly at the point at which the <BR> displays. As soon as the browser encounters a <BR> tag, it starts a new line with the text that follows the tag. This tag will be used later in this book.

Creating a List

Sometimes it is easier to explain your point with text formatted as a list, instead of in paragraph format. **Lists** structure your text in an outline format, which helps itemize information. Lists can be of two types: unordered and ordered.

Unordered lists also are known as **bulleted lists**. They format information as bullet points. Figure 1-15 shows text that has been formatted in an unordered, or bulleted, list and the HTML code that was used for this Web page.

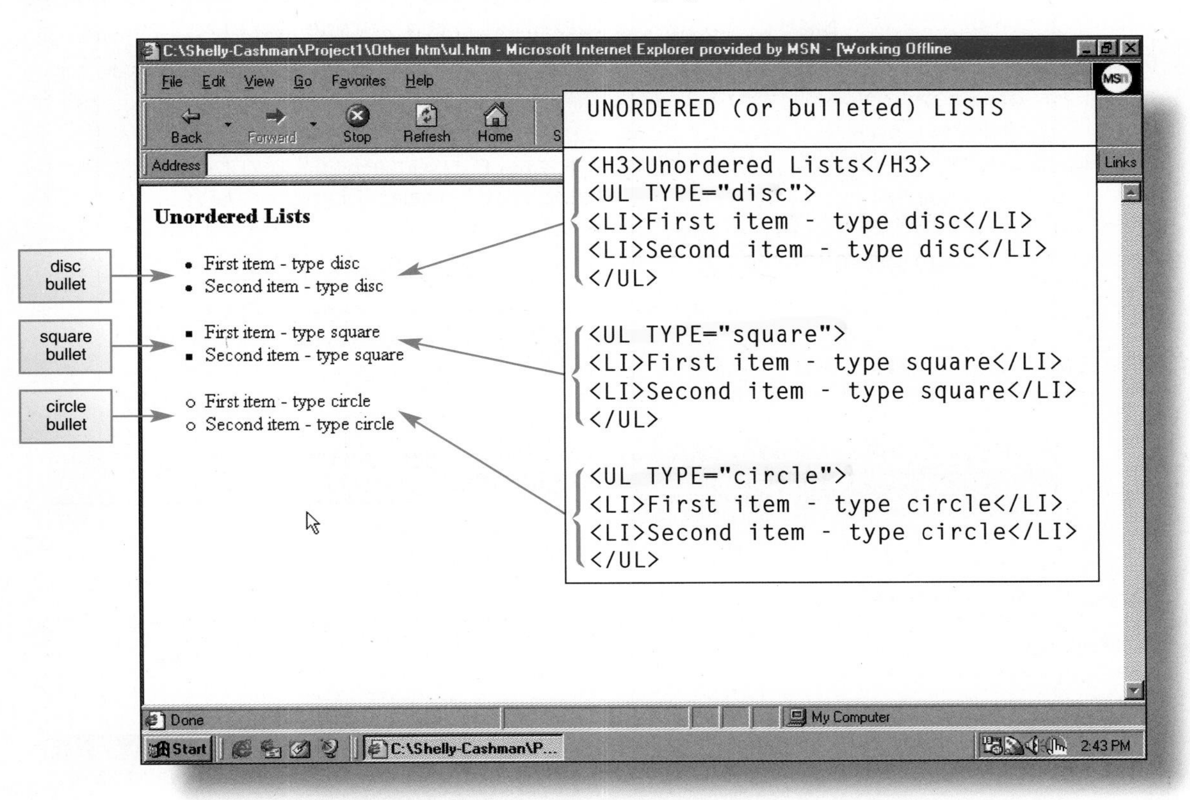

FIGURE 1-15

Ordered lists also are called **numbered lists**. The information in this type of list is shown as numbered or lettered points. Figure 1-16 on the next page shows a Web page formatted as an ordered, or numbered, list and the HTML tags and text used.

The <UL> and </UL> tags must be at the beginning and end of an unordered or bulleted list. The <OL> and </OL> tags are used at the beginning and end of an ordered or numbered list. Ordered and unordered lists have optional bullet and number types. You can create an ordered list using numbers, letters, or Roman numerals. The default option is to number the list. You also can select the type of bullet that you want in an unordered list. The bullet options for an unordered list are disc, square, or circle. If no type is identified, the default, disc, is used. The format of the tag without a type chosen is <UL> or <OL>. To change the default bullet or number type, you use the TYPE attribute within the <OL> or <UL> tags. The tag would be <UL TYPE=" "> or <OL TYPE=" "> where the selected type is found within the quotes.

The <LI> and </LI> tags define a list item within both ordered and unordered lists. After you have defined the type of list that you want (ordered or unordered), you then will precede each list item using the <LI> tag and end each list item with the </LI> tag. Each item in the list must have the <LI> tag in front of it and the </LI> tag at the end.

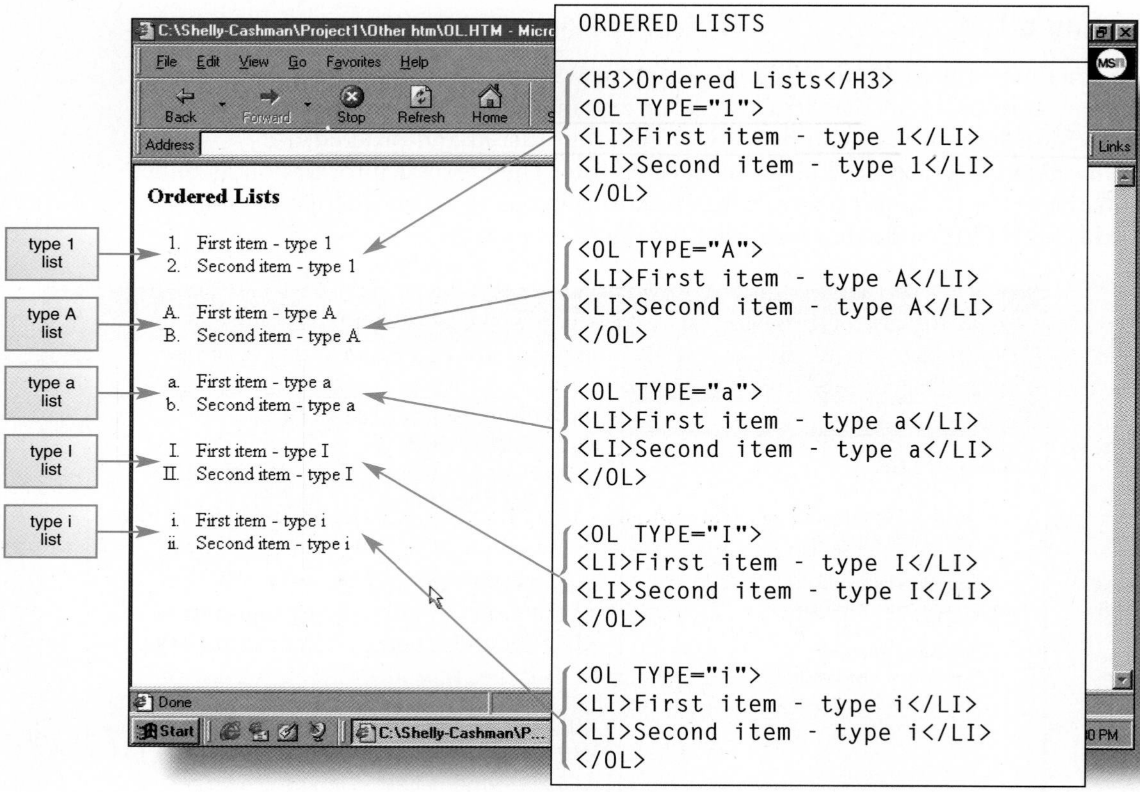
C:\Shelly-Cashman\Project1\Other htm\OL.HTM - Micro
File Edit View Go Favorites Help
Back Forward Stop Refresh Home
Address
Links
Ordered Lists
1. First item - type 1
2. Second item - type 1
A. First item - type A
B. Second item - type A
a. First item - type a
b. Second item - type a
I. First item - type I
II. Second item - type I
i. First item - type i
ii. Second item - type i
Done
Start
C:\Shelly-Cashman\P...
type 1 list
type A list
type a list
type I list
type i list
ORDERED LISTS
<H3>Ordered Lists</H3>
<OL TYPE="1">
<LI>First item - type 1</LI>
<LI>Second item - type 1</LI>
</OL>
<OL TYPE="A">
<LI>First item - type A</LI>
<LI>Second item - type A</LI>
</OL>
<OL TYPE="a">
<LI>First item - type a</LI>
<LI>Second item - type a</LI>
</OL>
<OL TYPE="I">
<LI>First item - type I</LI>
<LI>Second item - type I</LI>
</OL>
<OL TYPE="i">
<LI>First item - type i</LI>
<LI>Second item - type i</LI>
</OL>

FIGURE 1-16

Steps To Create a Bulleted List

1 **With the insertion point on line 11, type** <H2>Our services include:</H2> **and then press the ENTER key.**

2 **Type** <UL> **and then press the ENTER key. Type** <LI>A 100 seating capacity restaurant</LI> **and then press the ENTER key. Type** <LI>Take out orders</LI> **and then press the ENTER key. Type** <LI>Delivery services at no charge</LI> **and then press the ENTER key. Type** </UL> **as the tag.**

The HTML code displays in Notepad (Figure 1-17).

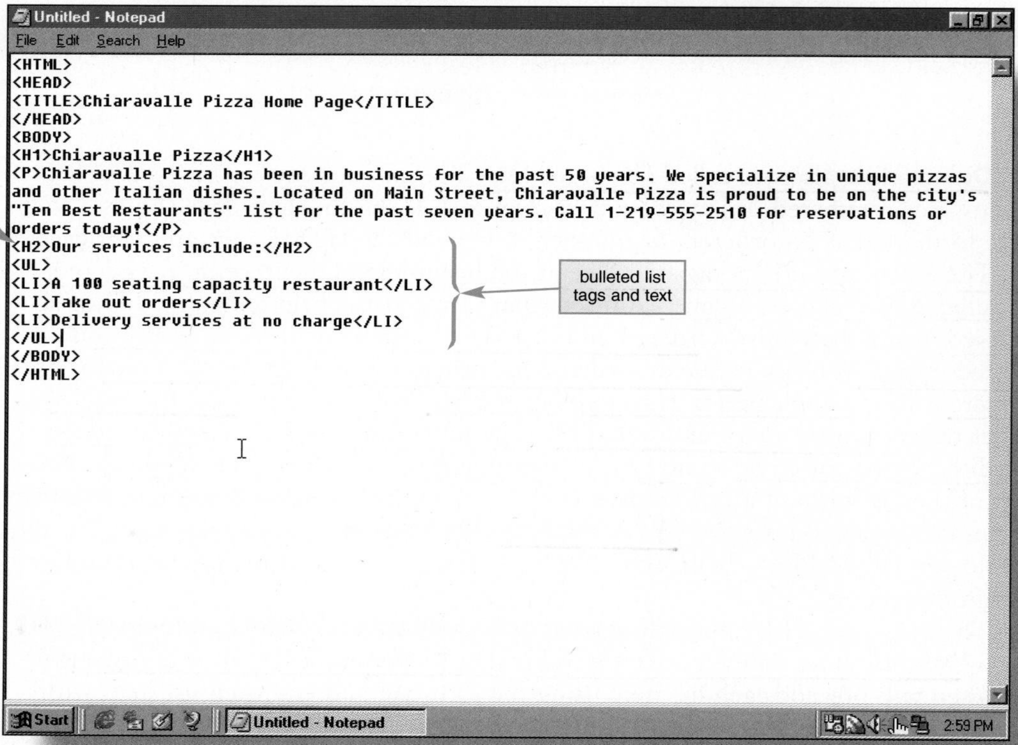
line 11
Untitled - Notepad
File Edit Search Help
<HTML>
<HEAD>
<TITLE>Chiaravalle Pizza Home Page</TITLE>
</HEAD>
<BODY>
<H1>Chiaravalle Pizza</H1>
<P>Chiaravalle Pizza has been in business for the past 50 years. We specialize in unique pizzas
and other Italian dishes. Located on Main Street, Chiaravalle Pizza is proud to be on the city's
"Ten Best Restaurants" list for the past seven years. Call 1-219-555-2510 for reservations or
orders today!</P>
<H2>Our services include:</H2>
<UL>
<LI>A 100 seating capacity restaurant</LI>
<LI>Take out orders</LI>
<LI>Delivery services at no charge</LI>
</UL>
</BODY>
</HTML>
bulleted list tags and text
Start
Untitled - Notepad
2:59 PM

FIGURE 1-17

Unordered (bulleted) and ordered (numbered) lists give a different look to text on a Web page. Lists are useful for information that is not suited to paragraph format. If you have a list of steps or items, it is appropriate to use a bulleted list as created in the previous steps or to use an ordered list as shown in Figure 1-16.

Saving the HTML File

You now will view the Web page in your browser to see what the Web page looks like up to this point. It is a good idea to view the Web page periodically as you develop it so you can see the effect of the HTML tags on the text. If you continue developing without ever viewing the page, you could be using tags that do not give the desired effect. In order to view your Web page in your browser, you first must save the HTML file.

Saving the HTML file is necessary so the corresponding Web page can be displayed using a browser. HTML files must end with an extension of .htm or .html. HTML files with an extension of .html can be viewed on Web servers running an operating system that allows long file names. Web servers with Windows 98, Windows 95, Windows NT, or Macintosh operating systems all allow long file names. For Web servers that run an operating system that does not accept long file names, you need the .htm extension. For the projects in this book, you will always use the .htm extension. Perform the following steps to save the HTML file.

HTML File Names

HTML files that can be viewed in a browser are indicated by an extension of .html or .htm. Generally, the home page of a Web site is called index.html or index.htm. Many service providers default to this name when selecting the first page of a Web site to display.

Steps: To Save the HTML File

1 With a floppy disk in drive A, click File on the menu bar and then point to Save As (Figure 1-18).

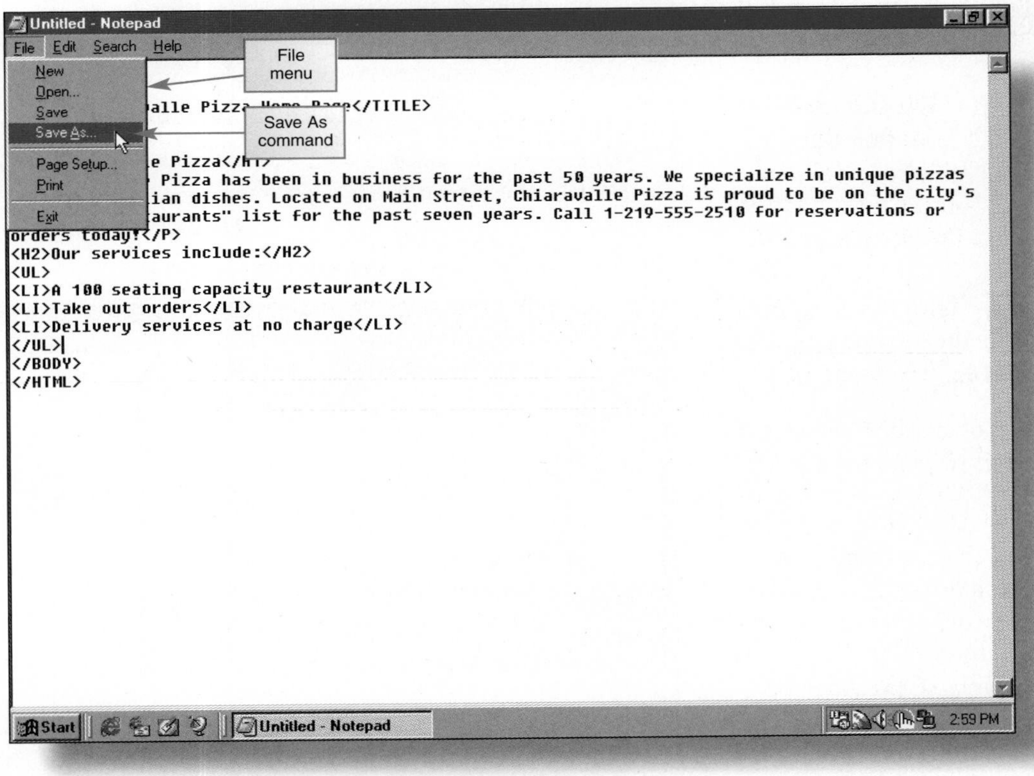

File menu

Save As command

FIGURE 1-18

2 **Click Save As.**

The Save As dialog box displays (Figure 1-19).

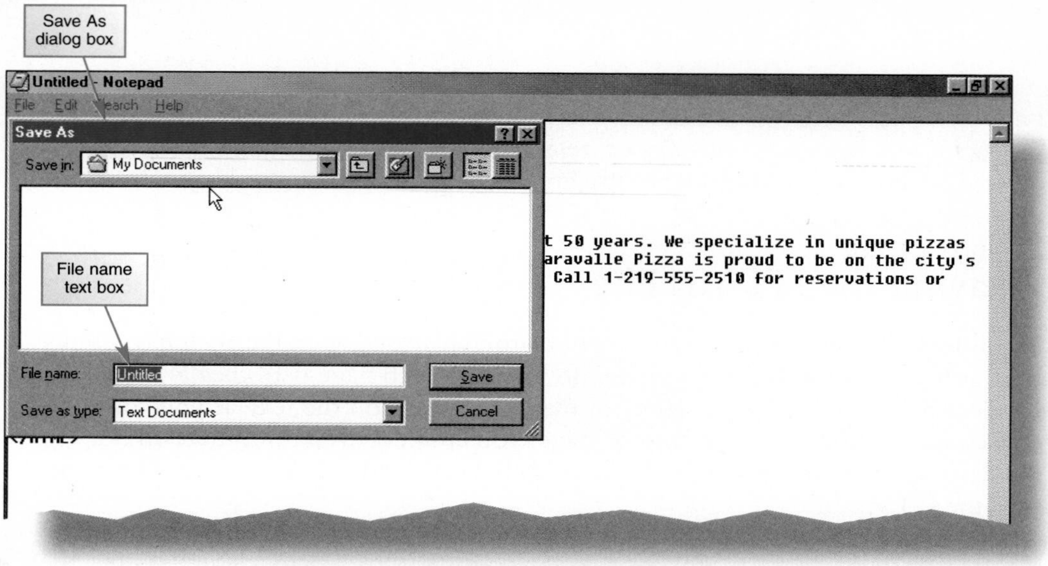

FIGURE 1-19

3 **Type** `page1.htm` **in the File name text box.**

The file name, page1.htm, replaces Untitled in the File name text box (Figure 1-20).

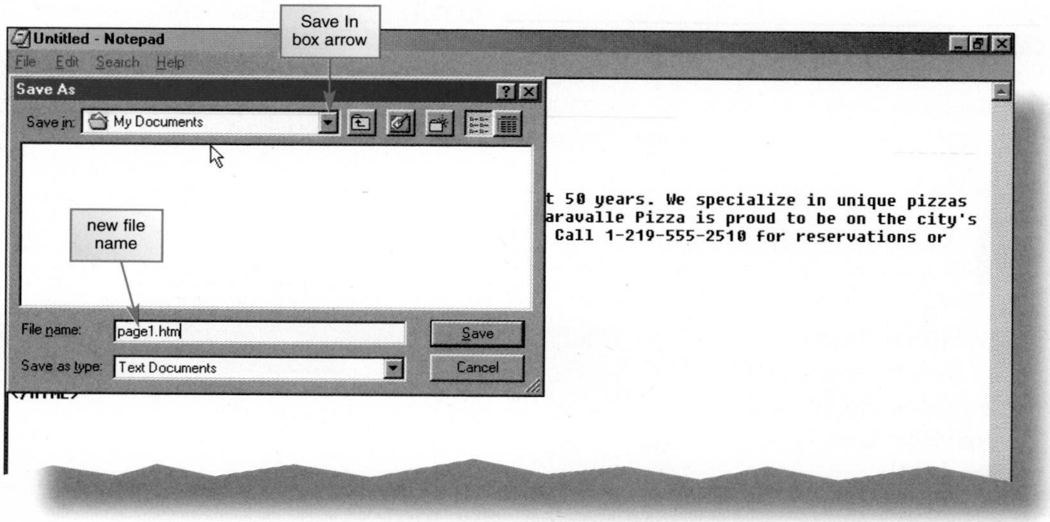

FIGURE 1-20

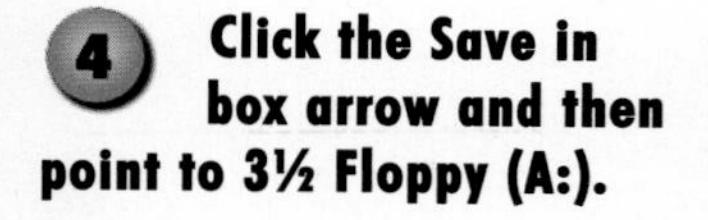

4 **Click the Save in box arrow and then point to 3½ Floppy (A:).**

A list of available drives and folders displays (Figure 1-21).

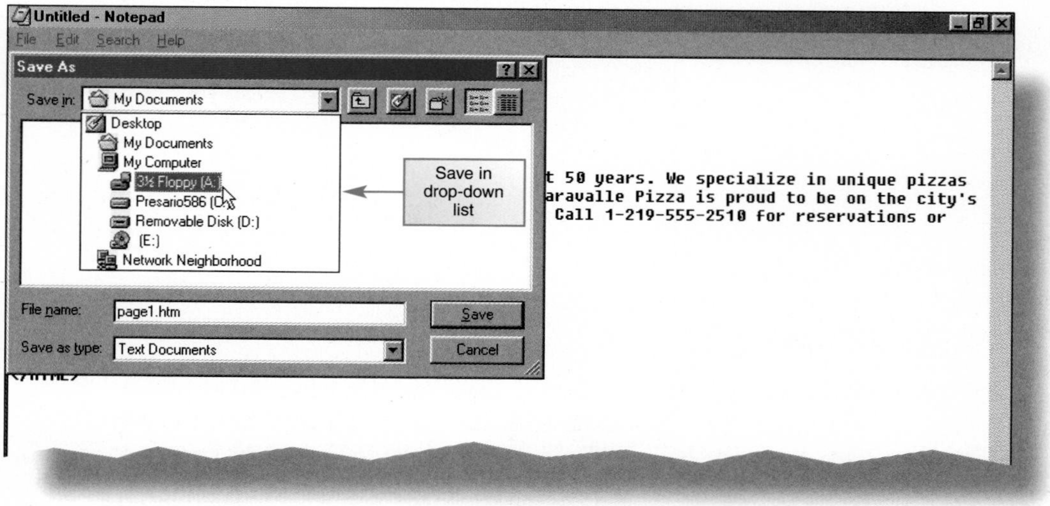

FIGURE 1-21

5 Click 3½ Floppy (A:) and then point to the Save button.

Drive A becomes the selected drive (Figure 1-22).

6 Click the Save button.

Notepad saves the HTML file on the floppy disk in drive A using the file name, page1.htm. After the save, page1.htm remains on the screen (Figure 1-23). The file name displays on the Notepad title bar.

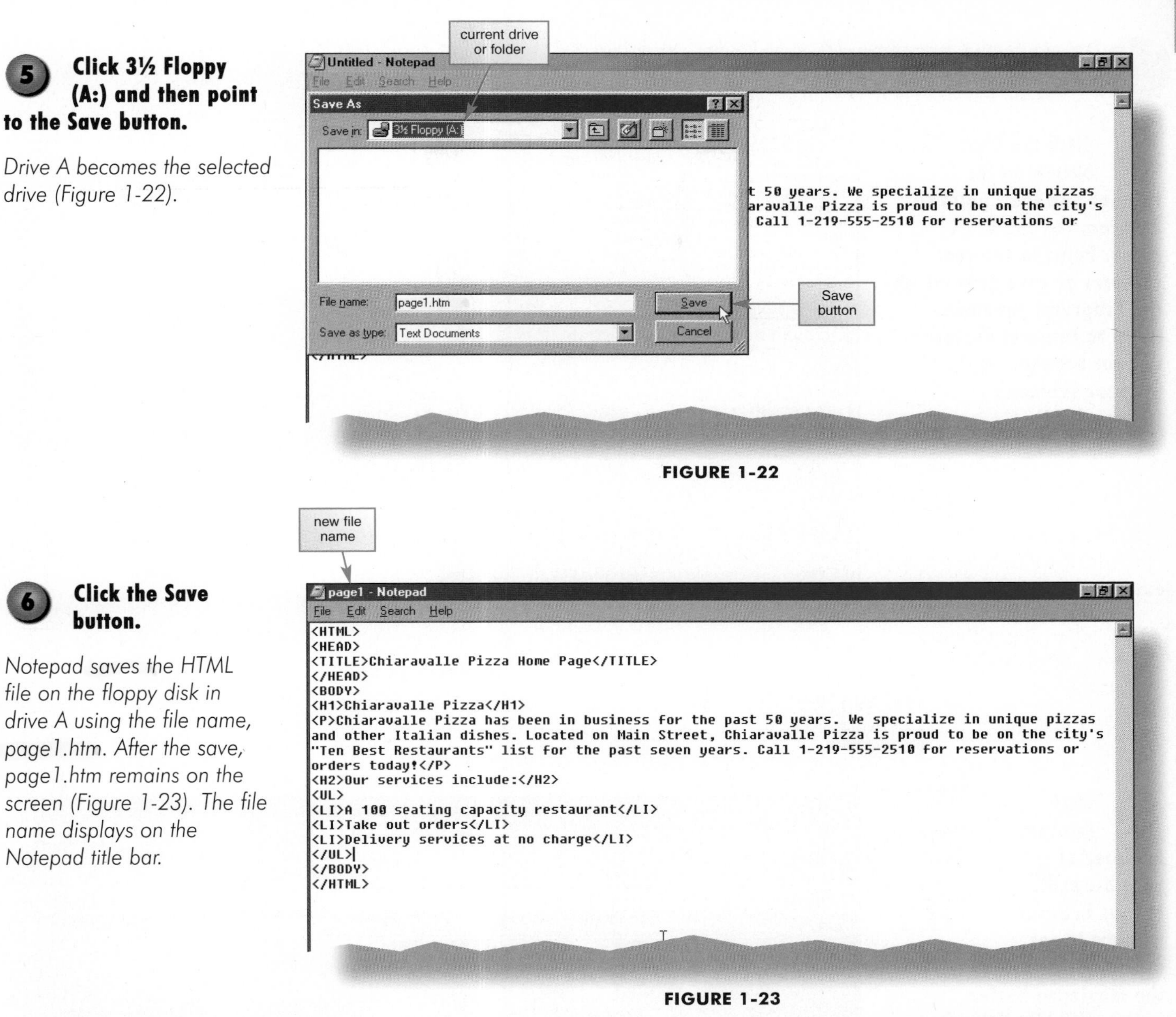

FIGURE 1-22

FIGURE 1-23

1. Press ALT+F, A

Using a Browser to View a Web Page

After you have saved the HTML file, you can use a browser to view your Web page. The HTML file displays in the browser just as it would if the file was published to the Web.

Starting Your Browser

An important feature of Windows is its capability of having one or more programs open at a time. With Notepad open for your Web page development, follow the steps on the next page to start your browser to view the corresponding Web page.

To Start Your Browser

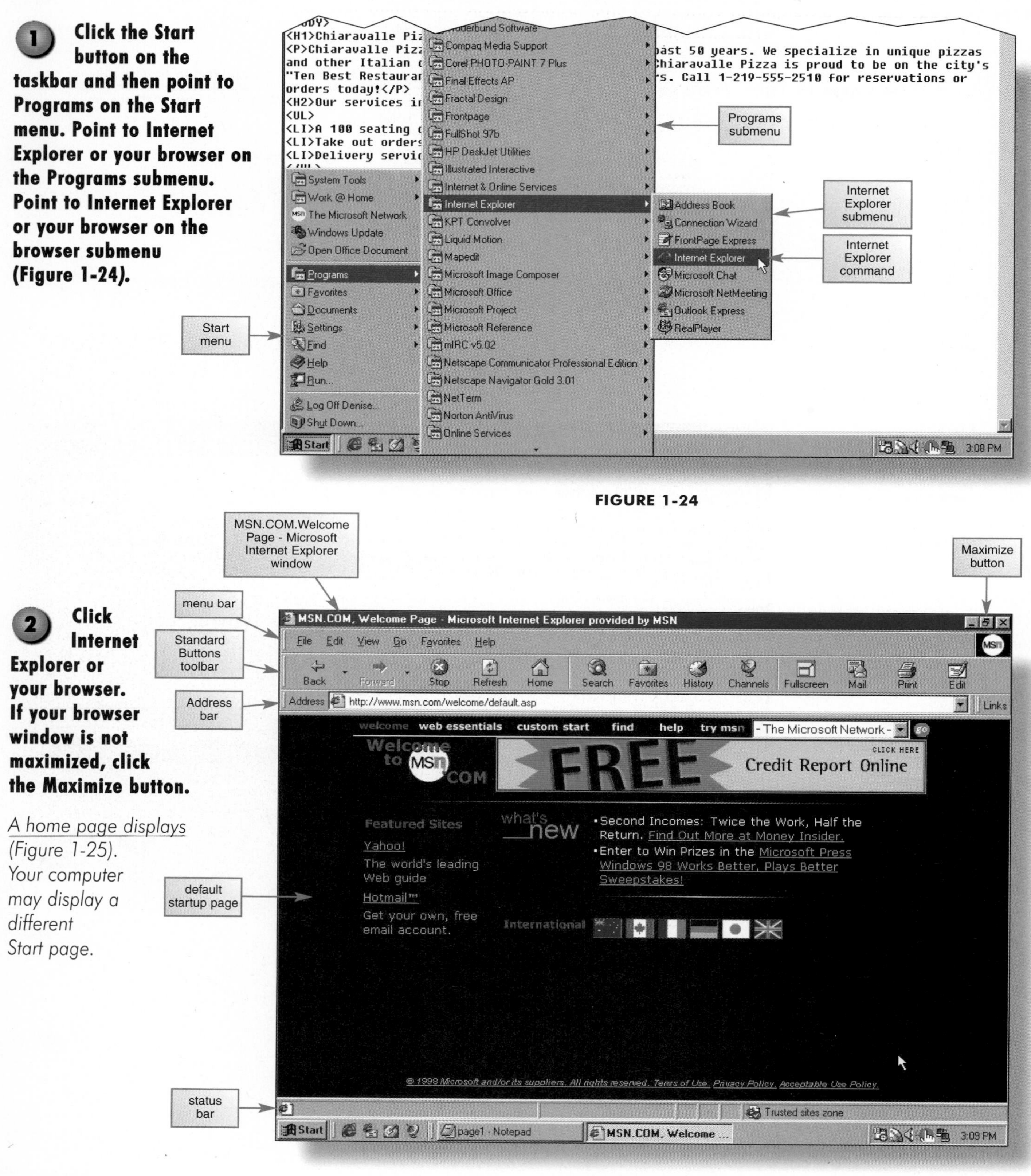

1 **Click the Start button on the taskbar and then point to Programs on the Start menu. Point to Internet Explorer or your browser on the Programs submenu. Point to Internet Explorer or your browser on the browser submenu (Figure 1-24).**

FIGURE 1-24

2 **Click Internet Explorer or your browser. If your browser window is not maximized, click the Maximize button.**

A home page displays (Figure 1-25). Your computer may display a different Start page.

FIGURE 1-25

Normally, when your browser starts, your computer is connected to a computer at the browser site. Because it is possible to change the page that displays, the initial page may be different on your computer. Some schools and organizations display their own home pages. The title of the Web page displays on the title bar.

Opening a Web Page in Your Browser

A browser allows you to open a file located on your PC and have full browsing capabilities. It gives you the same look and feel as if you actually had published your Web pages to a Web server on the Internet. This is the technique you will use to view the HTML file, page1.htm.

Steps To Open a Web Page in Your Browser

1 Click the Address bar.

The current URL is highlighted in the Address bar (Figure 1-26).

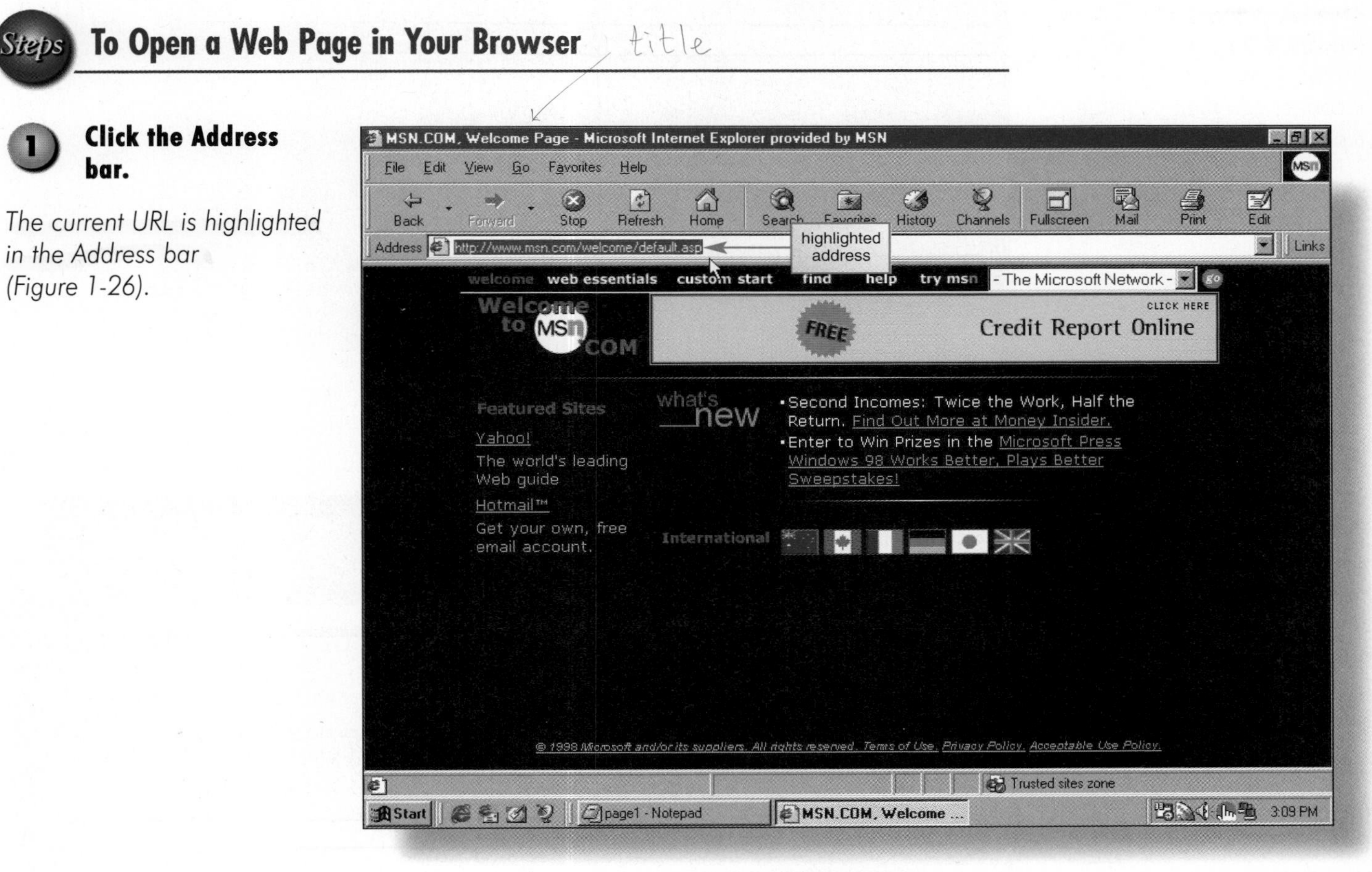

FIGURE 1-26

2 **Type** `a:\page1.htm` **in the Address text box.**

The new URL displays in the Address text box (Figure 1-27). If you type an incorrect letter or symbol in the Address text box and notice the error before you move on to the next step, you can use the BACKSPACE *key to erase all the characters back to and including the one that is incorrect and then continue typing.*

3 **Press the** ENTER **key.**

The browser displays the Web page, page1.htm (Figure 1-28).

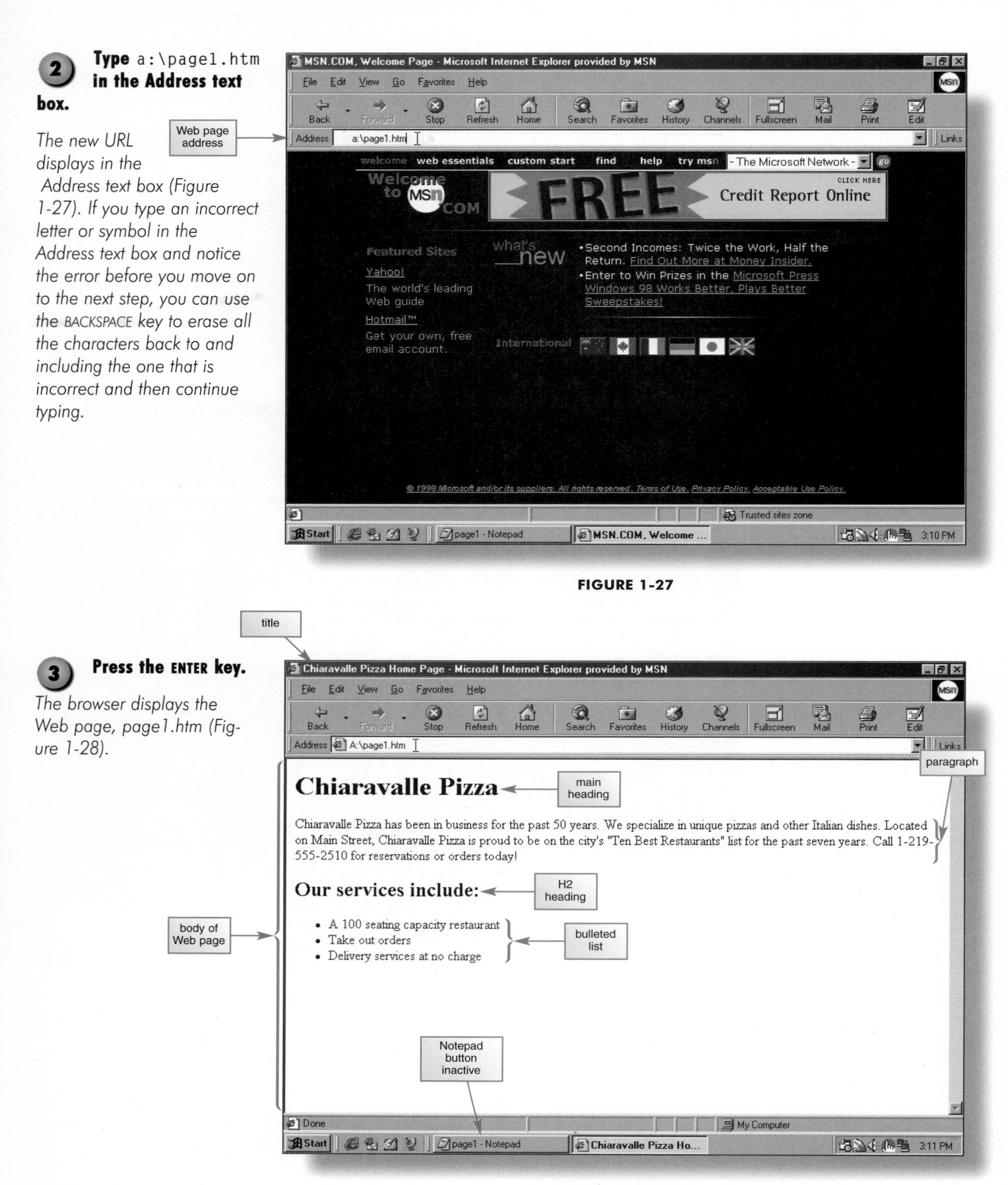

FIGURE 1-28

The Web page displays as it would if it had been published to the Web. Viewing your Web pages periodically during development will ensure that the Web pages will display in the manner you intend. It is interesting to compare your Web page as displayed in the browser to the HTML file in Notepad. The title bar, for example, displays Chiaravalle Pizza Home Page, which is the title that you entered on line three. The file name, page1.htm, displays in the Address text box showing the location of the file as well as its name.

All the information contained between the <BODY> and </BODY> tags now displays in the browser window. This is the body of the Web page. The heading, Chiaravalle Pizza, is larger because you tagged it as <H1>, whereas the heading, Our services include:, was tagged as <H2> and therefore is smaller. Your paragraph of text displays in the normal font size because you did not specify otherwise. You did not specify the type of bullet that you wanted in the bulleted list, so the default was used.

Activating Notepad

Next, you will modify your Web page by adding additional HTML tags. To continue editing, you first must return to Notepad. Perform the following step to return to Notepad.

TO ACTIVATE NOTEPAD

1. Click the Notepad button on the taskbar.

The maximized Notepad window becomes the active window (Figure 1-29).

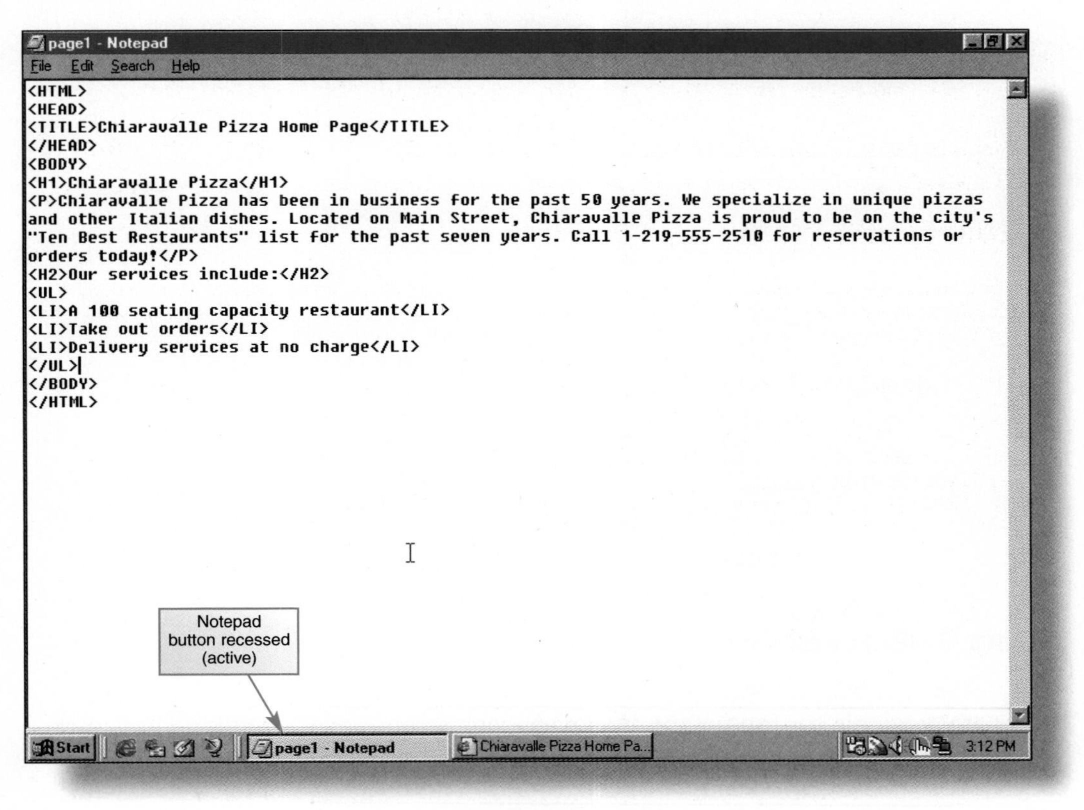

FIGURE 1-29

Improving the Appearance of Your Web Page

One goal in Web page development is to maintain the interest of the visitors. The Web page that you just developed is functional. You now will add some elements to the Web page that make it more interesting. In the next steps, you will modify your Web page from the one shown in Figure 1-30a to the one shown in Figure 1-30b by adding background color, text formatting, and a horizontal rule.

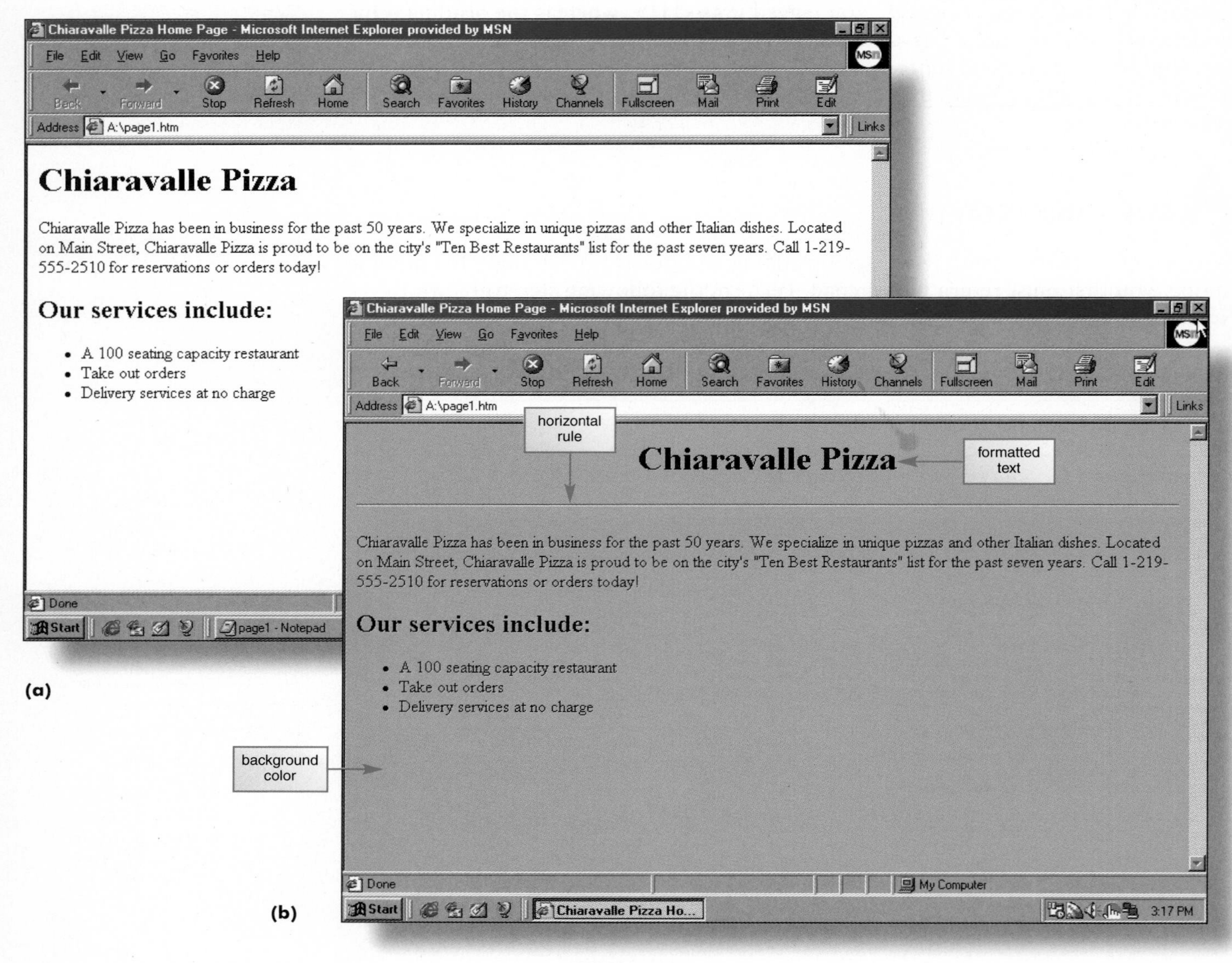

FIGURE 1-30

Adding Background Color

One way to help capture a Web page visitor's attention is to use color. Many colors are available for use for the Web page background, text, or links. The more common of those are shown in Table 1-2 with their corresponding six-digit number codes. These codes can be used for background, text, or links. In this project you will use a light blue color (#94D6E7) for the background of your Web page.

Table 1-2

COLORS IN HEX

Here is a table of common colors with their hexadecimal equivalents. Use the codes to define the desired color for the background, text, or links.

#FFC6A5	#FF9473	#FF6342	#FF3118	#FF0000	#D60000	#AD0000	#840000	#630000
#FFE7C6	#FFCE9C	#FFB573	#FF9C4A	#FF8429	#D66321	#AD4A18	#844D18	#632910
#FFFFC6	#FFFF9C	#FFFF6B	#FFFF42	#FFFF10	#D6C610	#AD9410	#847308	#635208
#F7FFCE	#EFEFAD	#E7F784	#DEF763	#D6EF39	#B5BD31	#8C9429	#6B6B21	#524A18
#DE93BD	#C6EF8C	#ADDE63	#94D639	#7BC618	#639C18	#527B10	#425A10	#314208
#CEEFBD	#A5DE94	#7BC66B	#52B552	#299C39	#218429	#186321	#184A18	#103910
#C6E7DE	#94D6CE	#63BDB5	#31ADA5	#089494	#087B7B	#006363	#004A4A	#003139
#C6EFF7	#94D6E7	#63C6DE	#31B5D6	#00A5C6	#0084A5	#006B84	#005263	#00394A
#BDC6DE	#949CCE	#6373B5	#3152A5	#083194	#082984	#08296B	#08215A	#00184A
#C6B5DE	#9C7BBD	#7B52A5	#522994	#31007B	#29006B	#21005A	#21004A	#180042
#DEBDDE	#CE84C6	#B552AD	#9C2994	#8C007B	#730063	#5A0052	#4A0042	#390031
#F7BDDE	#E78CC6	#DE5AAD	#D63194	#CE007B	#A50063	#840052	#6B0042	#520031
#FFFFFF	#E0E0E0	#BFBFBF	#A1A1A1	#808080	#616161	#404040	#212121	#000000

THE SIXTEEN PREDEFINED COLORS

(Because these colors belong to the RGB spectrum, they will look a bit different on screen.)

Silver	Gray	Maroon	Green	Navy	Purple	Olive	Teal
White	Black	Red	Lime	Blue	Magenta	Yellow	Cyan

To change the background color on a Web page, use BGCOLOR in the <BODY> tag. The **BGCOLOR** attribute lets you change the background color of the Web page. The following steps show how to add a colored background.

More About

Colors

All possible Web page colors are not listed in this table. There are many other colors that you can use for Web page backgrounds or text fonts. For more information about colors, visit the HTML More About page (http://www.scsite.com/html/more.htm) and click Colors.

Color Choices

You can use a numbered code or a color name as a background color choice. Table 1-2 lists several predefined color names that can be used for background or font colors. The HTML tag BACKGROUND="NAVY" uses one of the predefined color choices.

Steps To Add a Background Color

1 **Click after the Y in <BODY> on line 5 and then press the SPACEBAR.**

2 **Type** BGCOLOR=#94D6E7 **as the color code.**

The HTML code displays (Figure 1-31).

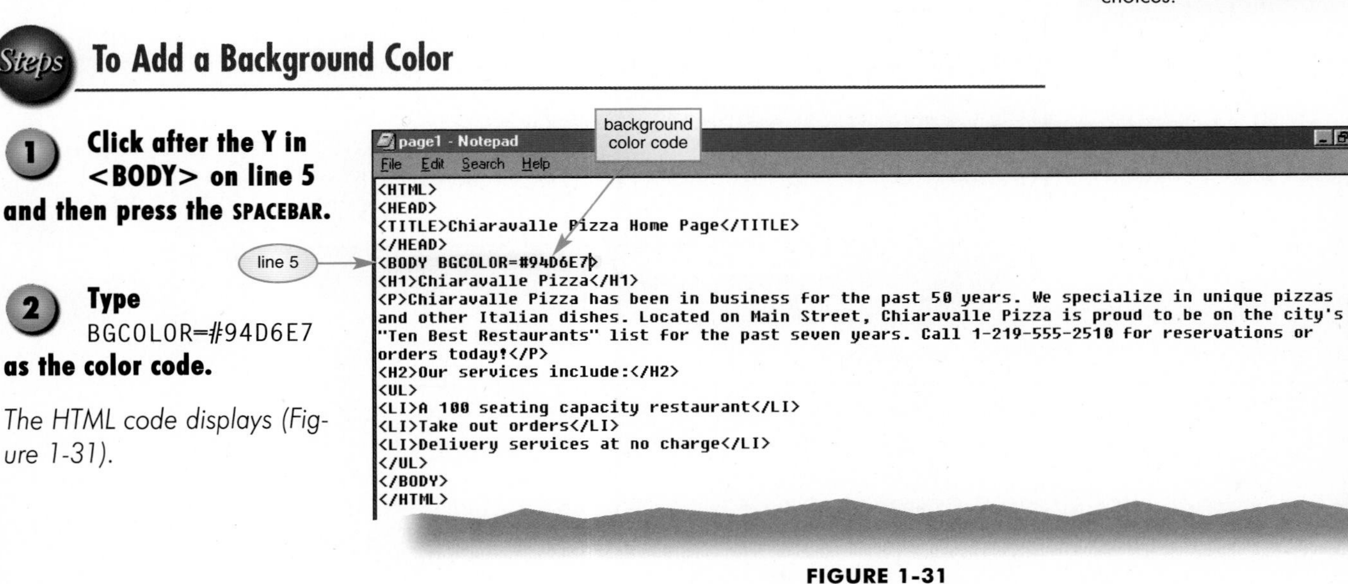

FIGURE 1-31

The color codes shown in Table 1-2 on page HTM 1.29 can be used for backgrounds, text, and link colors. For backgrounds, you used the BGCOLOR attribute as the keyword in the <BODY> tag. In later projects, you will use the TEXT and LINK attributes in the <BODY> tag to change colors for those elements.

Centering the Heading

Headings are used to separate new sections of text from each other. A main heading is used to indicate the beginning of the Web page. Generally, you use the Heading 1 style as the main heading. The heading, Chiaravalle Pizza, is the main heading and indicates the beginning of the Web page. You can highlight the beginning of the Web page further by aligning the text differently on the page. You can specify left-, right-, or center-alignment with the statements ALIGN="LEFT", ALIGN="RIGHT", or ALIGN="CENTER" in the heading tag. The default for headings is left-alignment. Because you did not specify an alignment, your heading was left-aligned. In the following steps, you will center-align the heading.

Steps To Center a Heading

1 **Click line 6 just after the 1 in the <H1> tag and then press the SPACEBAR.**

2 **Type** ALIGN="CENTER" **as the attribute.**

The insertion point is positioned before the > symbol (Figure 1-32).

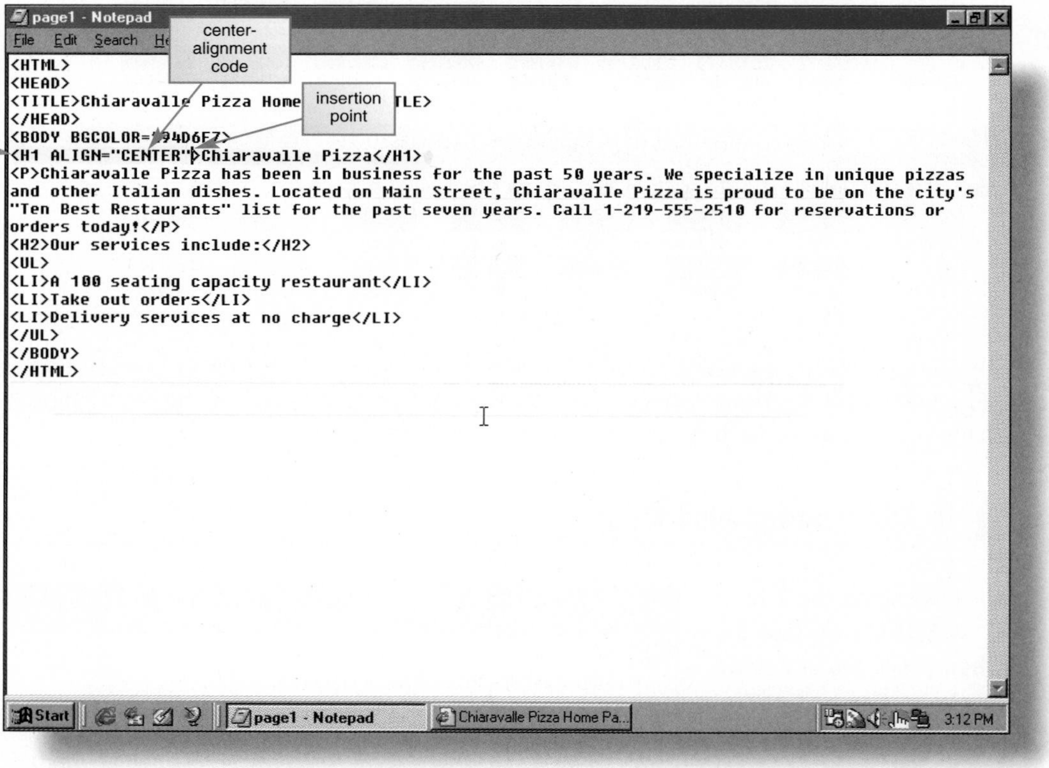

```
<HTML>
<HEAD>
<TITLE>Chiaravalle Pizza Home Page</TITLE>
</HEAD>
<BODY BGCOLOR=#94D6E7>
<H1 ALIGN="CENTER">Chiaravalle Pizza</H1>
<P>Chiaravalle Pizza has been in business for the past 50 years. We specialize in unique pizzas
and other Italian dishes. Located on Main Street, Chiaravalle Pizza is proud to be on the city's
"Ten Best Restaurants" list for the past seven years. Call 1-219-555-2510 for reservations or
orders today!</P>
<H2>Our services include:</H2>
<UL>
<LI>A 100 seating capacity restaurant</LI>
<LI>Take out orders</LI>
<LI>Delivery services at no charge</LI>
</UL>
</BODY>
</HTML>
```

center-alignment code

insertion point

line 6

FIGURE 1-32

Adding a Horizontal Rule

Horizontal rules are graphical images that act as dividers in a Web page. They give a visual separation of sections on the page. The HTML tag used to insert a horizontal rule is **<HR>**. Figure 1-33 shows the variety of horizontal rules available. The default horizontal rule is shown in the first line of the page. Dimension is added by increasing the number of pixels that will display. Another possibility is to turn the shading off using the NOSHADE option. The HTML tags used to create the HR sample page are shown in Figure 1-33.

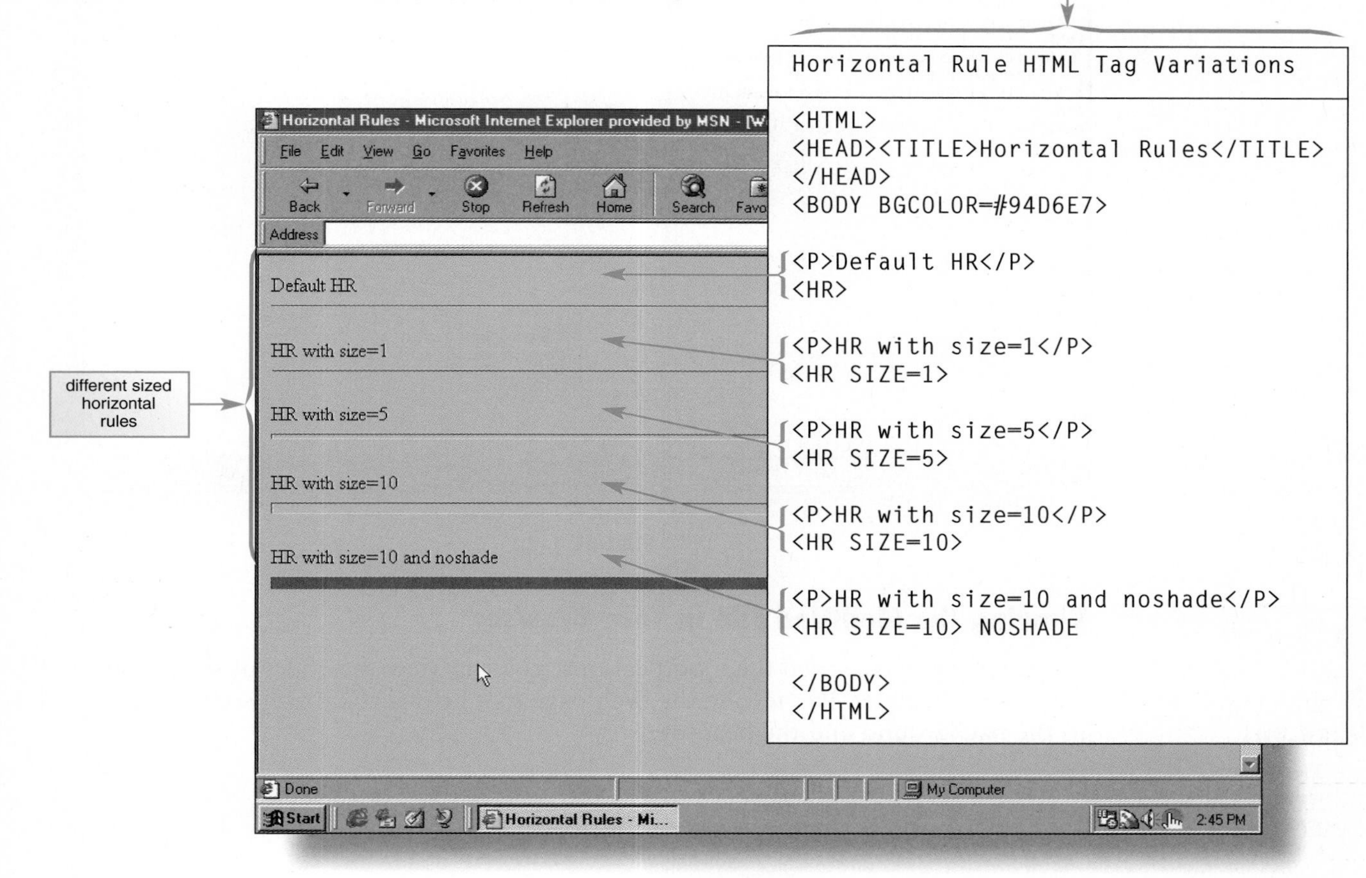

FIGURE 1-33

Horizontal rules are easy to insert. Perform the following steps to insert a horizontal rule.

TO INSERT A HORIZONTAL RULE

1. Click line 7 just before the < symbol in <P> and then press the ENTER key.
2. Position the insertion point on the blank line above <P>. Type <HR> as the HTML tag.
3. Click File on the menu bar and then click Save.

The page1 – Notepad window displays (Figure 1-34 on the next page).

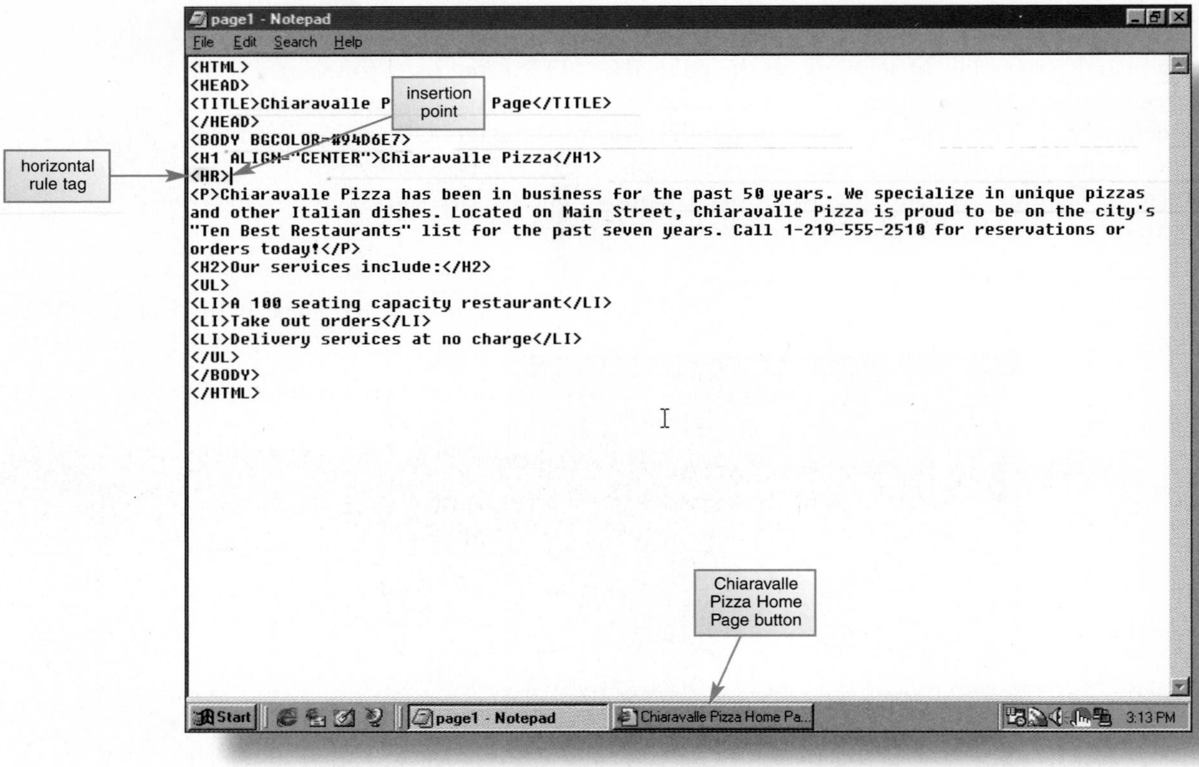
page1 - Notepad
File Edit Search Help
<HTML>
<HEAD>
<TITLE>Chiaravalle P Page</TITLE>
</HEAD>
<BODY BGCOLOR=#94D6E7>
<H1 ALIGN="CENTER">Chiaravalle Pizza</H1>
<HR>
<P>Chiaravalle Pizza has been in business for the past 50 years. We specialize in unique pizzas and other Italian dishes. Located on Main Street, Chiaravalle Pizza is proud to be on the city's "Ten Best Restaurants" list for the past seven years. Call 1-219-555-2510 for reservations or orders today!</P>
<H2>Our services include:</H2>
<UL>
<LI>A 100 seating capacity restaurant</LI>
<LI>Take out orders</LI>
<LI>Delivery services at no charge</LI>
</UL>
</BODY>
</HTML>
insertion point
horizontal rule tag
Chiaravalle Pizza Home Page button
Start
page1 - Notepad
Chiaravalle Pizza Home Pa...
3:13 PM

FIGURE 1-34

Viewing the Modified File in Your Browser

After you have saved the modifications, you can view the effect of the changes using your browser. By viewing the Web page in a browser you will see the changes to the background and the heading.

More About

Web Page Improvement

Web page development is an ongoing process. In Web page development, you create a Web page, view it in your browser, and then look for ways to improve the appearance of the page. For more information about Web page improvement, visit the HTML More About page (www.scsite.com/html/more.htm) and click Web Page Improvement.

Steps To Refresh the View in Your Browser

1. **Click the Chiaravalle Pizza Home Page button on the taskbar.**

2. **Click the Refresh button on the Standard Buttons toolbar.**

The latest version of page1.htm displays (Figure 1-35).

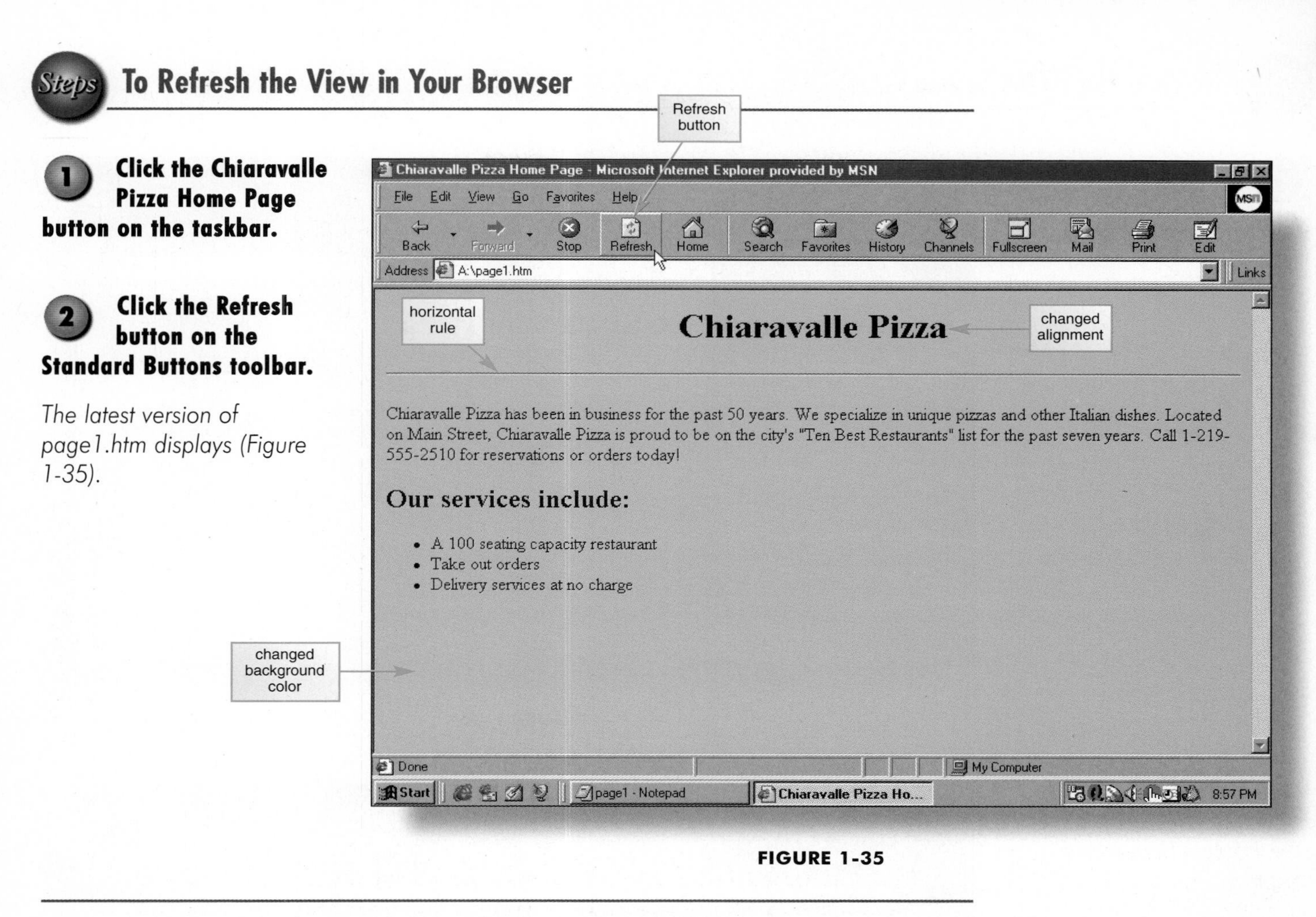

FIGURE 1-35

You can recall that Windows is a multitasking operating system. As such, you can have Notepad and your browser open at the same time. You can continue developing the HTML file in Notepad and viewing it in your browser by clicking the appropriate button on the taskbar, moving from one software package to another.

Viewing Your Web Page Source

You can view the HTML code on any Web page from within your browser. This feature allows you to see how other developers created their Web pages.

You might want to do this for a number of reasons. If a feature on a Web page is appropriate or appealing, you can view the source and then copy sections of the HTML code to put in your own Web pages. One reason Web development has become so popular is because developers can do this.

To View the HTML Source

1 Click View on the menu bar and then point to Source (Figure 1-36).

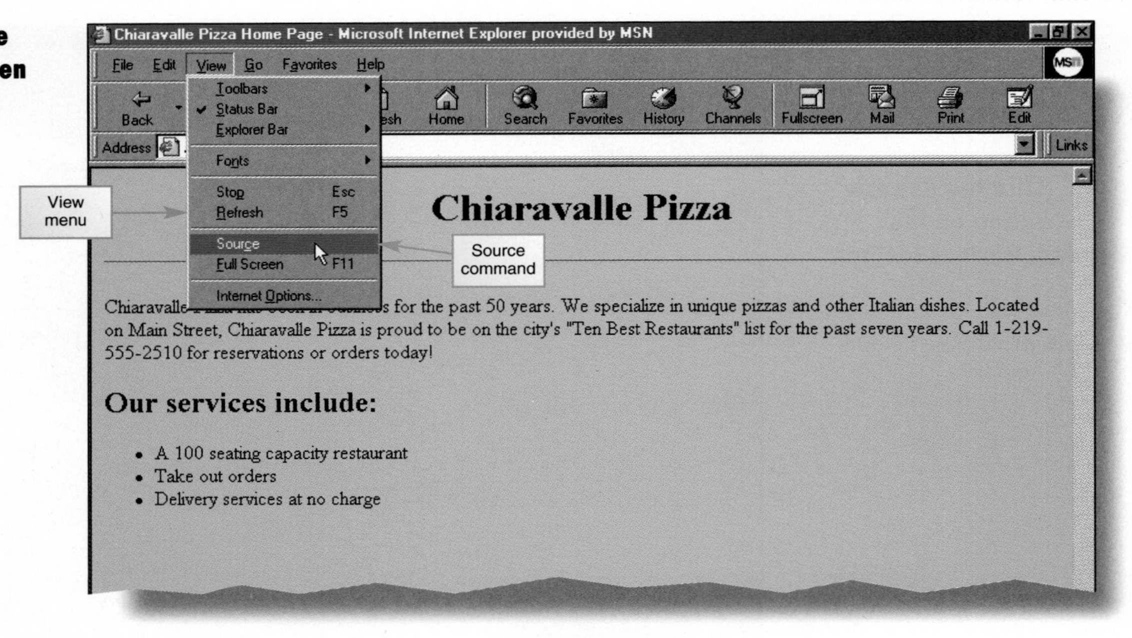

FIGURE 1-36

2 Click Source.

The HTML source code displays (Figure 1-37).

3 Click the Close button.

The Notepad window closes.

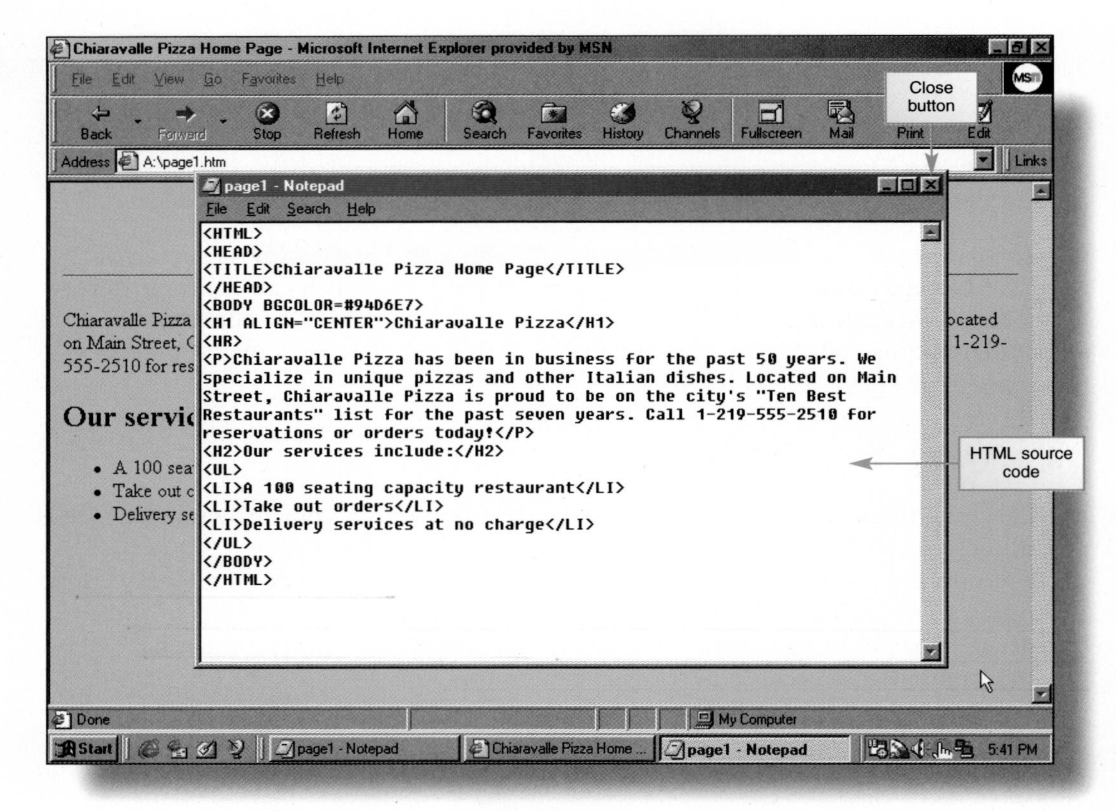

FIGURE 1-37

The HTML source code opens in the default text editor program when you view the source. Because Notepad was open, clicking View and then Source opened a second Notepad window.

Printing a Copy

After you have created the HTML file and saved it, you might want to print it. A printed version of the file is called a **hard copy** or **printout**.

Printouts are used for several reasons. First, to present the file to someone who does not have computer access, it must be in printed form. A printout, for example, can be handed out in a meeting at which you are discussing sample Web pages. In addition, persons other than those who prepare them often keep printed copies of HTML files and Web pages for reference. In many cases, HTML files and Web pages are printed and kept in binders for use by others. This section describes how to print an HTML file and its corresponding Web page.

To Print the Web Page and HTML File

1 Ready the printer according to the printer instructions. With the page1.htm Web page displaying in your browser window, click File on the menu bar and then click Print. Click the OK button in the Print dialog box.

2 When the printer stops printing the Web page, retrieve the printout (Figure 1-38).

Chiaravalle Pizza

Chiaravalle Pizza has been in business for the past 50 years. We specialize in unique pizzas and other Italian dishes. Located on Main Street, Chiaravalle Pizza is proud to be on the city's "Ten Best Restaurants" list for the past seven years. Call 1-219-555-2510 for reservations or orders today!

Our services include:

- A 100 seating capacity restaurant
- Take out orders
- Delivery services at no charge

FIGURE 1-38

3 **Click the Notepad button on the taskbar to activate the Notepad window.**

4 **Click File on the menu bar and then click Print.**

Notepad prints the HTML file (Figure 1-39).

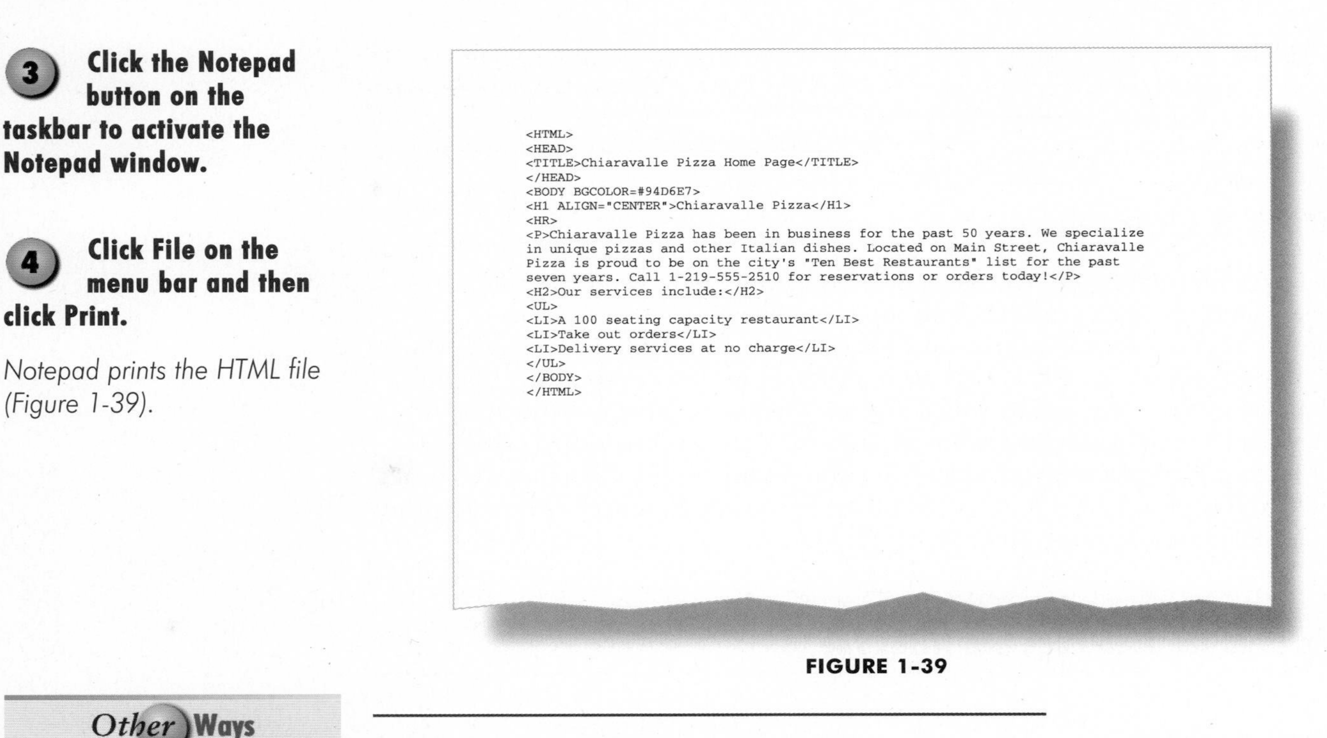

```
<HTML>
<HEAD>
<TITLE>Chiaravalle Pizza Home Page</TITLE>
</HEAD>
<BODY BGCOLOR=#94D6E7>
<H1 ALIGN="CENTER">Chiaravalle Pizza</H1>
<HR>
<P>Chiaravalle Pizza has been in business for the past 50 years. We specialize
in unique pizzas and other Italian dishes. Located on Main Street, Chiaravalle
Pizza is proud to be on the city's "Ten Best Restaurants" list for the past
seven years. Call 1-219-555-2510 for reservations or orders today!</P>
<H2>Our services include:</H2>
<UL>
<LI>A 100 seating capacity restaurant</LI>
<LI>Take out orders</LI>
<LI>Delivery services at no charge</LI>
</UL>
</BODY>
</HTML>
```

FIGURE 1-39

Other Ways

1. Press ALT+F, P

Having a printout of HTML code is an invaluable tool for beginning developers. A printed copy can help you immediately see the relationship between the HTML tags and the Web page that you view in the browser.

Quitting Notepad and Your Browser

The following steps show you how to quit Notepad and your browser.

Steps To Quit Notepad and Your Browser

1 **Point to the Close button on the Notepad title bar (Figure 1-40).**

Close button

page1 - Notepad

File Edit Search Help

```
<HTML>
<HEAD>
<TITLE>Chiaravalle Pizza Home Page</TITLE>
</HEAD>
<BODY BGCOLOR=#94D6E7>
<H1 ALIGN="CENTER">Chiaravalle Pizza</H1>
<HR>
<P>Chiaravalle Pizza has been in business for the past 50 years. We specialize in unique pizzas
and other Italian dishes. Located on Main Street, Chiaravalle Pizza is proud to be on the city's
"Ten Best Restaurants" list for the past seven years. Call 1-219-555-2510 for reservations or
orders today!</P>
<H2>Our services include:</H2>
<UL>
<LI>A 100 seating capacity restaurant</LI>
<LI>Take out orders</LI>
<LI>Delivery services at no charge</LI>
</UL>
</BODY>
</HTML>
```

FIGURE 1-40

2 **Click the Close button.**

The Notepad window closes and the Chiaravalle Pizza Home Page window displays (Figure 1-41).

3 **Click the Close button on the Chiaravalle Pizza Home Page title bar.**

The browser closes and the Windows desktop displays.

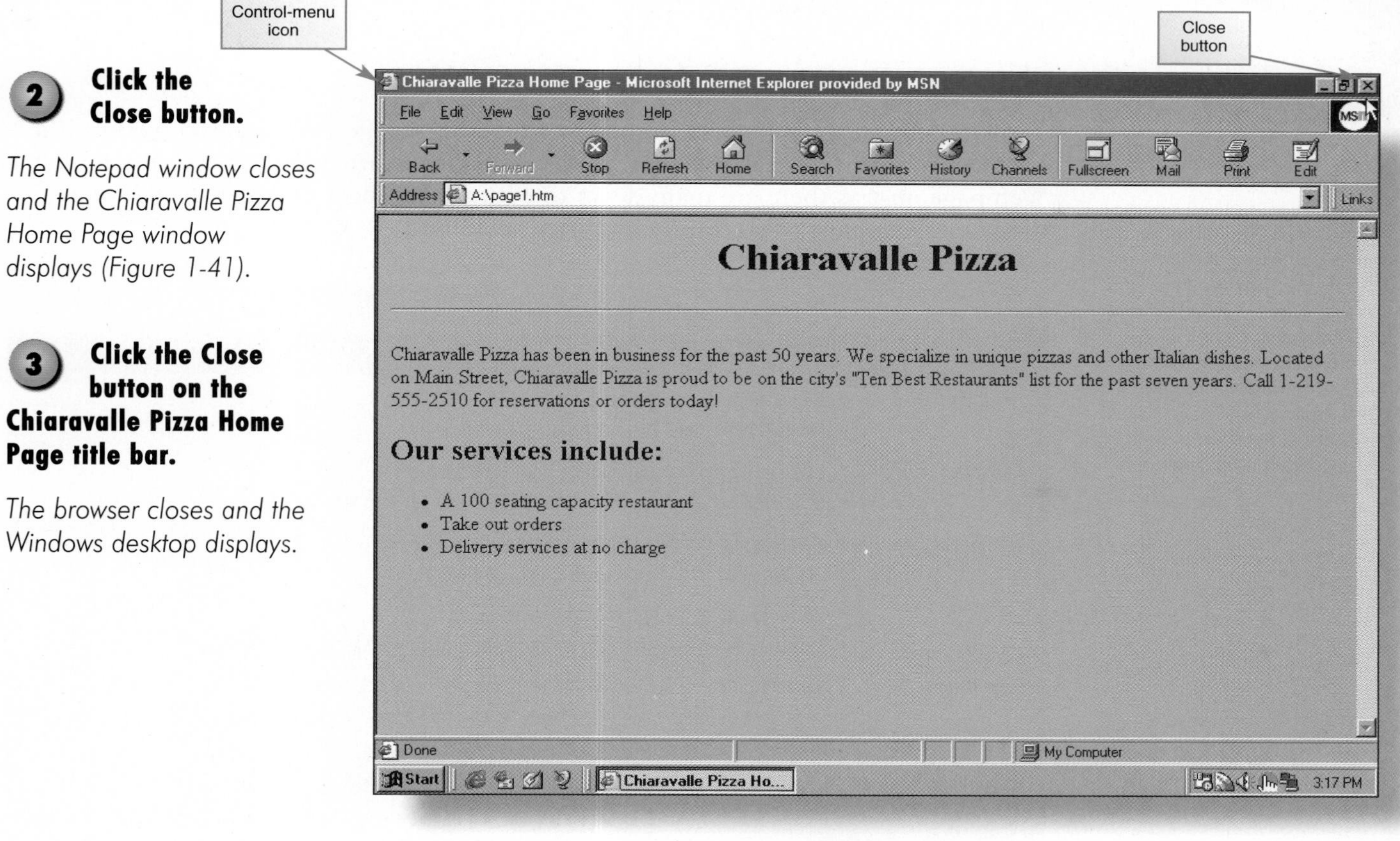

FIGURE 1-41

Other Ways

1. Double-click Control-menu icon
2. Click Close on File menu

Both the Close button on the right side of the title bar and the Control-menu icon on the left side of the title bar close the application.

Web Page Design

Published Web pages can be viewed by millions of people. As a Web page developer, it is important for you to consider good Web page design techniques and styles. A number of excellent design sources are available on the Internet. The following sections list some of the basic Web page design issues that you need to consider.

Purpose

People publish Web pages for many reasons. Professors publish to inform their students of course policies and requirements. Businesses publish to advertise their products or to give their customers 24-hour online support. Organizations create Web pages to keep their members informed of schedules and upcoming events or to recruit new members. Individuals develop Web pages to share their hobbies and knowledge or just to amuse others.

Web Design

When designing Web pages, you must consider many techniques and styles. A number of Web sites provide hints and tips that offer creative solutions and innovative design ideas. For more information about Web page design, visit the HTML More About page (www.scsite.com/html/more.htm) and click Web Design.

Web Page Organization

After you have defined the purpose of your Web page and gathered the specific content, you need to organize that information. There are many ways to organize a Web page, just as there are many ways to organize a report or paper. A few standards for Web page organization are listed in Table 1-3.

Table 1-3

ELEMENT	ORGANIZATIONAL STANDARD
Headings	• Use headings to separate main topics • Headings make your Web page easier to read
Horizontal rules	• Insert horizontal rules to separate topics or main ideas • HRs are an excellent, graphical way to break up your Web page
Paragraphs	• Use paragraphs to help divide large amounts of text • Turn your text into more readable, short sections of text
Lists	• Utilize lists when the text is conducive to bullets • Unordered or ordered lists also are great for organizing text
Page length	• Maintain suitable page lengths for your Web site • Six screens of information is too much for one Web page • Half of a screen is too little
Information	• Emphasize the most important information by placing it at the top of a Web page • WWW visitors are quick to peruse a page and do not always scroll to view the rest; they need to see the critical page information at the top of the page
Other	• Incorporate your e-mail address on your Web pages • Include date of last modification

Web Site Organization

A Web site is a collection of Web pages created and maintained by a specific group or an individual. Several different layouts are acceptable when you develop your Web site. You should select one of these layouts based on the information that you have and the manner that is best suited to display this information.

A **linear** Web site layout displays your Web pages in a straight line as shown in Figure 1-42. This is an appropriate layout if the information must be read one page after another. You would use a linear layout if the information on the first Web page was necessary for understanding information on the second Web page. You would have links from one Web page to another, and generally include a link on each page back to the home page.

A **hierarchical** Web site layout displays information in a tree-like structure as shown in Figure 1-43. This is a perfect format for information that has an index or table of contents. You would use this type of layout to display general information on the first pages and more details on the secondary pages.

A **webbed** Web site layout has no set structure as shown in Figure 1-44. This is good for information that does not need to be read in order. The World Wide Web itself is based on this type of design in which the Web visitors can link from one page to the next of their choice.

Most Web sites are a combination of the three layouts shown in Figures 1-42 through 1-44. Some information is displayed as nonintegrated, whereas other information needs to be read in a linear manner. Therefore, it is acceptable to mix the three layouts listed above.

Regardless of the layout(s) that you use, you should avoid Web sites that are too narrow (Figure 1-45) or too deep (Figure 1-46 on the next page). A **narrow Web site** is one in which the home page is the index (Figure 1-45). All other Web pages in this layout are individually linked to the home page. This forces the visitor to return to the home page in order to move from one Web page to another. This is time consuming for the Web site visitor. You need to present other navigation alternatives to the visitor besides returning to the home page for all movement.

A **deep Web site** is one in which the content Web pages are buried beneath many other Web pages (Figure 1-46). A deep Web site forces a visitor to link to several Web pages before reaching a Web page with content. This is not an effective layout because there are interim pages with little or no content. As a Web developer, you must exercise caution when designing your Web sites. The Web site visitor is looking for content; good design provides content with ease of navigation.

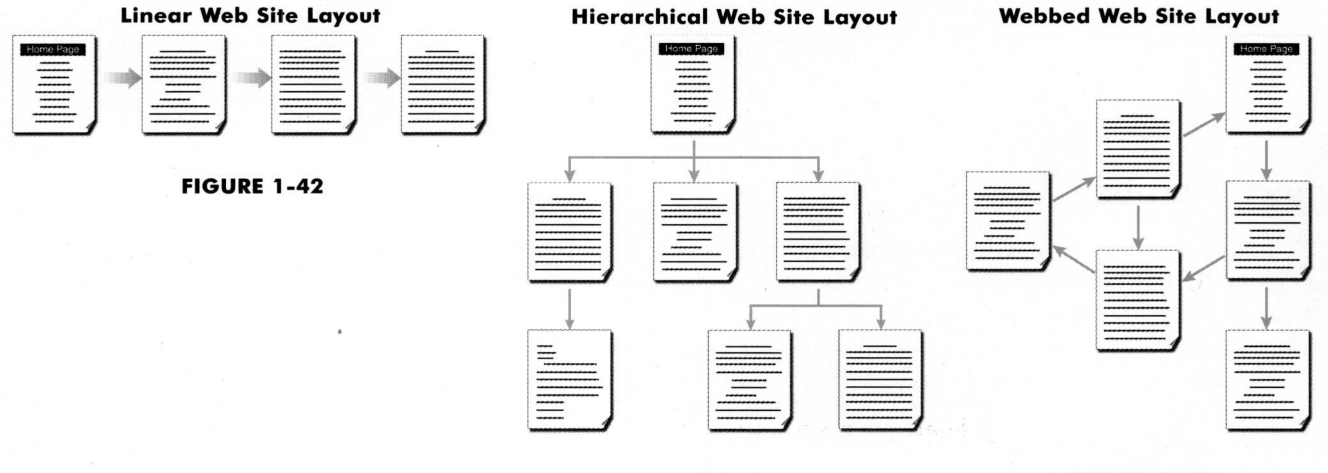

FIGURE 1-42

FIGURE 1-43

FIGURE 1-44

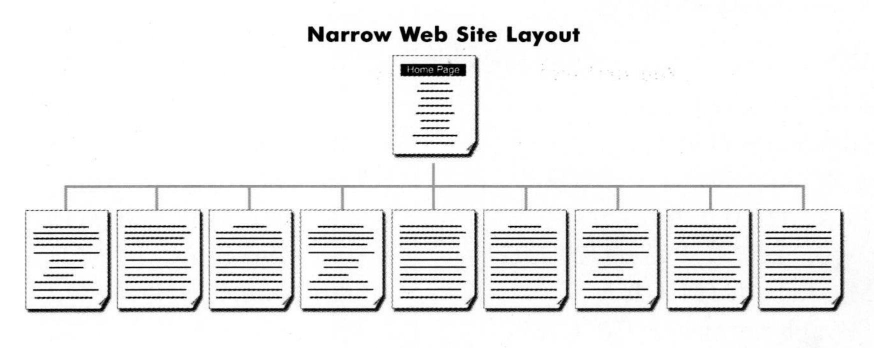

FIGURE 1-45

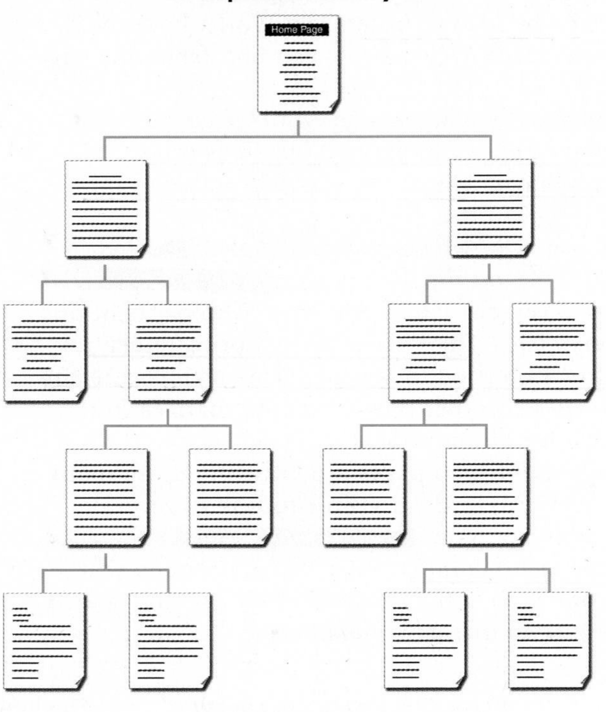

FIGURE 1-46

Project Summary

Project 1 introduced you to starting Notepad and creating an HTML text file. Prior to entering any text in the file, you gained a basic understanding of the Internet and World Wide Web, including terms and definitions. You learned about hypertext markup language, Web page development, and the elements of a Web page. Using Notepad, you entered HTML tags and text, and then you saved the file. You used a browser to view the Web page you created. Next, you edited the Web page and improved its appearance by using a background color, centering a heading, and adding a horizontal rule. Using your browser again, you refreshed the view to see the changes you made. After saving these changes, you learned how to print the Web page from the browser.

What You Should Know

Having completed this project, you now should be able to perform the following tasks.

- Activate Notepad *(HTM 1.27)*
- Add a Background Color *(HTM 1.29)*
- Center a Heading *(HTM 1.30)*
- Create a Bulleted List *(HTM 1.20)*
- Enter a Heading in the HTML File *(HTM 1.17)*
- Enter Initial HTML Tags *(HTM 1.15)*
- Enter Text in Paragraph Format *(HTM 1.18)*
- Insert a Horizontal Rule *(HTM 1.31)*
- Open a Web Page in Your Browser *(HTM 1.25)*
- Print the Web Page and HTML File *(HTM 1.35)*
- Quit Notepad and Your Browser *(HTM 1.36)*
- Refresh the View in Your Browser *(HTM 1.33)*
- Save the HTML File *(HTM 1.21)*
- Start Your Browser *(HTM 1.24)*
- Start Notepad *(HTM 1.12)*
- Turn on Word Wrap in Notepad *(HTM 1.13)*
- View the HTML Source *(HTM 1.34)*

Test Your Knowledge

1 True/False

Instructions: Circle T if the statement is true or F if the statement is false.

T F 1. The World Wide Web is a global-computer network.
T F 2. A Web site is a collection of Web pages created and maintained by one specific group or company.
T F 3. Hyperlinks connect one Web page to another.
T F 4. Hyperlinks can be created with a computer programming language called HTML.
T F 5. Tags are special instructions that tell a printer what format to use.
T F 6. Notepad is a text editor used to create Web pages.
T F 7. Links only can be created using text.
T F 8. HTML is case sensitive.
T F 9. The <TITLE> and </TITLE> tags indicate the beginning and end of the title that displays on the title bar of the Web browser.
T F 10. The <UL> and </UL> tags indicate the beginning and end of an unordered list.

2 Multiple Choice

Instructions: Circle the correct response.

1. The __________ is(are) used to break up sections of a Web page.
   a. body b. background c. title d. headings
2. The __________ of a Web page display(s) on the title bar of the browser that you use to view the Web page.
   a. body b. background c. title d. headings
3. The __________ of a Web page is(are) similar to the wallpaper in Windows.
   a. body b. background c. title d. headings
4. The __________ of the Web page contain(s) the information that displays in the browser window.
   a. body b. background c. title d. headings
5. Web page pictures and graphics are called __________
   a. GUI b. images c. pix d. links
6. There are __________ different heading sizes.
   a. three b. six c. nine d. twelve
7. The tags used to indicate an item in a list are __________ and __________.
   a. <OL>, </OL> b. <UL>, </UL> c.
, </BR> d. <LI>, </LI>
8. The __________ tag indicates the start of a paragraph.
   a. <PR> b. <HR> c. <P> d. <HEAD>
9. HTML files should have an extension of .htm or __________ in the file name.
   a. .doc b. .wks c. .txt d. .html
10. The tag that inserts a line across a Web page is __________.
   a. <P> b. <LI> c. <HR> d. <OL>

Test Your Knowledge

3 Understanding HTML

Instructions: Perform the following steps using a computer.

1. Start Notepad.
2. Open the page1.htm file created in Project 1.
3. Print the file.
4. Without looking at the book, circle the tag that inserts the horizontal rule across the Web page.
5. Without looking at the book, draw a line under the tag that will display the text on the title bar of the Web browser.
6. Without looking at the book, put a square around the tag that indicates a bulleted list.
7. Write your name and answers on the printout and hand it in to your instructor.

4 Editing HTML Files

Instructions: Perform the following tasks using a computer.

1. Start the browser.
2. Click the Address bar. Type `www.scsite.com/html/proj1.htm` and then press the ENTER key. When the Web page displays, scroll to Internet titles and then click proj1.htm.
3. When the Web page displays, click the link Project 1 - 4 Editing HTML Files.
4. Click View on the menu bar and then click Source to find the HTML code for a feature that was not used on the page1.htm Web page.
5. Highlight the code and copy it to the Clipboard (i.e., press CTRL+C).
6. Open the page1.htm file in Notepad.
7. Paste the Clipboard contents in the page1.htm file at an appropriate place.
8. Save the revised file on a floppy disk with page2.htm as the file name.
9. Print the revised document source.
10. Open page2.htm in your browser.
11. Print the Web page.
12. Write your name on both printouts and hand them in to your instructor.

Use Help

1 Notepad Help

Instructions: Perform the following tasks using a computer.

1. Start Notepad.
2. Click Help on the menu bar and then click Help Topics.
3. If necessary, click the Contents tab.
4. Double-click the Working with Text book.
5. Double-click the Wrapping text to the window size topic.
6. The Note explains what wrap text is. After reading the Note, write down reasons why you would wrap your text.
7. Include your name with your answers and hand them in to your instructor.

2 Web Page Design Ideas

Instructions: Perform the following tasks using a computer.

1. Start the browser.
2. Click the Address bar. Type `www.scsite.com/html/proj1.htm` and then press the ENTER key. When the Web page displays, scroll to Internet titles and then click the title of this book.
3. Click Yale, and then read the suggestions about the quality and the content of the Web pages that you create.
4. Write down some of the more important ideas.
5. Include your name with your answers and hand them in to your instructor.

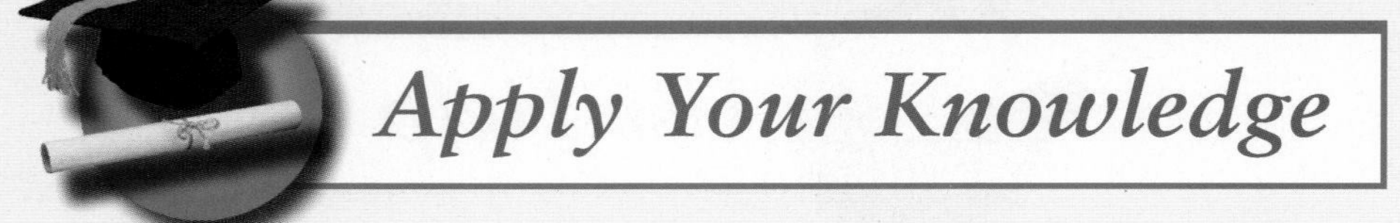

1 Editing the Apply Your Knowledge Web Page

Instructions: Start Notepad. Open the file, element.htm, on the HTML Data Disk. If you did not download the HTML Data Disk, see the inside back cover for instructions or see your instructor. Figure 1-47 shows the Apply Your Knowledge Web page as it should display in a browser. The element.htm file is a partially completed HTML file that contains some errors.

Perform the following steps using a computer.

1. Open the file in Notepad.
2. Open the file in your browser.
3. Examine the HTML file and its appearance in the browser.
4. Correct the HTML errors, making the Web page look similar to the one shown in Figure 1-47.
5. Add any HTML code necessary for additional features shown in the Web page.
6. Save the revised file on a floppy disk with element2.htm as the file name.
7. Print the revised document source.
8. Open the element2.htm file in your browser.
9. Print the Web page.
10. Write your name on both printouts and hand them in to your instructor.

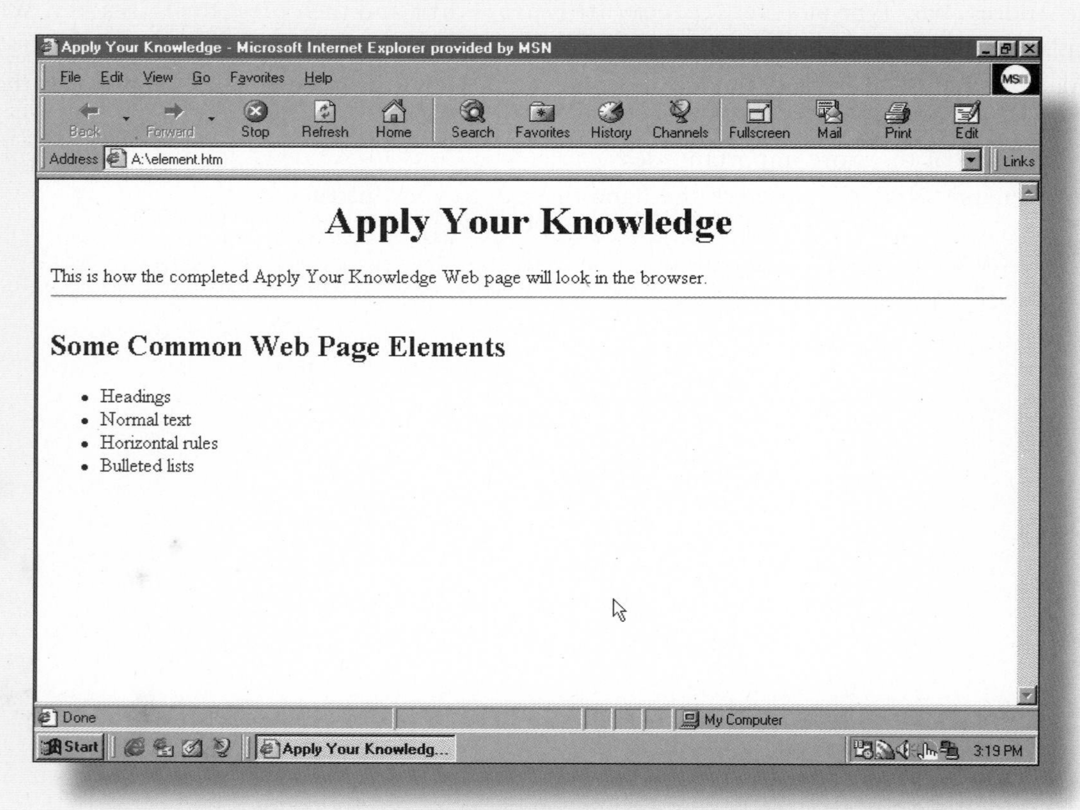

FIGURE 1-47

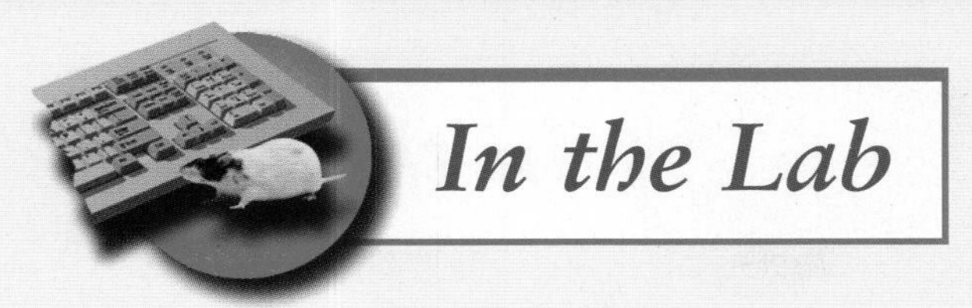

1 Creating a Personal Page

Problem: Your instructor would like to make the class syllabus available over the World Wide Web. You have been asked to create a Web page to display this information, similar to the one shown in Figure 1-48.

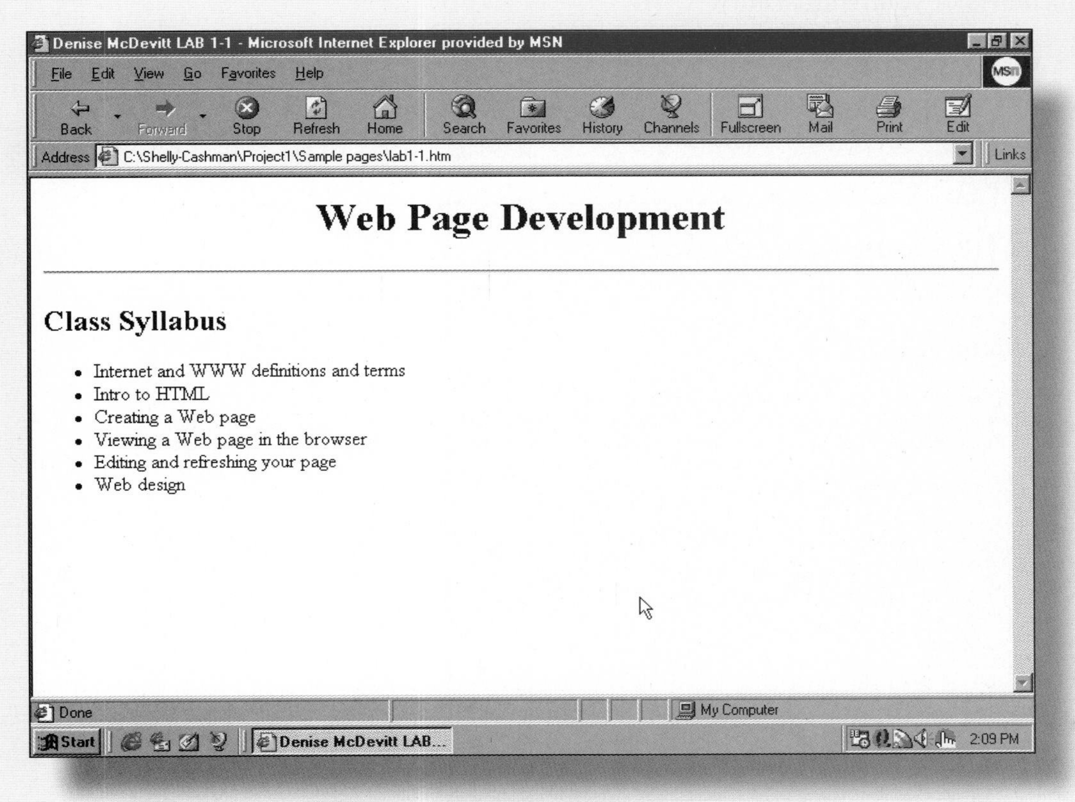

FIGURE 1-48

Instructions: Start Notepad. Perform the following steps using a computer.

1. Start a new HTML file with the title [your name] lab1-1 in the main heading section.
2. Begin the body section by adding a centered, Heading 1 style heading, Web Page Development.
3. Add a horizontal rule.
4. Add a Heading 2 style heading, Class Syllabus.
5. Add a bulleted list of the main topics of the class as shown in Figure 1-48.
6. Close the body, close the HTML file, and save the file using lab1-1.htm as the file name.
7. Print the lab1-1.htm file.
8. Open the lab1-1.htm file in the your browser.
9. Print the Web page.
10. Write your name on the printouts and hand them in to your instructor.

2 Creating an Information Page

Problem: You are the president of the Computer Club and decide to prepare a Web page announcement inviting new members such as the one shown in Figure 1-49. You decide to use paragraph format to inform prospective members of your club history.

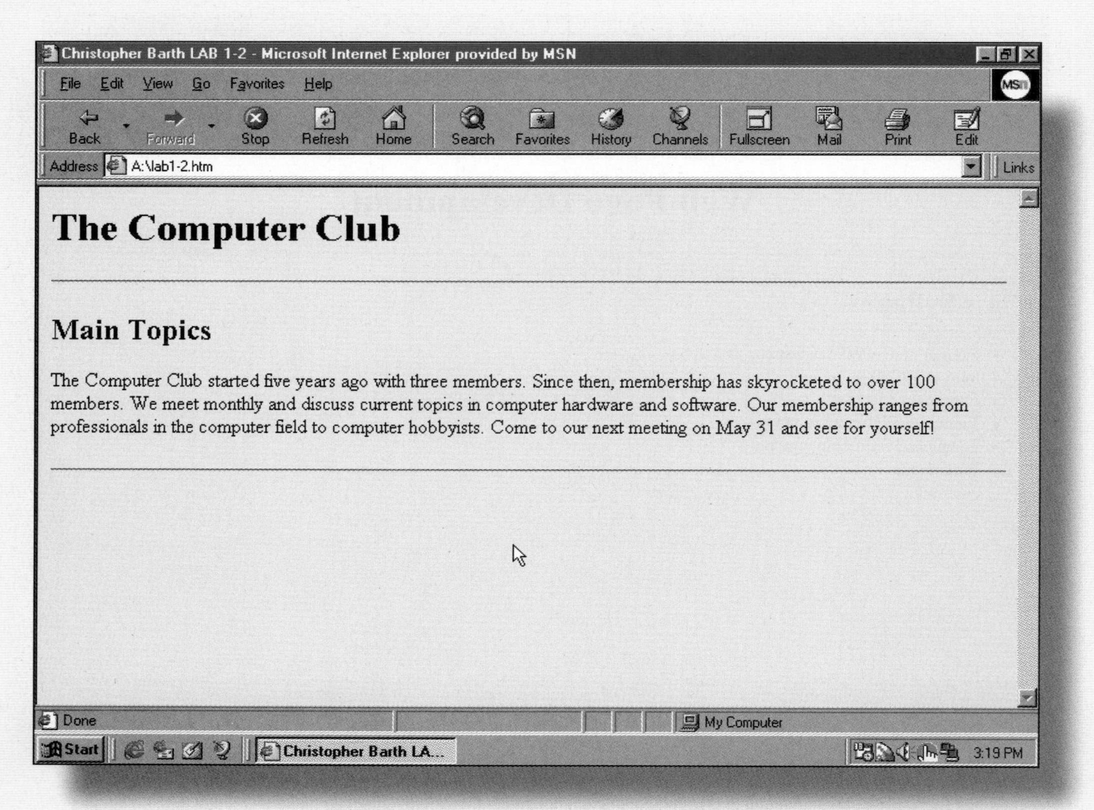

FIGURE 1-49

Instructions: Start Notepad. Perform the following steps using a computer.

1. Start a new HTML file with the title [your name] lab1-2 in the main heading section.
2. Add a colored background to the Web page using the #FFFFC6 color code.
3. Begin the body section by adding a left-aligned, Heading 1 style heading, The Computer Club.
4. Add a horizontal rule.
5. Add a left-aligned, Heading 2 style heading, Main Topics.
6. Add a paragraph of information as shown in Figure 1-49.
7. Add a horizontal rule; note the spacing from the previous line. (*Hint:* See <BR> tag.)
8. Close the body, close the HTML file, and save the file using lab1-2.htm as the file name.
9. Print the lab1-2.htm file.
10. Open the lab1-2.htm file in the your browser.
11. Print the Web page.
12. Write your name on the printouts and hand them in to your instructor.

3 Composing a Personal Web Page

Problem: You want to create a home page to tell people about yourself. You will use both paragraph and bullet formatting to list information as shown in Figure 1-50.

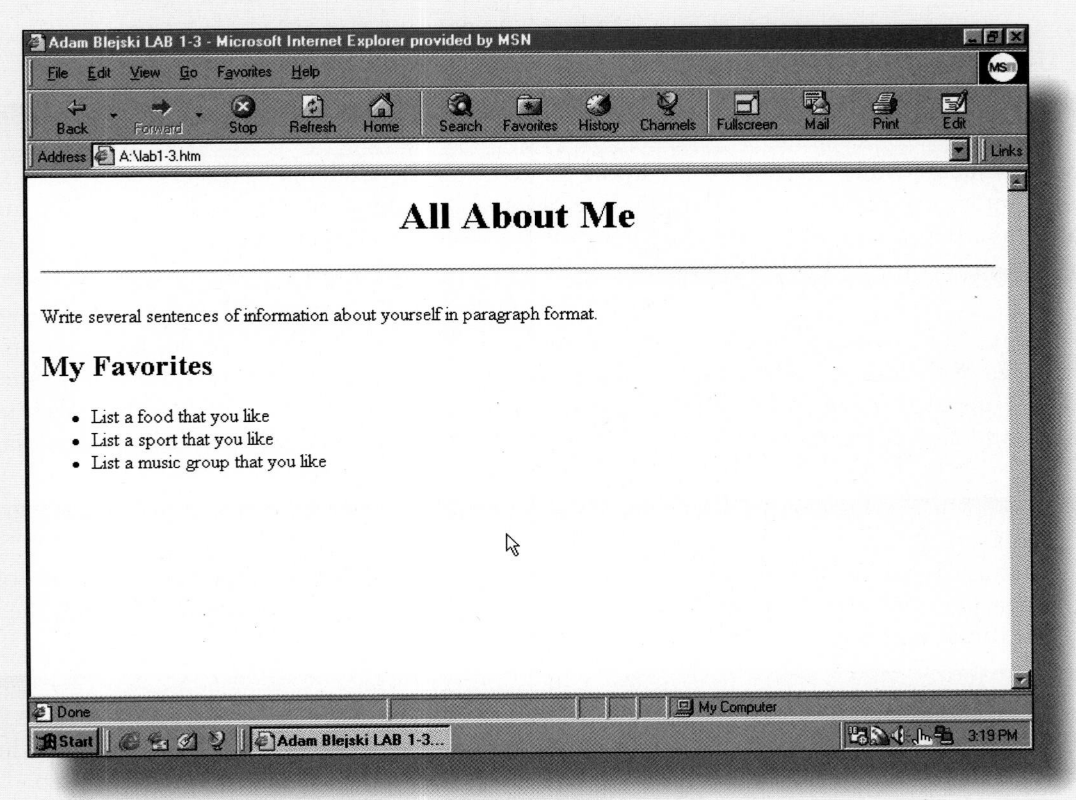

FIGURE 1-50

Instructions: Start Notepad. Perform the following steps using a computer.

1. Create a Web page about yourself similar to the one shown in Figure 1-50.
2. The title should be [your name] lab1-3.
3. Include a short paragraph of information and a bulleted list.
4. Save the Web page with the file name lab1-3.htm.
5. Print the Web page from your browser.
6. Write your name on the printout and hand it in to your instructor.

Cases and Places

The difficulty of these case studies varies:
◗ are the least difficult; ◗◗ are more difficult; and ◗◗◗ are the most difficult.

1 ◗ Mr. Smith likes your basic idea for the Chiaravalle Pizza Web page, but thinks it needs more information. Use Notepad to add some additional bullets and another paragraph.

2 ◗ Your instructor wants to publish the home pages of all the students in the class. She feels that you need to add more excitement to your pages. Use Notepad to add a colored background and another horizontal rule. By varying the size and style of the horizontal rule, you can produce different effects.

3 ◗◗ You are curious to see what other pizza places have Web pages. Start Internet Explorer and search for other pizza Web sites. View the source of a pizza place Web page that is especially interesting to you. Take note of one element of the Web page that you do not have in the Chiaravalle Pizza Web page. Use Notepad to add that component to a new Web page and insert specific information about Chiaravalle Pizza.

4 ◗◗ Think about local businesses in your area. Take the Chiaravalle Pizza Web page as a sample and insert information relative to any other business. You thereby can use your original HTML file as a template for other Web pages.

5 ◗◗◗ Your instructor is interested in seeing other student work published to the Internet. Take any report or paper that you have created using word processing software and copy the text into Notepad. Add the HTML tags necessary to make this report or paper into a Web page.

6 ◗◗◗ Browse some of the information on the Web page design sites listed in Project 1. Browse pages on the WWW and select three Web pages that you think are well-organized and three that are not. Print all six of those pages. Indicate on the printouts what you like about the well-organized pages. Indicate on the poorly organized pages what changes could be made to organize the information more efficiently.

7 ◗◗◗ HTML has many more tags than those discussed in Project 1. The number of available HTML tags continues to grow at a fast rate. Search the Internet for information about HTML tags. Learn about some of the tags that are not discussed in this project. Use at least three new tags to create a more complex Web page.

HTML

Creating a Web Site with Links

OBJECTIVES

You will have mastered the material in this project when you can:

- Describe linking terms and definitions
- Add a link to another Web page
- Create a home page
- Enhance a Web page using images
- Add bold, italics, and color to text
- Change bullet type
- Insert a background image
- Insert a horizontal rule image
- Add an e-mail link
- View the HTML file and test the links
- Edit the second Web page
- Insert an image and wrap text around an image
- Add a text link to another Web site
- Add an image link to another Web site
- Create links within a Web page
- Set link targets
- Add links to set targets
- Describe types of image files
- Control image sizing
- Locate images

Romeo & Juliet

...And They Lived Happily Ever After

Links Let Readers Choose the Plot

Romeo and Juliet drink poison and die for love. Dedalus and Bloom cross paths and spend a day in Dublin. Cinderella and Prince Charming marry and live a lifetime of happiness together. Have you ever read a book and then wished you could change the plot or ending? Well, now you can create your own cyberplot using hyperlinks. In this project, you will create a Web site with hyperlinks, or links, that allow Web surfers visiting your Web page to jump to another location on the page or to another Web site.

Similarly, cyberreaders can access published works on the Web by connecting to the Internet and opening a literary piece, such as a novel or poem, on their computers. They begin reading the hypertext words on their

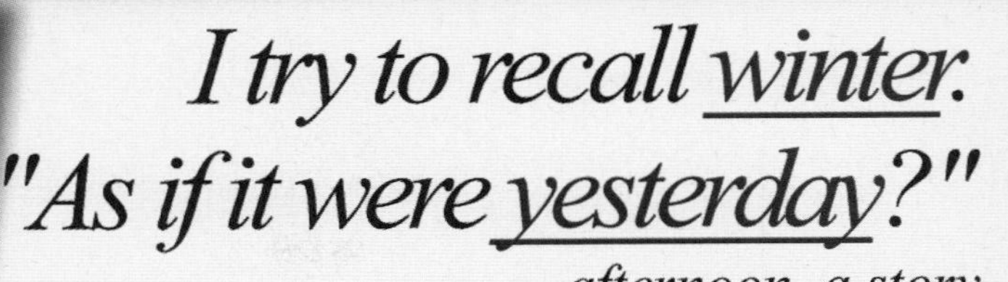

I try to recall winter.
"As if it were yesterday?"
–afternoon, a story

Storyspace

computer screens and then encounter a link, which resembles a fork in the road. Click the link, and they are transported to another scene. Ignore the link, and they continue along the initial path the author created.

afternoon, a story, is a hypertext novel written by literary pioneer Michael Joyce. The story was produced for the Storyspace authoring system and published in 1989 by Riverrun, one of the larger publishers of hypertext books. Since its Web publication, *afternoon* has established itself as a classic among hyperbooks. As readers progress through the pages of the book, links allow them to make the connection among events from chapter to chapter, with a simple click of the mouse.

When Joyce began writing *afternoon* in 1982, word processing software was in its infancy. Although the Web had not been invented, Professor Ted Nelson had coined the term hypertext, seventeen years earlier. Joyce realized that software could help readers navigate hypertext in the same way listeners may ask a speaker to clarify a point or repeat an earlier statement.

Joyce worked with Jay David Bolter, a professor at the Georgia Institute of Technology, and developed the Storyspace authoring software. Writers using Storyspace type their ideas in writing spaces, give these areas specific names, and then draw lines to connect and organize these spaces. Writers have used this software to create everything from dissertations to screenplays to government documents.

Did you ever sneak a peek at the answers in the appendix of your math textbook or the upside-down solution to the crossword puzzle in the newspaper? You cannot try this tactic with Storyspace if the author has set up *guard fields*. These protected areas are off limits until you have clicked and followed specific links. Only then can you discover the outcome or a connection to a decisive event.

As hypertext gains popularity and becomes easier to use, more authors and poets will be dabbling in this literary cyberworld. As you click and navigate through their works, you will invent your versions of literature. With your power, the characters can indeed live happily ever after.

HTML

Creating a Web Site with Links

PROJECT 2

CASE PERSPECTIVE

Resumes Unlimited is a company that specializes in resume writing. You want to advance your current position within the company by using your recently gained experience on the Internet. You can envision developing resumes as Web pages and then making the resumes accessible to people all over the world. Your customers' resumes will be online and instantly viewable as Web pages.

You know you will be able to convince your boss, Mark Mullet, that this idea will offer the company Internet exposure and marketing presence when you have the actual product to demonstrate. With this in mind, you will develop two Web pages using HTML. The first Web page consists of information about Resumes Unlimited, an e-mail hyperlink to the company, and a link to a second Web page. The second Web page contains a client resume and a link to a pertinent page on the World Wide Web. After these Web pages are completed, you can take them to Mark for the big sell.

Introduction

An important feature of the World Wide Web is its capability of allowing easy movement from one Web page to another in apparent continuity. An exciting aspect of Web page development is the ability to link Web pages together. In this project, you will learn how to connect Web pages using the following types of hyperlinks, or links.

- Links within a Web page
- Links to another Web page on the same Web site
- Links to another Web site
- E-mail links

You will identify the various links and learn how to use them, and then create a two-page Web site that uses each type of link.

Project Two — Web Res

In Project 1, you used HTML to create and edit a Web page. In this project, you will use HTML to create a new Web page for Web Res and its associated links (Figure 2-1a) and improve the appearance of the Sample Resume Web page that consists of the Marie M. Santos resume (Figure 2-1b) to which Web Res links.

The two completed Web pages shown in Figures 2-1a and 2-1b contain links to take the visitor from one page to the other. The first page is the Web Res home page. It displays information about Web Res and the services it offers. The second page is the Sample Resume page. This page contains internal links to allow visitors to move easily from section to section within the Web page. In addition, the Sample Resume page contains both text and image links to an outside Web site.

Using Notepad, you will create the Web Res page and edit the Sample Resume page. The unedited Sample Resume page is included on the HTML Data Disk. Then, using your browser, you will view the pages and follow the links you have created.

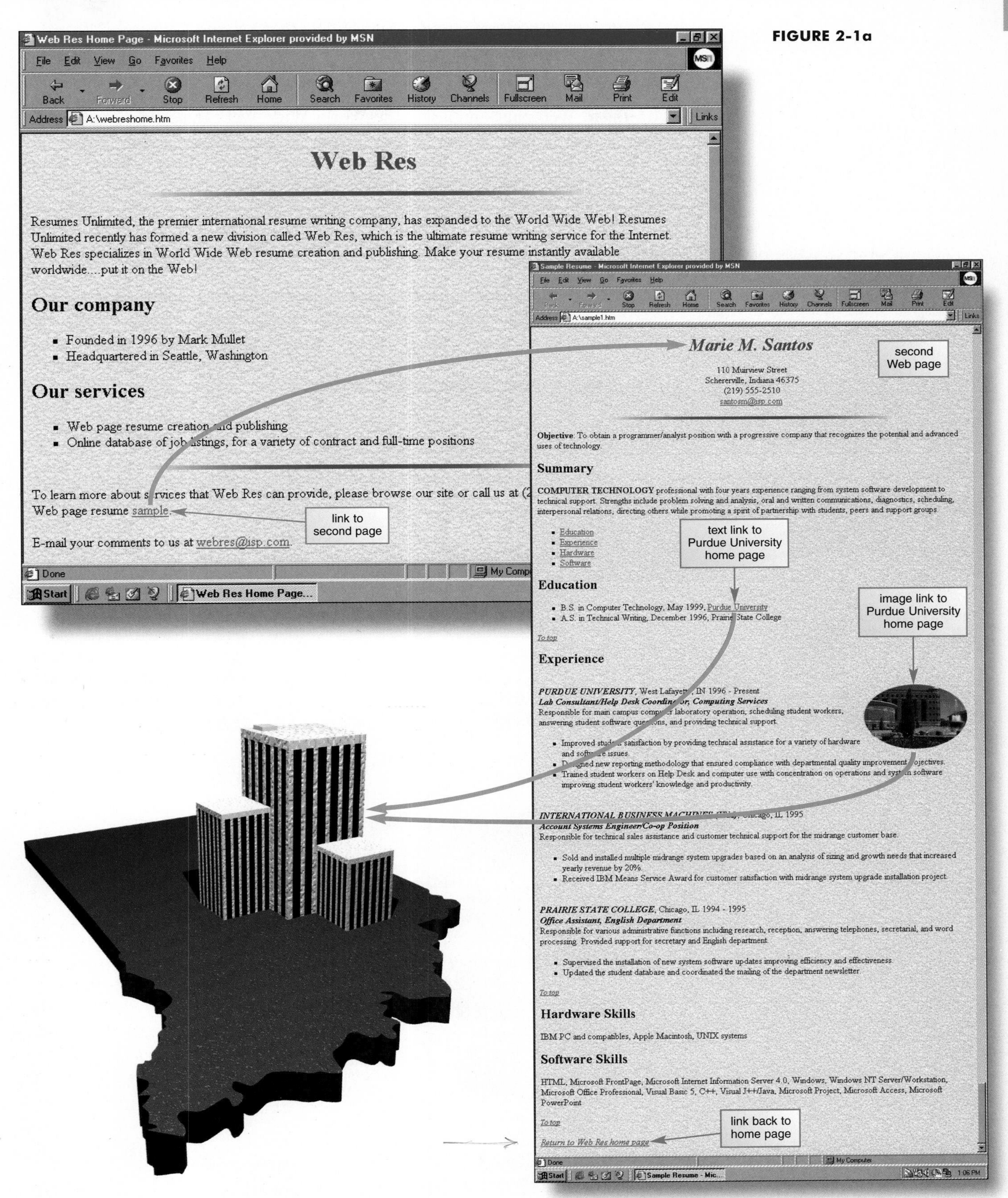

FIGURE 2-1a

FIGURE 2-1b

Introduction to Links

Millions of linked Web pages make up the World Wide Web. **Hyperlinks**, or **links**, are used to connect a Web page to another Web page on the same, or a different, Web server located anywhere in the world. Links can be created to allow a visitor to navigate to an area on the same Web page, to another Web page within a Web site, or to an entirely different Web site. Links also can be used to create an e-mail link easily. Visitors to a Web page can have immediate access to another Web page or a different section of the same Web page by clicking a link. The power of the Web centers on its linking capabilities.

You can use either text or an image as a hotspot for a link. A **hotspot** is an area of text or an image in which the mouse pointer changes when it is moved over the area. Generally, the mouse pointer changes to a pointing hand when it is moved over a hotspot. This change notifies the user that there is a link from that text or image. Additionally, text links generally are underlined and different in color to indicate their function. Figure 2-2 shows a sample of text used as a hotspot, and Figure 2-3 shows a sample of an image used as a hotspot. Moving the mouse pointer over the hotspot also displays the URL to which you will be moved on the status bar of the browser (Figure 2-3).

FIGURE 2-2

FIGURE 2-3

With text links, you always should use descriptive text as the clickable word(s). Avoid using the words, Click here, alone as the linking text because they do not give the visitor the purpose of the link.

Unless otherwise stated in the <BODY> tag, the color of text links use browser-dependent defaults throughout a Web page. The format of the tag used to change normal, visited, and active link colors from the default is <BODY LINK="color" VLINK="color" ALINK="color"> where color is a designated color code. Browsers generally have a standard default color for normal links but different active and visited link colors, according to the browser used. The same color defaults apply to the border color around an image link. If the image has no border, no color will display around the image. Table 2-1 lists the color control attributes that can be used in linking. In Figure 2-4 you can see samples of text links in all three states (normal, visited, and active).

More About

Linking Colors

You can change the link colors in popular browsers. In Microsoft Internet Explorer, you find color selections on the View menu using Internet Options. In Netscape Communicator, on the Edit menu, click Preferences. In both products, you change colors by clicking the color bars.

Table 2-1

ATTRIBUTE	FUNCTION
LINK	• Link color, without mouse over it or before having been visited • Controls the color of a normal link that has not been clicked • Default color usually is blue
VLINK	• Visited link • Controls the color of a link that has been clicked or visited • Default color usually is green or red
ALINK	• Active link • Controls the color of a link on which a mouse has been pressed but not clicked • Default color usually is green or red

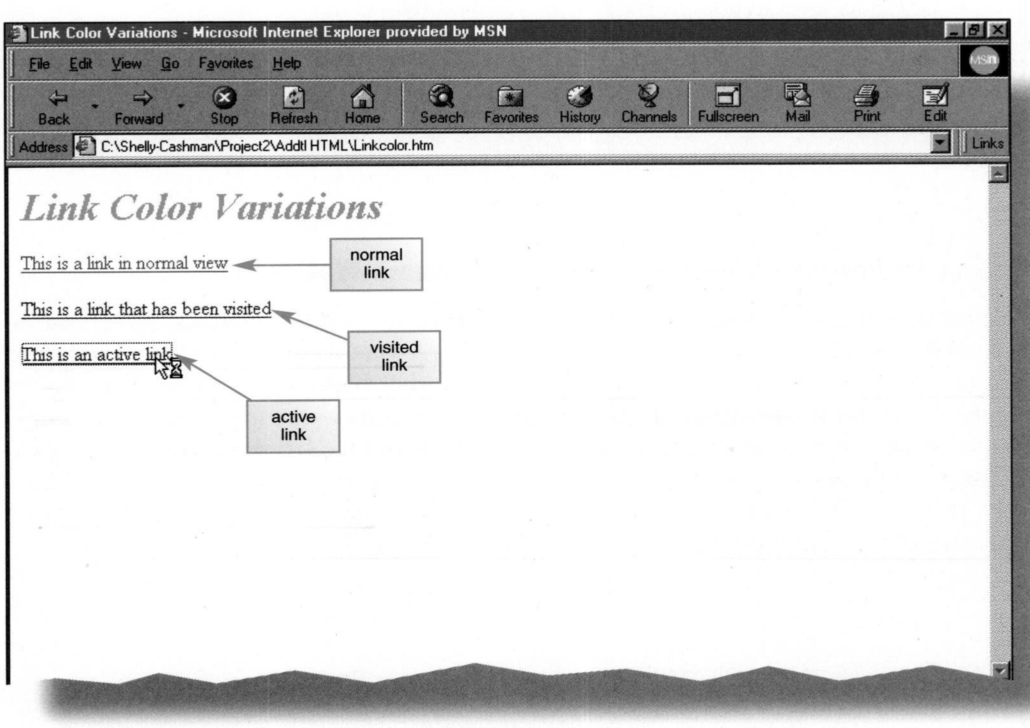

FIGURE 2-4

Linking within a Web Page

Links within a page allow visitors to move quickly from one section of the Web page to another. This is especially important in large Web pages. Your visitor can view the sections that are of interest without having to scroll entirely through the Web page. Developers often use links within a Web page as commands or a table of contents. Many Web pages contain a list at the top of the page that links to other sections within the same page, as shown in Figure 2-5. In this project, you will create this type of link to go from the top section of the resume to other sections.

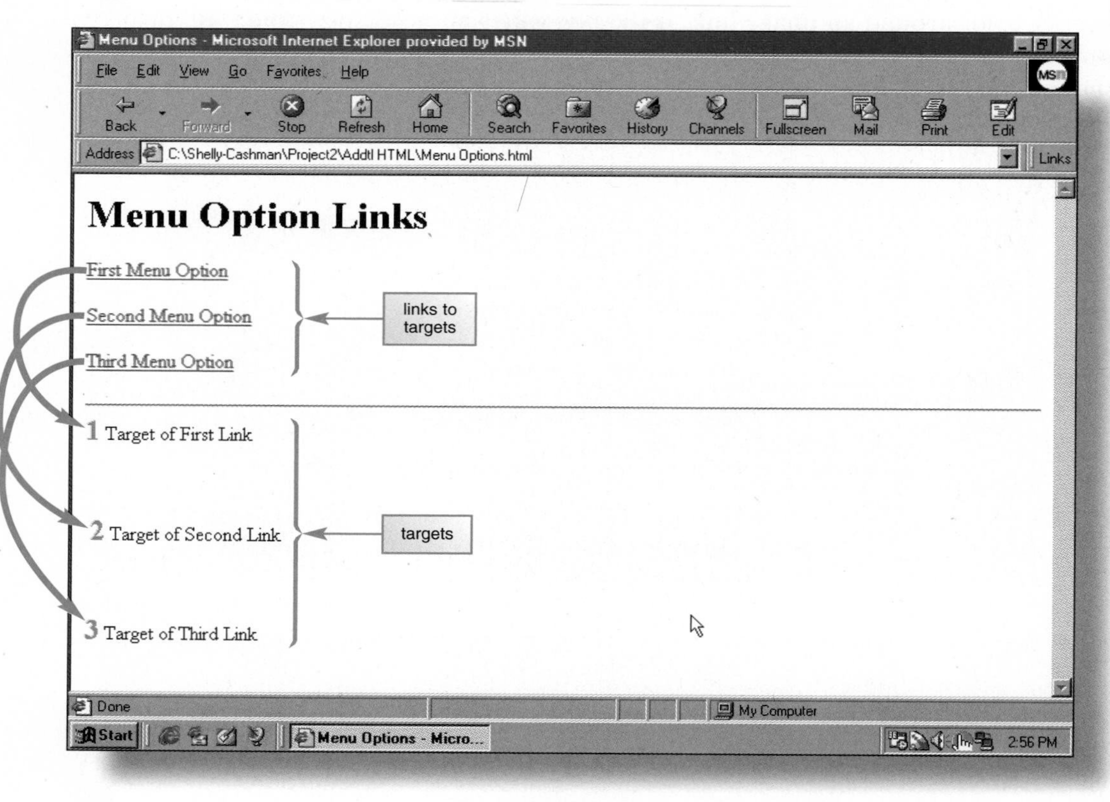

FIGURE 2-5

Linking to Another Web Page within the Same Web Site

The second type of link connects one Web page to another page within the same Web site. Figure 2-6 shows how these links work. A visitor clicks a link on the home page of a Web site (Figure 2-6a) and moves to another page on the same Web site (Figure 2-6b). Web sites generally use these types of links because a Web site usually consists of multiple pages, and visitors need a way to move from one Web page to another. In this project, you will create this type of link to move from the Web Res home page to the Sample Resume page. You then will have a reverse order link to allow the visitor to move from the Sample Resume page back to the home page.

More About

HTML Help

Many World Wide Web sites provide Help for new HTML developers. For more information about HTML Help, visit the HTML More About page (www.scsite.com/html/more.htm) and click HTML Help Desk.

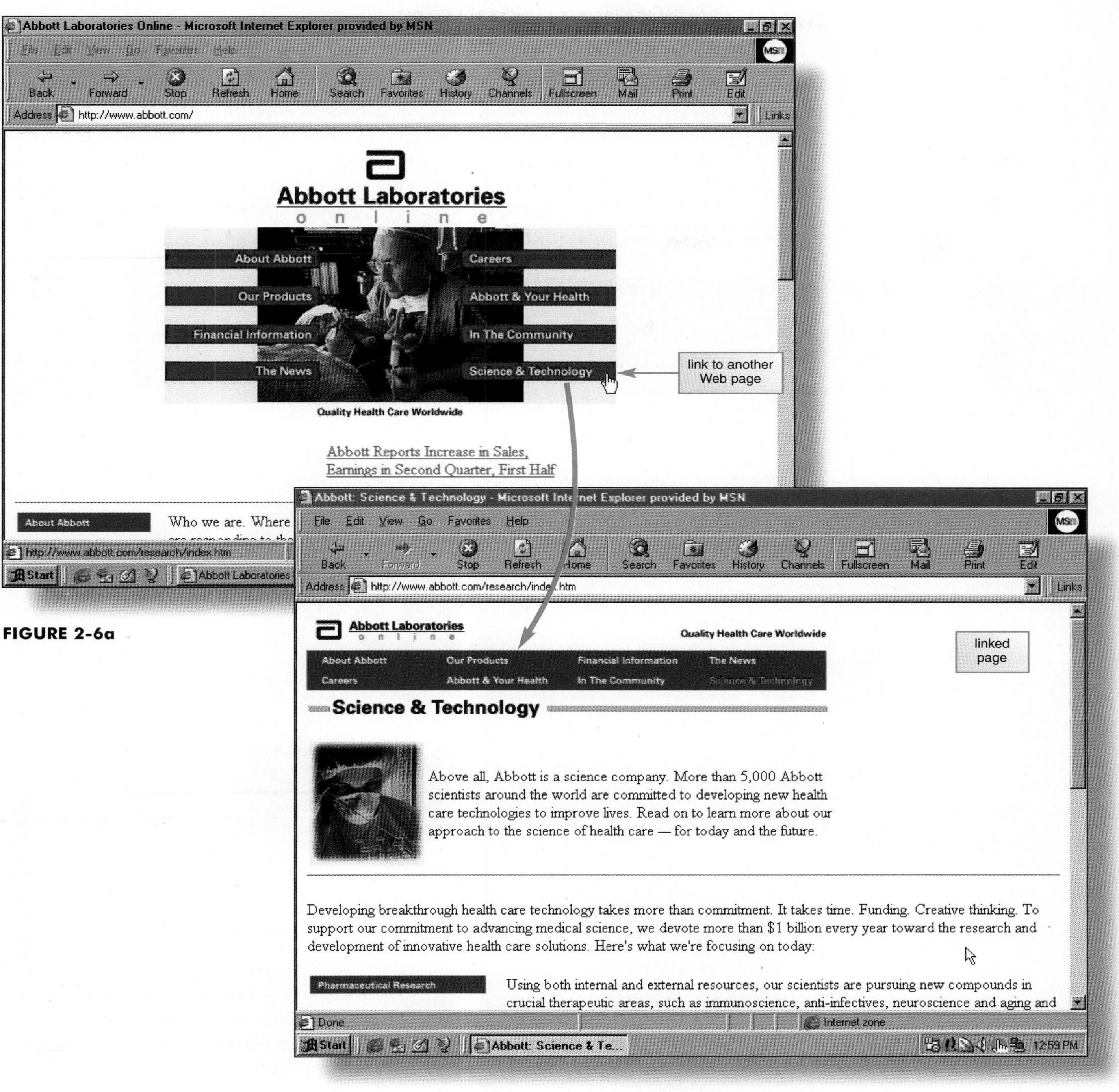

FIGURE 2-6a

FIGURE 2-6b

Linking to Another Web Site

A very important feature of the Web is the capability of linking one Web site to another. Web developers use these links to connect their Web sites to sites elsewhere containing information on the same topic. The same tag used to link within the same Web site is used to link to external Web sites. You will create this type of link in this project by linking to the university from which the student on the resume graduated. You will create two variations of the link. One will link from text; the other will link from an image of the university (Figure 2-7a). Clicking either the text link or the image link takes the visitor to the Purdue University Web page (Figure 2-7b).

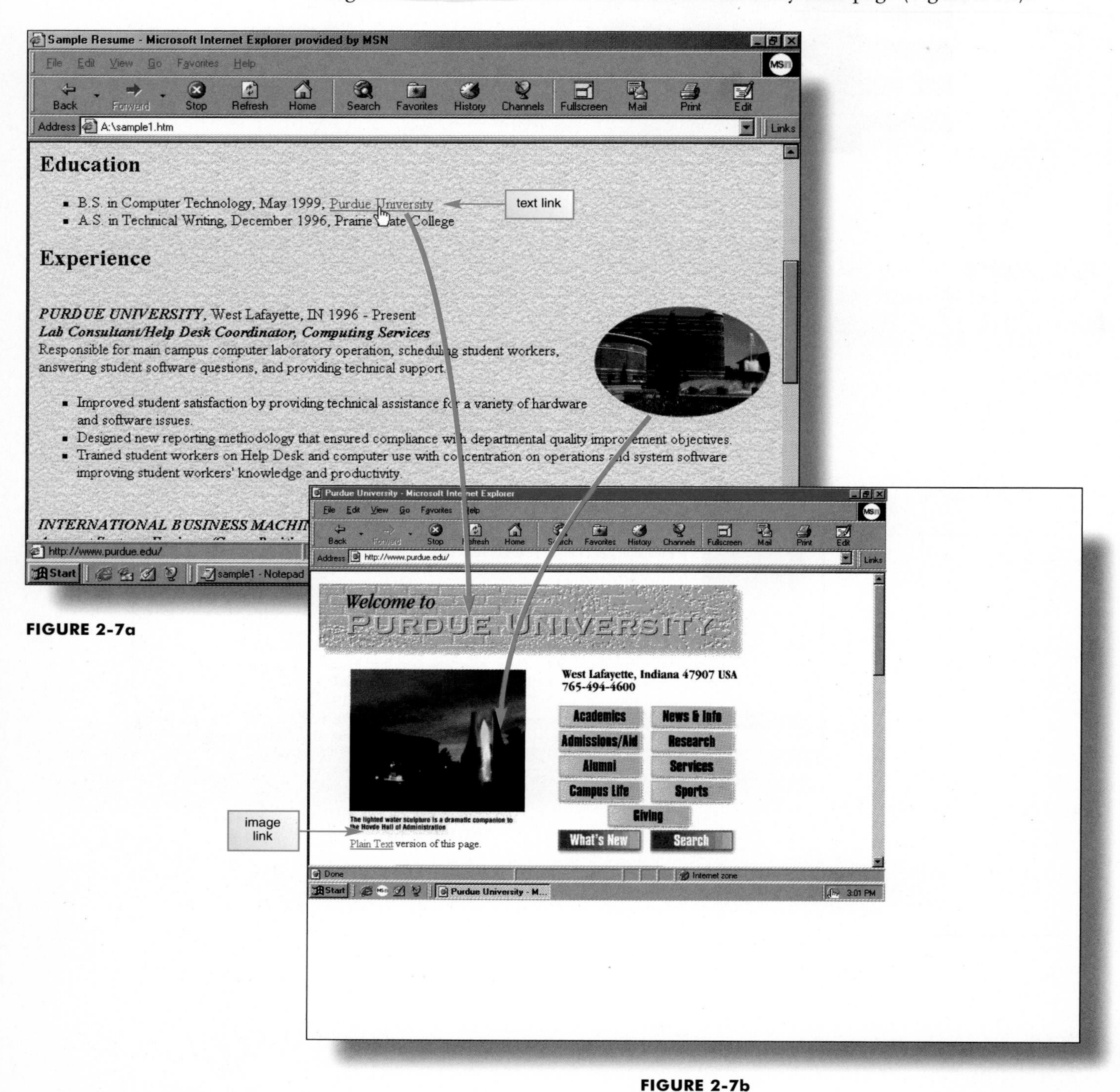

FIGURE 2-7a

FIGURE 2-7b

Linking to E-Mail

A well-designed Web page always provides a way for visitors to contact the Web developer. An easy way to do this is by providing an e-mail link somewhere on the Web site home page. Visitors use this link to contact the company to request additional information. Visitors also can comment on the Web site or notify the developer of a problem. Figures 2-8a and 2-8b are examples of an e-mail link.

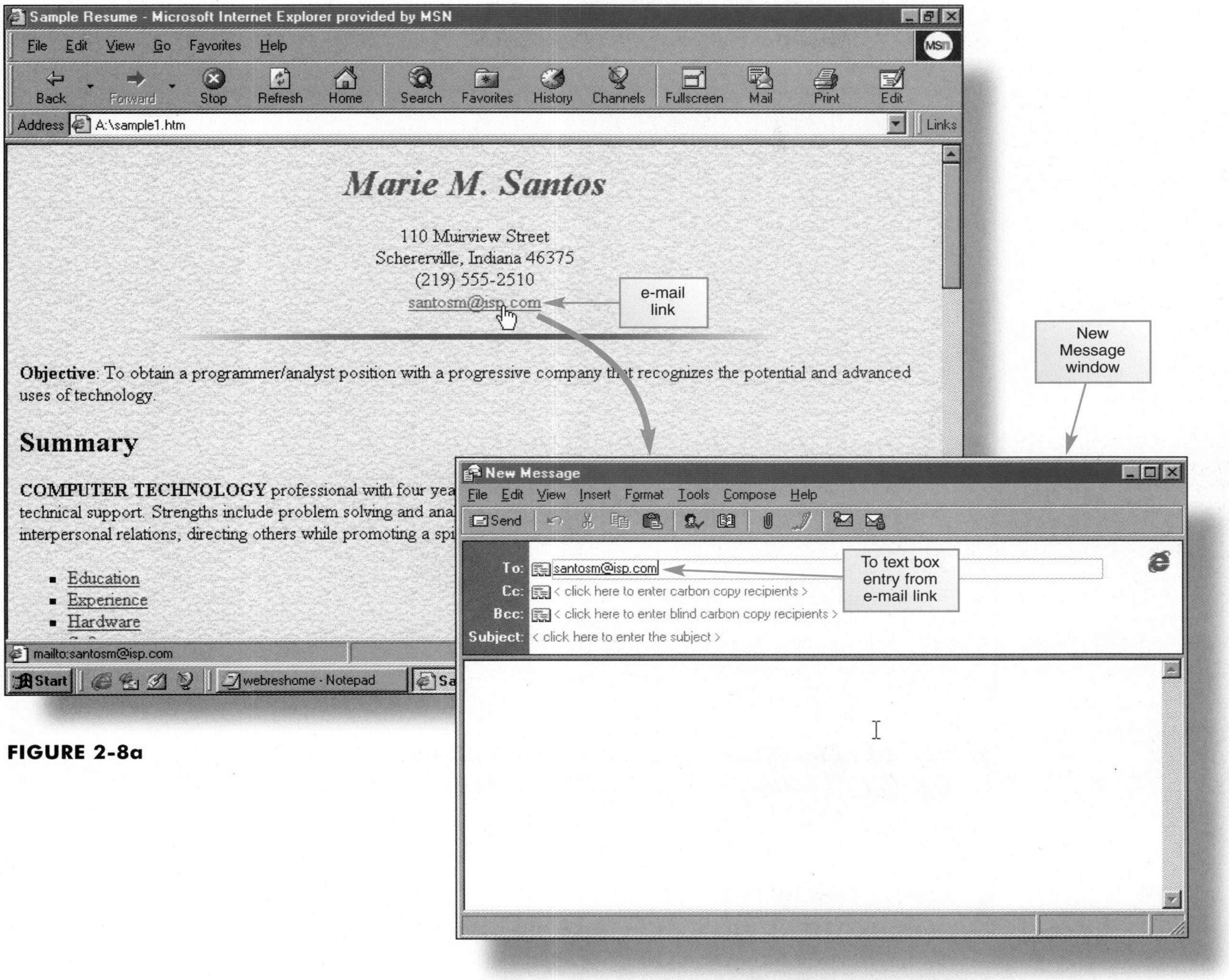

FIGURE 2-8a

FIGURE 2-8b

Starting Notepad

You will use Notepad as the text editor for the HTML files. Perform the following steps to start Notepad.

TO START NOTEPAD

1. Click the Start button on the taskbar and then point to Programs on the Start menu.
2. Point to Accessories on the Programs submenu and then point to Notepad on the Accessories submenu.
3. Click Notepad.

4. If necessary, click the Maximize button.

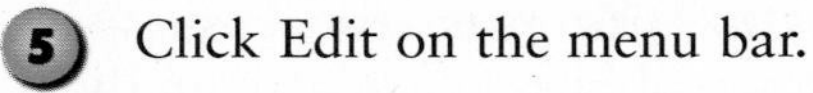

5. Click Edit on the menu bar.
6. If WordWrap is not checked, click WordWrap.

The Notepad window displays (Figure 2-9) and WordWrap is enabled.

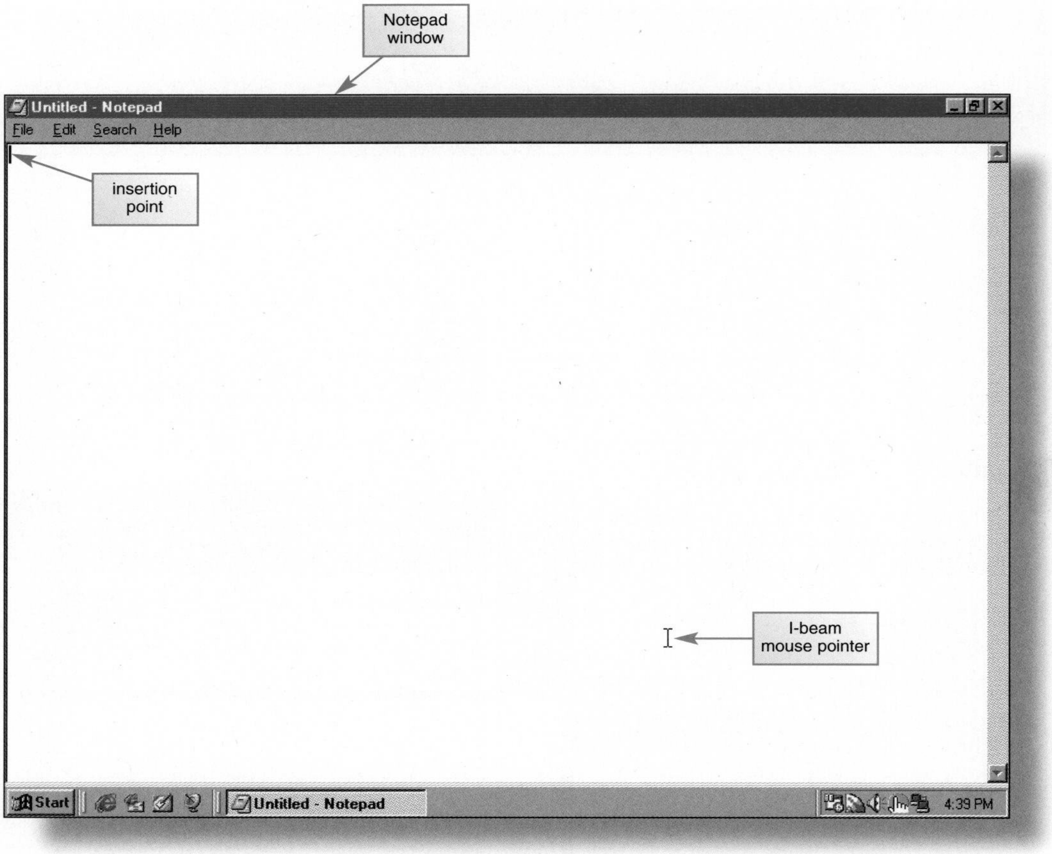

FIGURE 2-9

Creating a Home Page

A home page is the main page of a Web site. Visitors to a Web site generally will view the home page first. The home page that you develop in this project will have two links: a link to the second page and an e-mail link.

On the home page, it is important to identify the purpose of your Web site. You should state clearly what the Web site is about and how the visitor can move from one page on the site to another. The links from one Web page to another should be apparent. It is up to the Web developer to design the Web site in such a way that navigation is clear. It also is standard to include an e-mail link on the home page so visitors can e-mail you directly from the initial page.

Entering Initial HTML Tags

In Project 1, you entered an initial set of HTML tags. These tags define the overall structure of a standard Web page. The following steps show how to enter the initial HTML tags.

TO ENTER INITIAL HTML TAGS

1. Type `<HTML>` and then press the ENTER key.
2. Type `<HEAD>` and then press the ENTER key.
3. Type `<TITLE>Web Res Home Page</TITLE>` and then press the ENTER key.
4. Type `</HEAD>` and then press the ENTER key.
5. Type `<BODY>` and then press the ENTER key twice.
6. Type `</BODY>` and then press the ENTER key.
7. Type `</HTML>` as the final tag.
8. Position the insertion on the blank line between the <BODY> and </BODY> tags.

The HTML code displays (Figure 2-10).

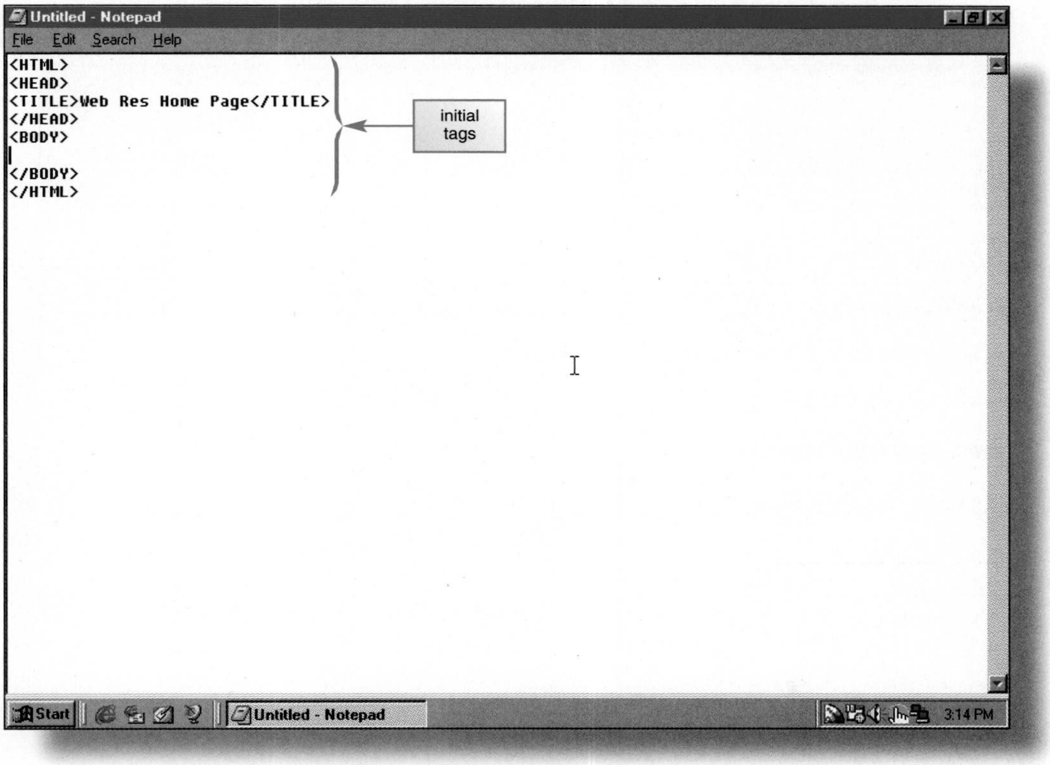

FIGURE 2-10

Entering a Heading

As discussed in Project 1, the <H1> tag assigns the largest possible size to a heading. Recall that the alignment attribute with the tag <H1 ALIGN="CENTER"> will center the heading. Using the <FONT> tag can enhance the heading further. Any text on a Web page can be altered to attract more attention with the beginning <FONT> and ending </FONT> tags. Table 2-2 lists the different FONT attributes that can be used to enhance standard text.

Table 2-2

ATTRIBUTE	FUNCTION
COLOR	• Changes the font color • Uses color codes
FACE	• Changes the font type • If the user does not specify a font, the text displays in the default font
SIZE	• Changes the font size • Choices range from 1 to 7, or relative values such as +2

The format that you will use to change the color of the text is <FONT COLOR=" "> with the color number code between the quotation marks. Figure 2-11 shows examples of some of these functions and how they affect the text.

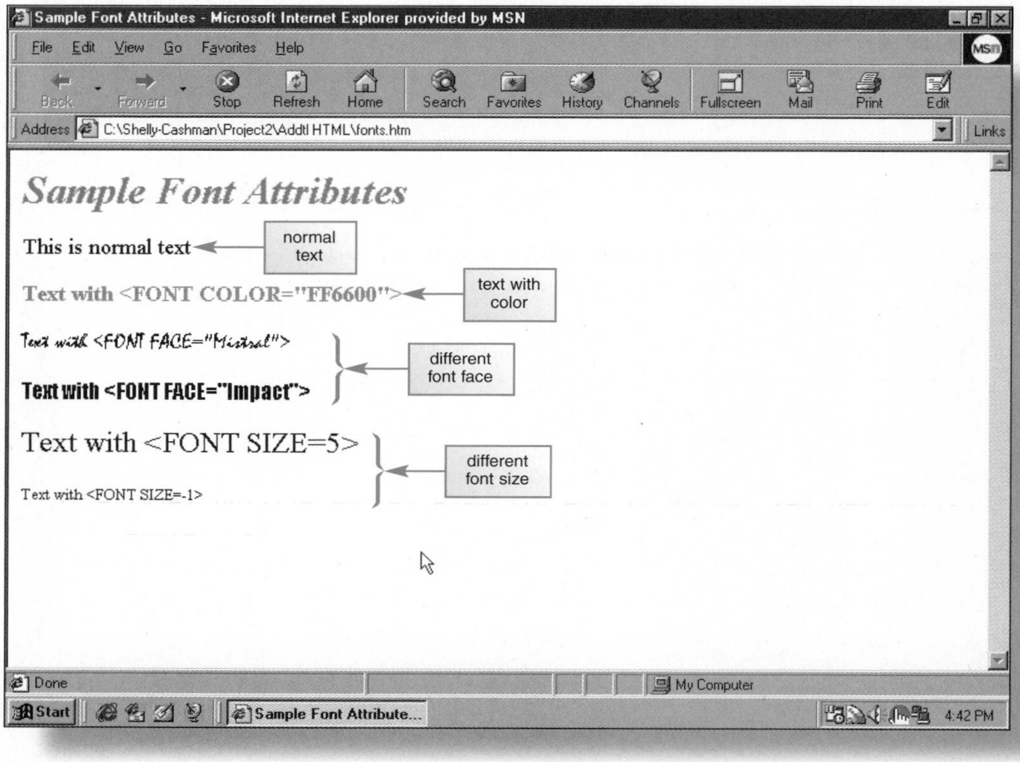

FIGURE 2-11

Steps To Enter a Heading

1 Click line 6 between the <BODY> and </BODY> tags, type `<H1 ALIGN="CENTER"><FONT COLOR="#000066">Web Res</FONT></H1>` **and then press the ENTER key.**

You always should end the tags in the opposite direction in which you started them. You started this line with the <H1> tag, and then used the <FONT> tag. You ended them the opposite way, inserting </FONT> first and then </H1> second (Figure 2-12).This technique is similar to math equations.

```
Untitled - Notepad
File  Edit  Search  Help
<HTML>
<HEAD>
<TITLE>Web Res Home Page</TITLE>
</HEAD>
<BODY>
<H1 ALIGN="CENTER"><FONT COLOR="#000066">Web Res</FONT></H1>

</BODY>
</HTML>
```

line 6

Start | Untitled - Notepad | 3:21 PM

FIGURE 2-12

Entering Text

In Project 1, you entered a paragraph of text using the <P> and </P> tags. Perform the following steps to enter text for this Web page.

More About

Font Sizes

The font attribute used most frequently is SIZE. The values of font sizes range from 1 to 7, with 3 being the default. You also can specify the font size as a relative value using a + or - sign. These relative values range from -3 to +4.

TO ENTER TEXT

1. With the insertion point on line 7, type `<P>Resumes Unlimited, the premier international resume writing company, has expanded to the World Wide Web! Resumes Unlimited recently has formed a new division called Web Res, which is the ultimate resume writing service for the Internet. Web Res specializes in World Wide Web resume creation and publishing. Make your resume instantly available worldwide....put it on the Web!</P>` as the first paragraph in the body.

2. Press the ENTER key.

The paragraph displays (Figure 2-13 on the next page).

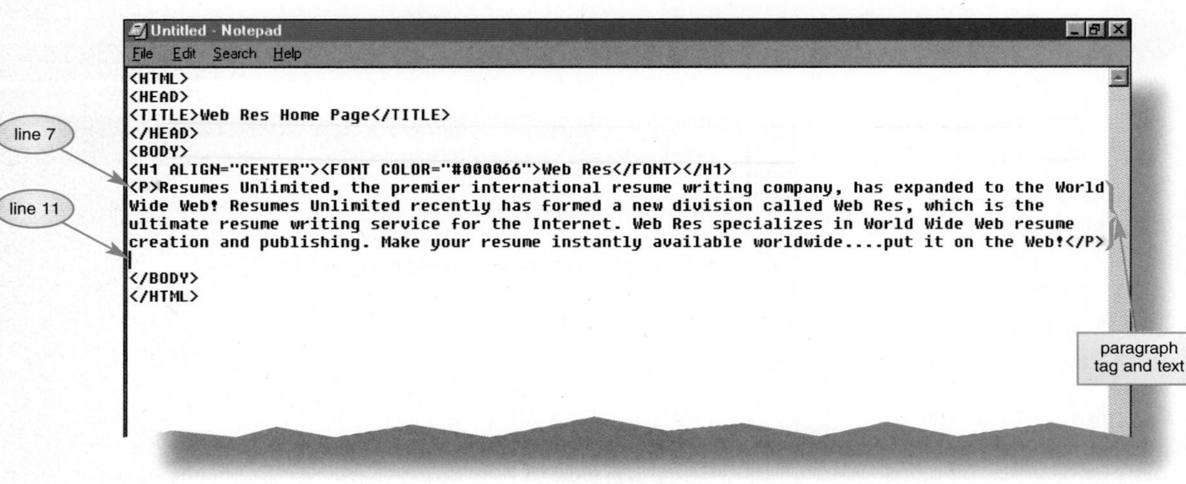
Untitled - Notepad
File Edit Search Help
<HTML>
<HEAD>
<TITLE>Web Res Home Page</TITLE>
</HEAD>
<BODY>
<H1 ALIGN="CENTER"><FONT COLOR="#000066">Web Res</FONT></H1>
<P>Resumes Unlimited, the premier international resume writing company, has expanded to the World Wide Web! Resumes Unlimited recently has formed a new division called Web Res, which is the ultimate resume writing service for the Internet. Web Res specializes in World Wide Web resume creation and publishing. Make your resume instantly available worldwide....put it on the Web!</P>
</BODY>
</HTML>
line 7
line 11
paragraph tag and text

FIGURE 2-13

Entering Bulleted Lists

In Project 1, you entered a bulleted list on the Web page. You did not specify bullet type, so the default, disc, was used. On this Web page, you will change the type of bullet used in the list to give the page a more distinctive look. You change the bullet type by using the TYPE="name" attribute, where name can be square or circle. If you want to use the default (circle, or disc), you need not specify it. The code to create the bulleted list is provided in Table 2-3.

Table 2-3

LINE	HTML TAG AND TEXT
11	<H2>Our company</H2>
12	<UL TYPE="square">
13	<LI>Founded in 1996 by Mark Mullet</LI>
14	<LI>Headquartered in Seattle, Washington</LI>
15	</UL>
16	<H2>Our services</H2>
17	<UL TYPE="square">
18	<LI>Web page resume creation and publishing</LI>
19	<LI>Online database of job listings, for a variety of contract and full-time positions</LI>
20	</UL>

Perform the following steps to enter the two bulleted lists that display on the Web Res home page.

To Enter Two Bulleted Lists

1. **If necessary, click line 11.**
2. **Enter the HTML code (Table 2-3).**
3. **Press the ENTER key.**

The HTML code displays (Figure 2-14).

Untitled - Notepad

File Edit Search Help

```
<HTML>
<HEAD>
<TITLE>Web Res Home Page</TITLE>
</HEAD>
<BODY>
<H1 ALIGN="CENTER"><FONT COLOR="#000066">Web Res</FONT></H1>
<P>Resumes Unlimited, the premier international resume writing company, has expanded to the World
Wide Web! Resumes Unlimited recently has formed a new division called Web Res, which is the
ultimate resume writing service for the Internet. Web Res specializes in World Wide Web resume
creation and publishing. Make your resume instantly available worldwide....put it on the Web!</P>
<H2>Our company</H2>
<UL TYPE="square">
<LI>Founded in 1996 by Mark Mullet</LI>
<LI>Headquartered in Seattle, Washington</LI>
</UL>
<H2>Our services</H2>
<UL TYPE="square">
<LI>Web page resume creation and publishing</LI>
<LI>Online database of job listings, for a variety of contract and full-time positions</LI>
</UL>

</BODY>
</HTML>
```

second bulleted list

FIGURE 2-14

Web Page Images

You can use images in many ways to enhance the look of a Web page. Images can be used as backgrounds, horizontal rules, or as pictures or graphics on any Web page. They make the Web pages more interesting and colorful. Images can be used to help clarify a point being made in the text or as links to other Web pages. They also can be directional symbols that allow the visitor to navigate through the Web site.

HTML Colors

Color is an important aspect of Web development. Visually appealing Web sites attract visitors. For more information about HTML color, visit the HTML More About page (www.scsite.com/html/more.htm) and click HTML Coloring Web Graphics.

Classes of Images

The two classes of images for Web pages are inline and external. **Inline images** are those that display on the Web page directly, together with the text. **External images** are stored separately from the Web page and are displayed only when the visitor clicks a link to display them. The purpose of the Web page determines which class of image you use.

Image Types

Three types of files can be used as images: JPEG, GIF, and PNG. In this project, you will use JPEG files. Joint Photographic Experts Groups (JPEG) files have an extension of .jpg, .jpe, or .jpeg. A **JPEG** (pronounced *JAY-peg*) is a graphic image that is saved using compression techniques to make it smaller for download on the Web. When you create a JPEG image, you can specify the image quality to reach a balance between image quality and file size. JPEG files often are used for photographs because they support millions of colors. These generally are more complex images.

You also can use Graphics Interchange Format (GIF) images on a Web page. These are files with an extension of .gif. A graphic image saved as a **GIF** (pronounced *jiff* or *giff*) also is saved using compression techniques to make it smaller for download on the Web. GIF supports more colors and resolutions than JPEG, making it especially effective for scanned photographs. The technique used to compress GIF files (called LZW compression), however, is patented, which means companies making products that use the GIF format must obtain a license. This does not apply to typical Web users or businesses that include GIFs in their Web pages. GIF images display one line at a time when loading. **Interlaced** GIF images load all at once, starting with a blurry look and becoming sharper as they load. This is a good technique to use for large images because the Web page visitor can see a blurred outline of what is to come as it loads.

The third type of image file is Portable Network Graphics (PNG), designated with a .png or .ping extension. A patent-free alternative to the GIF, the PNG format, has been developed and approved by the World Wide Web Consortium as an Internet graphics standard. The **PNG** (pronounced *ping*) format, also is a compressed file format that supports multiple colors and resolutions. At this time, not all browsers support PNG images.

If an image is not in one of these formats, you can use a paint program to convert the image to a Web image (.gif, .png, or .jpg) format. Many paint programs allow you to save a GIF image as interlaced. A number of paint programs are available in the marketplace today. Adobe Photoshop and Corel Draw are two popular paint programs.

Table 2-4

ATTRIBUTE	FUNCTION
ALIGN	• Controls alignment • Can select from bottom, middle, top, left, or right
ALT	• Alternative text to display when an image is being loaded
BORDER	• Defines the border width
HEIGHT	• Defines the height of the image • Improves loading time
HSPACE	• Defines the horizontal space that separates the image from the text
SRC	• Defines the URL of the image to be loaded
VSPACE	• Defines the vertical space that separates the image from the text
WIDTH	• Defines the width of the image • Improves loading time

Image Attributes

Table 2-4 lists the attributes that can be used with the <IMG> tag.

You will use three of these attributes in the <IMG> tags that you create in this project. The SRC attribute is used to define the URL that you want to load. The HEIGHT and WIDTH attributes will define the image size.

More About

Background Images

When choosing a background image, do not select one that overpowers the Web page. Assure that the background image does not make the text difficult to read. The World Wide Web has a variety of Web sites with background images. Many of these require that you name the Web site as a source for the image. For more information about background images, visit the HTML More About page (www.scsite.com/html/more.htm) and click Background Images.

Inserting Background and Horizontal Rule Images

In Project 1, you inserted a colored background and a default horizontal rule to give your Web page more pizzazz. In this project, you will use the <IMG> tag to insert images to be used as the background and horizontal rule. The two image files that you will use are stored on the HTML Data Disk. If you do not have a copy of the HTML Data Disk, see the inside back cover for instructions for downloading the HTML Data Disk, or see your instructor.

Inserting a Background Image

You use the **BACKGROUND** attribute to insert the background image on the Web page. The BACKGROUND attribute defines the source of the image. This statement tells the browser where to locate the image you want displayed.

To Insert a Background Image

1 Click immediately to the right of the Y in the <BODY> tag on line 5 to position the insertion point and then press the SPACEBAR.

2 Type BACKGROUND="greyback.jpg" **as the attribute.**

The HTML code displays (Figure 2-15). When displayed, the Web page background now has a grey, lightly textured look.

Untitled - Notepad

File Edit Search Help

```
<HTML>
<HEAD>
<TITLE>Web Res Home Page</TITLE>
</HEAD>
<BODY BACKGROUND="greyback.jpg">
<H1 ALIGN="CENTER"><FONT COLOR="#000066">Web Res</FONT></H1>
<P>Resumes Unlimited, the premier international resume writing company, has expanded to the World
Wide Web! Resumes Unlimited recently has formed a new division called Web Res, which is the
ultimate resume writing service for the Internet. Web Res specializes in World Wide Web resume
creation and publishing. Make your resume instantly available worldwide....put it on the Web!</P>
<H2>Our company</H2>
<UL TYPE="square">
<LI>Founded in 1996 by Mark Mullet</LI>
<LI>Headquartered in Seattle, Washington</LI>
</UL>
<H2>Our services</H2>
<UL TYPE="square">
<LI>Web page resume creation and publishing</LI>
<LI>Online database of job listings, for a variety of contract and full-time positions</LI>
</UL>

</BODY>
</HTML>
```

line 5

background image

FIGURE 2-15

Inserting a Horizontal Rule Image

In addition to the SRC attribute, you will use the HEIGHT and WIDTH attributes in the <IMG> tag to insert the horizontal rule image. Defining the height and width of an image helps the image display faster in the browser because the Web browser does not have to calculate the dimensions. Most paint programs will indicate the height and width of an image in pixels (number of dots). You can use the dimensions of the image itself or alter these dimensions within the <IMG> tag. Define image dimensions carefully. If you make an image too large, it will look grainy, as shown in Figure 2-16.

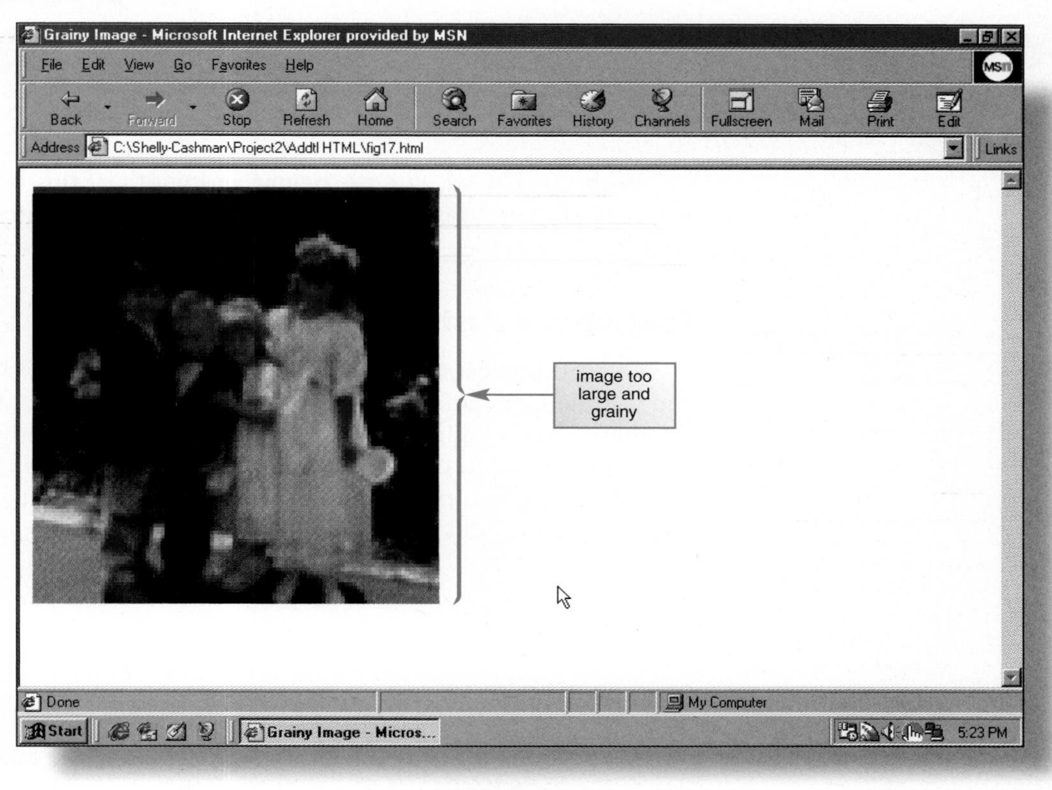

FIGURE 2-16

To Insert a Horizontal Rule Image

1 Click immediately to the right of the </H1> tag on line 6 and then press the ENTER key.

2 Type `<CENTER> <IMG SRC="bluebar.jpg" HEIGHT=5 WIDTH=500> </CENTER>` **as the tag.**

The HTML code displays (Figure 2-17).

Untitled - Notepad

File Edit Search Help

```
<HTML>
<HEAD>
<TITLE>Web Res Home Page</TITLE>
</HEAD>
<BODY BACKGROUND="greyback.jpg">
<H1 ALIGN="CENTER"><FONT COLOR="#000066">Web Res</FONT></H1>
<CENTER><IMG SRC="bluebar.jpg" HEIGHT=5 WIDTH=500></CENTER>
<P>Resumes Unlimited, the premier international resume writing company, has expanded to the World
Wide Web! Resumes Unlimited recently has formed a new division called Web Res, which is the
ultimate resume writing service for the Internet. Web Res specializes in World Wide Web resume
creation and publishing. Make your resume instantly available worldwide....put it on the Web!</P>
<H2>Our company</H2>
<UL TYPE="square">
<LI>Founded in 1996 by Mark Mullet</LI>
<LI>Headquartered in Seattle, Washington</LI>
</UL>
<H2>Our services</H2>
<UL TYPE="square">
<LI>Web page resume creation and publishing</LI>
<LI>Online database of job listings, for a variety of contract and full-time positions</LI>
</UL>

</BODY>
</HTML>
```

line 6

horizontal rule image

Start | Untitled - Notepad | 4:28 PM

FIGURE 2-17

With this HTML tag, the height and width of this horizontal rule image are enlarged slightly to make the horizontal rule more evenly dispersed across the Web page.

Copying and Pasting Text

One of the best features of Windows is the capability to copy and paste text. You can use the Copy and Paste commands to copy text from one area of a file to another, which eliminates the need to type the same command twice. You will use these commands to copy the horizontal rule image to another section of the Web page, resulting in a more balanced look. Because you have typed the image insert command once, you can just copy it to another section of the file.

Steps To Copy and Paste Text

1 **Position the mouse pointer immediately to the left of the <CENTER> tag in line 7.**

2 **Drag through the > in the </CENTER> tag.**

The text, <CENTER> <IMG SRC="bluebar.jpg" HEIGHT=5 WIDTH=500> </CENTER>, is highlighted (Figure 2-18).

```
Untitled - Notepad
File  Edit  Search  Help
<HTML>
<HEAD>
<TITLE>Web Res Home Page</TITLE>
</HEAD>
<BODY BACKGROUND="greyback.jpg">
<H1 ALIGN="CENTER"><FONT COLOR="#000066">Web Res</FONT></H1>
<CENTER><IMG SRC="bluebar.jpg" HEIGHT=5 WIDTH=500></CENTER>
<P>Resumes Unlimited, the premier international resume writing company, has expanded to the World
Wide Web! Resumes Unlimited recently has formed a new division called Web Res, which is the
ultimate resume writing service for the Internet. Web Res specializes in World Wide Web resume
creation and publishing. Make your resume instantly available worldwide....put it on the Web!</P>
<H2>Our company</H2>
<UL TYPE="square">
<LI>Founded in 1996 by Mark Mullet</LI>
<LI>Headquartered in Seattle, Washington</LI>
</UL>
<H2>Our services</H2>
<UL TYPE="square">
<LI>Web page resume creation and publishing</LI>
<LI>Online database of job listings, for a variety of contract and full-time positions</LI>
</UL>

</BODY>
```

line 7

highlighted text

FIGURE 2-18

3 **Click Edit on the menu bar and then point to Copy (Figure 2-19).**

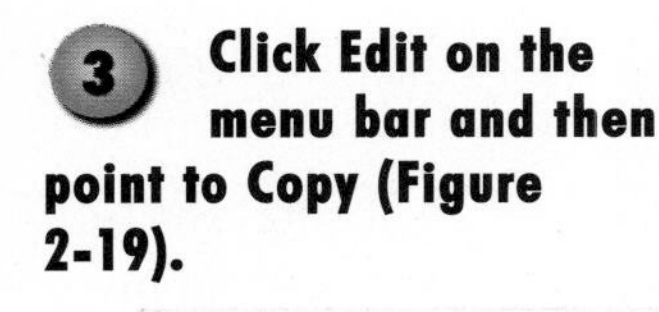

```
Untitled - Notepad
File  Edit  Search  Help
Undo        Ctrl+Z
Cut         Ctrl+X
Copy        Ctrl+C
Paste       Ctrl+V
Delete      Del
Select All
Time/Date   F5
✔ Word Wrap
Set Font...
```

Edit menu

Copy command

FIGURE 2-19

4 **Click Copy and then click line 22.**

5 **Click Edit on the menu bar and then point to Paste (Figure 2-20).**

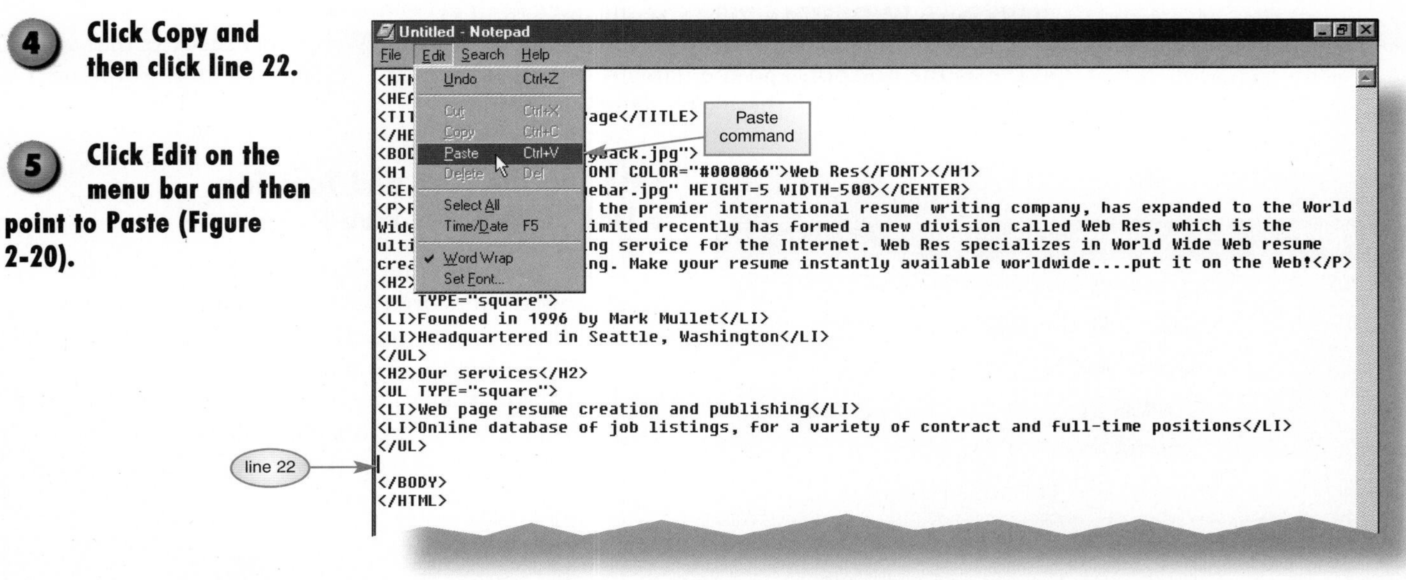
Untitled - Notepad
File
Edit
Search
Help
Undo Ctrl+Z
Cut Ctrl+X
Copy Ctrl+C
Paste Ctrl+V
Delete Del
Select All
Time/Date F5
Word Wrap
Set Font...
Paste command
line 22
<UL TYPE="square">
<LI>Founded in 1996 by Mark Mullet</LI>
<LI>Headquartered in Seattle, Washington</LI>
</UL>
<H2>Our services</H2>
<UL TYPE="square">
<LI>Web page resume creation and publishing</LI>
<LI>Online database of job listings, for a variety of contract and full-time positions</LI>
</UL>
</BODY>
</HTML>

FIGURE 2-20

Click Paste and then press the ENTER key.

The HTML code displays with the pasted text (Figure 2-21).

```
<HTML>
<HEAD>
<TITLE>Web Res Home Page</TITLE>
</HEAD>
<BODY BACKGROUND="greyback.jpg">
<H1 ALIGN="CENTER"><FONT COLOR="#000066">Web Res</FONT></H1>
<CENTER><IMG SRC="bluebar.jpg" HEIGHT=5 WIDTH=500></CENTER>
<P>Resumes Unlimited, the premier international resume writing company, has expanded to the World
Wide Web! Resumes Unlimited recently has formed a new division called Web Res, which is the
ultimate resume writing service for the Internet. Web Res specializes in World Wide Web resume
creation and publishing. Make your resume instantly available worldwide....put it on the Web!</P>
<H2>Our company</H2>
<UL TYPE="square">
<LI>Founded in 1996 by Mark Mullet</LI>
<LI>Headquartered in Seattle, Washington</LI>
</UL>
<H2>Our services</H2>
<UL TYPE="square">
<LI>Web page resume creation and publishing</LI>
<LI>Online database of job listings, for a variety of contract and full-time positions</LI>
</UL>
<CENTER><IMG SRC="bluebar.jpg" HEIGHT=5 WIDTH=500></CENTER>

</BODY>
</HTML>
```


FIGURE 2-21

Adding a Link to the Second Web Page

As discussed in Project 1, a Web site is a collection of Web pages created and maintained by a group or individual. One link used frequently in Web development is a link to another Web page within the same Web site. In this project, you will add a link from the Web Res home page to a Sample Resume page.

The <A> and </A> tags are used to create links. This often is called the **anchor tag** because it is used to create anchors for links within the same Web page, which is discussed later in this project. Table 2-5 shows some of the attributes associated with the <A> tag and their functions. You will use the Hypertext REFerence (HREF) attribute to link to another Web page within the same Web site. **HREF** indicates the name or URL of the file to which the link points. You will use the HREF attribute most often together with the <A> anchor tag in HTML coding.

You will need two items to create a link to another Web page: the text that will serve as the hotspot, and the name of the file to which you want to link. In the next steps, you will define these two items.

Table 2-5

ATTRIBUTE	FUNCTION
COORDS	Sets the size of the shape using pixel or percentage lengths
HREF	Defines the URL of the linked page
NAME	Defines an anchor
REL	Forward link types
REV	Reverse link types
TARGET	Determines where the page will display

Entering the Text and Tags for a Link to Another Web Page

Now you will enter a paragraph of text and select a word or words within the paragraph to use as the hotspot. Your selection should immediately tell the Web page visitor the purpose of the link. When the link on the home page is clicked, the browser will display the Sample Resume page. Because this text is in paragraph format, you will use the <P> and </P> tags, as discussed in Project 1.

Steps To Enter the Text and Tags for a Link to Another Web Page

1. **With the insertion point on line 23 just before the </BODY> tag, type** `<P>To learn more about services that Web Res can provide, please browse our site or call us at (206) 555-1Web. Preview our Web page resume sample.</P>` **and then press the ENTER key (Figure 2-22).**

```
Untitled - Notepad
File Edit Search Help
<HTML>
<HEAD>
<TITLE>Web Res Home Page</TITLE>
</HEAD>
<BODY BACKGROUND="greyback.jpg">
<CENTER><H1><FONT COLOR="#000066">Web Res</FONT></H1></CENTER>
<CENTER><IMG SRC="bluebar.jpg" HEIGHT=5 WIDTH=500></CENTER>
<P>Resumes Unlimited, the premier international resume writing company, has expanded to the World
Wide Web! Resumes Unlimited recently has formed a new division called Web Res, which is the
ultimate resume writing service for the Internet. Web Res specializes in World Wide Web resume
creation and publishing. Make your resume instantly available worldwide.....put it on the Web!<P>
<H2>Our company</H2>
<UL TYPE="square">
<LI>Founded in 1996 by Mark Mullet</LI>
<LI>Headquartered in Seattle, Washington</LI>
</UL>
<H2>Our services</H2>
<UL TYPE="square">
<LI>Web page resume creation and publishing</LI>
<LI>Online database of job listings, for a variety of contract and full-time positions</LI>
</UL>
<CENTER><IMG SRC="bluebar.jpg" HEIGHT=5 WIDTH=500></CENTER>
<P>To learn more about services that Web Res can provide, please browse our site or call us at
(206) 555-1Web. Preview our Web page resume sample.</P>

</BODY>
</HTML>

Start | Untitled - Notepad | 9:18 AM
```

line 23

new paragraph

FIGURE 2-22

2. **Click immediately before the s in sample on line 24. Type** `<A HREF="sample1.htm">` **to create the link destination.**

3. **Click immediately after the e in sample. Type** `</A>` **to end the tag.**

The HTML code displays (Figure 2-23). The </A> tag indicates the end of the hotspot text.

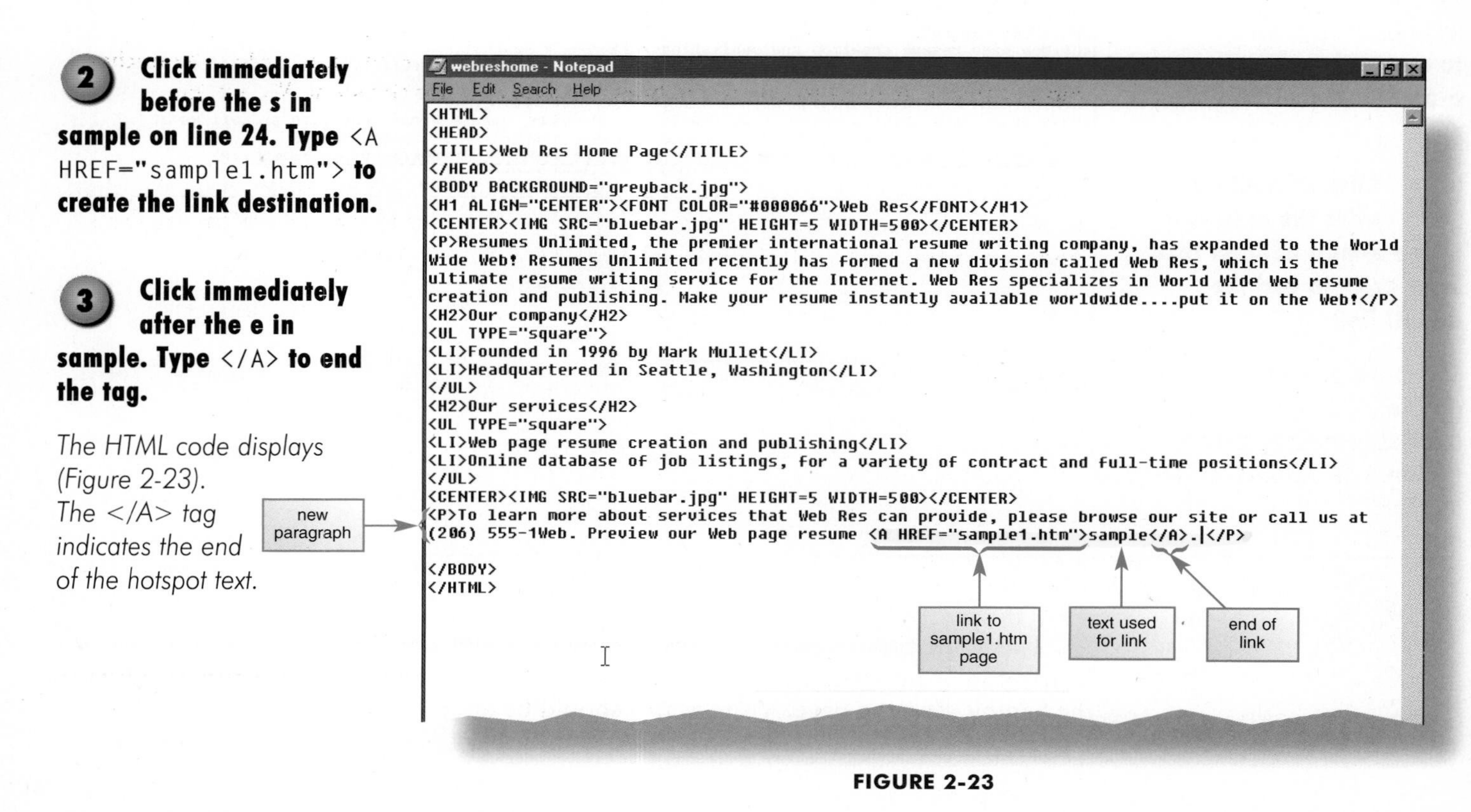
webreshome - Notepad
File Edit Search Help
<HTML>
<HEAD>
<TITLE>Web Res Home Page</TITLE>
</HEAD>
<BODY BACKGROUND="greyback.jpg">
<H1 ALIGN="CENTER"><FONT COLOR="#000066">Web Res</FONT></H1>
<CENTER><IMG SRC="bluebar.jpg" HEIGHT=5 WIDTH=500></CENTER>
<P>Resumes Unlimited, the premier international resume writing company, has expanded to the World
Wide Web! Resumes Unlimited recently has formed a new division called Web Res, which is the
ultimate resume writing service for the Internet. Web Res specializes in World Wide Web resume
creation and publishing. Make your resume instantly available worldwide....put it on the Web!</P>
<H2>Our company</H2>
<UL TYPE="square">
<LI>Founded in 1996 by Mark Mullet</LI>
<LI>Headquartered in Seattle, Washington</LI>
</UL>
<H2>Our services</H2>
<UL TYPE="square">
<LI>Web page resume creation and publishing</LI>
<LI>Online database of job listings, for a variety of contract and full-time positions</LI>
</UL>
<CENTER><IMG SRC="bluebar.jpg" HEIGHT=5 WIDTH=500></CENTER>
<P>To learn more about services that Web Res can provide, please browse our site or call us at
(206) 555-1Web. Preview our Web page resume <A HREF="sample1.htm">sample</A>.</P>
</BODY>
</HTML>
new paragraph
link to sample1.htm page
text used for link
end of link

FIGURE 2-23

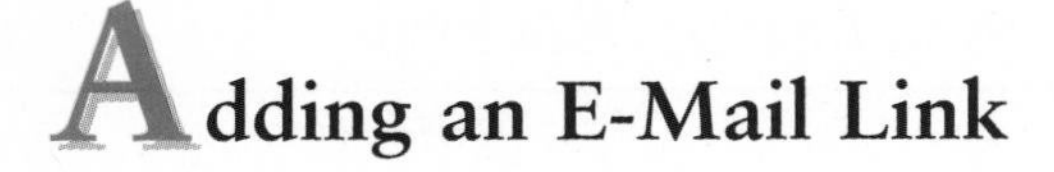

Adding an E-Mail Link

It is important for Web site visitors to be able to contact you for additional information or to comment on the Web page. Home pages that are developed properly include an e-mail link. The wording for this type of link also is important. Simply including an e-mail address and using it as the link provides no information. You need to instruct visitors to use the e-mail address to contact you with questions or comments.

The <A> and </A> tags also are used to create an e-mail link. The word, Mailto, is used for a link that creates electronic mail. When the browser recognizes a Mailto URL, it prompts the visitor for a subject and the body of the mail message.

To Add an E-Mail Link

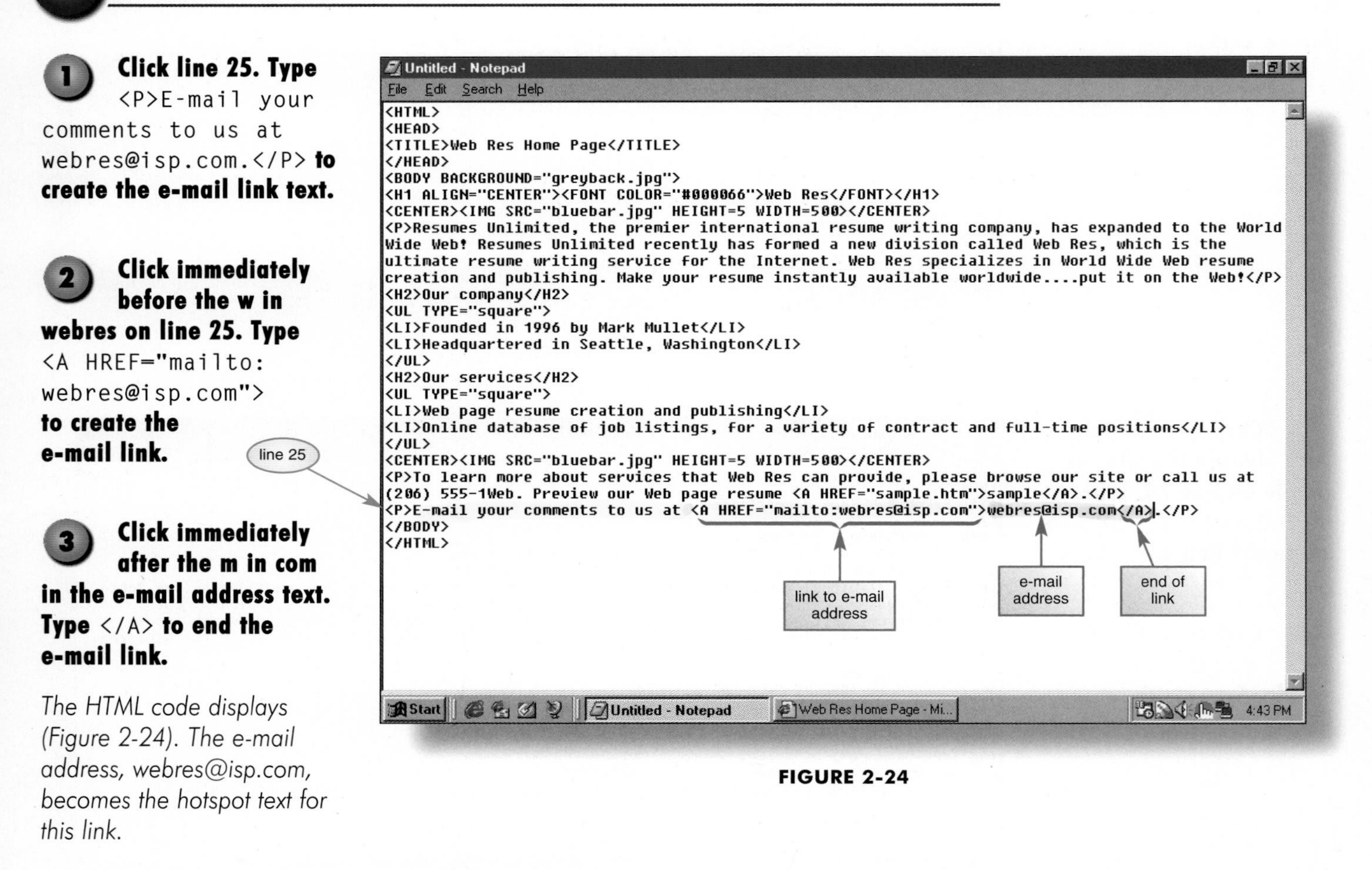
Untitled - Notepad
File Edit Search Help
<HTML>
<HEAD>
<TITLE>Web Res Home Page</TITLE>
</HEAD>
<BODY BACKGROUND="greyback.jpg">
<H1 ALIGN="CENTER"><FONT COLOR="#000066">Web Res</FONT></H1>
<CENTER><IMG SRC="bluebar.jpg" HEIGHT=5 WIDTH=500></CENTER>
<P>Resumes Unlimited, the premier international resume writing company, has expanded to the World
Wide Web! Resumes Unlimited recently has formed a new division called Web Res, which is the
ultimate resume writing service for the Internet. Web Res specializes in World Wide Web resume
creation and publishing. Make your resume instantly available worldwide....put it on the Web!</P>
<H2>Our company</H2>
<UL TYPE="square">
<LI>Founded in 1996 by Mark Mullet</LI>
<LI>Headquartered in Seattle, Washington</LI>
</UL>
<H2>Our services</H2>
<UL TYPE="square">
<LI>Web page resume creation and publishing</LI>
<LI>Online database of job listings, for a variety of contract and full-time positions</LI>
</UL>
<CENTER><IMG SRC="bluebar.jpg" HEIGHT=5 WIDTH=500></CENTER>
<P>To learn more about services that Web Res can provide, please browse our site or call us at
(206) 555-1Web. Preview our Web page resume <A HREF="sample.htm">sample</A>.</P>
<P>E-mail your comments to us at <A HREF="mailto:webres@isp.com">webres@isp.com</A>.</P>
</BODY>
</HTML>
line 25
link to e-mail address
e-mail address
end of link
Start
Untitled - Notepad
Web Res Home Page - Mi...
4:43 PM

1 **Click line 25. Type** <P>E-mail your comments to us at webres@isp.com.</P> **to create the e-mail link text.**

2 **Click immediately before the w in webres on line 25. Type** <A HREF="mailto: webres@isp.com"> **to create the e-mail link.**

3 **Click immediately after the m in com in the e-mail address text. Type** </A> **to end the e-mail link.**

The HTML code displays (Figure 2-24). The e-mail address, webres@isp.com, becomes the hotspot text for this link.

FIGURE 2-24

The home page is the first Web page that visitors see when they visit a Web site. It therefore is important to include relevant links, such as the one created to link to the Sample Resume page. Visitors also should be able to contact you via e-mail from the home page as well. These two links are necessary parts of Web development.

Saving and Printing the HTML File

You should save the HTML file and print it. A printed copy of the file also is important for your reference.

TO SAVE AND PRINT THE HTML FILE

1. Insert the HTML Data Disk in drive A. If you do not have a copy of the HTML Data Disk, see the inside back cover for instructions for downloading the HTML Data Disk, or see your instructor.
2. Click File on the menu bar and then click Save As. Type `webreshome.htm` in the File name text box. If necessary, click 3½ Floppy (A:) in the Save in list. Click the Save button in the Save As dialog box.
3. Click File on the menu bar and then click Print.

The HTML file prints (Figure 2-25).

```
webreshome

<HTML>
<HEAD>
<TITLE>Web Res Home Page</TITLE>
</HEAD>
<BODY BACKGROUND="greyback.jpg">
<H1 ALIGN="CENTER"><FONT COLOR="#000066">Web Res</FONT></H1>
<CENTER><IMG SRC="bluebar.jpg" HEIGHT=5 WIDTH=500></CENTER>
<P>Resumes Unlimted, the premier international resume writing company, has
expanded to the World Wide Web! Resumes Unlimited recently has formed a new
division called Web Res, which is the ultimate resume writing service for the
Internet. Web Res specializes in World Wide Web resume creation and publishing.
Make your resume instantly available worldwide....put it on the Web!</P>
<H2>Our company</H2>
<UL TYPE="square">
<LI>Founded in 1996 by Mark Mullet</LI>
<LI>Headquartered in Seattle, Washington</LI>
</UL>
<H2>Our services</H2>
<UL TYPE="square">
<LI>Web page resume creation and publishing</LI>
<LI>Online database of job listings, for a variety of contract and full-time
positions</LI>
</UL>
<CENTER><IMG SRC="bluebar.jpg" HEIGHT=5 WIDTH=500></CENTER>
<P>To learn more about services that Web Res can provide, please browse our site
or call us at (206) 555-1Web. Preview our Web page resume <A
HREF="sample1.htm">sample</A>.</P>
<P>E-mail your comments to us at <A
HREF="mailto:webres@isp.com">webres@isp.com</A>.</P>
</BODY>
</HTML>

Page 1
```

FIGURE 2-25

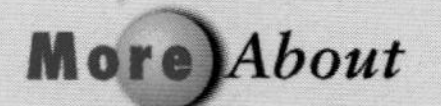

Web Page Testing

An important part of Web page development is testing Web page links. For more information about link testing, visit the HTML More About page (www.scsite.com/html/more.htm) and click Web Page Testing.

Viewing the Web Page and Testing the Links

Just as in Project 1, you should view the Web Page using a browser. It also is important to test the links to verify that they function as expected.

When the home page displays, you can click the e-mail hyperlink to verify that it works correctly. You also can test the link to the second page by clicking it. The second Web page, sample1.htm, will display, although it is not completed. In the remainder of this project, you add other features to sample1.htm to create the Web page shown in Figure 2-1b on page HTM 2.5.

TO VIEW THE WEB PAGE

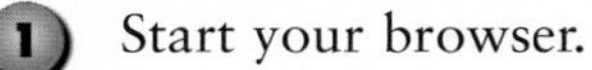

1. Start your browser.
2. If your browser window is not maximized, click the Maximize button.
3. Click the Address bar.
4. Type `a:\webreshome.htm` in the Address text box.
5. Press the ENTER key.

Your browser displays the Web page, webreshome.htm (Figure 2-26).

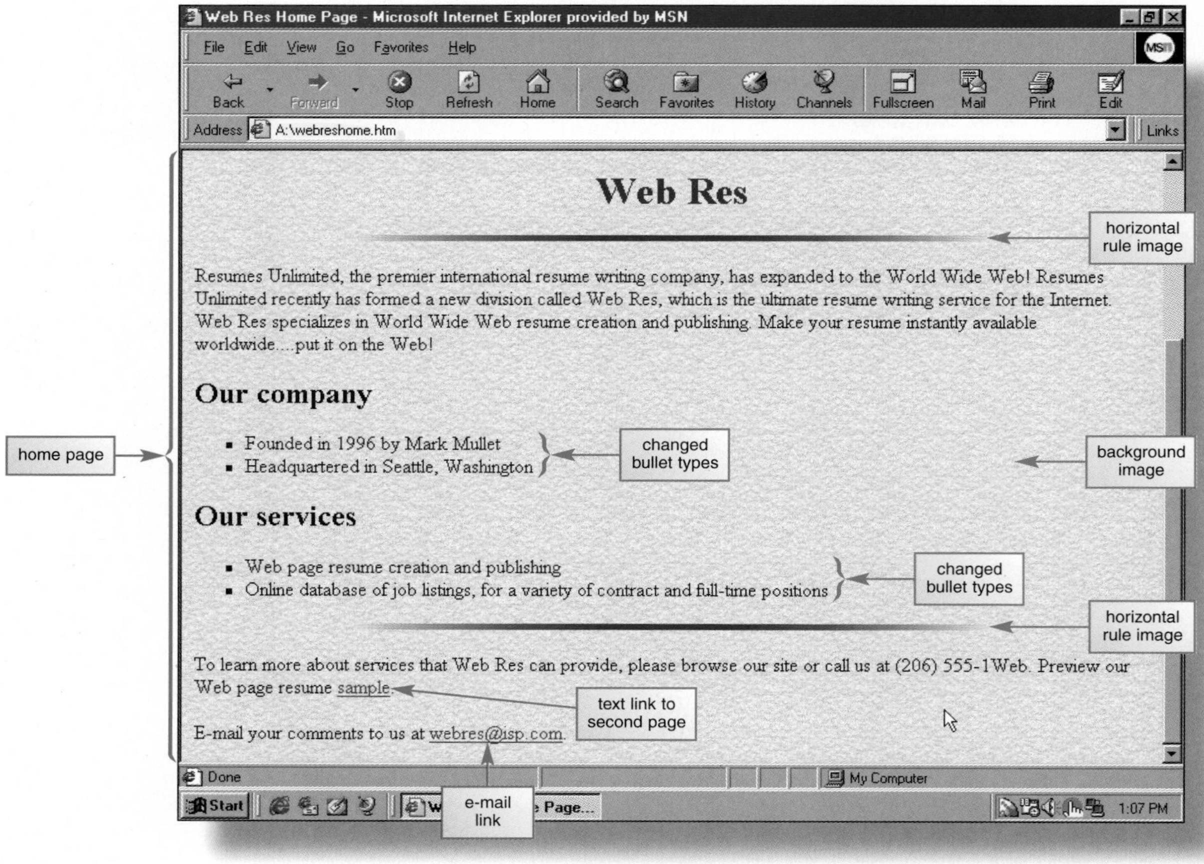

FIGURE 2-26

This page includes background and horizontal rule images and a different bullet type. This page also has two links. The first hotspot is the word, sample, and will link to the sample resume on the second Web page. The second hotspot is the e-mail address, webres@isp.com, and will link to a New Message window. Before testing the links, follow this step to print the Web page.

TO PRINT THE WEB PAGE

1. Click the Print button on the Standard Buttons toolbar.

The printed Web page displays (Figure 2-27).

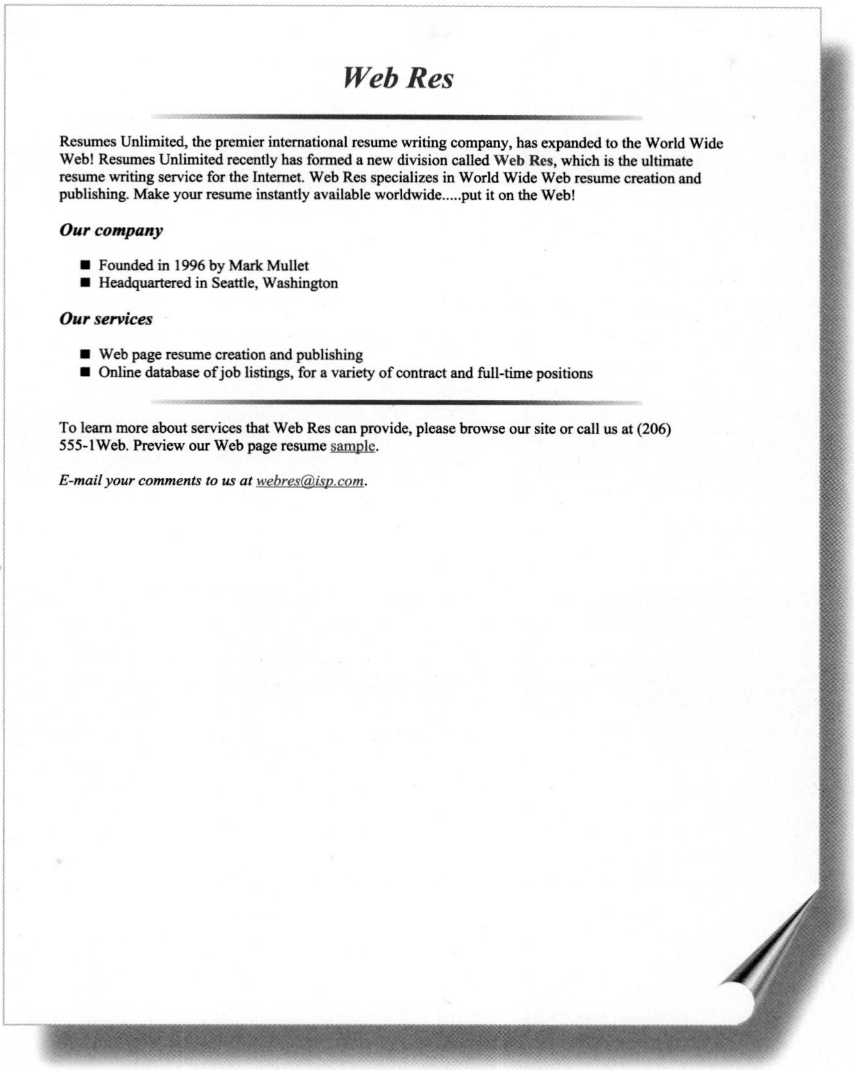

Web Res

Resumes Unlimited, the premier international resume writing company, has expanded to the World Wide Web! Resumes Unlimited recently has formed a new division called Web Res, which is the ultimate resume writing service for the Internet. Web Res specializes in World Wide Web resume creation and publishing. Make your resume instantly available worldwide.....put it on the Web!

Our company

- Founded in 1996 by Mark Mullet
- Headquartered in Seattle, Washington

Our services

- Web page resume creation and publishing
- Online database of job listings, for a variety of contract and full-time positions

To learn more about services that Web Res can provide, please browse our site or call us at (206) 555-1Web. Preview our Web page resume sample.

E-mail your comments to us at webres@isp.com.

FIGURE 2-27

Perform the steps on the next page to test the links in the Web Res Web page.

Steps To Test the Links

1 Point to the e-mail link, webres@isp.com.

The mouse pointer changes to a pointing hand (Figure 2-28).

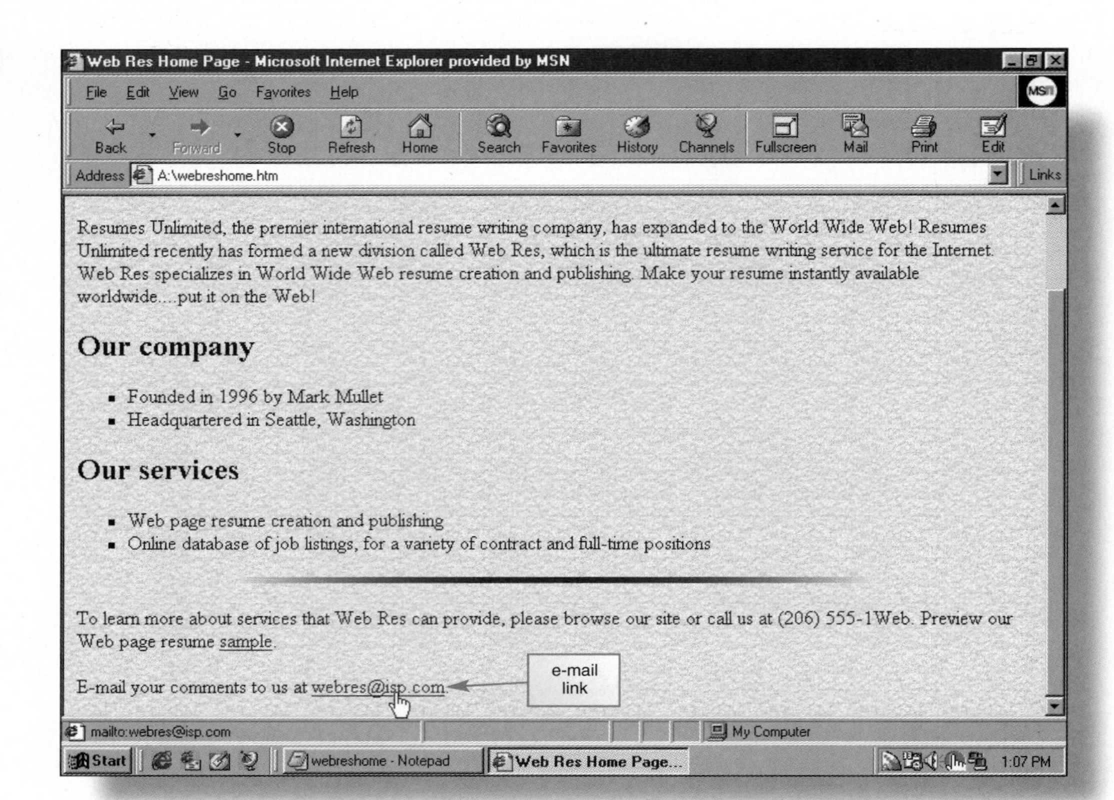

FIGURE 2-28

2 Click webres@isp.com.

A New Message window displays (Figure 2-29). The address, webres@isp.com, displays in the To text box.

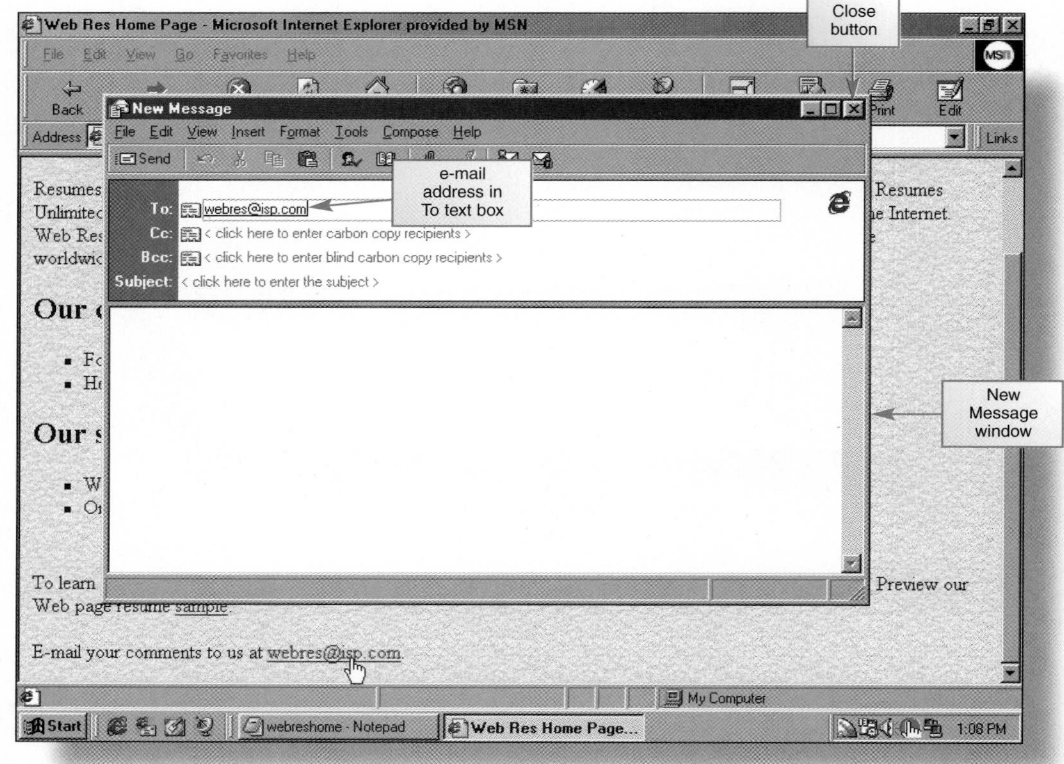

FIGURE 2-29

3 **Click the Close button in the New Message window.**

4 **With the HTML Data Disk in drive A, point to the link, sample.**

The mouse pointer changes to a pointing hand (Figure 2-30).

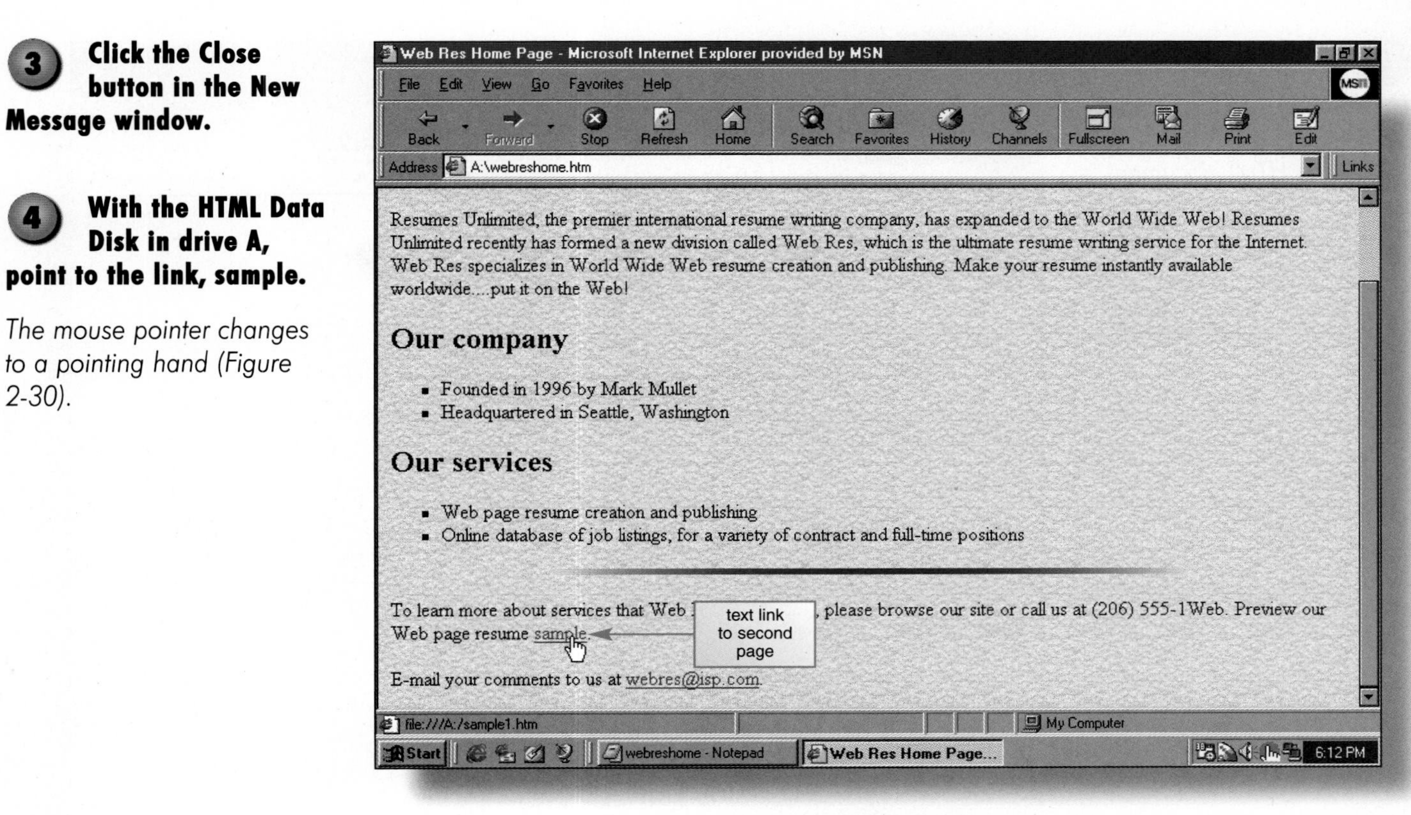

FIGURE 2-30

E-Mail Links

Although it is not common, you can assign more than one e-mail address to a mailto: tag. Use the form "mailto:first@isp.com, second@isp.com" in the <A HREF=> tag. Some older browsers may not support this tag.

(step continued on the next page)

5 Click sample.

The sample1.htm page displays (Figure 2-31). This Web page is an HTML document created for you and stored on the HTML Data Disk.

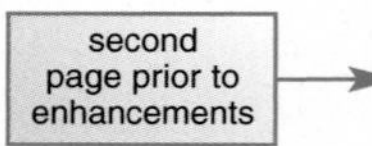

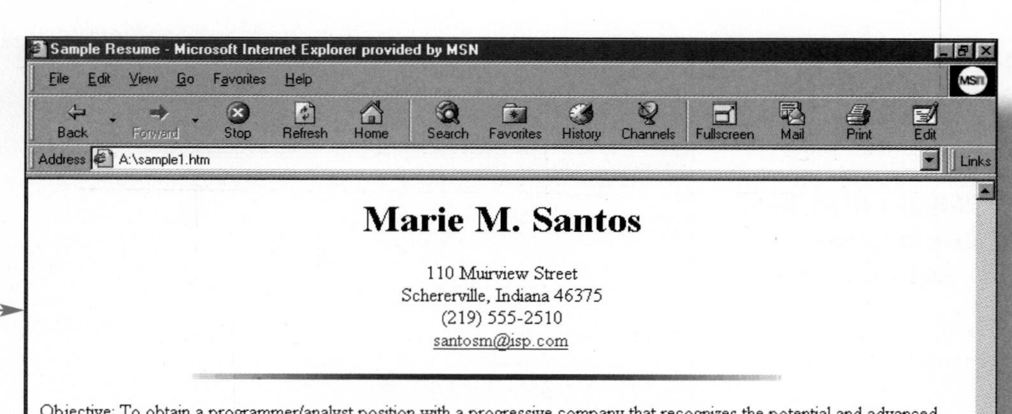

Objective: To obtain a programmer/analyst position with a progressive company that recognizes the potential and advanced uses of technology.

Summary

COMPUTER TECHNOLOGY professional with four years experience ranging from system software development to technical support. Strengths include problem solving and analysis, oral and written communications, diagnostics, scheduling, interpersonal relations, directing others while promoting a spirit of partnership with students, peers and support groups.

Education

- B.S. in Computer Technology, May 1999, Purdue University
- A.S. in Technical Writing, December 1996, Prairie State College

Experience

PURDUE UNIVERSITY, West Lafayette, IN 1996 - Present
Lab Consultant/Help Desk Coordinator, Computing Services
Responsible for main campus computer laboratory operation, scheduling student workers, answering student software questions, and providing technical support.

- Improved student satisfaction by providing technical assistance for a variety of hardware and software issues.
- Designed new reporting methodology that ensured compliance with departmental quality improvement objectives.
- Trained student workers on Help Desk and computer use with concentration on operations and system software improving student workers' knowledge and productivity.

INTERNATIONAL BUSINESS MACHINES (IBM), Chicago, IL 1995
Account Systems Engineer/Co-op Position
Responsible for technical sales assistance and customer technical support for the midrange customer base.

- Sold and installed multiple midrange system upgrades based on an analysis of sizing and growth needs that increased yearly revenue by 20%.
- Received IBM Means Service Award for customer satisfaction with midrange system upgrade installation project.

PRAIRIE STATE COLLEGE, Chicago, IL 1994 - 1995
Office Assistant, English Department
Responsible for various administrative functions including research, reception, answering telephones, secretarial, and word processing. Provided support for secretary and English department.

- Supervised the installation of new system software updates improving efficiency and effectiveness.
- Updated the student database and coordinated the mailing of the department newsletter.

Hardware Skills

IBM PC and compatibles, Apple Macintosh, UNIX systems

Software Skills

HTML, Microsoft FrontPage, Microsoft Internet Information Server 4.0, Windows, Windows NT Server/Workstation, Microsoft Office Professional, Visual Basic 5, C++, Visual J++/Java, Microsoft Project, Microsoft Access, Microsoft PowerPoint

Done | My Computer
Start | webreshome.htm - Notepad | Sample Resume - Mic... | 1:02 PM

FIGURE 2-31

Once you have verified that the two links work, scroll through the sample1.htm Web page to view its appearance. In the following section, you will add links within the sample1.htm page and a link to another Web site.

Editing the Second Web Page

The sample1.htm Web page has been created for you and stored on the HTML Data Disk. It is a sample of a resume with all previously discussed features, such as an e-mail link, headings, and bullets, already in place.

In this section, you will enhance the text by adding bold, italics, and color. You also will learn how to insert an image and wrap the text around it. You will add two other types of links within the same Web page and to another Web site. Finally, you will link the image and the text.

The browser in Figure 2-31 displays the current sample1.htm Web page. The same Web page with enhancements is shown in Figure 2-32.

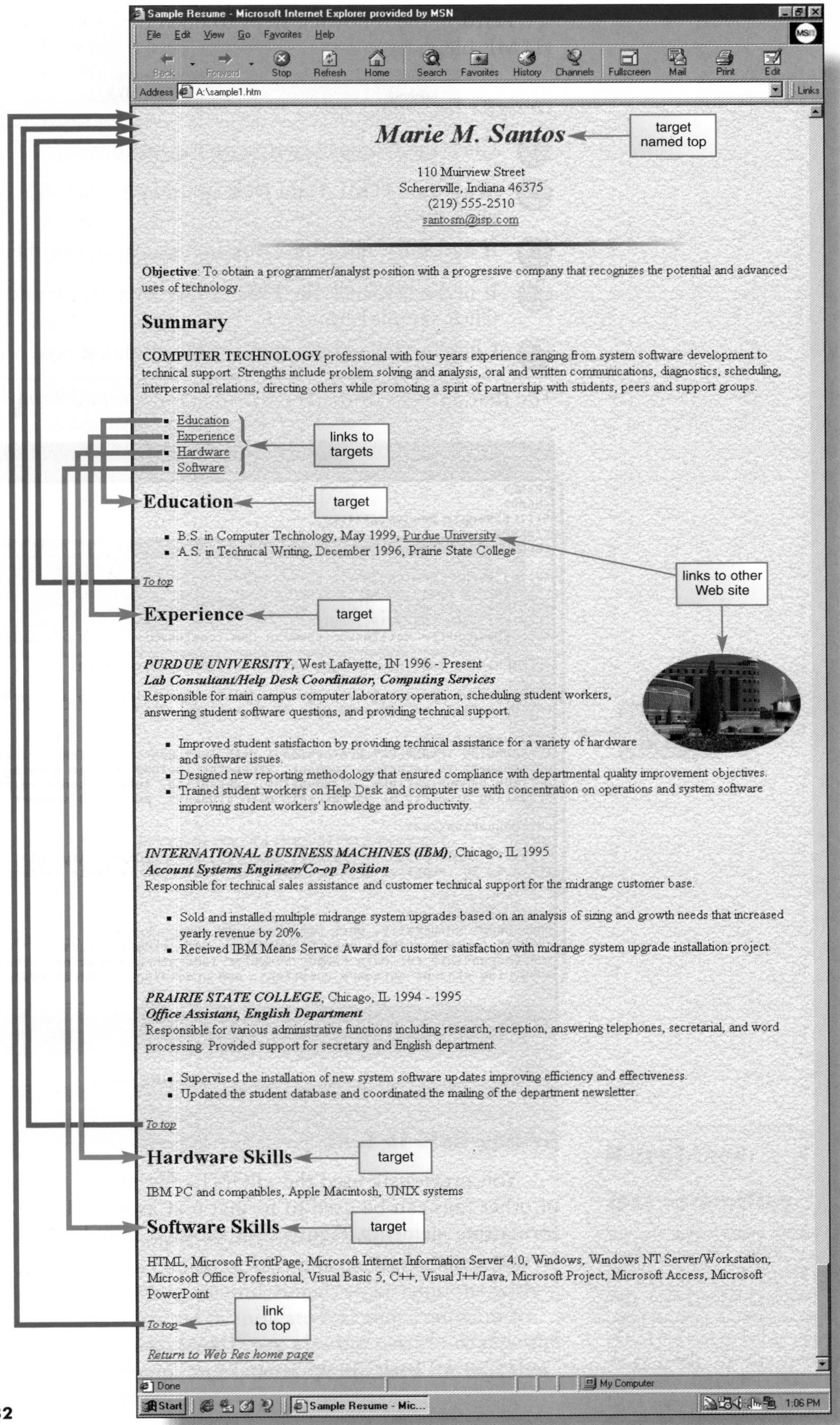

Sample Resume - Microsoft Internet Explorer provided by MSN

Address A:\sample1.htm

Marie M. Santos ← target named top

110 Muirview Street
Schererville, Indiana 46375
(219) 555-2510
santosm@isp.com

Objective: To obtain a programmer/analyst position with a progressive company that recognizes the potential and advanced uses of technology.

Summary

COMPUTER TECHNOLOGY professional with four years experience ranging from system software development to technical support. Strengths include problem solving and analysis, oral and written communications, diagnostics, scheduling, interpersonal relations, directing others while promoting a spirit of partnership with students, peers and support groups.

- Education
- Experience
- Hardware
- Software

(links to targets)

Education ← target

- B.S. in Computer Technology, May 1999, Purdue University
- A.S. in Technical Writing, December 1996, Prairie State College

(links to other Web site)

To top

Experience ← target

PURDUE UNIVERSITY, West Lafayette, IN 1996 - Present
Lab Consultant/Help Desk Coordinator, Computing Services
Responsible for main campus computer laboratory operation, scheduling student workers, answering student software questions, and providing technical support.

- Improved student satisfaction by providing technical assistance for a variety of hardware and software issues.
- Designed new reporting methodology that ensured compliance with departmental quality improvement objectives.
- Trained student workers on Help Desk and computer use with concentration on operations and system software improving student workers' knowledge and productivity.

INTERNATIONAL BUSINESS MACHINES (IBM), Chicago, IL 1995
Account Systems Engineer/Co-op Position
Responsible for technical sales assistance and customer technical support for the midrange customer base.

- Sold and installed multiple midrange system upgrades based on an analysis of sizing and growth needs that increased yearly revenue by 20%.
- Received IBM Means Service Award for customer satisfaction with midrange system upgrade installation project.

PRAIRIE STATE COLLEGE, Chicago, IL 1994 - 1995
Office Assistant, English Department
Responsible for various administrative functions including research, reception, answering telephones, secretarial, and word processing. Provided support for secretary and English department.

- Supervised the installation of new system software updates improving efficiency and effectiveness.
- Updated the student database and coordinated the mailing of the department newsletter.

To top

Hardware Skills ← target

IBM PC and compatibles, Apple Macintosh, UNIX systems

Software Skills ← target

HTML, Microsoft FrontPage, Microsoft Internet Information Server 4.0, Windows, Windows NT Server/Workstation, Microsoft Office Professional, Visual Basic 5, C++, Visual J++/Java, Microsoft Project, Microsoft Access, Microsoft PowerPoint

To top ← link to top

Return to Web Res home page

FIGURE 2-32

4 **Type the multiple tags** <B><I> **and** </I></B> **around Lab Consultant/Help Desk Coordinator on line 32, INTERNATIONAL BUSINESS MACHINES (IBM) on line 45, Account Systems Engineer/Co-op Position on line 46, PRAIRIE STATE COLLEGE on line 57, and Office Assistant, English Department on line 58.**

The bold and italic tags display (Figure 2-38).

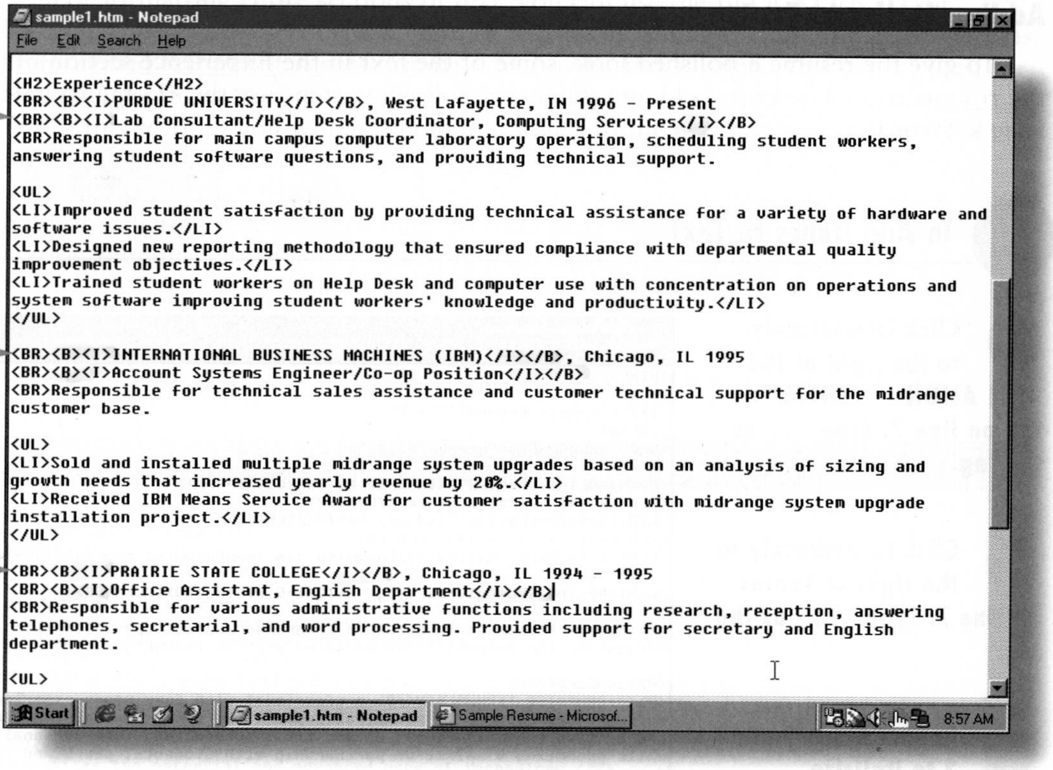

```
sample1.htm - Notepad
File  Edit  Search  Help

<H2>Experience</H2>
<BR><B><I>PURDUE UNIVERSITY</I></B>, West Lafayette, IN 1996 - Present
<BR><B><I>Lab Consultant/Help Desk Coordinator, Computing Services</I></B>     [line 32]
<BR>Responsible for main campus computer laboratory operation, scheduling student workers,
answering student software questions, and providing technical support.

<UL>
<LI>Improved student satisfaction by providing technical assistance for a variety of hardware and
software issues.</LI>
<LI>Designed new reporting methodology that ensured compliance with departmental quality
improvement objectives.</LI>
<LI>Trained student workers on Help Desk and computer use with concentration on operations and
system software improving student workers' knowledge and productivity.</LI>
</UL>

<BR><B><I>INTERNATIONAL BUSINESS MACHINES (IBM)</I></B>, Chicago, IL 1995     [line 45]
<BR><B><I>Account Systems Engineer/Co-op Position</I></B>
<BR>Responsible for technical sales assistance and customer technical support for the midrange
customer base.

<UL>
<LI>Sold and installed multiple midrange system upgrades based on an analysis of sizing and
growth needs that increased yearly revenue by 20%.</LI>
<LI>Received IBM Means Service Award for customer satisfaction with midrange system upgrade
installation project.</LI>
</UL>

<BR><B><I>PRAIRIE STATE COLLEGE</I></B>, Chicago, IL 1994 - 1995     [line 57]
<BR><B><I>Office Assistant, English Department</I></B>
<BR>Responsible for various administrative functions including research, reception, answering
telephones, secretarial, and word processing. Provided support for secretary and English
department.

<UL>

Start | sample1.htm - Notepad | Sample Resume - Microsof...    8:57 AM
```

FIGURE 2-38

Adding Color to Text

Changing the color of the text also can enhance its look. You will change the color of the heading to highlight it (Figure 2-32 on page HTM 2.31).

Steps To Change Text Color

1 **Click immediately to the right of the** <I> **tag on line 7. Type** <FONT COLOR="#000099"> **as the tag.**

2 **Click immediately to the right of Santos on line 7. Type** </FONT> **as the tag (Figure 2-39).**

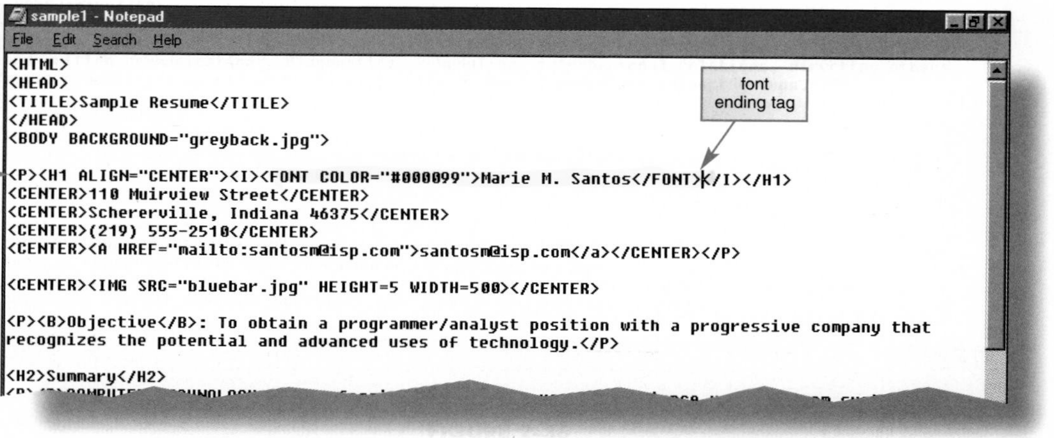

```
sample1 - Notepad
File  Edit  Search  Help
<HTML>
<HEAD>
<TITLE>Sample Resume</TITLE>
</HEAD>
<BODY BACKGROUND="greyback.jpg">

<P><H1 ALIGN="CENTER"><I><FONT COLOR="#000099">Marie M. Santos</FONT></I></H1>     [line 7; font ending tag]
<CENTER>110 Muirview Street</CENTER>
<CENTER>Schererville, Indiana 46375</CENTER>
<CENTER>(219) 555-2510</CENTER>
<CENTER><A HREF="mailto:santosm@isp.com">santosm@isp.com</a></CENTER></P>

<CENTER><IMG SRC="bluebar.jpg" HEIGHT=5 WIDTH=500></CENTER>

<P><B>Objective</B>: To obtain a programmer/analyst position with a progressive company that
recognizes the potential and advanced uses of technology.</P>

<H2>Summary</H2>
```

FIGURE 2-39

Font color #000099 will change the text from the default black color to a dark blue. Refer to Table 1-2 on page HTM 1.29 to see the list of possible color codes.

Changing the Default Bullet Type

The default type for a bulleted, or unordered, list is disc. In the Web Res home page, you changed the bullet type to square. To be consistent, subsequent pages in the site should have square bullets as well.

Steps To Change the Bullet Type

1 Click immediately to the right of the L in the <UL> tag on line 25. Press the SPACEBAR to insert a space and then type `TYPE="square"` **as the tag (Figure 2-40).**

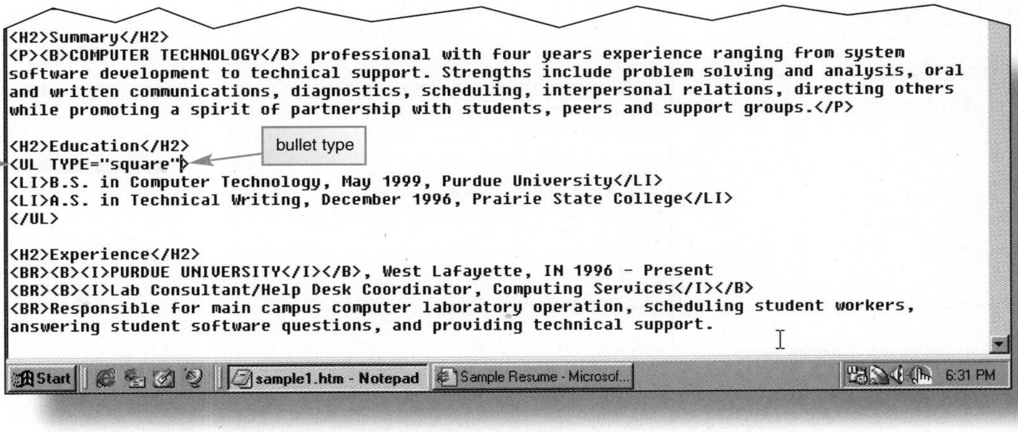

line 25

bullet type

```
<H2>Summary</H2>
<P><B>COMPUTER TECHNOLOGY</B> professional with four years experience ranging from system
software development to technical support. Strengths include problem solving and analysis, oral
and written communications, diagnostics, scheduling, interpersonal relations, directing others
while promoting a spirit of partnership with students, peers and support groups.</P>

<H2>Education</H2>
<UL TYPE="square">
<LI>B.S. in Computer Technology, May 1999, Purdue University</LI>
<LI>A.S. in Technical Writing, December 1996, Prairie State College</LI>
</UL>

<H2>Experience</H2>
<BR><B><I>PURDUE UNIVERSITY</I></B>, West Lafayette, IN 1996 - Present
<BR><B><I>Lab Consultant/Help Desk Coordinator, Computing Services</I></B>
<BR>Responsible for main campus computer laboratory operation, scheduling student workers,
answering student software questions, and providing technical support.
```

Start | sample1.htm - Notepad | Sample Resume - Microsof... | 6:31 PM

FIGURE 2-40

2 Repeat Step 1 to change the bullet types on lines 36, 50, and 63 (Figure 2-41).

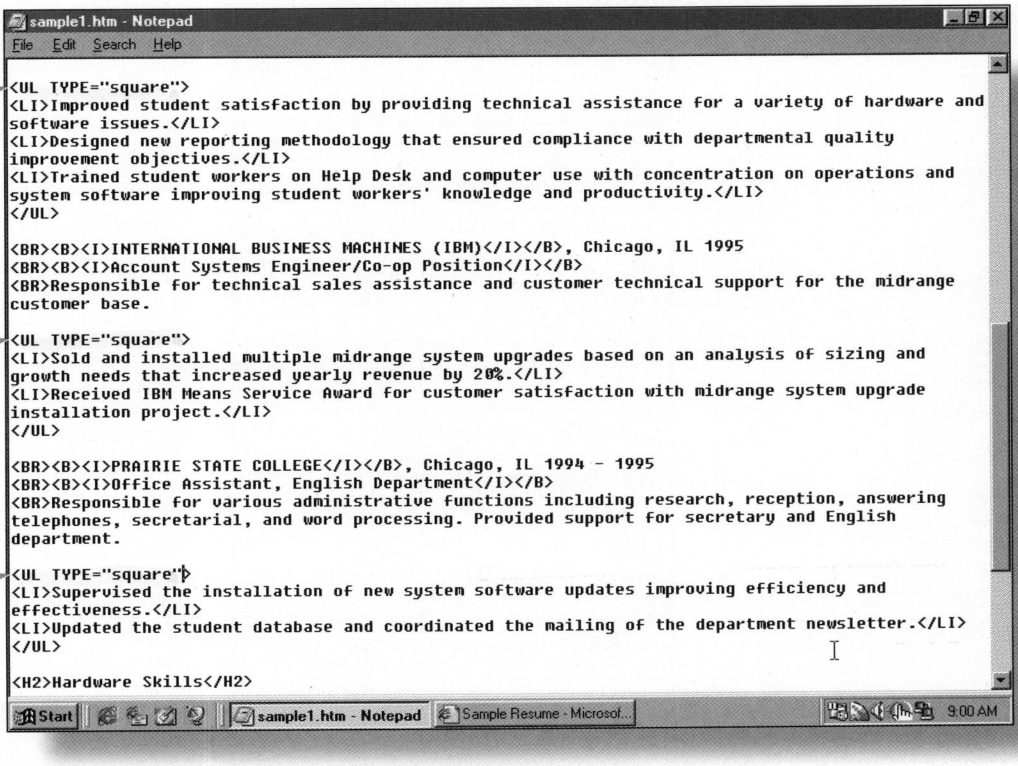

line 36

line 50

line 63

sample1.htm - Notepad

File Edit Search Help

```
<UL TYPE="square">
<LI>Improved student satisfaction by providing technical assistance for a variety of hardware and
software issues.</LI>
<LI>Designed new reporting methodology that ensured compliance with departmental quality
improvement objectives.</LI>
<LI>Trained student workers on Help Desk and computer use with concentration on operations and
system software improving student workers' knowledge and productivity.</LI>
</UL>

<BR><B><I>INTERNATIONAL BUSINESS MACHINES (IBM)</I></B>, Chicago, IL 1995
<BR><B><I>Account Systems Engineer/Co-op Position</I></B>
<BR>Responsible for technical sales assistance and customer technical support for the midrange
customer base.

<UL TYPE="square">
<LI>Sold and installed multiple midrange system upgrades based on an analysis of sizing and
growth needs that increased yearly revenue by 20%.</LI>
<LI>Received IBM Means Service Award for customer satisfaction with midrange system upgrade
installation project.</LI>
</UL>

<BR><B><I>PRAIRIE STATE COLLEGE</I></B>, Chicago, IL 1994 - 1995
<BR><B><I>Office Assistant, English Department</I></B>
<BR>Responsible for various administrative functions including research, reception, answering
telephones, secretarial, and word processing. Provided support for secretary and English
department.

<UL TYPE="square">
<LI>Supervised the installation of new system software updates improving efficiency and
effectiveness.</LI>
<LI>Updated the student database and coordinated the mailing of the department newsletter.</LI>
</UL>

<H2>Hardware Skills</H2>
```

Start | sample1.htm - Notepad | Sample Resume - Microsof... | 9:00 AM

FIGURE 2-41

3 **Click File on the menu bar and then click Save.**

4 **Activate your browser by clicking the Sample Resume button on the taskbar.**

5 **Click the Refresh button on the Standard Buttons toolbar.**

The Sample Resume Web page displays (Figure 2-42).

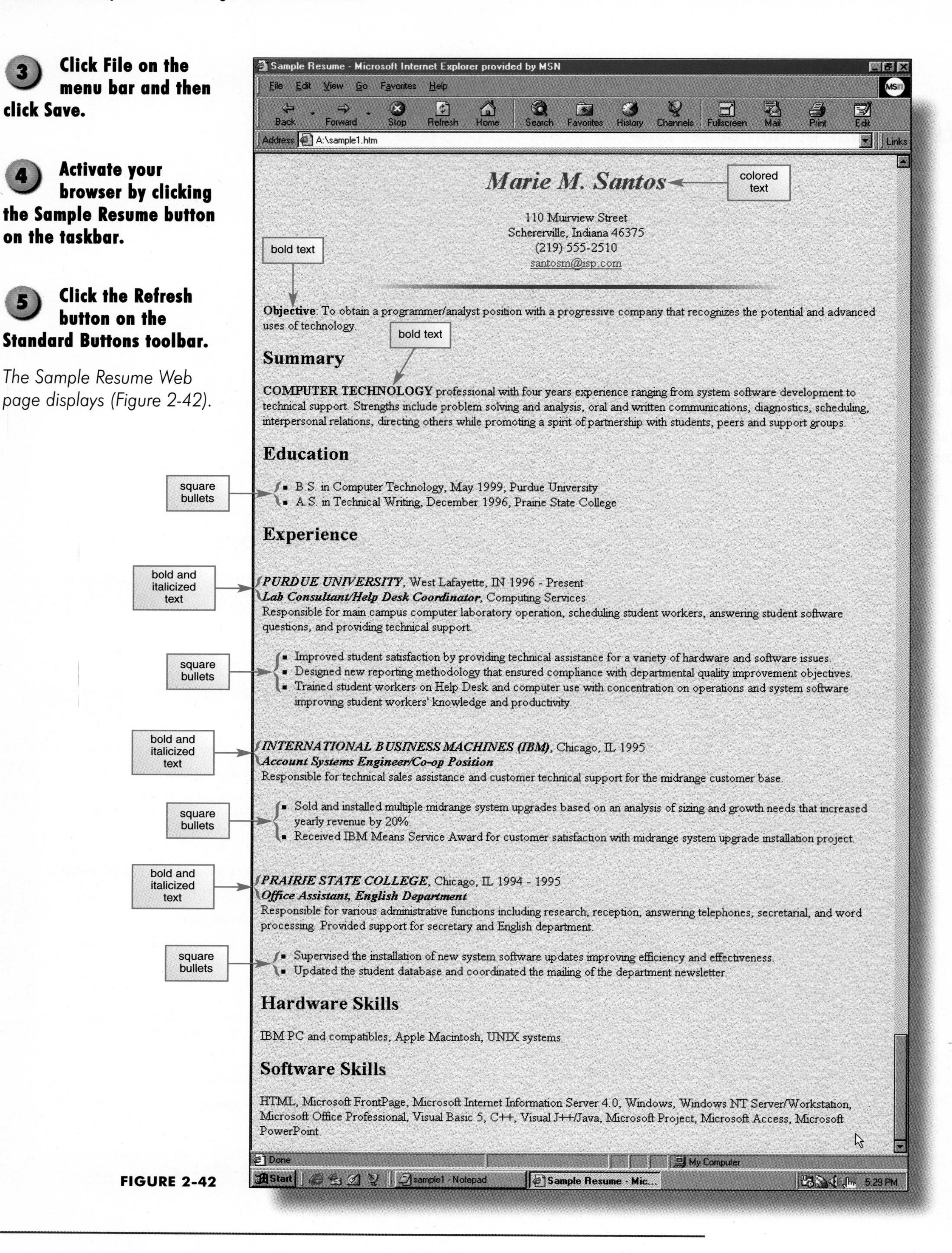

FIGURE 2-42

The bullets display as squares rather than discs as shown in Figure 2-42.

Inserting an Image and Wrapping Text

Table 2-4 on page HTM 2.18 lists the attributes available for use in the <IMG> tag. You previously used the HEIGHT and WIDTH attributes when you inserted the horizontal rule image. In this section, you will use the BORDER attribute to eliminate the border around an image. You also will use the ALIGN attribute to align text with the image.

A **border** on an image makes the image display as if it has a frame around it. This may be distracting if the image is used as a link. With a border around the image, the default (or selected) link colors display around the image when the link is normal, active, or visited. Figure 2-43 shows an image with a border and no linking (left), together with the same image with linking (center). Normal images and visited links display as indicated. The image on the right in Figure 2-43 shows the changed color when the link has been visited, giving the image an entirely different look.

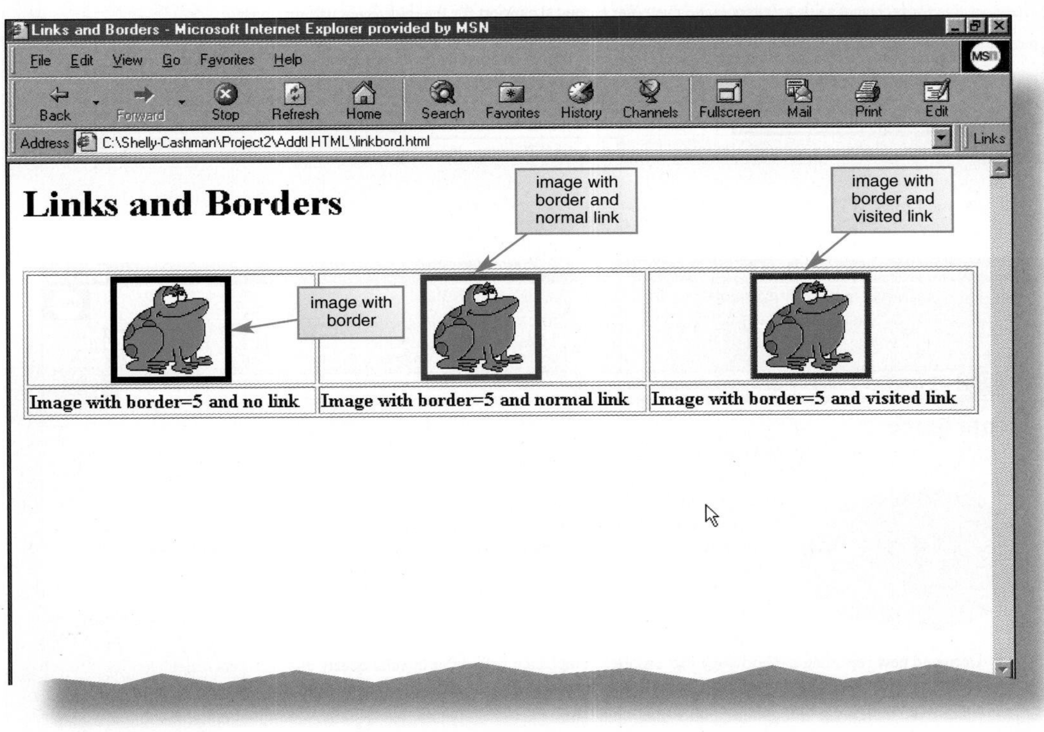

FIGURE 2-43

Alignment also is a key consideration when inserting an image. Alignment can give an image and surrounding text completely different looks. Figure 2-44 on the next page shows a Right alignment of the text, which wraps the text around the image. The format of that command is <IMG SRC="ovallaeb.gif" ALIGN=RIGHT>. You will use right alignment for the completed Web page as shown in Figure 2-32 on page HTM 2.31. To end right-aligned text wrap, use the <BR CLEAR=RIGHT> tag where you want the text to stop. Figure 2-45 on the next page shows a Left alignment of the text around an image. In the left-aligned example, you may want to use the <BR CLEAR=LEFT> tag before the first bullet, which would break the line and display all of the bullets beneath the image.

Inserting an Image with Wrapped Text

The following steps show how to insert an image with right-aligned, wrapped text, as shown in Figure 2-44 on page HTM 2.40. The image is contained on the HTML Data Disk.

Steps To Insert an Image with Wrapped Text

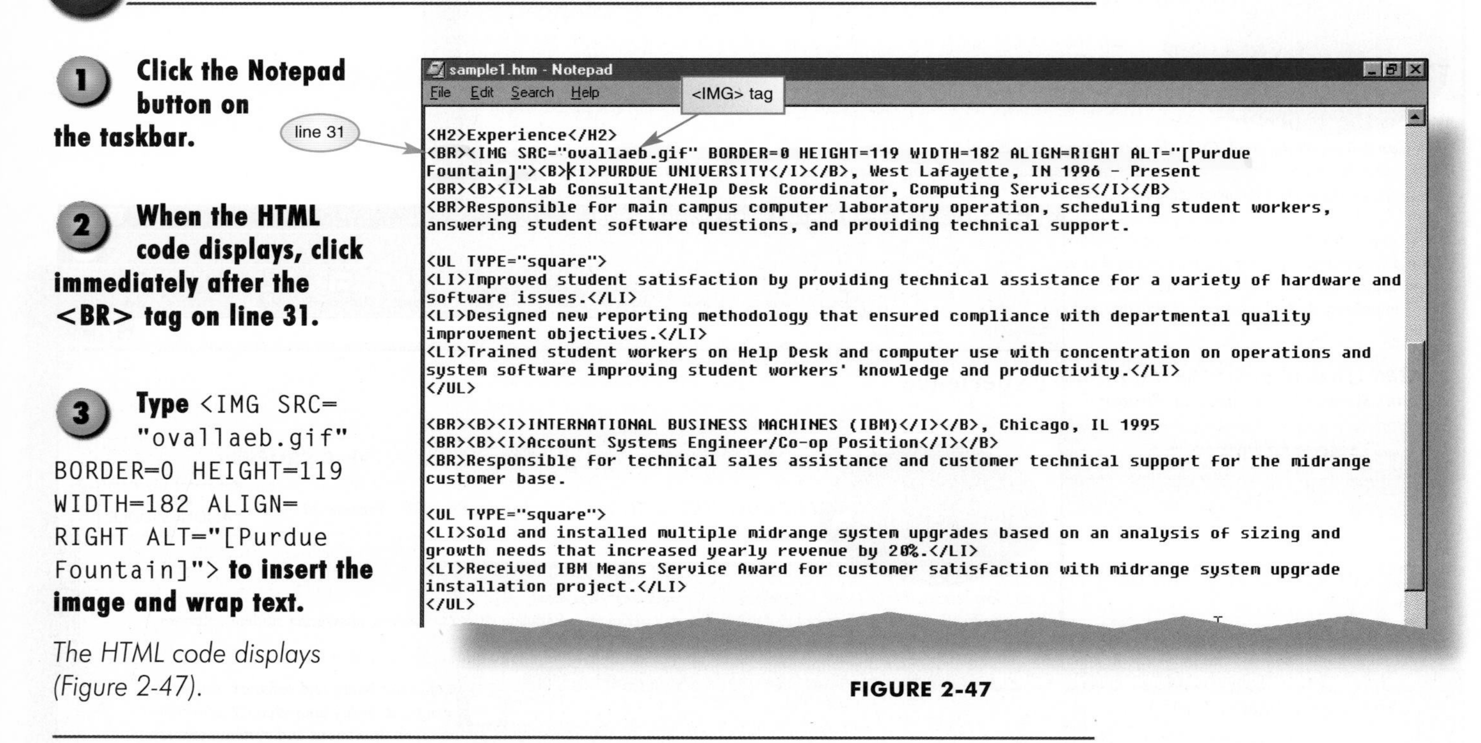

1. **Click the Notepad button on the taskbar.**

2. **When the HTML code displays, click immediately after the <BR> tag on line 31.**

3. **Type** `<IMG SRC="ovallaeb.gif" BORDER=0 HEIGHT=119 WIDTH=182 ALIGN=RIGHT ALT="[Purdue Fountain]">` **to insert the image and wrap text.**

The HTML code displays (Figure 2-47).

FIGURE 2-47

In the <IMG> tag added in the above steps, the SRC attribute indicates the file name of the image file, BORDER=0 will set no border around the image, the HEIGHT and WIDTH are in number of pixels, ALIGN=RIGHT will align the image to the right of the text, and the ALT will display the alternate text, Purdue Fountain, as the image is loading. The **ALT** attribute displays text while the image is loading. This helps to keep the visitor informed of what is going to display when the image has loaded completely. Figure 2-48 shows an example of what happens when an image is loading with the optional ALT attribute.

FIGURE 2-48

Adding Text and Image Links to Another Web Site

One of the most important features of the World Wide Web is the capability to link from one Web site to another Web site anywhere else in the world. In this section, you create a link to a Web site at Purdue University in West Lafayette, Indiana. You create a text link associated with the university, as well as an image link of the school.

Adding a Text Link to Another Web Site

In the following steps, you link the words, Purdue University, to the home page of the university Web site. You use the HREF attribute in the <A> tag to create this link. Between the quotation marks in the HREF attribute, you type the URL for Purdue University. You can link to any other Web site by typing in the full URL for the site.

To Add a Text Link to Another Web Site

1. **Click immediately to the left of Purdue on line 26.**
2. **Type** `<A HREF="http://www.purdue.edu">` **to insert the link.**
3. **Click immediately to the right of University on line 27.**
4. **Type** `</A>` **to end the tag.**

The HTML code displays (Figure 2-49).

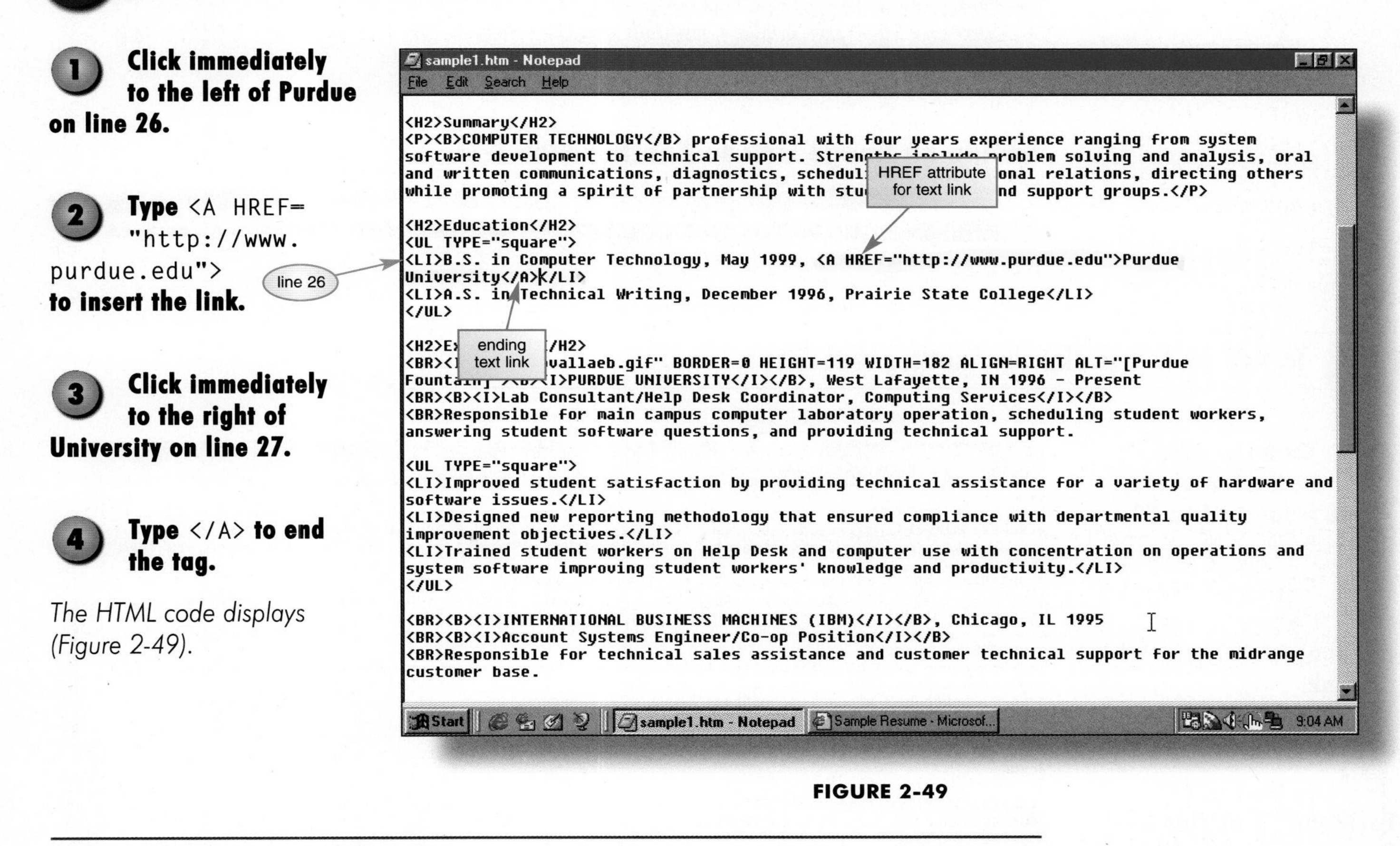

FIGURE 2-49

After adding this link, the Web page displays as shown in Figure 2-50 on the next page. You know that this is a text link because the text is blue and underlined. The mouse pointer also changes when moved over this hotspot.

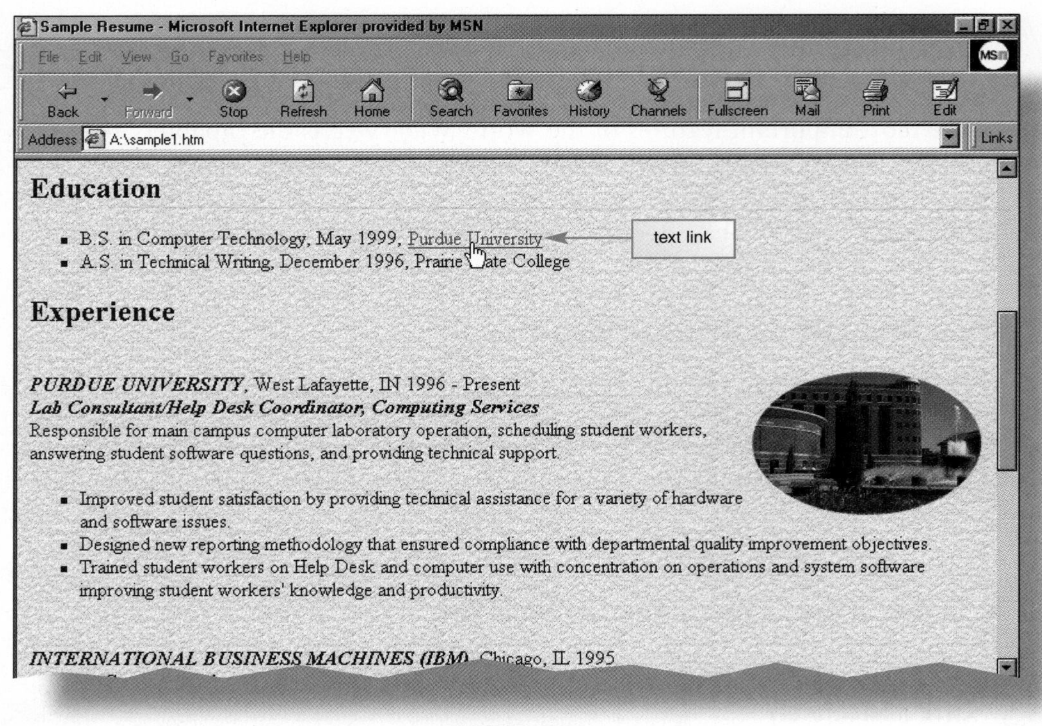

FIGURE 2-50

Adding an Image Link to Another Web Site

In the following steps, you insert the HTML tag to link the image inserted in the Experience section of the resume to the university Web site. You use the same <A> tag used above to create the image link.

Steps To Add an Image Link to Another Web Site

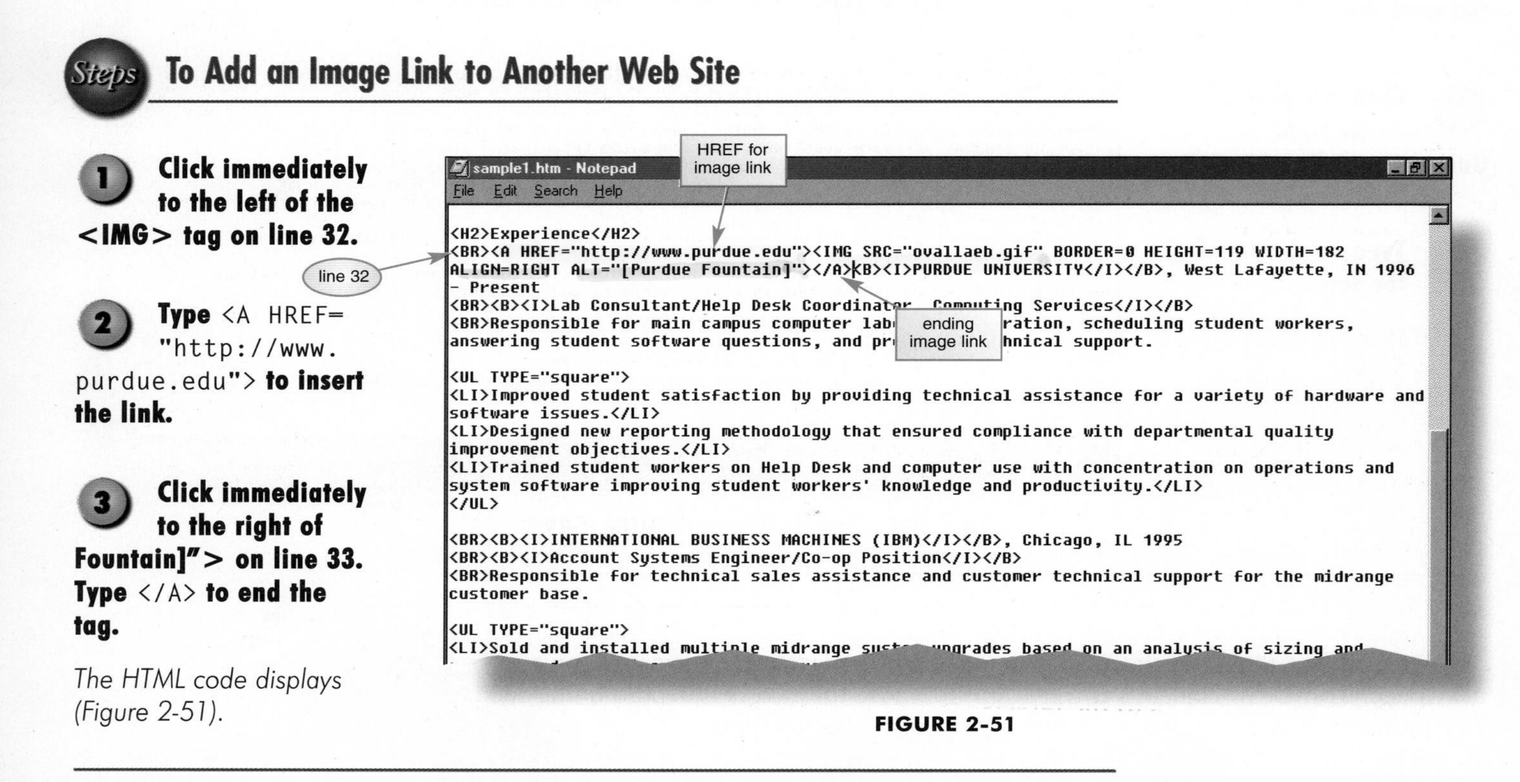

1. **Click immediately to the left of the <IMG> tag on line 32.**
2. **Type** `<A HREF="http://www.purdue.edu">` **to insert the link.**
3. **Click immediately to the right of Fountain]"> on line 33. Type** `</A>` **to end the tag.**

The HTML code displays (Figure 2-51).

FIGURE 2-51

Figure 2-52 shows you what this link will look like when displayed in the browser. You can tell that this is a link because the mouse pointer changes when moved over the image.

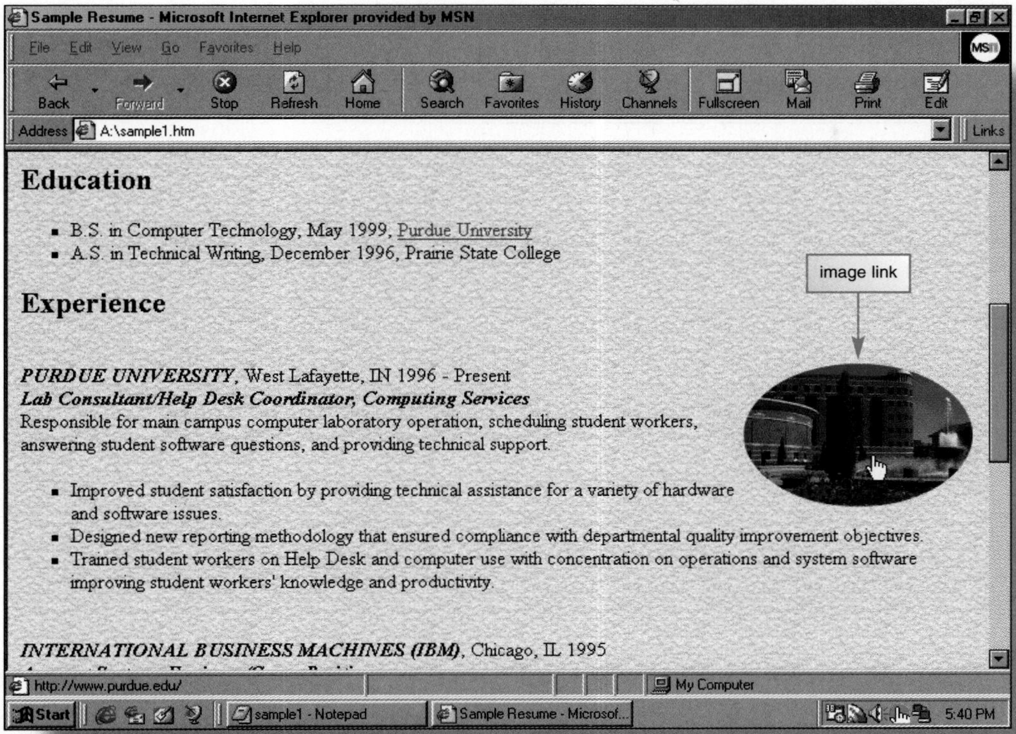

FIGURE 2-52

Creating Links within a Web Page

The final links that you will create in this project are links within the Sample Resume Web page. Because the Sample Resume is a long page, it would be easier for the visitors to have a menu or list at the top of the Web page so they could move immediately to another section. View the Web page in Figure 2-32 on page HTM 2.31 to see what these links will look like when completed.

Figure 2-53a on the next page shows an example of linking from the word, Education, at the top of the page, to the Education section in another part of the Web page (Figure 2-53b on the next page). When the mouse pointer is moved over the word, Education, and clicked (Figure 2-53a), the browser repositions, or links, the page to the Education target (Figure 2-53b).

To create links within the same Web page, you first set the targets for the links. A **target** is a section within a Web page to which you want to link. You have decided it would be easier for the Web page visitors to be able to go quickly from the top of the Sample Resume page to the Education, Experience, Hardware, and Software sections of the resume. You therefore set targets at the beginning of these four sections. You then create the links to these targets. To do this, you create a list of words that you will use as links. The bulleted list shown in Figure 2-53a provides the link text. When creating this bulleted list, you insert the <A> tag with a variation of the HREF attribute to provide the links to the targets.

More About

Links on a Web Page

An additional use of the anchor tag is to allow visitors to move within a single Web page. Use the NAME attribute to allow movement from one area of the Web page to another location on the same page. This linking technique is particularly useful on exceptionally long pages. An index of links also can provide easy access to various areas within the Web page.

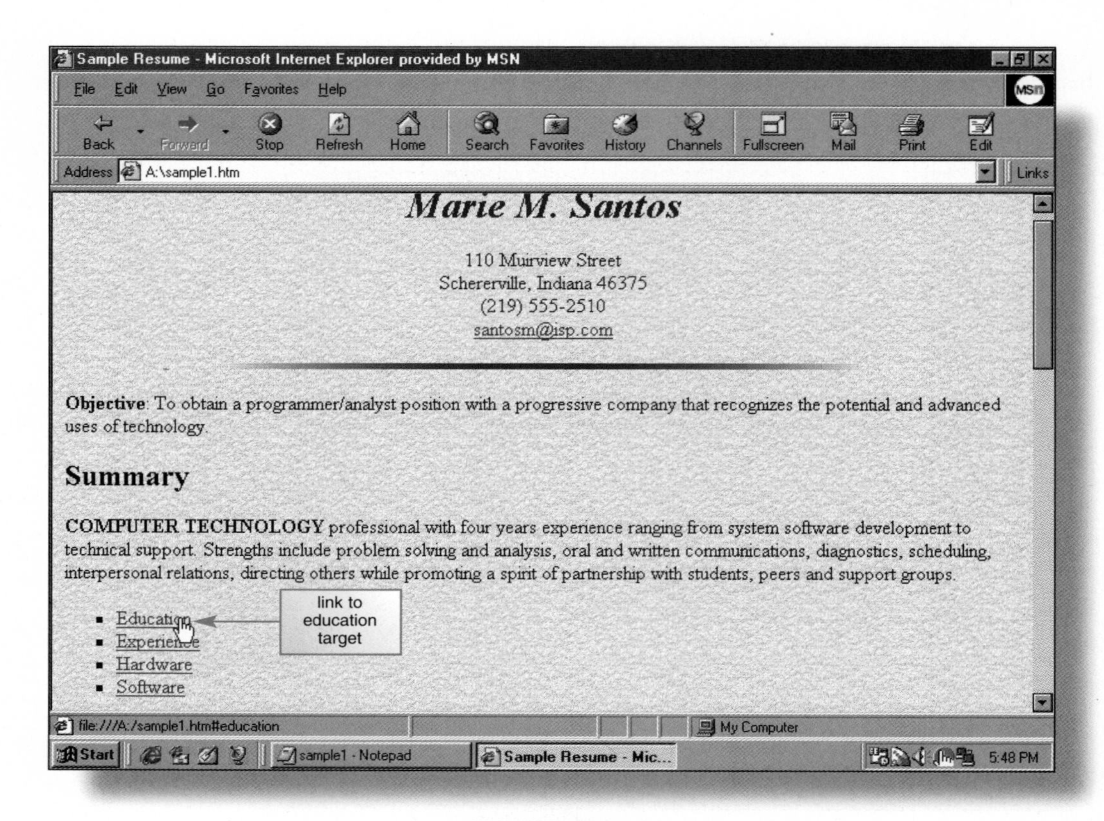

FIGURE 2-53a

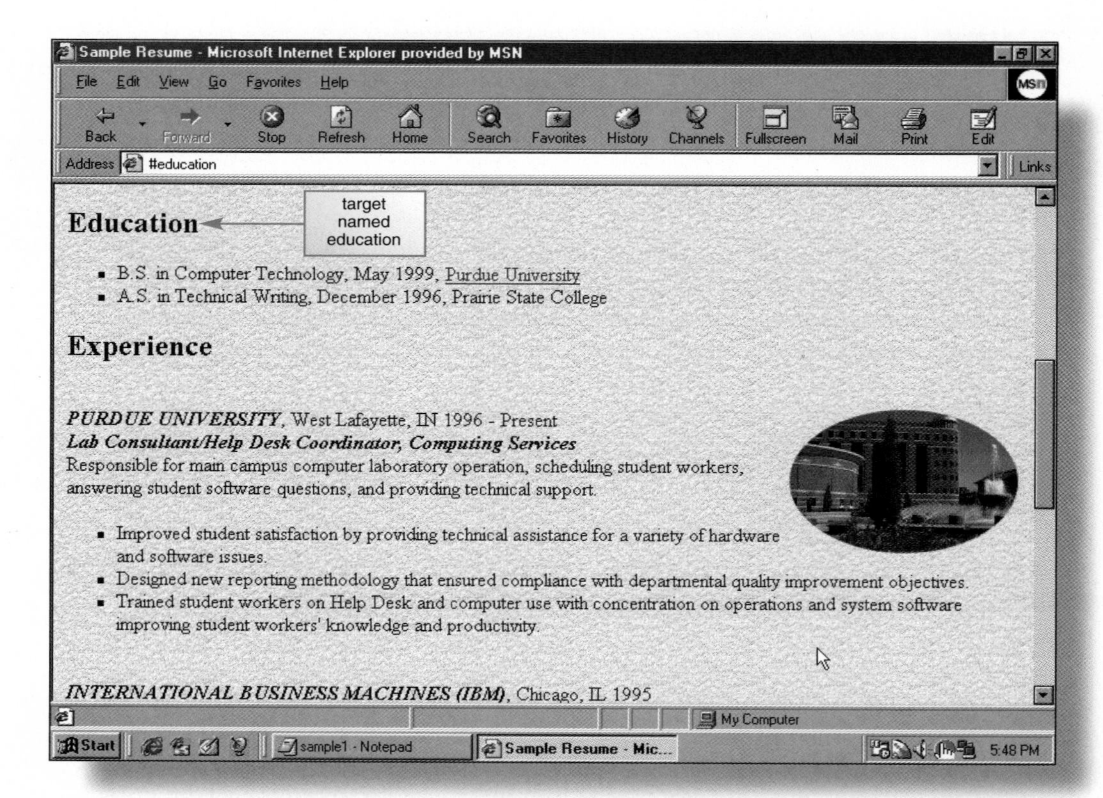

FIGURE 2-53b

Setting the Link Targets

To set link targets, you again use the <A> tag. You use the NAME attribute, rather than the HREF attribute used previously. When the visitor clicks a link to a specific section of the Web page, you want the visitor to be directed to that area of the Web page. In the following steps, you set the four link targets.

Steps To Set Link Targets

1. **Click immediately to the left of the <H2> tag on line 24.**
2. **Type** `<A NAME="education"></A>` **to create a target named education.**
3. **Click immediately to the left of the <H2> tag on line 31.**
4. **Type** `<A NAME="experience"></A>` **to create a target named experience.**

The HTML code displays (Figure 2-54).

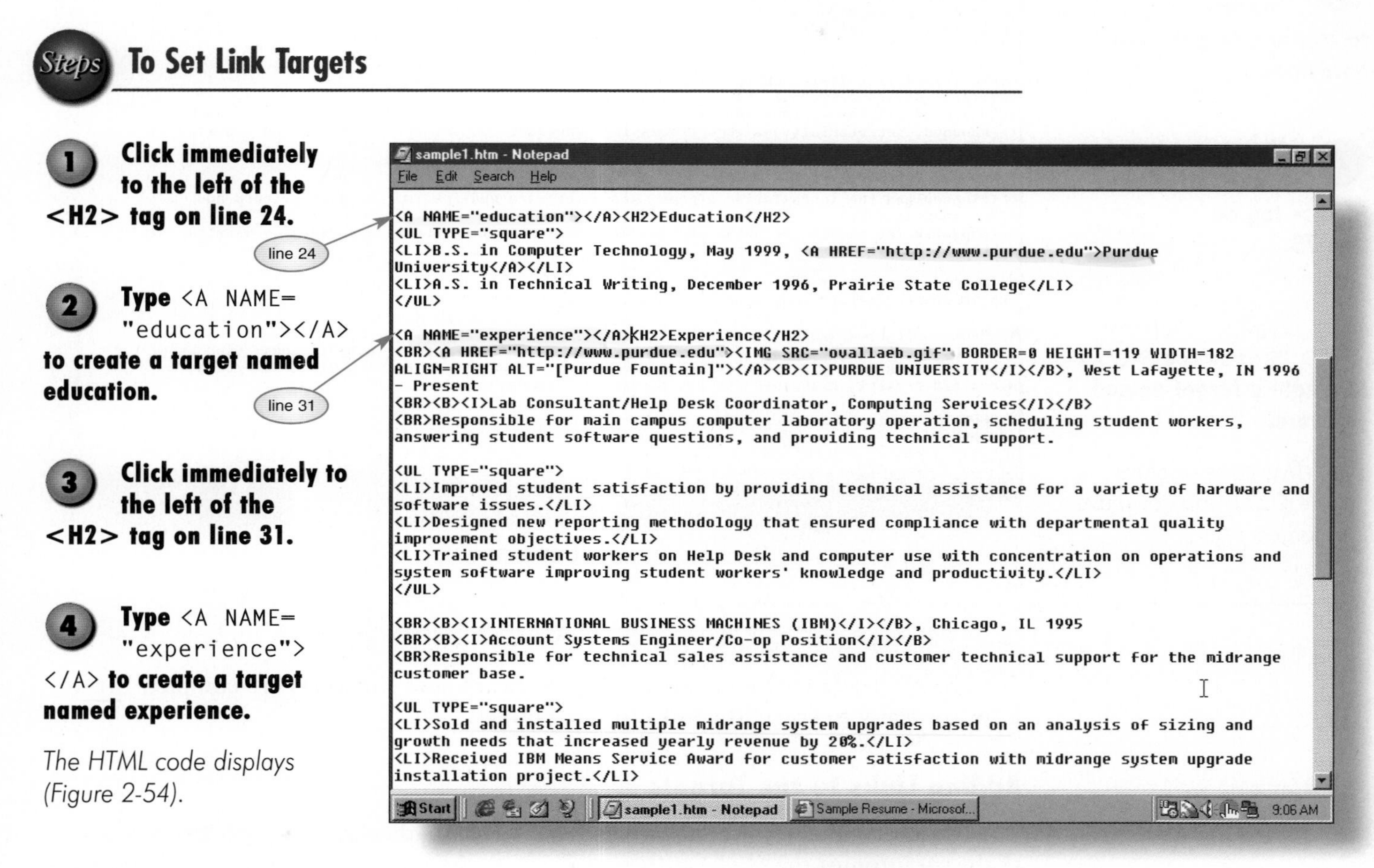

FIGURE 2-54

5) Click immediately to the left of the <H2> tag on line 72.

6) Type `<A NAME="hardware"></A>` **to create a target named hardware.**

7) Click immediately to the left of the <H2> tag on line 75.

8) Type `<A NAME="software"></A>` **to create a target named software.**

The HTML code displays (Figure 2-55). You now have four targets set.

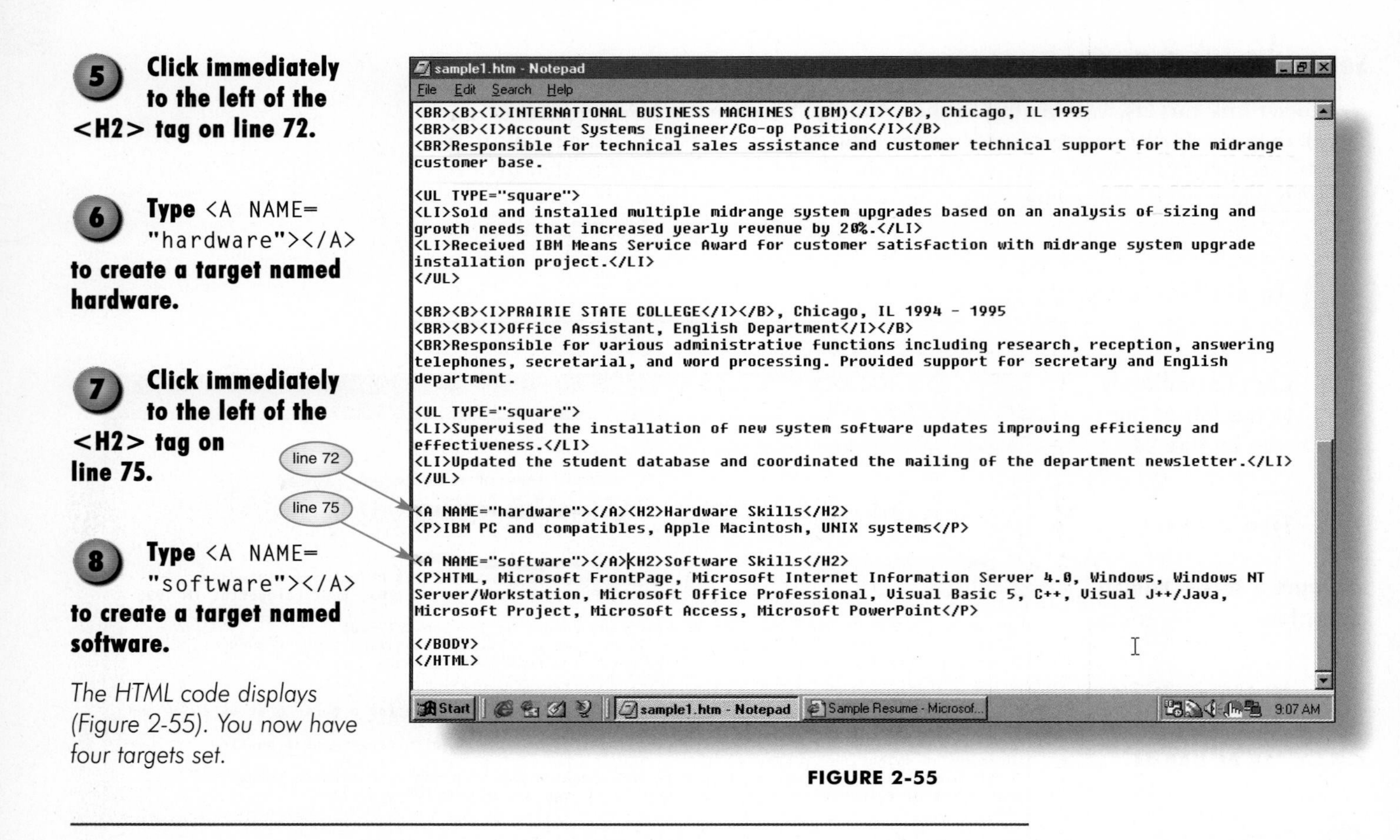

FIGURE 2-55

The targets (education, experience, hardware, and software) are complete. You now are ready to create the links to these targets.

Adding Links to the Targets

To create links to the four targets, you again use the <A> tag. You also use a slight variation of the HREF attribute. Perform the following steps to set the four link targets.

Steps To Add Links to the Targets

1 **Click immediately to the right of the </P> tag on line 22 and then press the ENTER key twice.**

2 **Type** `<UL TYPE="square">` **and then press the ENTER key.**

3 **Type** `<LI><A HREF="#education">Education</A></LI>` **and then press the ENTER key.**

The HTML code displays (Figure 2-56).

```
sample1 - Notepad
File  Edit  Search  Help
<CENTER>(219) 555-2510</CENTER>
<CENTER><A HREF="mailto:santosm@isp.com">santosm@isp.com</a></CENTER></P>

<CENTER><IMG SRC="bluebar.jpg" HEIGHT=5 WIDTH=500></CENTER>

<P><B>Objective</B>: To obtain a programmer/analyst position with a progressive company that
recognizes the potential and advanced uses of technology.</P>

<H2>Summary</H2>
<P><B>COMPUTER TECHNOLOGY</B> professional with four years experience ranging from system
software development to technical support. Strengths include problem solving and analysis, oral
and written communications, diagnostics, scheduling, interpersonal relations, directing others
while promoting a spirit of partnership with students, peers and support groups.</P>

<UL TYPE="square">
<LI><A HREF="#education">Education</A></LI>


<A NAME="education"></A><H2>Education</H2>
<UL TYPE="square">
<LI>B.S. in Computer Technology, May 1999, <A HREF="http://www.purdue.edu">Purdue
University</A></LI>
<LI>A.S. in Technical Writing, December 1996, Prairie State College</LI>
</UL>

<A NAME="experience"></A><H2>Experience</H2>
<BR><A HREF="http://www.purdue.edu"><IMG SRC="ovallaeb.gif" BORDER=0 HEIGHT=119 WIDTH=182
ALIGN=RIGHT ALT="[Purdue Fountain]"></A><B><I>PURDUE UNIVERSITY</B></I>, West Lafayette, IN 1996
- Present
<BR><B><I>Lab Consultant/Help Desk Coordinator</B></I>, Computing Services
<BR>Responsible for main campus computer laboratory operation, scheduling student workers,
answering student software questions, and providing technical support.

<UL TYPE="square">
<LI>Improved student satisfaction by providing technical assistance for a variety of hardware and
Start | sample1 - Notepad | Sample Resume - Microsof... | 5:50 PM
```

line 22

bulleted list for target menu

FIGURE 2-56

4 **Type** `<LI><A HREF="#experience">Experience</A></LI>` **and then press the ENTER key. Type** `<LI><A HREF="#hardware">Hardware</A></LI>` **and then press the ENTER key. Type** `<LI><A HREF="#software">Software</A></LI>` **and then press the ENTER key. Type** `</UL>`**.**

The HTML code displays (Figure 2-57).

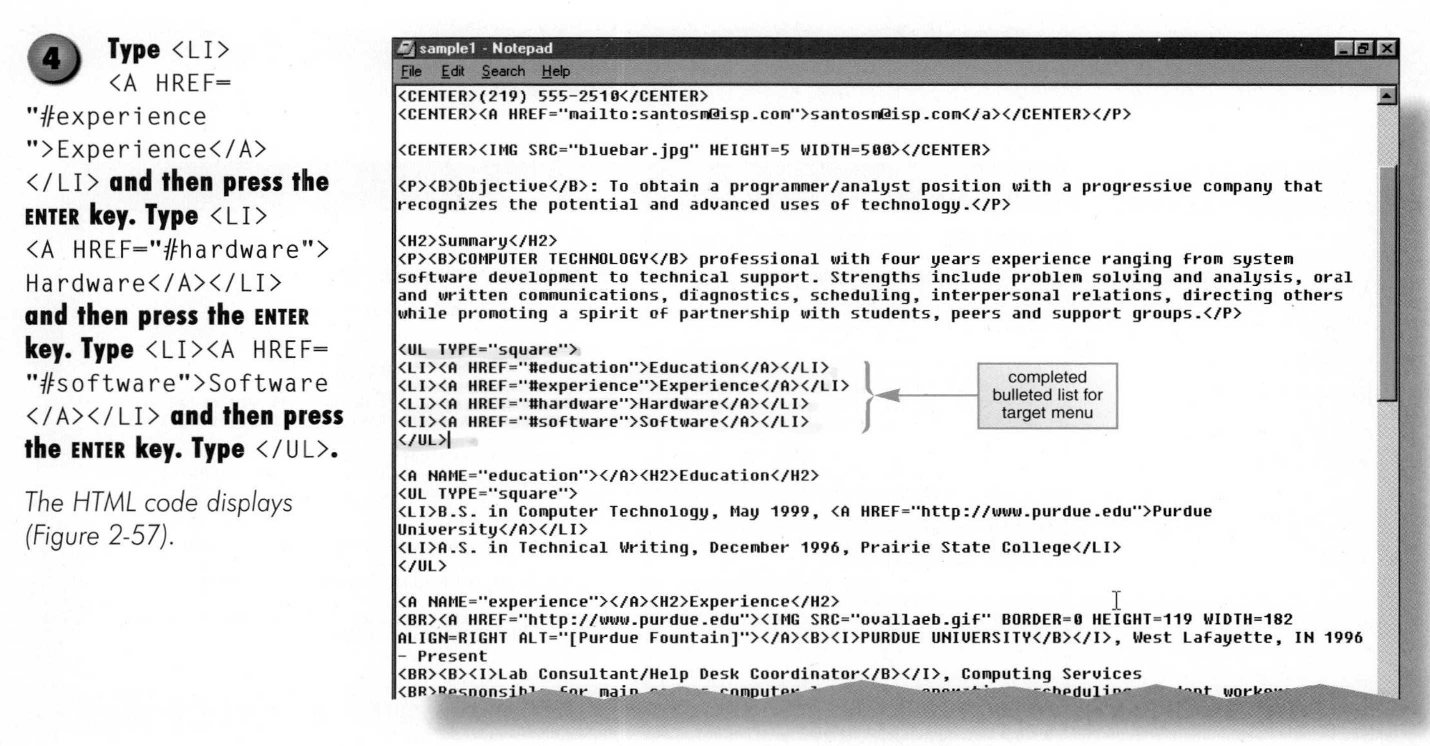

```
sample1 - Notepad
File  Edit  Search  Help
<CENTER>(219) 555-2510</CENTER>
<CENTER><A HREF="mailto:santosm@isp.com">santosm@isp.com</a></CENTER></P>

<CENTER><IMG SRC="bluebar.jpg" HEIGHT=5 WIDTH=500></CENTER>

<P><B>Objective</B>: To obtain a programmer/analyst position with a progressive company that
recognizes the potential and advanced uses of technology.</P>

<H2>Summary</H2>
<P><B>COMPUTER TECHNOLOGY</B> professional with four years experience ranging from system
software development to technical support. Strengths include problem solving and analysis, oral
and written communications, diagnostics, scheduling, interpersonal relations, directing others
while promoting a spirit of partnership with students, peers and support groups.</P>

<UL TYPE="square">
<LI><A HREF="#education">Education</A></LI>
<LI><A HREF="#experience">Experience</A></LI>
<LI><A HREF="#hardware">Hardware</A></LI>
<LI><A HREF="#software">Software</A></LI>
</UL>

<A NAME="education"></A><H2>Education</H2>
<UL TYPE="square">
<LI>B.S. in Computer Technology, May 1999, <A HREF="http://www.purdue.edu">Purdue
University</A></LI>
<LI>A.S. in Technical Writing, December 1996, Prairie State College</LI>
</UL>

<A NAME="experience"></A><H2>Experience</H2>
<BR><A HREF="http://www.purdue.edu"><IMG SRC="ovallaeb.gif" BORDER=0 HEIGHT=119 WIDTH=182
ALIGN=RIGHT ALT="[Purdue Fountain]"></A><B><I>PURDUE UNIVERSITY</B></I>, West Lafayette, IN 1996
- Present
<BR><B><I>Lab Consultant/Help Desk Coordinator</B></I>, Computing Services
```


FIGURE 2-57

Linking to the Top of the Page

Another link can make browsing easier for visitors. In several logical places on this Web page, you should provide links that quickly move the visitors to the top of the Web page. Look at the *To top* links in Figure 2-32 on page HTM 2.31 to see examples of these additional links. To create these links, you first need to set the target at the top of the page. Then you create three links to that target after the Education, Experience, and Software sections. Because the Hardware and Software sections are short, you do not need an additional *To top* link after the Hardware section.

Steps: To Link to the Top of the Page

1. **Click line 6 and then press the ENTER key.**

2. **Type** <A NAME= "top"></A> **as the tag.**

The target is set at the top of the Web page (Figure 2-58).

3. **Click line 39 and then press the ENTER key.**

4. **Type** <P><I> <FONT SIZE=-1> <A HREF="#top">To top</A></FONT></I> </P> **as the tag.**

The link is set to the top target (Figure 2-59).

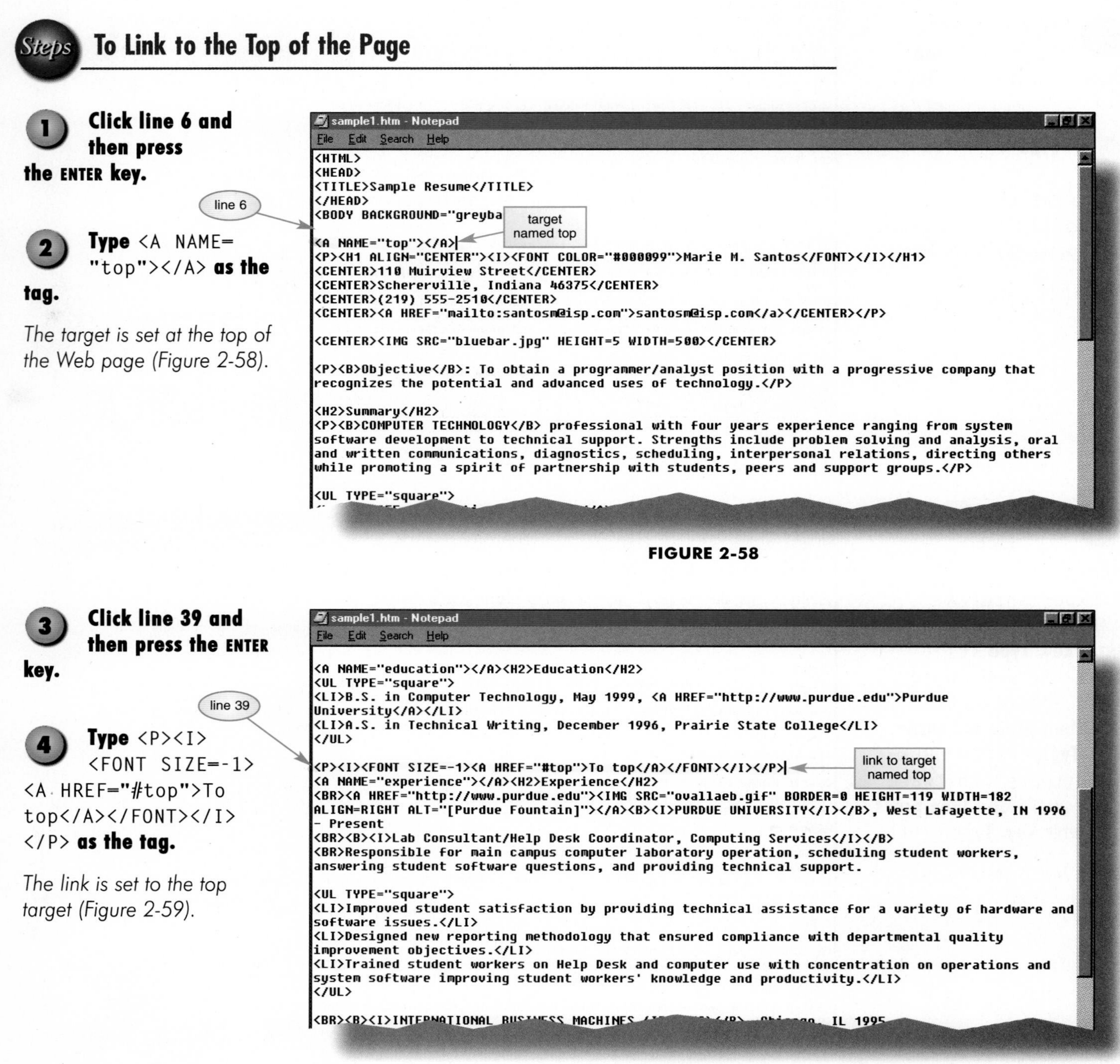

FIGURE 2-58

FIGURE 2-59

5 **Repeat Step 4 on line 80 to insert the tag and then press the ENTER key.**

6 **Repeat Step 4 on line 89 to insert the tag and then press the ENTER key.**

The HTML code displays (Figure 2-60).

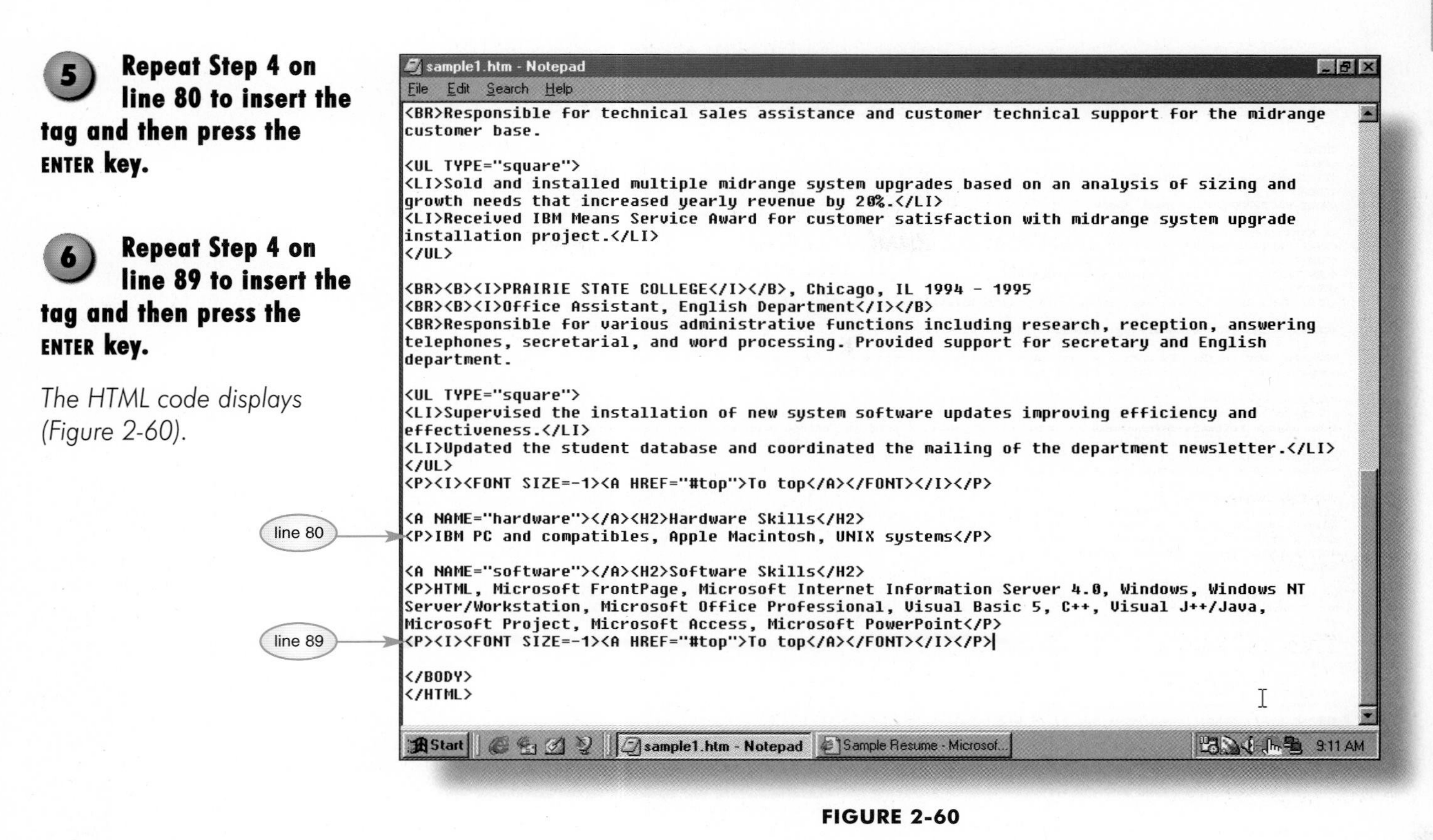


```
<BR>Responsible for technical sales assistance and customer technical support for the midrange
customer base.

<UL TYPE="square">
<LI>Sold and installed multiple midrange system upgrades based on an analysis of sizing and
growth needs that increased yearly revenue by 20%.</LI>
<LI>Received IBM Means Service Award for customer satisfaction with midrange system upgrade
installation project.</LI>
</UL>

<BR><B><I>PRAIRIE STATE COLLEGE</I></B>, Chicago, IL 1994 - 1995
<BR><B><I>Office Assistant, English Department</I></B>
<BR>Responsible for various administrative functions including research, reception, answering
telephones, secretarial, and word processing. Provided support for secretary and English
department.

<UL TYPE="square">
<LI>Supervised the installation of new system software updates improving efficiency and
effectiveness.</LI>
<LI>Updated the student database and coordinated the mailing of the department newsletter.</LI>
</UL>
<P><I><FONT SIZE=-1><A HREF="#top">To top</A></FONT></I></P>

<A NAME="hardware"></A><H2>Hardware Skills</H2>
<P>IBM PC and compatibles, Apple Macintosh, UNIX systems</P>

<A NAME="software"></A><H2>Software Skills</H2>
<P>HTML, Microsoft FrontPage, Microsoft Internet Information Server 4.0, Windows, Windows NT
Server/Workstation, Microsoft Office Professional, Visual Basic 5, C++, Visual J++/Java,
Microsoft Project, Microsoft Access, Microsoft PowerPoint</P>
<P><I><FONT SIZE=-1><A HREF="#top">To top</A></FONT></I></P>

</BODY>
</HTML>
```

FIGURE 2-60

This creates a new paragraph using the <P> and </P> tags, italicizes the text using the <I> and </I> tags, sets the font to a small size using the <FONT SIZE=-1> and the </FONT> tags, and sets the link to the top target <A HREF="#top"></A> using the anchor tag.

One final link is from the Sample Resume Web page back to the Web Res home page. In the following steps, you create a link at the bottom of this Web page that will take the visitor back to the home page.

TO COMPLETE THE LINK BACK TO THE HOME PAGE AND SAVE AND PRINT THE HTML FILE

1. If necessary, click the blank line just above the </BODY> tag.
2. Type `<P><I><A HREF="webreshome.htm">Return to Web Res home page</A></I></P>` as the tag and then press the ENTER key.
3. Save the HTML file by clicking File on the menu bar and then clicking Save.
4. Click File on the menu bar and then click Print.

The HTML file prints (Figure 2-61 on the next page).

```
sample1

<HTML>
<HEAD>
<TITLE>Sample Resume</TITLE>
</HEAD>
<BODY BACKGROUND="greyback.jpg">

<A NAME="top"></A>
<P><H1 ALIGN="CENTER"><I><FONT COLOR="#000099">Marie M. Santos</FONT></I></H1>
<CENTER>110 Muirview Street</CENTER>
<CENTER>Schererville, Indiana 46375</CENTER>
<CENTER>(219) 555-2510</CENTER>
<CENTER><A HREF="mailto:santosm@isp.com">santosm@isp.com</a></CENTER></P>

<CENTER><IMG SRC="bluebar.jpg" HEIGHT=5 WIDTH=500></CENTER>

<P><B>Objective</B>: To obtain a programmer/analyst position with a progressive
company that recognizes the potential and advanced uses of technology.</P>

<H2>Summary</H2>
<P><B>COMPUTER TECHNOLOGY</B> professional with four years experience ranging
from system software development to technical support. Strengths include problem
solving and analysis, oral and written communications, diagnostics, scheduling,
interpersonal relations, directing others while promoting a spirit of
partnership with students, peers and support groups.</P>

<UL TYPE="square">
<LI><A HREF="#education">Education</A></LI>
<LI><A HREF="#experience">Experience</A></LI>
<LI><A HREF="#hardware">Hardware</A></LI>
<LI><A HREF="#software">Software</A></LI>
</UL>

<A NAME="education"></A><H2>Education</H2>
<UL TYPE="square">
<LI>B.S. in Computer Technology, May 1999, <A
HREF="http://www.purdue.edu">Purdue University</A></LI>
<LI>A.S. in Technical Writing, December 1996, Prairie State College</LI>
</UL>

<P><I><FONT SIZE=-1><A HREF="#top">To top</A></FONT></I>
<A NAME="experience"></A><H2>Experience</H2>
<BR><A HREF="http://www.purdue.edu"><IMG SRC="ovallaeb.g
WIDTH=182 ALIGN=RIGHT ALT="[Purdue Fountain]"></A><B><I>
UNIVERSITY</I></B>, West Lafayette, IN 1996 - Present
<BR><B><I>Lab Consultant/Help Desk Coordinator</I></B>,
<BR>Responsible for main campus computer laboratory oper
student workers, answering student software questions, a
support.

<UL TYPE="square">
<LI>Improved student satisfaction by providing technical
variety of hardware and software issues.</LI>
<LI>Designed new reporting methodology that ensured comp
quality improvement objectives.</LI>
<LI>Trained student workers on Help Desk and computer us
operations and system software improving student workers
productivity.</LI>

Page 1
```

```
sample1

</UL>

<BR><B><I>INTERNATIONAL BUSINESS MACHINES (IBM)</I></B>, Chicago, IL 1995
<BR><B><I>Account Systems Engineer/Co-op Position</I></B>
<BR>Responsible for technical sales assistance and customer technical support
for the midrange customer base.

<UL TYPE="square">
<LI>Sold and installed multiple midrange system upgrades based on an analysis of
sizing and growth needs that increased yearly revenue by 20%.</LI>
<LI>Received IBM Means Service Award for customer satisfaction with midrange
system upgrade installation project.</LI>
</UL>

<BR><B><I>PRAIRIE STATE COLLEGE</I></B>, Chicago, IL 1994 - 1995
<BR><B><I>Office Assistant, English Department</I></B>
<BR>Responsible for various administrative functions including research,
reception, answering telephones, secretarial, and word processing. Provided
support for secretary and English department.

<UL TYPE="square">
<LI>Supervised the installation of new system software updates improving
efficiency and effectiveness.</LI>
<LI>Updated the student database and coordinated the mailing of the department
newsletter.</LI>
</UL>

<P><I><FONT SIZE=-1><A HREF="#top">To top</A></FONT></I></P>

<A NAME="hardware"></A><H2>Hardware Skills</H2>
<P>IBM PC and compatibles, Apple Macintosh, UNIX systems</P>

<A NAME="software"></A><H2>Software Skills</H2>
<P>HTML, Microsoft FrontPage, Microsoft Internet Information Server 4.0,
Windows, Windows NT Server/Workstation, Microsoft Office Professional, Visual
Basic 5, C++, Visual J++/Java, Microsoft Project, Microsoft Access, Microsoft
PowerPoint</P>
<P><I><FONT SIZE=-1><A HREF="#top">To top</A></FONT></I></P>

<P><I><A HREF="webreshome.htm">Return to Web Res home page</A></I></P>

</BODY>
</HTML>

Page 2
```

FIGURE 2-61

TO VIEW THE WEB PAGE

1. Click the Sample Resume button on the taskbar.
2. Click the Refresh button.

The enhanced Web page displays (Figure 2-32 on page HTM 2.31).

TO PRINT THE WEB PAGE

1. Click the Print button on the Standard Buttons toolbar.

The Web page prints (Figure 2-62).

Marie M. Santos

110 Muirview Street
Schererville, Indiana 46375
(219) 555-2510
santosm@isp.com

Objective: To obtain a programmer/analyst position with a progressive company
potential and advanced uses of technology.

Summary

COMPUTER TECHNOLOGY professional with four years experience rangin
development to technical support. Strengths include problem solving and analysi
communications, diagnostics, scheduling, interpersonal relations, directing other
of partnership with students, peers and support groups.

- Education
- Experience
- Hardware
- Software

Education

- B.S. in Computer Technology, May 1999, Purdue University
- A.S. in Technical Writing, December 1996, Prairie State College

To top

Experience

PURDUE UNIVERSITY, West Lafayette, IN 1996 - Present
Lab Consultant/Help Desk Coordinator, Computing Services
Responsible for main campus computer laboratory operation, scheduling student workers, answering student software questions, and providing technical support.

- Improved student satisfaction by providing technical assistance for a variety of hardware and software issues.
- Designed new reporting methodology that ensured compliance with depar
improvement objectives.
- Trained student workers on Help Desk and computer use with concentrati
system software improving student workers' knowledge and productivity.

INTERNATIONAL BUSINESS MACHINES (IBM), Chicago, IL 1995
Account Systems Engineer/Co-op Position
Responsible for technical sales assistance and customer technical support for the midrange customer base.

- Sold and installed multiple midrange system upgrades based on an analysis of sizing and growth needs that increased yearly revenue by 20%.
- Received IBM Means Service Award for customer satisfaction with midrange system upgrade installation project.

PRAIRIE STATE COLLEGE, Chicago, IL 1994 - 1995
Office Assistant, English Department
Responsible for various administrative functions including research, reception, answering telephones, secretarial, and word processing. Provided support for secretary and English department.

- Supervised the installation of new system software updates improving efficiency and effectiveness.
- Updated the student database and coordinated the mailing of the department newsletter.

To top

Hardware Skills

IBM PC and compatibles, Apple Macintosh, UNIX systems

Software Skills

HTML, Microsoft FrontPage, Microsoft Internet Information Server 4.0, Windows, Windows NT Server/Workstation, Microsoft Office Professional, Visual Basic 5, C++, Visual J++/Java, Microsoft Project, Microsoft Access, Microsoft PowerPoint

To top

Return to Web Res home page

FIGURE 2-62

The Web pages are complete. In this project, you created a home page for Web Res. This page contains an e-mail link so the Web page visitors can contact Web Res. It also contains a link to the second Web page in the Web site, sample1.htm. You then made enhancements to the sample1.htm Web page on the HTML Data Disk. You added bold and italics to text to vary the look within the page. You inserted an image and linked it to another Web site. You also linked text to another Web site.

Testing the Links

Testing all of these changes is very important. You should insure that all of the links work by clicking the links and verifying that each link takes you where it should. You also should test the Web pages in more than one browser to insure that the Web pages display as you expect.

More About Images

Images make Web pages more interesting. Inserting images on Web pages helps to attract visitors. You used several image attributes when inserting images in this project. Spacing between and around images and text also is important, as shown below. A good idea for very large images is discussed as well.

Horizontal and Vertical Space

HSPACE and **VSPACE** attributes control the amount of horizontal and vertical space around an image. If you wrap the text around an image, you may want to add some space so the text does not appear to run into the image. Figure 2-63 displays samples of the HSPACE and VSPACE attributes. Additional vertical space displays above and below the image where VSPACE=20. Additional horizontal space displays to the right and the left of the image where HSPACE=20.

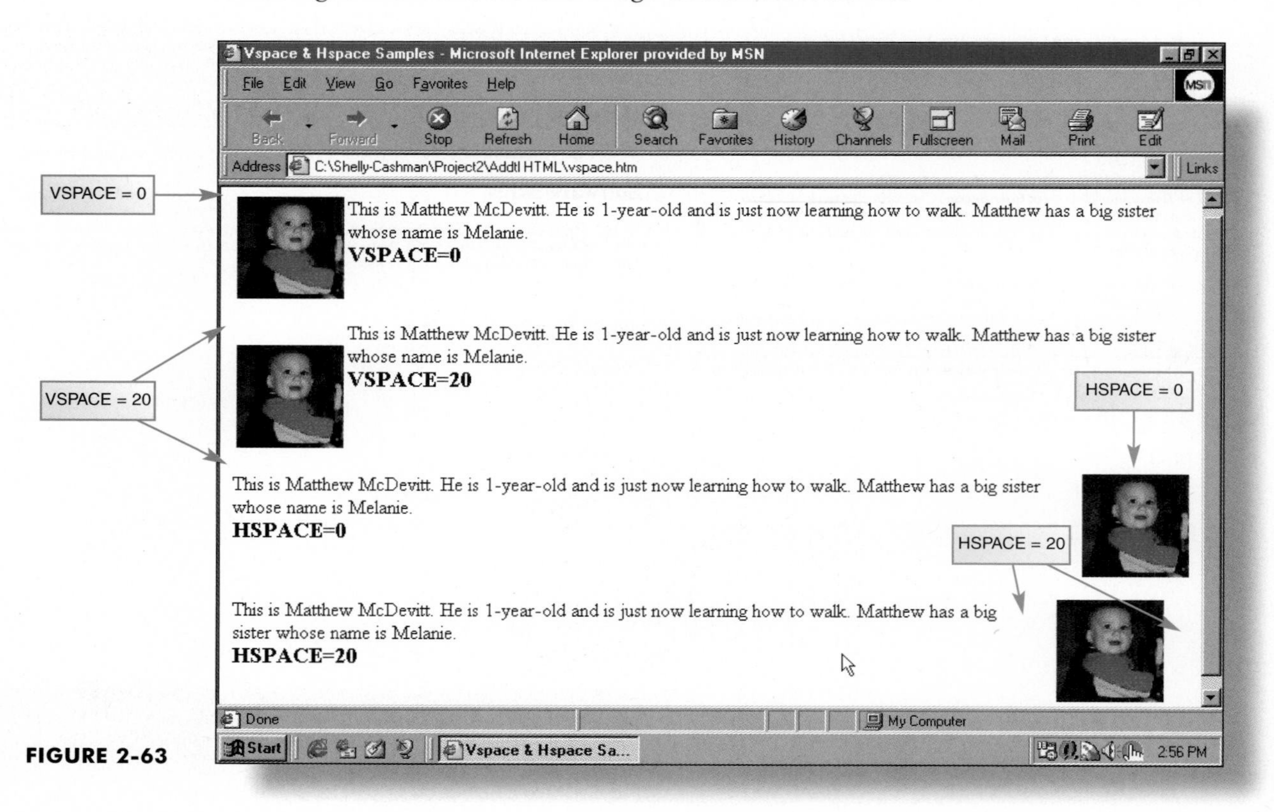

FIGURE 2-63

Thumbnail Images

Image loading is improved by many Web developers who use thumbnail images. A **thumbnail image** is a smaller version of the image itself. The thumbnail is used as a link that, when clicked, will load the full-sized image. Figure 2-64a shows an example of a thumbnail image that loads the full-sized image when clicked (Figure 2-64b). Loading images can take a long time, depending on the size and the complexity of the image. Visitors to the Web page may not want to wait. Web developers use thumbnail images to give the visitor the opportunity to decide whether or not they want to see the full-sized image. You can create a thumbnail version of the image by resizing the image in a paint program and saving it with a different file name. You then use the smaller version (thumbnail) of the image in the Web page with a link to the larger version of the image. The required tags are <A HREF="largeimage.gif"> <IMG SRC="thumbnail.gif"></A>, where largeimage.gif is the name of the full-sized image, and thumbnail.gif is the name of the smaller version of the image. If the visitor clicks the thumbnail image, he or she can use the Back button on the browser's Standard Buttons toolbar to return to the original Web page displaying the thumbnail image.

Clip Art

You do not have to be a graphics designer to create attractive Web pages. Free images are available on numerous Web sites. For more information about free images, visit the HTML More About page (www.scsite.com/html/more.htm) and click Clip Art.

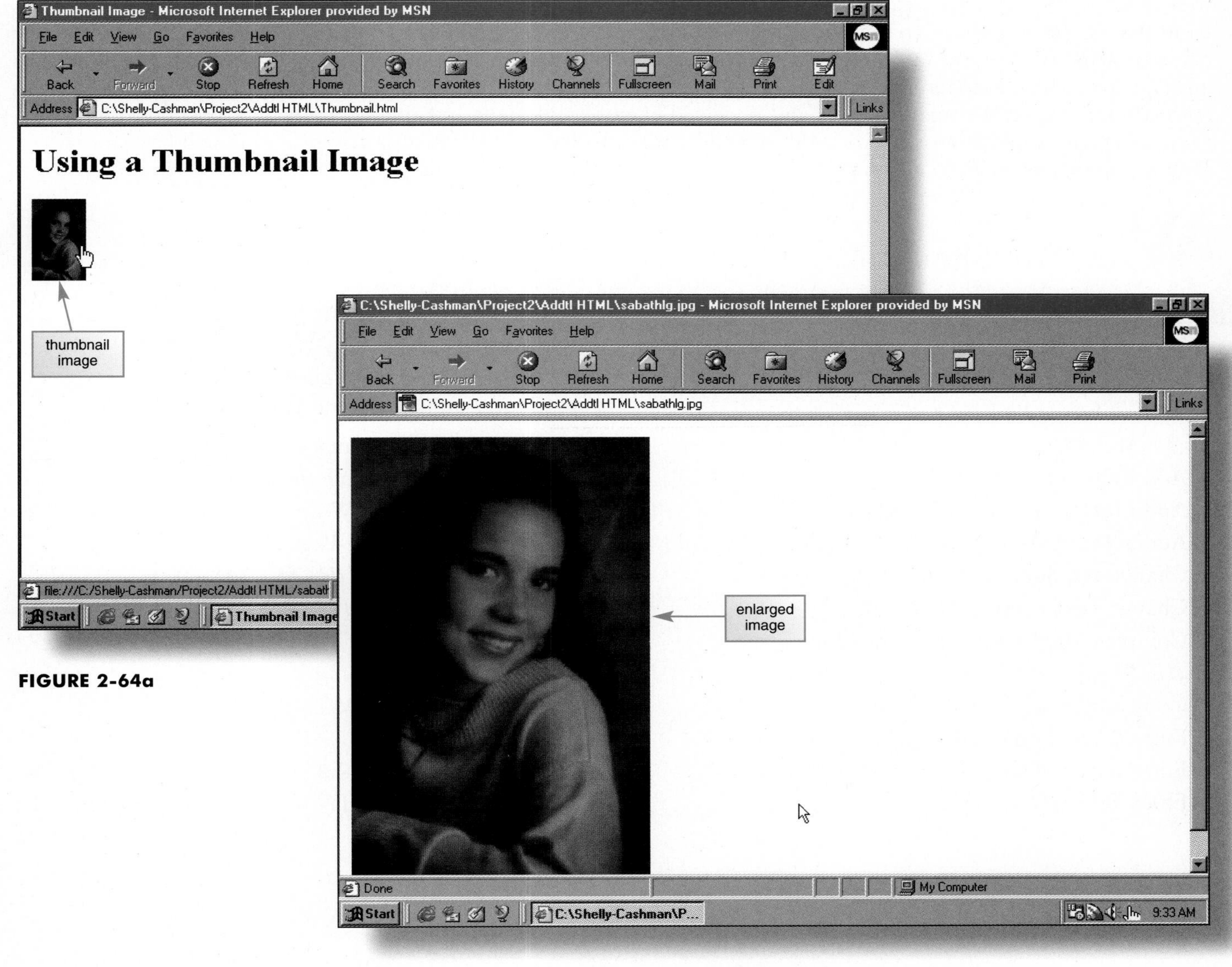

FIGURE 2-64a

FIGURE 2-64b

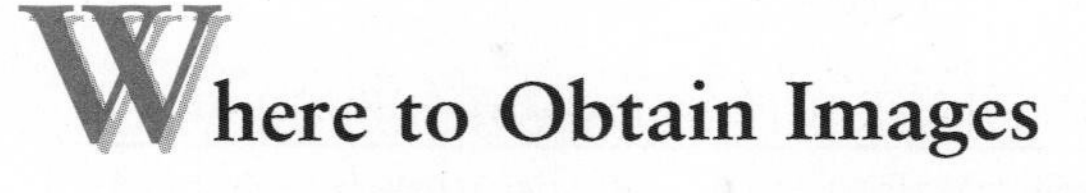

Where to Obtain Images

You can obtain images from a number of different sources. Clip art can be used on Web pages as well as images you create yourself with a paint program. You can scan images, pictures, or graphics with a scanner or use a digital camera to take pictures that can be read by the computer. You also can copy good images from the Internet. The Web contains thousands of image files on countless subjects that can be downloaded free and used for noncommercial purposes. Using one of the popular search engines, do a search on the words, Free GIFs, and see how many hits you get. You then can right-click an image that you want and save it. Regardless of where you get the images, always be aware of copyright rules and regulations.

Project Summary

In this project, you used Notepad to create and edit two HTML text files. You developed a two-page Web site that had links from each page to the other. You learned the terms and definitions of linking and used each of the four types of links in your pages. You created a link from the home page to the second page, together with one from the second page back to the home page. You created an e-mail link that, when clicked, opened up a New Message window. You set target links within the second page and then created a bulleted list to link to those targets. You also created a link to another Web site, and used both text and an image to link to the site. You learned more about Web page images and reviewed examples of many imaging techniques. You showed your two Web pages to your boss, Mark Mullet, and he was thrilled with the result. You probably will have more Web development work to do now.

What You Should Know

Having completed this project, you now should be able to perform the following tasks.

- Add Bold to Text *(HTM 2.34)*
- Add an E-Mail Link *(HTM 2.24)*
- Add an Image Link to Another Web Site *(HTM 2.44)*
- Add Italics to Text *(HTM 2.35)*
- Add Links to the Targets *(HTM 2.49)*
- Add a Text Link to Another Web Site *(HTM 2.43)*
- Change the Bullet Type *(HTM 2.37)*
- Change Text Color *(HTM 2.36)*
- Complete the Link Back to the Home Page *(HTM 2.51)*
- Copy and Paste Text *(HTM 2.21)*
- Enter a Heading *(HTM 2.15)*
- Enter Initial HTML Tags *(HTM 2.13)*
- Enter Text *(HTM 2.15)*
- Enter the Text and Tags for a Link to Another Web Page *(HTM 2.23)*
- Enter Two Bulleted Lists *(HTM 2.17)*
- Insert a Background Image *(HTM 2.19)*
- Insert a Horizontal Rule Image *(HTM 2.20)*
- Insert an Image with Wrapped Text *(HTM 2.42)*
- Link to the Top of the Page *(HTM 2.50)*
- Open the HTML File *(HTM 2.32)*
- Print the Web Page *(HTM 2.27, HTM 2.53)*
- Save and Print the HTML File *(HTM 2.25 HTM 2.51)*
- Set Link Targets *(HTM 2.47)*
- Start Notepad *(HTM 2.11)*
- Test the Links *(HTM 2.28)*
- View the Web Page *(HTM 2.26, HTM 2.53)*

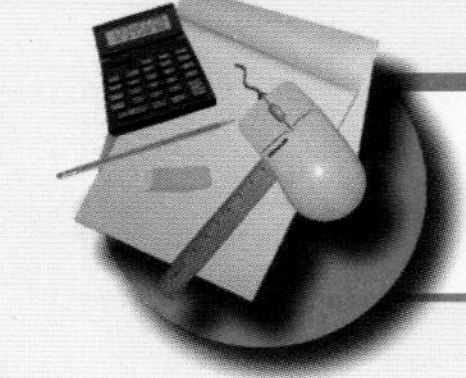

Test Your Knowledge

1 True/False

Instructions: Circle T if the statement is true or F if the statement is false.

T F 1. Hyperlinks allow you to move from one Web page to another.
T F 2. A hotspot is an area of a Web page in which no image can be inserted.
T F 3. You can create a link that generates a New Message window.
T F 4. Using the words, Click here, as a link is effective and descriptive link text.
T F 5. Visited link colors can be changed within the <A> tag.
T F 6. A home page is the very first page of a Web site.
T F 7. The <IMP> tag is used to insert images.
T F 8. The HREF attribute assigns a URL to a link.
T F 9. Targets are used for links that are created within a Web page.
T F 10. Any graphic file can be used as a Web page image.

2 Multiple Choice

Instructions: Circle the correct response.

1. The __________ attribute defines horizontal space between text and an image.
   a. HEIGHT b. HSPACE c. VSPACE d. WIDTH
2. The __________ attribute is used to define the URL of an image.
   a. SRC b. HEIGHT c. HREF d. ALT
3. To have no border on an image, the attribute would be __________.
   a. BORDER=NO b. NOBORDER c. BORDER=0 d. BORDER=-1
4. The __________ attribute defines an anchor.
   a. COORDS b. ANCH c. ALT d. NAME
5. __________ defines where the page will be displayed.
   a. COORDS b. TARGET c. HREF d. REL
6. To create bold text, use the __________ tag.
   a. <B> b. <BOLD> c. <BOLD=ON> d. <BL>
7. To italicize text, use the __________ tag.
   a. <ITALICS=ON> b. <IT> c. <I> d. <TT>
8. To underline text, use the __________ tag.
   a. <UNDERLINE=ON> b. <UN> c. <U> d. <UL>
9. The two types of files that can be used as Web page images are .gif and __________.
   a. .jpg b. .bmp c. .txt d. .img
10. A tag that would clear text wrapping around an image is __________.
    a. <WRAP=OFF> b. <BR CLEAR=OFF> c. <BR CLEAR=RIGHT> d. <IMG NOWRAP>

Test Your Knowledge

3 Understanding HTML

Instructions: Perform the following tasks using a computer.

1. Start Notepad.
2. Open the sample1.htm file created in Project 1.
3. Print the file and do the following without looking at the book:
   a. Circle the tag that prints alternate text while an image is loading.
   b. Draw a line under the two tags that will link to another site on the Web.
   c. Draw a square around the tag that indicates the To top target.
4. Write your name and answers on the printout and hand it in to your instructor.

4 Editing HTML Files

Instructions: Perform the following tasks using a computer.

1. Start your browser.
2. Enter `www.scsite.com/html/proj2.htm` in the Address text box. When the Web page displays, scroll to the Internet titles and then click the title of this book.
3. Click the link, Project 2 - 4 Editing HTML Files.
4. Click View on the menu bar and then click Source to find the HTML code for some feature that was not used on the sample1.htm Web page.
5. Highlight the code and copy it to the Clipboard (i.e., press CTRL+C).
6. Open the file, sample1.htm, in Notepad.
7. Paste the Clipboard contents in the sample1.htm file at an appropriate place.
8. Save the revised file on a floppy disk using the file name, sample2.htm.
9. Print the revised document source.
10. Open sample2.htm in your browser.
11. Print the Web page.
12. Write your name on both printouts and hand them in to your instructor.

1 Linking Help

Instructions: Perform the following tasks using a computer.

1. Start your browser.
2. Enter `www.scsite.com/html/proj2.htm` in the Address text box. When the Web page displays, scroll to the Internet titles and then click the title of this book.
3. Click Link Help, and then read the information about linking.
4. Write down some of the most important ideas about relative linking.
5. Write your name on the pages and hand them in to your instructor.

2 Web Page Design Ideas

Instructions: Perform the following tasks using a computer.

1. Start your browser.
2. Enter `www.scsite.com/html/proj2.htm` in the Address text box. When the Web page displays, scroll to the Internet titles and then click the title of this book.
3. Click Web Style Links, and then read the suggestions about links on the Web pages that you create.
4. Write down some of the most important ideas.
5. Write your name on the pages and hand them in to your instructor.

Apply Your Knowledge

1 Editing the Apply Your Knowledge Web Page

Instructions: Start Notepad. Open the apply2.htm file on the HTML Data Disk. Figure 2-65 on the next page shows the Apply Your Knowledge Web page as it should display in your browser. The apply2.htm file is a partially completed HTML file that contains some errors. Perform the following tasks.

1. Open the file in your browser.
2. Examine the HTML file in Notepad and its appearance as a Web page in the browser.
3. Correct the HTML errors, making the Web page look similar to the one shown in Figure 2-65, with all links working correctly.

(continued)

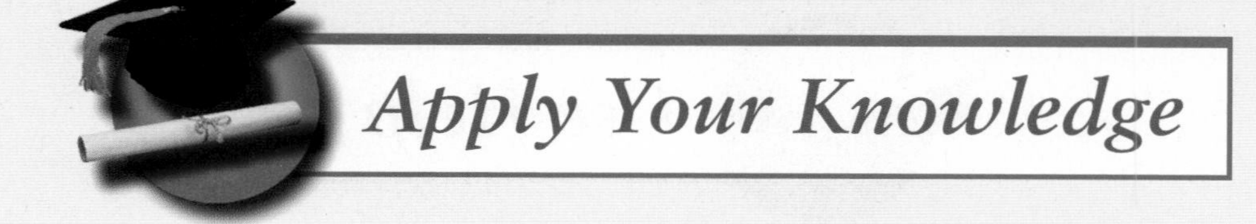

Editing the Apply Your Knowledge Web Page *(continued)*

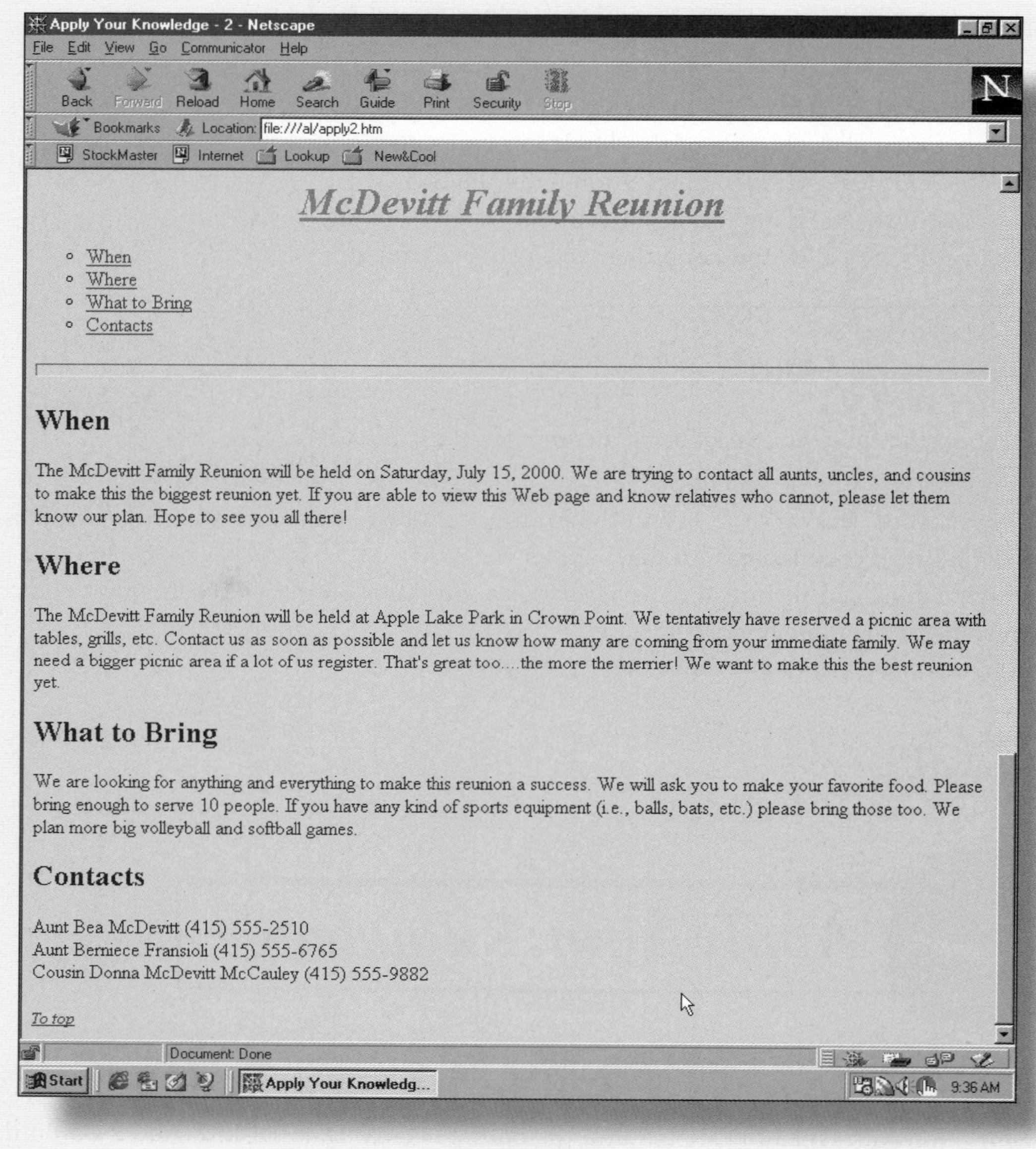

FIGURE 2-65

4. Add any HTML code necessary for additional features shown in the Web page.
5. Save the revised file using the file name, target.htm.
6. Print the revised document source.
7. Open the target.htm file in your browser.
8. Print the Web page.
9. Write your name on both printouts and hand them in to your instructor.

1 Creating a Web Page with Target Links

Problem: Your instructor wants you to create a Web page demonstrating your knowledge of target links. You have been asked to create a Web page to demonstrate this technique, similar to the one shown in Figure 2-66.

Instructions: Start Notepad. Perform the following tasks using a computer.

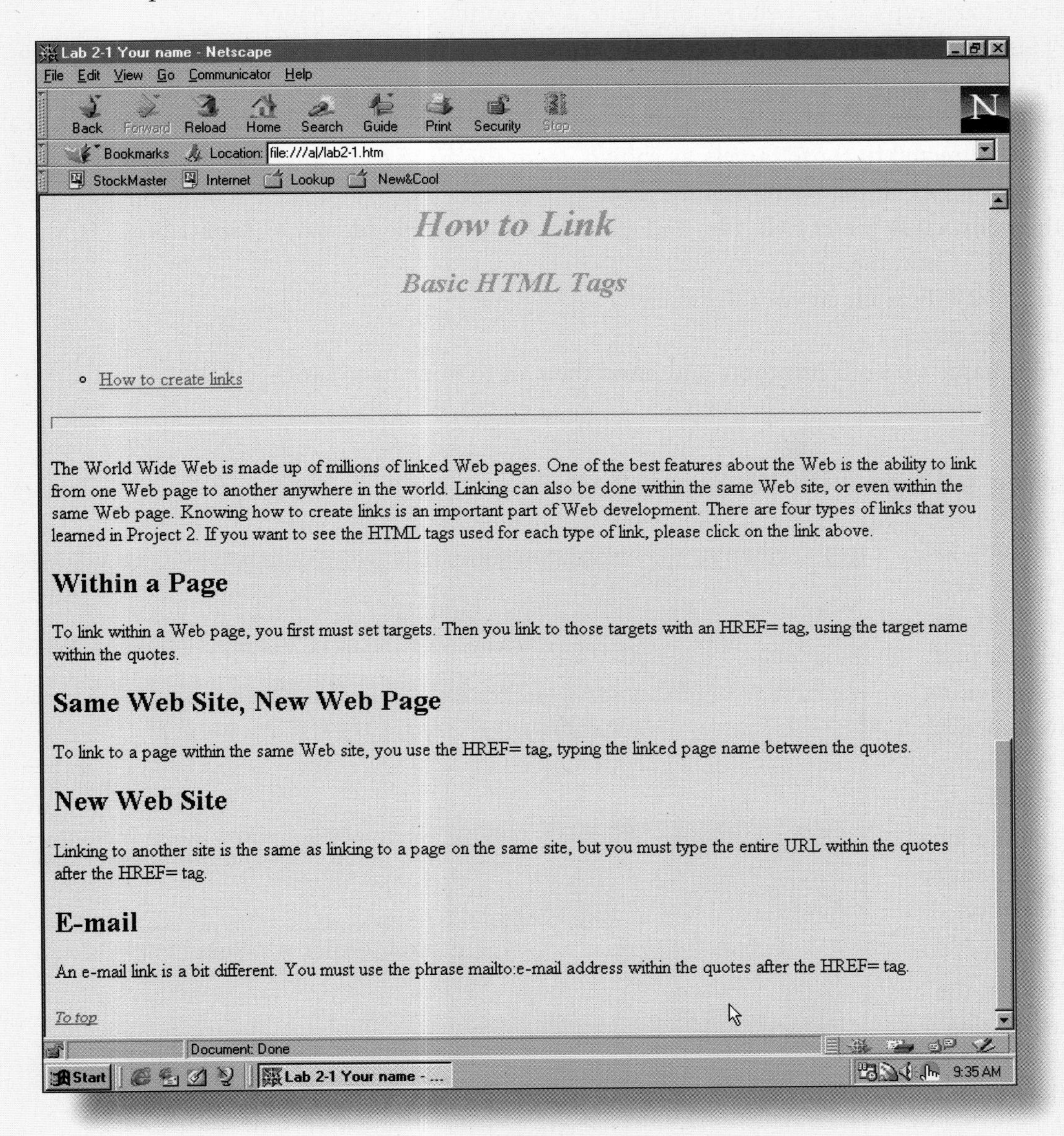

FIGURE 2-66

1. Create a new HTML file with the title, [your name] lab2-1, in the main heading section.
2. Begin the body section by adding a centered, Heading 1 style heading, How to Link. On the next line add a centered, Heading 2 style heading, Basic HTML Tags. Use font color #31B5D6 for both headings.

(continued)

Creating a Web Page with Target Links *(continued)*

3. Use background color #FFE7C6 for this page.
4. Add a bulleted list with the circle type of bullet.
5. Add a size 10 horizontal rule.
6. Type in the paragraph of text shown in Figure 2-66 on the previous page.
7. Add a Heading 2 style heading, Within a Page, and the paragraph as shown in the Figure 2-66.
8. Add all additional headings and paragraphs as shown in Figure 2-66.
9. Create a target at the top of the page called totop, and a target at the Within a Page heading called howto.
10. Create links directed to those targets as shown, from the *How to create links* toward the top of the page and the *To top* link at the bottom of the page.
11. Close the body, close the HTML file, and save the file using the file name, lab2-1.htm.
12. Print the lab2-1.htm file.
13. Open the lab2-1.htm file in your browser.
14. Print the Web page.
15. Write your name on both printouts and hand them in to your instructor.

2 Creating a Page with Wrapped Text

Problem: You are the head of a charity dance committee and decide to prepare a Web page announcement inviting people to the dance (Figure 2-67). You decide to use text wrapped around a left-aligned image to notify people of the dance.

Instructions: Start Notepad. Perform the following tasks using a computer.

1. Create a new HTML file with the title, [your name] lab 2-2, in the main heading section.

FIGURE 2-67

2. Begin the body section by adding a centered, italicized, Heading 1 style heading, SCHOOL CHARITY DANCE.
3. Add a colored background to the Web page using the #FFCCFF color code. Add a horizontal rule.
4. Add the image, school.jpg, left-aligned with horizontal space of 10, height of 226, and width of 324. Left-alignment will wrap text to the right of the image.
5. Add the paragraphs of information as shown in Figure 2-67.
6. Add an italicized e-mail sentence at the bottom of the paragraph and create the e-mail link.
7. Close the body, close the HTML file, and save the file using the file name, lab2-2.htm.
8. Print the lab2-2.htm file.
9. Open the lab2-2.htm file in your browser.
10. Print the Web page.
11. Write your name on the printouts and hand them in to your instructor.

3 Composing Two Linked Web Pages

Problem: You want to create a home page to tell people about yourself. You will use both paragraph and bulleted list formats to display information as shown in Figures 2-68a and 2-68b on the next page.

Instructions: Start Notepad. Perform the tasks on the next page using a computer.

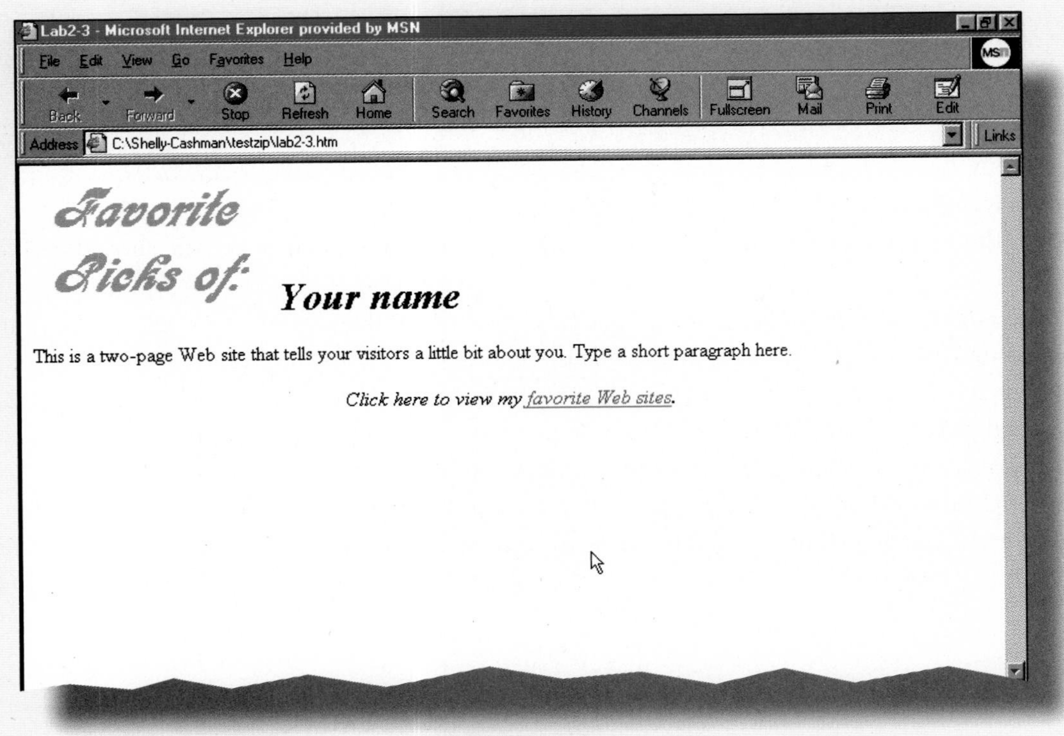

FIGURE 2-68a

(continued)

Composing Two Linked Web Pages *(continued)*

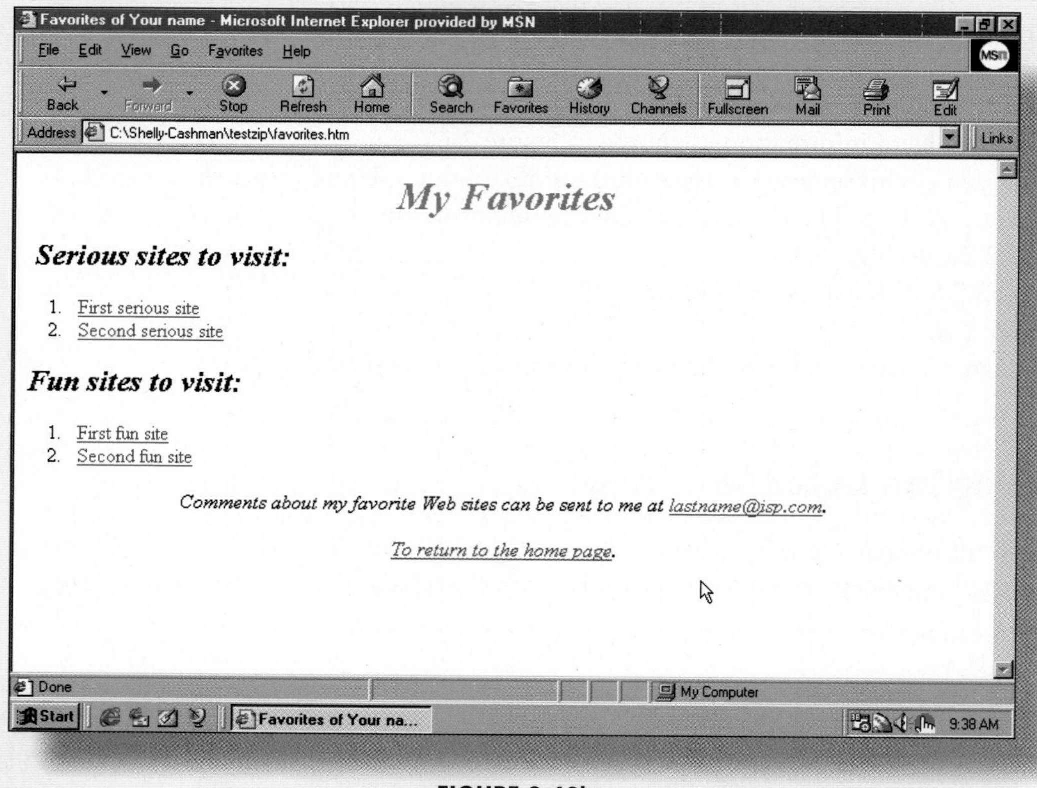

FIGURE 2-68b

1. Create two Web pages similar to the ones shown in Figures 2-68a and 2-68b.
2. The title on the home page should be [your name] lab2-3a. The second page title should be [your name] lab2-3b.htm.
3. On the home page, include the image, favtxt.gif, with horizontal space of 15, height of 105, and width of 164. Following that image, add your name using Heading style 1 and italics.
4. Create a link to a second page that will contain the text and numbered lists shown in Figure 2-68b.
5. To the second page add a link back to the home page as well as an e-mail link.
6. Save the pages using the file names, lab2-3a.htm and lab2-3b.htm, respectively.
7. Open the lab2-3a and lab2-3b files in your browser and then print the Web pages.
8. Write your name on the printouts and hand them in to your instructor.

Cases and Places

The difficulty of these case studies varies:
▶ are the least difficult; ▶▶ are more difficult; and ▶▶▶ are the most difficult.

1 Mr. Mullet likes your ideas for the Web Res Web site and now wants to expand on them. Use Notepad to add some additional bullets and another paragraph.

2 Your instructor wants to publish the linked Web pages that you created in In the Lab 3. He wants you to add more zip to the pages with a colored or textured background and a horizontal rule or image. Add these additional features to those pages.

3 You are interested to see if there are other Web-based resume companies. Start your browser and search for other Web sites specifically regarding Web resumes. View the source of a resume page that is especially interesting to you. Make note of one element on the Web page that you do not have in the Web Res site. Use Notepad to add that component to a new Web page and insert specific information about Web Res.

4 Create your own Web page resume using your original HTML file, sample1.htm, as a template. Add a link from the sample1.htm Web page to your resume. Change the link on the Web Res home page to say, samples, rather than sample.

5 Search the World Wide Web for hints and tips on resume writing. Find one Web page that lists some useful ideas about resume writing. Create a link from the Web Res home page to that Web page.

6 Browse some pages on the Web and choose two pages that show good examples of linking and two pages that show bad examples of linking. Print all four pages. Indicate on the printouts what you like about the pages with good examples. Indicate what changes could make the linking more user friendly on the bad example pages.

7 HTML linking is an important topic that you need to understand. Search the World Wide Web for information about HTML tags used for linking. Learn about some of the tags that are not discussed in this project. Use at least two new tags or tag attributes to create a more complex Web page.

HTML

Creating Tables in a Web Site

OBJECTIVES

You will have mastered the material in this project when you can:

- Define table elements
- Describe the steps used to plan, design, and code a table
- Create a borderless table with images only
- Create a list of links with text
- Create a borderless table with text only
- Create a menu bar with links
- Create a table with borders
- Change the horizontal alignment of text
- Add color to individual cells
- Add color to entire rows
- Insert a caption beneath a table
- Alter the spacing between cells using the CELLSPACING attribute
- Alter the spacing within cells using the CELLPADDING attribute
- Use the ROWSPAN attribute
- Use the COLSPAN attribute
- Use blank cells

CULTURAL ARTIFACTS

Add a Computer to Your Palette

Digital Art Moves to a Modern Museum

Walk through an art museum, and you likely will observe the works of Renoir, Monet, or Picasso. But walk through the San Francisco Museum of Modern Art (SFMOMA), and you likely will view computers and Intel logos alongside priceless masterpieces.

Digital art has found a home in the SFMOMA, thanks to David Ross, who joined the museum staff as director in 1998. One of his premier projects is, The American Century: Art and Culture 1900 - 2000, which is a $6 million exhibit of mixed media and commissioned computer art sponsored by Intel.

SFMOMA's move toward displaying digital art began prior to Ross's hiring. Curators had begun archiving particular Web sites as part

SAN FRANCISCO MUSEUM OF MODERN ART

PICASSO

DIGITAL ART

of its architecture and design collection. Ross initially thought these snapshots of the Internet destroyed the volatile and interactive nature of online images. He changed his mind, however, and decided that the museum and its patrons would benefit by capturing these images and displaying them as cultural artifacts.

The Museum's mission statement proclaims it "exists to collect, preserve, present, and interpret the best of contemporary and modern art for the purpose of enriching people's lives through aesthetic and learning experiences." Its multimedia education program presents the myriad of contexts influencing artists as they create their works.

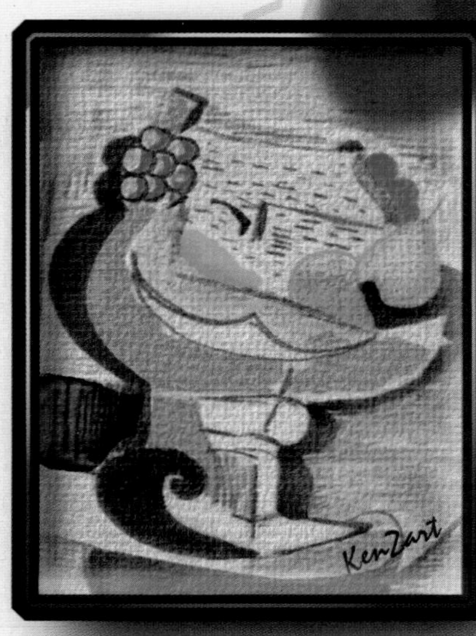

For example, its CD-ROM Voices & Images of California Art delves into the lives and motivations of eight Californian artists whose works are part of the Museum's permanent collection. It contains more than 75 photographs of the artists, 150 full-screen reproductions of their artworks, 40 rare video and audio clips, and 250 original newspaper clippings, handwritten letters, and diary entries.

Ross believes the attributes and definition of Internet art will change as the Net evolves. At a speech at the Art, Technology, and Culture Colloquium series sponsored by the University of California at Berkeley, he said that this digital art gathers and moves audiences and combines the product of writers and artists.

This Colloquium at the University of California features leading theorists, critics, and artists who discuss the effect of digital media on our Net-literate society. Its neatly organized Web site uses tables to describe its lecture series and speakers. Likewise, your Web pages in this project will use tables to organize data. With HTML tags, you will create tables, alter the vertical and horizontal alignment, add color, insert images, and add an e-mail link.

Similarly, the SFMOMA site contains tables that structure the page's components, such as the Museum's mission statement, a description of its history, and a virtual tour of its new building.

SFMOMA is at the forefront of exhibiting and promoting modern digital art. In its virtual gallery, you can view the masterpieces of the digital art community created by artists who have traded their paintbrush and canvas for a scanner and mouse.

<tr>

<td>Mu

</body>

</html>

HTML

Creating Tables in a Web Site

CASE PERSPECTIVE

The school's theater program is having trouble attracting students to its performances. As a result of this low attendance, the lack of funds is threatening to close the program completely. You are the head of advertising for the Theater Club and are trying to think of new ways to promote upcoming events. Your recommendation is to advertise the Theater Club on the World Wide Web. Advertising on the World Wide Web will increase the Theater Club's exposure to students.

On the Theater Club Web pages, you want to list club and membership information, as well as advertising the calendar of upcoming plays and special events. If students read about these events and the fellow students involved in them, they may come to future activities. You decide to develop the necessary Web pages with this information to show at the next Theater Club meeting.

Introduction

In Projects 1 and 2, you learned the key features of HTML programming. You learned how to use basic HTML tags and more advanced linking techniques. You learned about images and how to insert them in Web pages. You created Web pages that stood alone as well as pages that were linked together. You can create some very complex and interesting Web pages with the skills you developed in Projects 1 and 2. This project will add to your HTML knowledge by teaching you how to create tables.

One way to present information on a Web page is to create paragraphs and bulleted lists of text. A second way is to create tables with rows and columns of text and images. In this project, you will learn how to create and enhance tables using a variety of attributes and formats.

Project Three — Theater Club

Tables allow you to position elements easily on a Web page. Tables also help your Web pages look more organized and professional. In this project, you will use HTML to create two linked Web pages for the school's Theater Club, as shown in Figures 3-1a and 3-1b. You also will use HTML to improve the appearance of two other Web pages, as shown in Figures 3-1c and 3-1d.

At least one table displays on each Web page in this project. You will create a borderless table on the Theater Club home page into which you will insert images. You also will create another borderless table on the home page that will contain text and a link list. This list will serve as a menu bar and link to the other three pages. On the calendar.htm, members.htm, and anything.htm Web pages, you will use the header table created on the home page for consistency. On these pages, you also will create a menu bar just beneath the header for the links. On the members.htm Web page (Figure 3-1c), which is on the HTML Data Disk, you will add CELLSPACING and CELLPADDING attributes to give the page a different look. You also will add a caption to the members.htm Web page. On some of the Web pages, you will vary the vertical alignment and add color to specific cells. On the anything.htm Web page (Figure 3-1d), which also is on the HTML Data Disk, you will add headings that span several columns and rows.

You will use Notepad to edit the text and HTML tags to create and enhance the four Web pages. You also will use your browser to view Web pages as you develop them.

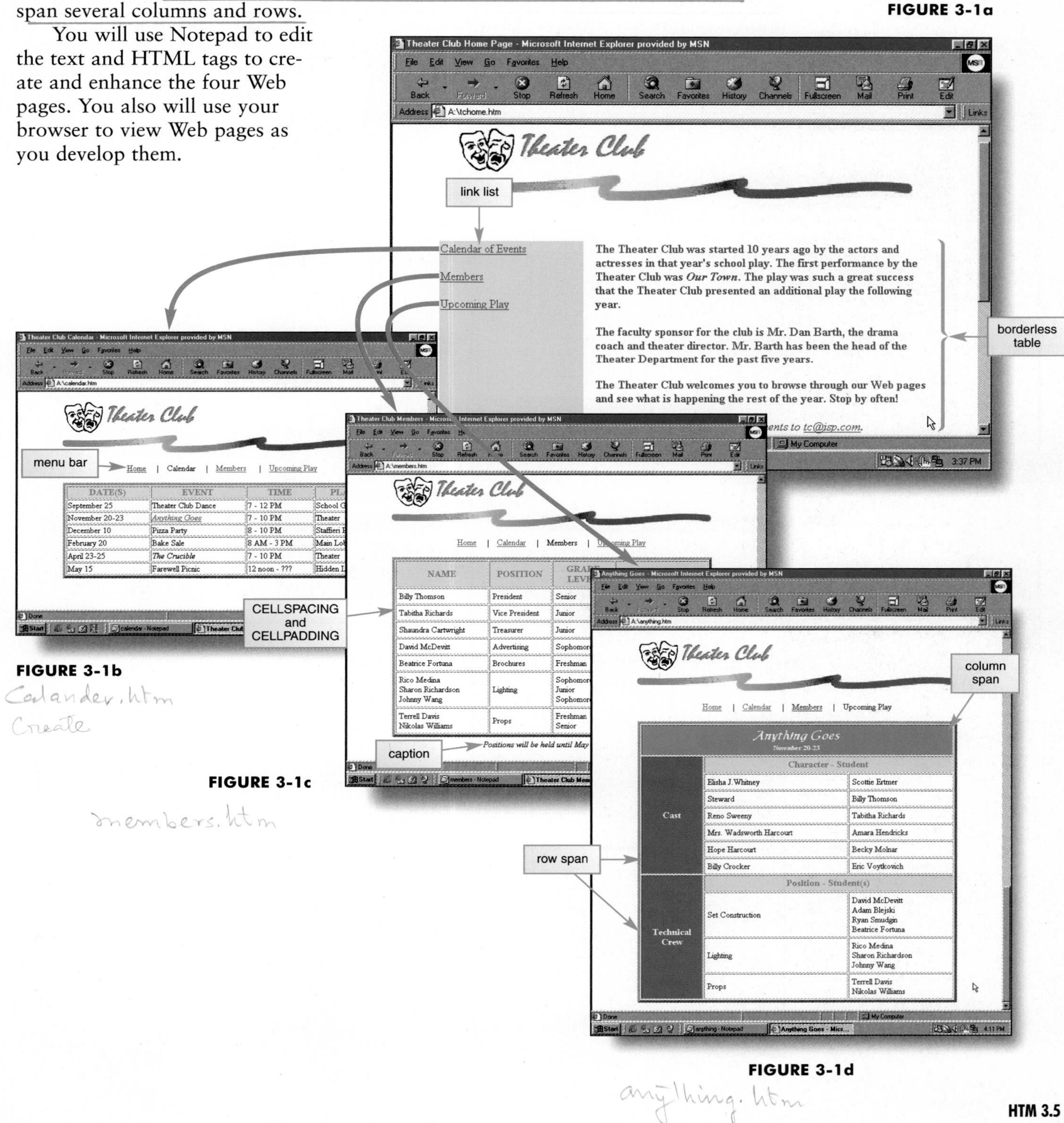

FIGURE 3-1a

FIGURE 3-1b

FIGURE 3-1c

FIGURE 3-1d

Creating Web Pages with Tables

Tables allow you to organize information on a Web page using HTML tags. **Tables** are useful when you want to arrange text and images into rows and columns, making the information straightforward and clear to the Web page visitor. You can use tables to display newspaper-type columns of text or lists of information. Web developers also use tables to create the appearance of a border around an image or text. Borders help to make the image or text stand out on the page, giving it a 3-dimensional effect. Tables can be complex (Figure 3-2a) or simple (Figure 3-2b). Tables can have a background color (Figure 3-2a) or just have color in certain cells (Figure 3-2b).

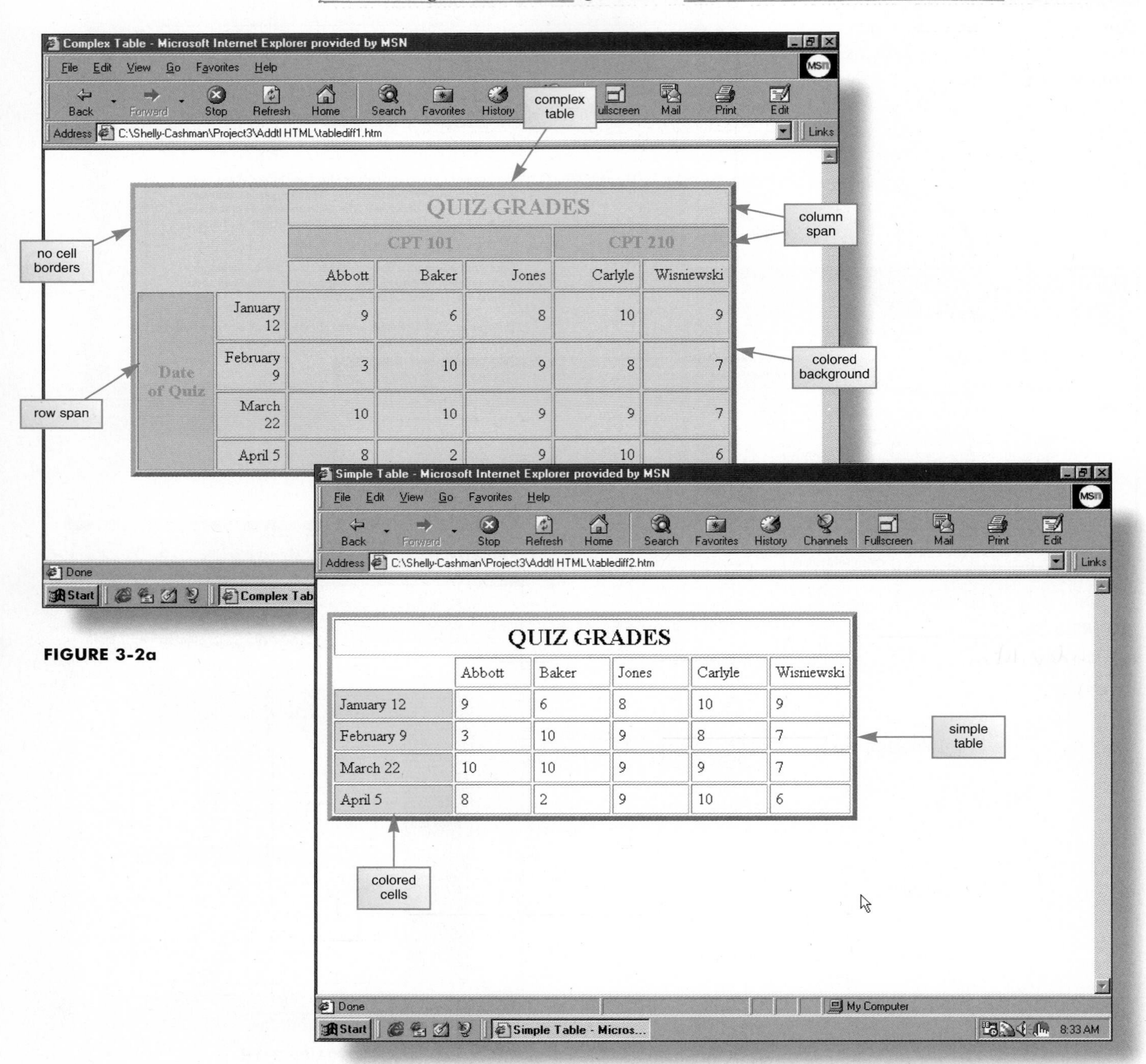

FIGURE 3-2a

FIGURE 3-2b

You can create a table with text only or insert images as shown in the borderless table in Figure 3-3. In Project 2, you learned how to wrap text around an image. You also can create a table to wrap text around an image. An advantage to using a table to insert images, instead of just wrapping the text around the image, is that you have more control over the placement of the text and image. Figure 3-4 shows the same images and information as Figure 3-3, but with the text wrapped to the right of the image. In Figure 3-3, you have the control to align the table in the middle 80% of the window's width. You cannot align in the middle of the window using wrapped text. The placement of the text can vary next to the image (i.e., center alignment of the heading, left alignment of the text) using a table with horizontal and vertical alignment attributes. Tables give you this flexibility. You also can add headings that span rows and columns, additional cellspacing or cellpadding, or captions that help make the Web pages clear, interesting, and easy to read.

More About

Tables

Tables are useful for a variety of purposes. They can store information in tabular form or create a layout on a Web page. Layouts created with tables give more flexibility to the Web developer. You have more control over the placement of information or images. Many popular Web sites use tables.

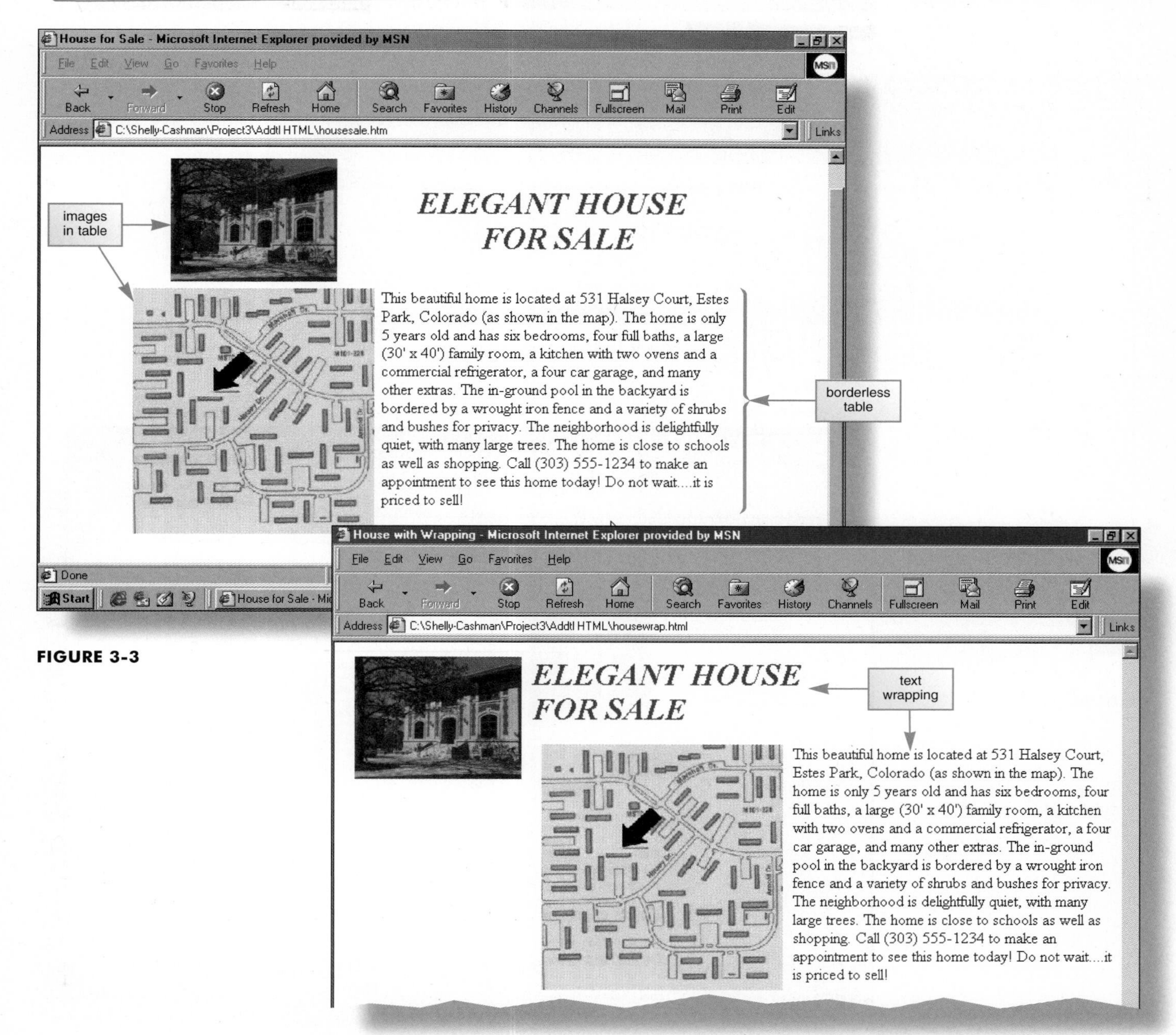

FIGURE 3-3

FIGURE 3-4

Table Elements

Tables consist of rows, columns, and cells, much like spreadsheets. A **row** is a horizontal line of information. A **column** is a vertical line of information. A **cell** is the intersection of a row and a column. Figure 3-5 shows examples of these three elements. In Figure 3-5a, one row in the table has a yellow background. In Figure 3-5b, the second column has a blue background. In Figure 3-5c, one cell (300 Crestwood) has a red background. These elements are important as you design and program tables using HTML.

You work with the row, column, and cell elements as you build a table. The attributes that you set are relative to these table elements. You can change certain attributes for an entire row of information. You also can set attributes for one or more cells within a row. Cells have two variations, heading and data. **Heading cells** display text as bold and center-aligned. In contrast, **data cells** display normal text that is left-aligned.

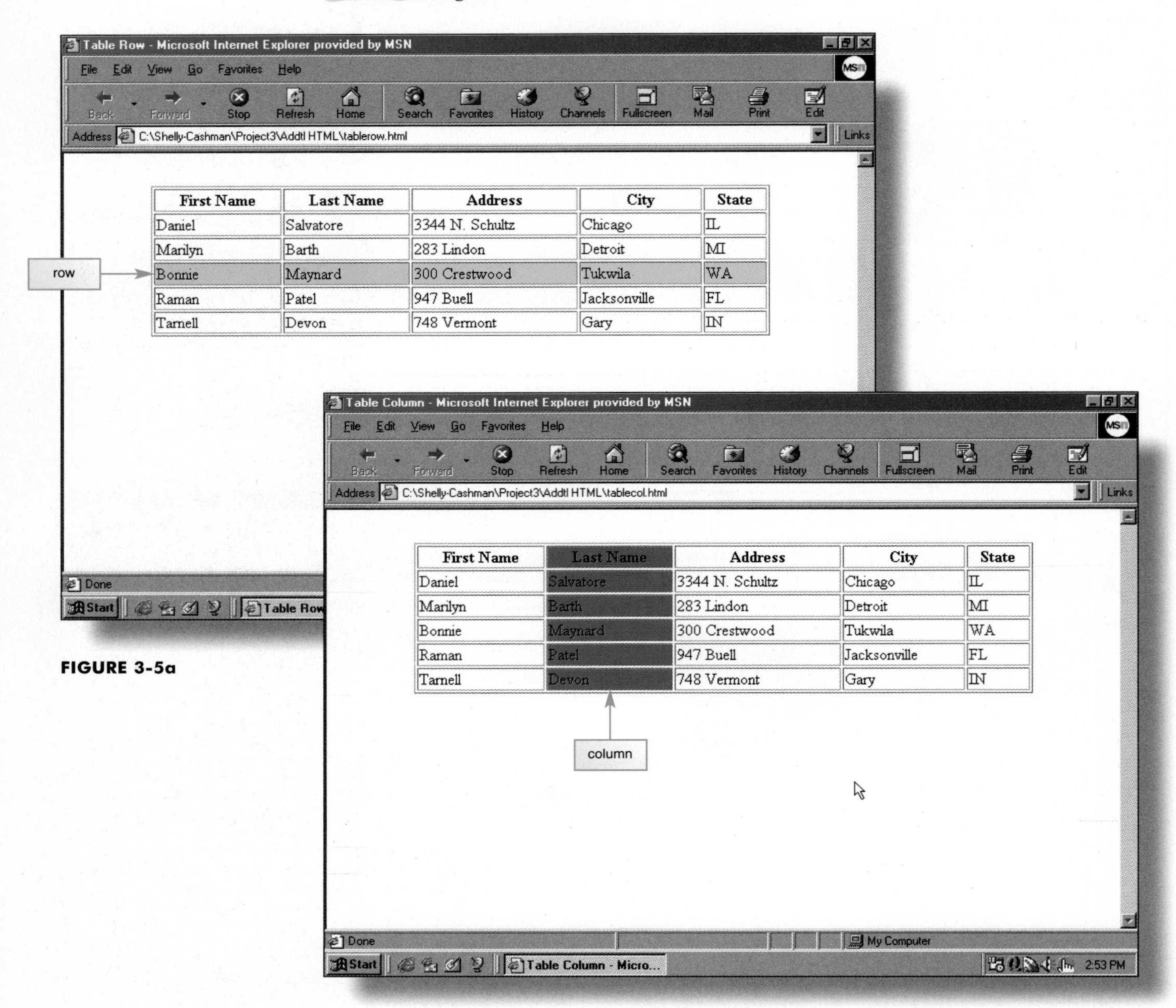

FIGURE 3-5a

FIGURE 3-5b

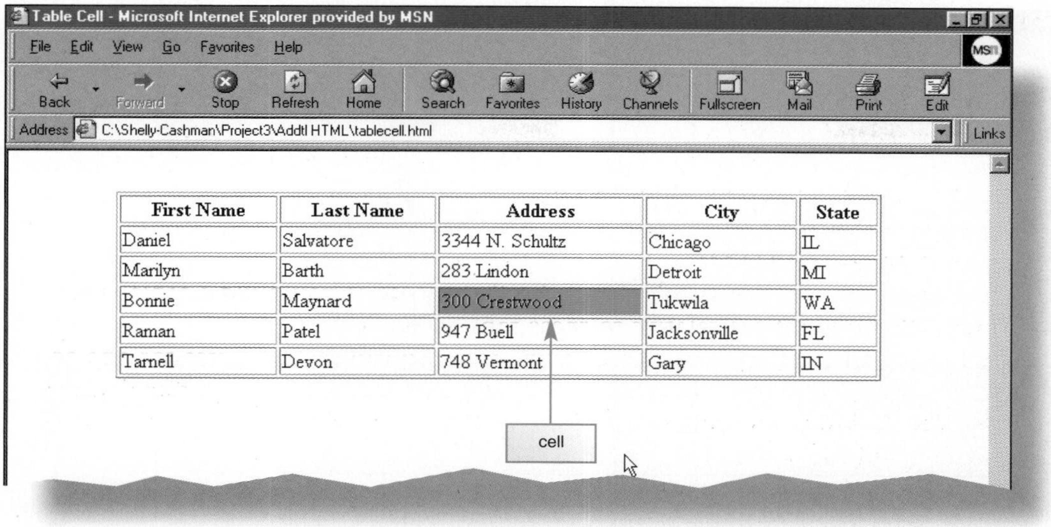

Table Cell - Microsoft Internet Explorer provided by MSN

File Edit View Go Favorites Help

Back Forward Stop Refresh Home Search Favorites History Channels Fullscreen Mail Print Edit

Address C:\Shelly-Cashman\Project3\Addtl HTML\tablecell.html Links

First Name	Last Name	Address	City	State
Daniel	Salvatore	3344 N. Schultz	Chicago	IL
Marilyn	Barth	283 Lindon	Detroit	MI
Bonnie	Maynard	300 Crestwood	Tukwila	WA
Raman	Patel	947 Buell	Jacksonville	FL
Tarnell	Devon	748 Vermont	Gary	IN

cell

FIGURE 3-5c

Other Table Parts

Other parts of a table include table borders, table headers, and table captions (Figure 3-6a). **Table borders** are lines that encompass the perimeter of the table. **Table headers** are bold text that indicate the purpose of the row or column. A **table caption** is descriptive text located above or below the table that further describes the purpose of the table. Tables can use each of these features or a combination of them. Tables also can be designed that use only one of these parts (Figure 3-6b on the next page). The purpose for the table dictates which of these parts you include.

For example, the table in Figure 3-6b lists columns of numbers. This may be acceptable if the goal is to display a list of numbers with no other information. If the goal is not to just list numbers but to explain their purpose, then you at least would need headers for each column (Figure 3-6a). To provide an additional explanation, you can add headings that span columns and rows (Figure 3-6c on the next page).

More About

Table Parts

Many Web sources discuss table parts, giving numerous examples and tips. For more information about HTML table parts, visit the HTML More About page (www.scsite.com/html/more.htm) and click HTML Table Parts.

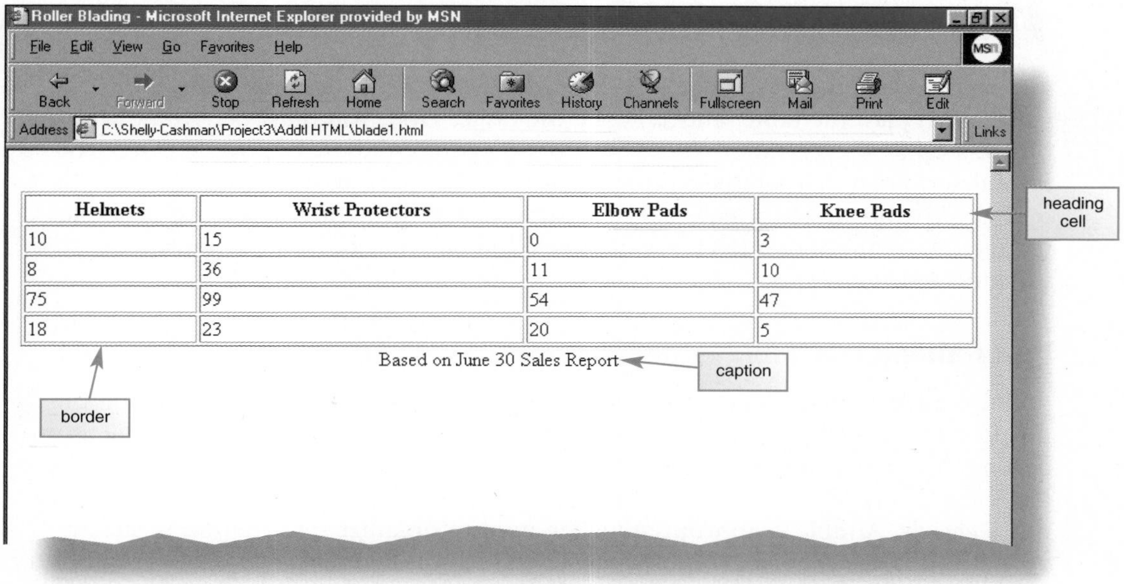

Roller Blading - Microsoft Internet Explorer provided by MSN

File Edit View Go Favorites Help

Back Forward Stop Refresh Home Search Favorites History Channels Fullscreen Mail Print Edit

Address C:\Shelly-Cashman\Project3\Addtl HTML\blade1.html Links

Helmets	Wrist Protectors	Elbow Pads	Knee Pads
10	15	0	3
8	36	11	10
75	99	54	47
18	23	20	5

Based on June 30 Sales Report

heading cell

caption

border

FIGURE 3-6a

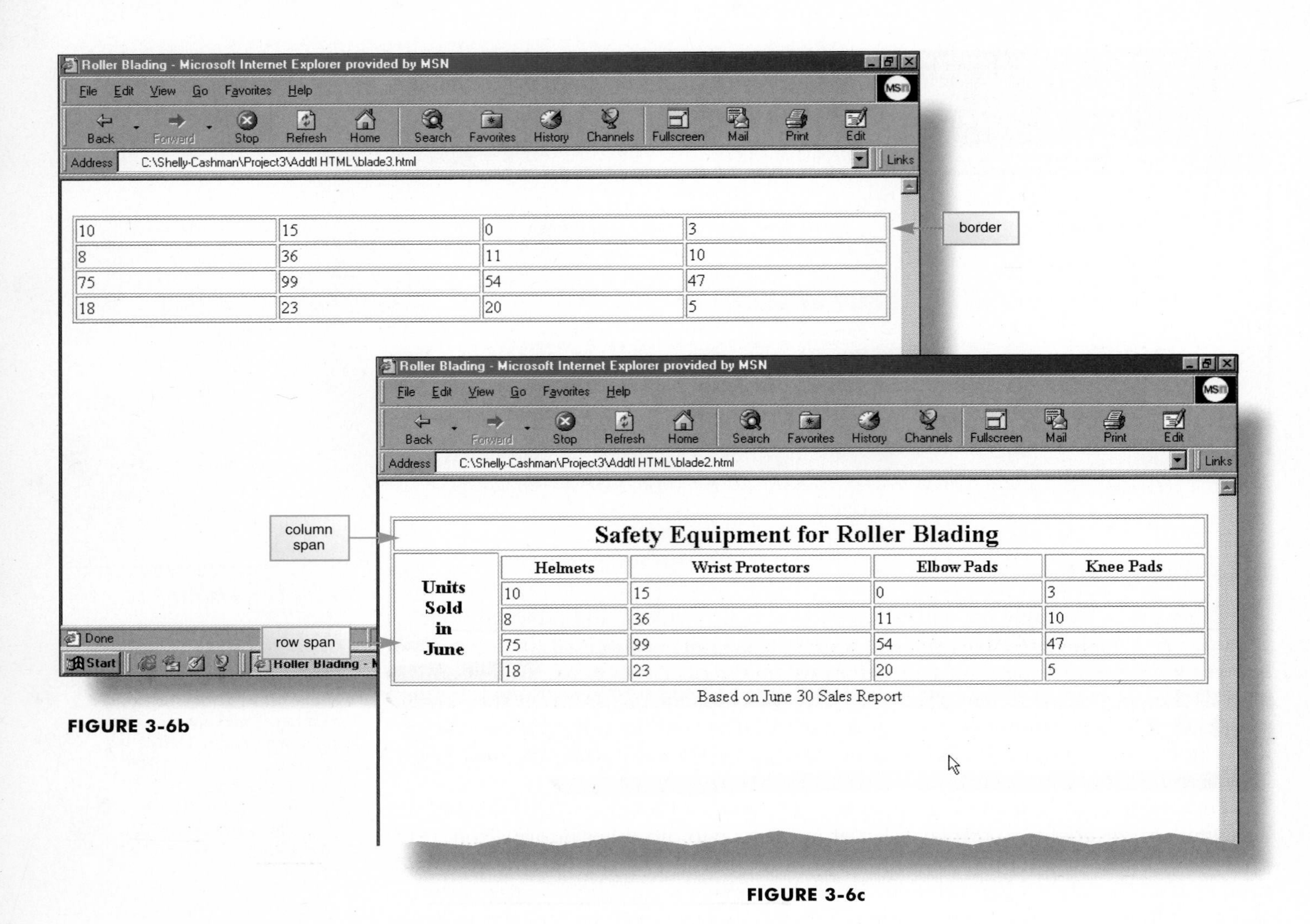

FIGURE 3-6b

FIGURE 3-6c

Planning, Designing, and Coding a Table

Creating tables for a Web page is a three-step process: (1) determine if a table is needed; (2) plan the table; and (3) code the table. First, you must determine whether or not a table is necessary. Not all Web pages require the use of a table. After you have determined that a table is necessary, then you must design the table, or lay it out. Good table design is necessary to display the information in a clear, readable manner. After those two tasks are completed, then you can begin to create the table using HTML.

Determining if a Table Is Needed

Not all Web page applications require the use of tables. If you can explain the purpose of the Web page using paragraphs and bulleted lists only, then a table is not needed. You have created three Web pages so far in Projects 1 and 2 without the use of tables. Those Web pages were interesting and attractive and explained their purposes clearly. A table is appropriate when used to organize information in such a way that it is easier for the Web page visitor to read. Figure 3-7 shows an example of information displayed as text in both a bulleted list and as a table. For this application, a table is the better choice. The table gives the Web page a more professional look and more clearly explains the topic.

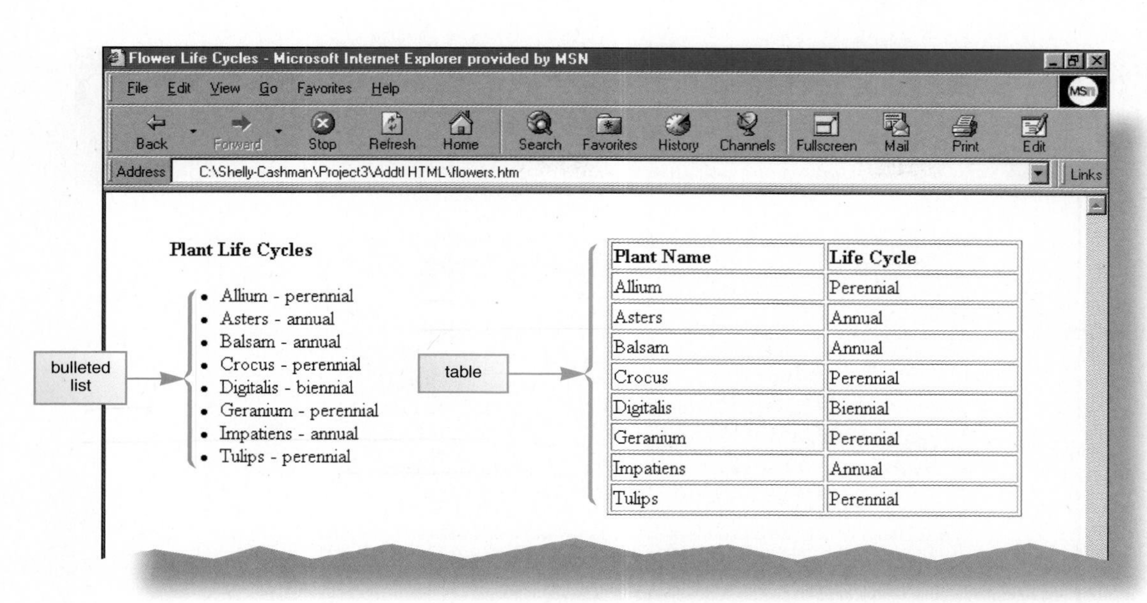

Plant Name	Life Cycle
Allium	Perennial
Asters	Annual
Balsam	Annual
Crocus	Perennial
Digitalis	Biennial
Geranium	Perennial
Impatiens	Annual
Tulips	Perennial

FIGURE 3-7

Planning the Table

In order to create effective tables, you must begin with a good design. You should sketch the table out on paper before writing the HTML code. Conceptualizing the table first on paper saves time trying to determine which HTML table tags to use. Once the table is on paper, you can see how many rows and columns you need, if you need headings or not, and if any of the headings span rows or columns. This will make it much easier to translate later to HTML tags.

If you want to create a simple table that lists the times run by various cross-country team members, you could create the table shown in Figure 3-8a. What if these runners participate in two different types of races though, such as 5K and 10K? You could include that information if you design a table as shown in Figure 3-8b. That table layout gives you only enough room to list one race, however. If you need to include more than one race, you may want to create a table such as the one shown in Figure 3-8c. To make the table easier for the Web page visitor to understand, you may want to include spanning headers as well as a caption. The resulting Web page would look like the one shown in Figure 3-9 on the next page. These design issues should be considered during the table planning stage of Web development.

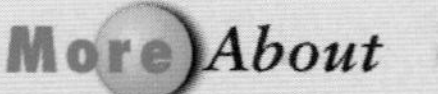

Table Tutorial

Table tutorials are available via online sources. Tutorials take you step by step through a creation process. For more information about HTML tables, visit the HTML More About page (www.scsite.com/html/more.htm) and click HTML Table Tutorial.

NAME1	NAME2	NAME3	NAME4
TIME	TIME	TIME	TIME

FIGURE 3-8a

5K		10K	
NAME1	NAME2	NAME3	NAME4
TIME	TIME	TIME	TIME

FIGURE 3-8b

5K			10K	
	NAME1	NAME2	NAME3	NAME4
MAY 5	TIME	TIME	TIME	TIME
MAY 12	TIME	TIME	TIME	TIME
MAY 19	TIME	TIME	TIME	TIME
MAY 26	TIME	TIME	TIME	TIME

FIGURE 3-8c

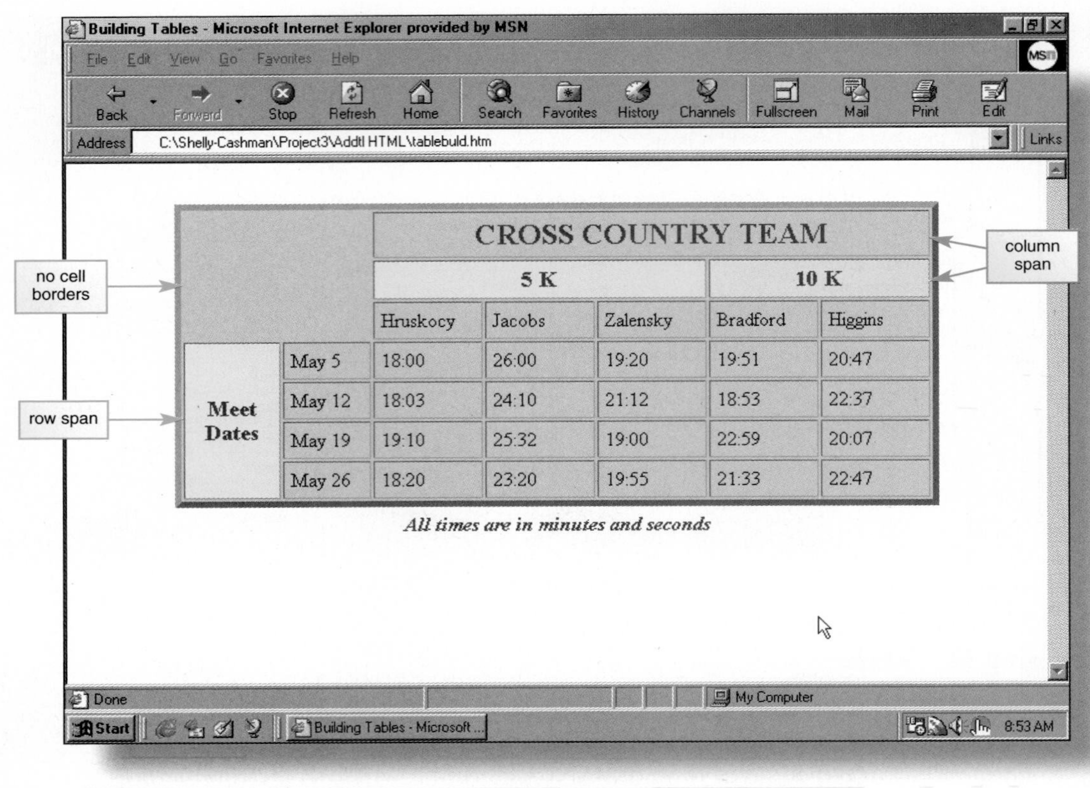

FIGURE 3-9

Coding the Table

After the design of the table is complete, you are ready to start coding the table with HTML tags. Table 3-1 shows the four main tags used for table creation. Each of these tags has a number of attributes, which are discussed later in this project.

Table 3-1

TAG	FUNCTION
<TABLE> </TABLE>	• Indicates the beginning and end of the table • All other tags will be inserted within these tags
<TR> </TR>	• Indicates the beginning and end of a table row • Rows consist of heading or data cells
<TH> </TH>	• Indicates the beginning and end of a table heading cell • Heading cells default to bold text and center alignment
<TD> </TD>	• Indicates the beginning and end of a table data cell • Data cells default to normal text and left alignment

Figure 3-10a shows an example of these tags used in an HTML file with the resulting Web page shown in Figure 3-10b.

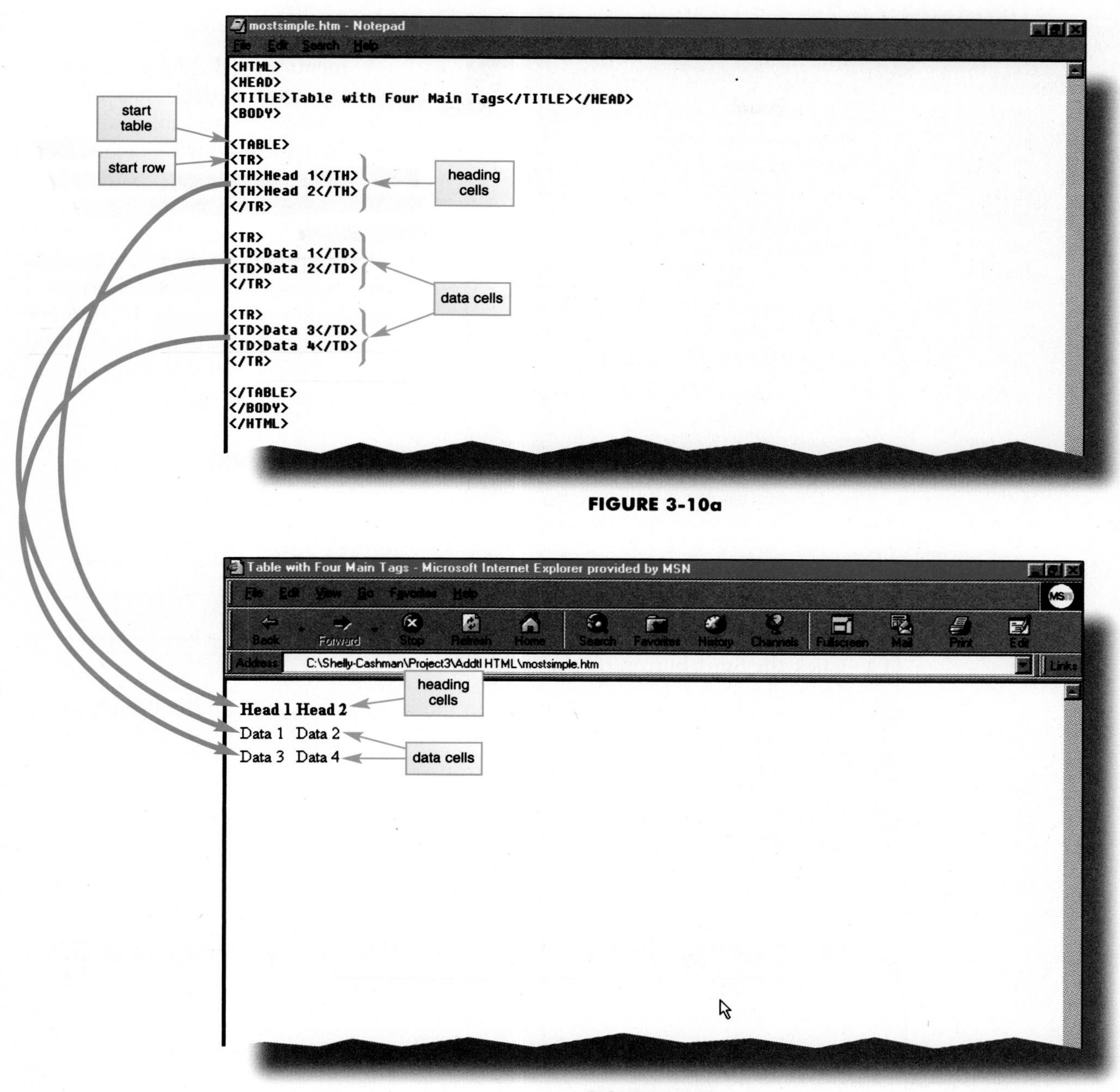

FIGURE 3-10a

FIGURE 3-10b

Looking at the table in Figure 3-10b, you see that it has three rows and two columns. The rows are indicated in the HTML file in Figure 3-10a with the beginning <TR> and ending </TR> tags. The columns are calculated automatically based on the number of cells within each row. You also can indicate the number of columns within the <TABLE> tag, as shown later in this project. In the table in Figure 3-10b, each row has two cells. In the first row, the cells are headings, indicated by the beginning <TH> and ending </TH> tags. In the second and third rows, the cells contain data, indicated by the beginning <TD> and ending </TD> tags. The first row is different from the other two rows. The text in the first row is bold and centered. The text in the data cells is left-aligned and normal. That is because of the use of the <TH> (header) and <TD> (data) tags, respectively. The table in Figure 3-10b is borderless because no border was indicated in the <TABLE> tag.

Table 3-2

TAG	ATTRIBUTE	FUNCTION
<TABLE> </TABLE>	ALIGN	• Controls table alignment (LEFT, CENTER, RIGHT)
	BGCOLOR	• Sets background color for table
	BORDER	• Sets width of table border in number of pixels
	CELLSPACING	• Spacing between cells
	CELLPADDING	• Spacing within cells
	COLS	• Number of columns
	WIDTH	• Table width relative to window width
<TR> </TR>	ALIGN	• Horizontally aligns row (LEFT, CENTER, RIGHT, JUSTIFY)
	BGCOLOR	• Sets background color for row
	VALIGN	• Vertically aligns row (TOP, MIDDLE, BOTTOM)
<TH> </TH> and <TD> </TD>	ALIGN	• Horizontally aligns cell (LEFT, CENTER, RIGHT, JUSTIFY)
	BGCOLOR	• Sets background color for cell
	COLSPAN	• Sets number of columns spanned by a cell
	ROWSPAN	• Sets number of rows spanned by a cell
	VALIGN	• Vertically aligns cell (TOP, MIDDLE, BOTTOM)

Table Attributes

As mentioned, the four main table tags have different attributes. Table 3-2 lists these tags and the main attributes associated with each. The <TH> and <TD> tags are both tags used for cells and have the same attributes.

Tables provide a useful method to display text and images in an organized, professional manner. A number of HTML tags and attributes are used to create tables. You use many of these tags in this project.

Starting Notepad

You use Notepad as the text editor for the HTML files. Perform the following steps to start Notepad.

TO START NOTEPAD

1. Click the Start button on the taskbar.
2. Point to Programs on the Start menu, point to Accessories on the Programs submenu, and then click Notepad.
3. If necessary, click the Maximize button.
4. Click Edit on the menu bar and, if necessary, click WordWrap to turn WordWrap on.

The maximized Notepad window displays (Figure 3-11).

FIGURE 3-11

Entering Initial HTML Tags

Just as in Project 2, you will initially create a home page for the Theater Club. A home page is the main page of a Web site. Visitors usually view the home page first. You use links to move from the home page to the other Web pages in the site. The home page that you develop in this project has three links to other pages: the calendar.htm, members.htm, and anything.htm Web pages. The home page also provides an e-mail link. In this project, you create two Web pages: tchome.htm and calendar.htm. Then you will open the members.htm and anything.htm files on the HTML Data Disk and add table tags and attributes to improve their appearance.

As described in Projects 1 and 2, the initial set of HTML tags define the overall structure of a Web page. Perform the following steps to enter the initial HTML tags.

TO ENTER INITIAL HTML TAGS

1. Type `<HTML>` and then press the ENTER key.
2. Type `<HEAD>` and then press the ENTER key.
3. Type `<TITLE>Theater Club Home Page</TITLE>` and then press the ENTER key.
4. Type `</HEAD>` and then press the ENTER key.
5. Type `<BODY>` and then press the ENTER key twice.
6. Type `</BODY>` and then press the ENTER key.
7. Type `</HTML>` as the final tag.
8. Click the blank line (line 6).

The HTML code displays (Figure 3-12).

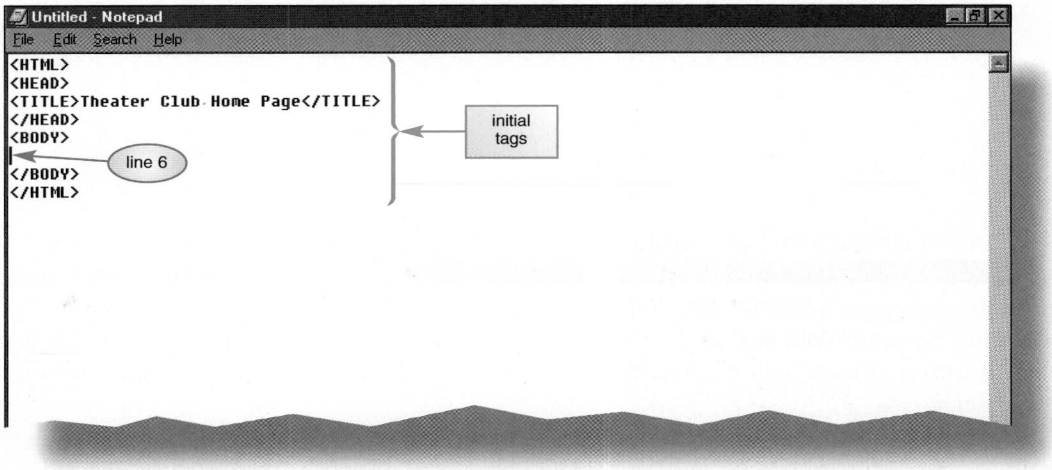

FIGURE 3-12

Adding a Borderless Header Table with Images

The next task is to create a borderless header table. This table contains the Theater Club logo and an attractive horizontal rule image (Figure 3-13 on the next page). You use a table for this header to give you more flexibility. With a table, you can insert a header that spans a percentage of the window's width. You also can vary the alignment of an image or text within a cell or row.

Table Borders

Table borders frame an image. You can insert a single image into a one-row, one-column table. Using a border gives the image a 3-D appearance, making the image appear to have a frame around it. A border of 1 pixel (BORDER=1) is too small to use as a frame, but BORDER=25 is too large.

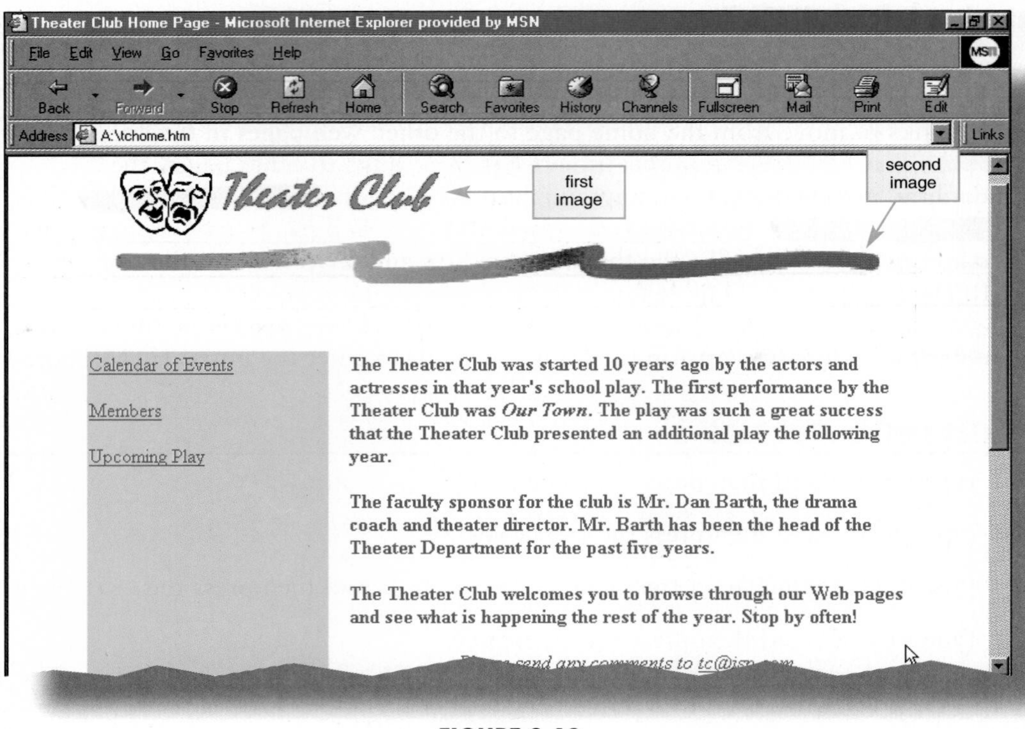

FIGURE 3-13

You employ four table attributes in the <TABLE> tag to create the header table in Figure 3-13.

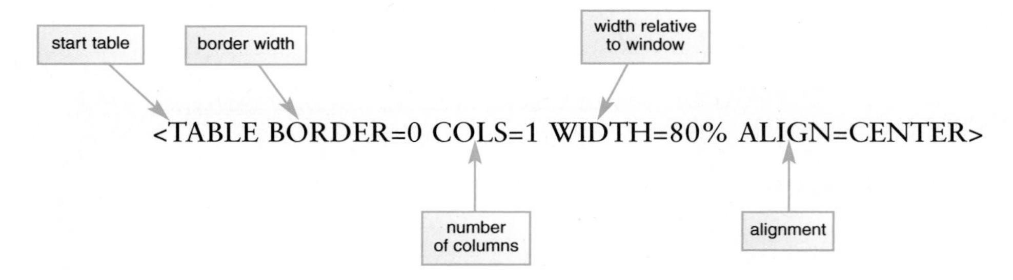

The ALIGN=CENTER attribute aligns the table in the center of the Web page. The BORDER=0 attribute creates a borderless table. The COLS=1 attribute indicates one column is in the table. The WIDTH=80% indicates that the table displays in 80% of the window's width. A benefit of using a percentage to set the table width is that it automatically will change the width of the table if the window is resized in the browser.

Figure 3-14a shows a sample of a table with the attributes as shown in the code above. Figure 3-14b shows the same table with ALIGN=RIGHT, BORDER=3, and WIDTH=100% attributes. Figure 3-14c shows the results of the <TABLE> tag with no attributes used. The default alignment is left. In Figure 3-14a the table is center-aligned, but it appears to be more left-aligned. Compare the table in Figure 3-14a to the left-aligned table in Figure 3-14c. You can tell that the table in Figure 3-14a is slightly to the right of the table in Figure 3-14c. Because you did not specify a column width, the table in Figure 3-14a displays in 80% of the window's width. In Figure 3-14b the width of the single column is more apparent because there is a border.

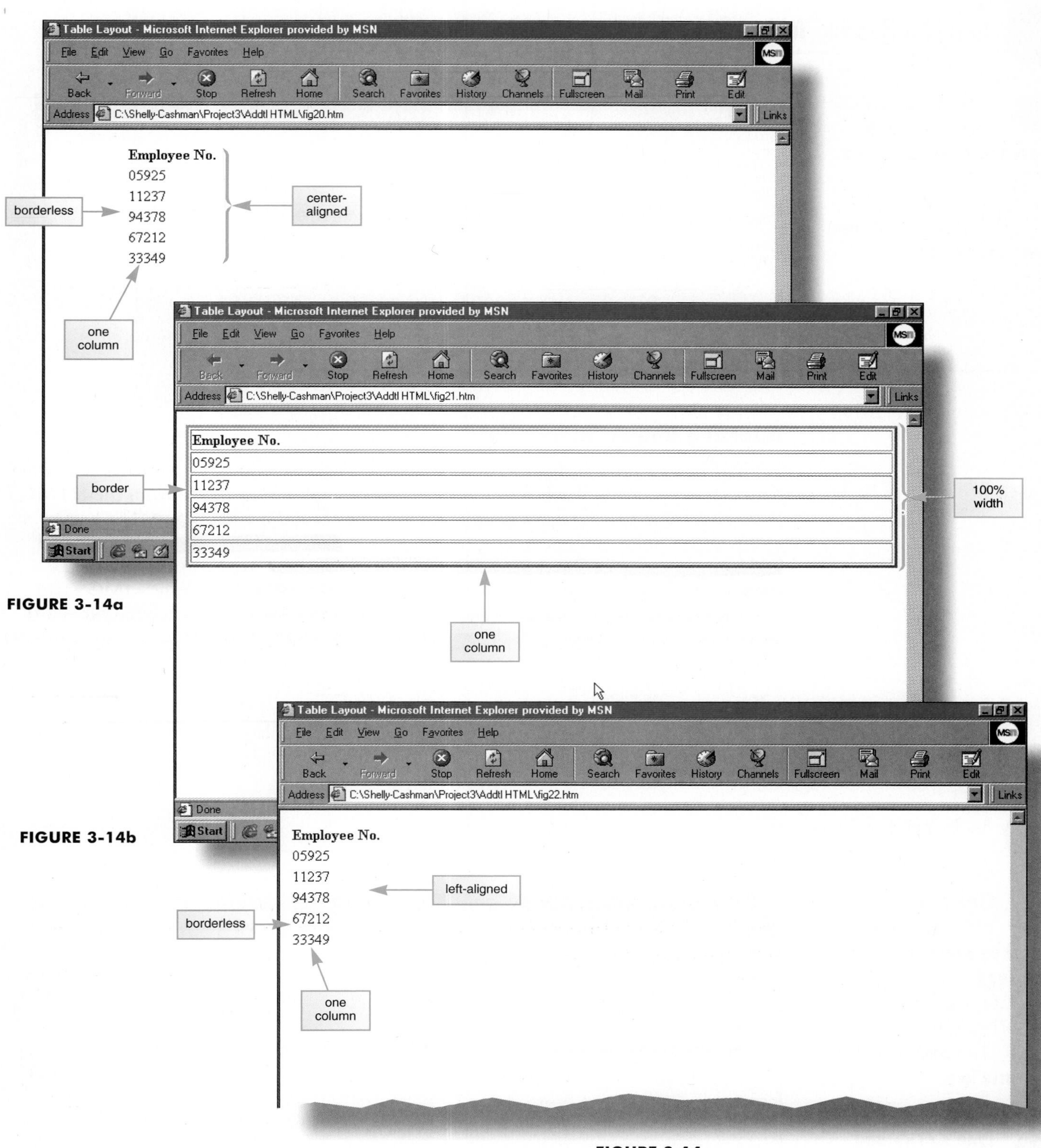

FIGURE 3-14a

FIGURE 3-14b

FIGURE 3-14c

Inserting the Heading Table

Using these attributes, perform the step on the next page to insert the heading table.

To Add a Heading Table

1 **With the insertion point on line 6, press the ENTER key. Type** `<TABLE BORDER=0 COLS=1 WIDTH=80% ALIGN=CENTER>` **and then press the ENTER key.**

The TABLE tag displays (Figure 3-15).

```
Untitled - Notepad
File Edit Search Help
<HTML>
<HEAD>
<TITLE>Theater Club Home Page</TITLE>
</HEAD>
<BODY>

<TABLE BORDER=0 COLS=1 WIDTH=80% ALIGN=CENTER>

</BODY>
</HTML>
```

line 6
TABLE tag

FIGURE 3-15

Inserting Images in a Table

The header table in Figure 3-13 on page HTM 3.16 contains two rows with one data cell in each row. Each of the two data cells contains an image from the HTML Data Disk. The first image is tclogo.jpg, and the second is hrcolor.jpg. The height and width of these images is indicated in pixels. You can determine the height and width of an image in the paint program used to create it. You also can adjust the height and width by using the HEIGHT and WIDTH attributes in the <IMG> tag.

To insert these two images, you need two sets of <TR> </TR> tags to begin and end the two rows. Between each set of <TR> </TR> tags, you insert one set of <TD> </TD> tags. The <TD> </TD> tags create the data cells within the rows. Recall that the <TR> tag means table row, and the <TD> tag means table data cell. You use data cell (<TD> </TD>) tags rather than header cell (<TH> </TH>) tags because these image files can be left-aligned in the cell. Perform the following steps to insert the logo image.

To Insert the Logo Image

1 **Click line 8, type** `<TR>` **as the tag and then press the ENTER key. Type** `<TD><IMG SRC="tclogo.jpg" HEIGHT=63 WIDTH=261></TD>` **and then press the ENTER key.**

2 **Type** `</TR>` **and then press the ENTER key twice.**

The HTML code displays (Figure 3-16).

```
Untitled - Notepad
File Edit Search Help
<HTML>
<HEAD>
<TITLE>Theater Club Home Page</TITLE>
</HEAD>
<BODY>

<TABLE BORDER=0 COLS=1 WIDTH=80% ALIGN=CENTER>
<TR>
<TD><IMG SRC="tclogo.jpg" HEIGHT=63 WIDTH=261></TD>
</TR>

</BODY>
</HTML>
```

line 8
data cell
end row

FIGURE 3-16

You created a borderless table and inserted an image, tclogo.jpg, from the HTML Data Disk. This image is shown in Figure 3-1a on page HTM 3.5. This completes the first row of the header table. Next, you insert the image for the second row of the table. Perform the following steps to insert the second image.

TO INSERT A HORIZONTAL RULE IMAGE

1. If necessary, click line 12. Type `<TR>` and then press the ENTER key. Type `<TD><IMG SRC="hrcolor.jpg" HEIGHT=35 WIDTH=607></TD>` and then press the ENTER key. Type `</TR>` and then press the ENTER key.
2. Type `</TABLE>` and then press the ENTER key twice.

The </TABLE> tag ends the first table. The HTML code displays (Figure 3-17).

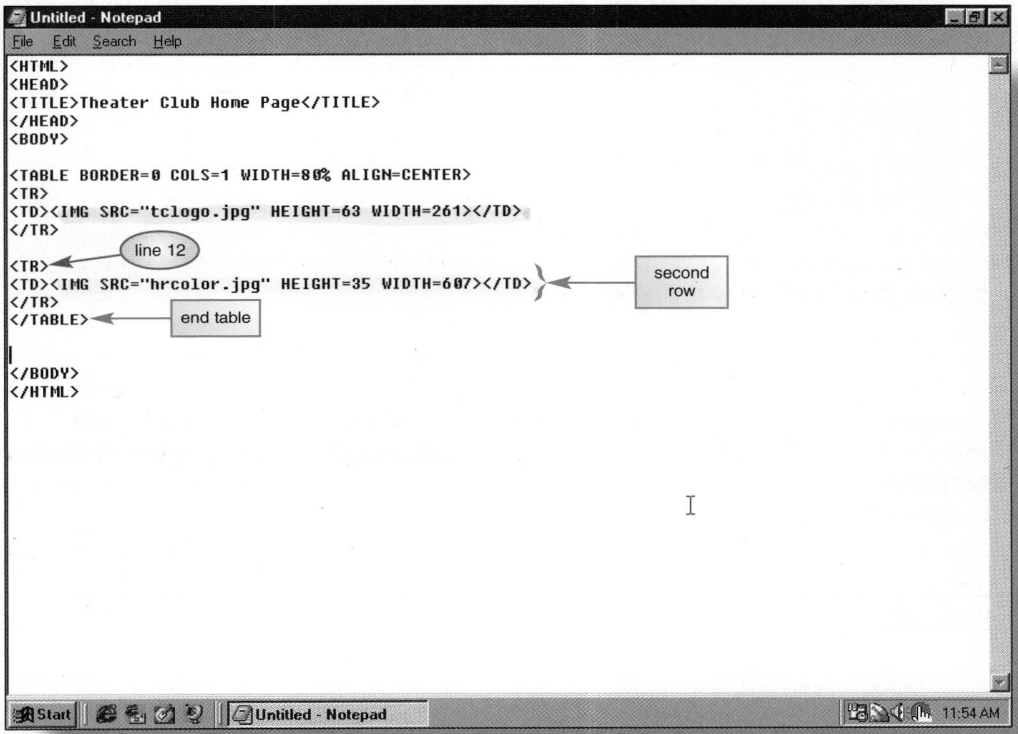

```
<HTML>
<HEAD>
<TITLE>Theater Club Home Page</TITLE>
</HEAD>
<BODY>

<TABLE BORDER=0 COLS=1 WIDTH=80% ALIGN=CENTER>
<TR>
<TD><IMG SRC="tclogo.jpg" HEIGHT=63 WIDTH=261></TD>
</TR>

<TR>
<TD><IMG SRC="hrcolor.jpg" HEIGHT=35 WIDTH=607></TD>
</TR>
</TABLE>

</BODY>
</HTML>
```

line 12 · second row · end table

FIGURE 3-17

The first borderless table on the Theater Club Home Page is complete. This table includes two images (Figure 3-13 on page HTM 3.16). You also use this same table to create the header on the other three Web pages.

Creating a List of Links with Text

The Web site that you are creating in this project consists of four Web pages. You need to move easily from any page to the other three pages. Providing links at the top of the page prevents the visitor from having to search the page for navigation links. You start with the home page. In the next section, you create a one row, two-column (or cell), borderless table (Figure 3-18a on the next page). In the left column of the table, you insert text describing the Theater Club. In the right column of the table, you insert text describing the Theater Club.

> **More About**
>
> **Navigation**
>
> Studies have been conducted to assess the best location on a Web page to place navigation bars and lists. The research results are varied, with indications that navigation options on the top, side, and bottom of a Web page show slight differences in visitor usability. The most important aspect of Web page navigation is to make the options easy enough to locate so visitors do not have to search for them.

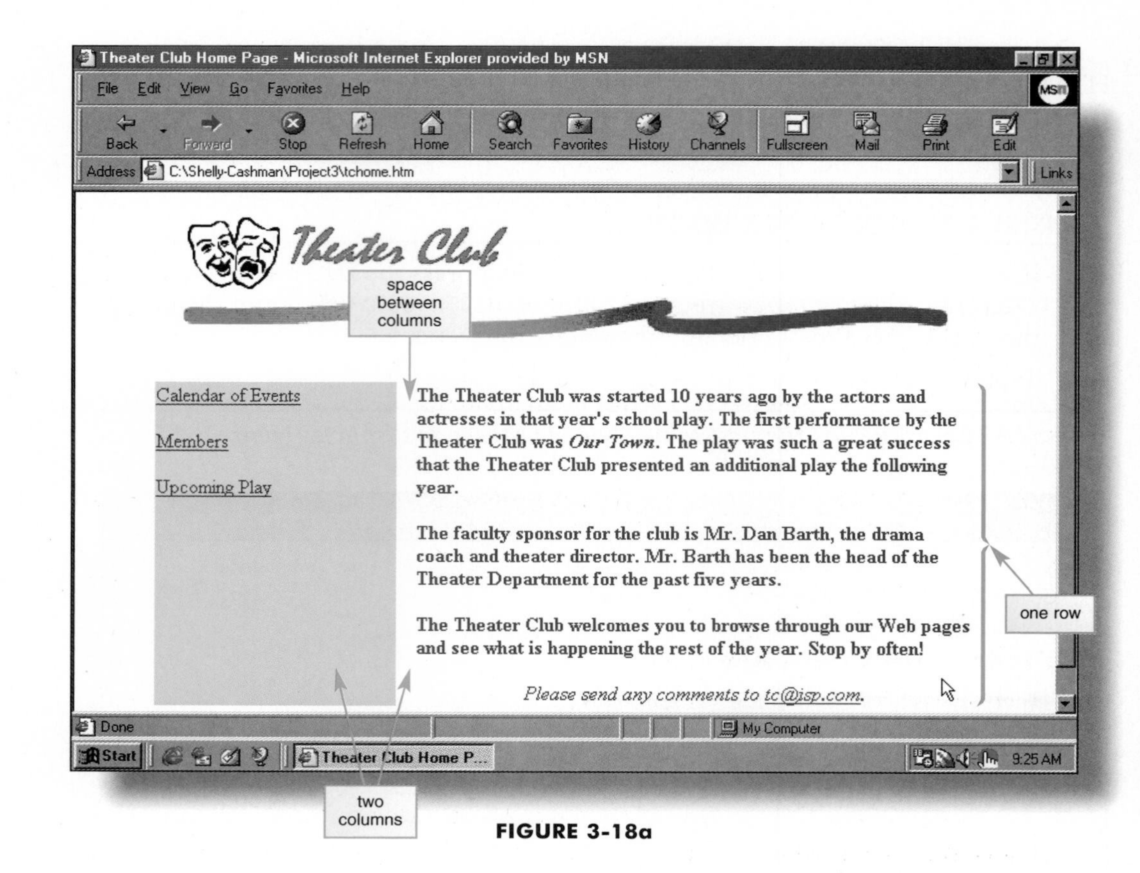

FIGURE 3-18a

Use the CELLSPACING attribute in the <TABLE> tag to insert some space between the left and right columns in the table. **Cellspacing** sets the amount of space between cells. Figure 3-18a shows the home page with cellspacing; Figure 3-18b shows the same page without cellspacing. If you have no cellspacing, the two columns are too close together. With cellspacing, you add some space in between the cells (or columns), which gives the Web page additional white space and a polished look.

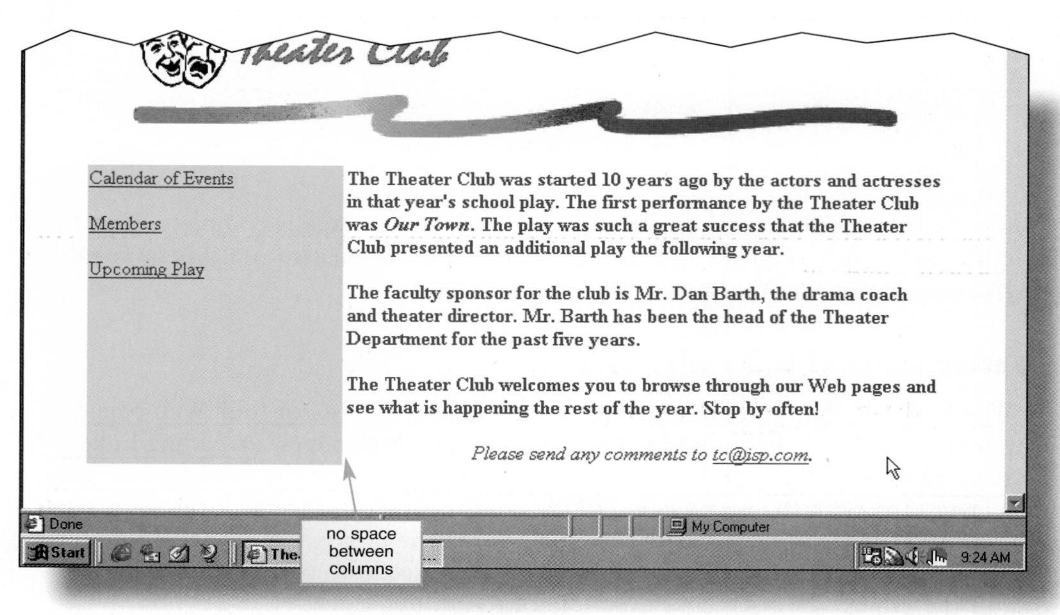

FIGURE 3-18b

You employ four table attributes in the <TABLE> tag for the text and link list table.

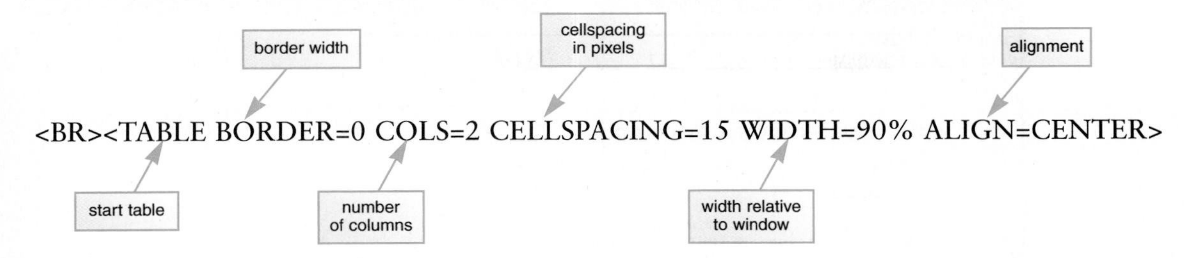

As in the first table, you use the WIDTH attribute to set the width of the entire table to a percentage of the window's width. You set this table at 90% so it is slightly larger than the heading table, which was set at 80%. The two columns that you are creating are data, not heading, cells. The default vertical alignment for data cells is centered. In this table, you want the text to align at the top of the cell. To change the alignment, insert the VALIGN=TOP attribute in the <TR> tag. This aligns the information at the top of the cell. Vertical alignment is the only attribute that you specify in this <TR> tag. The vertical alignment also can be set in each individual cell of a row by using the VALIGN attribute in the separate <TD> tags in the row. Because you want to set the vertical alignment for the entire row, you will insert the VALIGN attribute in the <TR> tag.

Use the BGCOLOR attribute within the <TD> tag for the first cell to set the background color for that cell only. You also can use the BGCOLOR attribute in the <TR> tag, but it would set the color for the entire row, instead of the specific cell.

Use the WIDTH attribute within the <TD> tag to indicate the width of each column relative to the entire table. These two columns of information do not have to be equal widths because the text entries vary in size. The column on the left-hand side of the table consists of short lines of text used as links. The right-hand column consists of paragraphs of text. The WIDTH attribute provides the flexibility to vary column widths in cases such as this. The WIDTH attribute allows you to set the width in number of pixels or as a percentage of the width of the table in the <TD> tag. Setting the width as a percentage is recommended. The finished table displays as shown in Figure 3-18a.

Perform the following steps to create the link list in the left-hand column of the borderless table.

Cellspacing

The CELLSPACING attribute adds pixels between cells. The purpose of cellspacing is to add additional space in the separation between the cells, whether or not a border exists. With a border, cellspacing increases the size of the border between the cells. Without a border, cellspacing increases the amount of white space between the cells.

TO CREATE A LIST OF LINKS IN A COLUMN

1. If necessary, click line 17 (see Figure 3-19 on the next page). Type `<BR><TABLE BORDER=0 COLS=2 CELLSPACING=15 WIDTH=90% ALIGN=CENTER>` and then press the ENTER key. Type `<TR VALIGN=TOP>` and then press the ENTER key. Type `<TD WIDTH="30%" BGCOLOR="#FFFF99">` and then press the ENTER key.
2. Type `<A HREF="calendar.htm">Calendar of Events</A>` and then press the ENTER key.
3. Type `<P><A HREF="members.htm">Members</A>` and then press the ENTER key. Type `<P><A HREF="anything.htm">Upcoming Play</A>` and then press the ENTER key. Type `</TD>` and then press the ENTER key twice.

These statements add three navigation links. The HTML code displays (Figure 3-19).

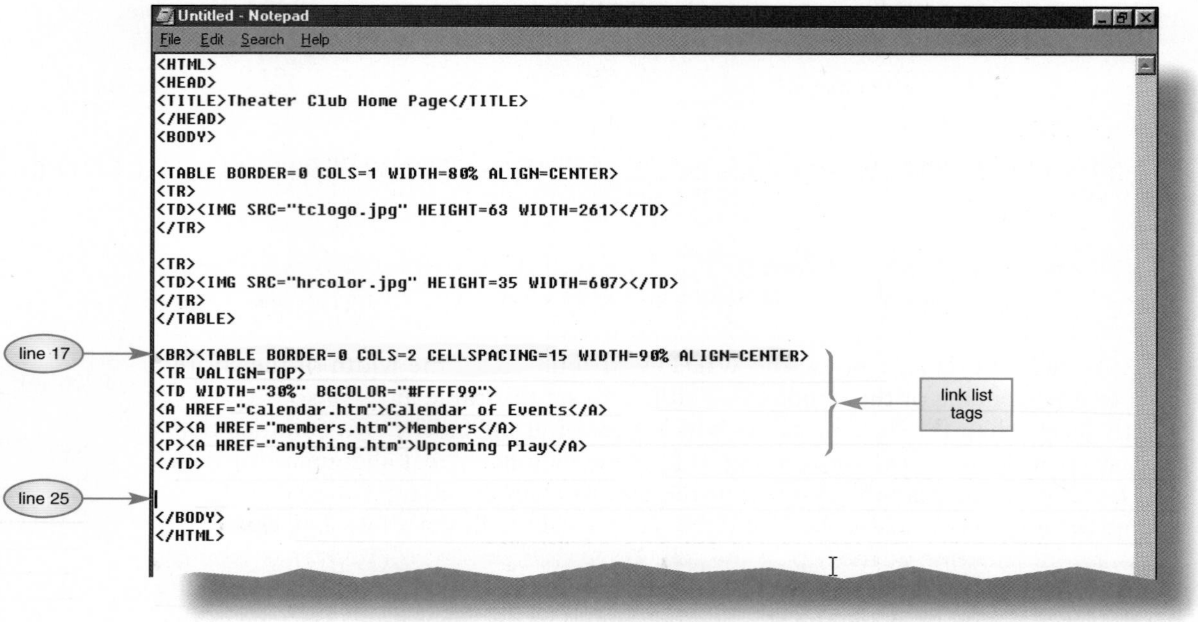

Untitled - Notepad

```
<HTML>
<HEAD>
<TITLE>Theater Club Home Page</TITLE>
</HEAD>
<BODY>

<TABLE BORDER=0 COLS=1 WIDTH=80% ALIGN=CENTER>
<TR>
<TD><IMG SRC="tclogo.jpg" HEIGHT=63 WIDTH=261></TD>
</TR>

<TR>
<TD><IMG SRC="hrcolor.jpg" HEIGHT=35 WIDTH=607></TD>
</TR>
</TABLE>

<BR><TABLE BORDER=0 COLS=2 CELLSPACING=15 WIDTH=90% ALIGN=CENTER>
<TR VALIGN=TOP>
<TD WIDTH="30%" BGCOLOR="#FFFF99">
<A HREF="calendar.htm">Calendar of Events</A>
<P><A HREF="members.htm">Members</A>
<P><A HREF="anything.htm">Upcoming Play</A>
</TD>

</BODY>
</HTML>
```

line 17

line 25

link list tags

FIGURE 3-19

In Step 1 on the previous page, you created a two-column, borderless table that is center-aligned and has cellspacing of 15. This table will fill 90% of the window's width. You also created one data cell with a different background color that fills 30% of the table's width. In Step 2, you inserted a link to the calendar.htm Web page that you create later in this project. The link is created with the <A HREF="calendar.htm"> tag. In Step 3, you created two new paragraphs of text that contain links to the members.htm and anything.htm Web pages. These two pages are stored on the HTML Data Disk and will be enhanced later in this project. The list of links in the left-hand column of this table allows the visitor to move from the home page to any other page quickly. Figure 3-20 shows what you have done so far.

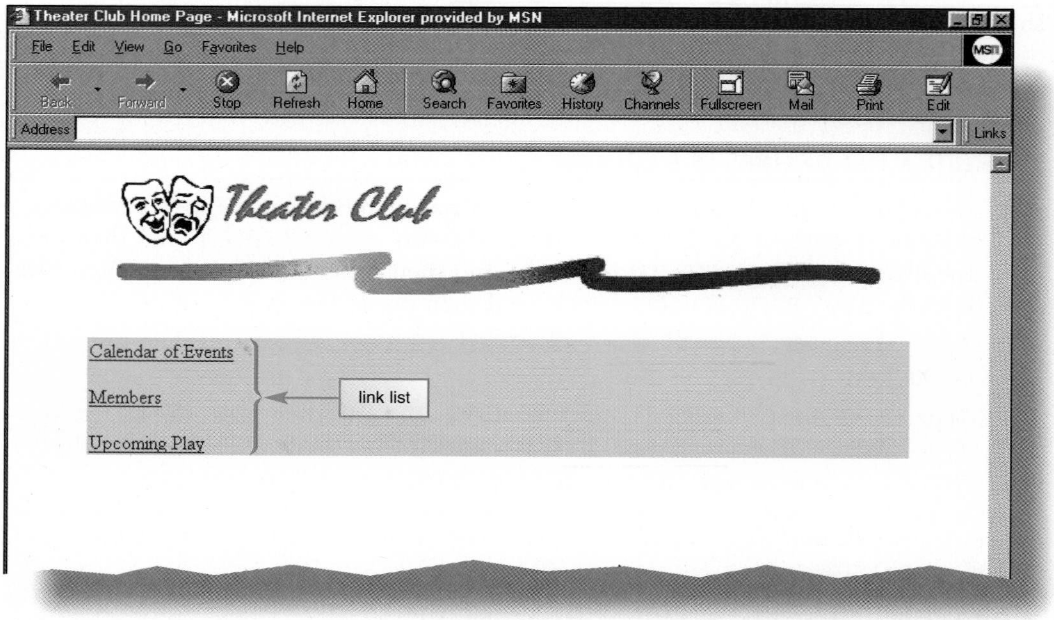

Theater Club Home Page - Microsoft Internet Explorer provided by MSN

Theater Club

Calendar of Events

Members

Upcoming Play

link list

FIGURE 3-20

Adding Text

You now add the text that displays in the right-hand column of the table in Figure 3-18a on page HTM 3.20. The tags are inserted within the same row as the <TD> </TD> tags inserted in the last sequence of steps on page HTM 3.21. Table 3-3 contains HTML tags and text. To create blank lines, as shown in lines 30, 34, and 37, press the ENTER key twice after typing lines 29, 33, and 36.

Table 3-3

LINE	HTML TAGS AND TEXT
25	`<TD WIDTH="70%"><B><FONT COLOR="#000099">The Theater Club was`
26	`started 10 years ago by the actors and actresses in that year's school`
27	`play. The first performance by the Theater Club was <I>Our Town</I>. The`
28	`play was such a great success that the Theater Club presented an additional`
29	`play the following year.`
30	
31	`<P>The faculty sponsor for the club is Mr. Dan`
32	`Barth, the drama coach and theater director. Mr. Barth has been the head`
33	`of the Theater Department for the past five years.</P>`
34	
35	`<P>The Theater Club welcomes you to browse through our Web pages and see`
36	`what is happening the rest of the year. Stop by often!</P></FONT></B>`
37	
38	`<P><CENTER><I>Please send any comments to`
39	`<A HREF="mailto:tc@isp.com>tc@isp.com">`
40	`</TD>`
41	`</TR>`
42	`</TABLE>`

Perform the following steps to add text to the HTML file.

TO ADD TEXT TO THE HTML FILE

1. If necessary, click line 25.
2. Enter the HTML code shown in Table 3-3.

The last three tags in Table 3-3 end the current cell, the current row, and the table. The HTML code displays (Figure 3-21 on the next page).

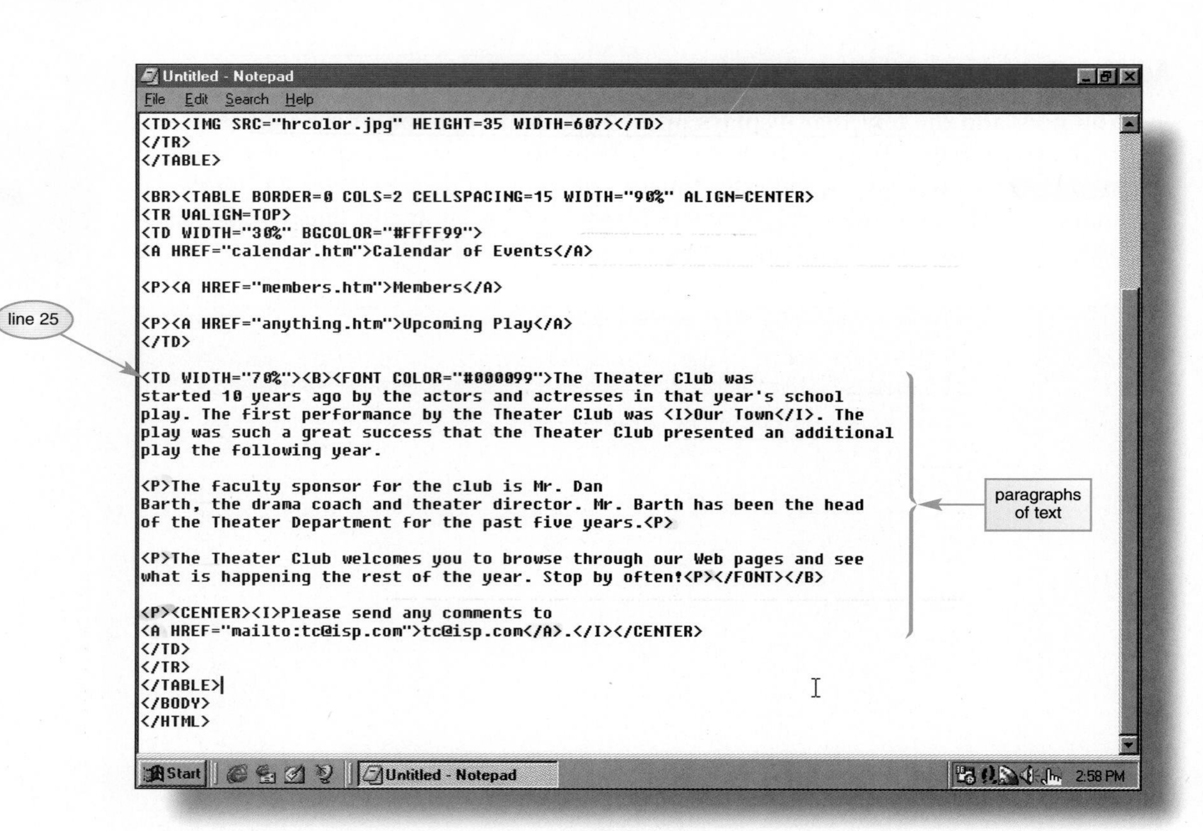


```
<TD><IMG SRC="hrcolor.jpg" HEIGHT=35 WIDTH=607></TD>
</TR>
</TABLE>

<BR><TABLE BORDER=0 COLS=2 CELLSPACING=15 WIDTH="90%" ALIGN=CENTER>
<TR VALIGN=TOP>
<TD WIDTH="30%" BGCOLOR="#FFFF99">
<A HREF="calendar.htm">Calendar of Events</A>

<P><A HREF="members.htm">Members</A>

<P><A HREF="anything.htm">Upcoming Play</A>
</TD>

<TD WIDTH="70%"><B><FONT COLOR="#000099">The Theater Club was
started 10 years ago by the actors and actresses in that year's school
play. The first performance by the Theater Club was <I>Our Town</I>. The
play was such a great success that the Theater Club presented an additional
play the following year.

<P>The faculty sponsor for the club is Mr. Dan
Barth, the drama coach and theater director. Mr. Barth has been the head
of the Theater Department for the past five years.<P>

<P>The Theater Club welcomes you to browse through our Web pages and see
what is happening the rest of the year. Stop by often!<P></FONT></B>

<P><CENTER><I>Please send any comments to
<A HREF="mailto:tc@isp.com">tc@isp.com</A>.</I></CENTER>
</TD>
</TR>
</TABLE>
</BODY>
</HTML>
```

FIGURE 3-21

The HTML code for the home page is complete. On line 25 in Figure 3-21, you inserted a new data cell and set it to 70% of the table's width. Next, you entered four paragraphs of text. In the fourth paragraph, you created a link to an e-mail address. You then ended the data cell, the row, and the table. The next step is to save and print the HTML file.

You have created two tables on this home page. The first is a two-row, one-column table containing two images. The second is a one-row, two-column table containing text. In the left-hand column, you altered the color of the background and created a list of links to the other pages in the Web site. The right-hand column contains text describing the Theater Club.

Perform the following steps to save and print the HTML file. It is most important that you save the HTML file on the HTML Data Disk because some of the images and Web pages referenced in this project are on the HTML Data Disk.

TO SAVE AND PRINT THE HTML FILE

1. Insert the HTML Data Disk in drive A. If you do not have a copy of the HTML Data Disk, see the inside back cover of this book or ask your instructor.
2. Click File on the menu bar and then click Save As.
3. Type `tchome.htm` in the File name text box. If necessary, click 3½ Floppy (A:) in the Save in list. Click the Save button in the Save As dialog box.

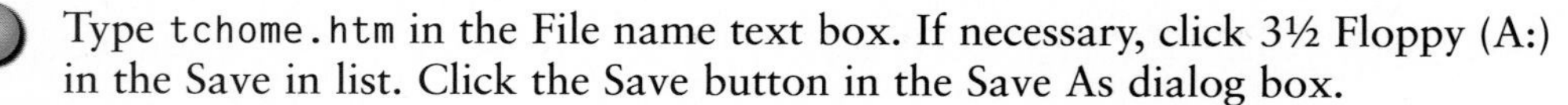

4. Click File on the menu bar and then click Print.

The HTML file prints (Figure 3-22).

```
tchome

<HTML>
<HEAD>
<TITLE>Theater Club Home Page</TITLE>
</HEAD>
<BODY>
<TABLE BORDER=0 COLS=1 WIDTH="80%" ALIGN=CENTER>
<TR>
<TD><IMG SRC="tclogo.jpg" HEIGHT=63 WIDTH=261></TD>
</TR>

<TR>
<TD><IMG SRC="hrcolor.jpg" HEIGHT=35 WIDTH=607></TD>
</TR>
</TABLE>

<BR><TABLE BORDER=0 COLS=2 CELLSPACING=15 WIDTH=90% ALIGN=CENTER>
<TR VALIGN=TOP>
<TD BGCOLOR="#FFFF99" WIDTH="30%">
<A HREF="calendar.htm">Calendar of Events</A>
<P><A HREF="members.htm">Members</A>
<P><A HREF="anything.htm">Upcoming Play</A>
</TD>

<TD WIDTH="70%"><B><FONT COLOR="#000099">The Theater Club was started
10 years ago by the actors and actresses in that year's school
play. The first performance by the Theater Club was <I>Our Town</I>. The
play was such a great success that the Theater Club presented an additional
play the following year.

<P>The faculty sponsor for the club is Mr. Dan
Barth, the drama coach and theater director. Mr. Barth has been the head
of the Theater Department for the past five years.</P>

<P>The Theater Club welcomes you to browse through our Web pages and see what is
happening
the rest of the year. Stop by often!</B>

<P><CENTER><I>Please send any comments to <A
HREF=mailto:tc@isp.com>tc@isp.com</A>.</I></CENTER>
</TD>
</TR>
</TABLE>

</BODY>
</HTML>

Page 1
```

FIGURE 3-22

As in previous projects, you now can view the Web page and print it using the browser. It is necessary to view what you have created and test the links that you inserted.

Viewing and Printing the Web Page Using the Browser

Just as in Projects 1 and 2, you should view the Web page file using the browser. When the home page displays, you can click the e-mail link to verify that it works correctly. You also can test the links to the third and fourth Web pages (members.htm and anything.htm) by clicking them. These two Web pages are stored on the HTML Data Disk. They display as they are developed thus far. Remember, you change the members.htm and anything.htm Web pages later in this project.

Perform the steps on the next page to view and print the Web page.

Steps To View the Web Page

1. **Start your browser.**

2. **Type** `a:\tchome.htm` **in the Address text box and then press the ENTER key.**

The tchome.htm Web page displays (Figure 3-23).

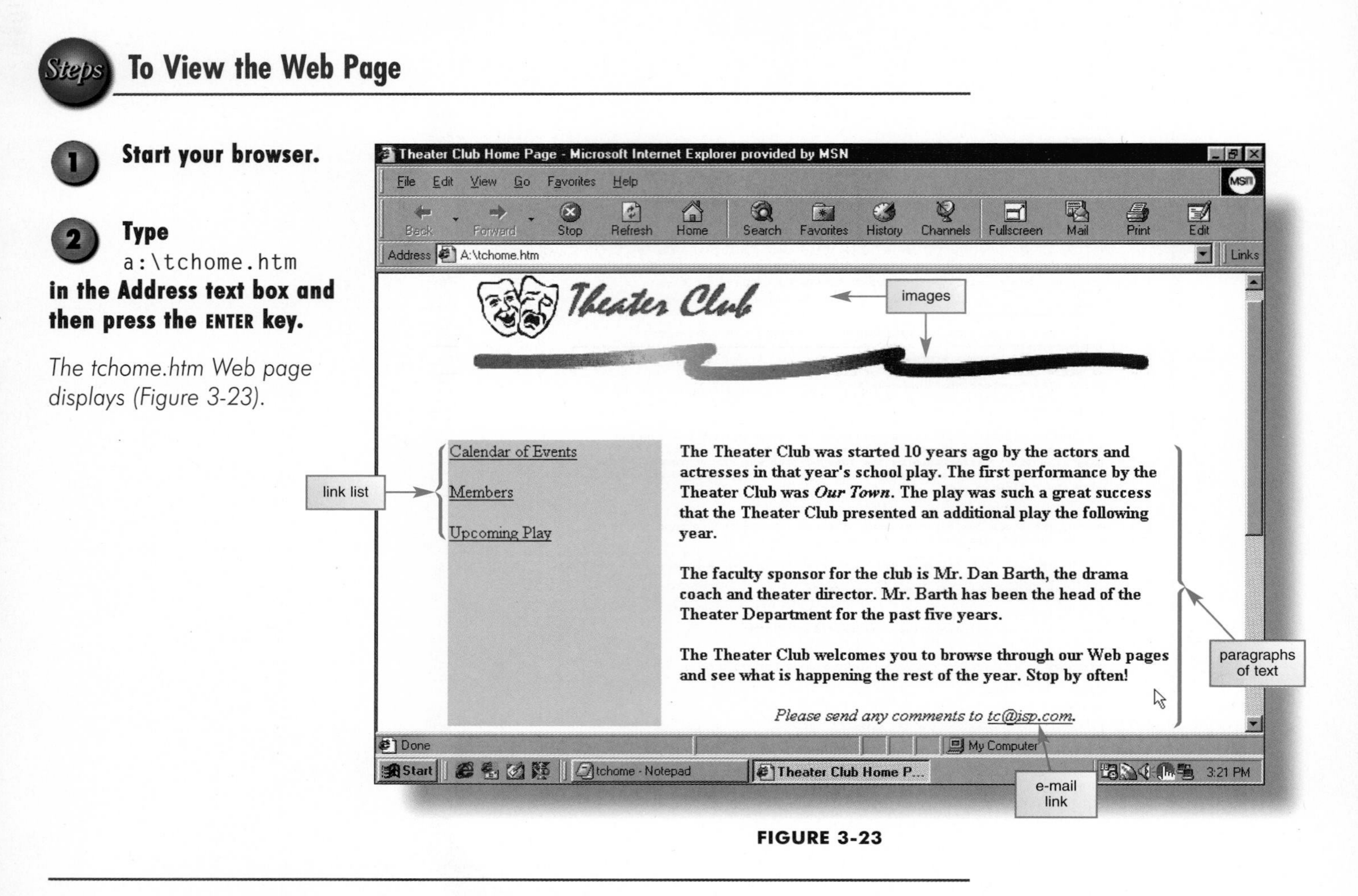

FIGURE 3-23

The next step is to use your browser to print the Web page.

TO PRINT THE WEB PAGE

1. Click the Print button on the Standard Buttons toolbar.

The home page prints (Figure 3-24).

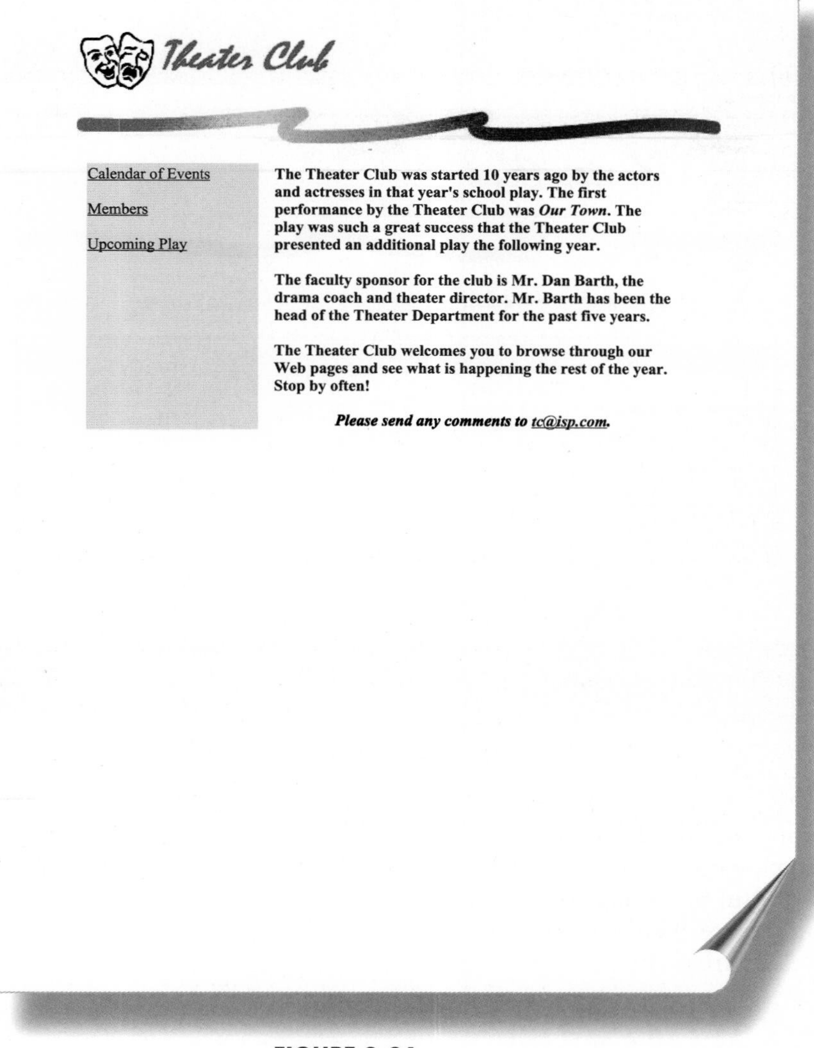

FIGURE 3-24

The home page is complete. The next step is to create a second Web page, calendar.htm. You can link to the calendar.htm Web page from the home page, using the link list created in the steps on page HTM 3.21.

Creating a Menu Bar on a Secondary Web Page

As mentioned earlier, it is important to give Web site visitors the option to move easily from one Web page to another without having to search for links. On the home page, you created a link list to address this need. On the three remaining Web pages, you create a menu bar, positioned toward the top of the Web page, just after the header table. Figure 3-25 on the next page illustrates a Web page with a menu bar. The menu bar lists the four Web pages — Home, Calendar, Members, and Upcoming Play — with a | symbol between the four links. A Web page should not contain a link to itself. For instance, it is unnecessary on the Calendar Web page to have a link set to Calendar.

Menu Bars

Many techniques are available to use when developing menu bars for navigation. Various Web sites contain some of the best ideas from current developers. For more information about menu bars, visit the HTML More About page (www.scsite.com/html/more.htm) and click Menu Bars.

Theater Club Calendar - Microsoft Internet Explorer provided by MSN

table copied from home page

Home | Calendar | Members | Upcoming Play

menu bar

DATE(S)	EVENT	TIME	PLACE
September 25	Theater Club Dance	7 - 12 PM	School Gym
November 20-23	*Anything Goes*	7 - 10 PM	Theater
December 10	Pizza Party	8 - 10 PM	Staffieri Pizza
February 20	Bake Sale	8 AM - 3 PM	Main Lobby
April 23-25	*The Crucible*	7 - 10 PM	Theater
May 15	Farewell Picnic	12 noon - ???	Hidden Lake

FIGURE 3-25

Before you insert the menu bar, initiate the second Web page. On the Theater Club home page, you created a borderless table with the Theater Club logo image and a colorful horizontal rule image. This table also displays at the top of the remaining three Web pages for consistency. Perform the following steps to copy the header table from the tchome.htm file to a new file.

TO COPY A TABLE TO A NEW FILE

1. Click the tchome - Notepad button on the taskbar (Figure 3-23 on page HTM 3.26).
2. Click immediately to the left of the < in the <HTML> tag on line 1. Drag through the first </TABLE> tag on line 15 to highlight lines 1 through 15.

3. Press CTRL+C to copy the selected lines to the Clipboard.
4. Click File on the menu bar and then click New.

5. Press CTRL+V to paste the contents from the Clipboard into a new file.

The HTML code for the new file displays (Figure 3-26).

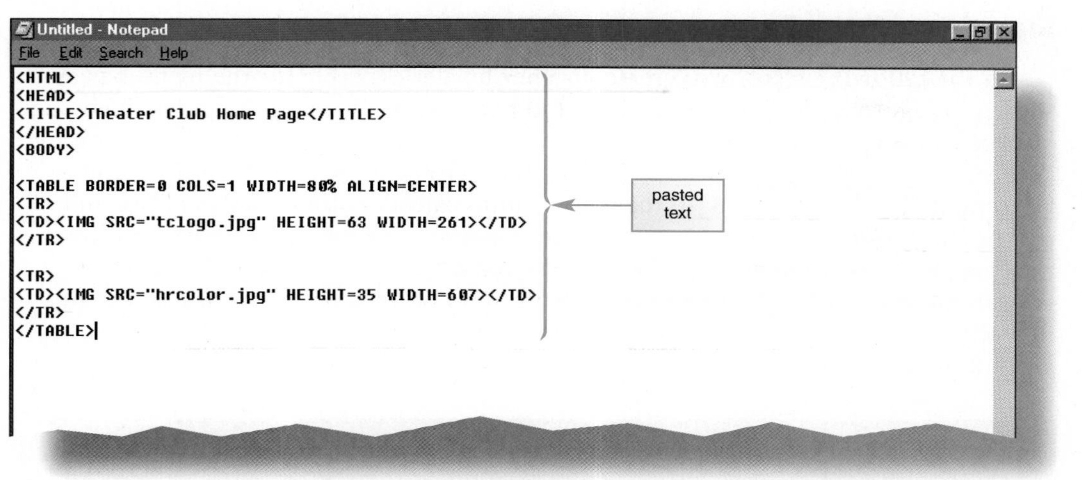

FIGURE 3-26

Changing the Title

The next step is to change the title of this page. The title of the tags and text that you copied is Theater Club Home Page. Change the title to Theater Club Calendar to reflect the current page. The title is important because it is the text that displays on the title bar of the Web browser. Perform the following steps to change the title of the new Web page to reflect the purpose of the Web page.

More About

Titles

A title is an important part of a Web page. Good titles are descriptive and indicate the content of the Web page. Visitors who bookmark a Web page should be able to return to the page based on the title. The title is not part of the text of the Web page itself. It may not contain anchors, paragraph marks, or highlighting. Because of limited room to display the title, the title must consist of not more than 64 characters. Titles that are too long will be truncated.

TO CHANGE THE TITLE

1. Highlight the words, Home Page, between the <TITLE> and </TITLE> tags on line 3. Type `Calendar` as the text.
2. Click immediately to the right of the </TABLE> tag on line 15. Press the ENTER key twice.
3. Type `</BODY>` and then press the ENTER key. Type `</HTML>` as the tag. Click line 16 and then press the ENTER key.

The HTML code displays (Figure 3-27).

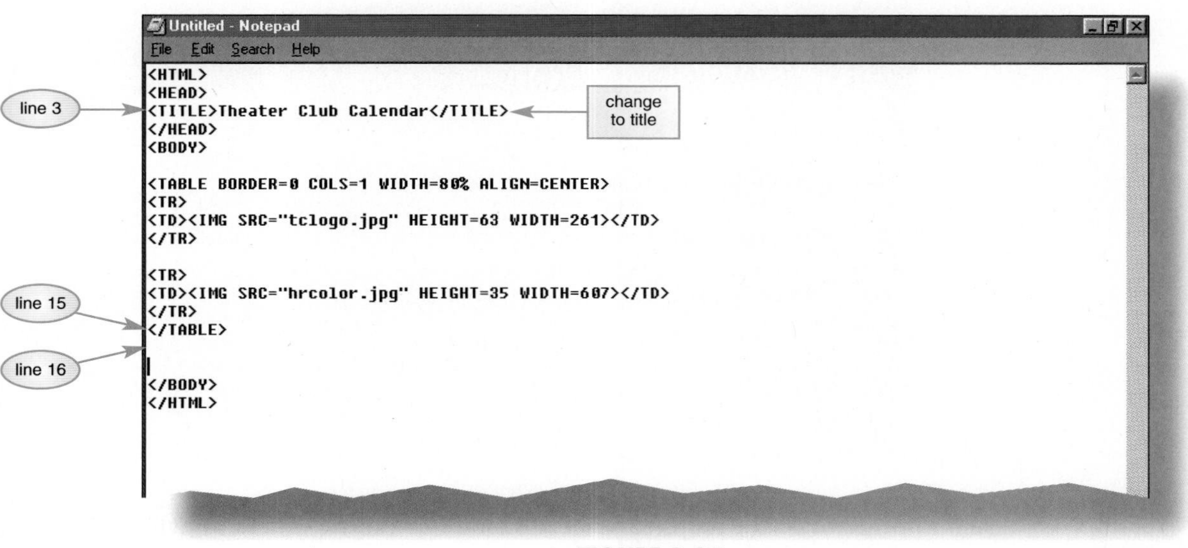

FIGURE 3-27

Inserting a Menu Bar

In the following steps, you create another borderless table for the menu bar as shown in Figure 3-28. The HTML tags and text are provided in Table 3-4. Web page visitors can use the menu bar to move easily from this Web page to any other on the Web site. The menu bar consists of four links — Home, Calendar, Members, and Upcoming Play — which link to the tchome.htm, calendar.htm, members.htm, and anything.htm Web pages, respectively. You insert a | symbol between the four links to separate them. You use a WIDTH of 1% for the | symbol because it does not require much space in the menu bar table. If you do not specify a width of 1% for this cell, all cells in the table will be spaced evenly. This makes the cell for the | symbol unnecessarily large.

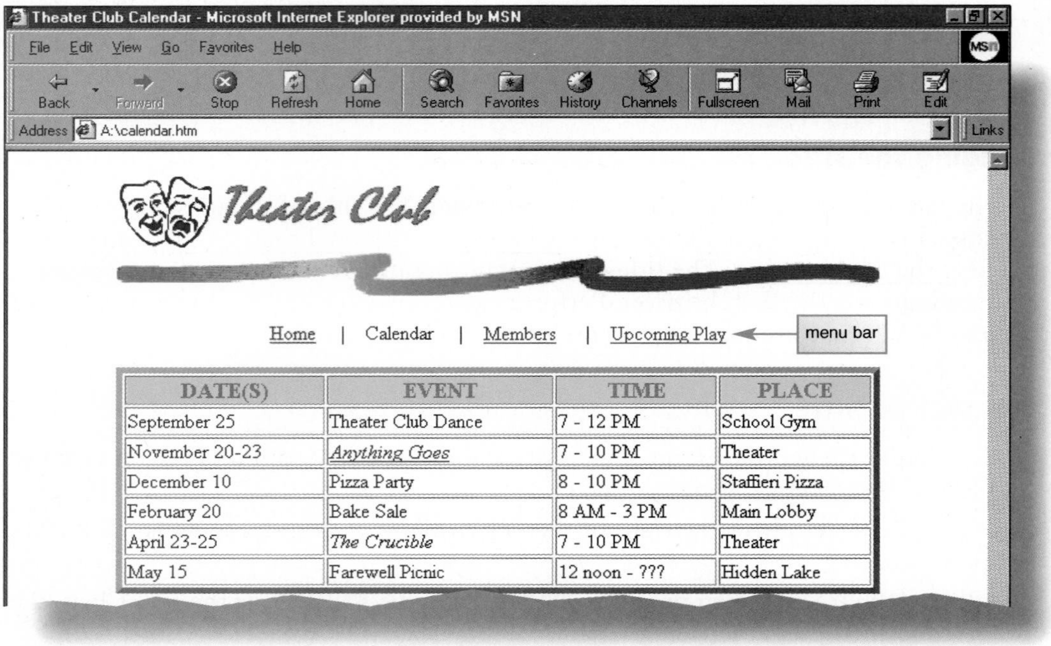

FIGURE 3-28

Table 3-4

LINE	HTML TAGS AND TEXT
17	` <TABLE ALIGN=CENTER BORDER=0 COLS=7 WIDTH="65%">`
18	`<TR ALIGN=CENTER>`
19	`<TD><A HREF="tchome.htm">Home</A></TD>`
20	`<TD WIDTH="1%">`|`</TD>`
21	`<TD>Calendar</TD>`
22	`<TD WIDTH="1%">`|`</TD>`
23	`<TD><A HREF="members.htm">Members</A></TD>`
24	`<TD WIDTH="1%">`|`</TD>`
25	`<TD><A HREF="anything.htm">Upcoming Play</A></TD>`
26	`</TR>`
27	`</TABLE>`

Perform the following steps to insert a menu bar on the Calendar Web page.

Steps To Insert a Menu Bar

1. **If necessary, click line 17.**
2. **Enter the HTML code shown in Table 3-4.**
3. **Press the ENTER key twice.**

The HTML code displays (Figure 3-29).

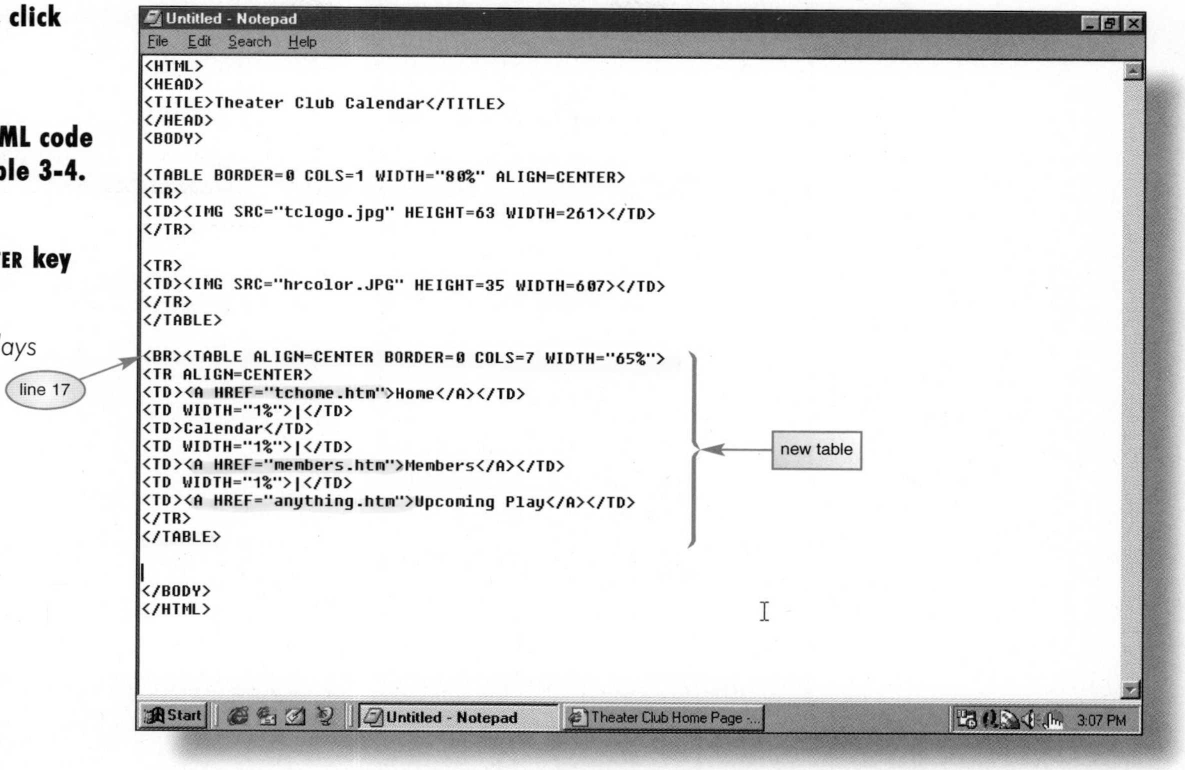

Untitled - Notepad

File Edit Search Help

```
<HTML>
<HEAD>
<TITLE>Theater Club Calendar</TITLE>
</HEAD>
<BODY>

<TABLE BORDER=0 COLS=1 WIDTH="80%" ALIGN=CENTER>
<TR>
<TD><IMG SRC="tclogo.jpg" HEIGHT=63 WIDTH=261></TD>
</TR>

<TR>
<TD><IMG SRC="hrcolor.JPG" HEIGHT=35 WIDTH=607></TD>
</TR>
</TABLE>

<BR><TABLE ALIGN=CENTER BORDER=0 COLS=7 WIDTH="65%">
<TR ALIGN=CENTER>
<TD><A HREF="tchome.htm">Home</A></TD>
<TD WIDTH="1%">|</TD>
<TD>Calendar</TD>
<TD WIDTH="1%">|</TD>
<TD><A HREF="members.htm">Members</A></TD>
<TD WIDTH="1%">|</TD>
<TD><A HREF="anything.htm">Upcoming Play</A></TD>
</TR>
</TABLE>


</BODY>
</HTML>
```

line 17

new table

Start | Untitled - Notepad | Theater Club Home Page -... | 3:07 PM

FIGURE 3-29

The HTML code for the menu bar is complete. In line 17 (Figure 3-29), you created a new, borderless table with seven columns that fills 65% of the window's width. You set the table's width smaller than the width of the heading table to improve the appearance. In line 19, you inserted one data cell with a link to the tchome.htm Web page. In line 21, you inserted the word, Calendar, but did not link it because that is the Web page currently under development. A link to the current calendar.htm Web page (Calendar) is pointless. You also created two other links to the members.htm (Members) and anything.htm (Upcoming Play) Web pages in lines 23 and 25. You separated all of these links with the | symbol as shown in lines 20, 22, and 24.

Creating a Table with Borders

Borderless tables are the best choices for some applications. In this project, a border around the header table would be distracting. In the second table on the home page, borders also would not enhance the look. In other instances, it is better to have borders on the tables. Borders can give a table a 3-dimensional appearance. For the Theater Club Calendar Web page, which has columns of information, a table with a border is more appropriate. Figure 3-30 on the next page shows the Calendar Web page with borders, and Figure 3-31 on the next page shows the same Web page without borders.

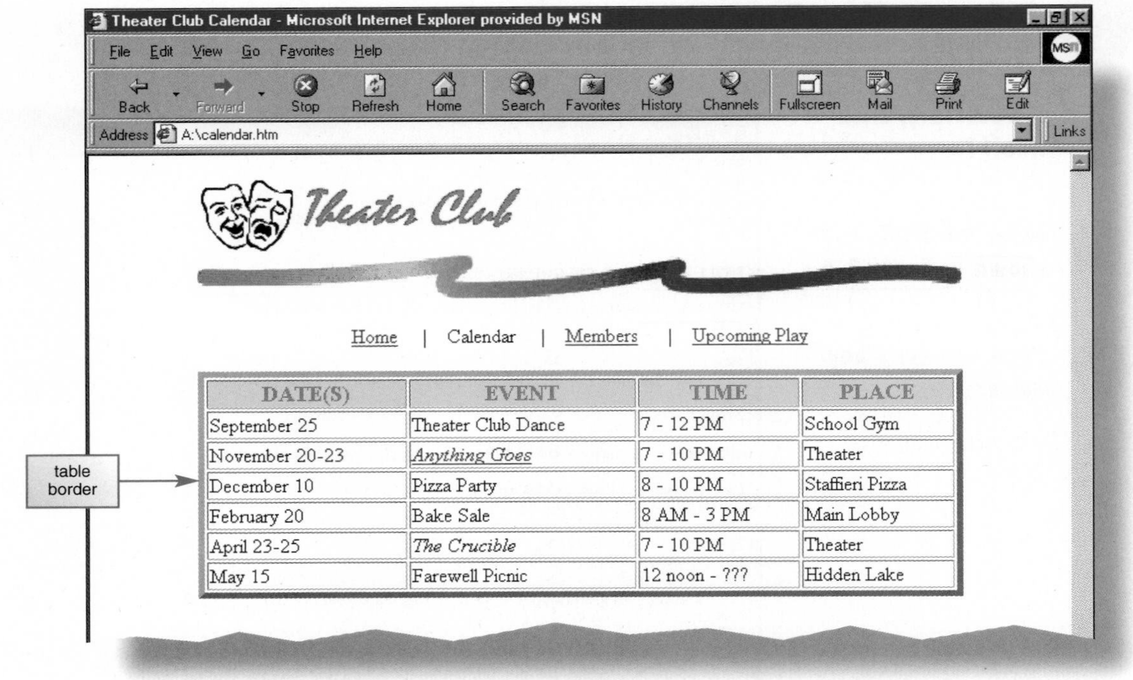

Theater Club Calendar - Microsoft Internet Explorer provided by MSN

Address A:\calendar.htm

Theater Club

Home | Calendar | Members | Upcoming Play

DATE(S)	EVENT	TIME	PLACE
September 25	Theater Club Dance	7 - 12 PM	School Gym
November 20-23	*Anything Goes*	7 - 10 PM	Theater
December 10	Pizza Party	8 - 10 PM	Staffieri Pizza
February 20	Bake Sale	8 AM - 3 PM	Main Lobby
April 23-25	*The Crucible*	7 - 10 PM	Theater
May 15	Farewell Picnic	12 noon - ???	Hidden Lake

table border

FIGURE 3-30

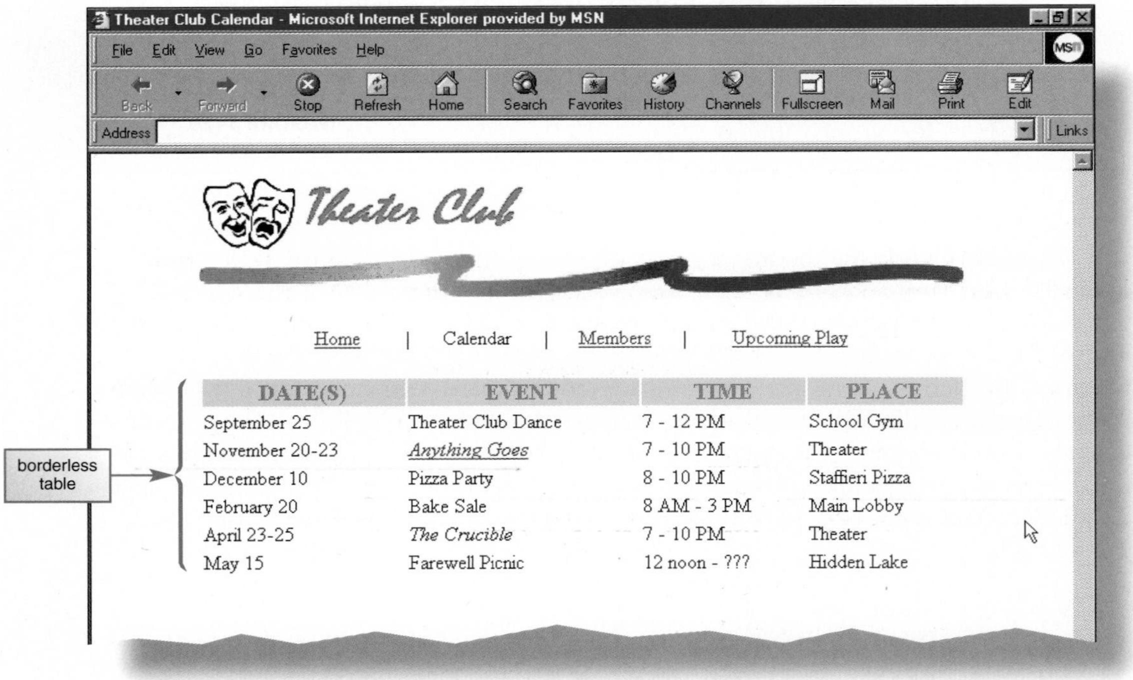

Theater Club Calendar - Microsoft Internet Explorer provided by MSN

Theater Club

Home | Calendar | Members | Upcoming Play

DATE(S)	EVENT	TIME	PLACE
September 25	Theater Club Dance	7 - 12 PM	School Gym
November 20-23	*Anything Goes*	7 - 10 PM	Theater
December 10	Pizza Party	8 - 10 PM	Staffieri Pizza
February 20	Bake Sale	8 AM - 3 PM	Main Lobby
April 23-25	*The Crucible*	7 - 10 PM	Theater
May 15	Farewell Picnic	12 noon - ???	Hidden Lake

borderless table

FIGURE 3-31

Inserting Text into Heading and Data Cells

In the next steps, you create a table with four columns and seven rows. One row is for headings; the other rows are for data. Heading cells differ from data cells in their appearance. Recall that text in a heading cell is bold and centered; text in a data cell is normal and left-aligned. Table 3-5 contains the HTML tags and text.

Table 3-5

LINE	HTML TAGS AND TEXT
30	 <TABLE BORDER=5 COLS=4 WIDTH="80%" ALIGN=CENTER>
31	<TR ALIGN=CENTER BGCOLOR="#FFFF99">
32	<TH><FONT COLOR="#FF0000" SIZE=+1>DATE(S)</FONT></TH>
33	<TH><FONT COLOR="#FF0000" SIZE=+1>EVENT</FONT></TH>
34	<TH><FONT COLOR="#FF0000" SIZE=+1>TIME</FONT></TH>
35	<TH><FONT COLOR="#FF0000" SIZE=+1>PLACE</FONT></TH>
36	</TR>
37	
38	<TR>
39	<TD>September 25</TD>
40	<TD>Theater Club Dance</TD>
41	<TD>7 - 12 PM</TD>
42	<TD>School Gym</TD>
43	</TR>
44	
45	<TR>
46	<TD>November 20-23</TD>
47	<TD><I><A HREF="anything.htm">Anything Goes</A></I></TD>
48	<TD>7 - 10 PM</TD>
49	<TD>Theater</TD>
50	</TR>

Peform the following steps to insert text into heading and data cells.

Steps To Insert Text into Heading and Data Cells

1. **If necessary, click line 30.**
2. **Enter the HTML code shown in Table 3-5.**
3. **Press the ENTER key twice.**

The HTML code displays (Figure 3-32).

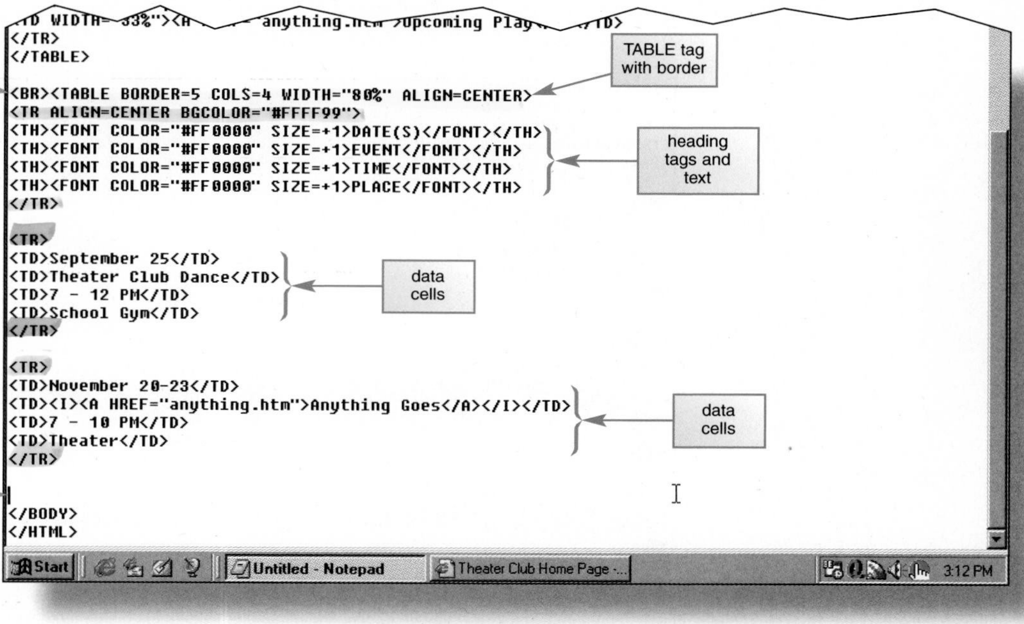

```
</TR>
</TABLE>

<BR><TABLE BORDER=5 COLS=4 WIDTH="80%" ALIGN=CENTER>
<TR ALIGN=CENTER BGCOLOR="#FFFF99">
<TH><FONT COLOR="#FF0000" SIZE=+1>DATE(S)</FONT></TH>
<TH><FONT COLOR="#FF0000" SIZE=+1>EVENT</FONT></TH>
<TH><FONT COLOR="#FF0000" SIZE=+1>TIME</FONT></TH>
<TH><FONT COLOR="#FF0000" SIZE=+1>PLACE</FONT></TH>
</TR>

<TR>
<TD>September 25</TD>
<TD>Theater Club Dance</TD>
<TD>7 - 12 PM</TD>
<TD>School Gym</TD>
</TR>

<TR>
<TD>November 20-23</TD>
<TD><I><A HREF="anything.htm">Anything Goes</A></I></TD>
<TD>7 - 10 PM</TD>
<TD>Theater</TD>
</TR>


</BODY>
</HTML>
```


FIGURE 3-32

Table 3-6

LINE	HTML TAGS AND TEXT
52	<TR>
53	<TD>December 10</TD>
54	<TD>Pizza Party</TD>
55	<TD>8 - 10 PM</TD>
56	<TD>Staffieri Pizza</TD>
57	</TR>
58	
59	<TR>
60	<TD>February 20</TD>
61	<TD>Bake Sale</TD>
62	<TD>8 AM - 3 PM</TD>
63	<TD>Main Lobby</TD>
64	</TR>
65	
66	<TR>
67	<TD>April 23-25</TD>
68	<TD><I>The Crucible</I></TD>
69	<TD>7 - 10 PM</TD>
70	<TD>Theater</TD>
71	</TR>
72	
73	<TR>
74	<TD>May 15</TD>
75	<TD>Farewell Picnic</TD>
76	<TD>12 noon - ???</TD>
77	<TD>Hidden Lake</TD>
78	</TR>
79	</TABLE>

On line 30, you created a four-column table with a border that is five pixels wide. The table will span 80% of the window's width. You inserted a row with a heading cell with a large size (+1) font on line 32. You added the remaining four headings on lines 33 through 35. On lines 38 through 50, you inserted text in the data cells located under the heading cells. You used the <TD> </TD> tags to create two rows with four data cells per row.

The code for the remaining data cell text is provided in Table 3-6. For each row of text, use the <TR> and </TR> tags. For each cell of text within that row, use the <TD> and </TD> tags. In this table, each row has four data cells, so four sets of <TD> </TD> tags are added per row. Perform the following steps to enter the remaining code.

TO ENTER REMAINING CODE

1. If necessary, click line 52 (see Figure 3-32 on the previous page).
2. Enter the HTML code shown in Table 3-6.

The HTML code displays (Figure 3-33).

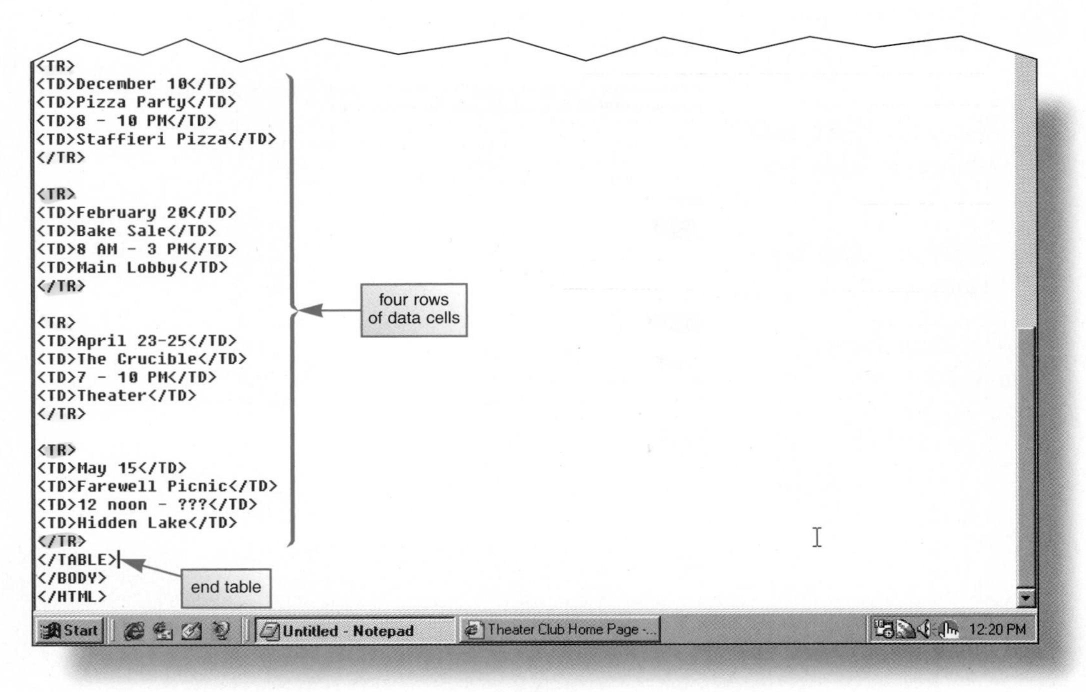

FIGURE 3-33

The HTML code for the table with borders is complete. On line 52, you started a new row of data cells using the <TR> (begin table row) tag. Additional rows were inserted on lines 59, 66, and 73. You ended each row with a </TR> (end table row) tag as shown on lines 57, 64, 71, and 78. You inserted all information into data cells between the <TR> and </TR> tags. In the following steps, you save the HTML file and print a hard copy.

TO SAVE AND PRINT THE HTML FILE

1. With the HTML Data Disk in drive A, click File on the menu bar and then click Save As.
2. Type `calendar.htm` in the File name text box. If necessary, click 3½ Floppy (A:) in the Save in list. Click the Save button in the Save As dialog box.
3. Click File on the menu bar and then click to Print.

The HTML file is saved on the HTML Data Disk in drive A and a hard copy prints (Figure 3-34).

```
calendar

<HTML>
<HEAD>
<TITLE>Theater Club Calendar</TITLE>
</HEAD>
<BODY>
<TABLE BORDER=0 COLS=1 WIDTH="80%" ALIGN=CENTER>
<TR>
<TD><IMG SRC="tclogo.jpg" HEIGHT=63 WIDTH=261></TD>
</TR>

<TR>
<TD><IMG SRC="hrcolor.jpg" HEIGHT=35 WIDTH=607></TD>
</TR>
</TABLE>

<BR><TABLE ALIGN=CENTER BORDER=0 COLS=7 WIDTH="65%">
<TR ALIGN=CENTER>
<TD><A H REF="tchome.htm">Home</A></TD>
<TD WIDTH="1%">|</TD>
<TD>Calendar</TD>
<TD WIDTH="1%">|</TD> <TD><A HREF="members.htm">Members</A></T
<TD WIDTH="1%">|</TD>
<TD><AHREF="anything.htm">Upcoming Play</A>
</TD>
</TR>
</TABLE>

<BR><TABLE BORDER=5 COLS=4 WIDTH="80%" ALIGN=CENTER>
<TR ALIGN=CENTER BGCOLOR="#FFFF99">
<TH><FONT COLOR="#FF0000" SIZE=+1>DATE(S)</FONT></TH>
<TH><FONT COLOR="#FF0000" SIZE=+1>EVENT<FONT></ TH >
<TH><FONT COLOR="#FF0000" SIZE=+1>TIME</FONT></ TH >
<TH><FONT COLOR="#FF0000" SIZE=+1>PLACE</FONT></ TH >
</TR>

<TR>
<TD>September 25</TD>
<TD>Theater Club Dance</TD>
<TD>7 - 12 PM</TD>
<TD>School Gym</TD>
</TR>

<TR>
<TD>November 20-23</TD>
<TD><I><A HREF="anything.htm">Anything Goes</A></I></TD>
 <TD>7 - 10 PM</TD>
<TD>Theater</TD>
</TR>

<TR>
<TD>December 10</TD>
<TD>Pizza Party</TD>
<TD>8 - 10 PM</TD>
<TD>Staffieri Pizza</TD>
</TR>

Page 1
```

```
calendar

</TR>
<TD>February 20</TD>
<TD>Bake Sale</TD>
<TD>8 AM - 3 PM</TD>
<TD>Main Lobby - 10 PM</TD>
</TR>

<TR>
<TD>April 23-25</TD>
<TD>The Crucible</TD>
<TD>7 - 10 PM</TD>
<TD>Theater</TD>
</TR>

<TR>
<TD>May 15</TD>
<TD>Farewell Picnic</TD>
<TD>12 noon - ???</TD>
<TD>Hidden Lake</TD>
</TR>
</TABLE>
</BODY>
</HTML>

Page 2
```

FIGURE 3-34

After saving and printing the HTML file, perform the following steps to view and print the Web page.

TO VIEW AND PRINT THE WEB PAGE USING THE BROWSER

1. Click the Theater Club Home Page button on the taskbar.
2. Click the Calendar of Events link on the Theater Club Home Page.
3. Click the Print button on the Standard Buttons toolbar.

The Calendar Web page displays (Figure 3-35).

Theater Club Calendar - Microsoft Internet Explorer provided by MSN

File Edit View Go Favorites Help

Back Forward Stop Refresh Home Search Favorites History Channels Fullscreen Mail Print Edit

Address A:\calendar.htm Links

Theater Club

images

Home | Calendar | Members | Upcoming Play

menu bar

DATE(S)	EVENT	TIME	PLACE
September 25	Theater Club Dance	7 - 12 PM	School Gym
November 20-23	*Anything Goes*	7 - 10 PM	Theater
December 10	Pizza Party	8 - 10 PM	Staffieri Pizza
February 20	Bake Sale	8 AM - 3 PM	Main Lobby
April 23-25	*The Crucible*	7 - 10 PM	Theater
May 15	Farewell Picnic	12 noon - ???	Hidden Lake

table with border

Done My Computer

Start calendar - Notepad Theater Club Calenda... 3:30 PM

FIGURE 3-35

In this section, you created three tables on the Calendar Web page: a two-row, one-column header table containing two images; a one-row, one-column table containing a menu bar with links to all other Web pages; and a seven-row, four-column table that contains the calendar information for the Theater Club.

To ensure the accuracy of the links, perform the following steps to test the links on the menu bar.

TO TEST THE LINKS

1. Click the Home link on the Calendar menu bar.

2. Click the Calendar of Events link on the home page to return.
3. Click the Upcoming Play link on the Calendar Web page.
4. Click the Members link on the Anything Goes Web page.

The Members Web page displays (Figure 3-36).

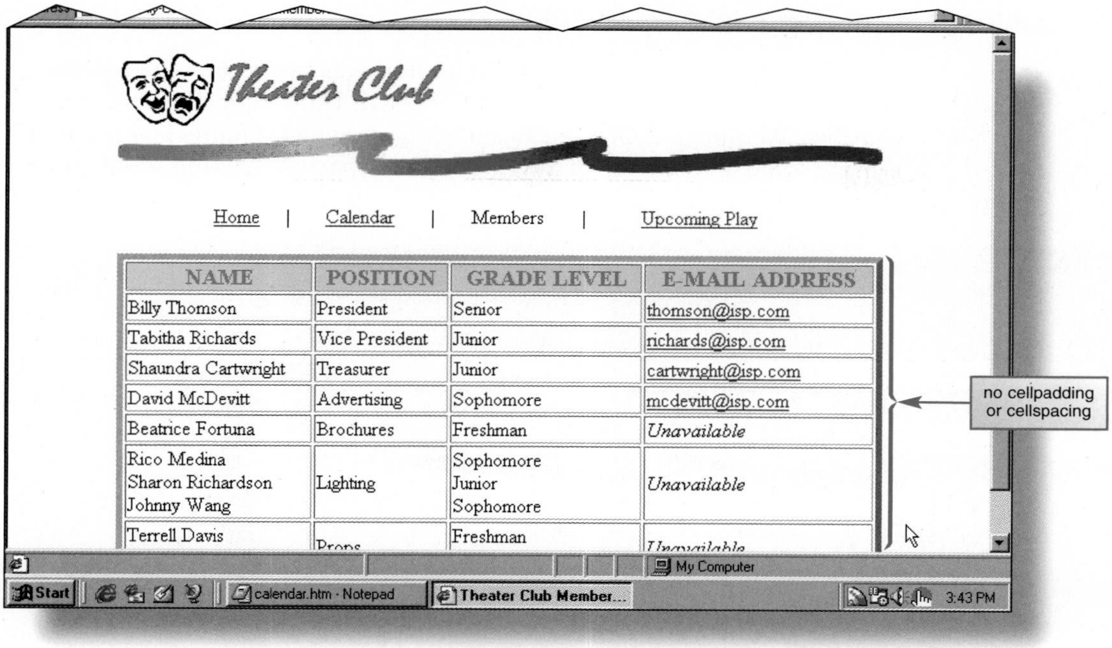

FIGURE 3-36

You have completed two of the Web pages in this project. The other two Web pages (members.htm and anything.htm) already are stored on the HTML Data Disk. They currently contain all the normal text on the Web pages. They also contain the heading table with two images and the menu bar. You enhance the appearance of the members.htm and anything.htm Web pages in the remainder of this project.

Spacing, Column Widths, and Captions

You did not add cellspacing or cellpadding to the table of information on the Calendar Web page. The size of each cell, therefore, was the minimum size needed for that text.

On the Web page, members.htm, you add cellspacing and cellpadding by adding the CELLSPACING and CELLPADDING attributes to the <TABLE> tag. **Cellspacing** is the number of pixels between cells. **Cellpadding** is the number of pixels within a cell. Figure 3-37 illustrates how cellspacing and cellpadding can affect the look of a table.

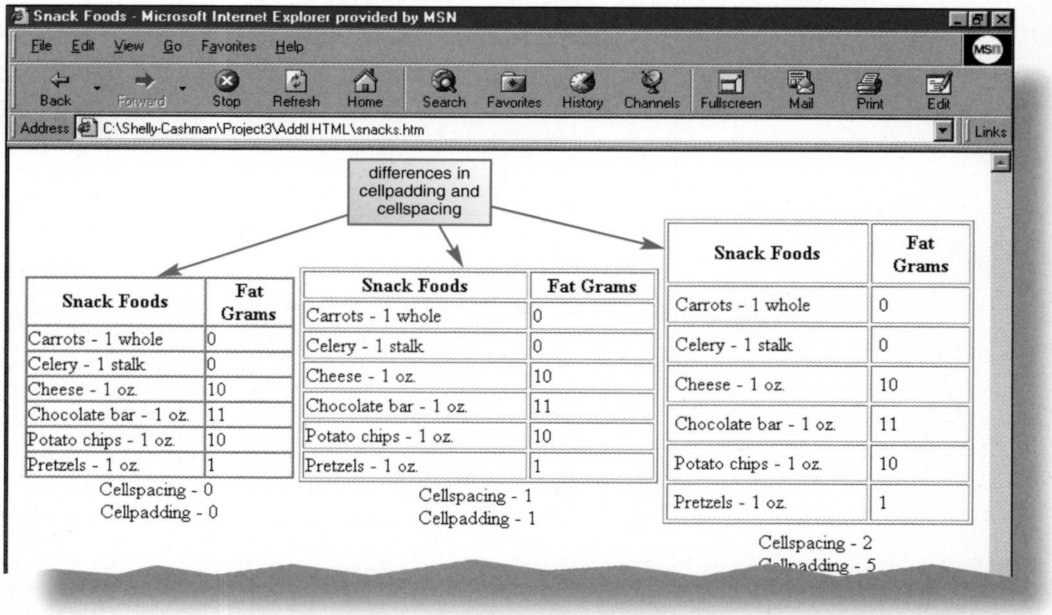

FIGURE 3-37

Adding Cellspacing and Cellpadding

The last link that you tested in the previous section was to the Members Web page. This is one of two Web pages stored on the HTML Data Disk. Figure 3-38a shows you what this Web page looks like as currently designed. Figure 3-38b shows what the Web page looks like after you have added the spacing, column width, and caption enhancements.

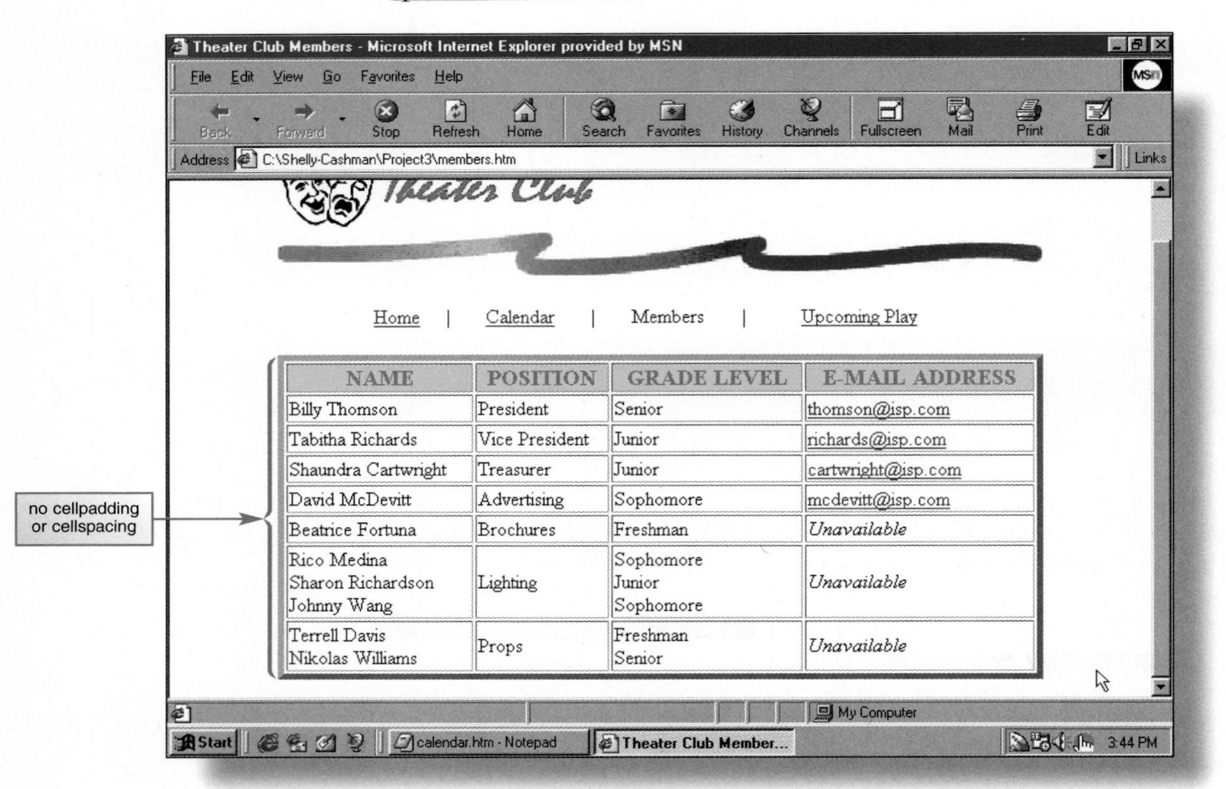

NAME	POSITION	GRADE LEVEL	E-MAIL ADDRESS
Billy Thomson	President	Senior	thomson@isp.com
Tabitha Richards	Vice President	Junior	richards@isp.com
Shaundra Cartwright	Treasurer	Junior	cartwright@isp.com
David McDevitt	Advertising	Sophomore	mcdevitt@isp.com
Beatrice Fortuna	Brochures	Freshman	*Unavailable*
Rico Medina Sharon Richardson Johnny Wang	Lighting	Sophomore Junior Sophomore	*Unavailable*
Terrell Davis Nikolas Williams	Props	Freshman Senior	*Unavailable*

FIGURE 3-38a

with cellpadding and cellspacing

NAME	POSITION	GRADE LEVEL	E-MAIL ADDRESS
Billy Thomson	President	Senior	thomson@isp.com
Tabitha Richards	Vice President	Junior	richards@isp.com
Shaundra Cartwright	Treasurer	Junior	cartwright@isp.com
David McDevitt	Advertising	Sophomore	mcdevitt@isp.com
Beatrice Fortuna	Brochures	Freshman	*Unavailable*
Rico Medina Sharon Richardson Johnny Wang	Lighting	Sophomore Junior Sophomore	*Unavailable*
Terrell Davis Nikolas Williams	Props	Freshman Senior	*Unavailable*

Positions will be held until May elections

FIGURE 3-38b

Follow the steps below to activate Notepad and open the member.htm file stored on the HTML Data Disk.

TO OPEN A FILE

1. Click the calendar – Notepad button on the taskbar (see Figure 3-35 on page HTM 3.36).
2. With the HTML Data Disk in drive A, click File on the menu bar and then click Open.
3. If necessary, click the Look in box arrow and then click 3½ Floppy (A:).
4. If necessary, click the Files of type box arrow and then click All files (*.*). Click members.htm.
5. Click the Open button in the Open dialog box.

The members.htm – Notepad window displays (Figure 3-39).

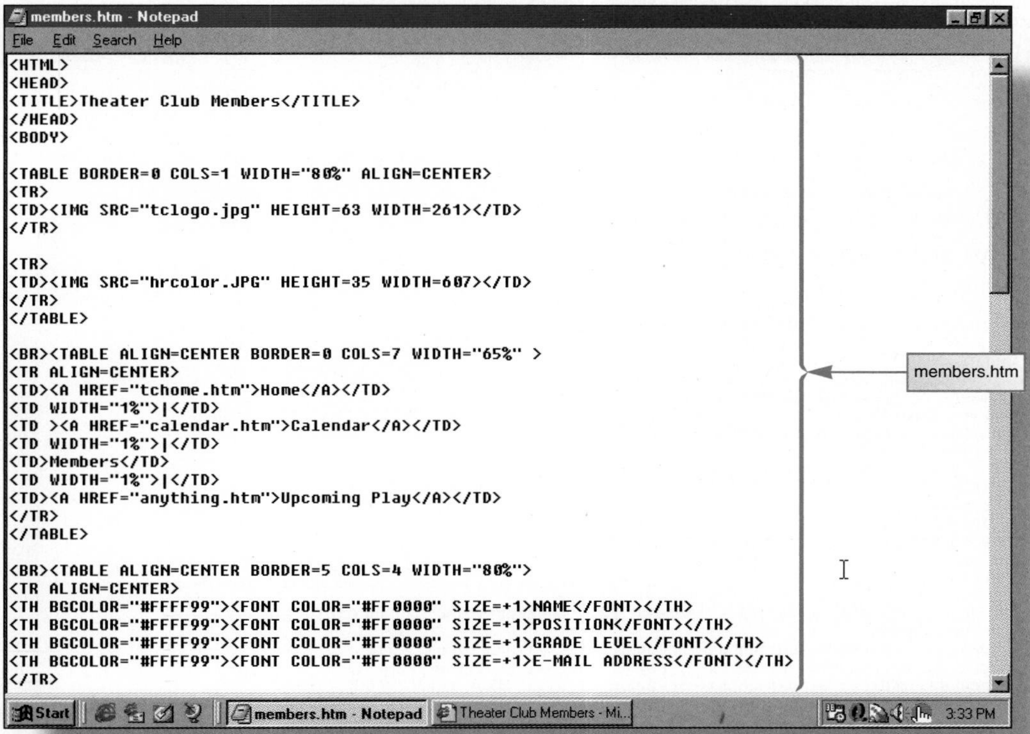

```
members.htm - Notepad
File  Edit  Search  Help
<HTML>
<HEAD>
<TITLE>Theater Club Members</TITLE>
</HEAD>
<BODY>

<TABLE BORDER=0 COLS=1 WIDTH="80%" ALIGN=CENTER>
<TR>
<TD><IMG SRC="tclogo.jpg" HEIGHT=63 WIDTH=261></TD>
</TR>

<TR>
<TD><IMG SRC="hrcolor.JPG" HEIGHT=35 WIDTH=607></TD>
</TR>
</TABLE>

<BR><TABLE ALIGN=CENTER BORDER=0 COLS=7 WIDTH="65%" >
<TR ALIGN=CENTER>
<TD><A HREF="tchome.htm">Home</A></TD>
<TD WIDTH="1%">|</TD>
<TD ><A HREF="calendar.htm">Calendar</A></TD>
<TD WIDTH="1%">|</TD>
<TD>Members</TD>
<TD WIDTH="1%">|</TD>
<TD><A HREF="anything.htm">Upcoming Play</A></TD>
</TR>
</TABLE>

<BR><TABLE ALIGN=CENTER BORDER=5 COLS=4 WIDTH="80%">
<TR ALIGN=CENTER>
<TH BGCOLOR="#FFFF99"><FONT COLOR="#FF0000" SIZE=+1>NAME</FONT></TH>
<TH BGCOLOR="#FFFF99"><FONT COLOR="#FF0000" SIZE=+1>POSITION</FONT></TH>
<TH BGCOLOR="#FFFF99"><FONT COLOR="#FF0000" SIZE=+1>GRADE LEVEL</FONT></TH>
<TH BGCOLOR="#FFFF99"><FONT COLOR="#FF0000" SIZE=+1>E-MAIL ADDRESS</FONT></TH>
</TR>

Start | members.htm - Notepad | Theater Club Members - Mi... | 3:33 PM
```

members.htm

FIGURE 3-39

With the member.htm file open, perform the steps on the next page to add cellspacing and cellpadding.

More About

Cellpadding

The CELLPADDING attribute adds pixels within a cell border. The purpose of cellpadding is to keep the content within each cell from looking too close to the content of another cell. Cellpadding will set a margin for the right, left, top, and bottom of the cell all at once with the specification of one tag.

To Add Cellspacing and Cellpadding

1 **Click immediately to the right of the 5 in BORDER=5 in line 29 and then press the SPACEBAR.**

The HTML code displays (Figure 3-40).

```
<TR>
<TD><IMG SRC="hrcolor.JPG" HEIGHT=35 WIDTH=607></TD>
</TR>
</TABLE>

<BR><TABLE ALIGN=CENTER BORDER=0 COLS=7 WIDTH="65%" >
<TR ALIGN=CENTER>
<TD><A HREF="tchome.htm">Home</A></TD>
<TD WIDTH="1%">|</TD>
<TD><A HREF="calendar.htm">Calendar</A></TD>
<TD WIDTH="1%">|</TD>
<TD>Members</TD>
<TD WIDTH="1%">|</TD>
<TD><A HREF="anything.htm">Upcoming Play
</TR>
</TABLE>

<BR><TABLE ALIGN=CENTER BORDER=5 COLS=4 WIDTH="80%">
<TR ALIGN=CENTER>
<TH BGCOLOR="#FFFF99"><FONT COLOR="#FF0000" SIZE=+1>NAME</FONT></TH>
<TH BGCOLOR="#FFFF99"><FONT COLOR="#FF0000" SIZE=+1>POSITION</FONT></TH>
<TH BGCOLOR="#FFFF99"><FONT COLOR="#FF0000" SIZE=+1>GRADE LEVEL</FONT></TH>
<TH BGCOLOR="#FFFF99"><FONT COLOR="#FF0000" SIZE=+1>E-MAIL ADDRESS</FONT></TH>
</TR>
```

insertion point

line 29

Start | members.htm - Notepad | Theater Club Members - Mi... | 12:34 PM

FIGURE 3-40

2 **Type** CELLSPACING =2 CELLPADDING=5 **as the attributes.**

The HTML code displays (Figure 3-41).

```
<TR>
<TD><IMG SRC="tclogo.jpg" HEIGHT=63 WIDTH=261></TD>
</TR>

<TR>
<TD><IMG SRC="hrcolor.JPG" HEIGHT=35 WIDTH=607></TD>
</TR>
</TABLE>

<BR><TABLE ALIGN=CENTER BORDER=0 COLS=7 WIDTH="65%" >
<TR ALIGN=CENTER>
<TD><A HREF="tchome.htm">Home</A></TD>
<TD WIDTH="1%">|</TD>
<TD><A HREF="calendar.htm">Calendar</A></TD>
<TD WIDTH="1%">|</TD>
<TD>Members</TD>
<TD WIDTH="1%">|</TD>
<TD><A HREF="anything.htm">Upcoming Play</A></TD>
</TR>
</TABLE>

<BR><TABLE ALIGN=CENTER BORDER=5 CELLSPACING=2 CELLPADDING=5 COLS=4 WIDTH="80%">
<TR ALIGN=CENTER>
<TH BGCOLOR="#FFFF99"><FONT COLOR="#FF0000" SIZE=+1>NAME</FONT></TH>
<TH BGCOLOR="#FFFF99"><FONT COLOR="#FF0000" SIZE=+1>POSITION</FONT></TH>
<TH BGCOLOR="#FFFF99"><FONT COLOR="#FF0000" SIZE=+1>GRADE LEVEL</FONT></TH>
<TH BGCOLOR="#FFFF99"><FONT COLOR="#FF0000" SIZE=+1>E-MAIL ADDRESS</FONT></TH>
</TR>
```

CELLSPACING attribute

CELLPADDING attribute

insertion point

Start | members.htm - Notepad | Theater Club Members - Mi... | 12:34 PM

FIGURE 3-41

By adding the CELLSPACING=2 and CELLPADDING=5 attributes, you added two pixels of spacing between cells and five pixels of spacing within the cells in the table. This is an adequate amount of spacing between and within cells.

Changing Column Widths

You can adjust the width of a column in any <TH> (heading cell) or <TD> (data cell) tag. The width can be indicated in number of pixels or as a percentage of the entire table. Using percentages is a better alternative because it accounts for different window sizes when viewed in the browser.

Next, perform the steps below to change the width of each cell in the first row, which then takes effect for the other rows. The first and fourth data cells (name and e-mail address) of each row contain more text than the second and third (position and grade level) data cells. You, therefore, set the width of the wider data cells (name and e-mail address) to 30%. You set the second and third data cells to 20% because they contain fewer characters.

Row and Column Spanning

Creating headings that span rows and columns defines tables more clearly. Many Web sites contain information about row and column spanning. For more information about row and column spanning, visit the HTML More About page (www.scsite.com/html/more.htm) and click Row and Column Spanning.

TO CHANGE THE COLUMN WIDTH

1. Click immediately to the right of the D in the first <TD> tag on line 38 and then press the SPACEBAR. Type `WIDTH="30%"` as the attribute.
2. Click immediately to the right of the D in the <TD> tag on line 39 and then press the SPACEBAR. Type `WIDTH="20%"` as the attribute.
3. Click immediately to the right of the D in the <TD> tag on line 40 and then press the SPACEBAR. Type `WIDTH="20%"` as the attribute.
4. Click immediately to the right of the D in <TD> tag on line 41 and then press the SPACEBAR. Type `WIDTH="30%"` as the attribute.

The HTML code displays (Figure 3-42).

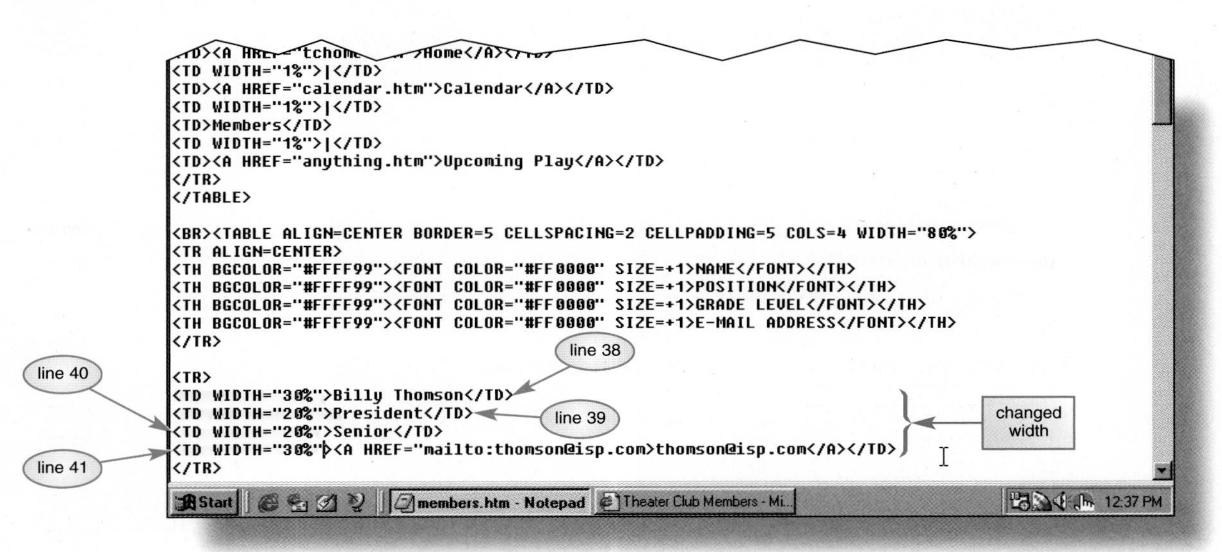

FIGURE 3-42

Adding a Caption

Captions sometimes help to clarify the purpose of a table. Some tables, such as the header and menu bar tables, do not need captions. Other tables, such as the Members table, benefit from a caption to clarify the contents of the table. A caption can be placed above or below the table using the ALIGN=ABOVE or ALIGN=BELOW attributes, respectively. Perform the steps on the next page to create a caption below the Members table.

Steps To Add a Caption

1. **With the HTML Data Disk in drive A, click immediately to the left of the </TABLE> tag on line 92 and type** `<CAPTION ALIGN=BOTTOM><I> Positions will be held until May elections</I> </CAPTION>` **as the tag.**

2. **Press the ENTER key.**

The HTML code displays (Figure 3-43).

```
members.htm - Notepad
File  Edit  Search  Help
<TD>Advertising</TD>
<TD>Sophomore</TD>
<TD><A HREF="mailto:mcdevitt@isp.com>mcdevitt@isp.com</A></TD>
</TR>

<TR>
<TD>Beatrice Fortuna</TD>
<TD>Brochures</TD>
<TD>Freshman</TD>
<TD><I>Unavailable</I></TD>
</TR>

<TR>
<TD>Rico Medina
<BR>Sharon Richardson
<BR>Johnny Wang</TD>
<TD>Lighting</TD>
<TD>Sophomore
<BR>Junior
<BR>Sophomore</TD>
<TD><I>Unavailable</I></TD>
</TR>

<TR>
<TD>Terrell Davis
<BR>Nikolas Williams</TD>
<TD>Props</TD>
<TD>Freshman
<BR>Senior</TD>
<TD><I>Unavailable</I></TD>
</TR>

<CAPTION ALIGN=BOTTOM><I>Positions will be held until May elections</I></CAPTION>
</TABLE>

Start | members.htm - Notepad | Theater Club Members - Mi... | 12:39 PM
```

line 92

FIGURE 3-43

The addition of the caption to the Members table completes the modifications to the members.htm file. The next step is to save and print the HTML file, and then view and print the Web page.

TO SAVE AND PRINT THE HTML FILE AND VIEW AND PRINT THE WEB PAGE

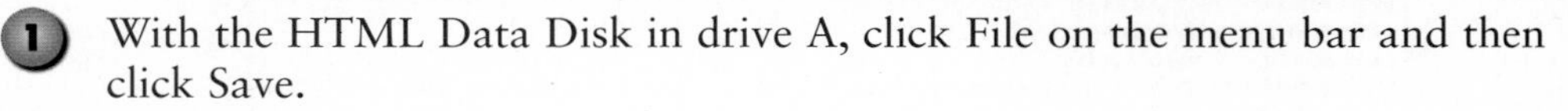

1. With the HTML Data Disk in drive A, click File on the menu bar and then click Save.

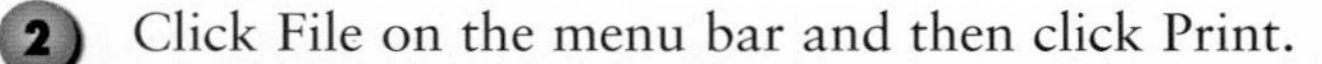

2. Click File on the menu bar and then click Print.

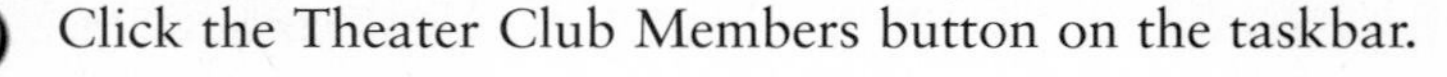

3. Click the Theater Club Members button on the taskbar.

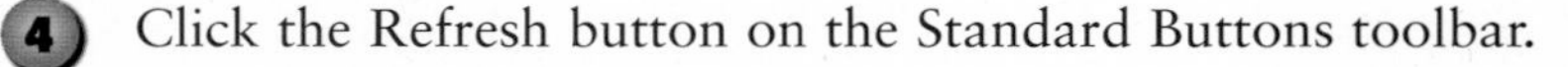

4. Click the Refresh button on the Standard Buttons toolbar.

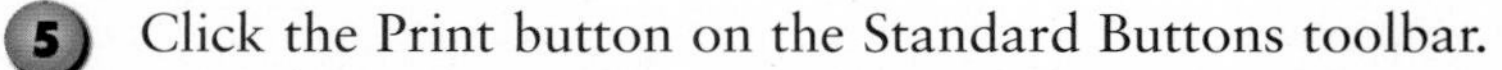

5. Click the Print button on the Standard Buttons toolbar.

Hard copy versions of the HTML file and Web page print. The Members Web page displays (Figure 3-44).

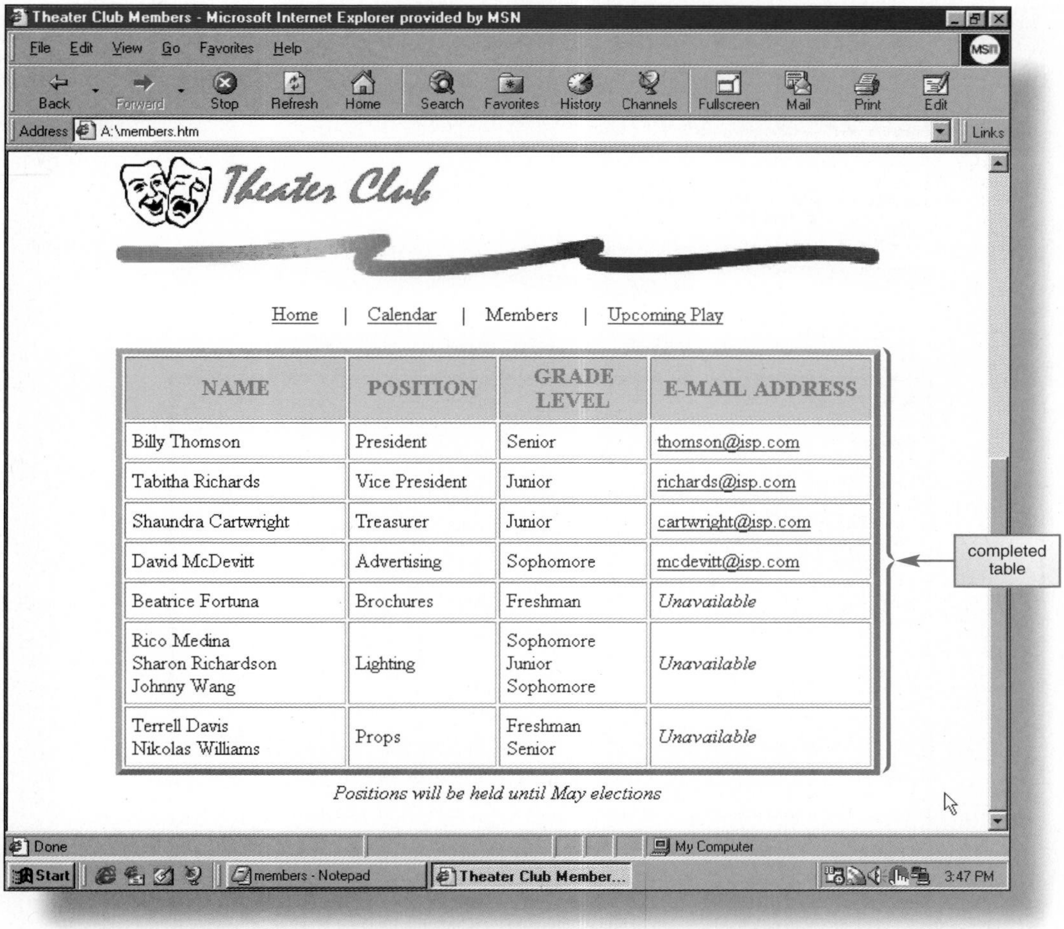
Theater Club Members - Microsoft Internet Explorer provided by MSN
File Edit View Go Favorites Help
Back Forward Stop Refresh Home Search Favorites History Channels Fullscreen Mail Print Edit
Address A:\members.htm
Links
Theater Club
Home | Calendar | Members | Upcoming Play
NAME
POSITION
GRADE LEVEL
E-MAIL ADDRESS
Billy Thomson
President
Senior
thomson@isp.com
Tabitha Richards
Vice President
Junior
richards@isp.com
Shaundra Cartwright
Treasurer
Junior
cartwright@isp.com
David McDevitt
Advertising
Sophomore
mcdevitt@isp.com
Beatrice Fortuna
Brochures
Freshman
Unavailable
Rico Medina
Sharon Richardson
Johnny Wang
Lighting
Sophomore
Junior
Sophomore
Unavailable
Terrell Davis
Nikolas Williams
Props
Freshman
Senior
Unavailable
Positions will be held until May elections
Done
My Computer
Start
members - Notepad
Theater Club Member...
3:47 PM
completed table

FIGURE 3-44

Spanning Rows and Columns

Spanning rows and columns is a frequently used technique that allows you to insert headings that go across rows or columns. You use the ROWSPAN and COLSPAN attributes within a <TH> or <TD> tag to do this. An example of the ROWSPAN and COLSPAN attributes can be seen in Figure 3-9 on page HTM 3.12.

The anything.htm Web page is located on the HTML Data Disk. Figure 3-45 on the next page shows what the Web page looks like when displayed in the browser. This table is incomplete because the Web page visitor cannot tell what the table means without headings of any kind. Next, you enhance the appearance of the anything.htm Web page. Adding headings that span rows and columns changes the table to look like the one shown in Figure 3-46 on page HTM 3.45.

The first step when deciding to span rows or columns is to lay out the table design on a piece of paper. Two main sections, Cast and Technical Crew, display in the body of the table in Figure 3-46. Within each of these main sections are subheadings. In the section for Cast, the subheadings are Character (of the play) and Student (playing that character). In the Technical Crew section, the subheadings are Position and the Student or Students who work in that capacity.

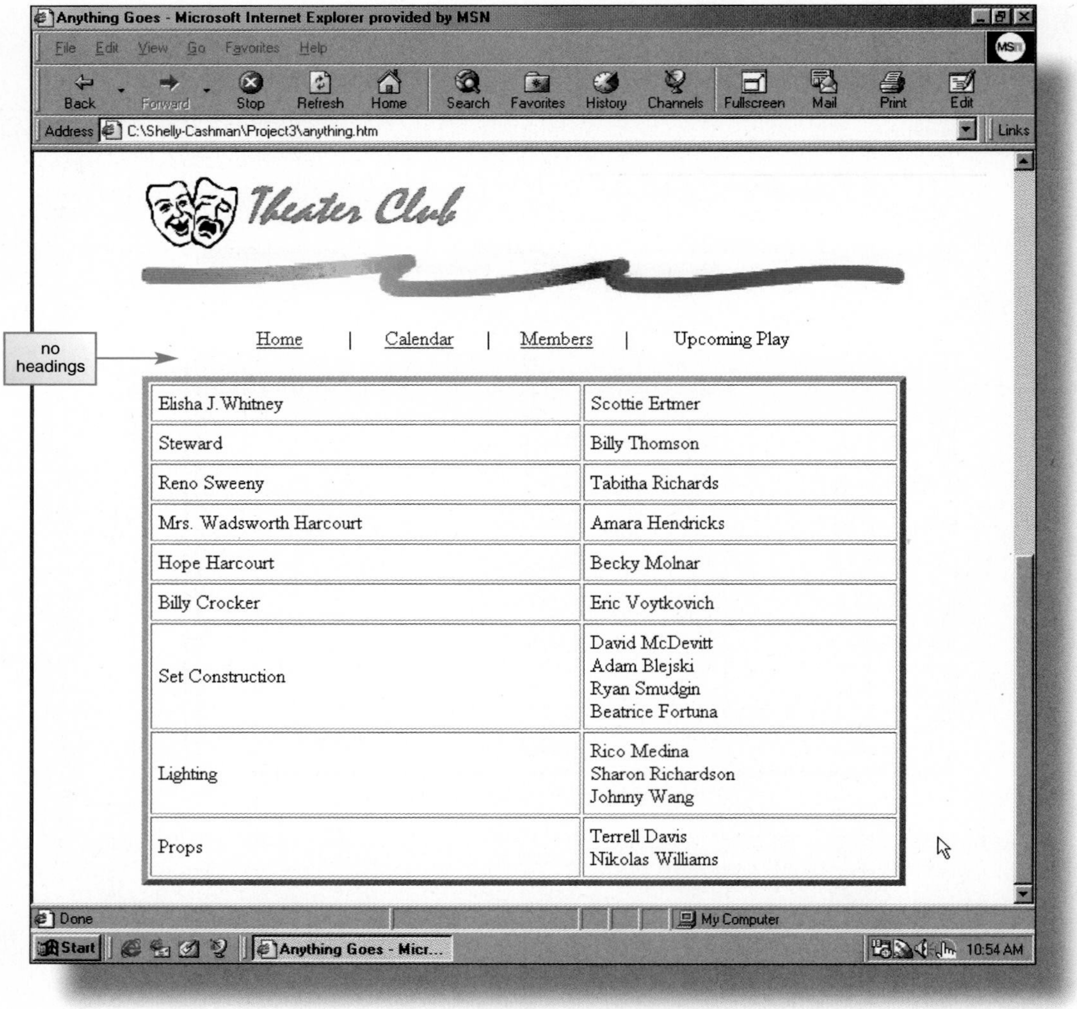
Anything Goes - Microsoft Internet Explorer provided by MSN
File Edit View Go Favorites Help
Back Forward Stop Refresh Home Search Favorites History Channels Fullscreen Mail Print Edit
Address C:\Shelly-Cashman\Project3\anything.htm
Links
Theater Club
no headings
Home | Calendar | Members | Upcoming Play
Elisha J. Whitney
Scottie Ertmer
Steward
Billy Thomson
Reno Sweeny
Tabitha Richards
Mrs. Wadsworth Harcourt
Amara Hendricks
Hope Harcourt
Becky Molnar
Billy Crocker
Eric Voytkovich
Set Construction
David McDevitt
Adam Blejski
Ryan Smudgin
Beatrice Fortuna
Lighting
Rico Medina
Sharon Richardson
Johnny Wang
Props
Terrell Davis
Nikolas Williams
Done
My Computer
Start
Anything Goes - Micr...
10:54 AM

FIGURE 3-45

TO LINK TO THE FINAL WEB PAGE

1. While in the browser, click the Upcoming Play link on the Members menu bar.

The anything.htm Web page displays (Figure 3-45). You will enhance this Web page next.

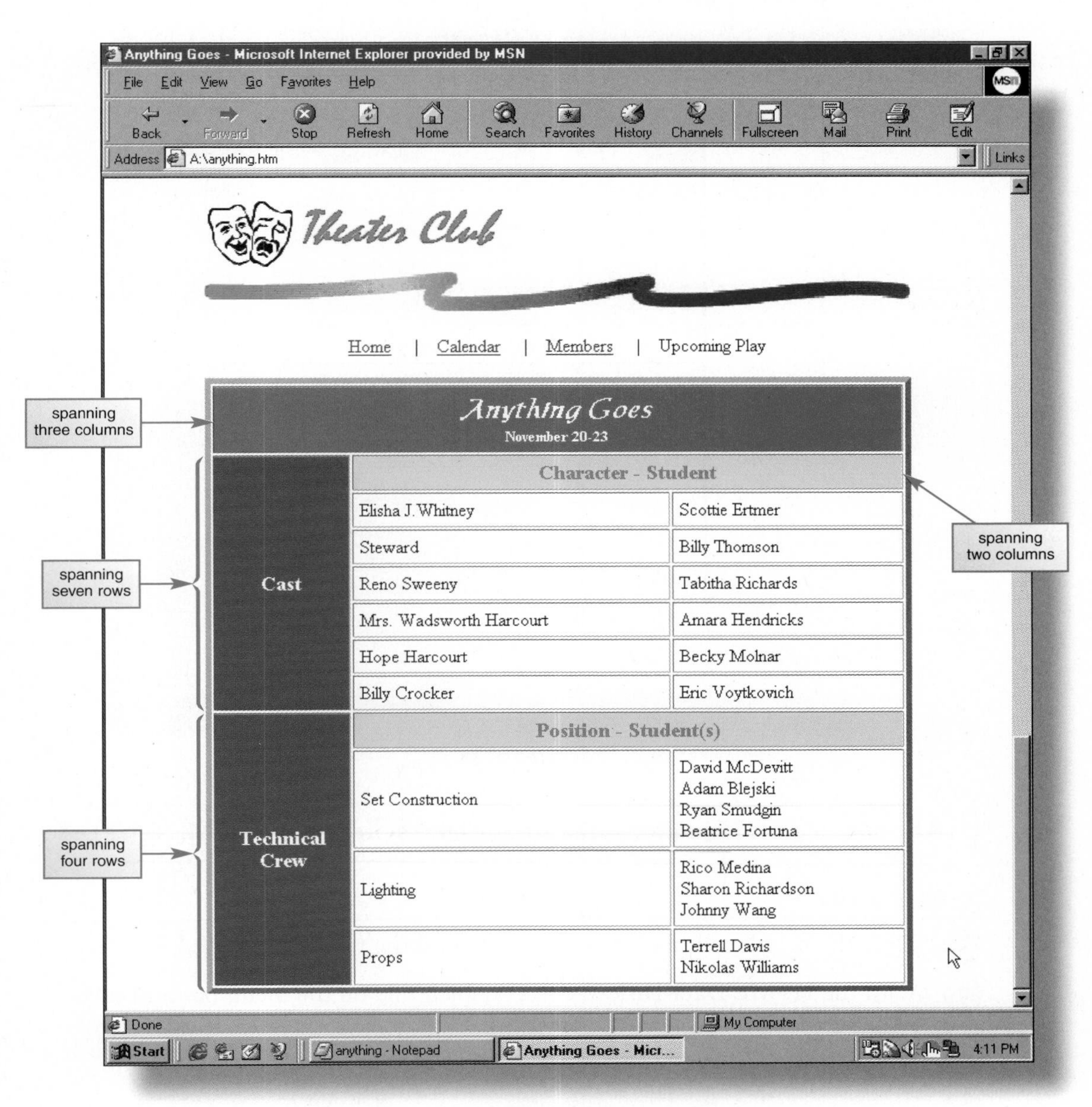

FIGURE 3-46

Now that you know the main sections, you need to determine how many rows or columns each heading requires. You need a heading for the first main section (Cast) that spans seven rows. The next heading (Technical Crew) spans four rows. Both the headings, Character - Student and Position - Student(s), span two columns. The final heading, Anything Goes, spans three columns (including the column that contains the Cast and Technical Crew headings). Figure 3-47 on the next page shows this layout as sketched on paper. You use the ROWSPAN and COLSPAN attributes to create these headings as shown in the steps on page HTM 3.47.

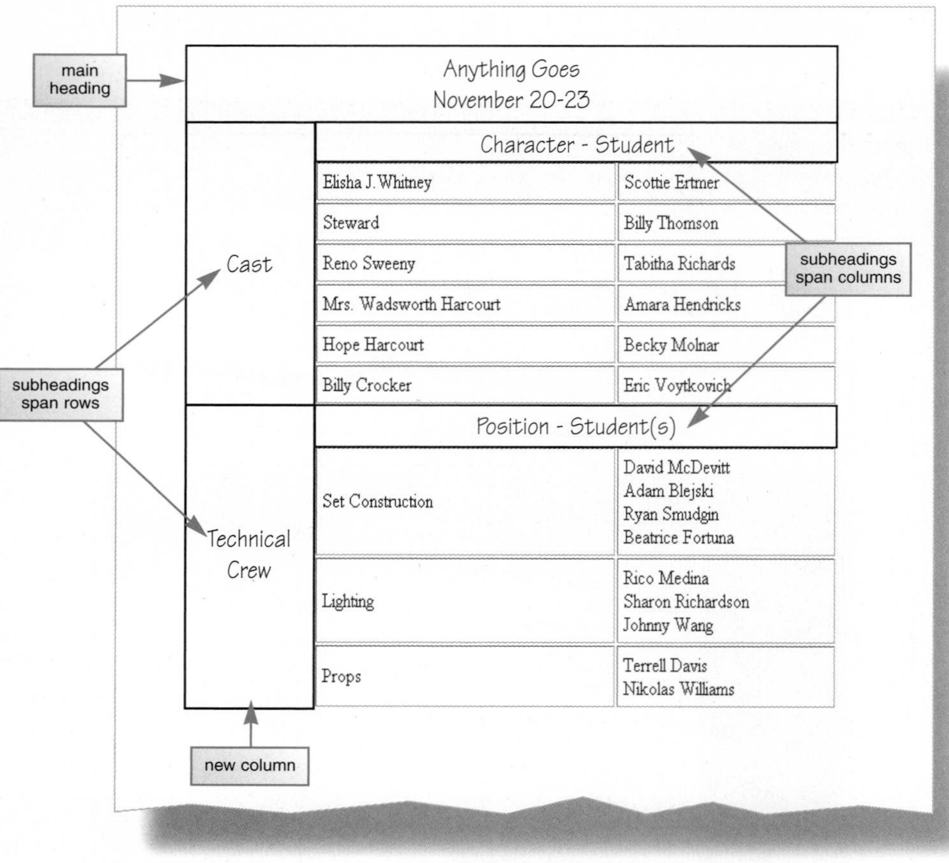

FIGURE 3-47

The first step is to open the file, anything.htm, stored on the HTML Data Disk.

TO OPEN A FILE

1. Click the members.htm - Notepad button on the taskbar.
2. With the HTML Data Disk in drive A, click File on the menu bar and then click Open.
3. If necessary, click the Look in box arrow and then click 3½ Floppy (A:).
4. If necessary, click the Files of type box arrow, click All files (*.*), and then click anything.htm.

5. Click the Open button in the Open dialog box.

Notepad displays the anything.htm file.

Spanning the Main Heading across All Columns

The main heading for the table is in a new row, above the first row of text that is currently in the table. The heading spans across both of the existing columns, as well as the new column that is created on the left (Figure 3-47). The main heading has two lines — Anything Goes on the first line, and November 20-23 on the second line.

To Span the Main Heading across All Columns

1 **Click line 31. Type** <TR> **and then press the ENTER key. Type** <TH COLSPAN="3" BGCOLOR="#009900"> <FONT COLOR= "#FFFFFF"><FONT FACE="Chaucer"><FONT SIZE=+2>Anything Goes</FONT></FONT> **and then press the ENTER key.**

2 **Type**
<FONT SIZE=-1>November 20-23</FONT> **and then press the ENTER key.**

The HTML code displays (Figure 3-48).

```
anything.htm - Notepad
File  Edit  Search  Help
<HEAD>
<TITLE>Anything Goes</TITLE>
</HEAD>
<BODY>

<CENTER><TABLE BORDER=0 COLS=1 WIDTH="80%" >
<TR>
<TD><IMG SRC="tclogo.jpg" HEIGHT=63 WIDTH=261></TD>
</TR>

<TR>
<TD><IMG SRC="hrcolor.JPG" HEIGHT=35 WIDTH=607></TD>
</TR>
</TABLE></CENTER>

<BR><TABLE ALIGN=CENTER BORDER=0 COLS=7 WIDTH="65%" >
<TR ALIGN=CENTER>
<TD><A HREF="tchome.htm">Home</A></TD>
<TD WIDTH="1%">|</TD>
<TD><A HREF="calendar.htm">Calendar</A></TD>
<TD WIDTH="1%">|</TD>
<TD><A HREF="members.htm">Members</A></TD>
<TD WIDTH="1%">|</TD>
<TD>Upcoming Play</TD>
</TR>
</TABLE>

<BR>
<TABLE ALIGN=CENTER BORDER=5 CELLSPACING=2 CELLPADDING=5 COLS=2 WIDTH="80%" >
<TR>
<TH COLSPAN="3" BGCOLOR="#009900"><FONT COLOR="#FFFFFF"><FONT FACE="Chaucer"><FONT
SIZE=+2>Anything Goes</FONT></FONT>
<BR><FONT SIZE=-1>November 20-23</FONT>

<TR>
Start | anything.htm - Notepad | Theater Club Members - Mi... 3:47 PM
```


FIGURE 3-48

3 **Type** </TH> **and then press the ENTER key. Type** </TR> **and then press the ENTER key twice.**

The HTML code displays (Figure 3-49).

```
<TD>Upcoming Play</TD>
</TR>
</TABLE>

<BR>
<TABLE BORDER=5 CELLSPACING=2 CELLPADDING=5 COLS=2 WIDTH="80%" ALIGN=CENTER>
<TR>
<TH COLSPAN="3" BGCOLOR="#009900"><FONT COLOR="FFFFFF"><FONT FACE="Chaucer"><FONT
SIZE=+2>Anything Goes</FONT></FONT>
<BR><FONT SIZE=-1>November 20-23</FONT>
</TH>
</TR>


<TR>
<TD>Elisha J. Whitney</TD>
<TD>Scottie Ertmer</TD>
</TR>

<TR>
Start | anything.htm - Notepad | Anything Goes - Microsoft I... 12:50 PM
```


FIGURE 3-49

In Step 1, the <TR> tag creates a new row. The <TH> tag creates a heading cell that will span three columns of the table. You changed the font to a large (+2) size and used the Chaucer font. In Step 2, you decreased the font size to -1, but used the same font face. You ended the heading and the row in Step 3. If you saved the HTML file at this point and viewed it in the browser, you would see the table as shown in Figure 3-50 on the next page.

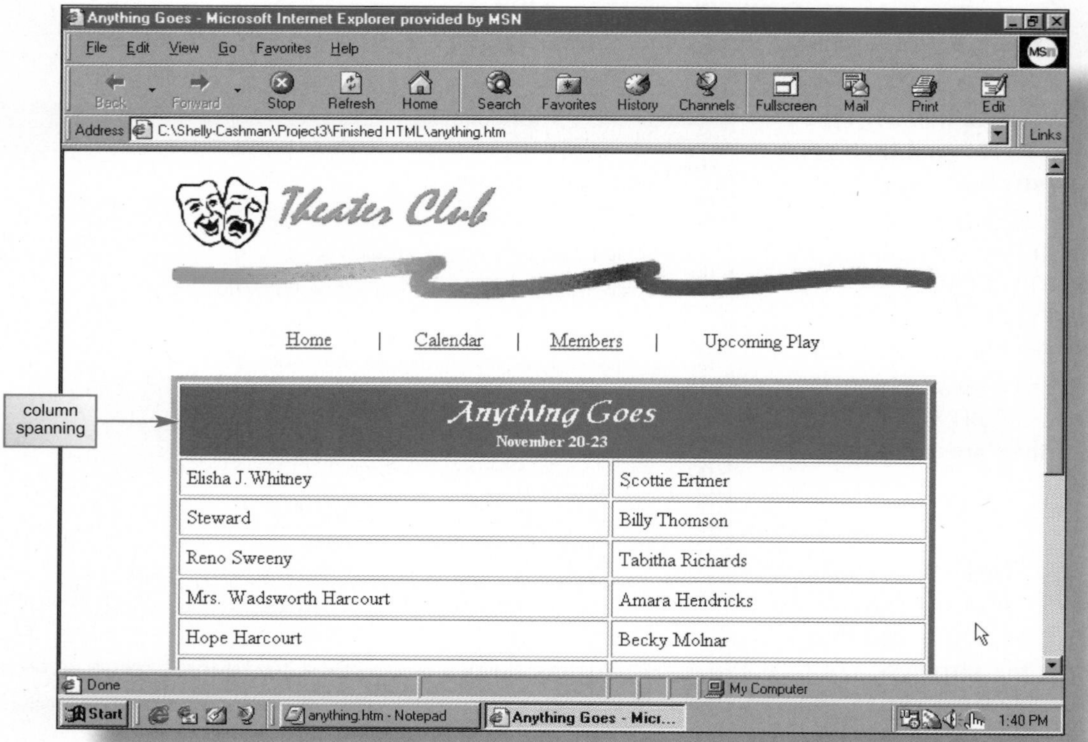

FIGURE 3-50

Creating Additional Headings that Span Rows and Columns

The next step is to create the heading that spans seven rows in the body of the table. Although only six rows contain cast member names, you also must account for an additional row for another heading (Character - Student), which you add later. The HTML code required to complete this task is shown in Table 3-7.

Table 3-7

LINE	HTML TAGS AND TEXT
38	`<TR ALIGN=CENTER BGCOLOR="#FFFFFF">`
39	`<TH ROWSPAN="7" WIDTH="20%" BGCOLOR="#3366FF">`
40	`<FONT COLOR="#FFFFFF"><FONT SIZE=+1>Cast</FONT></FONT>`
41	`</TH>`
42	`<TH COLSPAN="2" BGCOLOR="#FFFF99">`
43	`<FONT COLOR="FF0000"><FONT SIZE=+1>Character - Student</FONT></FONT>`
44	`</TH>`
45	`</TR>`

Perform the following steps to create the headings.

Steps To Create Headings that Span Rows and Columns

1 **If necessary, click line 38.**

2 **Enter the HTML code shown in Table 3-7. Press the ENTER key.**

The HTML code displays (Figure 3-51.)

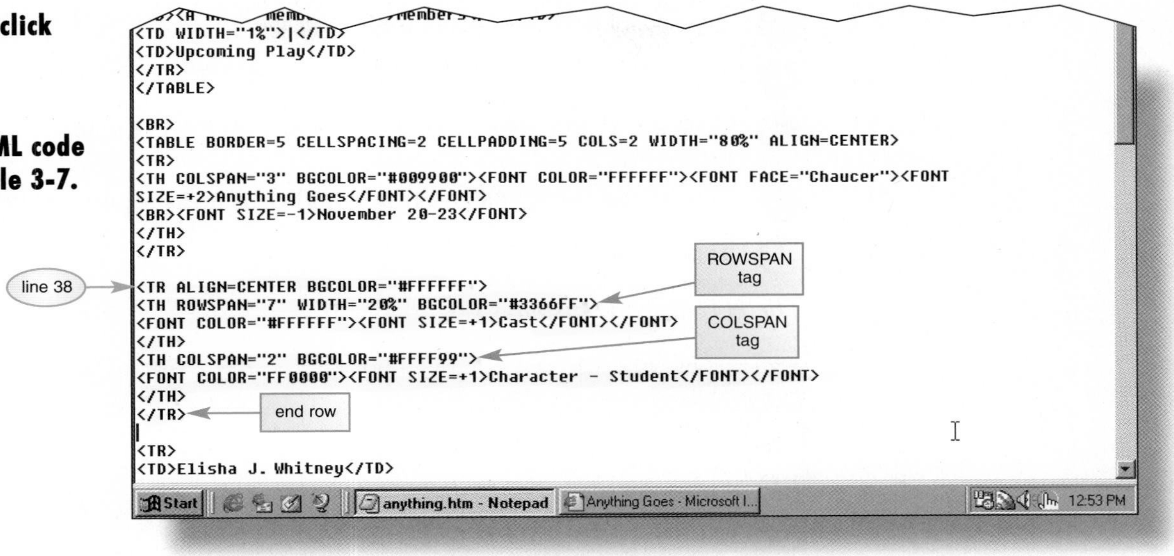

```
<TD WIDTH="1%">|</TD>
<TD>Upcoming Play</TD>
</TR>
</TABLE>

<BR>
<TABLE BORDER=5 CELLSPACING=2 CELLPADDING=5 COLS=2 WIDTH="80%" ALIGN=CENTER>
<TR>
<TH COLSPAN="3" BGCOLOR="#009900"><FONT COLOR="FFFFFF"><FONT FACE="Chaucer"><FONT
SIZE=+2>Anything Goes</FONT></FONT>
<BR><FONT SIZE=-1>November 20-23</FONT>
</TH>
</TR>

<TR ALIGN=CENTER BGCOLOR="#FFFFFF">
<TH ROWSPAN="7" WIDTH="20%" BGCOLOR="#3366FF">
<FONT COLOR="#FFFFFF"><FONT SIZE=+1>Cast</FONT></FONT>
</TH>
<TH COLSPAN="2" BGCOLOR="#FFFF99">
<FONT COLOR="FF0000"><FONT SIZE=+1>Character - Student</FONT></FONT>
</TH>
</TR>

<TR>
<TD>Elisha J. Whitney</TD>
```


FIGURE 3-51

The initial row and column spanning in the anything.htm Web page file is complete. You added a heading the spans seven rows of the table. This row had the width of 20% of the table. You inserted the heading, Cast, on line 40. On line 43, you added a heading, Character - Student, that spans two columns. If you saved the file and viewed the Web page at this point, it would look like the Web page shown in Figure 3-52.

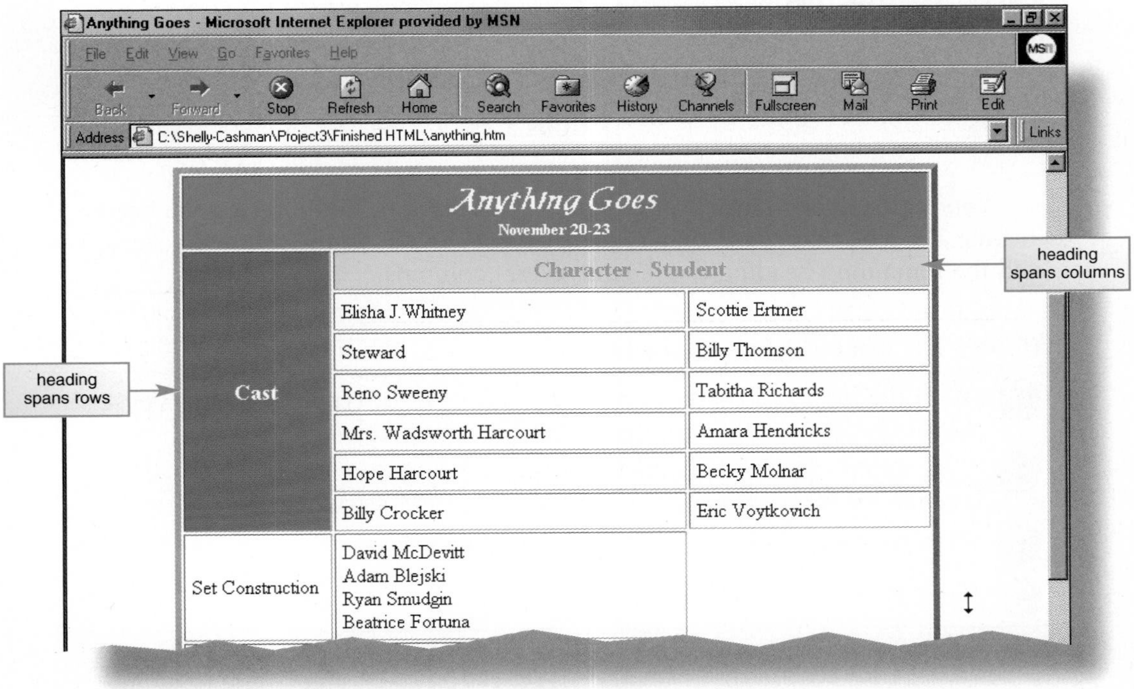

FIGURE 3-52

TO ADD THE REMAINING ROWSPAN TAG

1. Click line 76 and then press the ENTER key.
2. Type <TR> and then press the ENTER key.
3. Type <TH ROWSPAN="4" BGCOLOR="#3366FF"> and then press the ENTER key.
4. Type <FONT COLOR="#FFFFFF"><FONT SIZE=+1>Technical and then press the ENTER key.
5. Type
Crew</FONT></FONT> and then press the ENTER key.
6. Type </TH> and then press the ENTER key.

The HTML code displays (Figure 3-53).

```
anything.htm - Notepad
File  Edit  Search  Help
<TD>Eric Voytkovich</TD>
</TR>

<TR>
<TH ROWSPAN="4" BGCOLOR="#3366FF">
<FONT COLOR="#FFFFFF"><FONT SIZE=+1>Technical
<BR>Crew</FONT></FONT>
</TH>


<TR>
<TD>Set Construction</TD>
<TD>David McDevitt
<BR>Adam Blejski
<BR>Ryan Smudgin
<BR>Beatrice Fortuna</TD>
</TR>

<TR>
<TD>Lighting</TD>
<TD>Rico Medina
<BR>Sharon Richardson
<BR>Johnny Wang</TD>
</TR>

<TR>
<TD>Props</TD>
<TD>Terrell Davis
<BR>Nikolas Williams</TD>
</TR>
</TABLE>
```

line 76

HTML for row span

FIGURE 3-53

You added another row to the table in this section. You inserted the heading, Technical Crew, that spans four rows in Steps 4 and 5. In the following steps, you add the remaining heading that spans several columns.

TO ADD THE REMAINING COLSPAN TAG

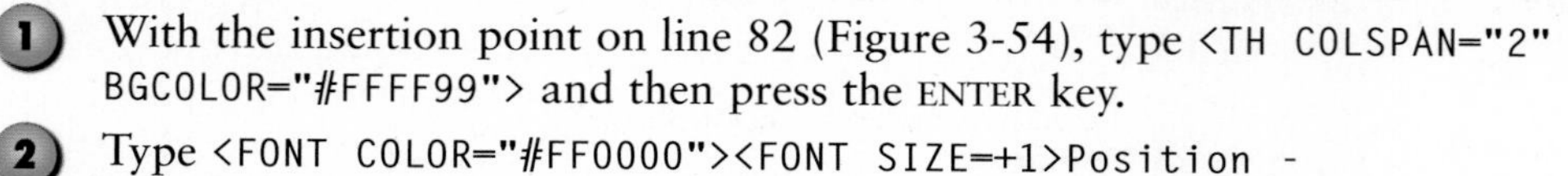

1. With the insertion point on line 82 (Figure 3-54), type <TH COLSPAN="2" BGCOLOR="#FFFF99"> and then press the ENTER key.
2. Type <FONT COLOR="#FF0000"><FONT SIZE=+1>Position - Student(s)</FONT></FONT> and then press the ENTER key.
3. Type </TH> and then press the ENTER key.
4. Type </TR> and then press the ENTER key.

The HTML code displays (Figure 3-54).

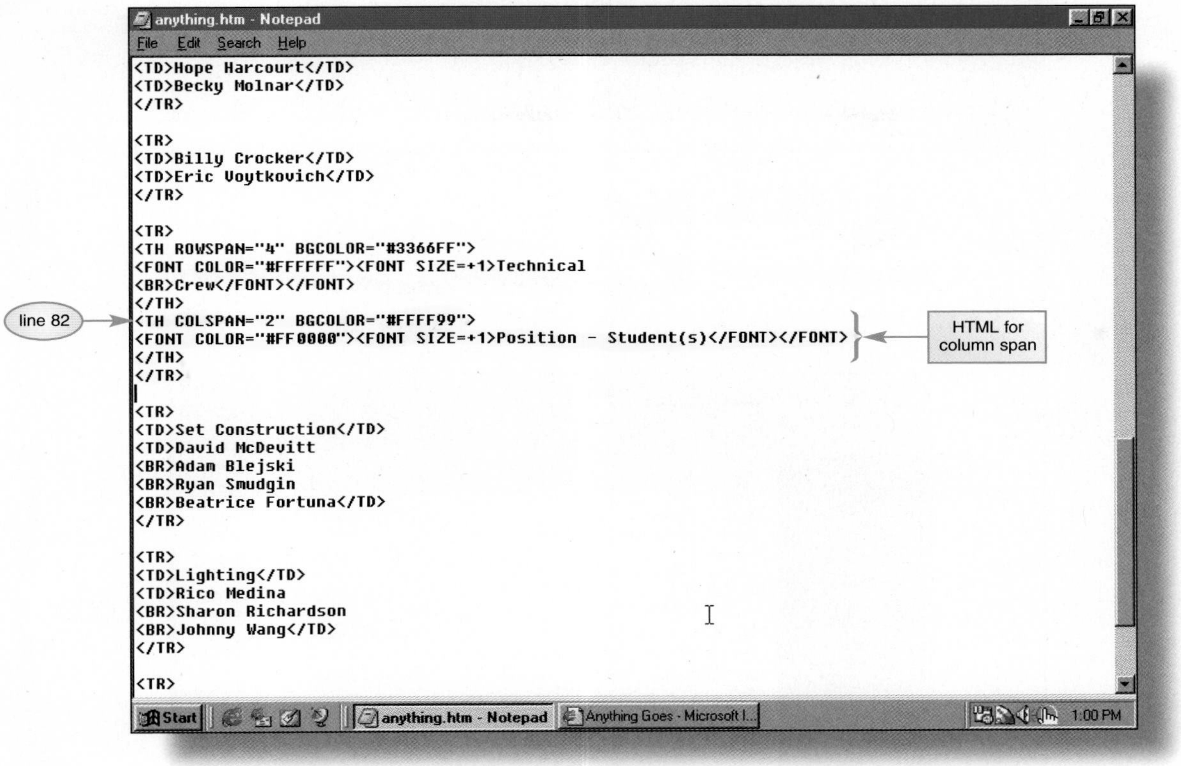

```
anything.htm - Notepad
File  Edit  Search  Help
<TD>Hope Harcourt</TD>
<TD>Becky Molnar</TD>
</TR>

<TR>
<TD>Billy Crocker</TD>
<TD>Eric Voytkovich</TD>
</TR>

<TR>
<TH ROWSPAN="4" BGCOLOR="#3366FF">
<FONT COLOR="#FFFFFF"><FONT SIZE=+1>Technical
<BR>Crew</FONT></FONT>
</TH>
<TH COLSPAN="2" BGCOLOR="#FFFF99">
<FONT COLOR="#FF0000"><FONT SIZE=+1>Position - Student(s)</FONT></FONT>
</TH>
</TR>

<TR>
<TD>Set Construction</TD>
<TD>David McDevitt
<BR>Adam Blejski
<BR>Ryan Smudgin
<BR>Beatrice Fortuna</TD>
</TR>

<TR>
<TD>Lighting</TD>
<TD>Rico Medina
<BR>Sharon Richardson
<BR>Johnny Wang</TD>
</TR>

<TR>
```


FIGURE 3-54

In Steps 1 and 2, you added another heading, Position - Student(s), that spans two columns. This completes the changes to the anything.htm file. You now save the file, print a hard copy, and view the Web page in the browser.

TO SAVE AND PRINT THE HTML FILE AND VIEW AND PRINT THE WEB PAGE

1. With the HTML Data Disk in drive A, click File on the menu bar and then click Save.
2. Click File on the menu bar and then click Print.
3. Click the Anything Goes button on the taskbar.
4. Click the Refresh button on the Standard Buttons toolbar.
5. Click the Print button on the Standard Buttons toolbar.

Hard copy versions of the HTML file and the Web page print. The anything.htm Web page displays (Figure 3-55 on the next page).

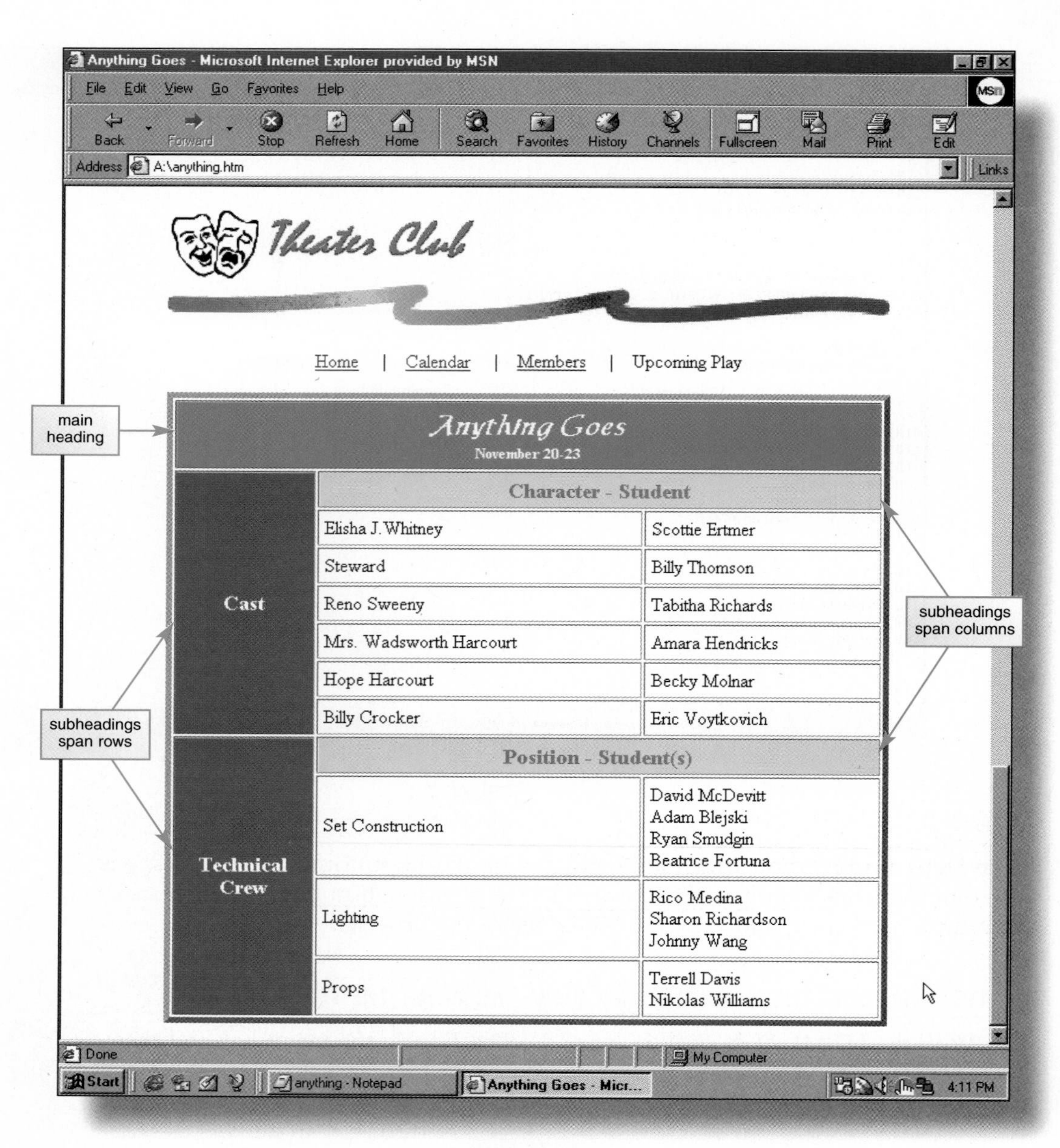

FIGURE 3-55

After viewing the Web page, you should verify all the links. Be sure to test the link to the Anything Goes Web page from the Calendar Web page. This completes the enhancement of the anything.htm file and the project. You now have two newly created Web pages (tchome.htm and calendar.htm) and two enhanced Web pages (members.htm and anything.htm).

Using Blank Cells

Although blank cells are not part of this project, sometimes you want a blank cell with borders to display indicating the cell is empty. Figure 3-56 shows you an example of this type of blank cell. Other times, you want the cell borders not to display when the cell is empty (Figure 3-57). In Figure 3-57, several headings span rows and columns. No cell borders display above the Date of Quiz heading in the top, left corner of the table. Although those are empty cells, it is not necessary to display the cell borders. Figure 3-57 contains the same HTML tags as Figure 3-56 with one difference. In Figure 3-56, a <BR> tag was inserted between the <TD> and </TD> tags.

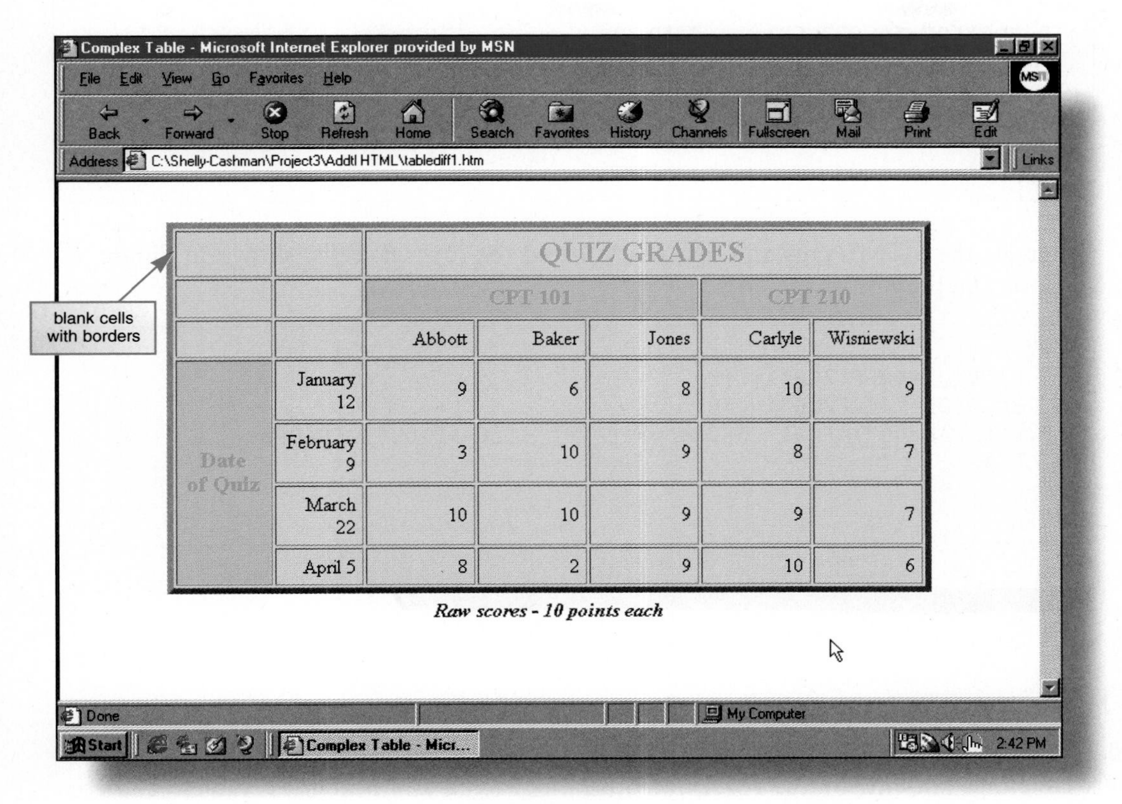

FIGURE 3-56

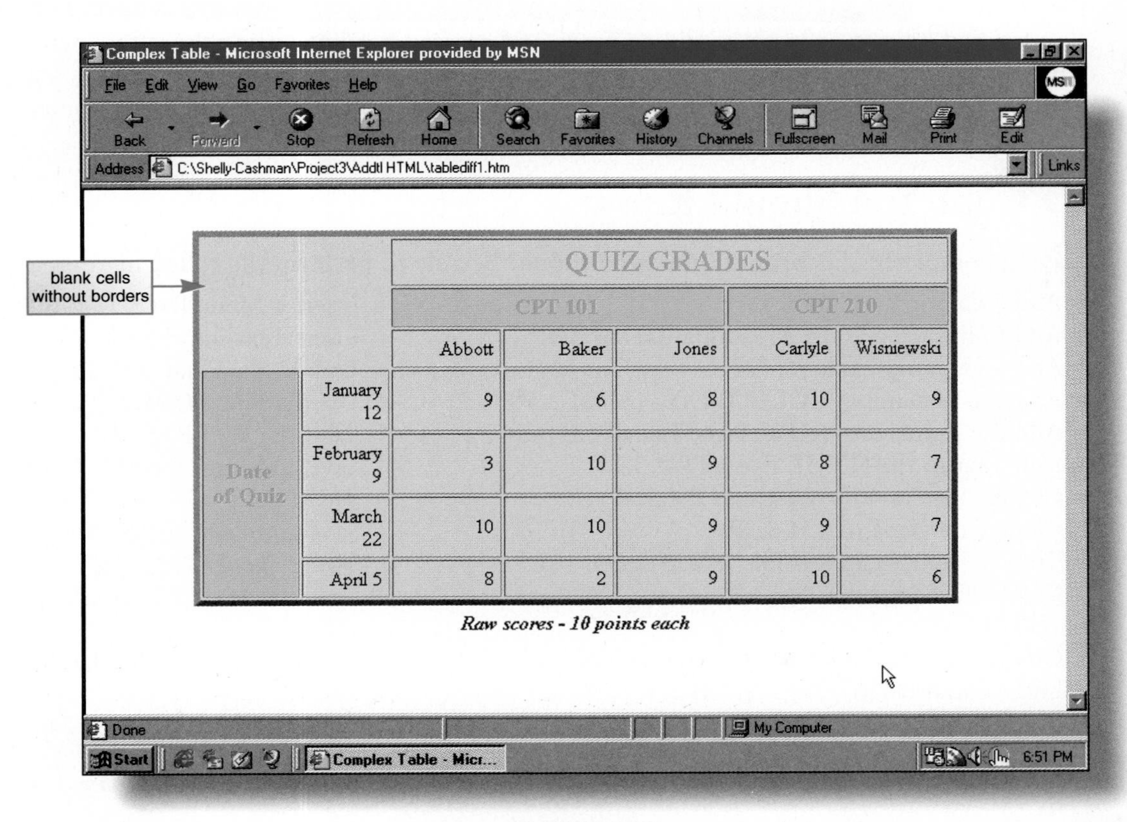

FIGURE 3-57

The HTML tags and text that created the top, left cells, shown in Figure 3-56 on the previous page, are:

```
<TR>
<TD BGCOLOR="#FFE7C6"><BR></TD>
<TD BGCOLOR="#FFE7C6"><BR></TD>
<TH COLSPAN="5"><FONT COLOR="#FF8429" SIZE=+2>QUIZ GRADES
</FONT>
</TH>
</TR>
```

Whereas, the HTML tags and text that created the top, left cells, shown in Figure 3-57 on the previous page, are:

```
<TR>
<TD BGCOLOR="#FFE7C6"></TD>
<TD BGCOLOR="#FFE7C6"></TD>
<TH COLSPAN="5"><FONT COLOR="#FF8429" SIZE=+2>QUIZ GRADES
</FONT>
</TH>
</TR>
```

The two <BR> tags give the cells borders in Figure 3-56.

Project Summary

In this project, you used Notepad to create and edit four HTML text files. You learned the terms and definitions of tables and used numerous table tags and attributes. You created both bordered and borderless tables. You created tables with images and tables with text. You developed a four-page Web site that had links from each page to the others. You created a link list on the home page and a menu bar on the other three Web pages for linking. You learned how to span rows and columns and created headings using those attributes. You created some tables with cellspacing and cellpadding and some without. The Theater Club Web site was a great success at the school. Not only did it generate more interest in students coming to the plays, but more students also joined the club.

What You Should Know

Having completed this project, you now should be able to perform the following tasks:

- Add a Caption *(HTM 3.42)*
- Add Cellspacing and Cellpadding *(HTM 3.40)*
- Add a Heading Table *(HTM 3.18)*
- Add the Remaining COLSPAN Tag *(HTM 3.50)*
- Add the Remaining ROWSPAN Tag *(HTM 3.50)*
- Add Text to the HTML File *(HTM 3.23)*
- Change the Column Width *(HTM 3.41)*
- Change the Title *(HTM 3.29)*
- Copy a Table to a New File *(HTM 3.28)*
- Create Headings that Span Rows and Columns *(HTM 3.49)*
- Create a List of Links in a Column *(HTM 3.21)*
- Enter Initial HTML Tags *(HTM 3.15)*
- Enter Remaining Code *(HTM 3.34)*
- Insert a Horizontal Rule Image *(HTM 3.19)*
- Insert the Logo Image *(HTM 3.18)*
- Insert a Menu Bar *(HTM 3.31)*
- Insert Text into Heading and Data Cells *(HTM 3.33)*
- Link to the Final Web Page *(HTM 3.44)*
- Open a File *(HTM 3.39, HTM 3.46)*
- Print the Web Page *(HTM 3.26)*
- Save and Print the HTML File *(HTM 3.24, HTM 3.35)*
- Save and Print the HTML File and View and Print the Web Page *(HTM 3.42, HTM 3.51)*
- Span the Main Heading Across All Columns *(HTM 3.47)*
- Start Notepad *(HTM 3.14)*
- Test the Links *(HTM 3.36)*
- View and Print the Web Page Using the Browser *(HTM 3.36)*
- View the Web Page *(HTM 3.26)*

Test Your Knowledge

1 True/False

Instructions: Circle T if the statement is true or F if the statement is false.

T F 1. The first step in good table development is to code the table in HTML.
T F 2. A table can be used to give a 3-D border to a single image on a Web page.
T F 3. You can add color to separate cells in a table, but not to individual rows.
T F 4. A column in a table is a horizontal line of information.
T F 5. The two types of cells are heading and data.
T F 6. A border is the line that runs around the outside of a table.
T F 7. Captions can be placed only on the bottom of a table.
T F 8. The </TABLE> tag is optional.
T F 9. There is no difference between how a <TH> tag and a <TD> tag displays.
T F 10. The <TR> tag is necessary at the start of a row.

2 Multiple Choice

Instructions: Circle the correct response.

1. The __________ attribute sets the background color of a row or a cell.
   a. ALIGN b. BGCOLOR c. BORDER d. WIDTH
2. The __________ attribute is used to define the dimensions of a column.
   a. ALIGN b. BGCOLOR c. BORDER d. WIDTH
3. To have a heading across cells, the attribute would be __________.
   a. COLSPAN b. ROWSPAN c. CELLPADDING d. CELLSPACING
4. To have a heading across rows, the attribute would be __________.
   a. COLSPAN b. ROWSPAN c. CELLPADDING d. CELLSPACING
5. __________ defines the space *between* cells.
   a. COLSPAN b. ROWSPAN c. CELLPADDING d. CELLSPACING
6. __________ defines the space *within* cells.
   a. COLSPAN b. ROWSPAN c. CELLPADDING d. CELLSPACING
7. The default horizontal alignment for a *heading* cell is __________.
   a. TOP b. BOTTOM c. CENTER d. LEFT
8. The default horizontal alignment for a *data* cell is __________.
   a. TOP b. BOTTOM c. CENTER d. LEFT
9. To create a table with no border, use the attribute __________.
   a. <BORDER=OFF> b. <BORDER=NO> c. <BORDER=NONE> d. <BORDER=0>
10. To resize a column, use the __________ attribute.
    a. SIZE b. WIDTH c. COLSPAN d. ALIGN

Test Your Knowledge

3 Understanding HTML

Instructions: Perform the following tasks using a computer.

1. Start Notepad.
2. Open the anything.htm file on the HTML Data Disk. If you did not work through the project, then complete the steps on pages HTM 3.47 through HTM 3.51.
3. Using a printout of the file, do the following:
   a. Circle the tag that creates a heading across several rows.
   b. Draw a line under the tag that creates a heading across several columns.
   c. Draw a square around the tag that indicates no border.
   d. Draw an asterisk next to the tag that specifies the width of a column.
4. Write your name and answers on the printout and hand it in to your instructor.

4 Editing HTML Files

Instructions: Perform the following tasks using a computer.

1. Start your browser.
2. Enter `www.scsite.com/html/proj3.htm` in the Address text box. When the Web page displays, scroll down to the Internet titles and click the title of this book.
3. Click the link Project 3 - 4 Editing HTML Files.
4. Click View on the menu bar and then click Source to find the HTML code for some feature that was not used on the calendar.htm Web page.
5. Highlight the code and copy it to the Clipboard (i.e., press CTRL+C).
6. Open the calendar.htm file in Notepad.
7. Paste the Clipboard contents in the calendar.htm file at an appropriate place.
8. Save the revised file on a floppy disk using the file name, calendar2.htm.
9. Print the revised document source.
10. Open the calendar2.htm file in your browser.
11. Print the Web page.
12. Write your name on both printouts and hand them in to your instructor.

1 Web Page Table Help

Instructions: Perform the following tasks using a computer.

1. Start your browser.
2. Enter www.scsite.com/html/proj3.htm in the Address text box. When the Web page displays, scroll down to the Internet titles and click the title of this book.
3. Click the link Project 3 - Help 1.
4. Read about the table attribute that allows you to turn off word wrapping within a cell.
5. Write down how that is done and how you would use it in a real Web page application.
6. Include your name with your answers and hand them in to your instructor.

2 More Table Ideas

Instructions: Perform the following tasks using a computer.

1. Start your browser.
2. Enter www.scsite.com/html/proj3.htm in the Address text box. When the Web page displays, scroll down to the Internet titles and click the title of this book.
3. Click the link Project 3 - Help 2.
4. Find one suggestion that you did not learn in Project 3.
5. Write down some information regarding that suggestion and discuss how you would use it in your own Web page development.
6. Include your name with your answers and hand them in to your instructor.

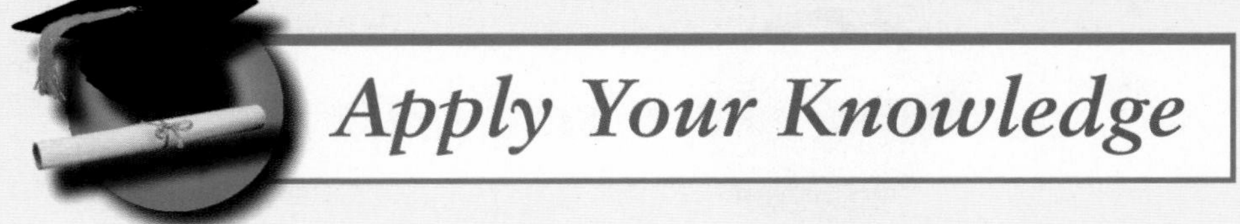

1 Editing the Apply Your Knowledge Web Page

Instructions: Start Notepad. Open the workoff.htm file on the HTML Data Disk. If you did not download the HTML Data Disk earlier, then see the inside back cover for instructions or see your instructor. Figure 3-58 shows the Apply Your Knowledge Web page as it should display in the browser. The workoff.htm file is a partially completed HTML file that contains some errors. Perform the following steps using a computer.

WORK OFF THE CALORIES					
	Running 7.5 mph	Swimming 2 mph	Bicycling 9.4 mph	Walking 3 mph	Aerobic Dancing
Cheesecake 6 oz.	34	56	71	118	68
Danish Pastry 3 oz.	21	34	43	72	42
Fruit Cake 1.5 oz.	12	20	25	42	24
Pecan Pie 5.5 oz.	44	72	91	152	88
Plain Donut 1.5 oz.	13	21	27	45	26
Pumpkin Pie 5.5 oz.	23	37	47	79	45

Minutes of exercise needed

FIGURE 3-58

1. Open the workoff.htm file in your browser.
2. Examine the HTML file and its appearance in the browser.
3. Correct the HTML errors, making the Web page look similar to the one shown in Figure 3-58.
4. Add any HTML code necessary for additional features shown in the Web page in Figure 3-58.
5. Save the revised file on a floppy disk using the file name, workoff2.htm.
6. Print the revised document source.
7. Open the workoff2.htm file in your browser.
8. Print the revised Web page.
9. Write your name on both printouts and hand them in to your instructor.

In the Lab

1 Creating Web Page Want Ads

Problem: The Theater Club needs to fill some open paid and volunteer positions. You decide to create a table on a Web page to advertise those jobs, such as the one shown in Figure 3-59.

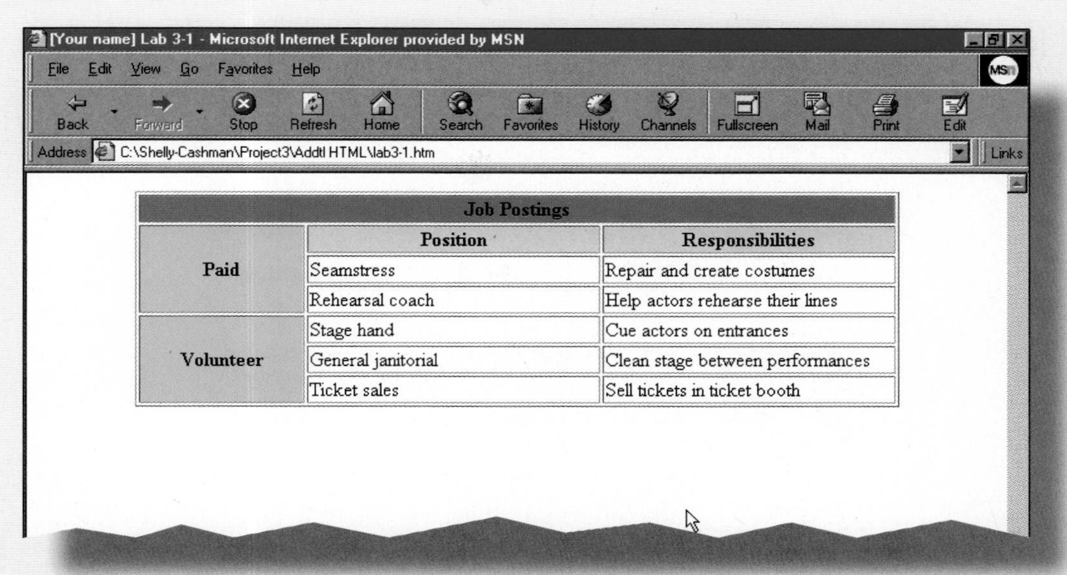

Job Postings		
	Position	**Responsibilities**
Paid	Seamstress	Repair and create costumes
	Rehearsal coach	Help actors rehearse their lines
Volunteer	Stage hand	Cue actors on entrances
	General janitorial	Clean stage between performances
	Ticket sales	Sell tickets in ticket booth

FIGURE 3-59

Instructions: Start Notepad. Perform the following steps using a computer.

1. Start a new HTML file with the title [your name] lab3-1 in the main heading section.
2. Begin the body section by adding a table with three columns and seven rows.
3. Add a background color of #00A5C6 to the first row.
4. Add two headings that span rows with a background color of #FFFF6B.
5. Add additional headings as found in Figure 3-59 with a background color of #C6EFF7.
6. Add all data cell information as shown in Figure 3-59.
7. Close the body, close the HTML file, and save the file using the file name, lab3-1.htm.
8. Print the lab3-1.htm file.
9. Open the lab3-1.htm file in your browser.
10. Print the Web page.
11. Write your name on the printouts and hand them in to your instructor.

2 Creating a Price List

Problem: Your instructor would like to market your Web development skills over the World Wide Web. You have been asked to create two Web pages, similar to the pages shown in Figures 3-60a and 3-60b on the next page. The first is a home page that displays information about Web Development, Inc., together with two links. The second Web page displays the pricing structure of the Web development phases.

Instructions: Start Notepad. Perform the following steps using a computer.

1. Start a new HTML file with the title [your name] lab3-2a in the main heading section.
2. Begin the project by creating an 80% wide, two-row, one-column borderless table with the heading shown in font type Bertram (or some other unusual font of your choice) in color #9C2994.

(continued)

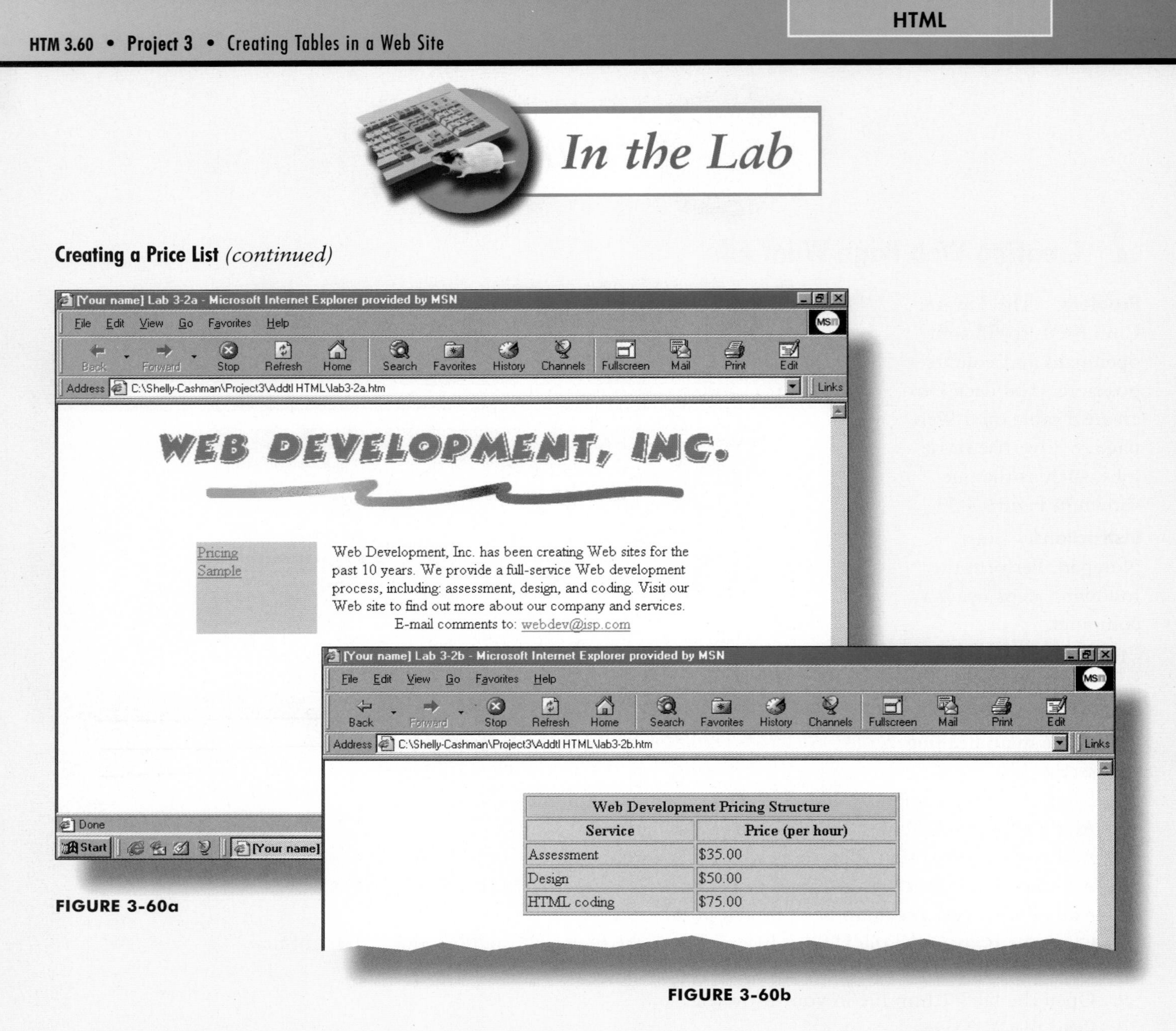

Creating a Price List *(continued)*

FIGURE 3-60a

FIGURE 3-60b

3. Insert the hrcolor.jpg image used in Project 3 into the second row.
4. The second table contains one row, two columns, and no border. The first column is 25% wide and color #DEBDDE. It contains the links Pricing (lab3-2b.htm) and Sample (tchome.htm).
5. The second column contains the text and an e-mail link as displayed in Figure 3-60a.
6. Close the body, close the HTML file, and save the file using the file name, lab3-2a.htm. Print the HTML file.
7. Start a new HTML file with the title [your name] lab3-2b in the main heading section.
8. The second Web page has one 70% wide, five-row, two-column table with a one-pixel border. The top row is color #DEBDDE and all other rows are color #E0E0E0.
9. Span the first heading as shown in Figure 3-60b across both columns.
10. Add the next row of headings and the information into data cells under Service and Price.
11. Close the body, close the HTML file, and save the file using the file name, lab3-2b.htm. Print the HTML file.
12. Open the lab3-2a.htm Web page in your browser and link to the lab3-2b.htm Web page.
13. Print both Web pages.
14. Write your name on all printouts and hand them in to your instructor.

3 Creating an Inventory List

Problem: You want to create two Web pages that list your household inventory and expenses. You will use a table format with headings that span several rows and columns. Your Web pages should look like the ones shown in Figures 3-61a and 3-61b.

[Your name] Lab 3-3 - Microsoft Internet Explorer provided by MSN

Address C:\Shelly-Cashman\Project3\Addtl HTML\lab3-3a.htm

| Expenses | Inventory |

HOUSEHOLD INVENTORY			
	Item	Location	Cost
Over $1,000	Item 1	Location 1	Cost 1
	Item 2	Location 2	Cost 2
Less than $1,000	Item 3	Location 3	Cost 3
	Item 4		
	Item 5		

FIGURE 3-61a

[Your name] Lab 3-3b - Microsoft Internet Explorer provided by MSN

Address C:\Shelly-Cashman\Project3\Addtl HTML\lab3-3b.htm

| Expenses | Inventory |

HOUSEHOLD EXPENSES		
	Expense	Cost
Monthly	House Payment	Cost 1
	Food	Cost 2
	Utilities	Cost 3
	Phone	Cost 4
Annually	Car Insurance	Cost 5
	Club Fees	Cost 6

FIGURE 3-61b

Instructions: Start Notepad. Perform the following steps using a computer.

1. Create Web pages similar to the ones shown in Figures 3-61a and 3-61b.
2. The titles should be [your name] lab3-3a and [your name] lab3-3b, respectively.
3. Include a one-pixel border table with a menu bar on both pages, with links as shown in Figures 3-61a and 3-61b.
4. Include the headings and data cells as shown in both pages, with valid information in the data cells.
5. Use colored backgrounds where you see fit.
6. Save the Web pages using the file names lab3-3a.htm (Inventory) and lab3-3b.htm (Expenses), respectively.
7. Print the pages from your browser.
8. Write your name on the printouts and hand them in to your instructor.

Cases and Places

The difficulty of these case studies varies:
▸ are the least difficult; ▸▸ are more difficult; and ▸▸▸ are the most difficult.

1 You are very pleased with the Theater Club Web site, but think the Calendar Web page could use some additional enhancements. Use Notepad to add some additional table tags or attributes to enhance the Calendar Web page.

2 Your instructor wants you to add more excitement to the Members Web page. Give the entire Members table a colored background. Also, find one area to use the ROWSPAN or COLSPAN attribute in that table.

3 You would like to add another theater-specific image to one of your Web pages. Start your browser and use a search engine to look for free images with a theater theme. Save the image and insert it into one of your tables. Remember to credit the Web site where you obtained the image, if required.

4 The Theater Club has benefitted greatly from the new Web site. Students are joining the club, volunteering to help with the plays, and coming to the activities. Think of another club or group at your school that could benefit from a Web site. Use your Theater Club Web pages as a Web-site template for this other club or group.

5 A Web site is rarely finished. Other Web pages always can be added to a site. Add other images or information about club members on separate Web pages. Link to those pages from the members.htm Web page.

6 Use a browser to look at other pages on the World Wide Web. Find three Web pages that contain borderless tables and three Web pages that contain tables with borders. To verify, you can check the page source from within the browser. Print all six pages and indicate if these are appropriate uses of each type of table and why.

7 Think of a topic that interests you and is conducive to a table layout. Create a table with the level of complexity of the table in Figure 3-2a on page HTM 3.6. Using your theme, put information into this complex table format. Print your Web page.

HTML

PROJECT 4

Creating an Image Map

OBJECTIVES

You will have mastered the material in this project when you can:

- Define terms relating to image mapping
- List the differences between server-side and client-side image maps
- Name the two components of an image map
- Describe the steps to implement an image map
- Distinguish between appropriate and inappropriate images for mapping
- Sketch hotspots on an image
- Describe how the x- and y-coordinates relate to vertical and horizontal alignment
- Open an image in Paint
- Use Paint to map the coordinates of an image
- Use the <MAP></MAP> tags to begin and end a map
- Insert an image into a table and use the USEMAP attribute to define a map
- Use the <AREA> tag to indicate the shape, coordinates, and URL for a mapped area
- Change link colors
- Create a link list
- Insert a chart into a table on a Web page

Modern-Day Silk Road

Marketing on the Web

In today's fast-paced World Wide Web, the word is marketing. Marketing on the Web has changed the way businesses advertise products and individuals purchase goods and services. Even marketing classes have encountered a change in the way students develop and present their final projects. Traveling from one exciting Web site to the next can make you feel as if you are a merchant-explorer in a new online world. Web sites are used to attract and keep customers interested, providing a new route for communication and commerce.

The World Wide Web links today's world: high-powered telephone lines connect thousands of servers around the globe, each containing pages of information. Long before the birth of the Web, the Silk Road connected the world. For 2,000 years, this road — a tenuous thread of communication and commerce that stretched from China to Europe — was a highway for caravans of merchants laden with silk, gold, and glass, trading goods and sharing culture along the way. Like the Web, the Silk Road was not merely a single route, it had many different branches that connected different towns.

Tim Berners-Lee, the father of the Web, was the first to travel the hyperlinks of the Web. While working at CERN, the European Particle Physics Laboratory in Switzerland in the 1980s, Berners-Lee wrote a program called Enquire, which stored information using random associations and used hypertext to move around the Internet. In 1989, Berners-Lee proposed the Web, and travel on the Web was underway.

Today, all you need is a modem, an Internet service provider, and a Web browser, and you are ready to explore this electronic Silk Road. Your Web browser is your golden tablet, providing passage between linked sites all over the world.

Browsing the World Wide Web is the Silk Road to learning essential Web site design. Looking at other's work, you quickly can recognize good and bad practices. The successful Web site must be innovative and effective to stand out. One way to achieve this effect is to use images and graphics in your Web page design. In good Web pages, images are not simply shown, they are integrated to furnish information, display pictures of goods and services, and permit navigation.

Assuming the role of Web site developer in this project, you will create an image map on the Web. Image maps are used for navigation. You will create links on a single image and divide it into multiple clickable areas as you develop a home page for the Surf's Up surf shop using HTML tags and attributes. Your Web page visitors will be able to link to the various pages to view product descriptions and sales figures.

With the techniques presented in this project, you can organize your site and be creative with the use of color and charts. Finally, you will test the site in your browser. All of these elements ensure your success in developing a Web site that attracts and influences those browsing the Web and gets you noticed.

Like the Silk Road, you can experience the wealth of the Web. In your Web travels, you can gather the richness of ideas, insight, and design that only browsing the Web can provide.

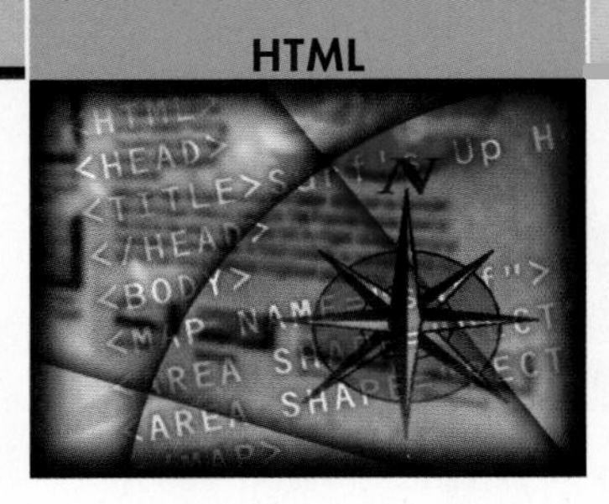

HTML

Creating an Image Map

CASE PERSPECTIVE

You are currently enrolled in a marketing class at school. Fifty percent of your grade for this class is based on the final project. In this project, you must determine a cost-effective way to publicize the monthly sales figures of a company that you create. Your instructor said grading will be based on organization of the information as well as creativity. Most of the students in the class are using spreadsheet software to track and chart the sales figures. You decide to use your HTML skills to create a Web site for this project.

You have used Web sites that utilize a technique called image mapping. With image mapping, a single image is divided into link areas. A Web page viewer can click a section of the image and link to other Web pages. The image mapping approach is a good way to creatively display different sales figures. You create a company named Surf's Up, which specializes in surfing equipment. You find a large image that symbolizes a company with this name. You divide the image into three rectangular areas, one for each of the Surf's Up stores. Each mapped area will link to another Web page that contains the monthly sales figures for that store.

Introduction

In Projects 2 and 3, you inserted images onto your Web pages by using the <IMG> tag. In Project 2, you also linked an image by using the <A> (anchor) tag. The link to this image transfers the Web page visitor to another Web site when the visitor clicks that image. When a link is embedded as part of an image, the entire image becomes the *clickable area*, or the *hotspot*. With an image map, the entire image does not have to be clickable. Instead, either a specific area or several areas serve as the hotspots.

Image maps give Web page developers significant flexibility. No longer do they have to rely on text-based links to route visitors to other locations. In this project, you will learn how to map images.

Project Four – Surf's Up

Image maps are used for navigation. Using an image map, a developer can create multiple links on a single image. A single image is divided into multiple clickable areas, or hotspots. Each hotspot, when clicked, sends the Web page visitor to another part of the same Web page or to a different Web page, either at the same site or a different site, based on which hotspot was clicked.

You will create the two Web pages shown in Figures 4-1a and 4-1b (surfhome.htm and hnbch.htm). The two Web pages shown in Figures 4-1c and 4-1d, (maui.htm and ftlaud.htm), are stored on the HTML Data Disk. First, you will create surfhome.htm, the home page of a company named Surf's Up, which has three stores that sell surfing gear (Figure 4-1a). The home page will include an image (surfmap.gif) that is divided into the three Surf's Up hotspots, one each to the Web pages for the Huntington Beach store (Figure 4-1b), the Maui store (Figure 4-1c), and the Fort Lauderdale store (Figure 4-1d).

The home page also will contain information about the company itself and text links associated with the image map links.

You then will create a Web page for the Huntington Beach store (hnbch.htm) (Figure 4-1b). This page will contain an image (hnbch.gif) for the store, text describing the store's location and sales history, and a chart (hnchart.jpg) reflecting its sales. Both the image and the chart are stored on the HTML Data Disk.

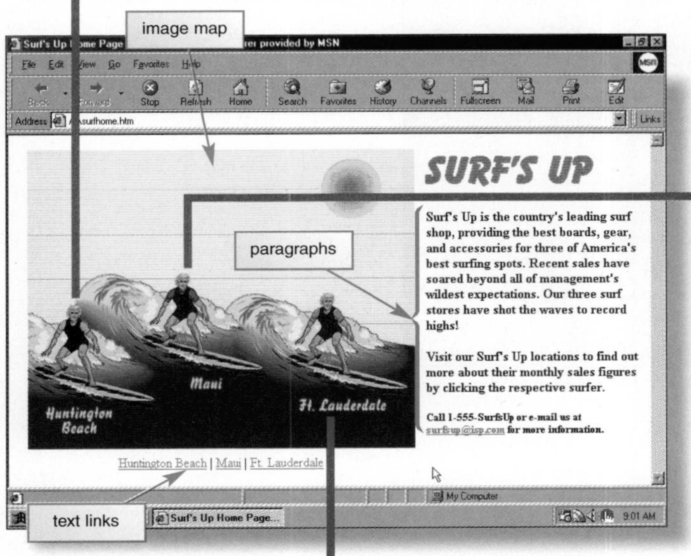

FIGURE 4-1a

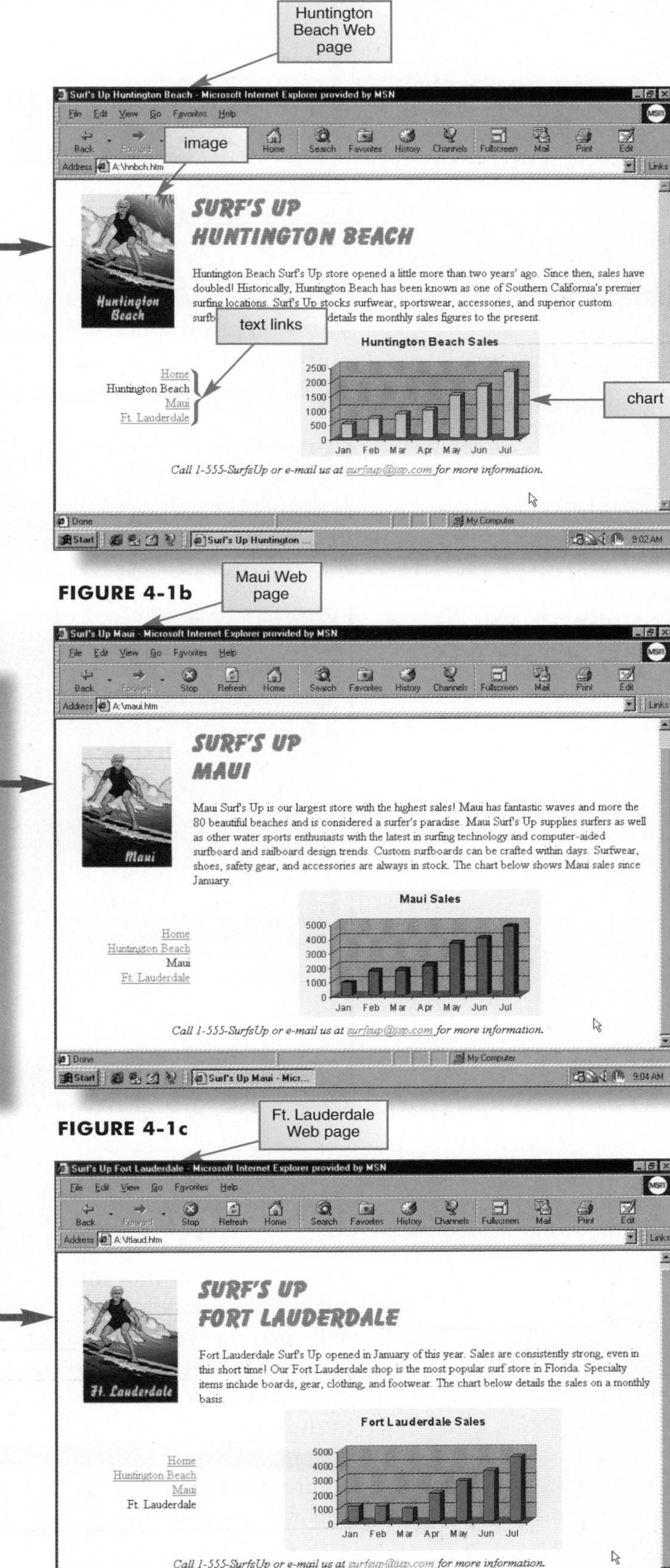

FIGURE 4-1d

To establish the hotspots, you will use a program called Paint to determine the screen pixel coordinates of each hotspot based on the horizontal and vertical axes on the home page image, surfmap.gif. You then will use HTML to create text-based links to the three hotspots, as shown in Figure 4-1a. The three hotspots on the image and the text link will link to the Web pages shown in Figures 4-1b, 4-1c, and 4-1d.

You will use Notepad to enter text and HTML tags to create the two Web pages, surfhome.htm and hnbch.htm. To create hotspots, you will enter the coordinates for each hotspot in the image map within the <AREA> tag. You will use your browser to view your Web pages as you develop them.

Introduction to Image Maps

In Project 1, a **hotspot** was defined as an area of an image that activates a function when selected. Web page visitors who click a hotspot are linked to another part of the same Web page or to another Web page on the same or another site. In addition, an **image map** was defined as a special type of inline image in which you define one or more areas as hotspots. Figure 4-2 is an example of each hotspot in an image map linking to a different Web page, for example, THINGS TO DO and RESEARCH. The Web is a graphic-intensive medium, so Web visitors expect to view many images on the Web pages that they visit. Images make Web pages more exciting and interesting to view. Image maps make the images useful for navigation.

Image Maps

Image maps are used frequently for Web site navigation. Many online HTML sources address the purposes of image maps and give suggestions for their use. An online style guide produced by Sun Microsystems is available for use by Web developers. For more information, visit the HTML More About page (www.scsite.com/html/more.htm) and click Image Maps.

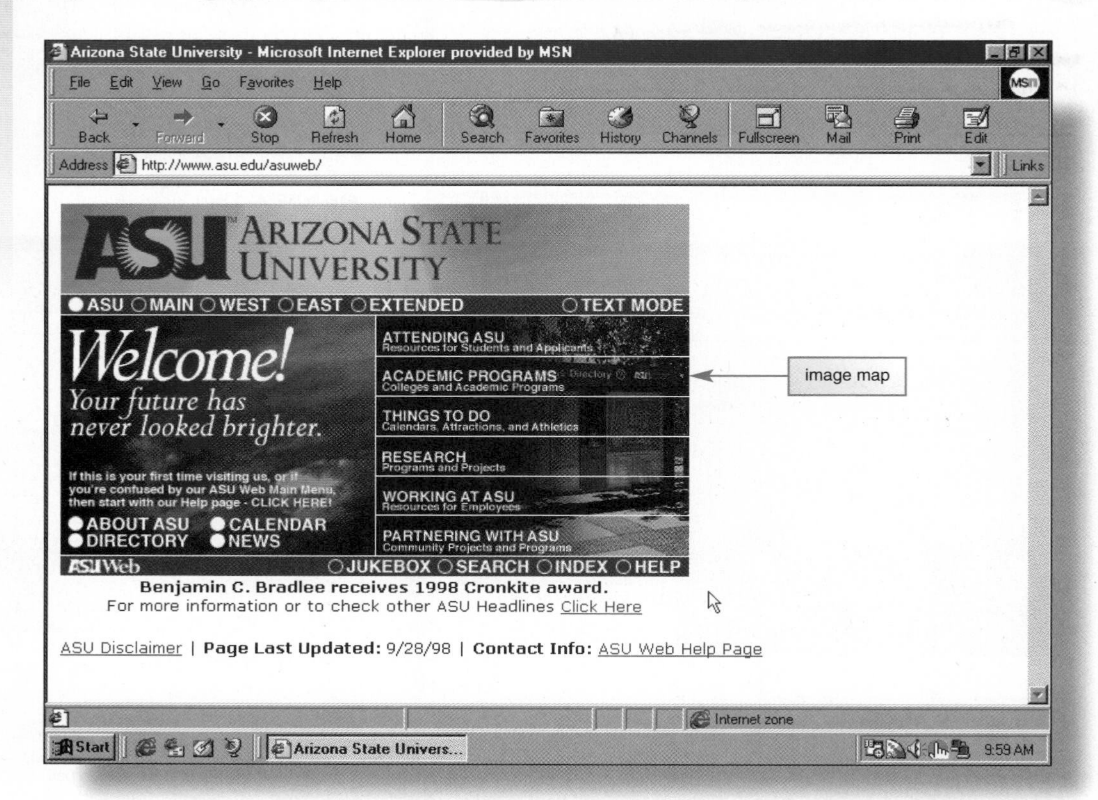

FIGURE 4-2

In Project 2, you created a link from an image on the sample resume page. Clicking anywhere in that image links the visitor to the specified URL. In this project, you will use an image map to create three links within a single image, as shown in Figure 4-1a on page HTM 4.5, each with its own clickable area. Each clickable area is rectangular in shape and positioned over a surfer, which is used as the hotspot. Figure 4-3a shows the borders of the three clickable areas. These outlines, although visible in the figure, are not visible on the Web page. A Web page visitor clicking anywhere within one of the rectangular clickable areas will link to the associated Web page. Figure 4-3b shows areas that are *not* part of the clickable areas. You will use HTML tags to create the image map that supports the three clickable areas in the image.

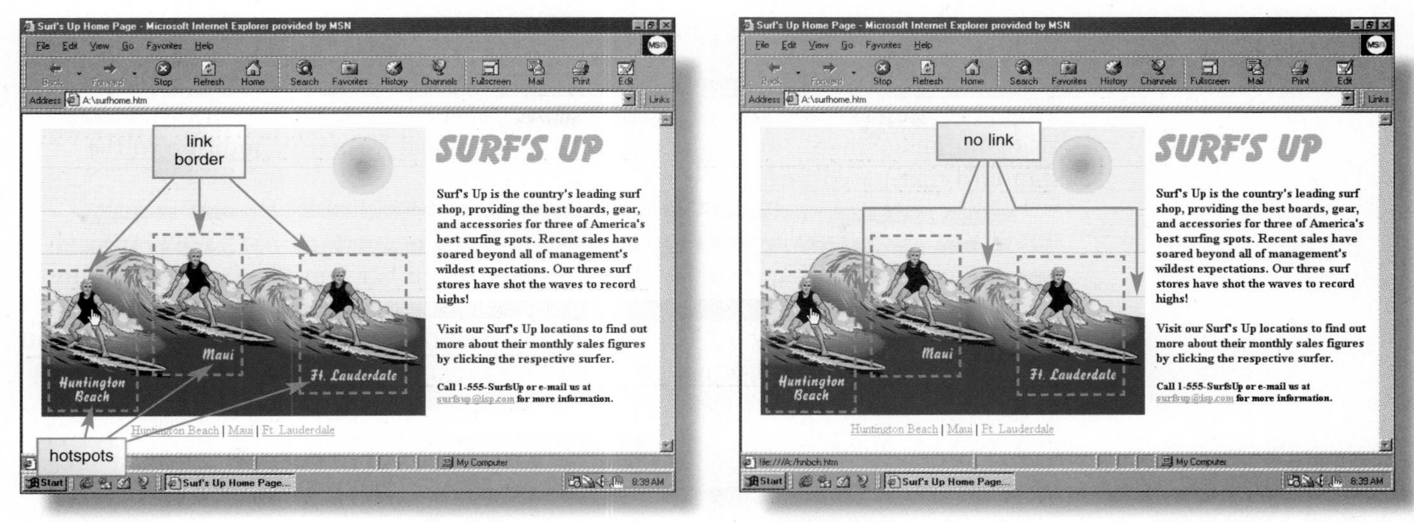

FIGURE 4-3a

FIGURE 4-3b

Image Map Caution

Image downloading has performance issues that many Web page visitors try to avoid. For example, the presence of images increases the amount of time required for pages to download. Some people turn off the viewing of images when they browse Web pages, electing to display only text in their browsers. This makes Web page browsing much faster. For this reason, on all Web pages that use image maps for navigation, you should include the text links to the URLs reflected in the image map, as shown in Figure 4-4a. In this way, a Web page visitor with images turned off, as shown in Figure 4-4b, can still link to associated Web pages by using the text links.

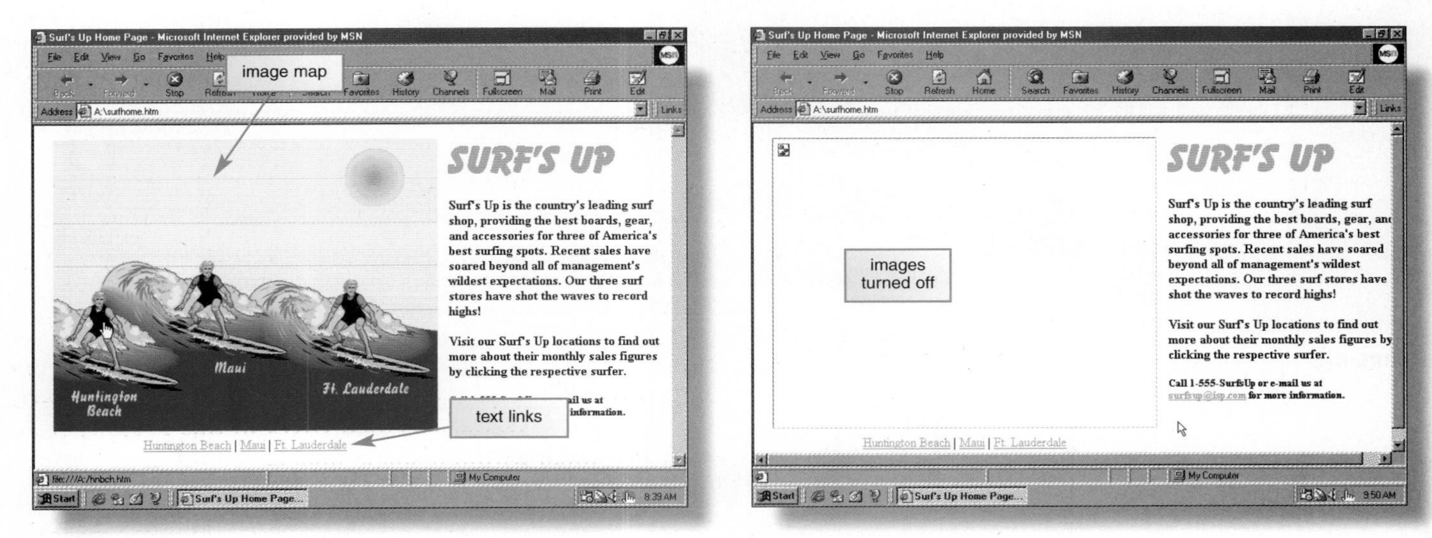

FIGURE 4-4a

FIGURE 4-4b

Image Map Uses

Image maps give you more flexibility as a Web developer. You can use one, instead of multiple, images to link to numerous Web sites from a single Web page. Using an image map, you can depict links in graphical format in addition to the standard text-based format.

Image maps can enhance the functionality and appeal of Web pages in many ways. You can use them for **image map button bars**, menu bars that have graphical images, as shown in Figure 4-5. This makes the menu bar a more attractive feature of the Web page. You also can use image maps to divide a geographical map into hotspots, as shown in Figure 4-6. A Web page visitor can click the area of choice and be linked to additional information about that geographical area. You further can use image maps for real estate applications, where a visitor can click a room within an image of a building (Figure 4-7a) and link to specifics about that room (Figure 4-7b).

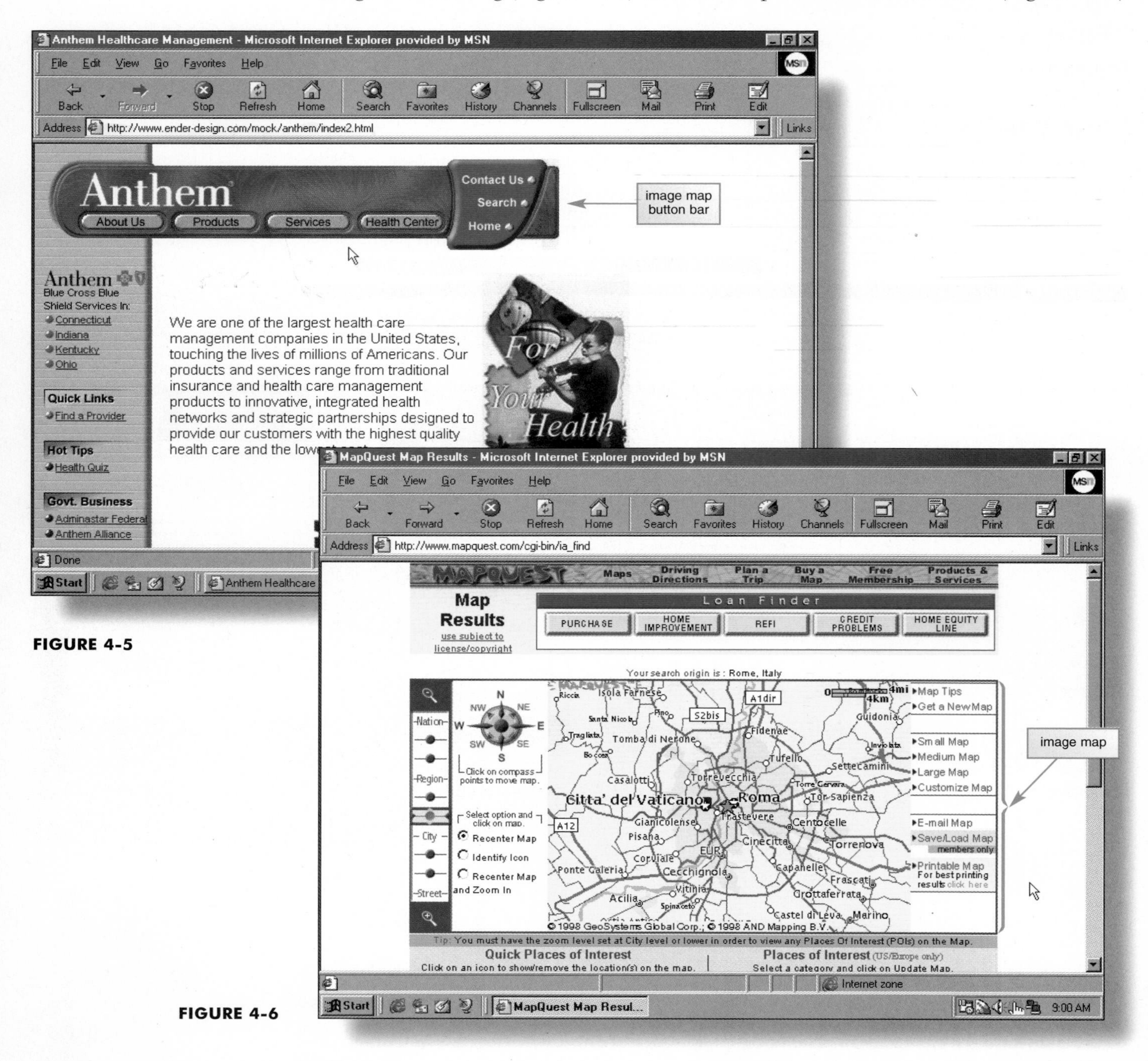

FIGURE 4-5

FIGURE 4-6

Images

Not all images are appropriate for image mapping. It is helpful to hear from Web development experts on things to consider when selecting or creating images. For some great tips and suggestions, visit the HTML More About page (www.scsite.com/html/more.htm) and click Images.

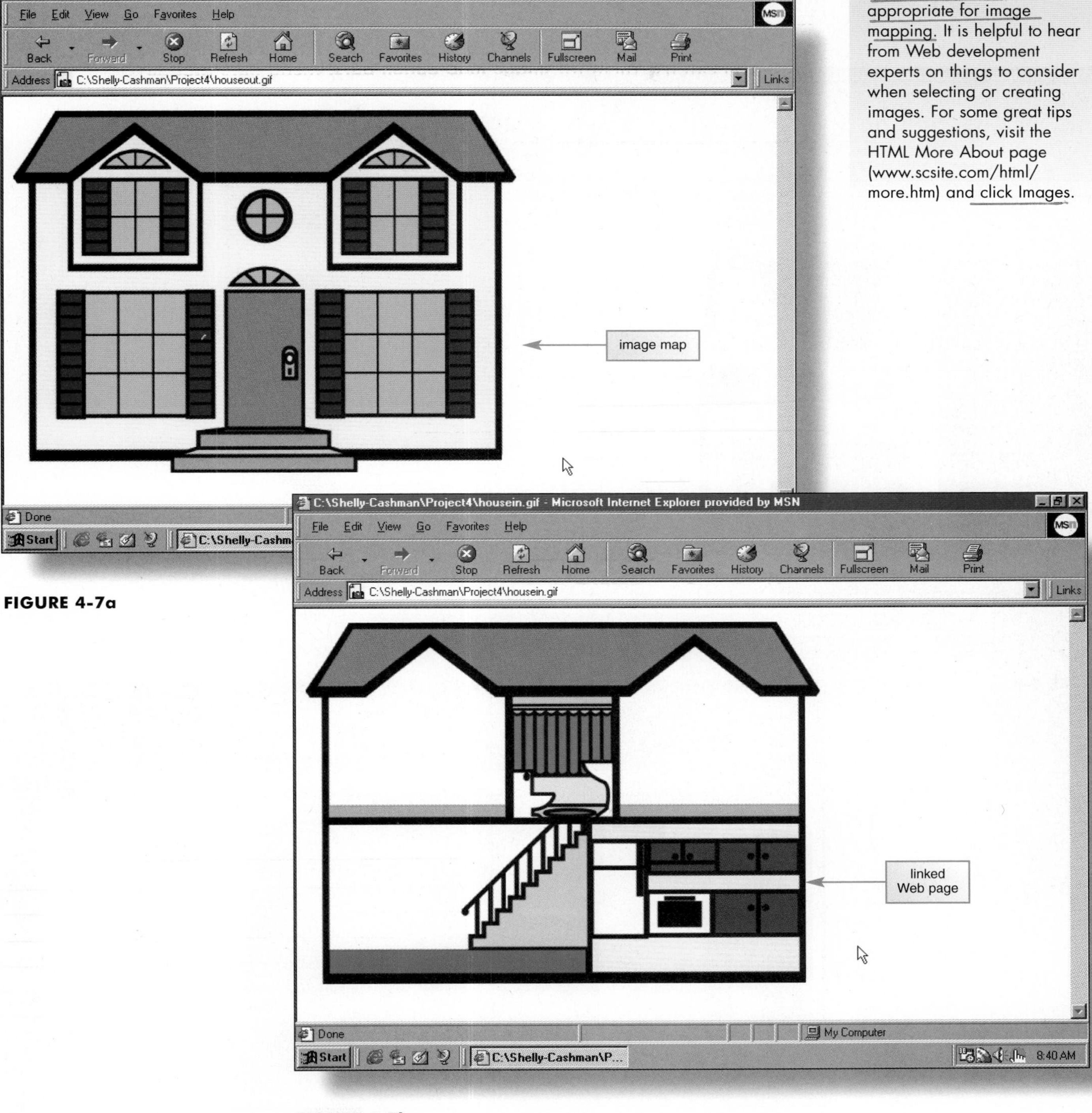

FIGURE 4-7a

FIGURE 4-7b

Companies use image maps to create hotspots that link different parts of a product, as shown in Figure 4-8, to Web pages that contain more information about a specific part. An image map such as a stack of books (Figure 4-9) can link to Web pages that contain specific course information. A company with an online ordering system can link from products stored on shelves and displayed on the Web page (Figure 4-10).

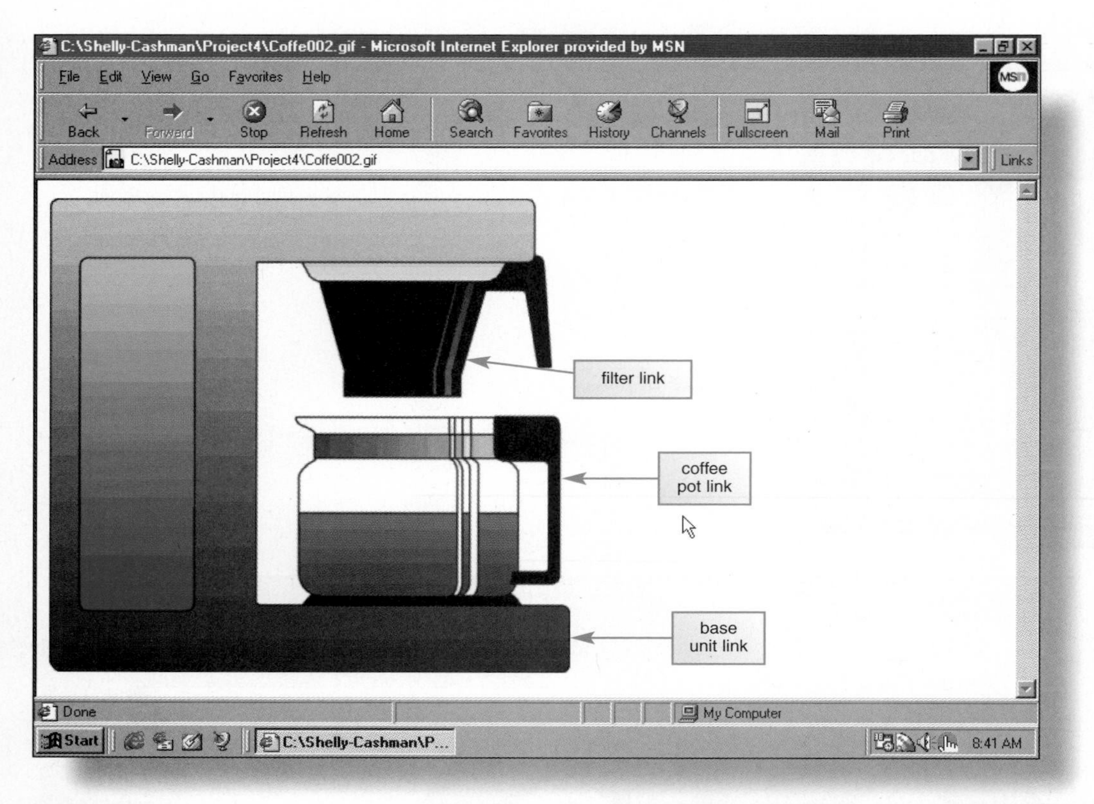

FIGURE 4-8

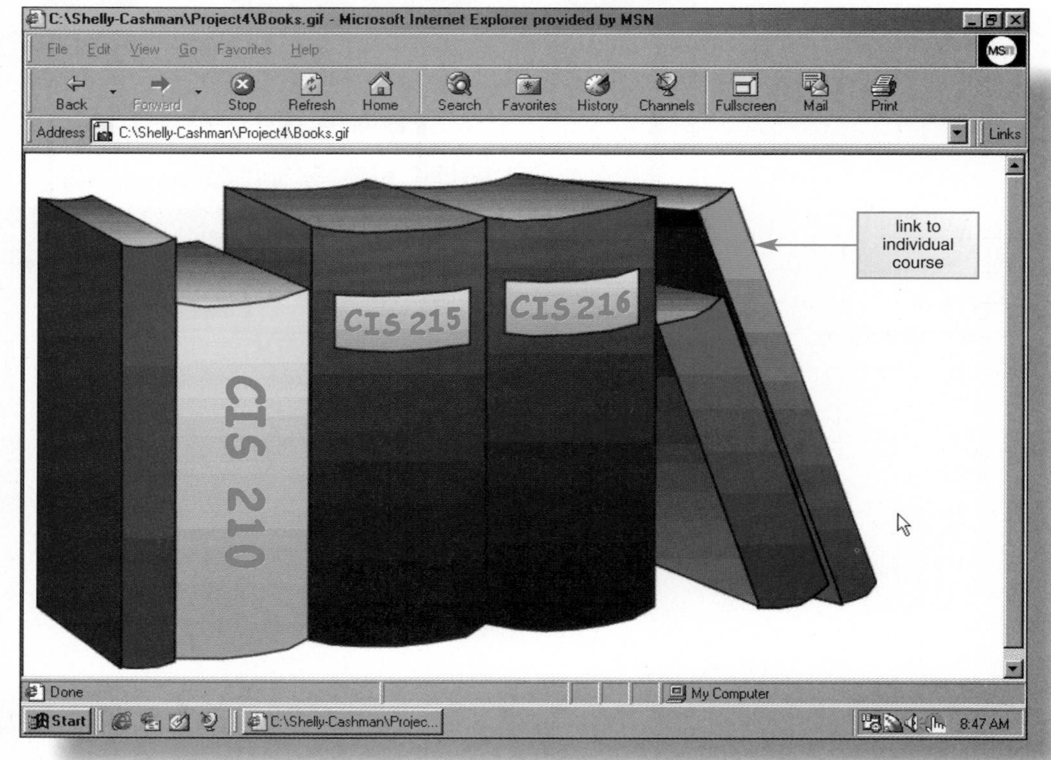

FIGURE 4-9

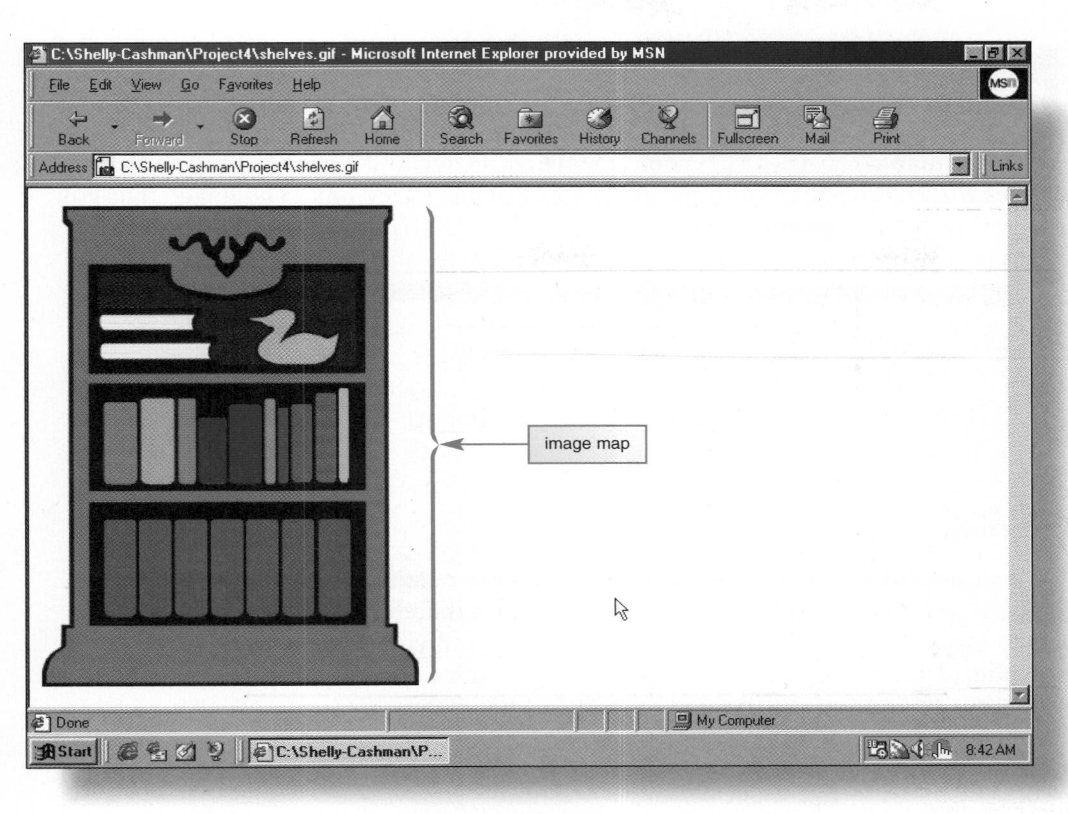

FIGURE 4-10

Server-Side versus Client-Side Image Maps

Two types of image maps exist: server-side and client-side. In a **server-side image map**, the image is displayed by the client (browser) and implemented by a program that runs on the Web server. When a Web page visitor clicks a link on a server-side image map, the browser sends the x- and y-coordinates of the mouse click to the Web server, which interprets them and then links the visitor to the site. Thus, the Web server does all of the work. Server-side image mapping has the advantage that it does not require a specific type or level of browser to support it.

Server-side image maps have disadvantages, however. They require that additional software runs on the Web server. Also, an image map available on a particular Web site's server must be registered to the server before it can be used. Although this process is simple, it must be done. Further, all changes to that registered image map must be coordinated with the Webmaster of that Web site; this reduces the Web developer's control over his or her image-mapped Web pages.

With a **client-side image map**, the browser does all of the work. It does not have to send the x- and y-coordinates of the mouse click to the Web server to be interpreted. Instead, the coordinates are included in the HTML file together with the URL (or location) of the link. In this project, you will create a client-side image map with three links on the Surf's Up home page.

More About

Server-Side versus Client-Side Maps

Web sites exist that provide information about server-side versus client-side image maps. To see an example of how image maps can be used for Web pages and which type is more efficient, visit the HTML More About Web page (www.scsite.com/html/more.htm) and click Maps.

Server-Side Image Maps

When a hotspot on an image map is clicked, a special image map program that is stored on the Web server is run. In addition, the browser also sends the x- and y-coordinates to the Web server for the position of the link on the image map. Most, if not all, browsers support server-side image map.

Image Map Components

An image map consists of two components: an image and a map definition that defines the linkable areas and the Web sites to which they link. The image that you use in this project (surfmap.gif) is stored on the HTML Data Disk. You add the HTML code necessary to define the map that creates the clickable areas.

Creating an image map for a Web page is a four-step process:

1. Select an image to use as an image map.
2. Sketch in the hotspots on the image.
3. Map the image coordinates for each hotspot.
4. Code the image map.

Selecting Images

Not all images are appropriate candidates for image mapping. An **appropriate image** is one that has obvious visual sections and therefore is a good choice as an image map. In Figure 4-11, you can easily select individual areas to serve as hotspots. The sections in this image are very distinct and easy to see. You can create numerous links from the varying sections of the image.

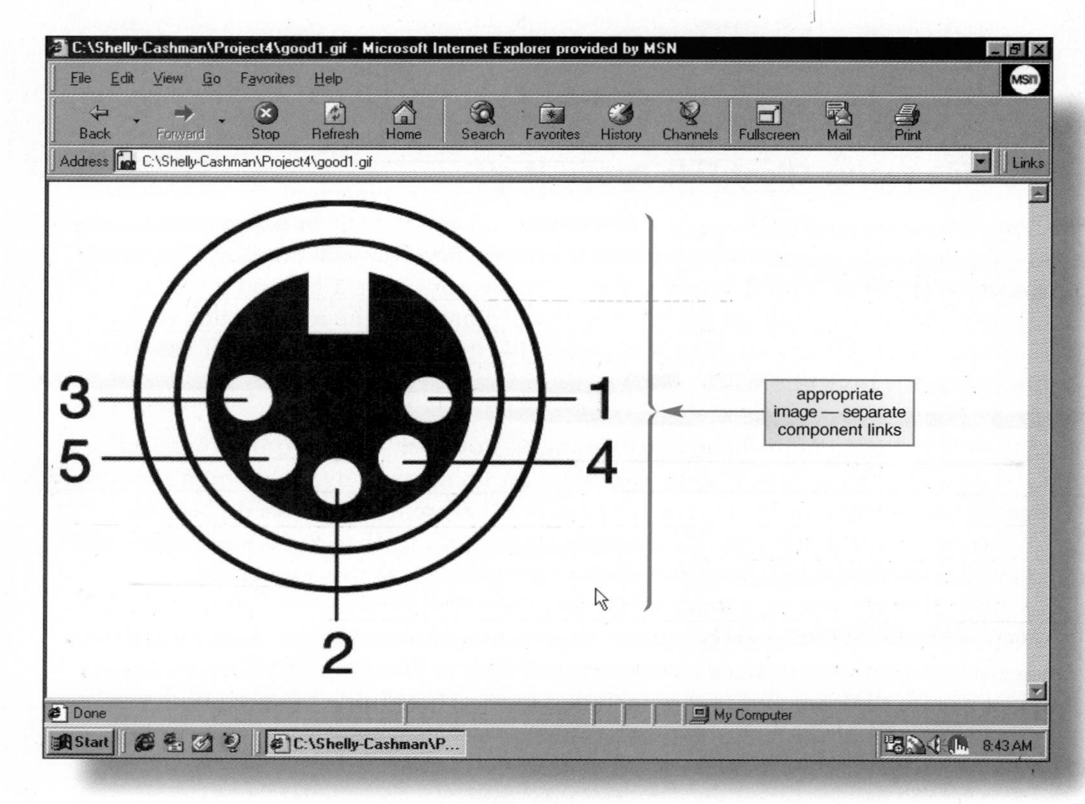

FIGURE 4-11

An **inappropriate image** is an image that does not have obvious visual sections and therefore is not a good choice as an image map. Figure 4-12 shows a sample of an image *not* suitable for image mapping because it has no distinct sections.

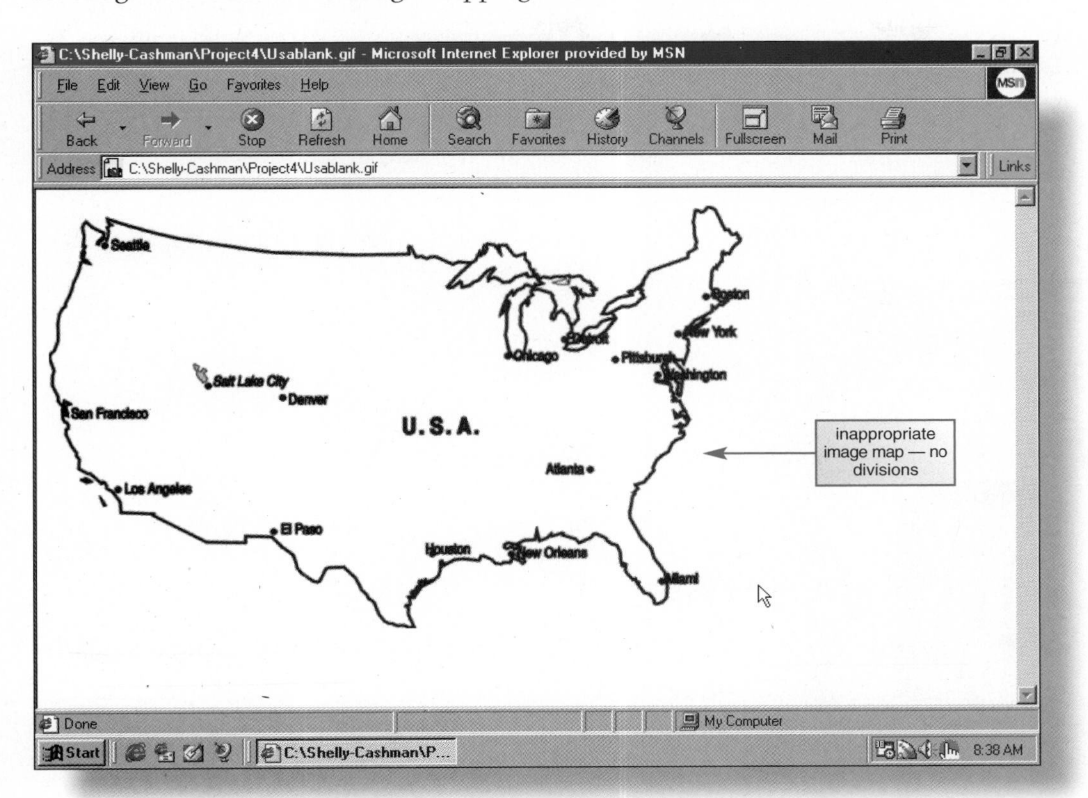

FIGURE 4-12

Sketching the Borders of Clickable Areas

After selecting an appropriate image for the Web page, sketch in the clickable areas within the image. Figure 4-13 on the next page shows an example of how a Web developer sketches in the areas of an image map. Here, a map of the United States is used, with each state serving as a different link. The image is divided into clickable areas that depict the various states.

Figure 4-14 on the next page is another example of sketching the various clickable areas to which links can be assigned. Each file drawer links to a different Web page, depending on the title of the drawer.

Figure 4-15 on the next page shows the image used for image mapping in this project, with the hotspots sketched in. This image, surfmap.gif, is stored on the HTML Data Disk. Each hotspot, represented by a surfer, will be a link to another Web page that contains information about the specific Surf's Up store. The x- and y-coordinates are determined from this initial sketch.

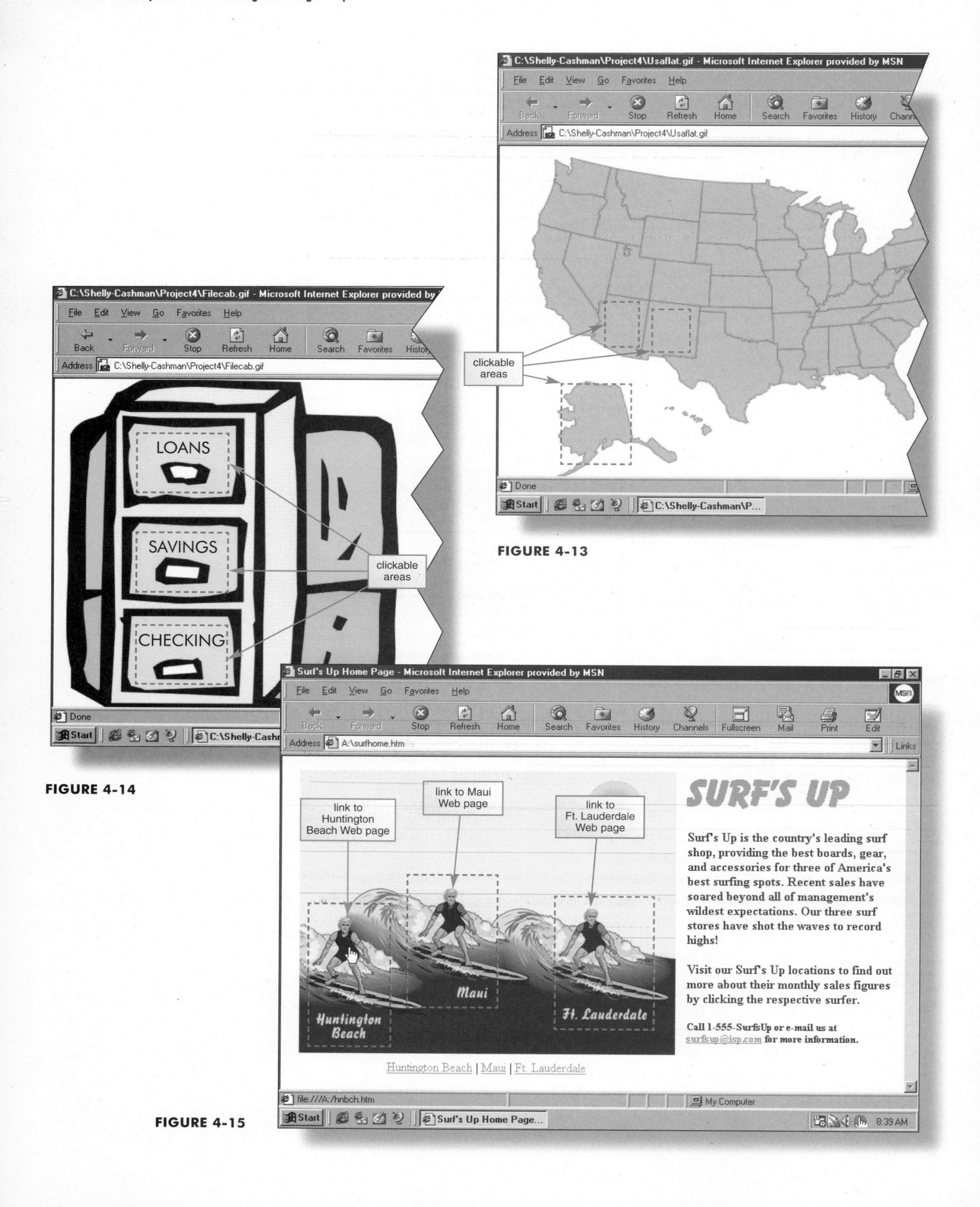

FIGURE 4-13

FIGURE 4-14

FIGURE 4-15

Mapping Coordinates

After you have determined how to divide the image into areas, you next find the x- and y-coordinates for those sections. These coordinates are relative to the x- and y-axes. The **x-axis** runs horizontally on the image, while the **y-axis** runs vertically. The top left-hand corner of the image in Figure 4-16 is coordinate point (0, 0). The first number of a **coordinate pair** is the x-coordinate, and the second number is the y-coordinate. Figure 4-16 shows some sample x- and y-coordinates in a Paint window that contains the image, surfmap.gif. The y-coordinate numbers increase as you move the mouse pointer down the image, and the x-coordinate numbers increase as you move the mouse pointer to the right on the image. As you move the mouse pointer, the coordinates of its position display in the status bar.

You may use a simple or a sophisticated paint program to determine these coordinates. In this project, you use Paint to find the x- and y-coordinates necessary to create the image map.

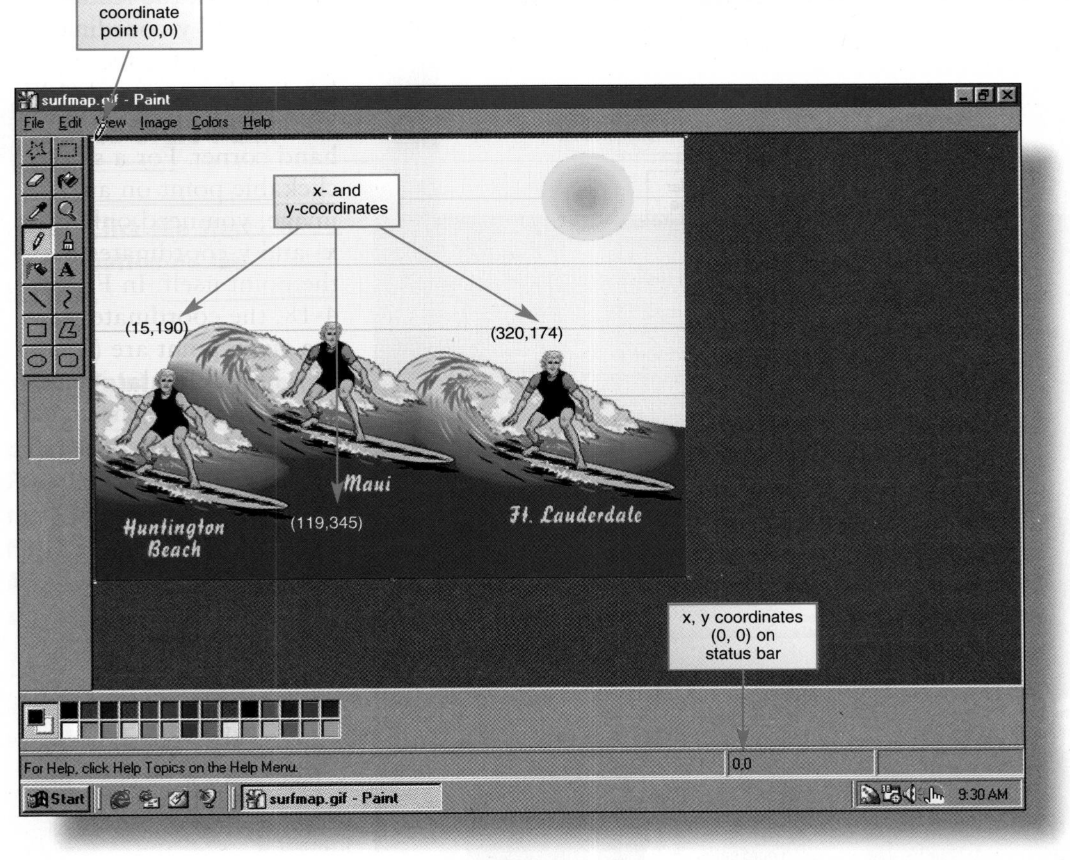

FIGURE 4-16

Coding the Map

The final step in image map creation is coding the map. The mapping tags <MAP> </MAP> and <AREA> are used in the HTML code. The map start tag (<MAP>) and map end tag (</MAP>) create a client-side image map. The <AREA> tag defines links and anchors. You use both of these tags, together with several attributes in this project. The x- and y-coordinates are inserted into the <AREA> tag with the COORDS attribute, within quotation marks and separated by commas.

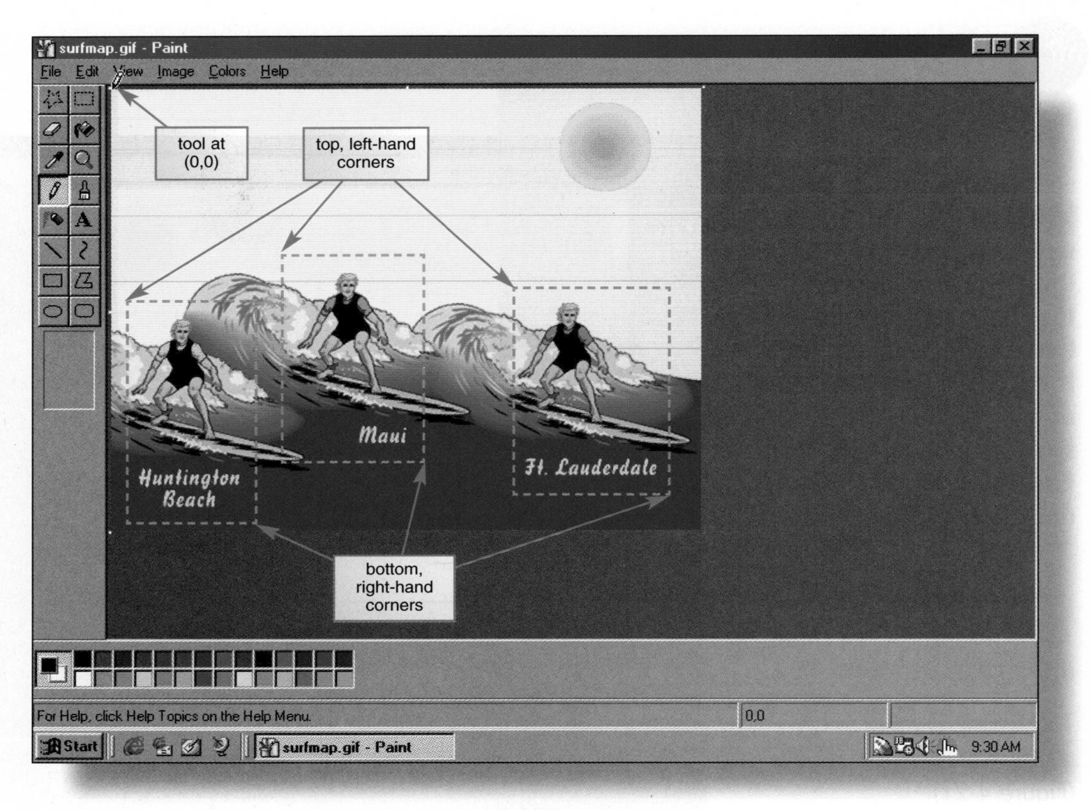

FIGURE 4-22

Table 4-1 shows the x- and y-coordinates for the top left-hand and bottom right-hand corners of all three rectangles. The first number is the x-coordinate, and the second number is the y-coordinate. For example, in the Huntington Beach rectangle, the top left-hand x-coordinate is 15 and the top left-hand y-coordinate is 190. The Huntington Beach bottom right-hand x-coordinate is 119 and the bottom right-hand y-coordinate is 345 (Table 4-1). These x- and y-coordinates (Figure 4-23) are used in the <AREA> tag necessary to build an image map.

Table 4-1

STORE LOCATION	*TOP LEFT-HAND X- AND Y-COORDINATES*	*BOTTOM RIGHT-HAND X- AND Y-COORDINATES*
Huntington Beach (points A and B)	(15, 190)	(119, 345)
Maui (points C and D)	(155,155)	(240, 292)
Ft. Lauderdale (points E and F)	(320, 174)	(438, 328)

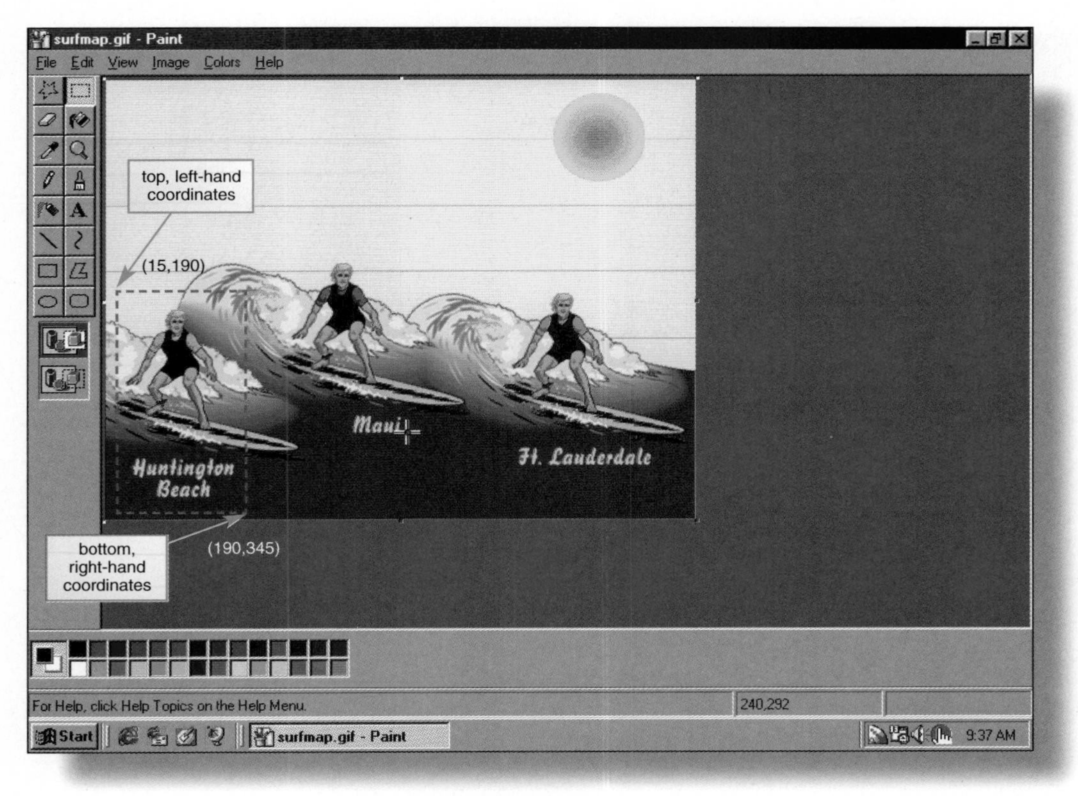

FIGURE 4-23

In the next steps, you practice locating the x- and y-coordinates of each clickable area by moving the mouse pointer to the corners as sketched. You will compare the coordinates with those in Table 4-1, which lists the exact coordinates that you use in the <AREA> tags.

To Locate the X- and Y-Coordinates

1 If necessary, click the Select button in the toolbox.

The Select button is indicated in Figure 4-24.

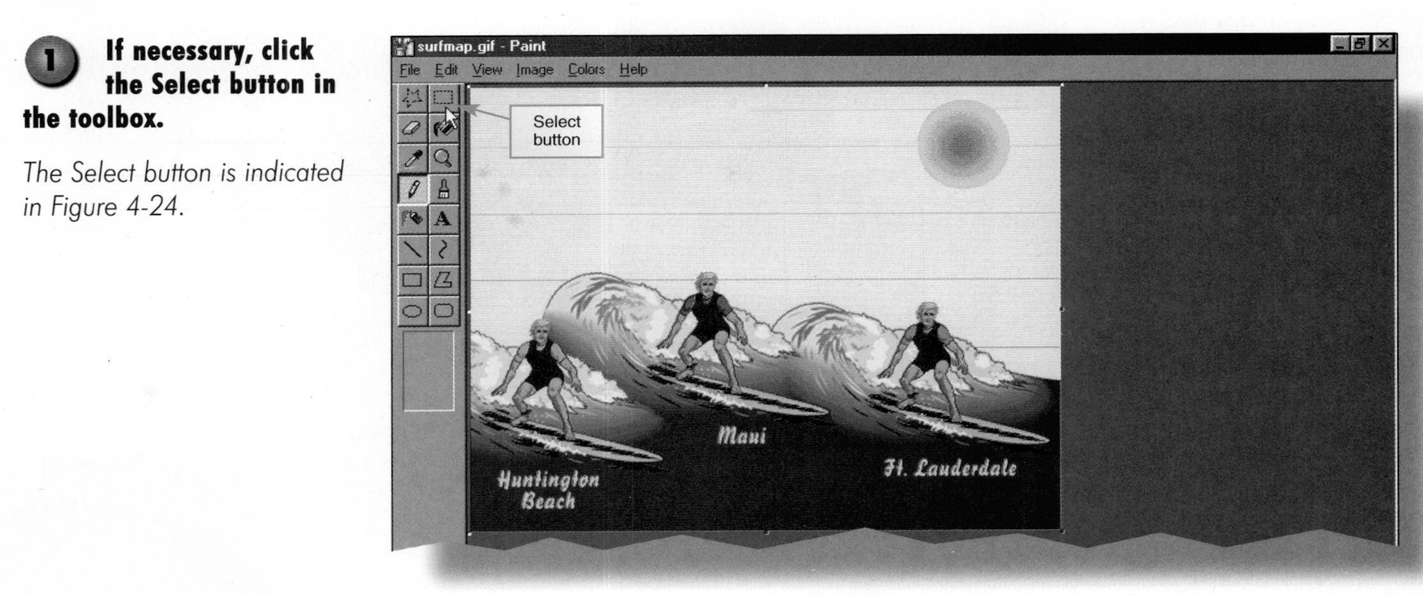

FIGURE 4-24

2 **Move the mouse pointer to coordinates (15, 190) as indicated in Figure 4-25. The x- and y-coordinates at the center of the mouse pointer display in the status bar and change as you move the mouse pointer within the drawing area.**

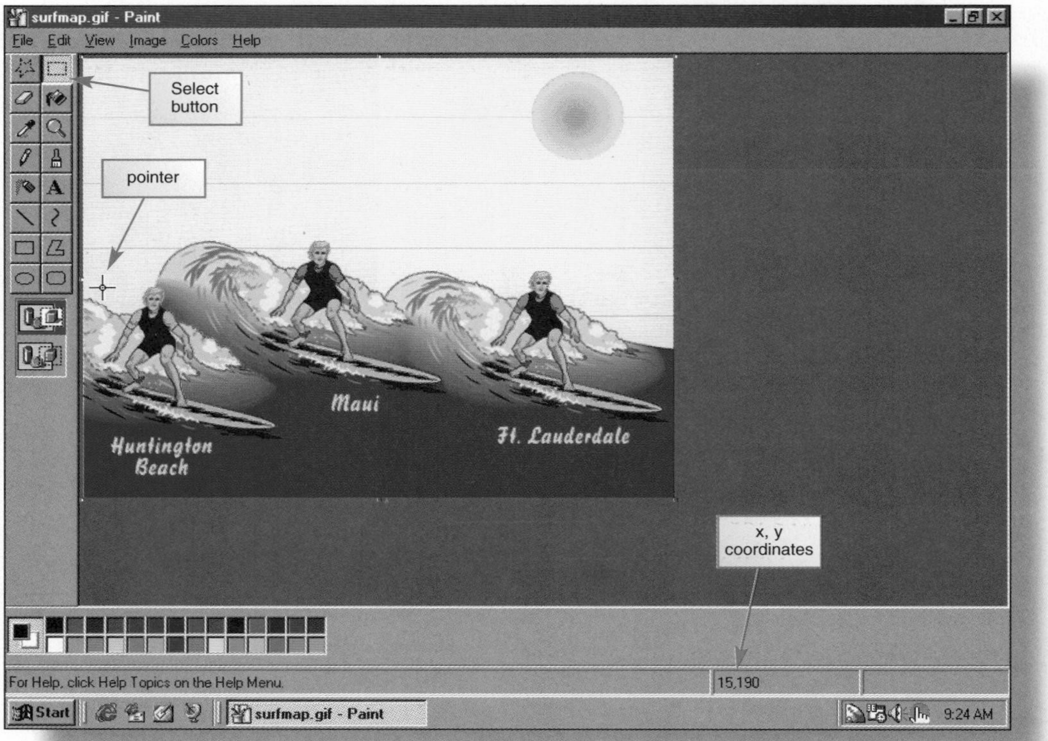

FIGURE 4-25

3 **Move the mouse pointer to coordinates (119, 345) as indicated in Figure 4-26.**

Point A indicates the top left-hand x- and y-coordinates, while point B indicates the bottom right-hand x- and y-coordinates (Figure 4-26).

4 **Move the mouse pointer to locations C, D, E, and F as indicated in Table 4-1 to verify the x- and y-coordinates.**

5 **To close Paint, click the Close button on the right-hand side of the title bar.**

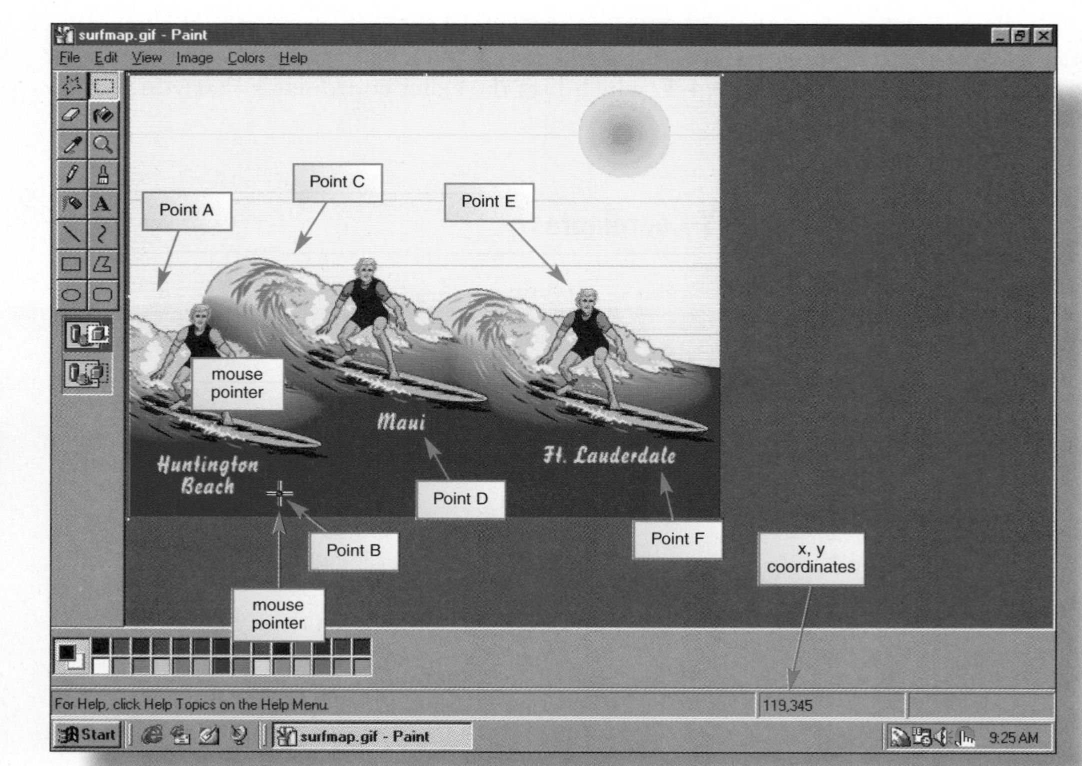

FIGURE 4-26

You have practiced locating the x- and y-coordinates given in Table 4-1 by moving the mouse to the top left-hand and bottom right-hand corners of the three sketched rectangles and compared the coordinates with those in the table. In later steps, you use these coordinates in the HTML code.

Coding the Image Map Using Tags and Attributes

After the design of the image map is complete, you are ready to start coding it using HTML tags. Table 4-2 shows the two main tags used for image mapping. Each of these has a number of attributes, which are discussed later in the project.

The <MAP></MAP> tags begin and end an image map. In the <AREA> tag, you insert the image shape (RECT in this project) and the x- and y-coordinates. An <AREA> tag is needed for each clickable area. The general syntax for the <AREA> tag is <AREA SHAPE=" " ALT=" " COORDS=" " HREF=" ">, where you define the shape of the clickable area, the alternate text, the x- and y-coordinates, and the URL for the link.

Table 4-2

TAG	*FUNCTION*
<MAP> </MAP>	• Creates a client-side image map
<AREA>	• Defines clickable areas within a <MAP> element • Defines links and anchors

Image Map Tag Attributes

The two main image mapping tags (<MAP></MAP> and <AREA>) have several attributes as given in Table 4-3. Also listed are the <IMG> tag attributes that are used in the creation of an image map.

In the following steps, Notepad is started and the HTML code is entered for the image map.

Table 4-3

TAG	*ATTRIBUTE*	*FUNCTION*
<MAP> </MAP>	NAME	• Defines the map's name
<AREA>	SHAPE	• Indicates the shape of the map area; possible values are RECT, POLY, CIRCLE, and POINT
	COORDS	• Indicates the points bounding the map area
	HREF	• Indicates the URL of the map area
	ALT	• Indicates the alternate text for image display
<IMG>	USEMAP	• Indicates the URL of a client-side image map
	ISMAP	• Indicates a server-side image map

Starting Notepad

Perform the following steps to start Notepad.

TO START NOTEPAD

1. Click the Start button on the taskbar.
2. Point to Programs on the Start menu, point to Accessories on the Programs submenu, and then click Notepad.
3. If necessary, click the Maximize button.
4. If necessary, click Edit on the menu bar and click WordWrap to turn on WordWrap.

The maximized Notepad window displays (Figure 4-27 on the next page).

HTML

In the following steps, you create the first row, which contains the surfmap.gif image map and the Surf's Up heading and text.

Steps To Create a Table

1 **If necessary, click line 6 and then press the ENTER key.**

2 **Type** `<TABLE ALIGN="LEFT" BORDER=0 COLS=2 ROWS=2>` **and then press the ENTER key.**

3 **Type** `<TR VALIGN="TOP">` **and then press the ENTER key.**

The HTML code displays (Figure 4-30) and the insertion point is on line 9.

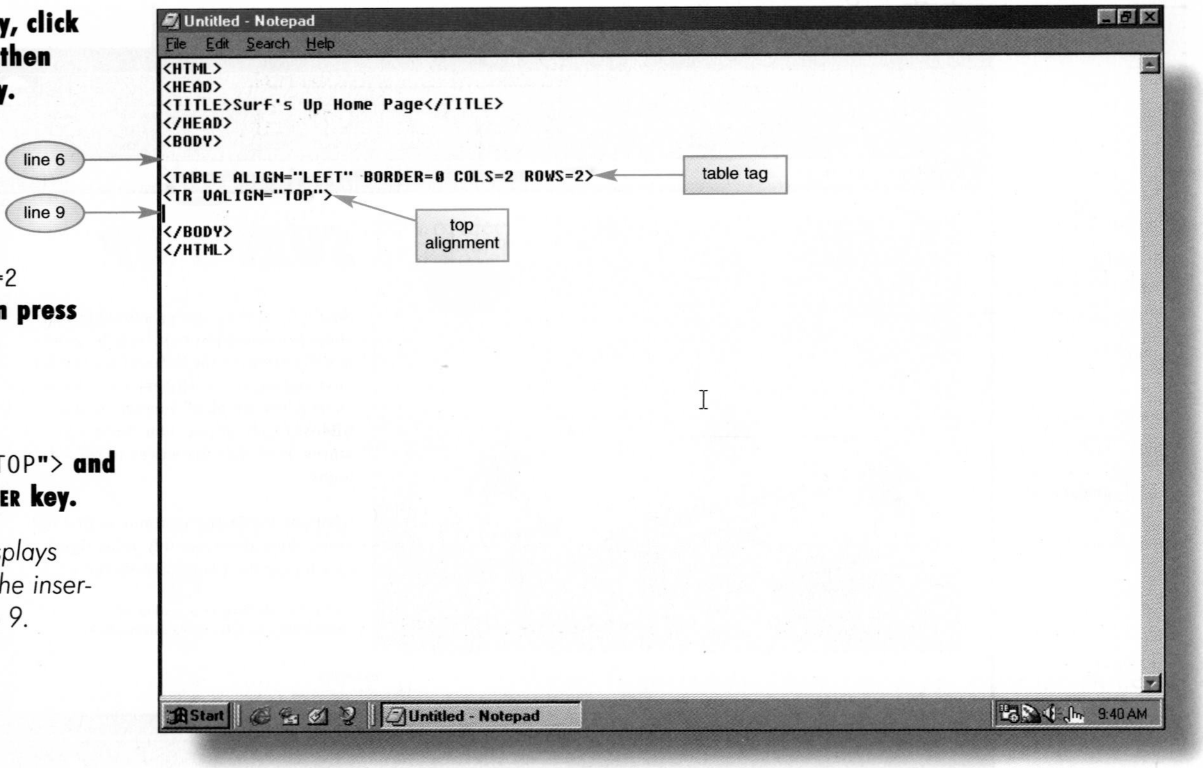

```
<HTML>
<HEAD>
<TITLE>Surf's Up Home Page</TITLE>
</HEAD>
<BODY>
<TABLE ALIGN="LEFT" BORDER=0 COLS=2 ROWS=2>
<TR VALIGN="TOP">

</BODY>
</HTML>
```

line 6
line 9
table tag
top alignment

FIGURE 4-30

You now have created a table and started to create the first row. You vertically aligned the text and image to the top of the cell in the first row, and therefore the top of the table, by using the <TR> tag. In the next set of steps, you insert the image that is used for the image map.

Inserting an Image

For the image map, use the surfmap.gif image on the HTML Data Disk. In later steps, you will divide this image into three link sections using the <AREA> tag. When you insert the image, you will use four attributes in the <IMG> tag — SCR, HSPACE, USEMAP, and BORDER — shown as follows:

```
<TD><IMG SRC="surfmap.gif" HSPACE="10" USEMAP="#surf" BORDER=0>
```

The HSPACE="10" attribute adds 10 pixels of horizontal space between the image and the text. If you do not insert this horizontal space, the text will run right up against the image, as shown in Figure 4-31.

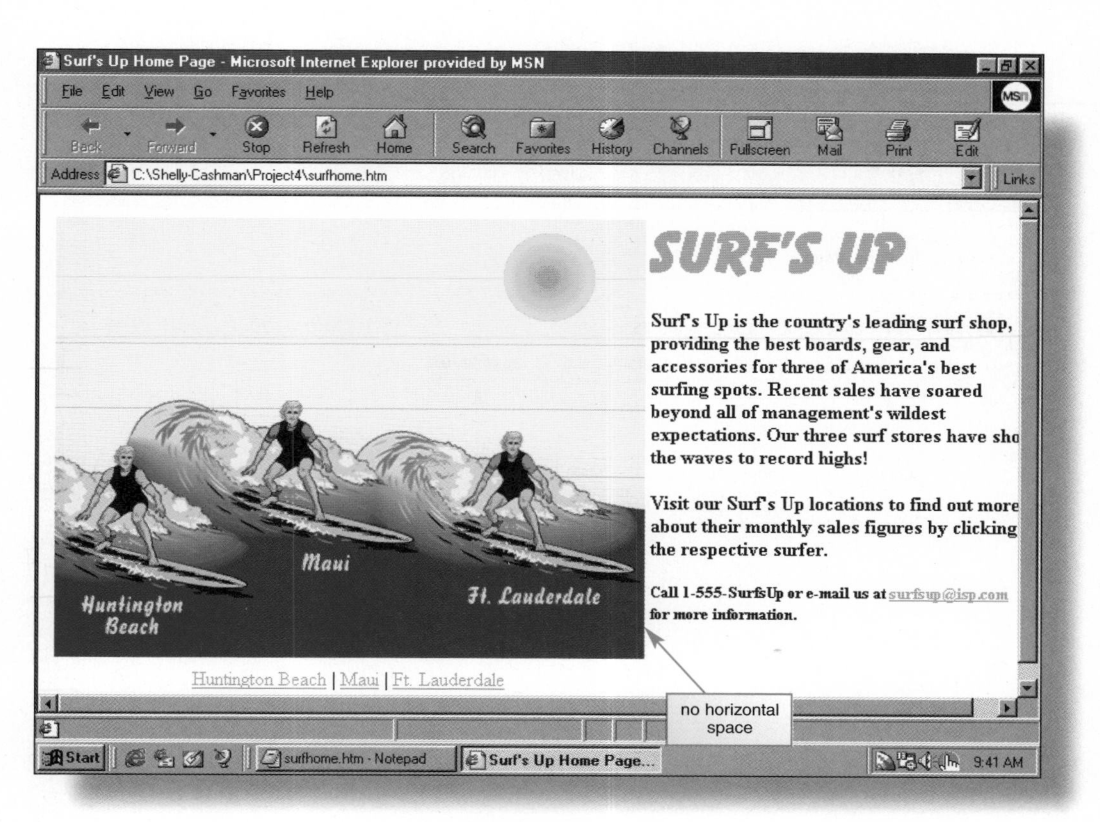

FIGURE 4-31

Generally speaking, the USEMAP attribute indicates the URL of a client-side image map. It tells the browser to use the map, called the *target*, which is defined later in the HTML code within the <MAP> tag. Later in this project, you will set a target named "surf" in the <MAP> tag by using <MAP NAME="surf">. USEMAP="surf" indicates that the browser should use the "surf" target as its image map source.

Finally, the BORDER=0 attribute creates a borderless image. A border is not needed for this table because the table simply allows flexibility in the design of the Web page.

Accessibility

Developers should utilize suggestions from accessibility guidelines when developing Web pages. With image maps, it is suggested that developers either use the ALT attribute with the <AREA> tag, or the MAP element with A elements (and other text) as content. Text can be output to speech synthesizers and braille displays, and can be presented visually on computer monitors and paper. For more information, visit the HTML More About page (www.scsite.com/html/more.htm) and click Accessibility.

Steps To Insert an Image

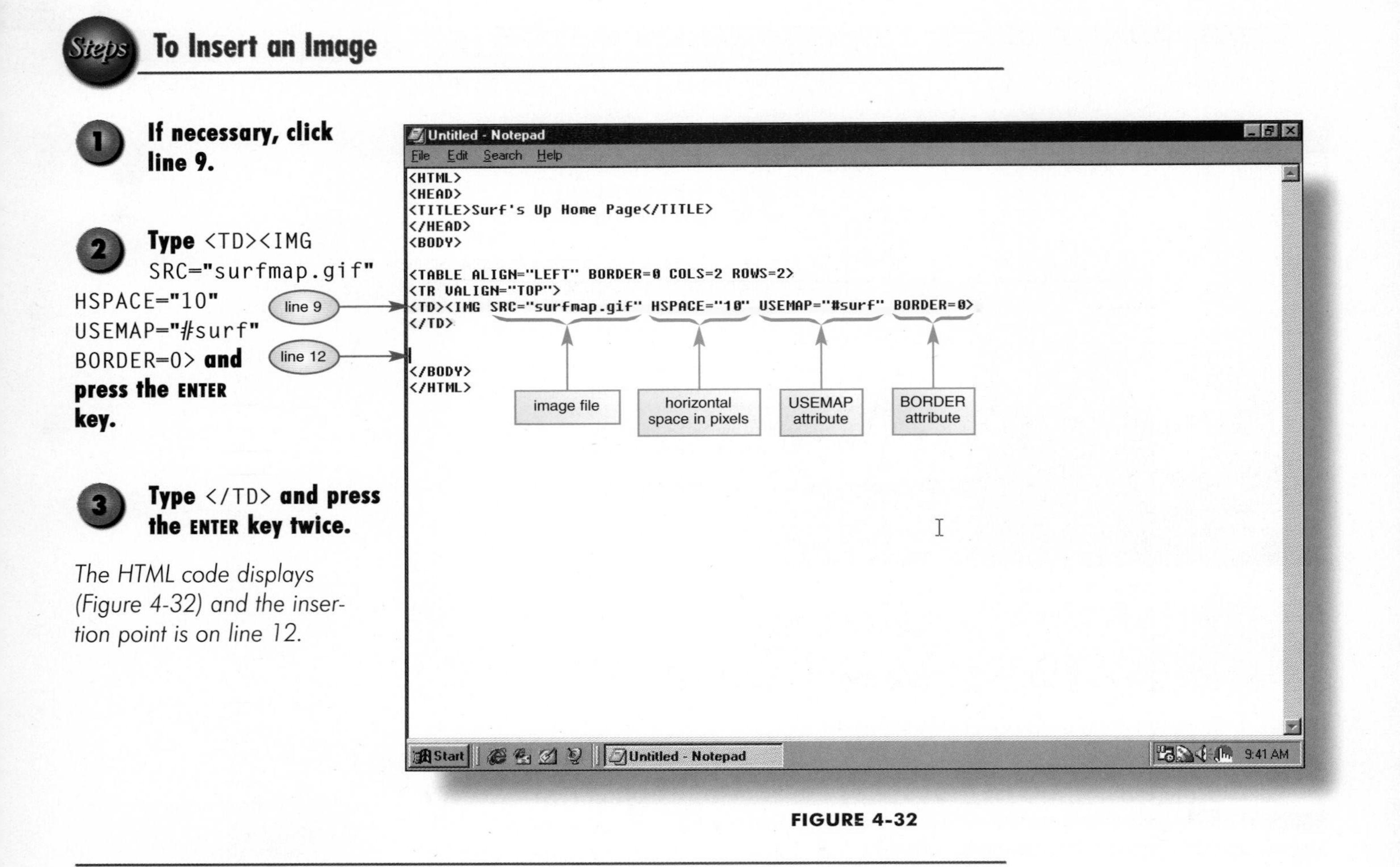

1. **If necessary, click line 9.**

2. **Type** `<TD><IMG SRC="surfmap.gif" HSPACE="10" USEMAP="#surf" BORDER=0>` **and press the ENTER key.**

3. **Type** `</TD>` **and press the ENTER key twice.**

The HTML code displays (Figure 4-32) and the insertion point is on line 12.

FIGURE 4-32

The image is inserted as a result of these steps, and the USEMAP target is specified. In later HTML code, you will set a target named "surf", to which USEMAP points. In the next steps, you use the <FONT> tag to create the Surf's Up heading, which is a large-sized font and a unique font face in an orange color.

Inserting a Heading

The <FONT> tag offers many different attributes. Some of these — SIZE, FACE, and COLOR — are used in the next set of steps. In addition, the heading is made boldfaced. Here is the HTML code:

```
<TD><B><FONT SIZE="+4" FACE="BAZOOKA" COLOR="#FF8429">SURF'S UP</FONT>
```

A heading should be more noticeable than the standard text. One simple way to distinguish text is to make it boldfaced. Another is to use a relative font size that is larger (+4 in this project) than the text. Relative font sizing is discussed in Project 2. Using a different font face or color or both also makes a heading stand out; in this project, you use the Bazooka font in an orange color. As mentioned in Project 2, if your system does not have the Bazooka font, it will default to the standard system font.

TO INSERT A HEADING

1. If necessary, click line 12.
2. Type <TD><B><FONT SIZE="+4" FACE="BAZOOKA" COLOR="#FF8429">SURF'S UP</FONT> and then press the ENTER key twice.

The HTML code displays (Figure 4-33) and the insertion point is on line 14.

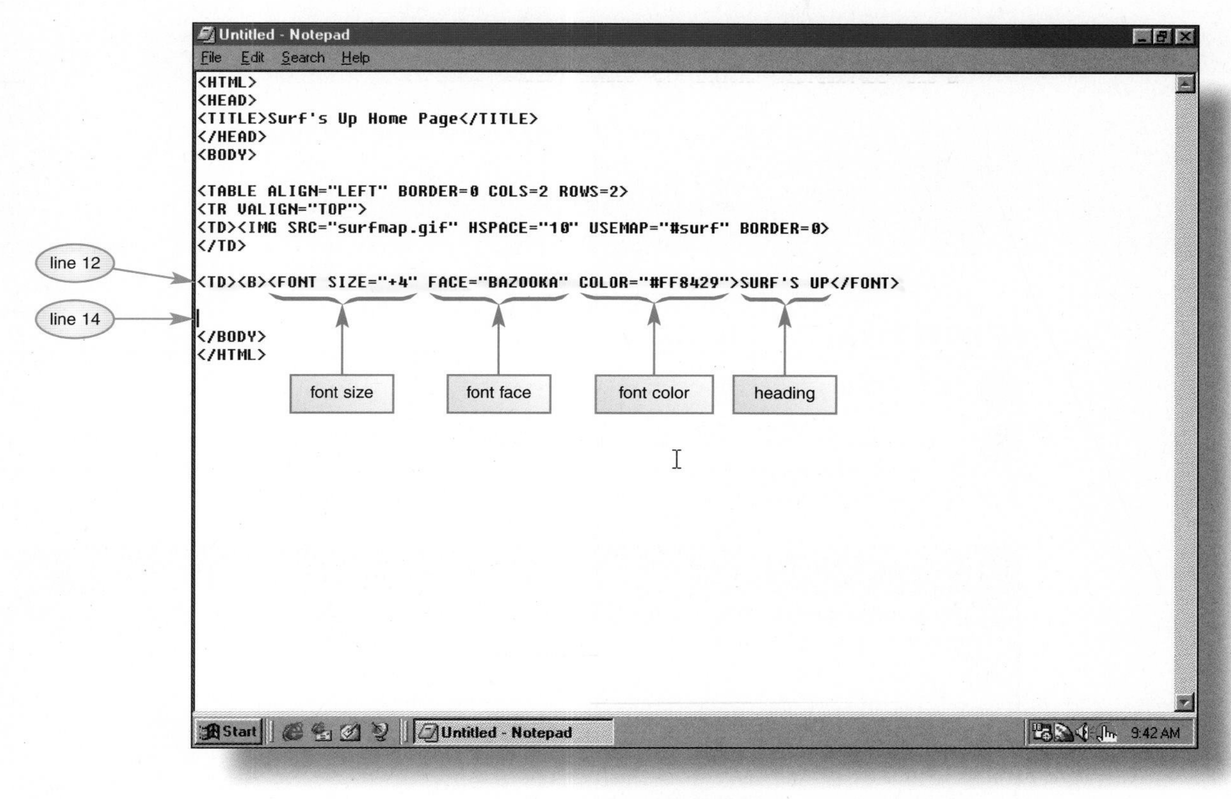

FIGURE 4-33

The </FONT> tag turns off all attributes, in this case size, face, and color, of the heading so that they do not apply to the text that follows. Any text entered after the </FONT> tag will be standard black text and of the size used for text on the page. Note that you explicitly need to turn off the bold by using the end tag, </B>. This was not done, so all text in the paragraphs that follow the heading will display boldfaced. The boldfacing is ended after the third paragraph (line 23 in Table 4-4 on the next page).

Inserting a Paragraph

The table on the Surf's Up home page contains three paragraphs of text in the right-hand column of the first row, as indicated by the three <P></P> tags (see Table 4-4). As mentioned in Project 2, you should always include an e-mail address on the home page for visitor contact. An e-mail link is included in the third paragraph. In the steps on the next page, you enter the tags and paragraphs of text given in Table 4-4.

Table 4-4

LINE	HTML TAGS AND TEXT
14	<P>Surf's Up is the country's leading surf shop, providing the best boards, gear, and
15	accessories for three of America's best surfing spots. Recent sales have soared beyond all of
16	management's wildest expectations. Our three surf stores have shot the waves to record
17	highs!</P>
18	
19	<P>Visit our Surf's Up locations to find out more about their monthly sales figures by
20	clicking the respective surfer.</P>
21	
22	<P><FONT SIZE="-1">Call 1-555-SurfsUp or e-mail us at
23	<A HREF="mailto:surfsup@isp.com">surfsup@isp.com</A> for more information.</FONT></P></B>
24	</TD>
25	</TR>

TO ENTER PARAGRAPHS OF TEXT

1. If necessary, click line 14.
2. Enter the HTML code shown in Table 4-4 and then press the ENTER key.

The HTML code displays (Figure 4-34) and the insertion point is on line 26.

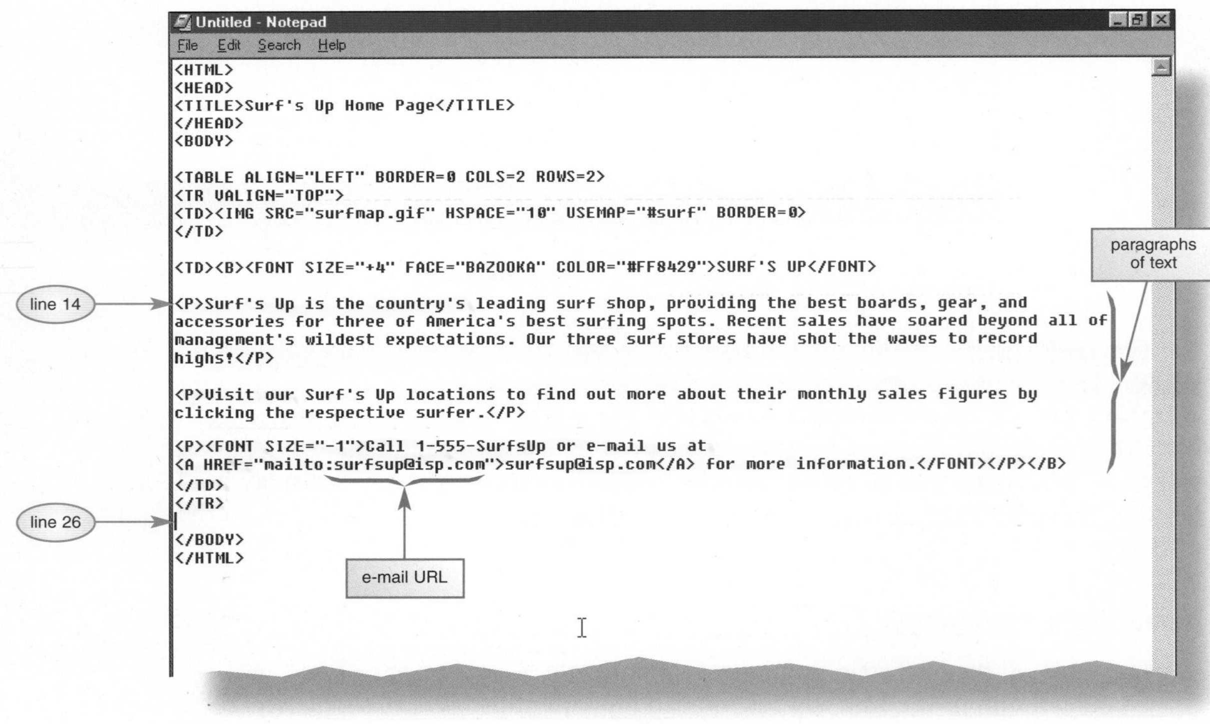

FIGURE 4-34

You created a borderless table and inserted in it an image, surfmap.gif, from the HTML Data Disk. This image is shown in Figure 4-1a on page HTM 4.5. You also entered a heading and paragraphs of text, including an e-mail link. This completes the first row of the table on the Surf's Up home page.

Creating Text Links

Next, you insert the text links in the second row of the table. Because some Web page visitors turn off the image display in their browsers in order to speed up Web page downloading, it is important that you provide text links to all URLs that have an image link. In the following steps, you create the three link sections on the image map and the three corresponding text links to the corresponding URLs. To separate the text links, you use the | symbol. Although it is not necessary to place each file name on a separate line, it does improve the readability of the HTML code. This is shown at the ends of lines 27 and 28 in Table 4-5. In the next steps, you enter the tags and paragraphs of text given in the table to create text links.

Table 4-5

LINE	HTML TAGS AND TEXT
26	<TR>
27	<TD ALIGN="CENTER"><A HREF="hnbch.htm">Huntington Beach</A> |
28	<A HREF="maui.htm">Maui</A> |
29	<A HREF="ftlaud.htm">Ft. Lauderdale</A>
30	</TD>
31	</TR>
32	</TABLE>

TO CREATE TEXT LINKS

1. If necessary, click line 26.
2. Enter the HTML code shown in Table 4-5 and press the ENTER key twice.

The HTML code displays (Figure 4-35) and the insertion point is on line 34.

```
<TR VALIGN="TOP">
<TD><IMG SRC="surfmap.gif" HSPACE="10" USEMAP="#surf" BORDER=0>
</TD>

<TD><B><FONT SIZE="+4" FACE="BAZOOKA" COLOR="#FF8429">SURF'S UP</FONT>

<P>Surf's Up is the country's leading surf shop, providing the best boards, gear, and
accessories for three of America's best surfing spots. Recent sales have soared beyond all of
management's wildest expectations. Our three surf stores have shot the waves to record
highs!</P>

<P>Visit our Surf's Up locations to find out more about their monthly sales figures by
clicking the respective surfer.</P>

<P><FONT SIZE=-1>Call 1-555-SurfsUp or e-mail us at
<A HREF="mailto:surfsup@isp.com">surfsup@isp.com</A> for more information.</FONT></P></B>
</TD>
</TR>
<TR>
<TD ALIGN=CENTER><A HREF="hnbch.htm">Huntington Beach</A> |
<A HREF="maui.htm">Maui</A> |
<A HREF="ftlaud.htm">Ft. Lauderdale</A>
</TD>
</TR>
</TABLE>


</BODY>
</HTML>
```

line 26

line 34

text links

Start | Untitled - Notepad | 9:45 PM

FIGURE 4-35

Lines 27, 28, and 29 create three links to the other Web pages on the Surf's Up site. The home page table ends with line 32. The borderless table on the Surf's Up home page is complete.

The image, surfmap.gif, already is specified in the <IMG> tag on line 9. The browser uses this image for the image map. The next set of steps creates three linkable areas from the surfmap.gif image by mapping the coordinates for the image map.

Creating an Image Map

The <AREA> tag has three attributes — SHAPE, COORDS, and HREF — shown as follows:

```
<AREA SHAPE="RECT" COORDS="15,190,119,345" HREF="hnbch.htm">
```

The SHAPE attribute with the RECT value defines the linkable section as a rectangle. Other possible values are CIRCLE, POLY(polygon), and POINT. The COORDS attribute sets the coordinates, with the coordinates separated by commas. In a rectangle, the first two numbers indicate the x- and y-coordinates of the top left-hand corner of the rectangle. The next two numbers denote the x- and y-coordinates of the bottom right-hand corner of the rectangle. In this example, a Web page visitor clicking anywhere within the rectangle bordered by x, y (15, 190) and x, y (119, 345) will link to the Web page hnbch.htm. Finally, the HREF attribute designates the URL of the link.

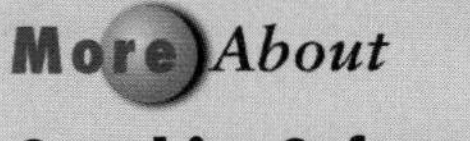

Graphics Software

Many graphics tools are available for advanced image creation and maintenance. One of the more popular tools is Adobe Photoshop. Photoshop allows you to create images that can be used as image maps or crop sections out of existing images. For more information, visit the HTML More About Web page (www.scsite.com/html/more.htm) and click Graphics Software.

If you had to insert the <AREA> tag for the circle, point, and polygon shapes shown in Figure 4-18 on page HTM 4.16, the tags would be as follows:

```
<AREA SHAPE="CIRCLE" COORDS="388,154,71" HREF="hnbch.htm">
<AREA SHAPE="POINT" COORDS="237,75" HREF="hnbch.htm">
<AREA SHAPE="POLY" COORDS="78,309,183,251,316,262,317,344,136,402"
HREF="hnbch.htm">
```

Three clickable areas are created in the image map on the Surf's Up home page for the three location links: Huntington Beach, Maui, and Ft. Lauderdale. All three clickable areas are rectangular in shape, as defined in Table 4-6. The x- and y-coordinates differ because each section is in a different area of the image. The coordinates are taken from Table 4-1 on page HTM 4.20. In the next steps, you enter the tags and paragraphs of text given in Table 4-6 to create the image map on the surfmap.gif image.

Table 4-6

LINE	HTML TAGS AND TEXT
34	`<MAP NAME="surf">`
35	`<AREA SHAPE="RECT" COORDS="15,190,119,345" HREF="hnbch.htm">`
36	`<AREA SHAPE="RECT" COORDS="155,155,240,292" HREF="maui.htm">`
37	`<AREA SHAPE="RECT" COORDS="320,174,438,328" HREF="ftlaud.htm">`
38	`</MAP>`

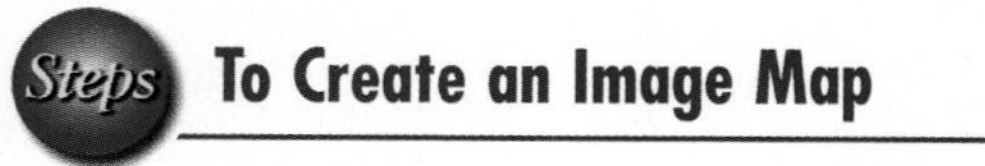

To Create an Image Map

1. **If necessary, click line 34.**
2. **Enter the HTML code shown in Table 4-6.**

The HTML code displays (Figure 4-36).

```
<TABLE ALIGN="LEFT" BORDER=0 COLS=2 ROWS=2>
<TR VALIGN="TOP">
<TD><IMG SRC="surfmap.gif" HSPACE="10" USEMAP="#surf" BORDER=0>
</TD>

<TD><B><FONT SIZE="+4" FACE="BAZOOKA" COLOR="#FF8429">SURF'S UP</FONT>

<P>Surf's Up is the country's leading surf shop, providing the best boards, gear, and
accessories for three of America's best surfing spots. Recent sales have soared beyond all of
management's wildest expectations. Our three surf stores have shot the waves to record
highs!</P>

<P>Visit our Surf's Up locations to find out more about their monthly sales figures by
clicking the respective surfer.</P>

<P><FONT SIZE="-1">Call 1-555-SurfsUp or e-mail us at
<A HREF="mailto:surfsup@isp.com">surfsup@isp.com</A> for more information.</P></B>
</TD>
</TR>
<TR>
<TD ALIGN="CENTER"><A HREF="hnbch.htm">Huntington Beach</A> |
<A HREF="maui.htm">Maui</A> |
<A HREF="ftlaud.htm">Ft. Lauderdale</A>
</TD>
</TR>
</TABLE>

<MAP NAME="surf">
<AREA SHAPE="RECT" COORDS="15,190,119,345" HREF="hnbch.htm">
<AREA SHAPE="RECT" COORDS="155,155,240,292" HREF="maui.htm">
<AREA SHAPE="RECT" COORDS="320,174,438,328" HREF="ftlaud.htm">
</MAP>
</BODY>
</HTML>
```


FIGURE 4-36

The image map is complete. On line 34 in Table 4-6, you named the map "surf," which can be used by the USEMAP attribute in the <IMG> tag. Lines 35 through 37 set three separate areas as hotspots by naming the top right-hand and the bottom left-hand x- and y-coordinates. A Web page visitor who clicks any of these hotspots will link to the appropriate URL as indicated by the HREF attribute. The map ends with the </MAP> tag on line 38. The next task is to change the color of the links to maintain consistent color throughout the Web page.

Changing Link Colors

Text link colors vary as the status of the link changes. The standard color of a normal (unvisited) link is blue in most browsers. A clicked (visited) link generally is green or purple. An active link varies in color depending on the browser. To maintain color consistency on this Web page, you change the colors of the links so that they always match the color of the heading (#FF8429). To do this, you make the color changes to the normal link (LINK), active link (ALINK), and visited link (VLINK) attributes in the <BODY> tag.

Steps To Change Link Colors

1 Click immediately to the right of the Y in <BODY> on line 5 and press the SPACEBAR.

2 Type `LINK="#FF8429" ALINK="#FF8429" VLINK="#FF8429"`**.**

The HTML code displays (Figure 4-37).

Untitled - Notepad

File Edit Search Help

```
<HTML>
<HEAD>
<TITLE>Surf's Up Home Page</TITLE>
</HEAD>
<BODY LINK="#FF8429" ALINK="#FF8429" VLINK="#FF8429">

<TABLE ALIGN="LEFT" BORDER=0 COLS=2 ROWS=2>
<TR VALIGN="TOP">
<TD><IMG SRC="surfmap.gif" HSPACE="10" USEMAP="#surf" BORDER=0>
</TD>

<TD><B><FONT SIZE="+4" FACE="BAZOOKA" COLOR="#FF8429">SURF'S UP</FONT>

<P>Surf's Up is the country's leading surf shop, providing the best boards, gear, and
accessories for three of America's best surfing spots. Recent sales have soared beyond all of
management's wildest expectations. Our three surf stores have shot the waves to record
highs!</P>
```

link color changes

FIGURE 4-37

surfhome.htm

```
<HTML>
<HEAD>
<TITLE>Surf's Up Home Page</TITLE>
</HEAD>
<BODY LINK="#FF8429" ALINK="#FF8429" VLINK="#FF8429">

<TABLE ALIGN="LEFT" BORDER=0 COLS=2 ROWS=2>
<TR VALIGN="TOP">
<TD><IMG SRC="surfmap.gif" HSPACE="10" USEMAP="#surf" BORDER=0>
</TD>

<TD><B><FONT SIZE="+4" FACE="BAZOOKA" COLOR="#FF8429">SURF'S
UP</FONT>

<P>Surf's Up is the country's leading surf shop, providing the
best boards, gear, and
accessories for three of America's best surfing spots. Recent
sales have soared beyond all of
management's wildest expectations. Our three surf stores have shot
the waves to record
highs!</P>

<P>Visit our Surf's Up locations to find out more about their
monthly sales figures by
clicking the respective surfer.</P>

<P><FONT SIZE="-1">Call 1-555-SurfsUp or e-mail us at
<A HREF="mailto:surfsup@isp.com">surfsup@isp.com</A> for more
information.</FONT></P></B>
</TD>
</TR>
<TR>
<TD ALIGN="CENTER"><A HREF="hnbch.htm">Huntington Beach</A> |
<A HREF="maui.htm">Maui</A> |
<A HREF="ftlaud.htm">Ft. Lauderdale</A>
</TD>
</TR>
</TABLE>

<MAP NAME="surf">
<AREA SHAPE="RECT" COORDS="15,190,119,345" HREF="hnbch.htm">
<AREA SHAPE="RECT" COORDS="155,155,240,292" HREF="maui.htm">
<AREA SHAPE="RECT" COORDS="320,174,438,328" HREF="ftlaud.htm">
</MAP>
</BODY>
</HTML>
```

Page 1

FIGURE 4-38

The HTML code for the Surf's Up home page is complete. The next step is to save and print the HTML file.

TO SAVE AND PRINT THE HTML FILE

1. With the HTML Data Disk in drive A, click File on the menu bar and then click Save As on the File menu.
2. Type `surfhome.htm` in the File name text box. If necessary, change to 3½ Floppy (A:) in the Save in box. Click the Save button in the Save As dialog box.
3. Click File on the menu bar and then click Print.

The HTML file is saved to drive A, and a hard copy prints (Figure 4-38).

Viewing and Printing the Web Page Using Your Browser

Just as you did in all previous projects, you should view the saved HTML file using your browser. When the home page displays, you can click the e-mail hyperlink to verify that it works correctly. You also can test the links to the Maui and Ft. Lauderdale Surf's Up locations by clicking the corresponding mapped areas of the image. These links work at this time because maui.htm and ftlaud.htm are stored on the HTML Data Disk. You can test both the hotspots and the text links at the bottom of the Web page. The link to Huntington Beach (hnbch.htm) cannot be tested because this is a Web page that you will create later in this project.

Steps: To View and Print the Web Page Using Your Browser

1. **Start your browser.**
2. **Type** `a:\surfhome.htm` **in the Address text box and then press the ENTER key.**

The browser displays the home page (Figure 4-39).

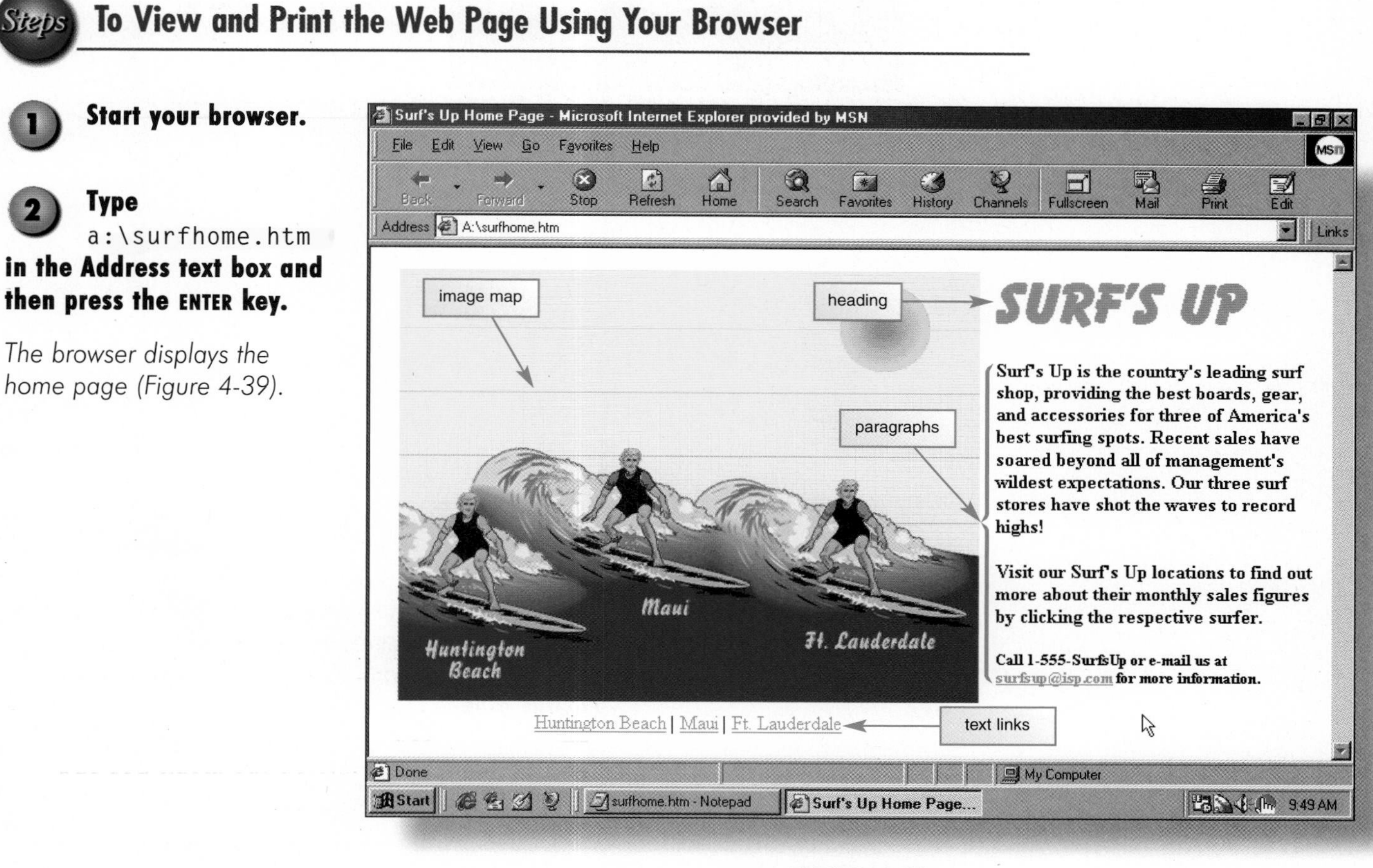

FIGURE 4-39

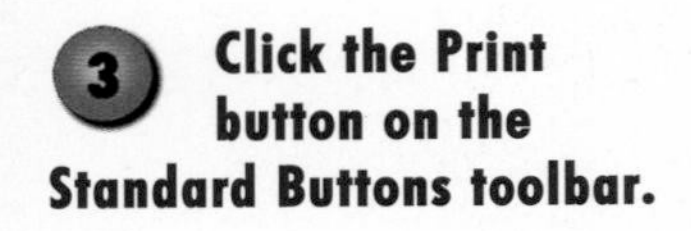

3 Click the Print button on the Standard Buttons toolbar.

The home page prints (Figure 4-40).

FIGURE 4-40

If there are any errors, double-check the spelling, symbols, and quotation marks in the HTML code. Then save the HTML file and redisplay the Web page using the Refresh button in your browser.

Creating a Second Web Page

Each Surf's Up store location (Huntington Beach, Maui, and Ft. Lauderdale) has a separate Web page that describes its products and lists its sales figures for the past seven months. The individual store location Web pages also have links to the home page, as well as to all other Web pages in the Web site. This section shows you how to create one of those Web pages (Huntington Beach), shown in Figure 4-41. The other two pages (Maui and Ft. Lauderdale) are both stored on the HTML Data Disk and are not altered.

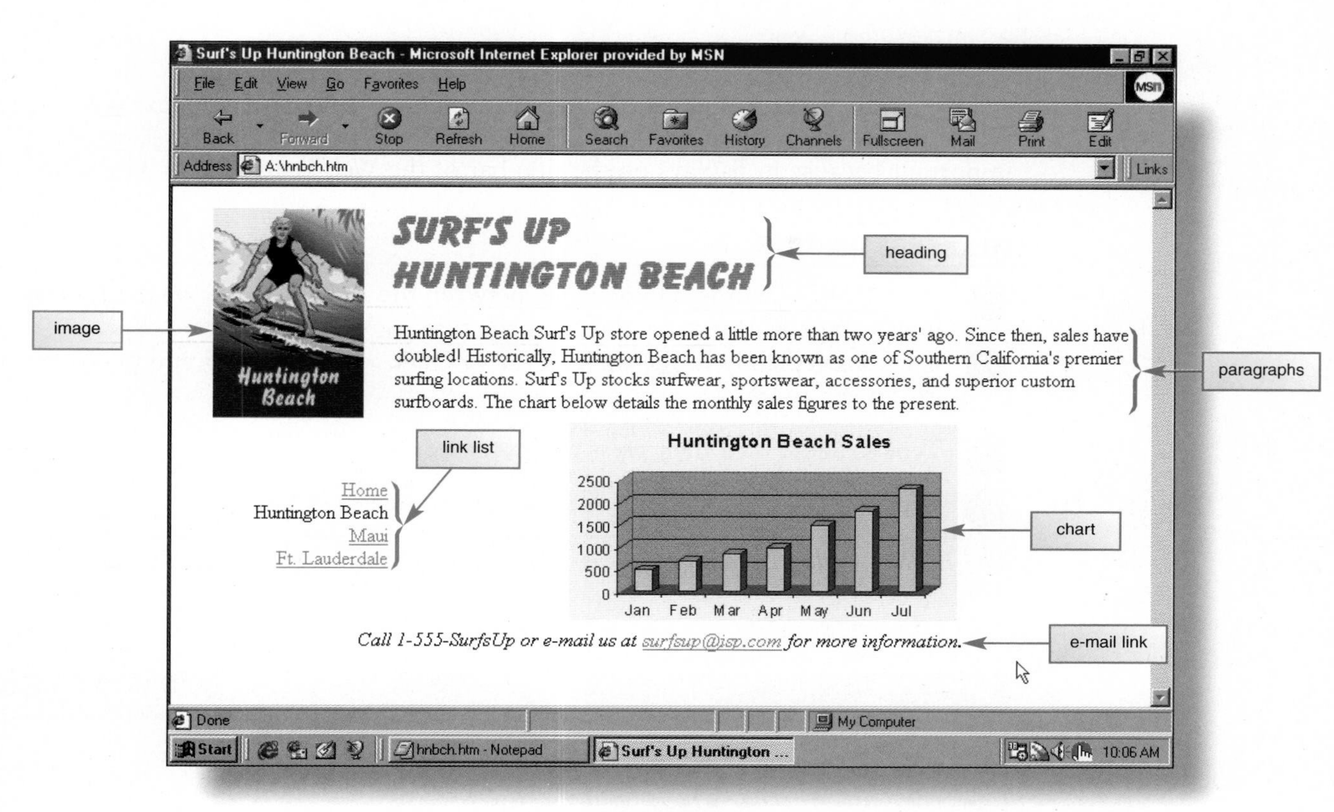

FIGURE 4-41

The easiest way to begin the second Web page is to copy applicable HTML tags from the home page to the second page. The first five lines of HTML code in the home page can be used in the second page, hnbch.htm.

TO COPY HTML CODE TO A NEW FILE

1. Click the Surf's Up Home Page button on the taskbar to minimize the browser window. The surfhome.htm file displays in the Notepad window.
2. Click immediately to the left of the < in the <HTML> tag on line 1. Drag through the first <BODY LINK="#FF8429" ALINK="#FF8429" VLINK="#FF8429"> tag on line 5 to highlight lines 1 through 5.
3. Press CTRL+C to copy the selected lines to the Clipboard.
4. Click New on the File menu.
5. Press CTRL+V to paste the contents of the Clipboard.

The HTML code displays in the new file (Figure 4-42).

Untitled - Notepad

```
<HTML>
<HEAD>
<TITLE>Surf's Up Home Page</TITLE>
</HEAD>
<BODY LINK="#FF8429" ALINK="#FF8429" VLINK="#FF8429">
```

pasted tags and text

FIGURE 4-42

Changing the Title

Next, you want to change the title of this page. The copied title text is Surf's Up Home Page. You need to change that to Surf's Up Huntington Beach. The title is important because it displays on the title bar of the Web browser and on the taskbar.

TO CHANGE THE TITLE

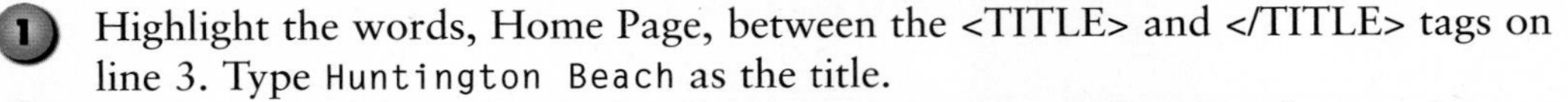

1. Highlight the words, Home Page, between the <TITLE> and </TITLE> tags on line 3. Type `Huntington Beach` as the title.
2. Click immediately to the right of the <BODY > tag on line 5 and press the ENTER key twice.
3. Type `</BODY>` and then press the ENTER key.
4. Type `</HTML>`, click line 6, and then press the ENTER key.

The HTML code displays (Figure 4-43) and the insertion point is on line 7.

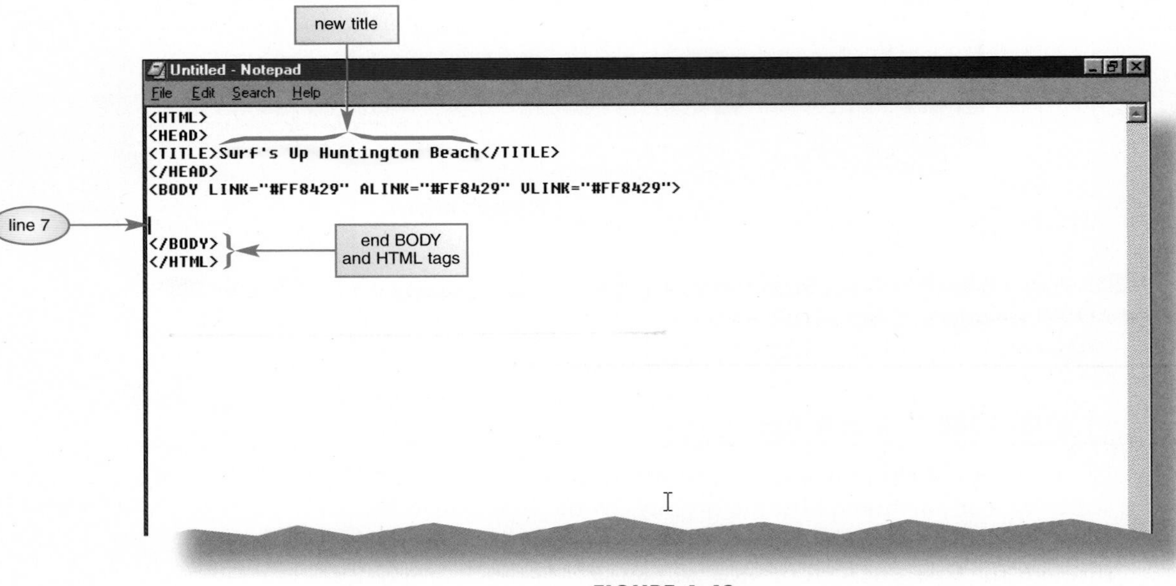

FIGURE 4-43

Inserting an Image

Next, you create a table with two rows and two columns. In Figure 4-41 on the previous page, column one of the first row contains an image (hnbch.gif) and column two contains a heading for the Huntington Beach store and a paragraph of text. In the second row, column one contains a link list for navigation and column two contains a chart (hnchart.jpg) that shows the sales for the Huntington Beach store.

As the first step in creating the table, you insert an image, hnbch.gif, of a single surfer who represents the Huntington Beach location. This image is stored on the HTML Data Disk. Five attributes are used in the <IMG> tag to insert this image — SRC, HSPACE, BORDER, ALIGN, and ALT — shown as follows:

```
<IMG SRC="hnbch.gif" HSPACE="20" BORDER=0 ALIGN="LEFT" ALT="Huntington Beach surfer">
```

The SRC attribute specifies the image file to use. The HSPACE="20" attribute inserts a horizontal space of 20 pixels to provide space between the image and the text. Without this space, the text will run too close to the image. The BORDER=0 attribute creates a borderless table. The ALIGN="LEFT" attribute aligns the image to the left of the Web page. The ALT attribute displays alternate text that gives the Web page visitor information about the image as the image is being loaded. In the next steps, you enter the tags and paragraphs of text given in Table 4-7 to insert an image.

Table 4-7

LINE	HTML TAGS AND TEXT
7	<TABLE>
8	<TR>
9	<TD>
10	<IMG SRC="hnbch.gif" HSPACE="20" BORDER=0 ALIGN="LEFT" ALT="Huntington
11	Beach surfer">
12	</TD>

Steps To Insert an Image

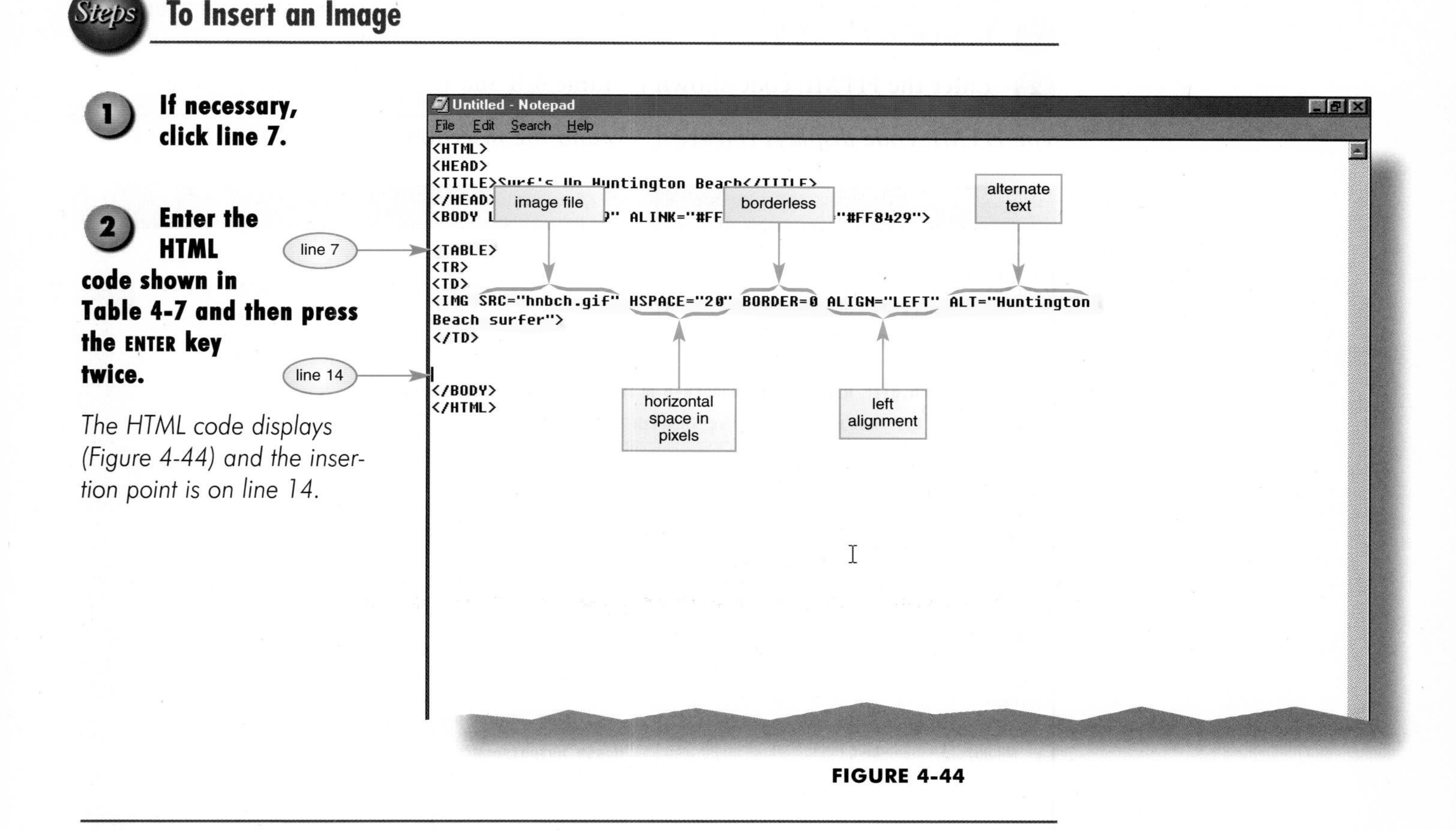

1 If necessary, click line 7.

2 Enter the HTML code shown in Table 4-7 and then press the ENTER key twice.

The HTML code displays (Figure 4-44) and the insertion point is on line 14.

FIGURE 4-44

You have created the table and positioned the surfer image in the first column of row one. The image aligns at the left margin in the table. You provided adequate spacing between the text and the image by using the HSPACE="20" attribute. As the Web page loads, the words "Huntington Beach surfer" (alternate text) display.

```
hnbch.htm

<HTML>
<HEAD>
<TITLE>Surf's Up Huntington Beach</TITLE>
</HEAD>
<BODY LINK="#FF8429" ALINK="#FF8429" VLINK="#FF8429">

<TABLE>
<TR>
<TD>
<IMG SRC="hnbch.gif" HSPACE="20" BORDER=0 ALIGN="LEFT" ALT="Huntin
gton
Beach surfer">
</TD>

<TD ALIGN="LEFT" VALIGN="TOP">
<B><FONT SIZE="+3" FACE="BAZOOKA" COLOR="#FF8429">SURF'S UP
<BR>Huntington Beach</FONT></B>

<P>Huntington Beach Surf's Up store opened a little more than two
years' ago. Since
then, sales have doubled! Historically, Huntington Beach has been
known as one of
Southern California's premier surfing locations. Surf's Up stocks
surfwear,
sportswear, accessories, and superior custom surfboards. The chart
 below details the
monthly sales figures to the present.</P>
</TD>
</TR>

<TR>
<TD ALIGN="RIGHT">
<A HREF="surfhome.htm">Home</A>
<BR>Huntington Beach
<BR><A HREF="maui.htm">Maui</A>
<BR><A HREF="ftlaud.htm">Ft. Lauderdale</A>
</TD>

<TD ALIGN="CENTER">
<IMG SRC="hnchart.jpg" ALT="Huntington Beach chart">
</TD>
</TR>
</TABLE>

<CENTER><I>Call 1-555-SurfsUp or e-mail us at
<A HREF="mailto:surfsup@isp.com">surfsup@isp.com</A>
for more information.</I></CENTER>
</BODY>
</HTML>

Page 1
```

FIGURE 4-49

More About

Testing

Especially with image maps, it is important to test the Web page thoroughly in the browser. If one incorrect number is typed in as an x- or y-coordinate, the entire image map can be wrong as a result. Make sure that the clickable area is exactly where you want it to be by testing.

TO CLOSE NOTEPAD

1. Click the Close button on the right-hand side of the title bar.

The Notepad window closes and the Windows desktop displays.

TO VIEW AND PRINT THE WEB PAGE USING YOUR BROWSER

1. Click the Surf's Up Home Page button on the taskbar to maximize the browser window.
2. Click the Huntington Beach link from the image map on the Surf's Up home page.

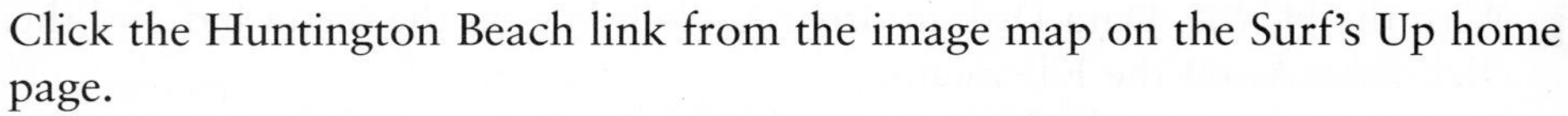

3. Click the Print button on the Standard Buttons toolbar.

The browser displays the Web page, hnbch.htm (Figure 4-50), and the Web page prints (Figure 4-51).

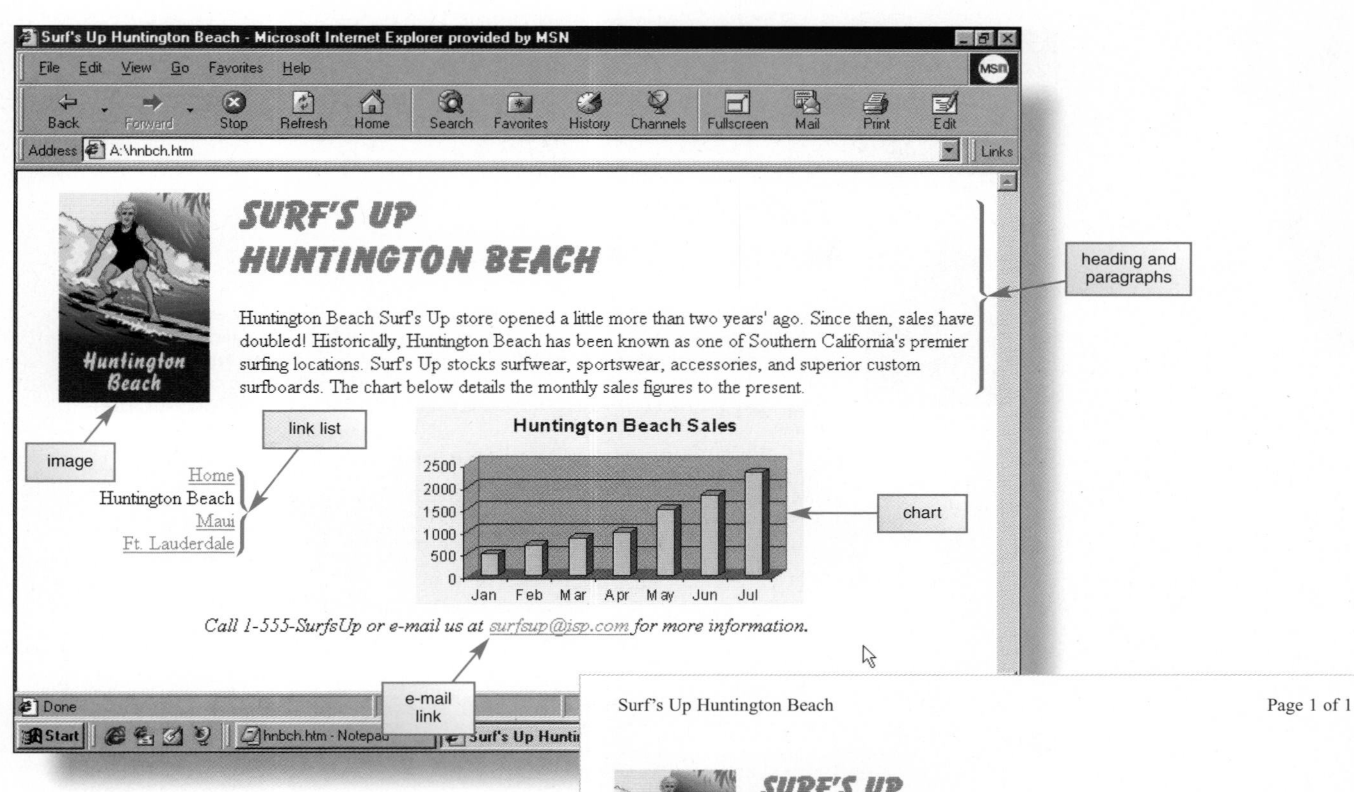

FIGURE 4-50

Surf's Up Huntington Beach Page 1 of 1

SURF'S UP
HUNTINGTON BEACH

Huntington Beach Surf's Up store opened a little more than two years' ago. Since then, sales have doubled! Historically, Huntington Beach has been known as one of Southern California's premier surfing locations. Surf's Up stocks surfwear, sportswear, accessories, and superior custom surfboards. The chart below details the monthly sales figures to the present.

Huntington Beach Sales

Home
Huntington Beach
Maui
Ft. Lauderdale

2500 2000 1500 1000 500 0
Jan Feb Mar Apr May Jun Jul

Call 1-555-SurfsUp or e-mail us at surfsup@isp.com for more information.

FIGURE 4-51

One table was created on this Web page. It contains an image and text in the first row and a link list and a chart in the second row. The Surf's Up Web site is complete.

Testing the Links

The next step in Web development is to test the links. Links must be tested from the image map on the home page, as well as from the link list on each of the other pages.

TO TEST THE LINKS

1. Click the Home link on the Huntington Beach Web page.
2. Click the Ft. Lauderdale link on the home page.
3. Click the Huntington Beach link on the Ft. Lauderdale Web page.
4. Click the Maui link on the Huntington Beach Web page.

The Maui Web page displays (Figure 4-52 on the next page).

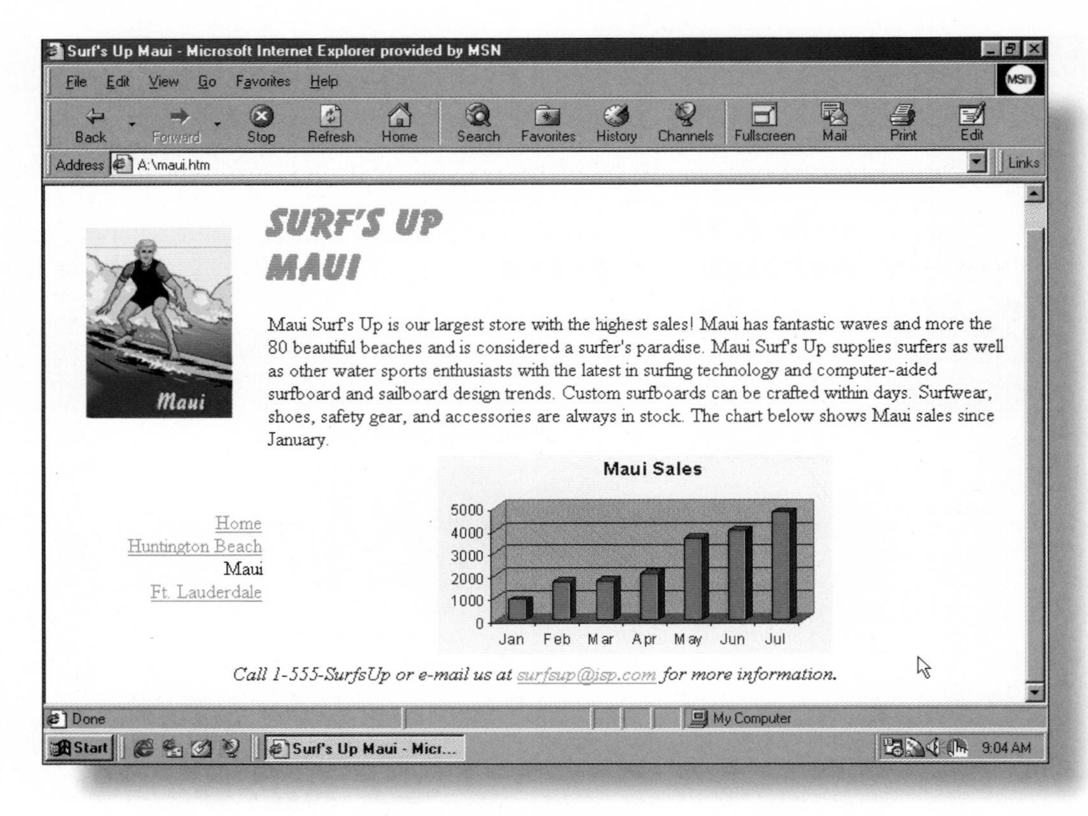

FIGURE 4-52

If the links fail, modify the HTML code and then retest the links.

TO CLOSE YOUR BROWSER

1. Click the Close button on the right-hand side of the title bar of the browser window.

The browser closes and the Windows desktop displays.

Image Mapping Software

Earlier in this project, you opened the image, surfmap.gif, in Paint and located the x- and y-coordinates of the top left-hand corner point and the bottom right-hand corner point as indicated in Table 4-1 on page HTM 4.20. Although that was relatively easy to do, several image map-making software tools are available that simplify this process. These tools generate the x- and y-coordinates based on the clickable areas that you select on the image by using the mouse. Several of these tools are listed in Table 4-12.

Image Mapping Software

In Project 4, you used Paint to determine the x- and y-coordinates of an image. Software is available that makes that process much simpler. You select the areas that are to be hotspots, and the software takes care of the rest. Visit the Web sites in Table 4-12 for free trial versions of image mapping software.

Table 4-12

TOOL	PLATFORM	URL
Mapedit	Windows/UNIX/Mac	www.scsite.com/mapedit
LiveImage	Windows	www.scsite.com /liveimage
Imaptool	Linux/X-Window	www.scsite.com /imaptool

Project Summary

In this project, you used Notepad to create two HTML text files, surfhome.htm and hnbch.htm. You learned image mapping terms and definitions and used numerous image map tags and attributes. You created borderless tables to contain the images. You mapped a single image into three different link areas. You developed a four-page Web site with links from each page to the others. You created a link list on the home page that corresponded with the links in the image map. You created a navigational list on the second Web page for linking. You inserted a chart into the second Web page. The Surf's Up Web site was a great success, and you received an A for your marketing class project.

What You Should Know

Having completed this project, you now should be able to perform the following tasks.

- Change Link Colors *(HTM 4.34)*
- Change the Title *(HTM 4.38)*
- Close Notepad *(HTM 4.44)*
- Close Your Browser *(HTM 4.46)*
- Copy HTML Code to a New File *(HTM 4.37)*
- Create an E-Mail Link *(HTM 4.43)*
- Create an Image Map *(HTM 4.33)*
- Create a Link List *(HTM 4.41)*
- Create a Table *(HTM 4.26)*
- Create Text Links *(HTM 4.31)*
- Enter Initial HTML Tags *(HTM 4.24)*
- Enter Paragraphs of Text *(HTM 4.30)*
- Insert a Chart *(HTM 4.42)*
- Insert a Heading *(HTM 4.29)*
- Insert an Image *(HTM 4.28, HTM 4.39)*
- Insert a Paragraph of Text *(HTM 4.40)*
- Locate the X- and Y-Coordinates *(HTM 4.21)*
- Open an Image File *(HTM 4.19)*
- Save and Print the HTML File *(HTM 4.34, HTM 4.43)*
- Start Notepad *(HTM 4.23)*
- Start Paint *(HTM 4.17)*
- Test the Links *(HTM 4.45)*
- View and Print the Web Page Using Your Browser *(HTM 4.35, HTM 4.44)*

Test Your Knowledge

1 True/False

Instructions: Circle T if the statement is true or F if the statement is false.

T F 1. The last step in image map development is to code the table in HTML.
T F 2. An image map can be used to link to multiple URLs within a single image on a Web page.
T F 3. Images with nonobvious visual sections are the best to use for image mapping.
T F 4. The x-axis runs vertically on a Web page.
T F 5. The y-axis runs horizontally on a Web page.
T F 6. The shape choices for image mapping are rectangle, circle, polygon, and point.
T F 7. Multiple images make up an image map.
T F 8. The <AREA> tag is optional in an image map application.
T F 9. The <MAP> tag is used to create the image map name.
T F 10. Server-side and client-side image maps are the same in all ways.

2 Multiple Choice

Instructions: Circle the correct response.

1. The __________ tag is used to create a client-side image map.
   a. MAP b. AREA c. ISMAP d. ITMAP
2. The __________ tag defines clickable areas.
   a. MAP b. AREA c. ISMAP d. ITMAP
3. The attribute in the <IMG> tag used to target an image map is __________.
   a. MAP b. TOMAP c. MAPIT d. USEMAP
4. __________ is the attribute used to increase horizontal space.
   a. HORIZONTAL=OFF
   b. HORIZONTAL=ON
   c. HSPACE
   d. VSPACE
5. The __________ -axis runs vertically on the image.
   a. x b. y c. z d. n
6. The __________ -axis runs horizontally on the image.
   a. x b. y c. z d. n
7. The coordinates used for a circular shape consist of __________.
   a. top and bottom
   b. center point and diameter
   c. center point and radius
   d. center point only
8. The coordinates used for a polygon shape consist of __________.
   a. center point, radius
   b. top and bottom x and y
   c. x and y for all corners
   d. x and y for every other corner

Test Your Knowledge

9. The __________ attribute indicates the x- and y-coordinates for an image map.
   a. SHAPE　　b. COORDS　　c. SIZE　　d. HREF
10. The __________ attribute indicates the form of the clickable area that is used for any URL.
   a. SHAPE　　b. COORDS　　c. SIZE　　d. HREF

3 Understanding HTML

Instructions: Perform the following tasks using a computer.

1. Start Notepad.
2. Open the surfhome.htm file created in Project 4.
3. Print the file and do the following without looking at the book:
   a. Circle the tag that creates an image map target name.
   b. Draw a line under the tag that creates coordinates for the Maui store.
   c. Put a square around the tag that indicates the image map to use.
   d. Put an asterisk next to the tag that specifies the horizontal space between the image and adjoining text.
4. Write your name on the printout and hand the printout in to your instructor.

4 Editing HTML Files

Instructions: Perform the following tasks using a computer.

1. Start your browser.
2. Enter `www.scsite.com` in the Address text box. When the Web page displays, scroll down to the Internet titles and click the title of this book.
3. Click the link, Project 4 - 4 Editing HTML Files.
4. Click View on the menu bar. Then click Source to find the HTML code for some feature that was not used on the surfhome.htm Web page.
5. Highlight the code, and copy it to the Clipboard (press CTRL+C).
6. Open the file, surfhome.htm, in Notepad.
7. Paste the Clipboard contents into the surfhome.htm file at an appropriate place.
8. Save the revised file on a floppy disk with shome2.htm as the file name.
9. Print the revised document source.
10. Open shome2.htm in your browser.
11. Print the Web page.
12. Write your name on both printouts and hand them in to your instructor.

1 Web Page Image Map Help

Instructions: Perform the following tasks using a computer.

1. Start your browser.
2. Enter `www.scsite.com/html/proj4.htm` in the Address text box. When the Web page displays, scroll down to the Internet titles and click the title of this book.
3. Click the link, Project 4 - Help1.
4. You can create a client-side image map with an equivalent server-side map to support browsers that are not capable of displaying client-side image maps.
5. Write down how to create a client-side image map that falls back to server-side support if needed, using the ISMAP attribute.
6. Include your name with your answers and hand them in to your instructor.

2 More Image Map Ideas

Instructions: Perform the following tasks using a computer.

1. Start your browser.
2. Enter `www.scsite.com/html/proj4.htm` in the Address text box. When the Web page displays, scroll down to the Internet titles and click the title of this book.
3. Click the link, Project 4 - Help2.
4. Find one suggestion that you did not learn in Project 4.
5. Write down some information from that suggestion and discuss how you would use it in your own Web page development.
6. Include your name with your answers and hand them in to your instructor.

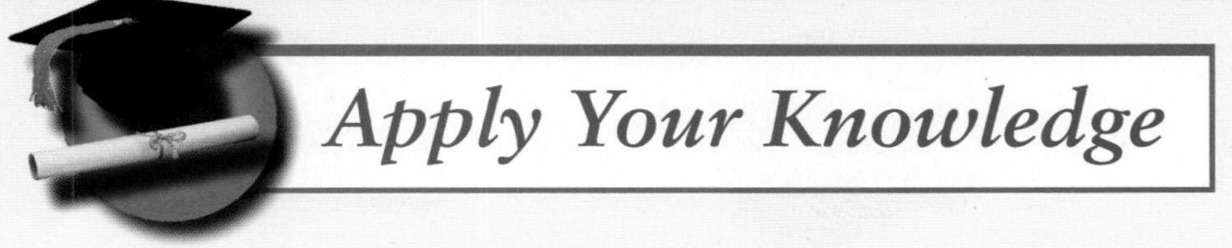

1 Editing the Apply Your Knowledge Web Page

Instructions: Start Paint, Notepad, and your browser. Open in Notepad the file, apply4.htm, on the HTML Data Disk. This file is a partially completed HTML file for the Apply Your Knowledge Web page and contains errors. Figure 4-53 shows the page as it should appear in your browser. Perform the following tasks using a computer.

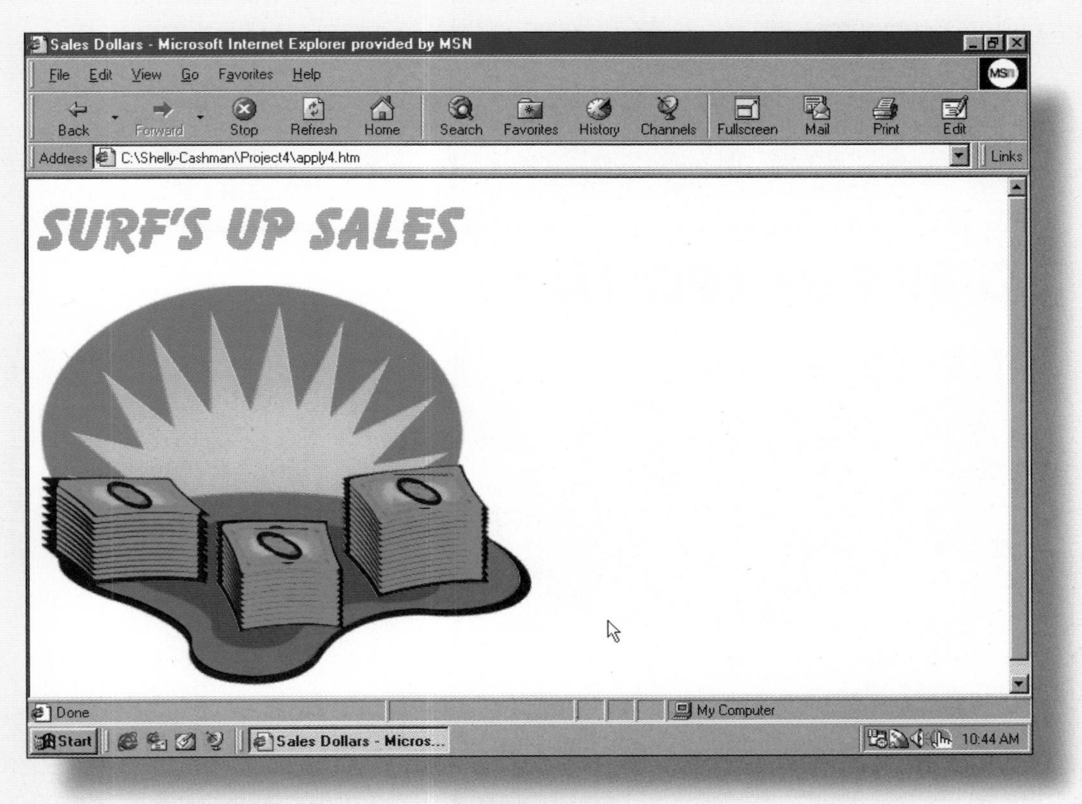

FIGURE 4-53

1. Open the apply4.htm file in your browser.
2. Examine the HTML file in Notepad and its appearance in the browser.
3. Open the money.gif file in Paint. Determine the x- and y-coordinates necessary to create three clickable areas, one for each stack of money.
4. Add any HTML code necessary to the apply4.htm file to create the image map necessary for links from each stack of money to hnchart.gif, mchart.gif, and flchart.gif, respectively.
5. Save the revised apply4.htm file on a floppy disk, using money.htm as the file name.
6. Print the revised document source for money.htm.
7. Open money.htm in your browser.
8. Print the Web page.
9. Write your name on both printouts and hand them in to your instructor.

1 Creating a Map

Problem: Surf's Up wants a new look to its home page. You decide to create an image map on the United States map named uslab1.gif and stored on the HTML Data Disk. The home page should look like the one shown in Figure 4-54.

Instructions: Start Paint and open the uslab1.gif file. This is the image that will be mapped. Perform the following tasks using a computer.

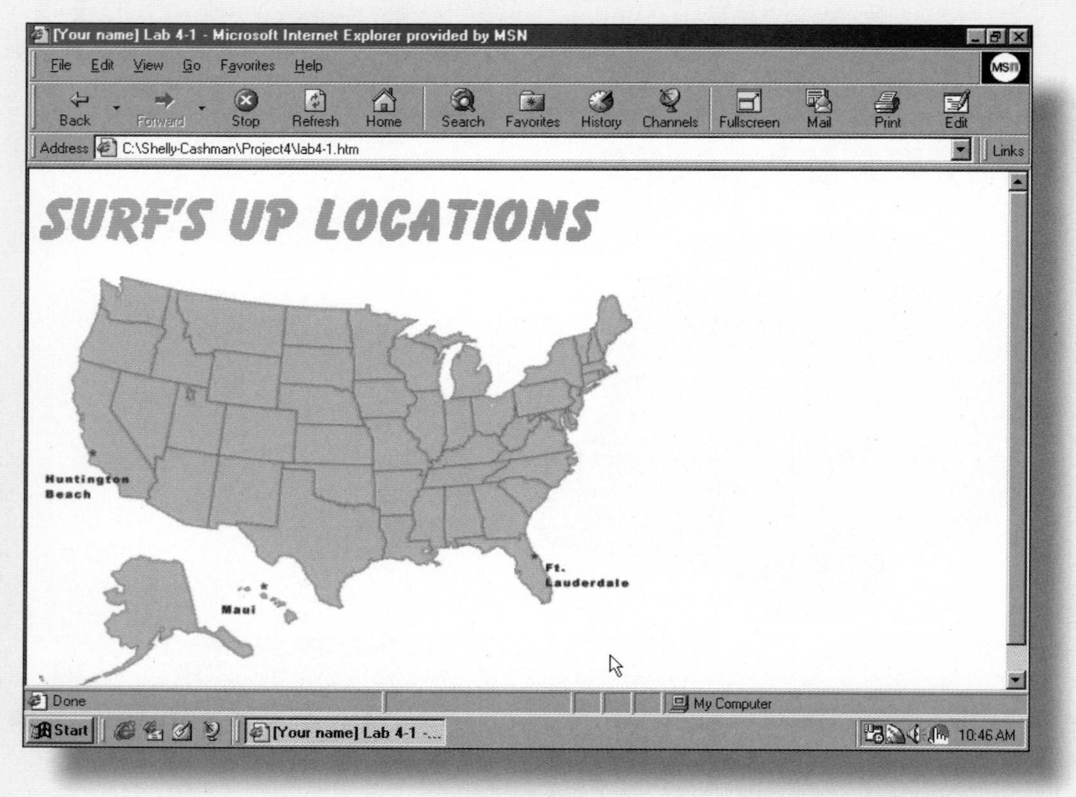

FIGURE 4-54

1. Determine the x- and y-coordinates of the points in the center of the asterisks at each location: Huntington Beach, Maui, and Ft. Lauderdale. Write down those coordinates for use later.
2. Start Notepad and create a new HTML file with the title, [your name] Lab4-1, in the title section.
3. Begin the body section by adding the same Surf's Up heading as found in Figure 4-1a on page HTM 4.5.
4. Insert the image, uslab1.gif, after the heading. Make sure to use the USEMAP attribute in the <IMG> tag.
5. Use the <MAP> tag to set the target for the USEMAP.
6. Create the necessary <AREA> tags to support the x- and y-coordinates that you plotted in Step 1 of this exercise. The links should be the same as those in Project 4.
7. Close the body, close the HTML file, and save the file using lab4-1.htm as the file name.

8. Print the lab4-1.htm file.
9. Open the lab4-1.htm file in your browser.
10. Print the Web page.
11. Write your name on the printouts and hand them in to your instructor.

2 Creating a Shopping Cart

Problem: You want to use your image mapping skills to create a Web page for shopping. You create one Web page with the image, shop.gif, shown in Figure 4-55. Table 4-13 on the next page shows the links for each item in the shopping cart.

Instructions: Start Paint and open the shop.gif file on the HTML Data Disk. This is the image that will be mapped. Perform the following tasks using a computer.

FIGURE 4-55

1. Each separate item in the shopping cart has a distinct shape. Determine the x- and y-coordinates needed for each shape. Write down those coordinates for later use.
2. Start Notepad and create a new HTML file with the title, [your name] lab4-2, in the main heading section.
3. Insert the shop.gif image, making sure to include the USEMAP attribute.

(continued)

Creating a Shopping Cart *(continued)*

4. Use the <MAP> tag to set the target for the USEMAP.
5. Create the necessary <AREA> tags to support the x- and y-coordinates that you plotted in Step 1 of this exercise. Table 4-13 contains the links' URLs.
6. Save the HTML file with the file name, lab4-2.htm.
7. Print the HTML file.
8. Print the Web page from your browser.
9. Write your name on the printouts and hand them in to your instructor.

Table 4-13

ITEM IN SHOPPING CART	URL
Books	http://www.amazon.com
Computers	http://www.egghead.com

3 Creating a Government Services Web Page

Problem: You want to create a Web page that gives you easy access to important government Web sites. You use the image, starlab3.gif, on the HTML Data Disk for your image map. Your Web page should look like Figure 4-56.

Instructions: Start Paint and Notepad and perform the following tasks using a computer.

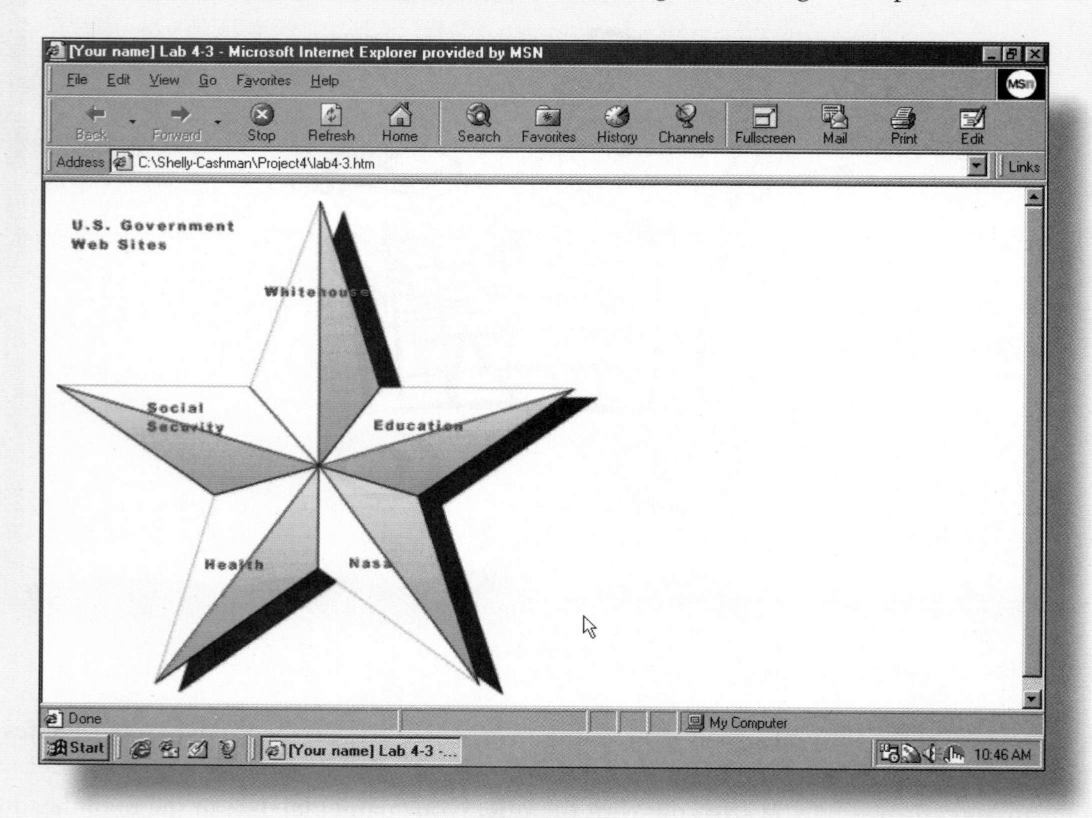

FIGURE 4-56

In the Lab

1. Create a Web page similar to the one shown in Figure 4-56.
2. Each separate link area is a polygonal-shaped point in the star. Determine the x- and y-coordinates of all corners in each polygon shape. Table 4-14 contains the links' URLs.
3. Include in the HTML file the necessary <MAP> and <AREA> tags to support the polygons.
4. Save the HTML file with the file name, lab4-3.htm. Print the HTML file.
5. Print the Web page from your browser.
6. Write your name on the printouts and hand them in to your instructor.

Table 4-14

TITLE	URL
White House	http://www.whitehouse.gov
Department of Education	http://www.ed.gov
Social Security Administration	http://www.ssa.gov
NASA	http://www.nasa.gov
Department of Health & Human Services	http://www.dhhs.gov

Cases and Places

The difficulty of these case studies varies:
◗ are the least difficult; ◗◗ are more difficult; and ◗◗◗ are the most difficult.

1 ◗ Using the Web or a graphics program, find two images that are appropriate for image mapping and two images that are not appropriate. Analyze what makes these images appropriate or inappropriate for image maps. Print each image. On the appropriate printouts, note what sections of the images can be utilized for link areas. Write a one-page paper telling why you categorized each image as you did.

2 ◗ Using one of the appropriate images from Case 1, determine how this image can be used as an image map. Print the image and then use a pencil to sketch in sections on it that can be used as linkable areas. Utilize all available shapes (rectangle, circle, polygon, and point) in your sketch, making sure that no areas overlap. Using Paint, determine the x- and y-coordinates of all points in your sketch. Note those coordinates on the printed copy of the image.

3 ◗◗ As mentioned in this project, some Web page visitors turn off images while browsing. This reduces the time to download Web pages from the Web server. Connect to the Internet and browse for three Web pages that have image maps. To determine if a page uses image maps, use View Source. Track the amount of time that it takes to download each Web page. Also, determine whether each page has text links associated with the links on the image map. Now turn images off in your browser, and track the time that it takes to download each page. Review what the Web pages look like now.

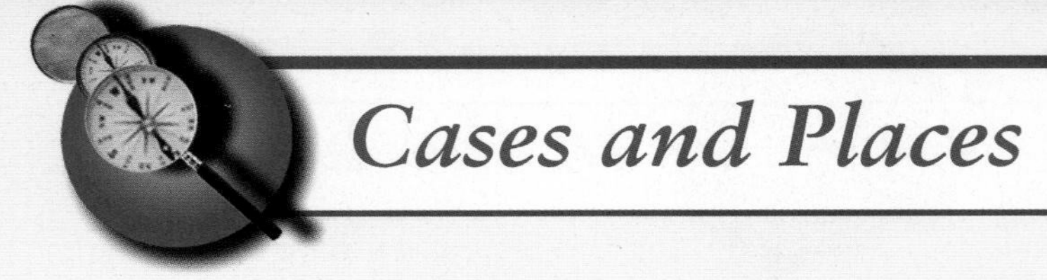

4 ▶▶ Visit three Web sites that contain information about HTML. Several are mentioned in the projects in this series. Read additional information about image mapping. Compare what these sources say about the advantages and disadvantages of image mapping. What suggestions do they make regarding the use of image maps in Web page development? Write a two-page paper containing information that you read in this project and the advantages and disadvantages discussed in the sources that you found.

5 ▶▶▶ Visit the Web sites of the image mapping software tools listed in Table 4-12 on page HTM 4.46. Read the information about each tool, including its cost, availability, and ease of use. Print information from the Web site of each tool. Write a four-page paper describing all of the products and how each could be used to improve image mapping.

6 ▶▶▶ Determine which image mapping software tool from Table 4-12 on page HTM 4.46 is available for your platform. Visit the Web site for that tool and determine whether a free trial version is offered. If one is, download the software and use it to create an image map. Compare the technique of using this tool to writing the HTML code necessary for image mapping. Does the tool make image mapping easier or more difficult to do? Discuss your findings in a four-page paper.

7 ▶▶▶ HTML tables (Project 3) can be used in the same way as image maps (this project) for linking. A more thorough test of image mapping versus tables can be accomplished by using both techniques to serve the same purpose. Using the image and the sketch completed in Case 2, create an image map. Use any of the URLs listed in either Table 4-13 or Table 4-14 as the links for the clickable areas. Create a similar Web page using tables, with links to the same URLs. Print each page, noting in a two-page paper the times that each Web page took to download initially. Explain which of these techniques is more viable to use for the Web page and why.

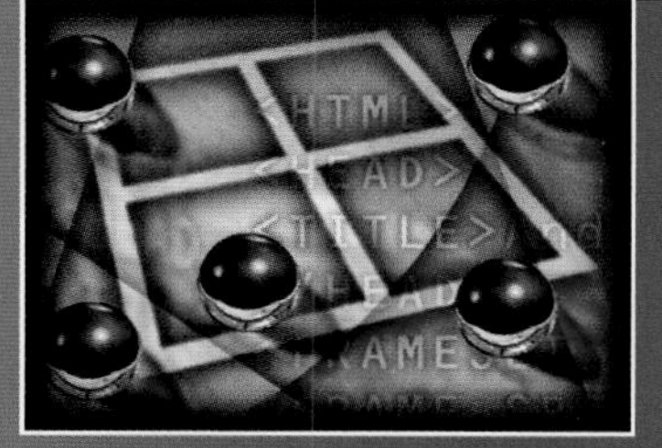

HTML

Creating Frames on a Web Page

You will have mastered the material in this project when you can:

OBJECTIVES

- Define terms related to frames
- Describe the steps used to design a frame structure
- Plan and lay out frameset
- Create a frame definition file
- Use the <FRAMESET> tag
- Use the <FRAME> tag
- Change frame scrolling options
- Name a frame content target
- Identify Web pages to display at start-up
- Set frame rows
- Set frame columns
- Create a header page with an image and text
- Create a navigation page
- Create a home page

It's Just Fun to Know

Locate Long-Lost Classmates Online

As a class reunion approaches or you happen to come across an old yearbook, do you ever wonder what happened to your high school class president, the cheerleading captain, your best friend in homeroom, or a childhood sweetheart? It would be fun to know.

Now, you may be able to find a former classmate with the help of ClassMates™, a unique service on the Internet. The site is the brainchild of Randy Conrads, who devised the concept while perusing the list of America Online and Prodigy subscribers in search of former classmates. He found the name of a friend he had not seen in many years, and the two subsequently met. Then, in Conrads's words, he became "the first spammer" in 1995 by contacting every AOL and Prodigy subscriber and asking for participants in his alumni matching project.

The response was overwhelming, and Conrads found himself trying to manage the thousands of people expressing an interest. As a nonprogrammer setting up a Web site, he encountered many of the same development issues you have

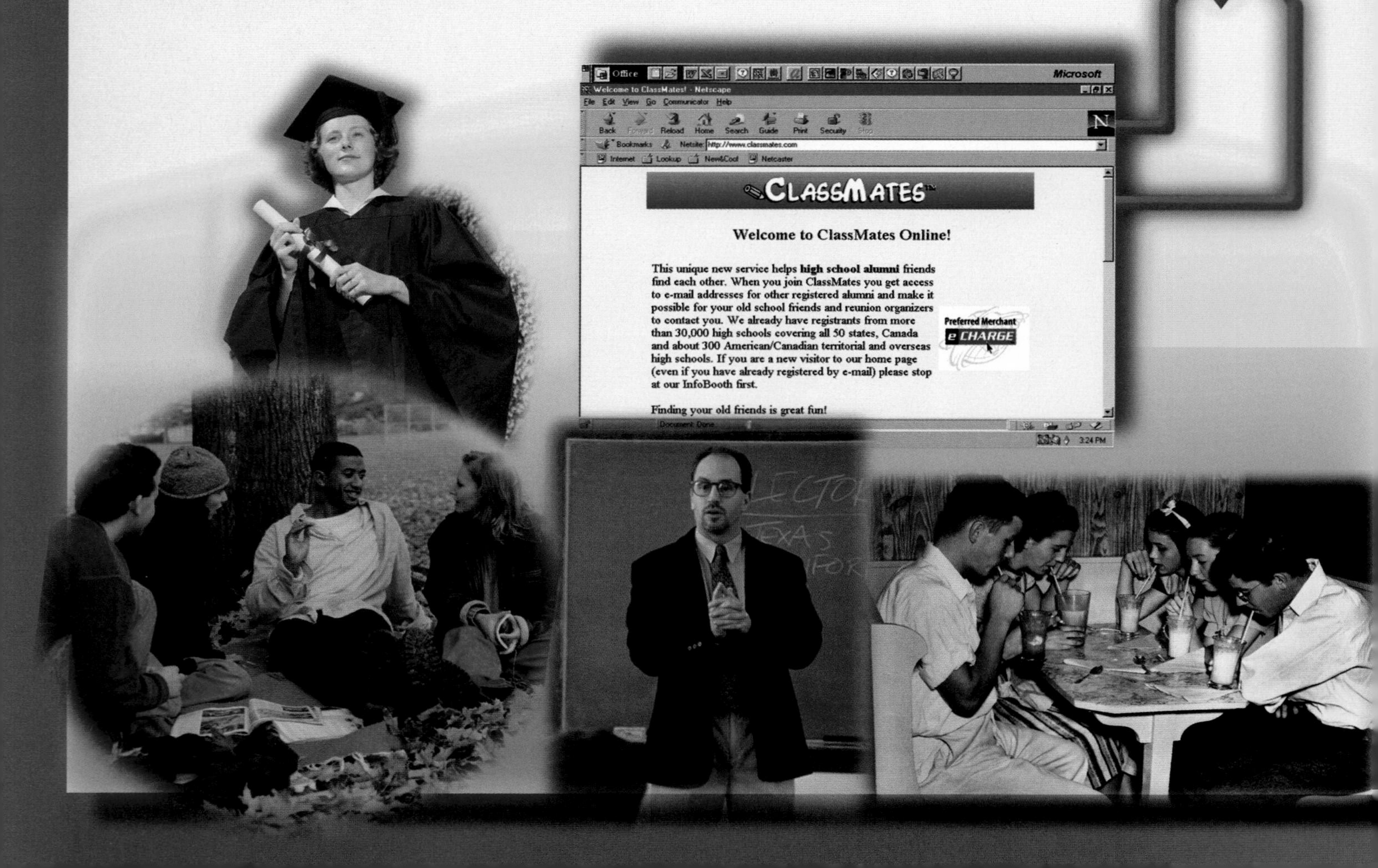

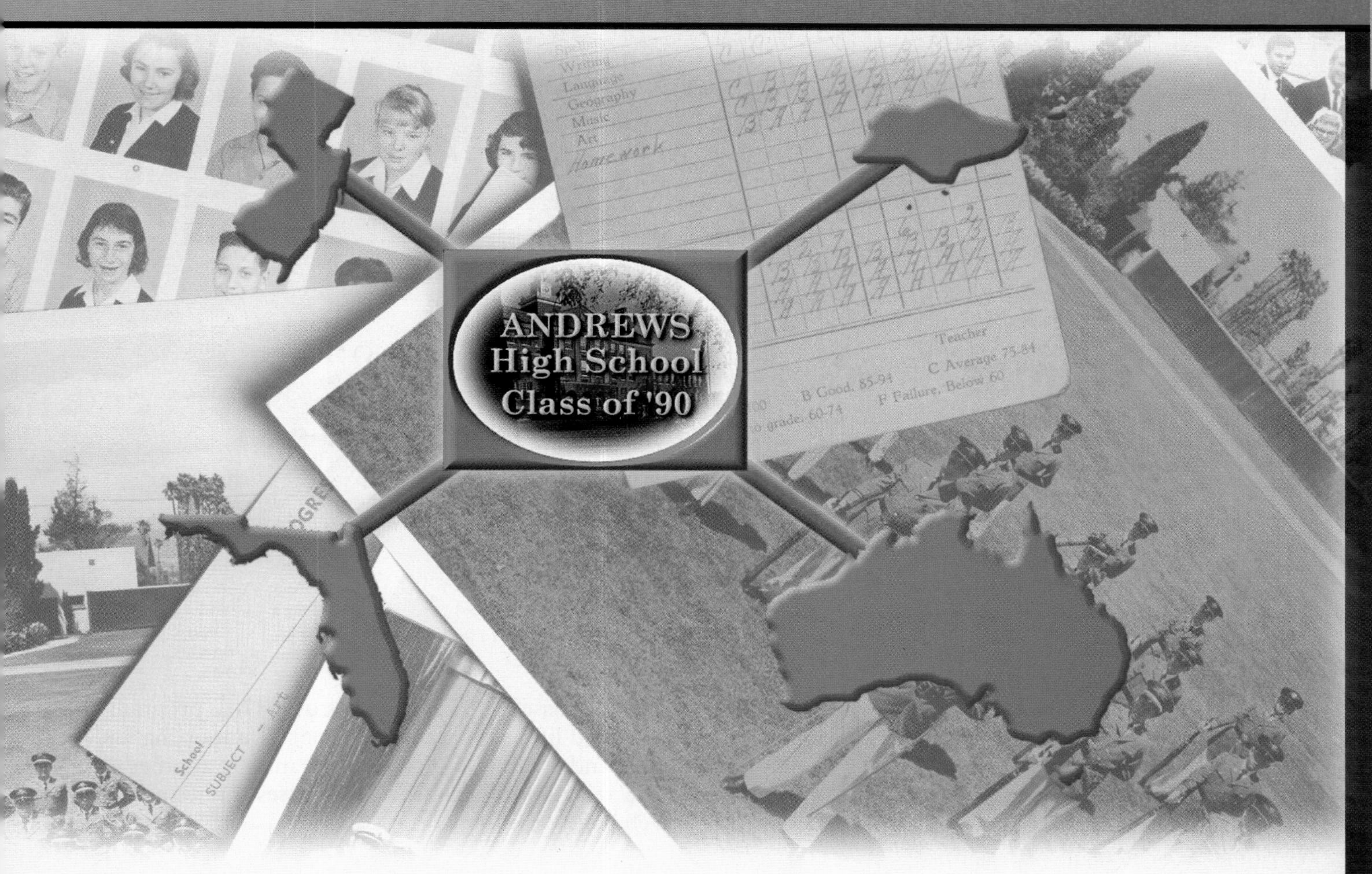

faced using HTML as you have created and edited Web pages, and created links, tables, and image maps. Now in Project 5, you will create frames on a Web page. The benefits of using frames are that Web site visitors can view more than one Web page at a time and navigation is made easier.

Today, more than 50,000 Web surfers use ClassMates™ each month, and nearly 2,000 people join daily. One million graduates from more than 30,000 high schools in North America and 300 overseas schools have registered free for this service. Registration allows users to scan the database to search for familiar names from a particular graduating class. Registrants must become members to contact any of the registered alumni, and membership access requires a small fee.

When registering, users enter data in interactive forms resembling the forms you will create in Project 6. The ClassMates.com Web pages contain text boxes to capture the registrant's name, high school, year of graduation, and 250-character personal biography.

Conrads is very concerned about attempts to exploit members and to invade their privacy. He does not allow advertisers to sell products to members, nor does he allow the members to distribute the data for any commercial purpose, except for planning a class reunion.

While a traditional class reunion involves face-to-face contact, ClassMates.com schedules online virtual class reunions for alumni scattered throughout the world. For example, one such reunion for a Miami high school included participants dialing in from a New Jersey hotel, a military base in Australia, and Singapore.

The site includes message boards that allow former schoolmates to reminisce about high school experiences, friends, teachers, and hangouts. This feature is popular for graduates who have moved to different parts of the country or world.

Conrads calls business on the Web, "a tremendous opportunity field," even for computer users with little Web page development experience.

Each day he receives hundreds of letters and e-mail messages from members delighted with the service. Three classmates have reunited and then married, and Conrads even attended one of these weddings. Judging from this positive response, the site's motto — It's Just Fun to Know! — is indeed true.

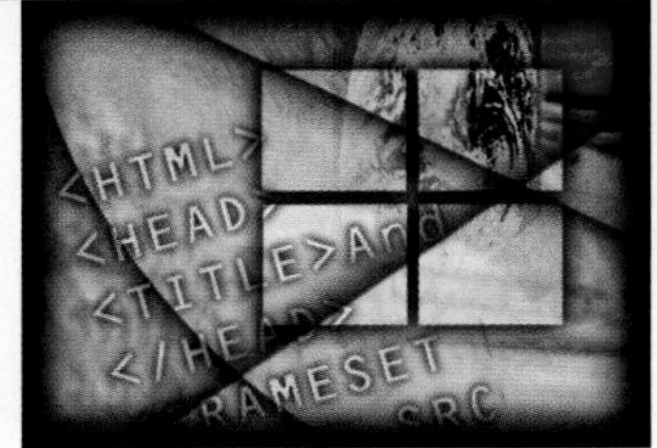

HTML

Creating Frames on a Web Page

CASE PERSPECTIVE

It is hard to believe, but the Andrews High School ten-year class reunion is coming up next year. It will be exciting to see old friends again and catch up on all that has happened since graduation. You and a few high school friends decide to form a reunion committee and begin work on the ten-year reunion plans. During one of the committee meetings, Danielle Staffieri, the president of the Reunion Committee, brought up the idea of creating a Web site for the reunion.

A Web site would enable reunion information to be available online to anyone in the world. A reunion Web site could eliminate the need to mail updates to graduates, thereby saving the committee money. Information also could be easily updated and displayed on the Web instantaneously.

Danielle knows that you have done some Web development. She asks you to form a subcommittee that will create the AHS Class of '90 Web site. When your Web site is completed, you will show it to the committee for its approval.

Introduction

Previous projects discussed the key features of HTML programming. These included linking to other Web pages, importing and mapping images, and creating tables. Using frames is another common HTML technique. This project discusses frames and their use in Web page development.

Project Five — Andrews High School Class Reunion

A **frame** is a rectangular area — a window — in which text or graphics can appear. You use frames to divide a Web page into more than one window. Each frame displays a different, individual Web page, with multiple pages able to interact with each other. Web pages that include frames look and act differently than the Web pages created in previous projects. You can use frames to replace tables and menu bars, giving your Web site an organized look. You also can use them to organize your Web pages by displaying more than one page on the same screen.

In this project, you will use HTML to create a frame definition file. A **frame definition file** contains the layout of the frames on the Web page and specifies their Web page contents. It is the frame definition file that opens when the visitor enters the URL of the Web site in the Address text box. Based on the information in this file, various Web pages display at start-up and when links are clicked. This file is the Web site home page and in this project is named framedef.htm. In the definition file, framedef.htm, that you create for this project, you will specify the layout for three frames and their contents. You also will create three Web pages (header.htm, menu.htm, and home.htm) for the AHS ten-year class reunion that will display in those frames and form the AHS Web site home page. Figure 1-5a shows the display area divided into three frames in which the three separate Web pages will display.

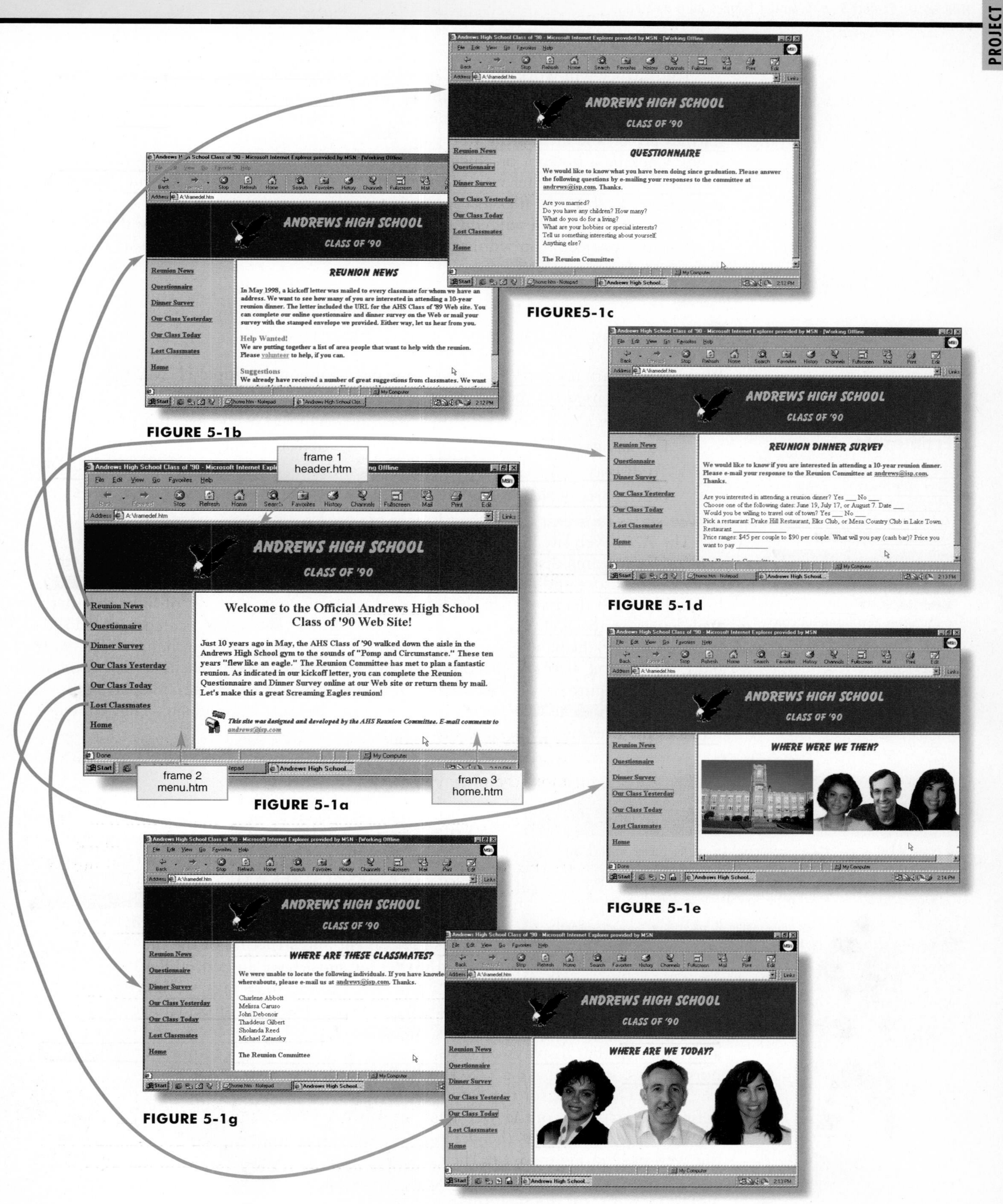

FIGURE 5-1a

FIGURE 5-1b

FIGURE5-1c

FIGURE 5-1d

FIGURE 5-1e

FIGURE 5-1f

FIGURE 5-1g

You further will work with six other files (news.htm, survey1.htm, survey2.htm, yesterday.htm, today.htm, and lost.htm), which are stored on the HTML Data Disk and are shown in Figures 5-1b through 5-1g on the previous page. Links from these six files are on the menu.htm Web page (frame 2 of Figure 5-1a on the previous page). Clicking a hotspot on this page causes the corresponding linked Web page to display in one of the other frames, replacing that frame's previous content. You will change two of these six files in Project 6.

Using Notepad, you will edit the text and HTML tags used to create the Web pages in this project. You will use your browser to view your Web pages as they are developed.

Creating Web Pages with Frames

When frames are used, the web site home page contains multiple HTML files. Frames can be used for the following:

- To allow a Web site visitor to view more than one Web page at a time
- For navigation, as a replacement for such objects as menu lists and menu bars
- To display banners or other information that needs to remain on the screen as other parts of the Web page change

A Web site is more versatile when frames are used for site organization.

The AHS Web site home page in Figure 5-1a shows a Web page with three frames. Each frame displays a different Web page. Frame 1 contains a banner with the school mascot and heading for the Andrews High School Class of '90. Frame 2, located beneath the banner in the left-hand column, contains a list of links to other Web pages on the Web site and is used for navigation. Frame 3, located beneath the banner in the right-hand column, is the only frame whose content changes. The Web page, home.htm, displays in frame 3 at start-up, that is, when the site is first accessed by a visitor (Figure 5-1a). When a link in frame 2 is clicked, frame 3 displays the content of the linked Web page, also located on the AHS reunion site. That content replaces the previous content of the frame.

Framesets

A frameset can be thought of as a window with various windowpanes. Within each windowpane is a separate Web page. The frame definition file is the HTML file that defines the Web pages that display in the individual windowpanes. Every Web page used in a frameset can be viewed independently in the browser as well as within the frameset.

Using Frames

To use frames, you create a frame definition file in HTML, using a combination of three tags and several attributes to specify the layout. The tags, shown in Table 5-1, are <FRAMESET>, <FRAME>, and <NOFRAME>. A **frameset** is used to define the layout of the frames when displayed on the screen. A pair of <FRAMESET> tags contains the content and structure of the file. Each start <FRAMESET> tag must have an end </FRAMESET> tag. Within a pair of <FRAMESET> tags, <FRAME> tags define the frames; each frame must be defined by a <FRAME> tag. No </FRAME> end tag is used. <NOFRAMES> is used to specify alternate text that displays on a visitor's screen if the visitor's browser does not support frames. It must have a </NOFRAMES> end tag.

Table 5-1

TAG	FUNCTION
<FRAMESET> </FRAMESET>	• Defines the structure of the frames within a window. • Required end tag when creating frames.
<FRAME>	• Defines a given frame. Required for each frame.
<NOFRAMES> </NOFRAMES>	• Alternate content if the browser does not support frames. Supported by multiple types and versions of browsers.

The HTML code for the definition file, framedef.htm, shown in Figure 5-2, defines the structure of the Web page in Figure 5-1a on page HTM 5.5. The code defines three HTML files (header.htm, menu.htm, and home.htm) that are used for the Web page in Figure 5-1a. The three Web pages corresponding to the three HTML files each display in one of the three frames. These are shown in Figures 5-2b, 5-2c, and 5-2d and form the Web site home page.

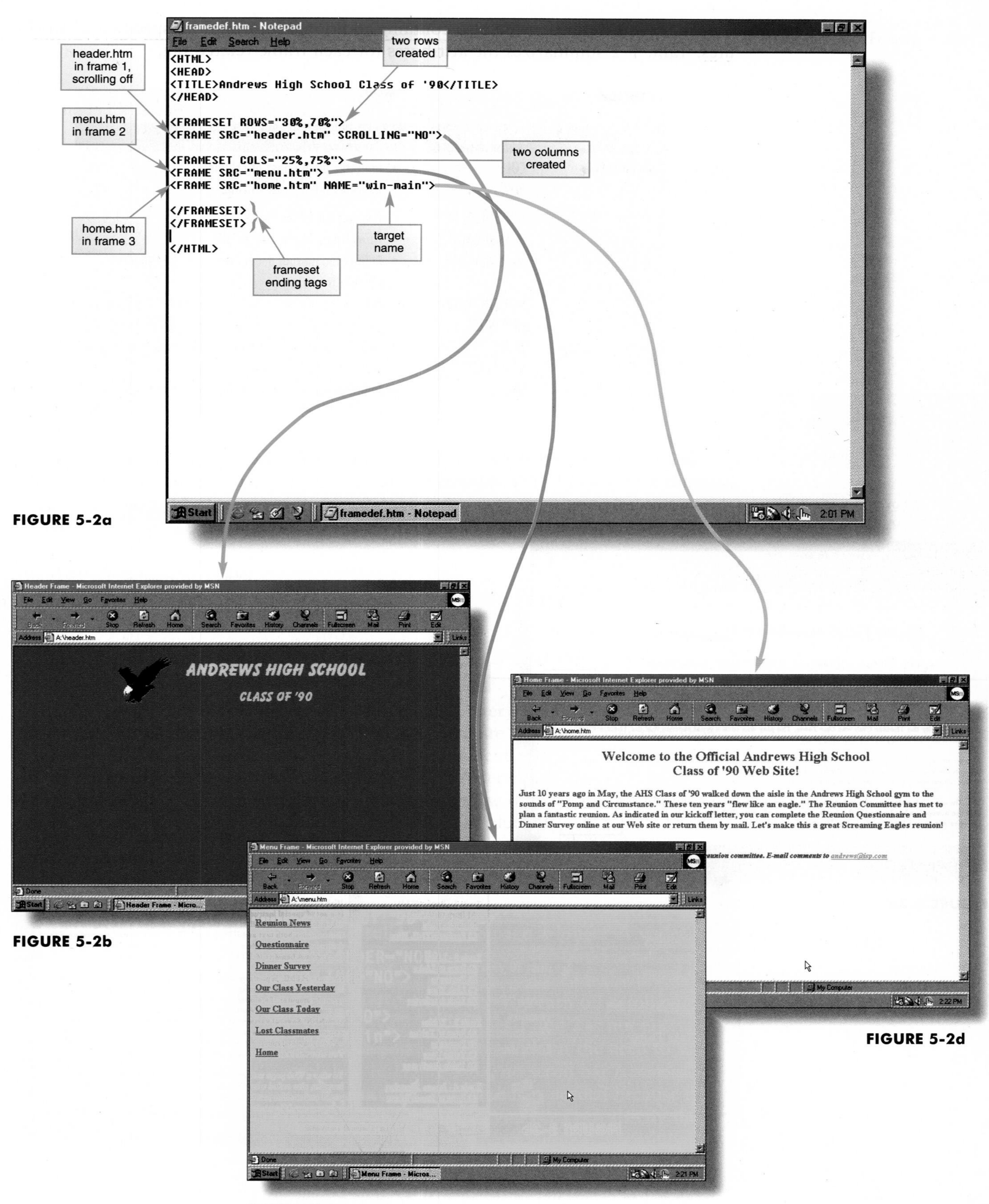

FIGURE 5-2a

FIGURE 5-2b

FIGURE 5-2c

FIGURE 5-2d

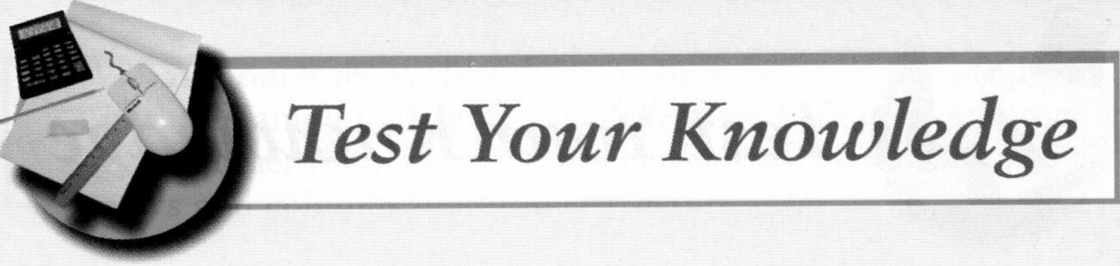

3 Understanding HTML

Instructions: Perform the following steps using a computer.

1. Start Notepad.
2. Open the framedef.htm file you created in Project 5.
3. Print the file.
4. Circle the tag that defines the structure of the frames.
5. Draw a line under the tag that defines a given frame.
6. Put a square around the tag that indicates no scrolling.
7. Put an asterisk next to the tag that specifies the number of columns.
8. Include your name with your answers and hand them in to your instructor.

4 Editing HTML Files

Instructions: Perform the following tasks using a computer.

1. Start your browser.
2. Enter `www.scsite.com` in the Address text box. When the Web page displays, scroll down to the Internet titles and click the title of this book.
3. Click the link, Project 5 - 4 Editing HTML Files.
4. Click View on the menu bar and then click Source to find the HTML code for some feature that was not used in the framedef.htm frame definition file.
5. Highlight the code and copy it to the Clipboard (i.e., press CTRL+C).
6. Open the framedef.htm file in Notepad.
7. Paste the Clipboard contents in the framedef.htm file at an appropriate place.
8. Save the revised file on a floppy disk using the file name, framedef2.htm.
9. Print the revised document source.
10. Open the framedef2.htm file in your browser.
11. Print the Web page.
12. Include your name with the printouts and hand them in to your instructor.

Use Help

1 Web Page Frame Help

Instructions: Perform the following tasks using a computer.

1. Start your browser.
2. Enter `www.scsite.com/html/proj5.htm` in the Address text box. When the Web page displays, scroll down to the Internet titles and click the title of this book.
3. Click the link, Project 5 — Help1.
4. Read about the frameset attribute that allows you to turn off frames.
5. Write down how that is done and how you would use it in a real Web page.
6. Include your name with your answers and hand them in to your instructor.

2 More Frames Ideas

Instructions: Perform the following tasks using a computer.

1. Start your browser.
2. Enter `www.scsite.com/html/proj5.htm` in the Address text box. When the Web page displays, scroll down to the Internet titles and click the title of this book.
3. Click the link, Project 5 — Help2.
4. Find one suggestion that you did not learn in Project 5.
5. Write down some information from that suggestion and discuss how you would use it in your own Web page development.
6. Include your name with your answers and hand them in to your instructor.

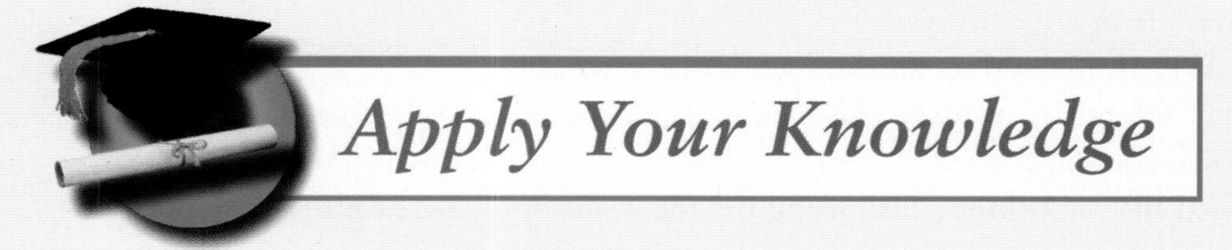

Apply Your Knowledge

1 Editing the Apply Your Knowledge Web Page

Instructions: Start Notepad. Open the apply5.htm file on the HTML Data Disk. The apply5.htm file is a partially completed HTML file for the Apply Your Knowledge Web page that contains some errors. Figure 5-28 on the next page shows the Apply Your Knowledge Web page as it should display in the browser. If you did not download the HTML Data Disk earlier, then see the inside back cover for instructions or see your instructor. Perform the tasks on the next page using a computer.

(continued)

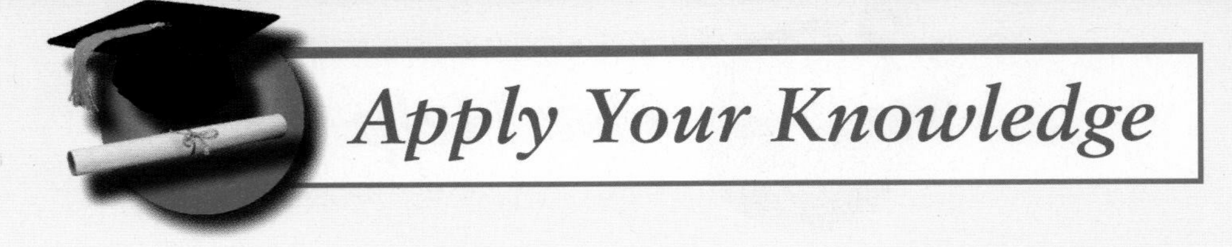

Editing the Apply Your Knowledge Web Page *(continued)*

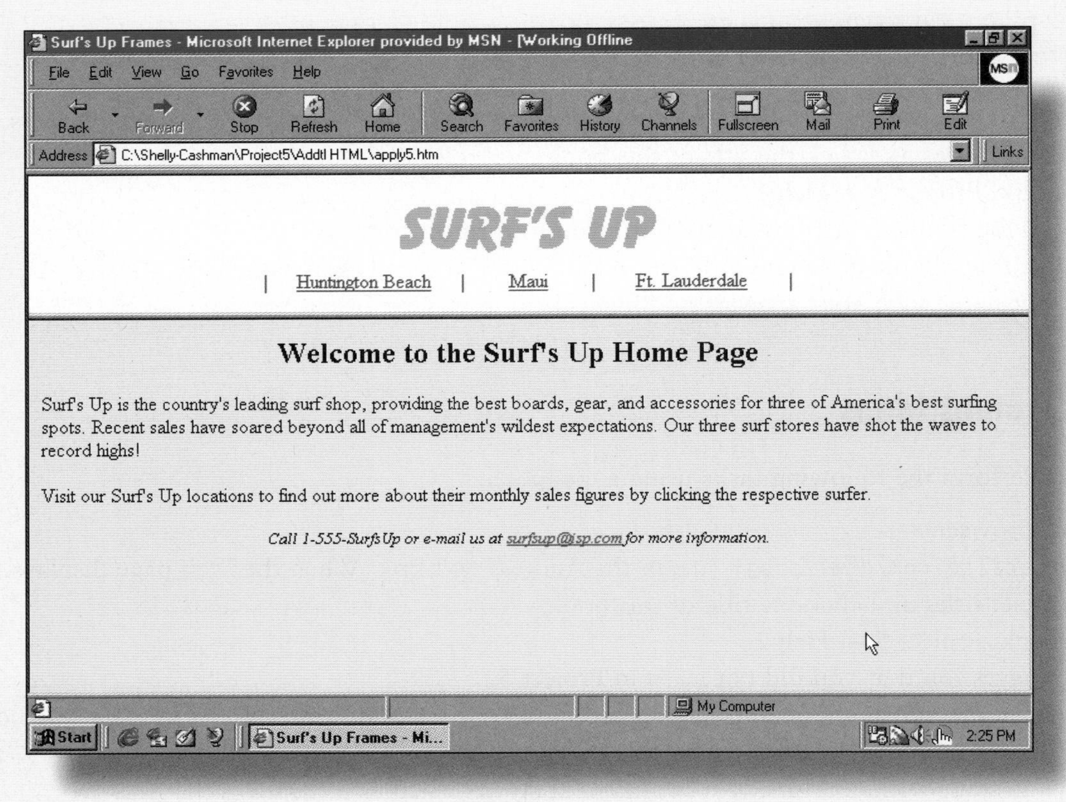

FIGURE 5-28

1. Open the file, apply5.htm, in Notepad.
2. Open the same file in your browser.
3. Examine the HTML file and its appearance in the browser.
4. Correct the HTML errors to make the Web page look similar to the one shown in Figure 5-28.
5. Add any HTML code necessary to create additional features shown in the Web page.
6. Save the revised file on a floppy disk using the file name apply5-2.htm.
7. Print the revised document source.
8. Open the apply5-2.htm file in your browser.
9. Print the Web page.
10. Write your name on the printouts and hand them in to your instructor.

1 Restructuring the AHS Web Site

Problem: The Reunion Committee wants to try a different frame structure for the Web site. You decide to create a new frame definition, such as the one shown in Figure 5-29.

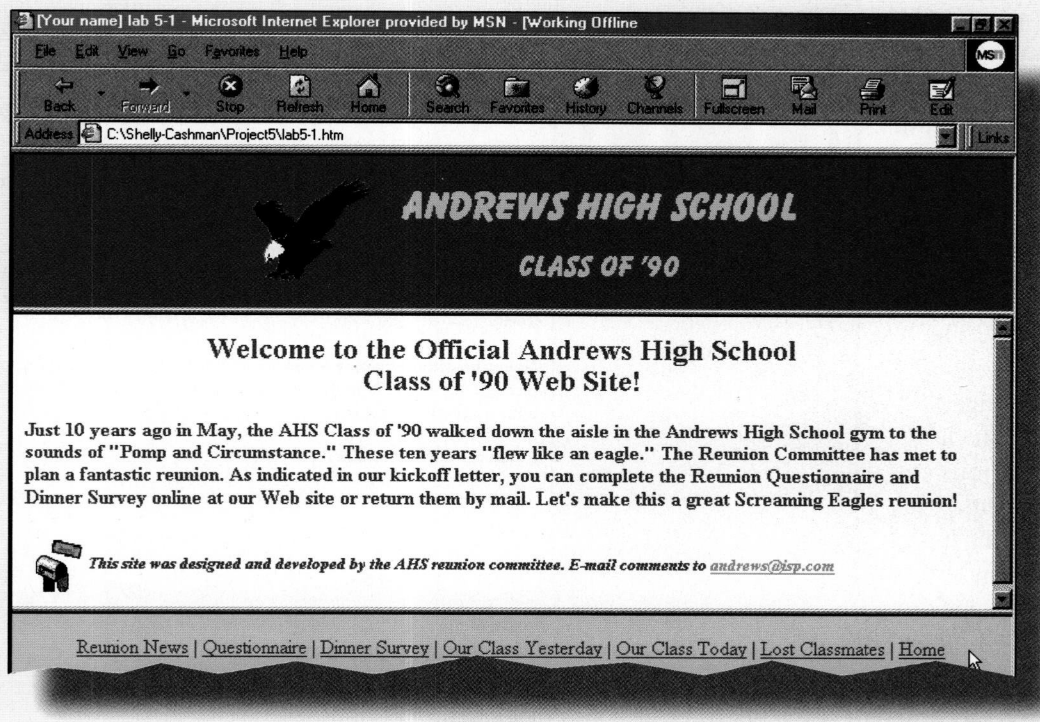

FIGURE 5-29

Instructions: Start Notepad. Perform the following tasks using a computer.

1. Start a new HTML file with the title, [your name] lab5-1, in the main heading section.
2. Begin the frame definition file by specifying three rows:
   a. The first row contains the header.htm file with a background color of navy.
   b. The second row contains the home.htm file created in Project 5.
   c. The last row contains a Web page similar to menu.htm, except that it is horizontal rather than vertical. Use the file name, menu5-1.htm, in the frame definition file for this frame.
3. Save the frame definition file as lab5-1.htm.
4. Open menu.htm and save it as menu5-1.htm.
5. Change this file to have horizontal links rather than vertical links. Remember to put a dividing line between links, using the | symbol.
6. Save the file using the file name, menu5-1.htm.
7. Print the lab5-1.htm and menu5-1.htm files.
8. Open the lab5-1.htm file in your browser and test all links.
9. Print the Web page.
10. Write your name on the printouts and hand them in to your instructor.

2 Creating an Online Bank

Problem: The $ Bank has decided to do banking online over the Internet. You have been asked to create a Web page containing two frames, similar to those shown in Figure 5-30. First, you need to create a frame definition file that specifies a two-column structure, with columns set to 30% and 70%. The left-hand column (frame) holds a page, menu5-2.htm, that displays links to various options and information about the bank. The right-hand column (frame) holds a home page named home5-2.htm.

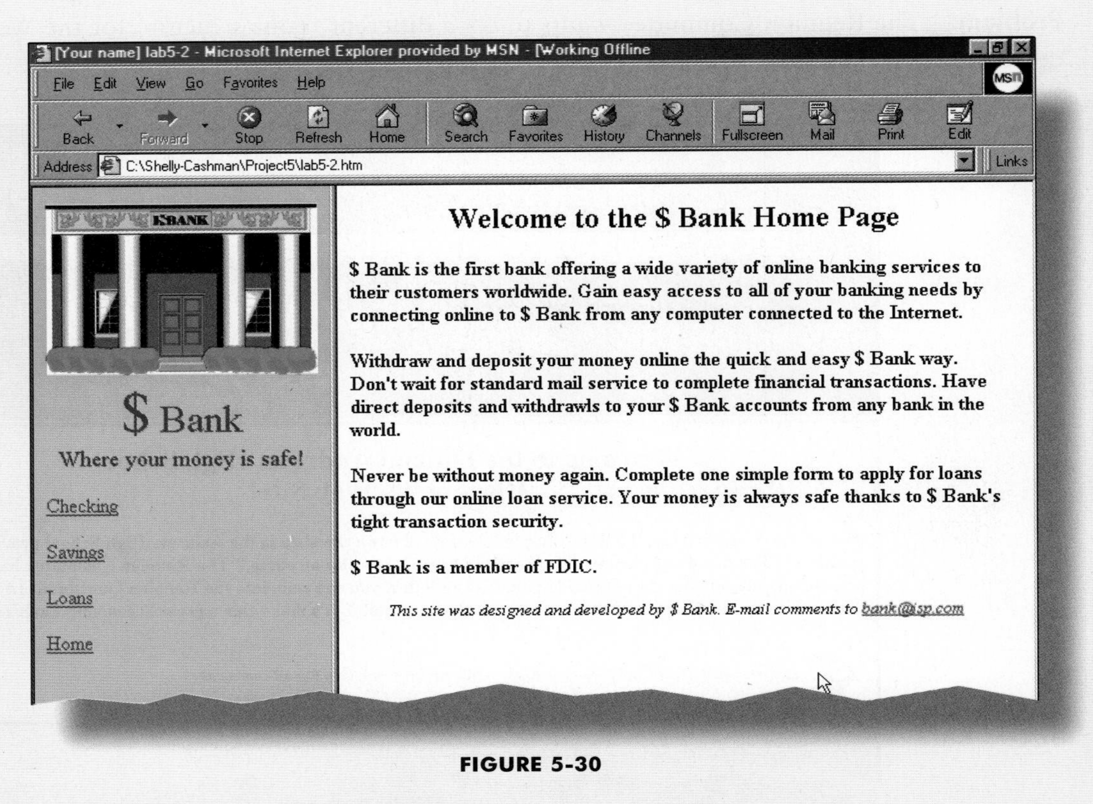

FIGURE 5-30

Instructions: Start Notepad. Perform the following tasks using a computer.

1. Start a new HTML file with the title, [your name] lab5-2, in the main heading section.
2. Begin the project by creating a frame definition file that specifies a structure with two columns, 30% and 70%.
3. For the Web page in the left-hand column (frame), create a new file and do the following:
   a. Set a background color of #FFCC00.
   b. Insert the image, bank.gif, from the HTML Data Disk.
   c. Enlarge the $ in the name, $ Bank, as needed to make it larger than the rest of the text for that line.
   d. Create four links on the page. Link the Home button to home5-2.htm. Use any of the Web pages on the HTML Data Disk for the other three links: Checking, Savings, Loans.
   e. Save the file as menu5-2.htm.
4. For the right-hand column (frame), create a third file that contains the text shown in Figure 5-30.
   a. Make the text all bold except for the last line (the e-mail address line).
   b. Make the e-mail address line italic.
   c. Make the link colors (normal, active, and visited) green.
   d. Save this file as home5-2.htm.
5. Open the lab5-2.htm file in your browser.
6. Print the Web page.
7. Print the three HTML files.
8. Write your name on the printouts and hand them in to your instructor.

3 Creating a Four-Frame Structure

Problem: You want to create a four-frame structure to promote the Web development work that you have done in previous projects. Your Web page should look like the one shown in Figure 5-31. Use any image stored on the HTML Data Disk as your logo. Use any of the Web pages previously created and stored on the HTML Data Disk to display in the bottom, right-hand frame.

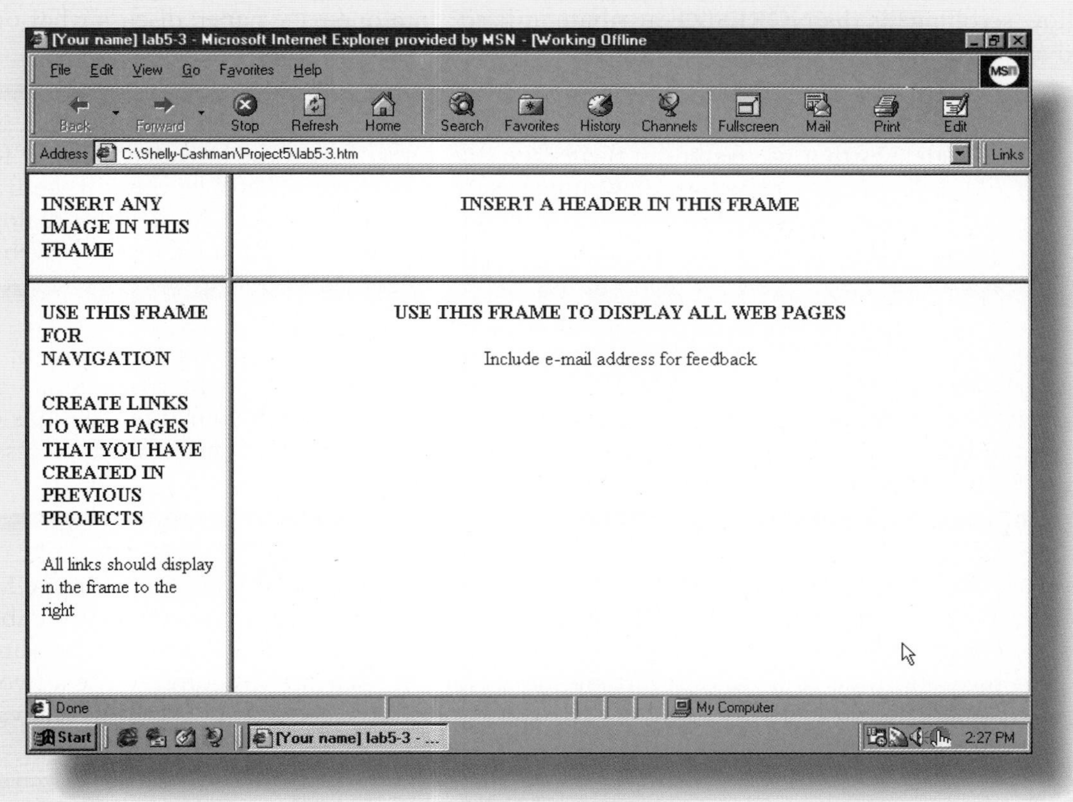

FIGURE 5-31

Instructions: Start Notepad. Perform the following tasks using a computer.

1. Create a frame definition file and three Web pages similar to those sketched in Figure 5-31. The title of the frame definition file should be [your name] lab5-3. Name the other files logo5-3.htm for the logo frame, hdr5-3.htm for the header frame, and menu5-3.htm for the navigation frame.
2. Insert in the logo frame (logo5-3.htm) any image stored on the HTML Data Disk.
3. Include in the header frame (hdr5-3.htm) a heading that has a unique color and font face.
4. Include in the navigation frame (menu5-3.htm) links to several Web pages.
5. Use scroll bars where you think they are necessary.
6. Use colored backgrounds where you see fit.
7. Save the Web pages using the file names lab5-3.htm, logo5-3.htm, hdr5-3.htm, and menu5-3.htm, respectively.
8. Print the pages from your browser.
9. Write your name on the printouts and hand them in to your instructor.

Cases and Places

The difficulty of these case studies varies:
▶ are the least difficult; ▶▶ are more difficult; and ▶▶▶ are the most difficult.

1 ▶ Find one Web site that utilizes frames. View the HTML source code for that page, and see what frame options were used on the page. Is the scrolling turned off, or is the default used? How many frames allow scrolling? Is the NORESIZE attribute utilized? In a one-page paper, discuss what options were used and whether you agree with them.

2 ▶ Locate two Web sites that use frames in their page structures. Assess the intended purpose for using this structure and decide whether the overall Web pages are more or less useful because of the frames. Print each overall Web page (remember to use the As laid out on screen option in the Print dialog box). Write a one-page paper discussing the use of frames for the intended purpose for those two Web sites.

3 ▶▶ Find one Web site that does not use frames but that you think could. Assess the purpose of the Web site and determine what frame layout would be best. Design two frame layouts that you think enhance the functionality of the Web site. Print the Web page that you found. Sketch your frame designs on another sheet of paper. In a one-page paper, discuss why your designs provide better/easier access to information on the Web site.

4 ▶▶ Visit three Web sites that contain information about HTML. Several are mentioned in the More Abouts in this project. Others are indicated in previous projects. Read additional information about frames. Compare what these sources have to say about the advantages and disadvantages of using frames. What suggestions do they make regarding the use of this Web site structure? Write a two-page paper containing information that you read in this project, as well as the advantages and disadvantages discussed in the sources that you found.

5 ▶▶▶ Find a Web site that does not currently use frames and is, in your opinion, inappropriate for their use. Draw a sketch of the page with two possible frame layouts. In a two-page paper, discuss the disadvantages of frames for that particular Web site. State why the current design (that is, no frames) is a more appropriate Web site structure, as opposed to the use of frames for the information displayed.

6 ▶▶▶ Many Web sites appear to utilize frames but really do not (check the site's HTML source code to verify). Often, these have a header across the top of the page and a navigation bar along the left-hand side, giving the illusion of a frame structure. Find one Web site that uses a technique other than frames but gives the appearance of a frame structure. In a four-page paper, discuss why the Web site is better the way it is or how it could be improved with the use of frames.

HTML

Creating Forms on a Web Page

OBJECTIVES

You will have mastered the material in this project when you can:

- Define terms related to forms
- Describe the different form controls and their uses
- Use the <FORM> tag
- Use the <INPUT> tag
- Create radio buttons
- Create a text field
- Create a textarea field
- Use the <SELECT> tag
- Use the <OPTION> tag
- Create a selection menu
- Insert options into a selection menu
- Create a Submit button
- Create a Reset button

Information Give and Take

Using Online Forms

Initially, these three best-selling authors, Allen Ginsberg, American poet known as the spokesman for the Beat Generation; Ernest Hemingway, American novelist and short-story writer whose style is characterized by crispness, concise dialog, and emotional understatement; and Alex Haley, American author who helped popularize the study of black history and genealogy, appear to have little in common with each other or with creating online forms using HTML, as you will do in this project. The three authors wrote unique works for distinct audiences at historical literary moments. Yet, despite these apparent differences, each author was highly regarded for his literary contribution.

As an author of Web pages, you have the opportunity to make your contribution in Web publishing circles. As well as providing appeal and interest for Web page visitors, you can offer functionality and purpose for sites you develop. You are an author of a unique work in the online age of Web publishing.

In traditional publishing, an author writes a manuscript and an editor marks up the pages with instructions for layout. The designer, in conjunction with the markups, lays out the pages accordingly. Adjustments are made by the editor and the author, and the designer revises the layout until it is complete.

In Web publishing, the author writes the text file and marks up the words with HTML tags to indicate the various formatting features. He or she is involved in all aspects of the development, design, and layout.

This project illustrates using forms to create an environment that invites people to return to the site. All forms are designed to allow visitors to interact easily with the owners of the Web site by submitting information in an online format. HTML makes it possible to convert text-based Web pages to Web page forms for gathering information as well as for information sending.

As authors interact with their audience through their characters and stories, you can use a form to interact with your Web page audience, with the added advantage of instant feedback. Receiving a response about the Web page or other areas of interest; finding out who visits the Web pages; selling products or services; and acting as a guest book are just some of the ways in which you can interact with your visitors using forms.

As you conclude the projects in this book, you now have a working knowledge of the HTML creation and editing processes, linking Web pages, using tables, working with image maps, and creating frames and forms to convey your purpose and achieve your results.

While your work may not win a Pulitzer Prize, as an aspiring Web page developer, you you have a distinct advantage over the literary authors: you are author, editor, and designer.

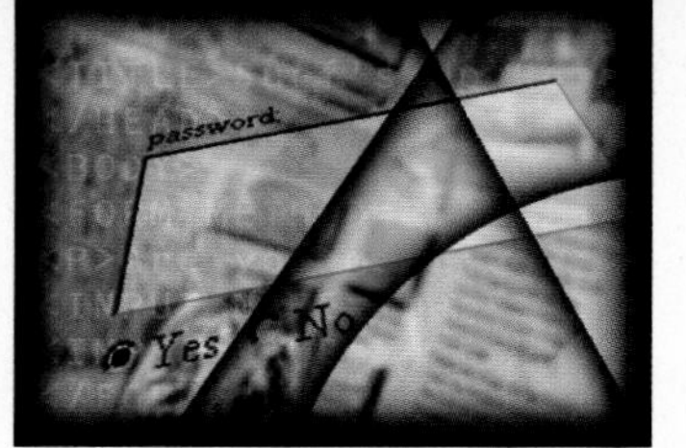

HTML

Creating Forms on a Web Page

CASE PERSPECTIVE

The Andrews High School reunion Web site created in the previous project has been a great success. Many graduates of the class have found out important information about the AHS Class of '90 reunion through the Web site. Two survey forms are included on the site. Although this is a great idea, it has been difficult to collect the data. Graduates have to print the survey, complete it, and e-mail the responses to the Reunion Committee. An online data collection solution would be more beneficial and easier to use for both the graduates and the committee.

Danielle Staffieri, the president of the Reunion Committee, has asked you to convert the paper survey forms on the reunion Web site to online forms by using HTML. Graduates then will be able to fill in the forms on the Web page and submit them to an e-mail address for collection.

Introduction

The goal of projects completed thus far has been to deliver information to a Web page visitor. Getting information from the visitor is another important aspect of good Web page development and is vital to good communication between the Web site owner and Web page visitors.

Two Web pages created with HTML tags are stored on the HTML Data Disk. These Web pages were designed as text-only surveys to solicit information from visitors to the AHS Class of '90 reunion Web site. The Web pages have no areas in which a Web site visitor can enter information. So the Web page visitor must print the survey, complete it, and e-mail the responses to the intended recipient. Although information gathering like this can work, a better approach is to create an HTML form that contains the capability for online submission, as described in this project.

Project Six – Andrews High School Class Reunion Survey Forms

One challenge of Web site development is to create an environment that invites people to return to the site. Including forms on your site helps you do this. Web sites use forms for a variety of purposes, such as collecting visitor feedback about the Web site or gathering information that can be used to market products. All forms are designed to allow visitors to interact easily with the owners of the Web site by submitting information in an online format.

In this project, you will use HTML to convert two text-based Web pages (Figures 6-1a and 6-1b) to Web page forms (Figures 6-1c and 6-1d). These forms are used to gather information for the AHS ten-year class reunion.

AHS '90 Questionnaire - Microsoft Internet Explorer provided by MSN

Address A:\survey1.htm

QUESTIONNAIRE

We would like to know what you have been doing since graduation. Please answer the following questions by e-mailing your responses to the committee at andrews@isp.com.

Are you married?
Do you have any children? How many?
What have you been doing since graduation?
What are your hobbies or special interests?
Tell us something interesting about yourself.

Thank you for taking the time to answer our Questionnaire.
The Reunion Committee

text-based questions

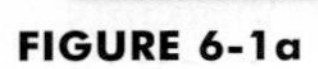

FIGURE 6-1a

AHS '90 Dinner Survey - Microsoft Internet Explorer provided by MSN

Address A:\survey2.htm

REUNION DINNER SURVEY

We would like to know if you are interested in attending a 10-year reunion dinner. Please answer the following questions by e-mailing your response to the Reunion Committee at andrews@isp.com.

Are you interested in attending a reunion dinner? Yes ___ No ___
Choose one of the following dates: June 19, July 17, or August 7. Date ___
Would you be willing to travel out of town? Yes ___ No ___
Pick a restaurant: Drake Hill Restaurant, Elks Club, or Mesa Country Club in Lake Town. Restaurant ___
Price ranges: $45 per couple to $90 per couple. What will you pay (cash bar)? Price you want to pay ___

Thank you for your input.
The Reunion Committee

text-based questions

FIGURE 6-1b

AHS '90 Questionnaire - Microsoft Internet Explorer provided by MSN

Address A:\survey1.htm

QUESTIONNAIRE

We would like to know what you have been doing since graduation. Please answer the following questions and send your responses to the Reunion Committee by using the Submit button below.

Are you married? Yes No
Do you have any children? Yes No
How many?
What have you been doing since graduation?
What are your hobbies or special interests?
Tell us something interesting about yourself.

Submit the Form | Reset the Form

Thank you for taking the time to answer our Questionnaire.
The Reunion Committee

radio buttons
text field
textarea field
text field
textarea field
Submit button
Reset button

FIGURE 6-1c

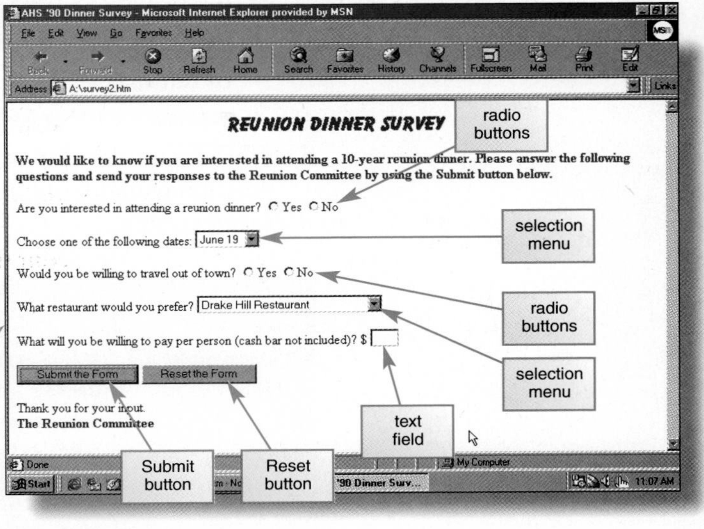

FIGURE 6-1d

Creating Web Page Forms

When forms are included on a Web page, the page can be used for more than information sending; it can be used for information gathering. You can use a form to interact with your Web page visitors in various ways, including the following:

- Get feedback about the Web page or other areas of interest
- Find out who is visiting the Web page
- Sell products or services
- Act as a guestbook

Forms

A number of HTML guides on the Internet discuss the use of forms on Web pages. Many of those sites are created and maintained at universities. The guides give practical tips on the purpose and use of HTML tags and attributes. To view one HTML guide, visit the HTML More About page (www.scsite.com/html/more.htm) and click Forms.

Figures 6-1c and 6-1d show sample Web page forms. Each form is designed to request specific information from the Web page visitor. A Web page form has three main components:

1. Input controls
2. FORM tag, which contains the information necessary to process the form
3. Submit button, which sends the data to be processed

Input Controls

An **input control** is any type of input mechanism on a form. A form may contain any of a variety of input controls classified as data or text input controls. A **data input control** is either a radio button (RADIO), a check box (CHECKBOX), a submit button (SUBMIT), a reset button (RESET), or a selection (drop-down) menu (SELECT). A **text input control** is either

- a text field (TEXT), in which the visitor may enter small amounts of text,
- a textarea field (TEXTAREA), in which the visitor may enter larger amounts of data, or
- a password text field (PASSWORD), in which the visitor may enter a password.

The forms you develop in this project use many types of input controls.

Of the available input controls, the seven listed in Table 6-1 are used most often in form creation.

Table 6-1

CONTROL	FUNCTION	REMARKS
TEXT	• Creates a single-line field for a relatively small amount of text.	• Indicates both the size of the field and the total maximum length.
PASSWORD	• Identical to text fields used for single-line data entry.	• Echoes (or masks) back the entered text as asterisks or bullets.
TEXTAREA	• Creates a multiple-line field for a relatively large amount of text.	• Indicates the number of rows and columns for the area.
SELECT	• Creates a menu of choices from which a visitor selects.	• Indicates the width of the list in number of rows.
CHECKBOX	• Creates a list item.	• More than one item in a list may be chosen.
RADIO	• Creates a list item.	• Only one item in a list may be chosen.
SUBMIT	• Submits a form for processing.	• Tells the browser to send the data on the form to the server.
RESET	• Resets the form.	• Returns all input controls to the default status.

Figures 6-2 through 6-5 show examples of the controls listed in Table 6-1.

A **TEXT control** creates a text field that is used for a single line of input (Figure 6-2). The TEXT control has two attributes:

1. SIZE, which determines the number of characters that display on the form
2. MAXLENGTH, which specifies the maximum length of the input field

The maximum length of the field may exceed the size of the field that displays on the form. For example, consider a field size of three characters and a maximum length of nine characters. If a Web page visitor types in more characters than the size of the text field (three characters), the characters scroll to the left, to a maximum of nine characters entered.

A **PASSWORD control** creates a text field the same as a regular text field, that is, a single-line input field (Figure 6-2), except that the characters display as asterisks or bullets. A password text field holds the password entered by a visitor. A password always appears as a series of characters, asterisks or bullets as determined by the Web developer, one per character in the password entered. This feature is designed to help protect the visitor's password from being observed by others as it is being entered.

FIGURE 6-2

A **TEXTAREA control** creates a field that allows multiple lines of input (Figure 6-3). Textarea fields are useful when an extensive amount of input from the Web page visitor is required or desired. The TEXTAREA control has two primary attributes:

1. ROWS, which specifies the number of rows in the textarea field
2. COLS, which specifies the number of columns in the textarea field

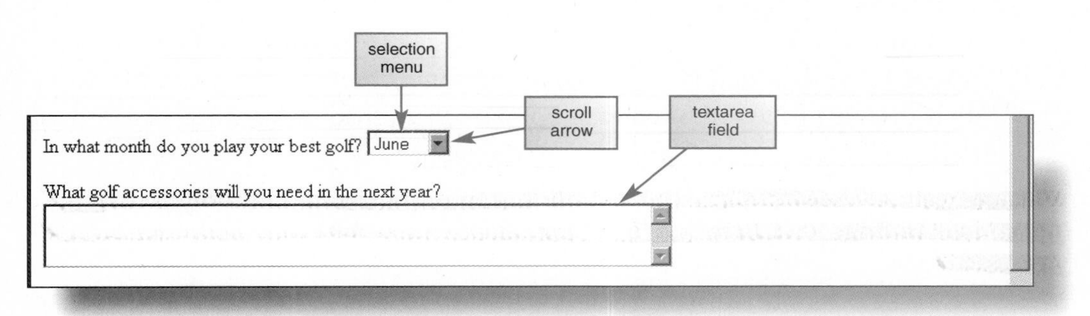

FIGURE 6-3

A **SELECT control** creates a selection menu from which the visitor selects one or more choices (Figure 6-3). This eliminates the visitor's having to type information into a text or textarea field. This type of control is suitable when a limited number of choices are available.

A **CHECKBOX control** allows a Web page visitor to select more than one choice from a list of choices (Figure 6-4 on the next page). Each choice in a check box list can be either on or off. By default, all check boxes are deselected. However, you may change the default so that a particular check box is pre-selected as the default.

Form Tutorial

What better way to learn more about the HTML form tag than using a tutorial on the Web? Lessons are grouped by topic, starting with initial HTML tags. An index is provided for ease of use. The tutorial uses illustrative examples to teach the important points of HTML to create Web pages. For more information, visit the HTML More About Web page (www.scsite.com/html/more.htm) and click Form Tutorial.

A **RADIO control** limits the Web page visitor to only one choice from a list of choices (Figure 6-4). Each choice is preceded by a **radio button,** typically an open circle. When the visitor selects one of the radio buttons, all other radio buttons in the list are automatically deselected. By default, all radio buttons are deselected. However, you can change the default so that a particular button is pre-selected as the default.

radio buttons with yes/no options

check box list

Do you like to golf? ○ Yes ○ No

Which course(s) do you like to play?
☐ Kapalua
☐ St. Andrews
☐ Muirfield
☐ La Paloma

FIGURE 6-4

The **RESET** and **SUBMIT controls** create the Reset and Submit buttons (Figure 6-5). The **Reset button** clears any input that was entered in the form, resetting the input controls back to the defaults. The **Submit button** sends the information to the appropriate location for processing. A Web page form must include a Submit button. Most also include a Reset button.

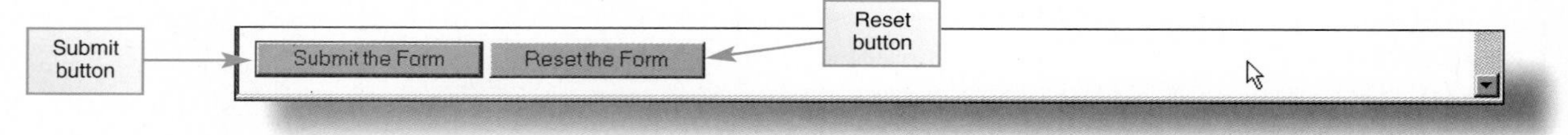

FIGURE 6-5

The type of information desired dictates what controls you use. If it varies substantially, use a text or textarea field. To limit the number of choices for a selection, use radio buttons, check boxes, or selection menus.

Each input control has one or two attributes:

1. NAME. The **NAME attribute** identifies the specific information that is being sent. All controls have a NAME.
2. VALUE. All controls except TEXTAREA also have a **VALUE attribute**. The **VALUE** is the data that is contained in the named input control (i.e., the data that the Web page visitor enters). For a textarea field, no VALUE attribute is possible because of the variability of the input.

When a Web page visitor clicks the Submit button on the form, both the NAME of the control and the VALUE of the data contained within that control are sent to be processed.

Form Tags

Input controls are either tags or attributes of tags. For example, the SELECT and TEXTAREA controls are HTML tags that are used as input controls. Other input controls are attributes of HTML tags. For example the tags <INPUT> or <SELECT>, include a number of attributes, including CHECKBOX, RADIO, and SUBMIT, that are used as input controls. Several form-related tags are used to create the interactive Web pages in this project. These are listed in Table 6-2. You define some of the controls used in a form using the <INPUT> tag. The default type for the <INPUT> tag is a text field. Therefore, if the TYPE attribute is not used in the <INPUT> tag, the type is text.

Table 6-2

TAG	FUNCTION	REMARKS
<FORM> </FORM>	• Creates a form that allows user input.	• Required when creating forms.
<INPUT>	• Defines the controls used in the form, using a variety of attributes.	• Required for input controls.
<SELECT> </SELECT>	• Creates a menu of choices from which a visitor selects.	• Required for selection choices.
<OPTION> </OPTION>	• Specifies a choice in a <SELECT> tag.	• Required, one per choice.
<TEXTAREA> </TEXTAREA>	• Creates a multiple-line input area.	• Required for large input areas.

Form statements begin with the <FORM> tag and end with the </FORM> tag. The <INPUT> tag is vital because it creates several of the input controls, including radio buttons, check boxes, and text fields. The Submit and Reset buttons are also created with the <INPUT> tag. The <SELECT> and <OPTION> tags create selection menus. Multiple lines of input can be inserted using the <TEXTAREA> tag. Any combination of these elements creates a Web page form.

Form Tag Attributes

The five primary tags have several attributes. Table 6-3 lists the tags and their main attributes.

Table 6-3

TAG	ATTRIBUTE	FUNCTION
<FORM> </FORM>	ACTION METHOD TARGET	• URL for action completed by the server. • HTTP method (POST). • Location at which the resource will display.
<INPUT>	TYPE NAME VALUE CHECKED DISABLED READONLY SIZE MAXLENGTH SRC ALT TABINDEX	• Type of input control (text, password, checkbox, radio, submit, reset, file, hidden, image, button). • The name of the control. • Value submitted if a control is selected (required for radio and checkbox controls). • Sets a radio button to a checked state (only one can be checked). • Disables a control. • Used for text passwords. • Number of characters that display on the form. • Maximum number of characters that can be entered. • URL to an image control. • Alternate text for an image control. • Sets tabbing order among control elements.
<SELECT> </SELECT>	NAME SIZE MULTIPLE DISABLED TABINDEX	• Name of the element. • Number of options visible when Web page is first opened. • Allows for multiple selections. • Disables a control. • Sets the tabbing order among control elements.
<OPTION> </OPTION>	SELECTED DISABLED VALUE	• Specifies if an option is selected. • Disables a control. • Value submitted if a control is selected.
<TEXTAREA> </TEXTAREA>	NAME ROWS COLS DISABLED READONLY TABINDEX	• Name of the control. • Width in number of rows. • Height in number of columns. • Disables a control. • Used for text passwords. • Sets the tabbing order among control elements.

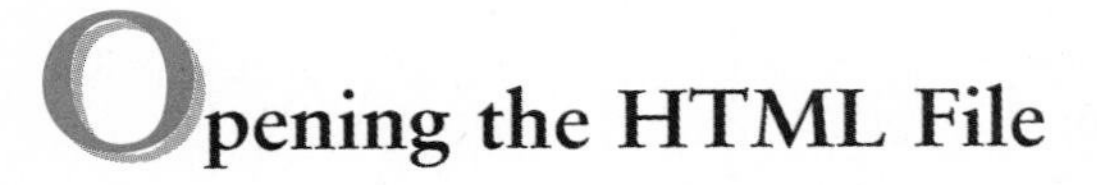

Opening the HTML File

In this project, you will makes changes to the two text-based Web pages stored on the HTML Data Disk, survey1.htm and survey2.htm. The file, survey1.htm, currently contains text only and no controls (Figure 6-1a on page HTM 6.5). This is an inconvenient way for the Web page visitor to respond to the survey. The visitor must print the survey, complete it, and then e-mail that information to the address listed in the opening paragraph of text. You will convert this Web page to the Web page form shown in Figure 6-1c on page HTM 6.5.

Perform the following steps to start Notepad and open the HTML file, survey1.htm.

TO START NOTEPAD AND OPEN THE HTML FILE

1. Start Notepad.
2. Insert the HTML Data Disk in drive A, click File on the menu bar, and then click Open.
3. Type `survey1.htm` in the File name text box and then click the Open button in the Open dialog box.

The HTML code displays as shown in Figure 6-6.

survey1.htm file

survey1.htm - Notepad

File Edit Search Help

```
<HTML>
<HEAD>
<TITLE>AHS '90 Questionnaire</TITLE>
</HEAD>
<BODY>

<CENTER><FONT COLOR="navy"><FONT FACE="Bazooka" SIZE=+2>Questionnaire
</FONT></CENTER>

<P><B>We would like to know what you have been doing since graduation.
Please answer the following questions
by e-mailing your responses to the committee at
<A HREF="mailto:andrews@isp.com">andrews@isp.com</A>.
</B></FONT></P>

<P>Are you married?
<BR>Do you have any children? How many?
<BR>What have you been doing since graduation?
<BR>What are your hobbies or special interests?
<BR>Tell us something interesting about yourself.</P>

<P>Thank you for taking the time to answer our Questionnaire.
<BR><B><FONT COLOR="navy">The Reunion Committee</FONT></B></P>

</BODY>
</HTML>
```

initial text and HTML tags

text-based questionnaire

FIGURE 6-6

Margin CGI Scripts

Using CGI scripts to process forms is a much more efficient way to handle the data that is sent from a form. Many Web sites have free sample CGI scripts for Web developers to use. To view an interactive Web site with a multitude of information and free samples, visit the HTML More About page (www.scsite.com/html/more.htm) and click CGI.

<FORM: METHOD GET, POST>

Creating a Form Having Text, Radio Button, and Textarea Controls

When creating a form, you begin by identifying how the form will be sent and processed when it is submitted. The <FORM> tag designates a Web page as a form. Between the <FORM> and </FORM> tags, you use various form controls to request different types of information. You can use as many controls as desired.

Identifying the Form Process

The <FORM> attribute, METHOD, specifies the manner in which the form is sent to the server to be processed. Two primary ways are used in HTML: the GET method and the POST method. The GET method sends the name-value pairs to the end of the URL indicated in the ACTION attribute. The POST method sends a separate data file with the name-value pairs to the URL indicated in the ACTION attribute. The POST method is used for the forms in this project.

The <FORM> attribute, ACTION, specifies the action that will be taken when the form is submitted. Information on forms can be sent by e-mail to a central e-mail address or can be used to update a database. Although the e-mail option is functional, many Web sites process information from forms using Common Gateway Interface (CGI) scripting. A CGI script is a program written in a programming language (such as Perl) that communicates with the Web server. The CGI script sends the information input on the Web page form to the server for processing. This type of processing involves programming tasks that are beyond the scope of this book. Therefore, the information from the forms in this project will be submitted in a file to an e-mail address. E-mail is specified as the ACTION in the <FORM> tag.

The HTML code shown in Figure 6-7 creates a form using the POST method. When the form is submitted, a file containing the input data will be sent as an attachment to an e-mail to the e-mail address, ahs@isp.com.

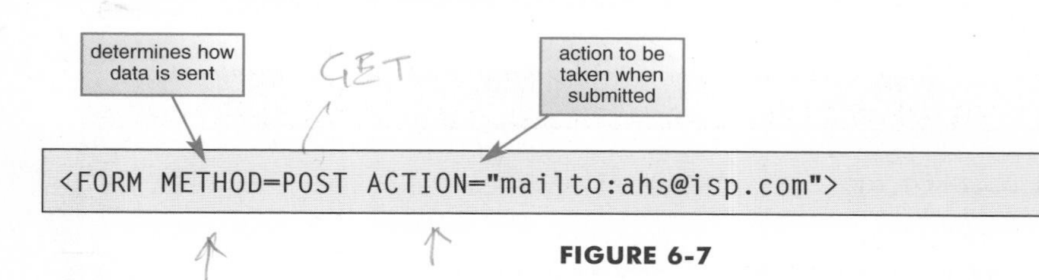

FIGURE 6-7

Perform the following steps to create the form structure.

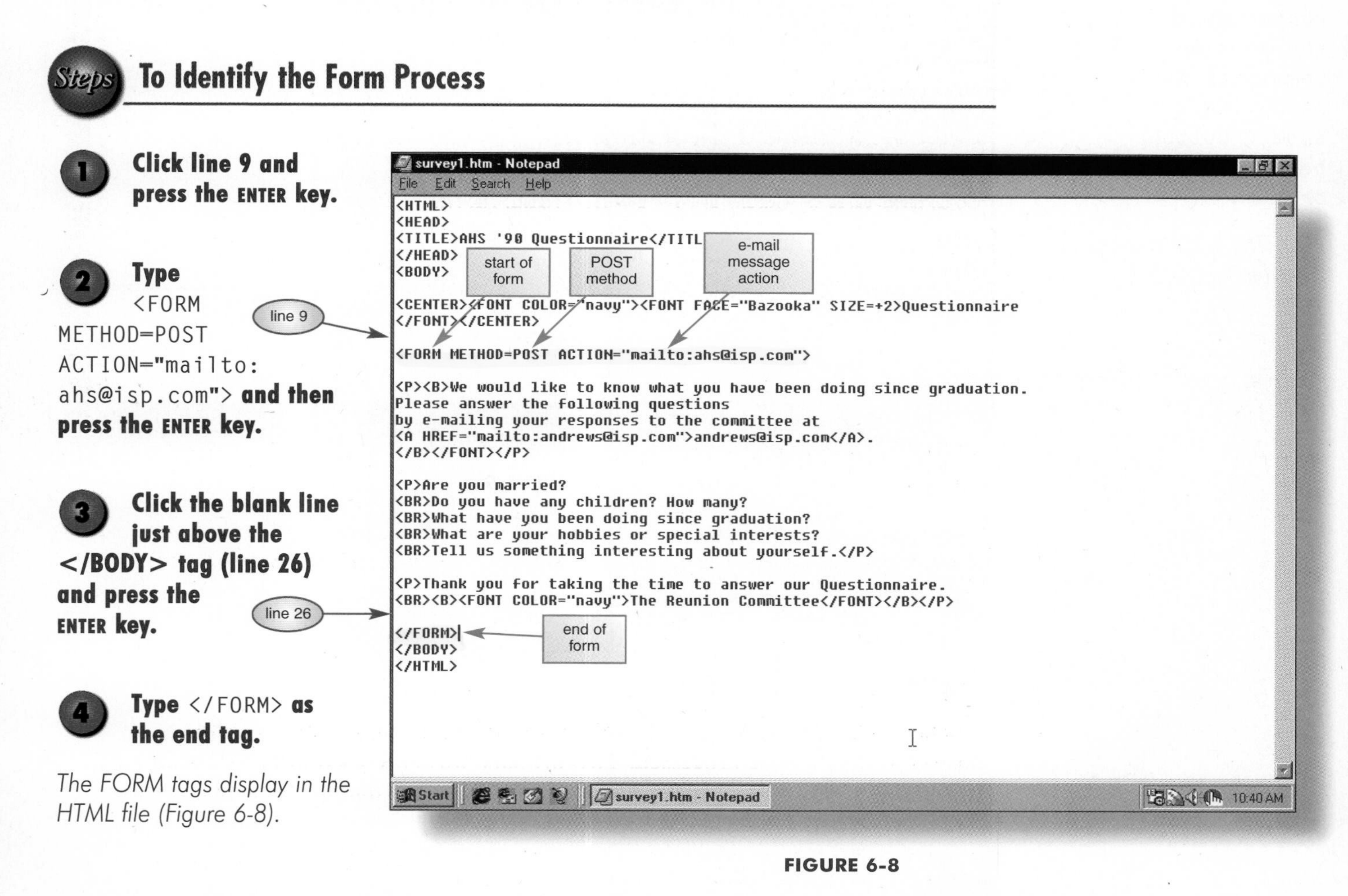

Steps To Identify the Form Process

1. **Click line 9 and press the ENTER key.**

2. **Type** `<FORM METHOD=POST ACTION="mailto:ahs@isp.com">` **and then press the ENTER key.**

3. **Click the blank line just above the </BODY> tag (line 26) and press the ENTER key.**

4. **Type** `</FORM>` **as the end tag.**

The FORM tags display in the HTML file (Figure 6-8).

FIGURE 6-8

The <FORM METHOD=POST ACTION="mailto:ahs@isp.com"> tag designates that the form will use the POST method to send the data. The form will be sent in a file to the e-mail address, ahs@isp.com. The </FORM> tag just above the </BODY> tag ends the Web page form.

Changing the Text Message

The next step in the conversion is to alter the text that tells the visitor to submit the questionnaire via e-mail. Perform the following steps to change the text to a more appropriate message.

Steps To Change the Text

1 Select lines 14 and 15 and then press the DELETE key.

2 With the insertion point on line 14, type `and send your responses to the Reunion Committee by using the Submit button below.` **as the new text.**

The HTML code displays as shown in Figure 6-9.

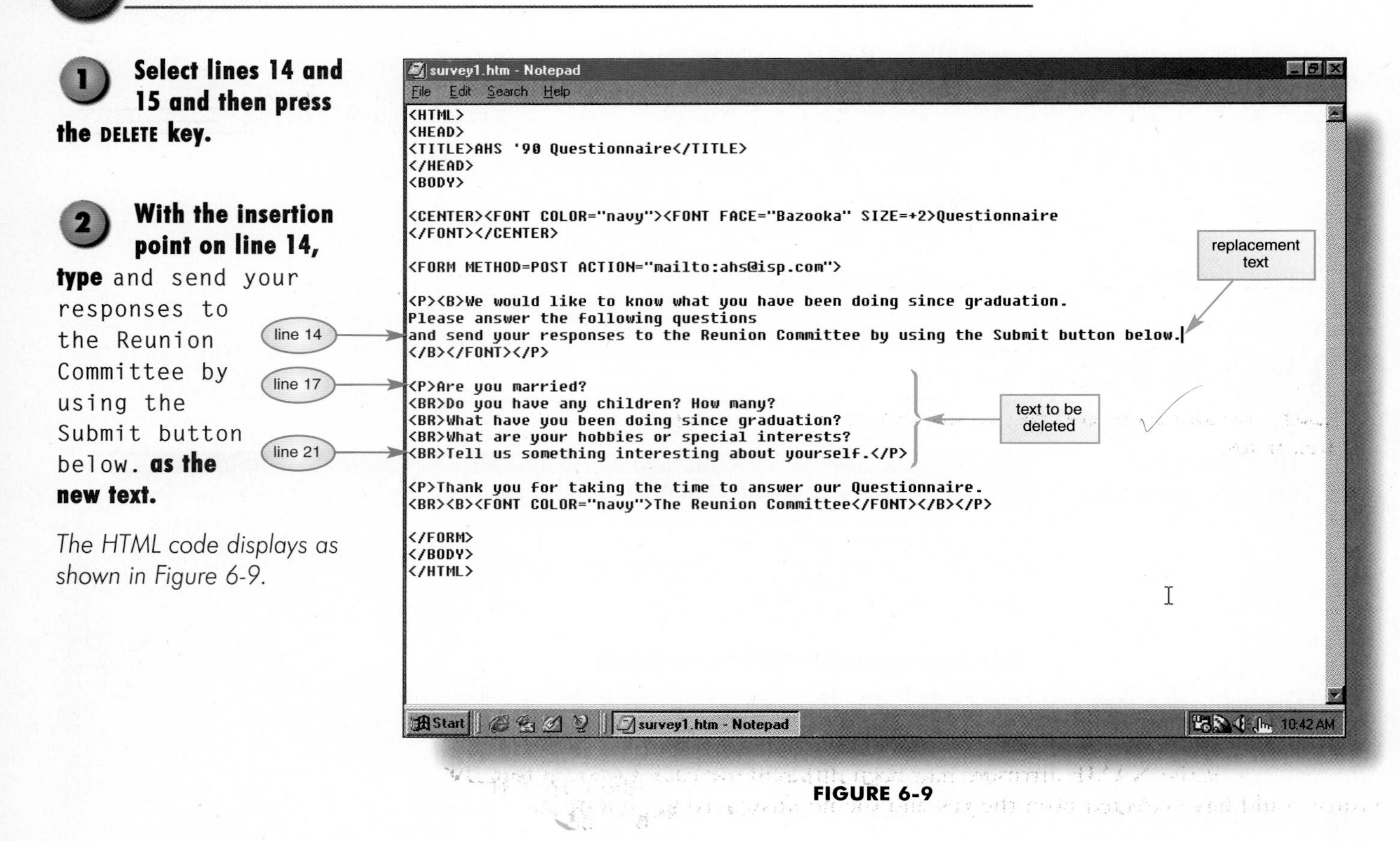

FIGURE 6-9

3 Highlight lines 17 through 21 and then press the DELETE key.

The HTML code displays as shown in Figure 6-10 and the insertion point is on line 17.

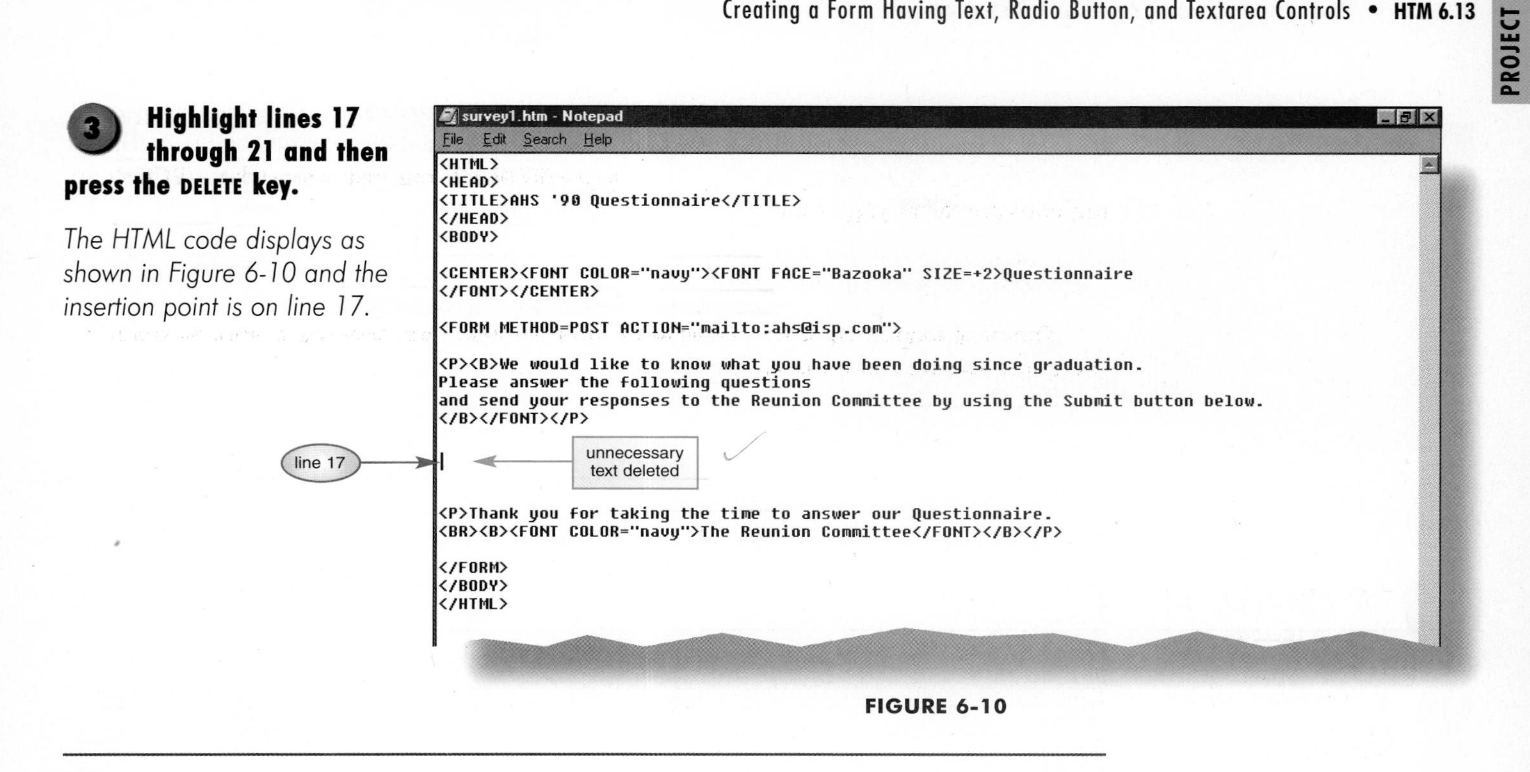


```
<HTML>
<HEAD>
<TITLE>AHS '90 Questionnaire</TITLE>
</HEAD>
<BODY>

<CENTER><FONT COLOR="navy"><FONT FACE="Bazooka" SIZE=+2>Questionnaire
</FONT></CENTER>

<FORM METHOD=POST ACTION="mailto:ahs@isp.com">

<P><B>We would like to know what you have been doing since graduation.
Please answer the following questions
and send your responses to the Reunion Committee by using the Submit button below.
</B></FONT></P>

|

<P>Thank you for taking the time to answer our Questionnaire.
<BR><B><FONT COLOR="navy">The Reunion Committee</FONT></B></P>

</FORM>
</BODY>
</HTML>
```

FIGURE 6-10

The visitor now is directed to submit the questionnaire via the Submit button that you will create later at the bottom of the Web page form. Some of the text currently contained in the original Web page (survey1.htm) will be reinserted as the file is being converted to a Web page form.

Next, you add input controls to survey1.htm: radio buttons, text fields, and textarea fields.

Radio Buttons

Old-time car radios were operated by a row of large black plastic buttons. Push one button, and you get one preset radio station. You could only push one button at a time. Radio buttons on forms work the same way as the old-time radio buttons — one button at a time. With check boxes, more than one option can be selected at a time.

Adding Radio Buttons

The first items you add to the Web page form are two sets of radio buttons. Radio buttons allow the Web page visitor to select only one option from a list of items. Figure 6-11 shows two of the HTML tags that you will use to create two radio buttons.

The TYPE="radio" attribute specifies that the type of control is RADIO, the radio button. In Figure 6-11, a yes or no question is asked; the visitor may select only Yes or No. You specify this by using the same NAME attribute, "married", for both buttons. If the NAME attribute had been different for each radio button, the visitor could have selected both the yes and the no answer to the question.

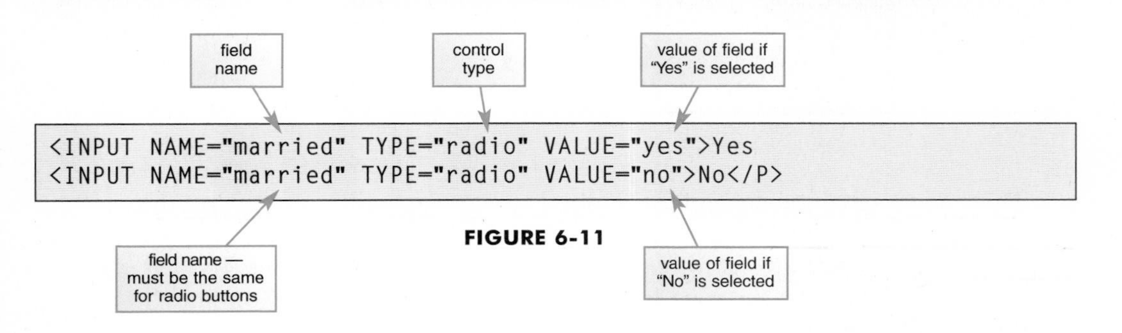


```
<INPUT NAME="married" TYPE="radio" VALUE="yes">Yes
<INPUT NAME="married" TYPE="radio" VALUE="no">No</P>
```

FIGURE 6-11

Table 6-4

LINE	HTML TAGS AND TEXT
17	<P>Are you married?
18	<INPUT NAME="married" TYPE="radio" VALUE="yes">Yes
19	<INPUT NAME="married" TYPE="radio" VALUE="no">No</P>
20	
21	<P>Do you have any children?
22	<INPUT NAME="children" TYPE="radio" VALUE="yes">Yes
23	<INPUT NAME="children" TYPE="radio" VALUE="no">No

The VALUE attribute defines the value of the radio button option. The value (for example, yes or no) is the text that is sent to be processed when the visitor selects an option, and is associated with the field name. If a Web page visitor checked yes under married, the text string, married=yes, is sent to be processed. The VALUE attribute is required for the RADIO input control.

Table 6-4 contains the HTML code that creates the first two sets of radio buttons, one for marital status and the other regarding children. In the following steps, you enter the HTML code given in Table 6-4.

Perform the following steps to specify two sets of radio buttons.

To Add Radio Buttons

1 **If necessary, click line 17.**

2 **Enter the HTML code shown in Table 6-4 and then press the ENTER key.**

The HTML code displays as shown in Figure 6-12 and the radio buttons display on the Web page form as shown in Figure 6-1c on page HTM 6.5. The insertion point is on line 24.

```
<HTML>
<HEAD>
<TITLE>AHS '90 Questionnaire</TITLE>
</HEAD>
<BODY>

<CENTER><FONT COLOR="navy"><FONT FACE="Bazooka" SIZE=+2>Questionnaire
</FONT></CENTER>

<FORM METHOD=POST ACTION="mailto:ahs@isp.com">

<P><B>We would lik... since graduation.
Please answer the ... qu...
and send your resp... the ... Comm... sing the Submit button below.
</B></FONT></P>

<P>Are you married?
<INPUT NAME="married" TYPE="radio" VALUE="yes">Yes
<INPUT NAME="married" TYPE="radio" VALUE="no">No</P>

<P>Do you have any children?
<INPUT NAME="children" TYPE="radio" VALUE="yes">Yes
<INPUT NAME="children" TYPE="radio" VALUE="no">No

<P>Thank you for taking the time to answer our Questionnaire.
<BR><B><FONT COLOR="navy">The Reunion Committee</FONT></B></P>

</FORM>
</BODY>
</HTML>
```

survey1.htm - Notepad; callouts: field name, control type, value if selected, line 17, first set of radio buttons, second set of radio buttons

FIGURE 6-12

This completes the definition of the first two sets of radio buttons on the survey1.htm form. The Web page visitor can answer either yes or no to both questions asked. The buttons for each set display next to each other. To have the radio buttons display on separate lines, precede the <INPUT> tags on lines 19 and 23 with a <BR> tag.

The next step is to add a text field.

Adding a Text Field

A text field allows for a single line of input. The <INPUT> tag used to set a text field in survey1.htm is shown in Figure 6-13. The NAME of a text field, "chilnum" in this case, is associated with the text that the visitor enters. You specify the size of the text field that appears on the form with the SIZE attribute. Here, SIZE="2" means that the text field is two characters in length. That is, two characters will appear, although more characters may be entered. The maximum number of characters that may be entered in the text field is specified by the MAXLENGTH attribute. In Figure 6-13, the MAXLENGTH attribute specifies the same number of characters (2) as the SIZE attribute (2). The input therefore cannot exceed two characters. If you specify a maximum number of characters that is greater than the number of characters specified in the SIZE attribute, the additional characters will scroll to the left in the text field.

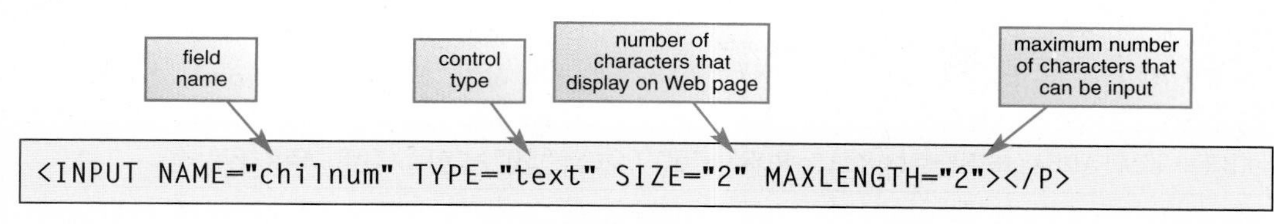

FIGURE 6-13

Perform the following steps to add a text field.

Steps To Add a Text Field

1. **If necessary, click line 24.**

2. **Type** `<BR>How many?` **and then press the ENTER key.**

3. **Type** `<INPUT NAME="chilnum" TYPE="text" SIZE="2" MAXLENGTH="2"></P>` **and press the ENTER key twice.**

The HTML code displays as shown in Figure 6-14 and the insertion point is on line 27.

survey1.htm - Notepad

File Edit Search Help

```
<HTML>
<HEAD>
<TITLE>AHS '90 Questionnaire</TITLE>
</HEAD>
<BODY>

<CENTER><FONT COLOR="navy"><FONT FACE="Bazooka" SIZE=+2>Questionnaire
</FONT></CENTER>

<FORM METHOD=POST ACTION="mailto:ahs@isp.com">

<P><B>We would like to know what you have been doing since graduation.
Please answer the following questions
and send your responses to the Reunion Committee by using the Submit button below.
</B></FONT></P>

<P>Are you married?
<INPUT NAME="married" TYPE="radio" VALUE="yes">Yes
<INPUT NAME="married" TYPE="radio" VALUE="no">No</P>

<P>Do you have any children?
<INPUT NAME="children" TYPE="radio" VALUE="yes">Yes
<INPUT NAME="children" TYPE="radio" VALUE="no">No
<BR>How many?
<INPUT NAME="chilnum" TYPE="text" SIZE="2" MAXLENGTH="2"></P>

<P>Thank you for taking the time to answer our Questionnaire.
<BR><B><FONT COLOR="navy">The Reunion Committee</FONT></B></P>

</FORM>
</BODY>
</HTML>
```

line 24

line 27

text field specified

field name

control type

number of characters that display on Web page

maximum number of characters that can be input

Start | survey1.htm - Notepad | 10:47 AM

FIGURE 6-14

You now have created two sets of radio buttons and one text field. In the next section, you will add several textarea fields to the form. Textarea fields are similar to text fields, except that they allow multiple lines of text input.

Adding Textareas

A single line of text is appropriate for some input, such as the number of children in the previous example. For this input, a TEXT control works well. Often, you will need to provide more space to accommodate a larger amount of input. For these cases, a TEXTAREA control is more appropriate. Note that the <TEXTAREA> tag requires an end tag, </TEXTAREA>. Two of the controls you enter next on the form ask questions that are difficult to answer in a single line, so you will create textarea fields for input. Figure 6-15 shows the attributes used in this tag.

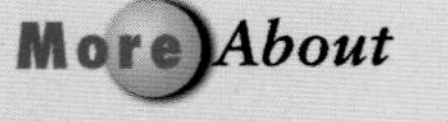

Textareas

To create a textarea, the Web developer specifies the number of rows and columns in which the Web page visitor can enter information. The maximum number of characters for a textarea is 32,700. It is a good rule of thumb to keep the number of columns in a textarea to 50 or less. Using that as a limit, the textarea will fit on most screens.

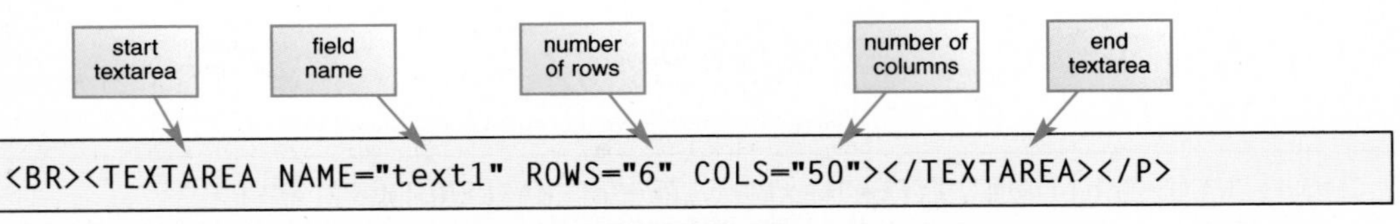

FIGURE 6-15

The NAME attribute gives the TEXTAREA input control a name to identify the information that is entered data in a textarea field. To define the size of a textarea field, you specify the number of rows (ROWS) and columns (COLS) that should display on the form. In this example, 6 rows and 50 columns will display.

In the next steps, you also will insert a variation of the TEXT control, one with a SIZE attribute of 50 and a MAXLENGTH attribute of 200 characters. After the first 50 characters, the text will scroll to the left in the text field.

Table 6-5 contains the tags and text to specify two TEXTAREA controls for multiple-line input and one TEXT control for single-line input. The text field is added for information that may not exceed one line. In the next steps, you enter the tags and text given in Table 6-5.

Table 6-5

LINE	HTML TAGS AND TEXT
27	<P>What have you been doing since graduation?
28	 <TEXTAREA NAME="text1" ROWS="6" COLS="50"></TEXTAREA></P>
29	
30	<P>What are your hobbies or special interests?
31	 <INPUT NAME="text2" TYPE="text" SIZE="50" MAXLENGTH="200"></P>
32	
33	<P>Tell us something interesting about yourself.
34	 <TEXTAREA NAME="text3" ROWS="4" COLS="50"></TEXTAREA></P>

Perform the following steps to insert two TEXTAREA controls and one TEXT control.

Steps To Add a Textarea Field

1. **If necessary, click line 27.**

2. **Enter the HTML code shown in Table 6-5 and then press the ENTER key twice.**

The HTML code displays (Figure 6-16) and the insertion point is on line 36.

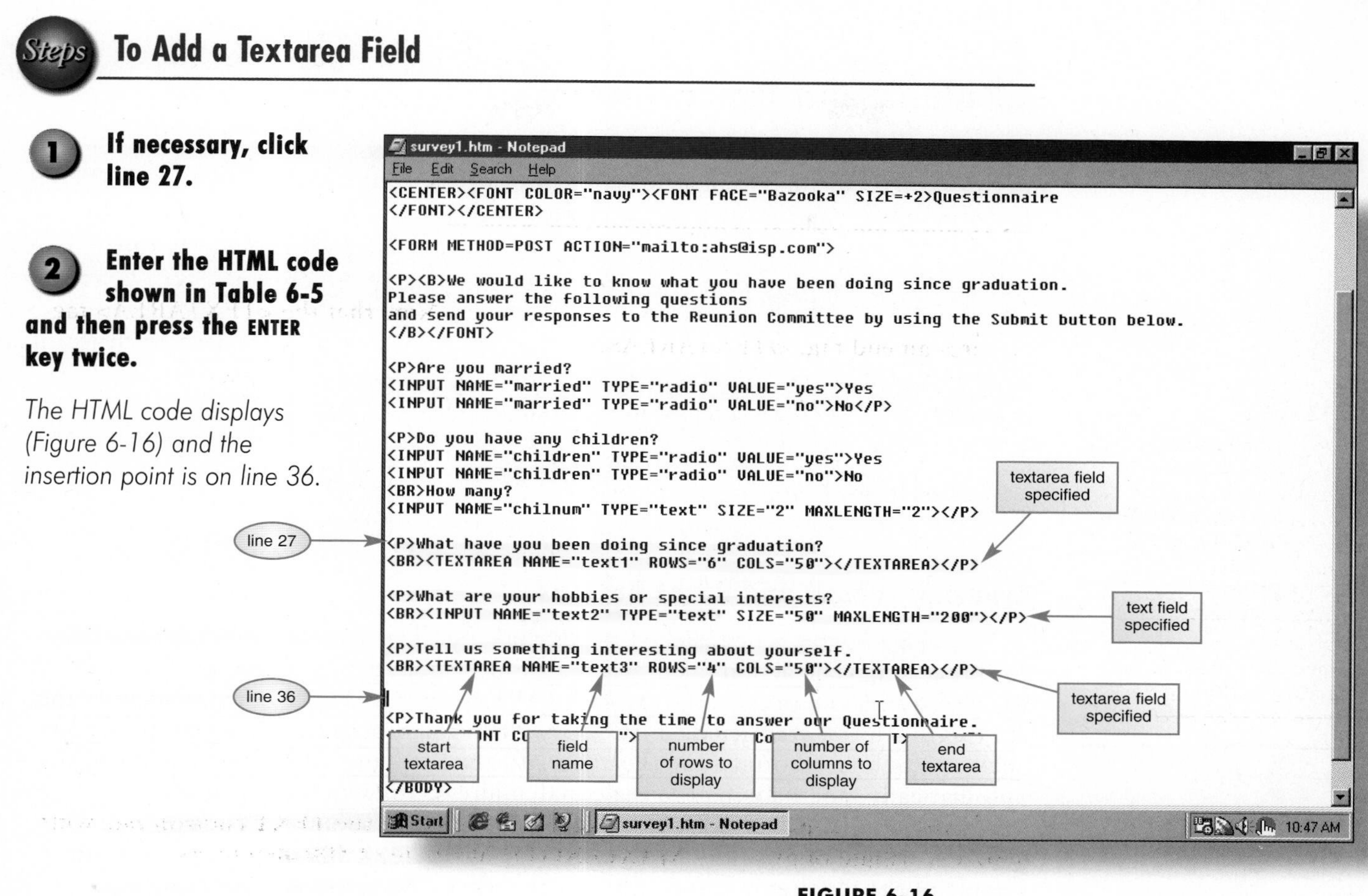

FIGURE 6-16

In the last steps, you added three input controls. Each control includes a question on lines 27, 30, and 33. The textarea and text fields display directly under their respective question without a blank line between the question and field. This is because the <BR> tag was used on lines 28, 31, and 34. The three sections of input controls have a blank line in between them because of the <P> tags used in lines 27, 30, and 33.

You now have added all of the input controls to the Web page form. First, you added two sets of radio buttons that followed yes/no questions. You also added two text fields for single-line input and two textarea fields. These controls provide different types of input areas for various types of questions.

The form controls are useless unless something can be done with the information entered in the form. Your next step is to create two buttons at the bottom of the Web page form. The first button, Submit the Form, is for submitting the form. When the visitor clicks this button, the data input on the form is sent to the appropriate location for processing. The second button, Reset the Form, clears any input that was entered in the form.

Submit and Reset Buttons

Input controls are not useful unless something is done with the data that is entered. Forms need to be submitted in order to be of value. Figure 6-17 shows the <INPUT> tags used to specify the Submit and Reset buttons.

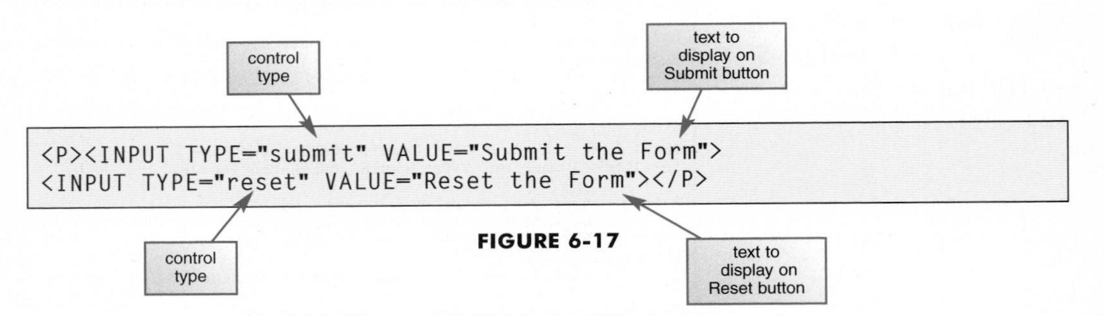

FIGURE 6-17

Creating Submit and Reset Buttons

A **Submit button**, when clicked, sends the input data to the appropriate location for processing. The action taken when a form is submitted is based on what the ACTION attribute in the <FORM> tag specifies. In the <FORM> tag used at the start of this form, you specified ACTION="mailto:ahs@isp.com". When the visitor clicks the Submit button, a file (Postdata.att) that contains all of the input data is automatically sent via e-mail to the e-mail address, ahs@isp.com. You specify a Submit button by using the attribute, TYPE="submit", in an <INPUT> tag and the text that displays on the button by using the VALUE attribute. Figure 6-18 shows a sample of the file that is sent to the e-mail address. The ampersand (&) strings together all of the form responses.

More About

Submit Buttons

A simplistic, default button is created when you use the TYPE="submit" attribute within the <INPUT> tag. The <BUTTON> tag also can be used to create a submit button. The <BUTTON> tag gives you the option of using an image for the button, rather than use the default button style. The appearance of the button text can be changed with the STYLE tag. These tags give you more flexibility when creating submit or reset buttons.

```
married=yes&children=yes&chilnum=2&text1=Went to college&text2=Reading
and golf&text3=I am currently working for CompTech, a computer
software company, and travel to Europe often.
```

FIGURE 6-18

In this sample, the Web page visitor selected yes for married, yes for children, and 2 for the number of children. After graduation from Andrews High School, the visitor went to college. This is indicated in the first TEXTAREA control (text1). The visitor listed reading and golfing as hobbies, as indicated in the TEXT control (text2). Finally, the visitor works for CompTech and travels to Europe, as indicated in the second TEXTAREA control (text3).

The **Reset** button also is an important part of any form. Resetting the form deletes any data previously typed into text or textarea fields, as well as resets radio buttons and check boxes to their initial values. You specify a Reset button by using the attribute, TYPE="reset", in an <INPUT> tag. The text that displays on the button is defined by using the VALUE attribute.

Perform the following steps to create a Submit button and a Reset button.

Steps To Create Submit and Reset Buttons

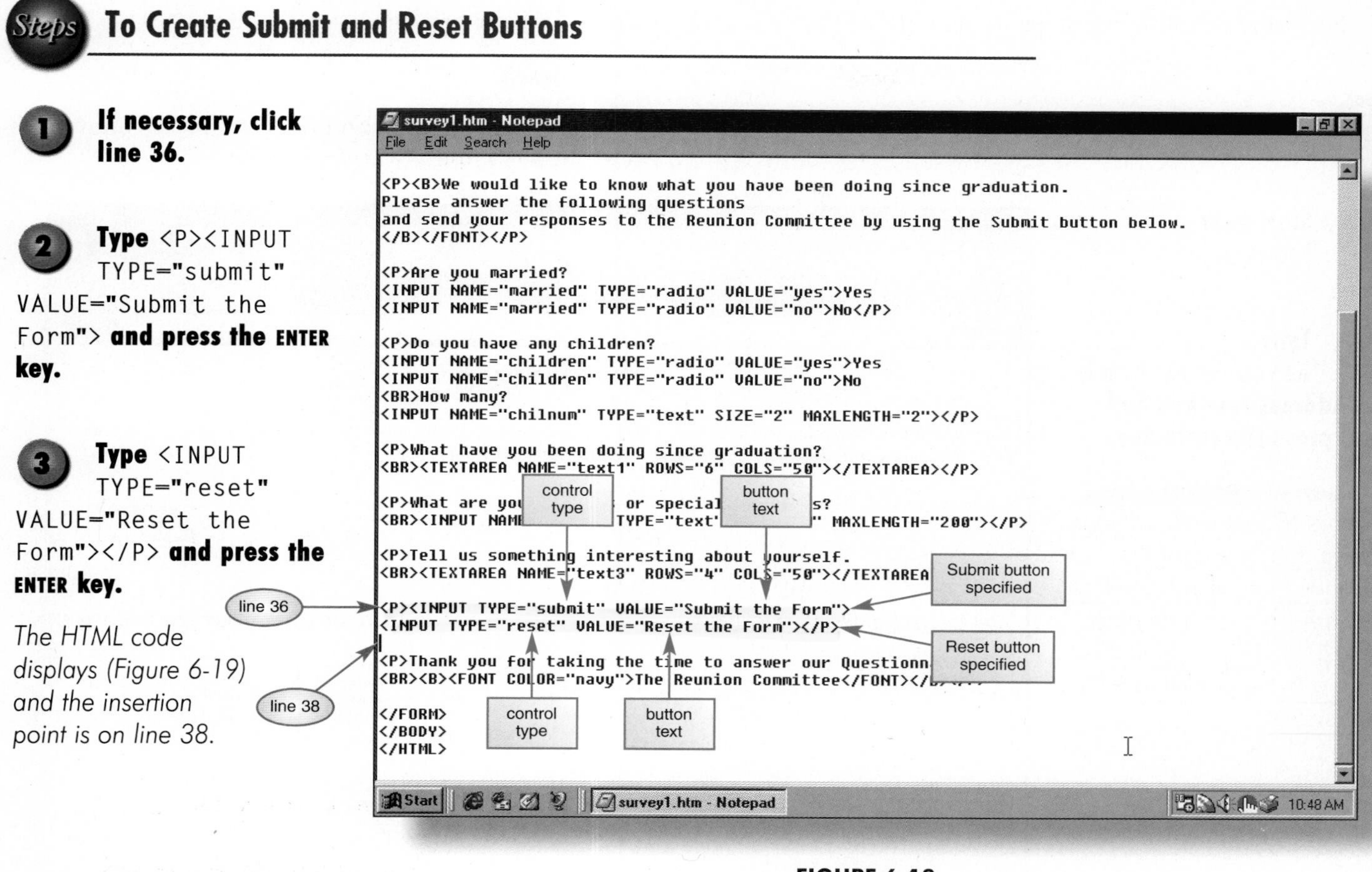

1. **If necessary, click line 36.**

2. **Type** `<P><INPUT TYPE="submit" VALUE="Submit the Form">` **and press the ENTER key.**

3. **Type** `<INPUT TYPE="reset" VALUE="Reset the Form"></P>` **and press the ENTER key.**

The HTML code displays (Figure 6-19) and the insertion point is on line 38.

FIGURE 6-19

The Web page form, survey1.htm, is complete. It contains two questions with radio button options, two text fields, and two textarea fields. It also contains a Submit button that will send a file containing the form's input to the e-mail address, ahs@isp.com, and a Reset button that clears any input that was entered in the form. Next, you need to save and view the HTML file in the browser.

Saving the HTML File

Perform the following steps to save the survey1.htm file to the HTML Data Disk.

TO SAVE THE HTML FILE

1. Save the file on the HTML Data Disk with survey1.htm as the file name.

The updated version of survey1.htm is saved to the HTML Data Disk.

Viewing, Testing, and Printing the Web Page and HTML File

As in earlier projects, you should view and print the Web page using your browser and print the saved HTML file. You also need to test the controls in the browser to see that they work as specified.

Perform the following steps to view the HTML file, survey1.htm, in your browser.

To View the HTML File in the Browser

1 Start your browser.

2 Type a:\survey1.htm **in the Address text box and then press the ENTER key.**

The survey1.htm Web page displays (Figure 6-20). If your system does not have the Bazooka font (as indicated on line 7 in Figure 6-6 on page HTM 6.10), the heading displays with the default font for your system.

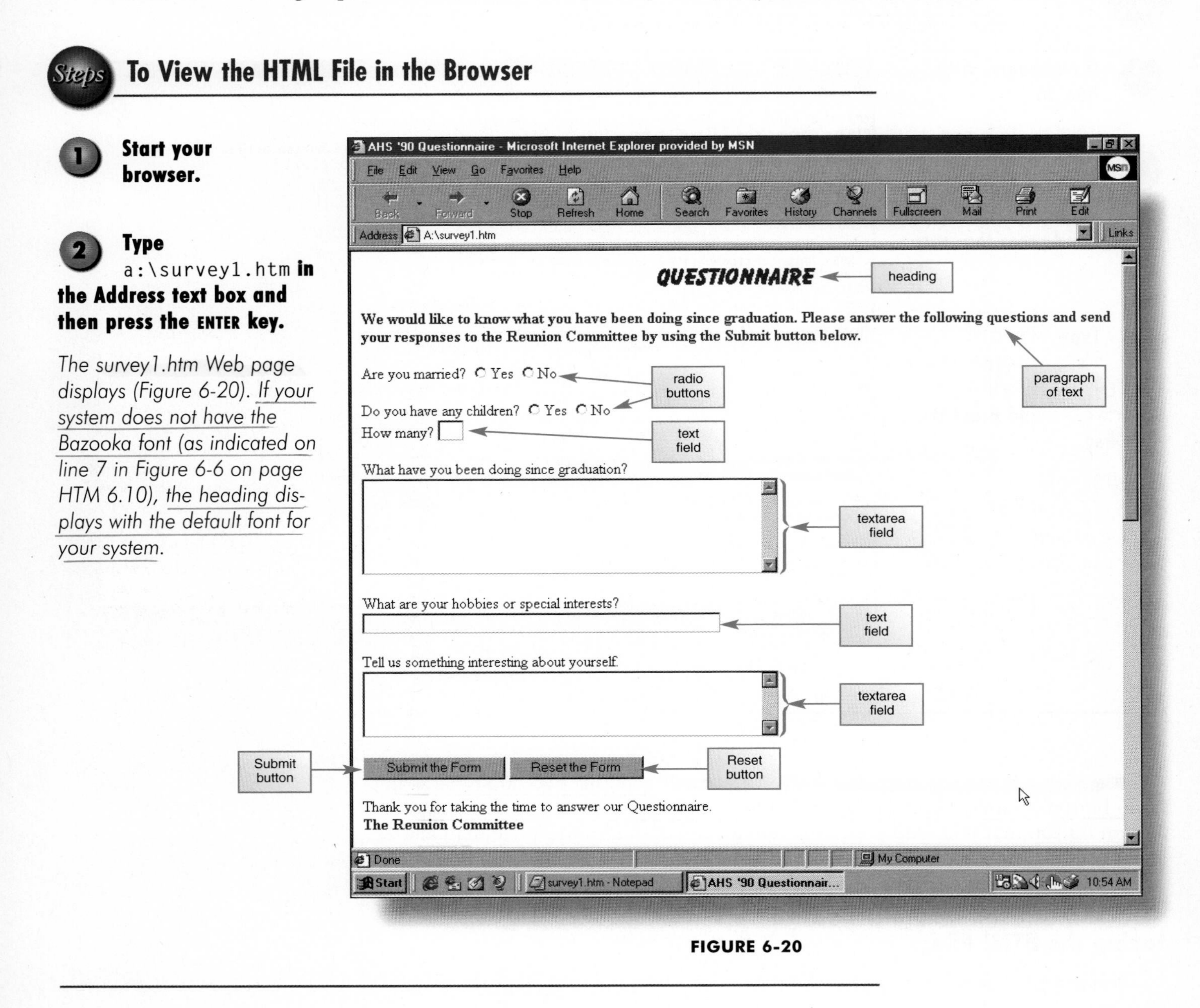

FIGURE 6-20

Compare Figure 6-19 on the previous page to Figure 6-20. Step through Figure 6-19 to see if you can pick out the lines that correspond to each control on the form.

Next, use your browser to print the Web page. Notice that all controls used on the form are printed, as well as the Submit and Reset buttons.

TO PRINT THE WEB PAGE

1. Click the Print button on the Standard Buttons toolbar.

The Web page prints (Figure 6-21).

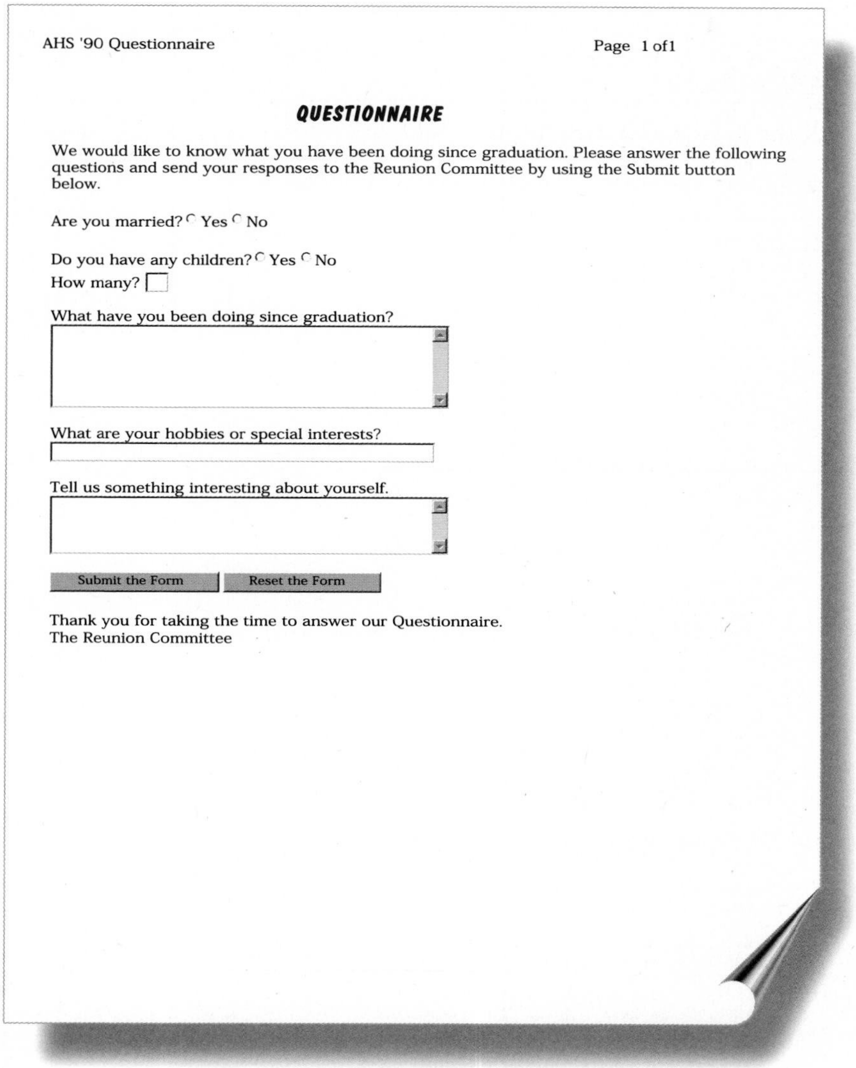

AHS '90 Questionnaire Page 1 of1

QUESTIONNAIRE

We would like to know what you have been doing since graduation. Please answer the following questions and send your responses to the Reunion Committee by using the Submit button below.

Are you married? Yes No

Do you have any children? Yes No
How many?

What have you been doing since graduation?

What are your hobbies or special interests?

Tell us something interesting about yourself.

Submit the Form | Reset the Form

Thank you for taking the time to answer our Questionnaire.
The Reunion Committee

FIGURE 6-21

More About

Fonts

The font Bazooka was selected for the titles in this project by using the FONT FACE tag and attribute. Not all Web page visitors have the Bazooka font on their computers, however. If a visitor does not have the font used by the Web developer for a Web page, the text displays in the default font.

You also should test the buttons and fields to ensure they operate correctly.

- Click the radio buttons to test them. You should be able to choose only one choice (yes or no). Then click the Reset button. The selected radio button should reset to its initial (clear) state.
- Test the text field that asks how many children the visitor has. You should be able to see only two characters.
- Test the text field under the question about hobbies and special interests. It should allow more characters to be entered than are shown because of the difference between the SIZE and the MAXLENGTH attribute values.
- Test the Reset button again. It should clear all fields.

You cannot test the Submit button because it automatically generates an e-mail to ahs@isp.com, which is a nonexistent e-mail address.

After you have verified that all controls on the Web page form work correctly, print the HTML file in Notepad. This printed file is a good source of reference for HTML form input controls. If a problem with the form is discovered during testing, you should return to Notepad and make the corrections before printing the file.

Frame Feedback

One good use of forms is to get feedback from your visitors. Suggestions from visitors can not only help improve the Web site, but give your visitors the feeling that you care about their opinions. Taking visitor feedback into account provides for better customer satisfaction. For more information about customer feedback, visit the HTML More About page (www.scsite.com/html/more.htm) and click Feedback.

TO PRINT THE HTML FILE

1. Click the Notepad button on the taskbar.
2. Click File on the menu bar and then click Print.

The HTML file prints (Figure 6-22).

```
survey1.htm

<HTML>
<HEAD>
<TITLE>AHS '90 Questionnaire</TITLE>
</HEAD>
<BODY>

<CENTER><FONT COLOR="navy"><FONT FACE="Bazooka" SIZE=+2>Questionnaire
</FONT></CENTER>

<FORM METHOD=POST ACTION="mailto:ahs@isp.com">

<P><B>We would like to know what you have been doing since
graduation. Please
answer the following questions and send your responses to the Reunion
Committee by using the Submit button below.</B></FONT>

<P>Are you married?
<INPUT NAME="married" TYPE="radio" VALUE="yes">Yes
<INPUT NAME="married" TYPE="radio" VALUE="no">No</P>

<P>Do you have any children?
<INPUT NAME="children" TYPE="radio" VALUE="yes">Yes
<INPUT NAME="children" TYPE="radio" VALUE="no">No
<BR>How many?
<INPUT NAME="chilnum" TYPE="text" SIZE="2" MAXLENGTH="2"></P>

<P>What have you been doing since graduation?
<BR><TEXTAREA NAME="text1" ROWS="6" COLS="50"></TEXTAREA></P>

<P>What are your hobbies or special interests?
<BR><INPUT NAME="text2" TYPE="text" SIZE="50" MAXLENGTH="200"></P>

<P>Tell us something interesting about yourself.
<BR><TEXTAREA NAME="text3" ROWS="4" COLS="50"></TEXTAREA></P>

<P><INPUT TYPE="submit" VALUE="Submit the Form">
<INPUT TYPE="reset" VALUE="Reset the Form"></P>

<P>Thank you for taking the time to answer our Questionnaire.
<BR><B><FONT COLOR="navy">The Reunion Committee</FONT></B></P>

</FORM>
</BODY>
</HTML>

Page 1
```

FIGURE 6-22

You have completed the changes to the first form, survey1.htm. The next step is to convert the second HTML file (survey2.htm) that is stored on the HTML Data Disk to a form. You will be adding selection menus to this form.

Creating a Form with Selection Menus

Another method for inputting information onto a Web page is to use a SELECT control, which creates a **selection menu**, or list. This control works well when you want to limit the number of choices from which the Web page visitor can choose. Figure 6-23 shows examples of four types of selection menus.

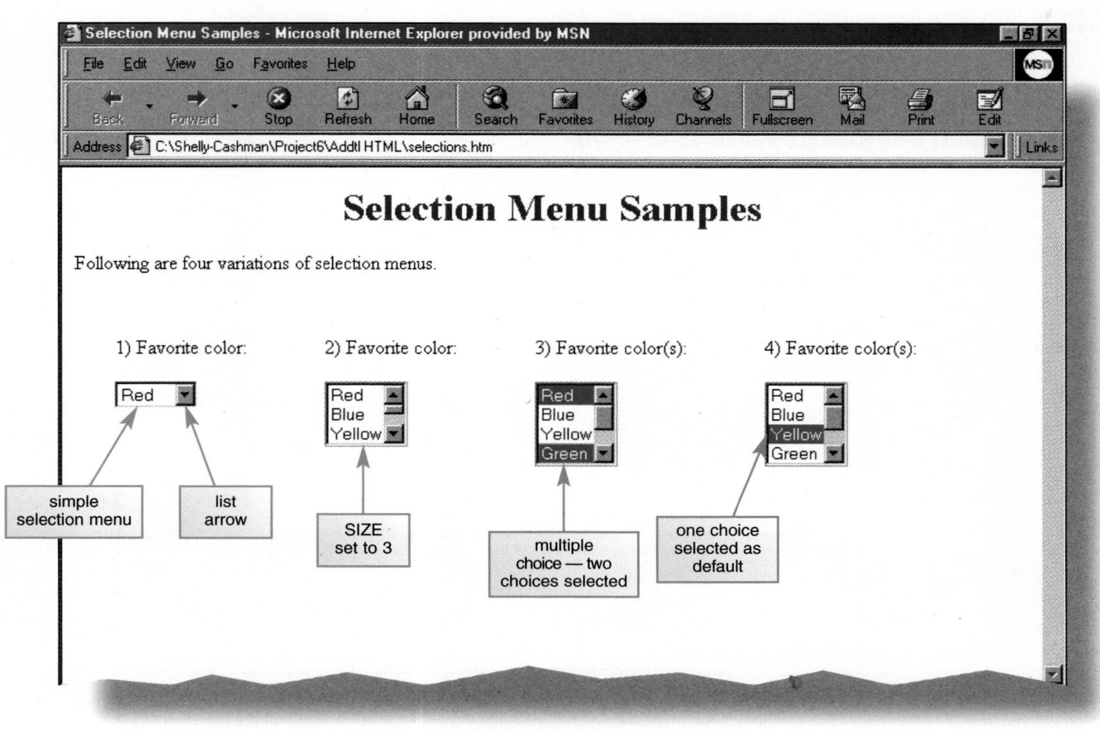

FIGURE 6-23

Selection menu 1 displays only one option at a time in the selection list. The visitor clicks the list arrow to see other choices. The default appears first and is shown highlighted to indicate it is selected. Selection menu 2 shows a list that has three choices, with all three choices showing. Selection menu 3 shows a list that has specified multiple options. This allows the Web page visitor to select more than one choice in a selection menu. Selection menu 4 shows a selection menu in which one of the choices (Yellow) is selected as the default. When the page displays, Yellow is selected (or highlighted).

Opening the HTML File

The second HTML file for the AHS Web site that you will change in this project, survey2.htm, is on the HTML Data Disk. First, you need to open the file in order to change it. Perform the following steps to open the file.

TO OPEN THE HTML FILE

1. Click File on the menu bar and then click Open.
2. Type `survey2.htm` in the File name text box and click the Open button in the Open dialog box.

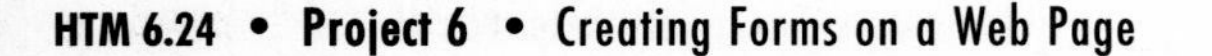

The HTML file opens, ready to be converted to a Web page form. Figure 6-24a shows the original Web page. Figure 6-24b shows what it will look like after it is converted to a Web page form.

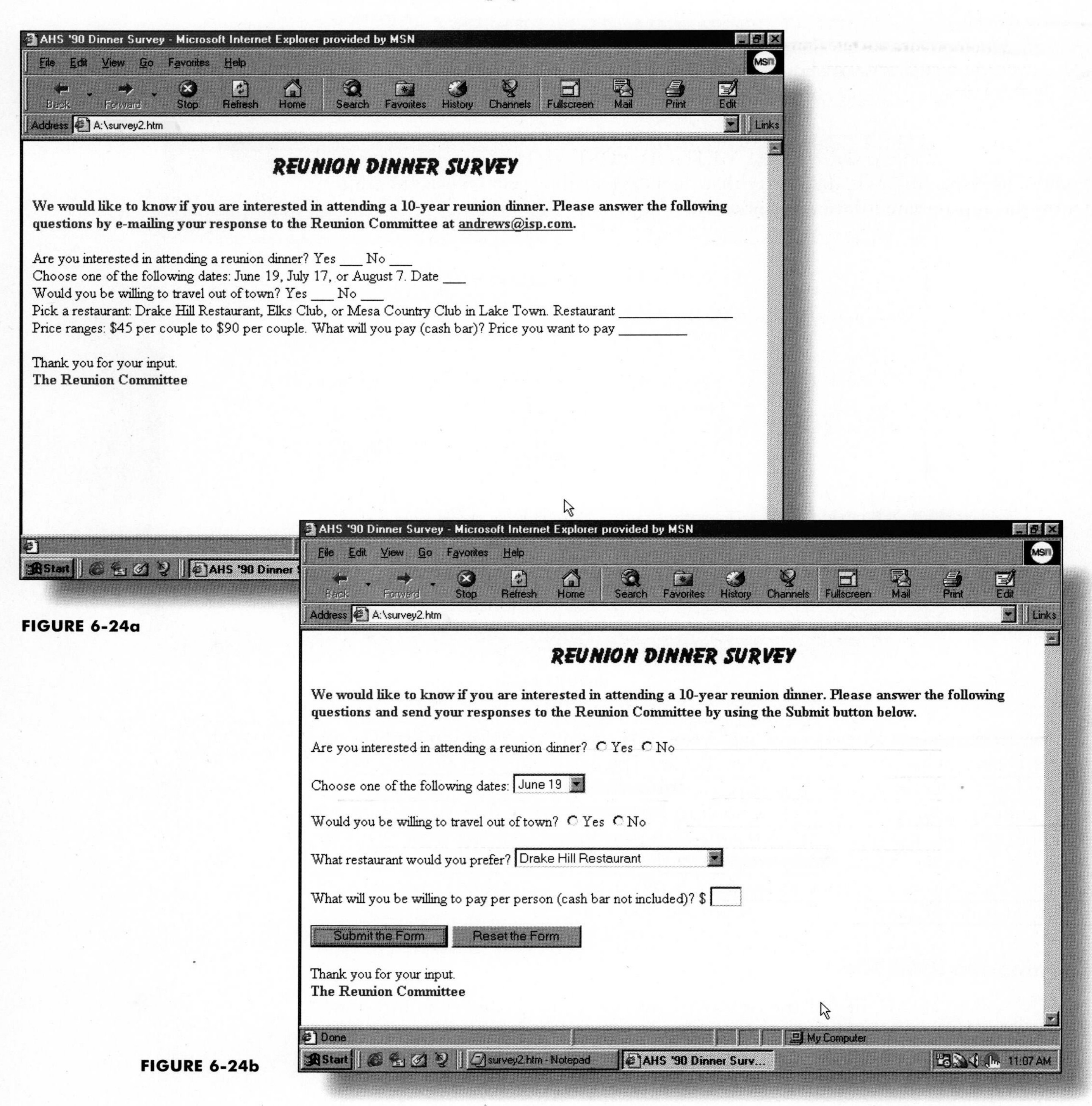

FIGURE 6-24a

FIGURE 6-24b

As mentioned earlier in the project, the first step in Web page form conversion is to identify the method and action that are used for processing the form. Perform the following steps to do that.

TO IDENTIFY THE FORM PROCESS

1. Click line 9 and press the ENTER key.
2. Type `<FORM METHOD=POST ACTION="mailto:ahs@isp.com">` and then press the ENTER key.
3. Click the blank line just above the </BODY> tag (line 28) and press the ENTER key.
4. Type `</FORM>` as the tag.

As with survey1.htm, the <FORM METHOD=POST ACTION= “mailto:ahs@isp.com”> tag designates that the POST method will be used to send data to the appropriate location for processing. The form automatically will be sent to the e-mail address, ahs@isp.com, when submitted. The </FORM> tag just above the </BODY> tag ends the Web page form.

Changing the Initial Text

Next, you need to alter the text that directs the visitor to submit the questionnaire via e-mail. In the following steps, you change the text that specifies e-mail submission to a more appropriate message.

Perform the following steps to change the text message.

TO CHANGE THE TEXT

1. Highlight lines 14 and 15 and then press the DELETE key.
2. With the insertion point on line 14, type `and send your responses to the Reunion Committee by using the Submit button below.` as the text.
3. Highlight lines 17 through 23 and then press the DELETE key.

The HTML code displays as shown in Figure 6-25 and the insertion point is on line 17.

survey2.htm - Notepad

File Edit Search Help

```
<HTML>
<HEAD>
<TITLE>AHS '90 Dinner Survey</TITLE>
</HEAD>
<BODY>

<CENTER><FONT COLOR="navy"><FONT FACE="Bazooka" SIZE=+2>Reunion Dinner Survey
</FONT></CENTER>

<FORM METHOD=POST ACTION="mailto:ahs@isp.com">

<P><B>We would like to know if you are interested in attending a 10-year
reunion dinner. Please answer the following questions
and send your responses to the Reunion Committee by using the Submit button below.
</B></FONT></P>



<P>Thank you for your input.
<BR><B><FONT COLOR="navy">The Reunion Committee</FONT></B></P>

</FORM>
</BODY>
</HTML>
```

line 17

deleted text

FIGURE 6-25

The visitor has been directed to submit the questionnaire by clicking the Submit button that you create later at the bottom of the Web page.

Adding Radio Buttons to the Second Form

As done to the previous Web page form, you will add radio buttons to this form. These radio buttons will capture yes or no data about interest in a reunion dinner. Table 6-6 contains the HTML code that creates these radio buttons. In the next steps, you enter the tags and text given in Table 6-6.

Table 6-6

LINE	HTML TAGS AND TEXT
17	<P>Are you interested in attending a reunion dinner?
18	<INPUT NAME="attend" TYPE="radio" VALUE="yes">Yes
19	<INPUT NAME="attend" TYPE="radio" VALUE="no">No</P>

These radio buttons have yes or no options, as well as the same name, so the visitor may select only one choice (yes or no). Perform the following steps to create these radio buttons.

Steps To Add Radio Buttons

1. **If necessary, click line 17 and then press the ENTER key.**

2. **Enter the HTML code shown in Table 6-6 and press the ENTER key.**

The HTML code displays as shown in Figure 6-26 and the insertion point is on line 20.

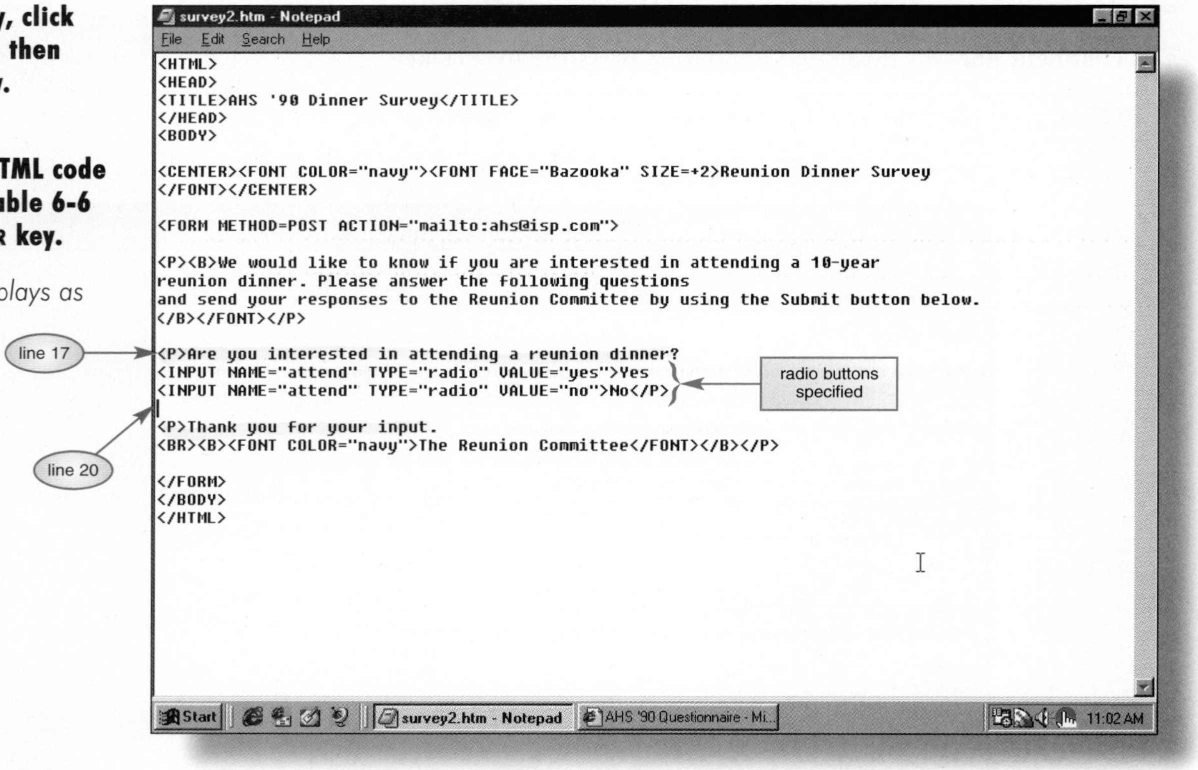

```
<HTML>
<HEAD>
<TITLE>AHS '90 Dinner Survey</TITLE>
</HEAD>
<BODY>

<CENTER><FONT COLOR="navy"><FONT FACE="Bazooka" SIZE=+2>Reunion Dinner Survey
</FONT></CENTER>

<FORM METHOD=POST ACTION="mailto:ahs@isp.com">

<P><B>We would like to know if you are interested in attending a 10-year
reunion dinner. Please answer the following questions
and send your responses to the Reunion Committee by using the Submit button below.
</B></FONT></P>

<P>Are you interested in attending a reunion dinner?
<INPUT NAME="attend" TYPE="radio" VALUE="yes">Yes
<INPUT NAME="attend" TYPE="radio" VALUE="no">No</P>

<P>Thank you for your input.
<BR><B><FONT COLOR="navy">The Reunion Committee</FONT></B></P>

</FORM>
</BODY>
</HTML>
```

FIGURE 6-26

All necessary text has been changed and radio buttons have been added to this second form. Your next step is to add selection controls.

Creating Selection Controls

For questions with a limited number of choices, use a SELECT control, which creates a selection menu. Figure 6-23 on page HTM 6.23 shows a variety of SELECT control menus. To specify a selection menu, you use the <SELECT> and <OPTION> tags. The <SELECT> tag is used to start a selection control (Figure 6-27) and requires an end tag </SELECT>. All options are contained within the <SELECT> and </SELECT> tags.

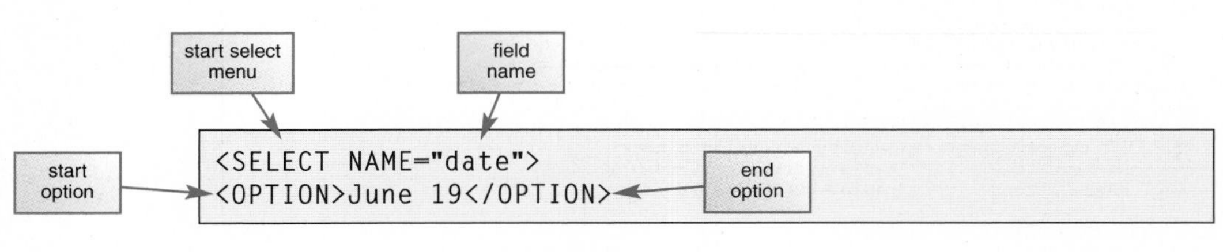

FIGURE 6-27

Table 6-3 on page HTM 6.9 lists five attributes for the <SELECT> tag. With the SIZE attribute, you can specify the number of options that should be displayed initially. The default is one line of text with a list menu. In this case, the visitor may select one option from the menu. To allow the visitor to select more than one option, use the MULTIPLE attribute. The DISABLED attribute disables the input control. The HTML code needed for these advanced control techniques is discussed later in this project.

As with the <INPUT> and <TEXTAREA> tags, the attribute, NAME, assigns a name to a control. The first SELECT control in this form is named "date." When the form is submitted to the e-mail address, the field is called "date," and the value associated with that field can be distinguished from other fields by that name.

The <OPTION> tag defines the text options that are possible and displayed in the menu. Each possible option is enclosed within a pair of <OPTION> and </OPTION> tags. The first selection menu created in this form contains three date options: June 19, July 17, and August 7. In Figure 6-27, the first option (June 19) is used as an example. The SIZE attribute is not specified, so only one option will display, along with a menu list arrow.

Table 6-7 shows the HTML tags and text that are used to create the first selection menu, with three dates (June 19, July 17, and August 7) as the menu choices. In the following steps, you enter the text and tags given in Table 6-7.

More About

Options

The <SELECT> and <OPTION> tags are useful when you have a limited number of choices from which a Web page visitor can select. If the number of options becomes too large, however, the list is difficult to read. A better idea might be to group like options together into submenus. You can use the <OPTGROUP> tag before the first <OPTION> tag in the first group that you want to use in a submenu. After the last option in that group, use the </OPTGROUP> tag.

Table 6-7

LINE	HTML TAGS AND TEXT
21	<P>Choose one of the following dates:
22	<SELECT NAME="date">
23	<OPTION>June 19</OPTION>
24	<OPTION>July 17</OPTION>
25	<OPTION>August 7</OPTION>
26	</SELECT></P>

Perform the following steps to insert a selection menu on the Web page form.

To Add a Selection Menu

1 **If necessary, click line 20 and then press the ENTER key.**

2 **Enter the HTML code shown in Table 6-7 on the previous page and then press the ENTER key.**

The HTML code displays as shown in Figure 6-28 and the insertion point is on line 27.

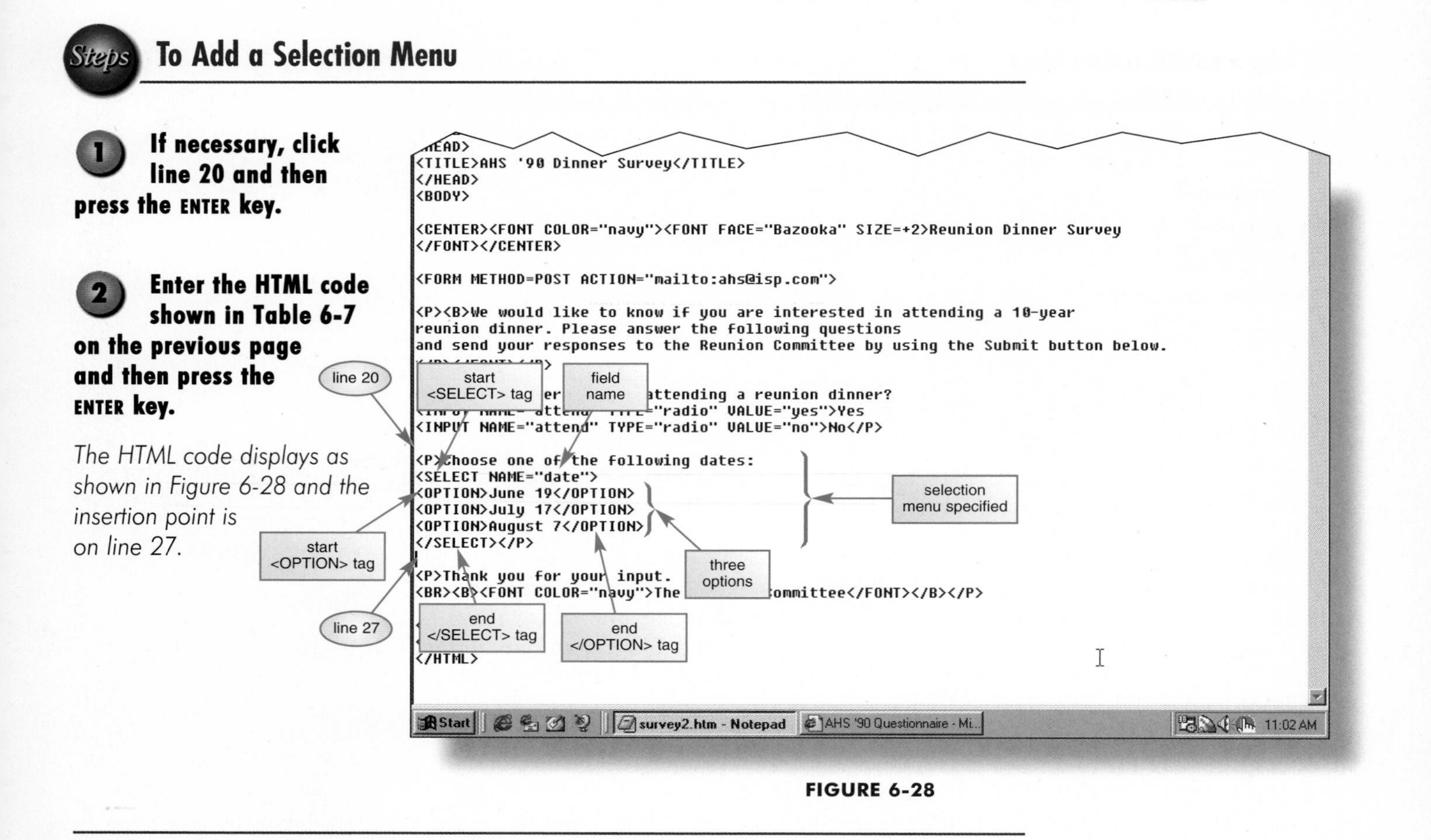

FIGURE 6-28

You have now completed the HTML tags that change the original text message, added one set of radio buttons, and added one selection menu. In the selection menu, the SIZE attribute default of one option only was specified, so only one choice displays, along with a list arrow to view other available choices on the menu. The Web page visitor will be allowed to select only one choice because the MULTIPLE attribute was not used. In the following steps, you will add a second set of radio buttons and a second selection menu.

Table 6-8

LINE	HTML TAGS AND TEXT
28	<P>Would you be willing to travel out of town?
29	<INPUT NAME="travel" TYPE="radio" VALUE ="yes">Yes
30	<INPUT NAME ="travel" TYPE="radio" VALUE="no">No</P>
31	
32	<P>What restaurant would you prefer?
33	<SELECT NAME="restaurant">
34	<OPTION>Drake Hill Restaurant</OPTION>
35	<OPTION>Elks Club</OPTION>
36	<OPTION>Mesa Country Club in Lake Town</OPTION>
37	</SELECT></P>

Adding More Radio Buttons and a Selection Menu

Table 6-8 contains the HTML code needed to add a second set of radio buttons and another selection menu. In the following steps, you enter the tags and text given in Table 6-8.

As before in this project, the radio buttons are yes/no options. The selection menu contains three choices, and only the first displays because no SIZE attribute is used. The Web page visitor may select only one choice in the selection menu because the MULTIPLE attribute is not used in the <SELECT> tag on line 33.

Perform the following steps to add another set of radio buttons and an additional selection menu.

Steps To Add Radio Buttons and a Selection Menu

1 **If necessary, click line 27 and then press the ENTER key.**

2 **Enter the HTML code shown in Table 6-8 and press the ENTER key.**

The HTML code displays as shown in Figure 6-29 and the insertion point is on line 38.

```
<P>Choose one of the following dates:
<SELECT NAME="date">
<OPTION>June 19</OPTION>
<OPTION>July 17</OPTION>
<OPTION>August 7</OPTION>
</SELECT></P>

<P>Would you be willing to travel out of town?
<INPUT NAME="travel" TYPE="radio" VALUE ="yes">Yes
<INPUT NAME ="travel" TYPE="radio" VALUE="no">No</P>

<P>What restaurant would you prefer?
<SELECT NAME="restaurant">
<OPTION>Drake Hill Restaurant</OPTION>
<OPTION>Elks Club</OPTION>
<OPTION>Mesa Country Club in Lake Town</OPTION>
</SELECT></P>

<P>Thank you for your input.
<BR><B><FONT COLOR="navy">The Reunion Committee</FONT></B></P>

</FORM>
</BODY>
</HTML>
```

line 27
line 38
options
field name
radio buttons specified
selection menu specified
Start | survey2.htm - Notepad | AHS '90 Questionnaire - Mi... | 11:03 AM

FIGURE 6-29

The HTML code for the radio button and selection controls on the second form are complete. You next need to add a text field.

Inserting a Text Field

The last item needed to complete the input areas of the form is a text field. A text field is used rather than a textarea field because the visitor needs to enter only a few characters. Perform the following steps to create the new text field.

1. If necessary, click line 38 and then press the ENTER key.
2. Type `<P>What will you be willing to pay per person (cash bar not included)? $` and then press the ENTER key.
3. Type `<INPUT NAME="amount" TYPE="text" SIZE="3" MAXLENGTH="3"></P>` and then press the ENTER key twice.

The HTML code displays as shown in Figure 6-30 and the insertion point is on line 42.

```
<OPTION>Drake Hill Restaurant</OPTION>
<OPTION>Elks Club</OPTION>
<OPTION>Mesa Country Club in Lake Town</OPTION>
</SELECT></P>

<P>What will you be willing to pay per person (cash bar not included)? $
<INPUT NAME="amount" TYPE="text" SIZE="3" MAXLENGTH="3"></P>

<P>Thank you for your input.
<BR><B><FONT COLOR="navy">The Reunion Committee</FONT></B></P>

</FORM>
</BODY>
```

line 38
line 42
text field specified
Start | survey2.htm - Notepad | AHS '90 Questionnaire - Mi... | 11:05 AM

FIGURE 6-30

In this text field, the SIZE and MAXLENGTH attributes are the same. A space for three characters displays on the form and only three characters of information may be entered.

You have now added all of the controls to the second form. The last step is to add the Submit and Reset buttons.

Adding the Submit and Reset Buttons

Perform the following steps to add the Submit and Reset buttons.

TO CREATE SUBMIT AND RESET BUTTONS

1. If necessary, click line 42.
2. Type <P><INPUT TYPE="submit" VALUE="Submit the Form"> and press the ENTER key.

3. Type <INPUT TYPE="reset" VALUE="Reset the Form"></P> and press the ENTER key.

The HTML code displays as shown in Figure 6-31.

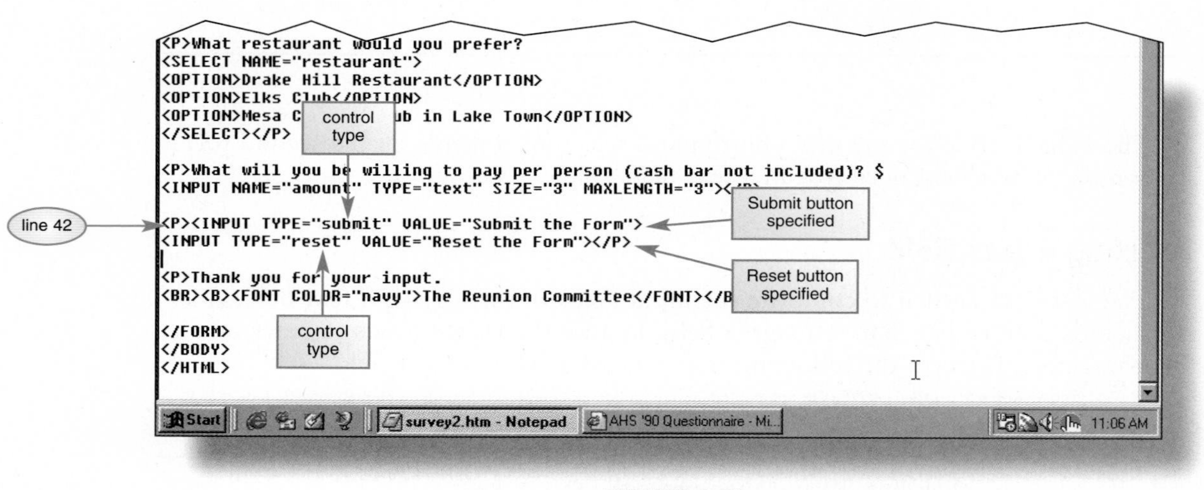

FIGURE 6-31

You have now completed the HTML code for the second Web page form. Next, you need to save and view the file in the browser, as well as test all buttons, fields, and selections.

Saving, Viewing, Testing, and Printing the HTML File

As with the first form, survey1.htm, you need to save, view, and print the survey2.htm file using your browser, as well as print the HTML in Notepad. You also must test all buttons, fields, and selections to ensure that they operate properly.

Perform the following step to save the HTML file.

TO SAVE THE HTML FILE

1. Save the file on the HTML Data Disk with survey2.htm as the file name.

Next, view the HTML file in your browser.

TO VIEW THE HTML FILE IN THE BROWSER

1. Start your browser.
2. Type `a:\survey2.htm` in the Address text box and then press the ENTER key.

The survey2.htm Web page displays (Figure 6-32). If your system does not have the Bazooka font (specified on line 7 in Figure 6-6 on page HTM 6.10), the heading displays with the default font for your system.

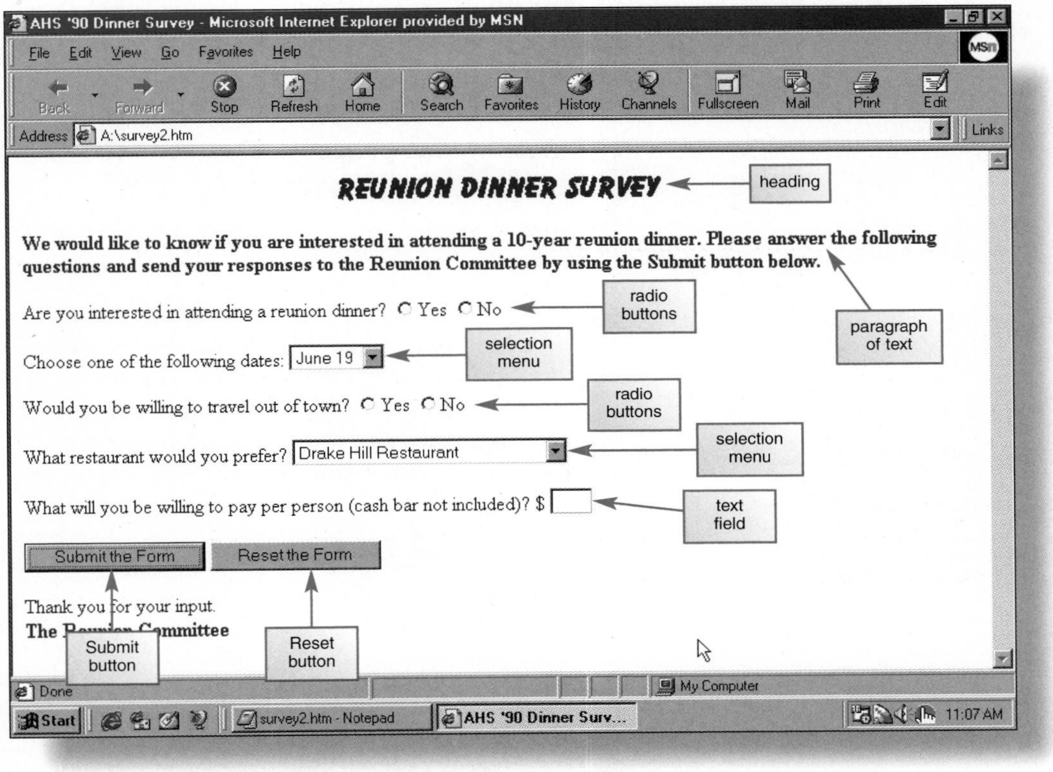

FIGURE 6-32

When the initial Web page displays, verify that no options have initially been selected. That is because the CHECKED attribute was not used in any of the radio buttons. Because SELECTED was not specified in the <OPTION> tags, the selection menus also do not have a choice selected by default. Select various choices on the form and click the Reset button to ensure that all options are reset.

You have now completed the conversion of the second HTML file stored on the HTML Data Disk to a Web page form. The next step is to use your browser to print the Web page.

TO PRINT THE WEB PAGE

1. Click the Print button on the Standard Buttons toolbar.

The Web page prints (Figure 6-33 on the next page).

Discussion Forums

Other HTML resources include a USENET newsgroup where HTML authoring issues are discussed. Among other things, visitors can ask "How To" questions here. Many issues related to forms and CGI are discussed. To find out more about this newsgroup, visit the HTML More About Web page (www.scsite.com/html/more.htm) and click Newsgroup.

AHS '90 Dinner Survey Page 1 of 1

REUNION DINNER SURVEY

We would like to know if you are interested in attending a 10-year reunion dinner. Please answer the following questions and send your responses to the Reunion Committee by using the Submit button below.

Are you interested in attending a reunion dinner? Yes No

Choose one of the following dates: June 19

Would you be willing to travel out of town? Yes No

What restaurant would you prefer? Drake Hill Restaurant

What will you be willing to pay per person (cash bar not included)? $

Submit the Form | Reset the Form

Thank you for your input.
The Reunion Committee

FIGURE 6-33

```
survey2.htm

<HTML>
<HEAD>
<TITLE>AHS '90 Dinner Survey</TITLE>
</HEAD>
<BODY>

<CENTER><FONT COLOR="navy"><FONT FACE="Bazooka" SIZE=+2>Reunion Dinner Survey
</FONT></CENTER>

<FORM METHOD=POST ACTION="mailto:ahs@isp.com">

<P><B>We would like to know if you are interested in attending a 10-year
reunion dinner. Please answer the following questions
and send your responses to the Reunion Committee by using the Submit button
below.
</B></FONT></P>

<P>Are you interested in attending a reunion dinner?
<INPUT NAME="attend" TYPE="radio" VALUE="yes">Yes
<INPUT NAME="attend" TYPE="radio" VALUE="no">No</P>

<P>Choose one of the following dates:
<SELECT NAME="date">
<OPTION>June 19</OPTION>
<OPTION>July 17</OPTION>
<OPTION>August 7</OPTION>
</SELECT></P>

<P>Would you be willing to travel out of town?
<INPUT NAME="travel" TYPE="radio" value="yes">Yes
<INPUT name="travel" TYPE="radio" VALUE="no">No</P>

<P>What restaurant would you prefer?
<SELECT NAME="restaurant">
<OPTION>Drake Hill Restaurant</OPTION>
<OPTION>Elks Club</OPTION>
<OPTION>Mesa Country Club in Lake Town</OPTION>
</SELECT></P>

<P>What will you be willing to pay per person (cash bar not included)? $
<INPUT NAME="amount" TYPE="text" SIZE="3" MAXLENGTH="3"></P>

<P><INPUT TYPE="submit" VALUE="Submit the Form">
<INPUT TYPE="reset" VALUE="Reset the Form"></P>

<P>Thank you for your input.
<BR><B><FONT COLOR="navy">The Reunion Committee</FONT></B></P>

</FORM>
</BODY>
</HTML>

Page 1
```

FIGURE 6-34

Next, you print the HTML file using Notepad. This printed file acts as a good source for HTML formats. If a problem with the form is discovered during testing, return to Notepad and make the corrections before printing the file.

TO PRINT THE HTML FILE

1. Click the Notepad button on the Taskbar.
2. Click File on the menu bar and then click Print.

The HTML file prints (Figure 6-34).

The conversion of two HTML files to Web page forms is complete. You opened two HTML files previously stored on the HTML Data Disk and converted both to Web page forms. In the first form, you added radio buttons, text fields, and textarea fields for input. In the second form, you added two selection menus in addition to radio buttons and a text field. Each control used in the two forms served a different purpose. The radio buttons provided a choice of a yes or no answer to simple questions. The text fields provided single-line input areas. In two text fields, the size and maximum length were the same, so no characters could be added beyond what could be seen on the form. In another text field, the maximum length was greater than the size, so additional characters could be added beyond what could be seen on the form.

You created Submit and Reset buttons on both forms. The Submit button is used to send the form to the server to be processed. The Reset button is used to clear all input from the form.

Testing the Submit Buttons

In both survey1.htm and survey2.htm, ACTION="mailto:ahs@isp.com" was used as the processing action that took place when the Submit button was clicked. You were not able to test the Submit buttons because the e-mail address, ahs@isp.com, was nonexistent.

To test the Submit buttons, open survey1.htm and survey2.htm in Notepad and insert your own e-mail address in place of ahs@isp.com. Save the files again to the HTML Data Disk and then open them in your browser. Test the Submit button on each form by clicking it. An e-mail message should transfer to your e-mail address. It should contain a file similar to the one shown in Figure 6-18 on page HTM 6.18. The name and value pairs from the form are inserted into the file. You can view the file using Notepad.

Advanced Selection Menus

Selection menus have many variations. A selection menu can display multiple choices or only one. A Web page visitor can select only one or multiple choices. One choice can be selected as the default. Figure 6-35 shows samples of selection menus.

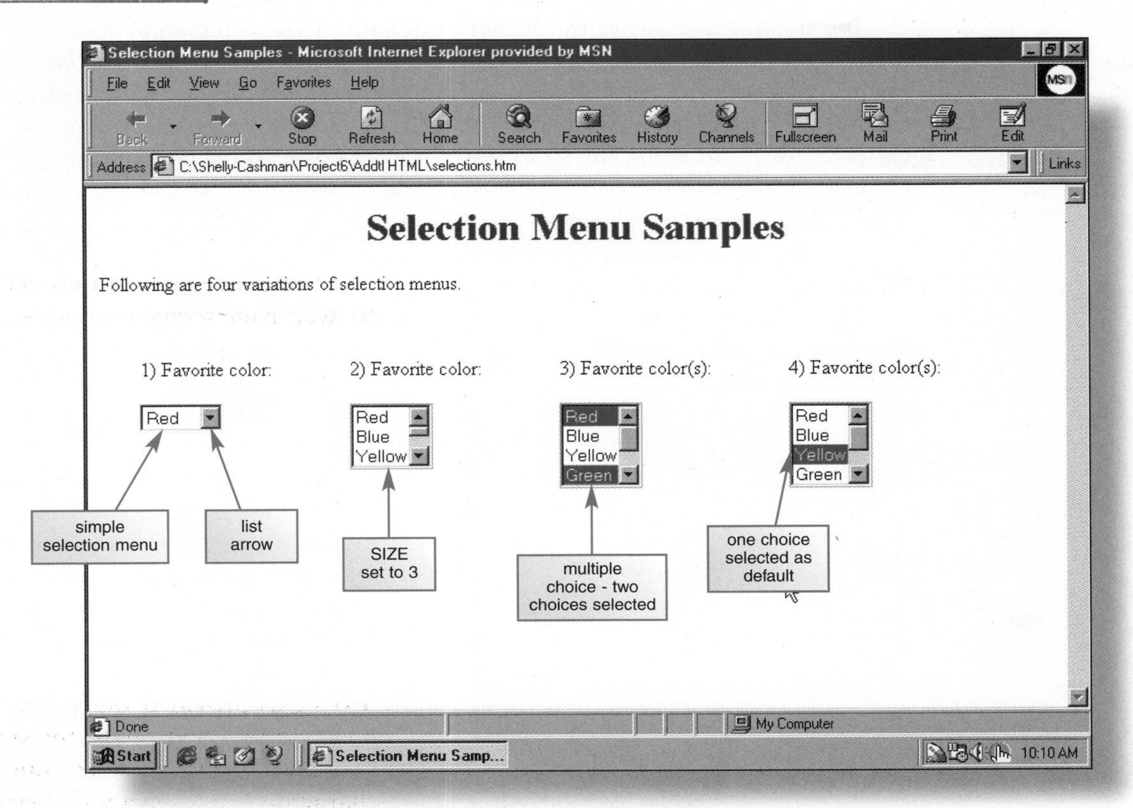

FIGURE 6-35

The HTML code used for each option in Figure 6-35 is shown in Figure 6-36.

(1) FAVORITE COLOR:

no size or multiples designated

```
<BR>
<SELECT NAME="color">
<OPTION>Red</OPTION>
<OPTION>Blue</OPTION>
<OPTION>Yellow</OPTION>
<OPTION>Green</OPTION>
<OPTION>Black</OPTION>
<OPTION>White</OPTION>
</SELECT>
```

(2) FAVORITE COLOR:

three choices display as default

```
<BR>
<SELECT NAME="color" SIZE="3">
<OPTION>Red</OPTION>
<OPTION>Blue</OPTION>
<OPTION>Yellow</OPTION>
<OPTION>Green</OPTION>
<OPTION>Black</OPTION>
<OPTION>White</OPTION>
</SELECT>
```

(3) FAVORITE COLOR(S):

multiple choices possible for selection

```
<BR>
<SELECT NAME="color" MULTIPLE>
<OPTION>Red</OPTION>
<OPTION>Blue</OPTION>
<OPTION>Yellow</OPTION>
<OPTION>Green</OPTION>
<OPTION>Black</OPTION>
<OPTION>White</OPTION>
</SELECT>
```

(4) FAVORITE COLOR(S):

multiple choices possible for selection

Yellow as default with SELECTED attribute

```
<BR>
<SELECT NAME="color"" MULTIPLE>
<OPTION>Red</OPTION>
<OPTION>Blue</OPTION>
<OPTION SELECTED>Yellow</OPTION>
<OPTION>Green</OPTION>
<OPTION>Black</OPTION>
<OPTION>White</OPTION>
</SELECT>
```

FIGURE 6-36

Selection menu 1 uses the selection default. This results in a single choice in a list menu. Selection menu 2 offers several choices displayed at start-up. This is accomplished by using the SIZE attribute. Selection menu 3 offers multiple choices because the MULTIPLE attribute is used. The Web page visitor can select choices in a row by choosing one and using the SHIFT key to select consecutive choices. Noncontiguous choices can be selected by using the CTRL key. Selection menu 4 also contains the MULTIPLE attribute, so numerous choices can be selected. It also is an example of one choice (Yellow) being selected at start-up. That choice is highlighted because the SELECTED attribute is used in the <OPTION> tag for that choice.

The purpose of the selection menu will dictate the HTML code that is used for that control. Using these basic tags and attributes, you can create any number of selection menus.

Project Summary

In Project 6, you used Notepad to convert two HTML text files to Web page forms. You learned the terms and definitions relating to forms and used numerous form tags and attributes. You created several sets of radio buttons on both forms. You also created several text fields for single-line input and textarea fields for multiple-line input. Finally, you created selection menus for limited choices. The Andrews High School Class of '90 Web site was an even greater success with the inclusion of Web page forms. The forms made it much easier for the graduates of the class of '90 to send information to the Reunion Committee.

What You Should Know

Having completed this project, you now should be able to perform the following tasks.

- Add Radio Buttons *(HTM 6.14, HTM 6.26)*
- Add Radio Buttons and a Selection Menu *(HTM 6.29)*
- Add a Selection Menu *(HTM 6.28)*
- Add a Text Field *(HTM 6.15, HTM 6.29)*
- Add a Textarea Field *(HTM 6.17)*
- Change the Text *(HTM 6.12, HTM 6.25)*
- Create Submit and Reset Buttons *(HTM 6.19, HTM 6.30)*
- Identify the Form Process *(HTM 6.11, HTM 6.25)*
- Open the HTML File *(HTM 6.23)*
- Print the HTML File *(HTM 6.22, HTM 6.32)*
- Print the Web Page *(HTM 6.21, HTM 6.31)*
- Save the HTML File *(HTM 6.19, HTM 6.30)*
- Start Notepad and Open the HTML File *(HTM 6.10)*
- View the HTML File in the Browser *(HTM 6.20, HTM 6.31)*

Test Your Knowledge

1 True/False

Instructions: Circle T if the statement is true or F if the statement is false.

T F 1. Text fields are used for multiple line input.
T F 2. Selection menus can allow single or multiple choices.
T F 3. Radio buttons always allow more than one choice.
T F 4. Check boxes are used for multiple choice selections.
T F 5. The SIZE attribute of the text field determines the maximum number of characters that may be entered.
T F 6. The <SELECT> tag is used to add choices to a list.
T F 7. The size of a textarea field is determined by specifying the number of rows and of columns.
T F 8. A RADIO control does not have a VALUE option.
T F 9. A choice that has the CHECKED attribute applied is the default.
T F 10. The ACTION attribute specifies the URL for the processing that is to be done.

2 Multiple Choice

Instructions: Circle the correct response.

1. The __________ attribute sets the default.
   a. NAME b. VALUE c. CHECKED d. SRC
2. The __________ attribute is used to define the identification of the field whose data is sent for processing.
   a. NAME b. VALUE c. CHECKED d. SRC
3. To indicate the contents of the input control that is sent, use the __________ attribute.
   a. NAME b. VALUE c. CHECKED d. SRC
4. The __________ tag is required for form creation.
   a. <FORM> b. <INPUT> c. <SELECT> d. <TEXTAREA>
5. The __________ tag defines a multiple-line input area.
   a. <FORM> b. <INPUT> c. <SELECT> d. <TEXTAREA>
6. The __________ tag defines a list of choices.
   a. <FORM> b. <INPUT> c. <SELECT> d. <TEXTAREA>
7. The __________ tag is used to define Submit and Reset buttons.
   a. <FORM> b. <INPUT> c. <SELECT> d. <TEXTAREA>
8. To display more than one option in a list menu, use the __________ attribute.
   a. NAME b. VALUE c. SIZE d. MULTIPLE
9. To allow a visitor to select more than one choice, use the __________ attribute.
   a. NAME b. VALUE c. SIZE d. MULTIPLE
10. The __________ tag specifies a choice in a selection menu.
   a. <FORM> b. <OPTION> c. <SELECT> d. <CHOICE>

Test Your Knowledge

3 Understanding HTML

Instructions: Perform the following tasks using a computer.

1. Start Notepad.
2. Open the survey2.htm file created in Project 6.
3. Print the file.
4. Circle the tags that define the processing structure of the form.
5. Draw a line under the tag that defines the name given to a radio button.
6. Put a square around the tag that indicates the second option in the selection menu.
7. Put an asterisk next to the tag that specifies the input control that resets the form.
8. Write your name and answers on the printout and hand it in to your instructor.

4 Editing HTML Files

Instructions: Perform the following tasks using a computer.

1. Start your browser.
2. Enter `www.scsite.com` in the Address text box. When the Web page displays, scroll down to the Internet titles and click the title of this book.
3. Click the link, Project 6 - 4 Editing HTML Files.
4. Click View on the menu bar and then click Source to find the HTML code for some feature that was not used on the survey1.htm Web page.
5. Highlight the code and copy it to the Clipboard (i.e., press CTRL+C).
6. Open the survey1.htm file in Notepad.
7. Paste the Clipboard contents into the survey1.htm file at an appropriate place.
8. Save the revised file on a floppy disk using the file name, survey1b.htm.
9. Print the revised document source.
10. Open the survey1b.htm file in your browser.
11. Print the Web page.
12. Write your name on both printouts and hand them in to your instructor.

1 Web Page Table Help

Instructions: Perform the following tasks using a computer.

1. Start your browser.
2. Enter `www.scsite.com/html/proj6.htm` in the Address text box. When the Web page displays, scroll down to the Internet titles and click the title of this book.
3. Click the link, Project 6 - Help1.
4. Read about the form attribute that allows the Web page visitor to select more than one choice.
5. Write down how that is done and how you would use it in a real Web page application.
6. Include your name with your answers and hand them in to your instructor.

2 More Forms Ideas

Instructions: Perform the following tasks using a computer.

1. Start your browser.
2. Enter `www.scsite.com/html/proj6.htm` in the Address text box. When the Web page displays, scroll down to the Internet titles and click the title of this book.
3. Click the link, Project 6 - Help2.
4. Find one suggestion that you did not learn in Project 6.
5. Write down some information from that suggestion and discuss how you would use it in your own Web page development.
6. Include your name with your answers and hand them in to your instructor.

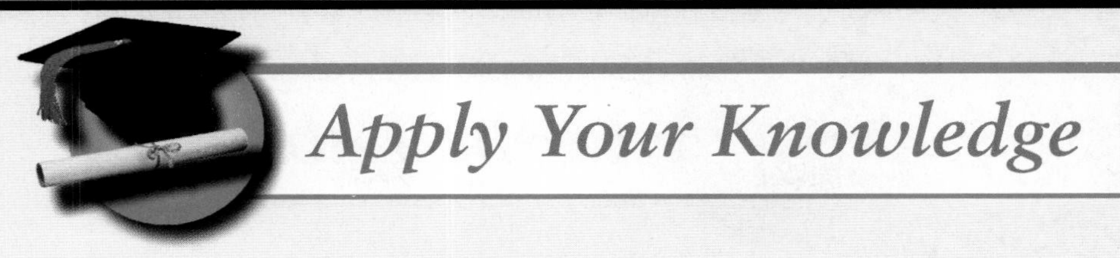

1 Editing a Web Page

Instructions: Start Notepad. Open the apply6.htm file on the HTML Data Disk. If you did not download the HTML Data Disk earlier, then see the inside back cover for instructions or see your instructor. The apply6.htm file is a partially completed HTML file that contains some errors. Figure 6-36 shows the Apply Your Knowledge Web page as it should display in the browser. Perform the following tasks using a computer.

FIGURE 6-36

1. Open the file in Notepad.
2. Open the file in your browser.
3. Examine the HTML file and its appearance in the browser.
4. Correct the HTML errors, making the Web page look similar to the one shown in Figure 6-36.
5. Add any HTML code necessary to include any additional features shown on the Web page.
6. Save the revised file on a floppy disk using the file name, apply6-2.htm.
7. Print the revised document source code.
8. Open the apply6-2.htm file in your browser.
9. Print the Web page.
10. Write your name on both printouts and hand them in to your instructor.

1 Surveying Bookstore Habits

Problem: The owners of Arnie's Bookstore are considering developing a Web site for online book buying. They want to survey the students at the college to find out whether Internet shopping is feasible for their products. They want you to create a Web page form that contains the questions shown in Figure 6-37.

FIGURE 6-37

Instructions: Start Notepad. Perform the following tasks using a computer.

1. Start a new HTML file with the title, [your name] lab6-1, in the main heading section.
2. Begin the form processing structure by using the POST method with the ACTION attribute set to email@isp.com.
3. Insert in the first row text fields for first name, last name, and e-mail address.
4. Insert in the second row a text field for an address.
5. Insert in the third row text fields to contain city, state, and ZIP code.
6. Create radio buttons for the next survey question.
7. In the next row create a selection menu with the first option (Arnie's Books) plus two other options.
8. Insert a second radio button control for the next question.
9. Specify a five-row, 50-column textarea field for the input.
10. Create Submit and Reset buttons at the bottom of the Web page form.
11. Save the file as lab6-1.htm.

12. Print the lab6-1.htm file.
13. Open the lab6-1.htm file in your browser and test all controls (except the Submit button).
14. Print the Web page.
15. Write your name on the printouts and hand them in to your instructor.

2 ALCO Records Music Questionnaire

Problem: ALCO Records is trying to determine the music listening habits of people in the Chicago area. Its management decided that a World Wide Web survey could be used to provide a low-cost analysis. You need to create the survey shown in Figure 6-38 using a variety of input controls.

[Your name] lab6-1 - Microsoft Internet Explorer provided by MSN

File Edit View Go Favorites Help

Back Forward Stop Refresh Home Search Favorites History Channels Fullscreen Mail Print Edit

Address C:\Shelly-Cashman\Project6\Addtl HTML\lab6-2.htm Links

ALCO Records Music Questionnaire

Please give us your name: E-mail address:

Do you frequently listen to music? Yes No

What type(s) do you prefer?
Jazz
Rock
Easy Listening
Country

What radio station(s) do you listen to?
WAMM - 90.6
WCBC - 98.6
WKPZ - 99.8
WLSS - 101
WYC - 103.4

Why do you tune in to those stations?

Submit the Form Reset the Form

Thank you for your input.

Done My Computer

Start [Your name] lab6-1 - ... 10:01 AM

FIGURE 6-38

(continued)

ALCO Records Music Questionnaire *(continued)*

Instructions: Start Notepad. Perform the following tasks using a computer.

1. Start a new HTML file with the title, [your name] lab6-2, in the main heading section.
2. Insert a <FORM> tag with attributes similar to those in Project 6. Next, create two text fields for input.
3. Insert radio buttons for yes/no music listening habits.
4. Insert check boxes for multiple choice input.
5. Insert a selection menu that will initially displays five rows and allows multiple input.
6. Insert a 5-row, 60-column textarea field.
7. Add a Submit button to email@isp.com and a Reset button.
8. Save this file as lab6-2.htm.
9. Print the lab6-2.htm file.
10. Open the lab6-2.htm file in your browser.
11. Print the Web page.
12. Write your name on the printouts and hand them in to your instructor.

3 Creating a Form within a Table Structure

Problem: You want to create a form that utilizes a table structure like the one shown in Figure 6-39. With a table structure, you have more control over the placement of the form controls in that you are not limited to placing controls beneath one another. This should be a borderless table.

Instructions: Start Notepad. Perform the following tasks using a computer.

1. Create a borderless table similar to the one shown in Figure 6-39.
2. The title of the form should be [your name] lab6-3.
3. Insert text fields for name and e-mail address information.
4. Insert at least one set of radio buttons and one set of check boxes on this form.
5. Insert two textarea fields of varying sizes.
6. Insert two selection menus that have multiple choices, one of which has a selected default option.
7. Add any other controls as you see fit.
8. Save the Web page using the file name, lab6-3.htm.
9. Print the page from your browser.
10. Write your name on the printout and hand it in to your instructor.

In the Lab

[Your name] lab6-3 - Microsoft Internet Explorer provided by MSN

File Edit View Go Favorites Help

Back Forward Stop Refresh Home Search Favorites History Channels Fullscreen Mail Print Edit

Address C:\Shelly-Cashman\Project6\Addtl HTML\lab6-3.htm Links

Controls within a Table

Your name: E-mail address:

Your question here: Choice 1 Choice 2

Your question here: Choice 1 Choice 2 Choice 3 Choice 4

Your question here:

Your question here:

Your question here: Option 1 Option 2 Option 3 Option 4

Your question here: Option 1 Option 2 Option 3 Option 4

Submit the Form Reset the Form

Done My Computer

Start [Your name] lab6-3 - ... 10:00 AM

FIGURE 6-39

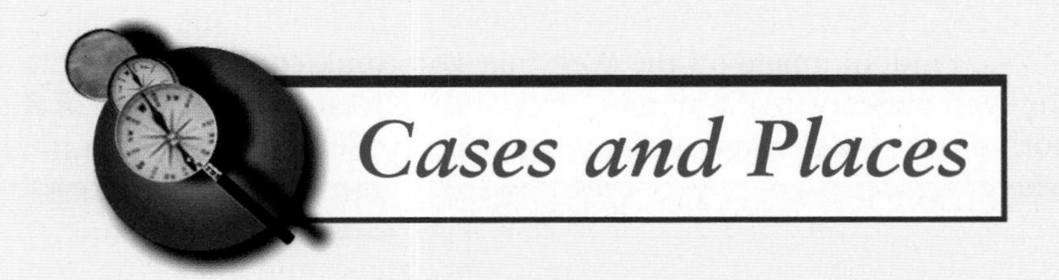

Cases and Places

The difficulty of these case studies varies:
▶ are the least difficult; ▶▶ are more difficult; and ▶▶▶ are the most difficult.

1 ▶ Find one Web site that uses text fields on a form in which the size of the text field is much smaller than the maximum length possible in the field. How many characters are allowed in the maximum length of the text field? Is it a problem if the maximum length is greater than the size on this form? Would this control have been better as a textarea field? Create a Web page form that contains a text field with the same size and maximum length. Also insert a textarea field that contains the same amount of character space. Test both fields to determine which is easier to use.

Cases and Places

2 ▶ Look for two Web sites that use forms ineffectively. Determine if the forms are well thought out and be able to support your answer. Print each Web page. Decide what other input controls might have been better to use. Draw your changes on a separate sheet of paper. Create the forms that you sketched on paper, utilizing your ideas for enhancing the original Web page form.

3 ▶▶ You want to convince the head of Web development at your company that Web page forms can be used to collect important information from the visitors to the company's Web site. Search the Internet for one Web site that does not use forms but that you think should. Assess the purpose of the Web site and determine what form structure you would use. You are now the Web developer for that Web site. What sort of information gathered from visitors could be helpful? What controls would be appropriate? Print the home page of the Web site that you found. Design a form that you think enhances the functionality of the Web site. Sketch your form design on another sheet of paper. Develop the Web page form that you think would help gather valuable information from the Web site visitors.

4 ▶▶ Do a Web search for two Web sites that contain information about forms. Several are mentioned in the More Abouts in this project. Read additional information about forms. Compare what these sources have to say about the advantages and disadvantages of using forms. What suggestions do they make regarding the use of forms? What controls are recommended? What is the best way to handle form submits? Create a Web page form that utilizes some of the suggestions from these Web sites. Include input controls that were not discussed in Project 6.

5 ▶▶▶ You are the Web developer for a graphics design company. Graphical images are important to your field. Such images often are used in forms. Find a Web site that utilizes images on its forms as input control features. How are the images used and how do they benefit the site? How could the form have been designed without the use of images? Create a Web page form without an image that contains at least five input controls. Find an image on the Web that you think could enhance the appearance and functionality of your Web page form. Copy that image to the form. Print a copy of the HTML files that you created. Test both pages to determine if the image helped the Web page form in any way.

6 ▶▶▶ You are a Web site developer for a small company in your community. You are interested in learning the latest programming techniques so that you can stay current with the technology. Project 6 mentioned CGI scripts and the Perl programming language. Find out what other options besides these two can be used to transfer information from the form to the Web server. Locate Web sites that discuss more advanced form topics for data transfer. In a four-page paper, discuss what options are available for data transfer. Locate Web sites that discuss advanced form topics for data transfer. Which options are better for more advanced developers?

7 ▶▶▶ In your search to learn as much as possible about Web development, you decide to use CGI scripts to enhance Web page forms that you had previously created. In Project 6, data from a form was sent in a file to an e-mail address. A better, more secure method is to use a CGI script to transfer information. Learn enough about a scripting language to write a simple script that can be used in lieu of an e-mail submission. Write a three-page paper that discusses how CGI scripts can be used to send information from a form. What problems did you have writing a simple script? Is information on CGI scripting readily available on the Internet?

Index